REA's Test Prep Books Are The Best!
(a sample of the <u>hundreds of letters</u> REA receives each year)

" I did well because of your wonderful prep books... I just wanted to thank you for helping me prepare for these tests. "

Student, San Diego, CA

" My students report your chapters of review as the most valuable single resource they used for review and preparation. "

Teacher, American Fork, UT

" Your book was such a better value and was so much more complete than anything your competition has produced (and I have them all!) "

Teacher, Virginia Beach, VA

" Compared to the other books that my fellow students had, your book was the most useful in helping me get a great score. "

Student, North Hollywood, CA

" Your book was responsible for my success on the exam, which helped me get into the college of my choice... I will look for REA the next time I need help. "

Student, Chesterfield, MO

" Just a short note to say thanks for the great support your book gave me in helping me pass the test... I'm on my way to a B.S. degree because of you! "

Student, Orlando, FL

(more on next page)

(continued from front page)

" I am writing to congratulate you on preparing an exceptional study guide. In five years of teaching this course, I have never encountered a more thorough, comprehensive, concise and realistic preparation for this examination. "
Teacher, Davie, FL

" I have found your publications, *The Best Test Preparation...*, to be exactly that. "
Teacher, Aptos, CA

" I used your book to prepare for the test and found that the advice and the sample tests were highly relevant... Without using any other material, I earned very high scores and will be going to the graduate school of my choice. "
Student, New Orleans, LA

" I used your *CLEP Introductory Sociology* book and rank it 99% – thank you! "
Student, Jerusalem, Israel

" Your GMAT book greatly helped me on the test. Thank you. "
Student, Oxford, OH

" I recently got the French SAT II Exam book from REA. I congratulate you on first-rate French practice tests. "
Instructor, Los Angeles, CA

" Your AP English Literature and Composition book is most impressive. "
Student, Montgomery, AL

" The REA LSAT Test Preparation guide is a winner! "
Instructor, Spartanburg, SC

THE BEST TEST PREPARATION FOR THE
ADVANCED PLACEMENT EXAMINATION

Mathematics
CALCULUS AB

with CD-ROM for both
Windows & Macintosh
REA's Interactive AP Calculus AB TEST*ware*®

Donald E. Brook
Mathematics Instructor
Mount San Antonio College, Walnut, California

Donna M. Smith
Mathematics Instructor
American River College, Sacramento, California

Tefera Worku
Mathematics Instructor
SUNY-Albany, Albany, New York

Research & Education Association
61 Ethel Road West Piscataway, New Jersey 08854

**The Best Test Preparation for the
ADVANCED PLACEMENT EXAMINATION
IN MATHEMATICS: CALCULUS AB**
with CD-ROM for both Windows & Macintosh
REA's Interactive AP Calculus AB TEST*ware*®

Year 2000 Printing

Printed in the United States of America

Library of Congress Catalog Card Number 98-65432

International Standard Book Number 0-87891-113-8

TEST*ware*® is a trademark of
Research & Education Association, Piscataway, NJ 08854.
Windows™ is a trademark of Microsoft® Corporation.
Macintosh™ is a trademark of Apple Computer, Inc.

Research & Education Association
61 Ethel Road West
Piscataway, New Jersey 08854

REA supports the effort to conserve and
protect environmental resources by
printing on recycled papers.

CONTENTS

ABOUT RESEARCH & EDUCATION ASSOCIATION

Research & Education Association (REA) is an organization of educators, scientists, and engineers specializing in various academic fields. Founded in 1959 with the purpose of disseminating the most recently developed scientific information to groups in industry, government, high schools, and universities, REA has since become a successful and highly respected publisher of study aids, test preps, handbooks, and reference works.

REA's Test Preparation series includes study guides for all academic levels in almost all disciplines. Research & Education Association publishes test preps for students who have not yet completed high school, as well as high school students preparing to enter college. Students from countries around the world seeking to attend college in the United States will find the assistance they need in REA's publications. For college students seeking advanced degrees, REA publishes test preps for many major graduate school admission examinations in a wide variety of disciplines, including engineering, law, and medicine. Students at every level, in every field, with every ambition can find what they are looking for among REA's publications.

Unlike most test preparation books—which present only a few practice tests that bear little resemblance to the actual exams—REA's series presents tests that accurately depict the official exams in both degree of difficulty and types of questions. REA's practice tests are always based upon the most recently administered exams, and include every type of question that can be expected on the actual exams.

REA's publications and educational materials are highly regarded and continually receive an unprecedented amount of praise from professionals, instructors, librarians, parents, and students. Our authors are as diverse as the fields represented in the books we publish. They are well-known in their respective disciplines and serve on the faculties of prestigious universities throughout the United States.

ACKNOWLEDGMENTS

In addition to our authors, we would like to thank Dr. Max Fogiel, President, for his overall guidance, which brought this publication to its completion; Carl Fuchs, Director of Educational Software Publishing, Larry B. Kling, Quality Control Manager of Books in Print, and John Paul Cording, Manager of Educational Software Publishing, for their supervision of the production of this revised edition, and Amy Jamison for her technical and editorial contributions.

Advanced Placement Examination in Calculus AB

INDEPENDENT STUDY SCHEDULE

ADVANCED PLACEMENT CALCULUS AB
INDEPENDENT STUDY SCHEDULE

The following study schedule allows for thorough preparation for the AP Calculus AB Examination. Although it is designed for six weeks, it can be reduced to a three-week course by collapsing each two-week period into one. Be sure to set aside enough time (at least two hours each day) to study. But no matter which study schedule works best for you, the more time you spend studying, the more prepared and relaxed you will feel on the day of the exam.

It is important for you to discover the time and place for studying that works best for you. Some students may set aside a certain number of hours every morning to study, while others may choose to study at night before going to sleep. Only you will be able to know when and where your studying is most effective. Keep in mind that the most important factor is consistency. Use your time wisely. Work out a study routine and stick to it!

Week	Activity
Week 1	Acquaint yourself with the AP Calculus AB Test by reading the Preface and About the Test. Take AP Calculus AB Diagnostic Software Exam I. This is the same as Test 4 in your book, but it is highly recommended that you take the exam first on computer for maximum study benefits. After the computer scores your exam, read through all the detailed explanations carefully (not just those for your incorrect answers). Make a note of any sections that were difficult for you, or any questions that were still unclear after reading the explanations. Review the specific field of difficulty in the AP course review included with this book, or by using the appropriate textbooks and notes.
Weeks 2 and 3	Carefully read and study the AP Calculus AB Review included in this book. Do not study too much at any one time. Pace yourself, so that you can better comprehend what you are reading. Remember that cramming is not an effective means of study.

Week 4	Take AP Calculus AB Diagnostic Software Exams II & III. These are the same as Tests 5 and 6 in your book. After the computer scores your exams, read through all the detailed explanations (not just those for your incorrect answers). Make a note of any sections that were difficult for you, or any questions that were still unclear after reading the explanations. Review those subjects by studying again the appropriate section of the AP Calculus AB Review.
Week 5	Take Tests 1 and 2 in your book, and after scoring your exam, review carefully all incorrect answer explanations. If there are any types of questions or particular subjects that seem difficult to you, review those subjects by studying again the appropriate section of the AP Calculus AB Review.
Week 6	Take Test 3 in your book, and after scoring your exam, review carefully all incorrect answer explanations. Study any areas you consider to be your weaknesses by using the AP Calculus AB Review and any other study resources you have on hand. Review the practice tests one more time to be sure you understand the problems that you originally answered incorrectly.

Advanced Placement Examination in Calculus AB

INTRODUCTION

ABOUT THIS BOOK AND TEST*ware* ®

This book and the accompanying software (AP Calculus AB TEST*ware*®) provide an accurate and complete representation of the Advanced Placement Examination in Mathematics: Calculus AB. The six practice tests provided are based on the format of the most recently administered Advanced Placement Calculus AB Exams. Each test is three hours and 15 minutes in length and includes every type of question that can be expected on the actual exam. Following each test is an answer key complete with detailed explanations designed to clarify the material for the student. By completing all six tests and studying the explanations which follow, students will discover their strengths and weaknesses and become well prepared for the actual exam.

Exams 4, 5, and 6 of the book are also on computer disk in our special interactive AP Calculus AB TEST*ware*®. By taking these exams on the computer you will have the additional study features and benefits of enforced timed conditions, individual diagnostic analysis of what subjects need extra study, and instant scoring. Many features are included that you will find helpful as you prepare for the AP Calculus AB Test. For your convenience, our interactive AP Calculus AB TEST*ware*® has been provided for you in both Windows and Macintosh formats. For instructions on how to install and use our software, please refer to the appendix at the back of this book.

ABOUT THE TEST

The Advanced Placement Calculus AB Examination is offered each May at participating schools and multi-school centers throughout the world.

The Advanced Placement Program is designed to allow high school students to pursue college-level studies while attending high school. The participating colleges, in turn, grant credit and/or advanced placement to students who do well on the examinations.

The Advanced Placement Calculus courses cover college-level mathematics; they are intended for students with a strong background in college-preparatory mathematics, including algebra, axiomatic geometry, trigonometry, and analytic geometry. The courses cover graphical, numerical, analytic, and verbal calculus, along with overarching concepts like derivatives, integrals, limits, applications and modeling, and approximation.

The AP Calculus AB exam has two sections:

Section I) **Multiple-choice**: composed of 45 multiple-choice questions, designed to measure the student's abilities in a wide range of mathematical topics. These questions vary in difficulty and complexity. This section is broken into two parts. Part A consists of 28 questions for which a calculator *cannot* be used. Part B contains 17 questions, some of which will *require* the use of a graphing calculator. One hour and forty-five minutes is allowed for this section of the exam.

Section II) **Free-response**: composed of six free-response questions that test how well and how accurately the student is able to recall and utilize knowledge of calculus. Between 0 and 9 points are awarded for each question based on the work shown and whether or not the solution given is correct. Partial credit is given for answers that are correct in format, yet incorrect in the solution. Therefore, it is strongly recommended that all work is written down. Each of these two sections counts for 50% of the student's total exam grade. Because the exam contains such a vast array of material, it is a foregone conclusion that all students will not be able to answer all the questions correctly.

These calculators have been approved by the College Board for use on the AP Calculus AB exam; bring one with you when you take the test:

Casio	Sharp	Radio Shack	Hewlett-Packard
fx-6000 series	EL-5200	EC-4033	HP-28 series
fx-6200 series	EL-9200 series	EC-4034	HP-48 series
fx-6300 series	EL-9300 series	EC-4037	HP-38G
fx-6500 series	EL-9600 series		
fx-7000 series			
fx-7300 series	**Texas Instruments**	**Other**	
fx-7400 series	TI-73	Micronta	
fx-7500 series	TI-80	Smart^2	
fx-7700 series	TI-81		
fx-7800 series	TI-82		
fx-8000 series	TI-83		
fx-8500 series	TI-85		
fx-8700 series	TI-86		
fx-8800 series	TI-89		
fx-9700 series			
fx-9750 series			
cfx-9800 series			
cfx-9850 series			
cfx-9950 series			
cfx-9970 series			

The sample tests in this book provide calculator questions with explanations that include the steps necessary with the calculator. These steps are illustrated after the word *calculator,* listing the keystrokes that should be used.

ABOUT THE REVIEW SECTION

This book contains review material that students will find useful as a study aid while preparing for the AP Calculus AB Examination. This review—in a handy outline format—provides information that will most likely appear on the actual test. Included in this section are the following topics:

Elementary Functions — Covers the Properties of Functions, the Properties of Particular Functions, and Limits.

Differential Calculus — Covers Derivatives and Application of the Derivative.

Integral Calculus — Covers Anti-Derivatives, Applications of Anti-Derivatives, the Law of Exponential Change, Techniques of Integration, the Definite Integral, and Applications of the Integral.

SCORING THE TEST

SCORING THE MULTIPLE-CHOICE SECTION

For the multiple choice section, use this formula to calculate your raw score:

$$\underline{\hspace{1.5cm}} - (\underline{\hspace{1.5cm}} \times 1/4) = \underline{\hspace{1.5cm}}$$

number right   number wrong*   raw score (round to nearest whole #)

* DO NOT INCLUDE UNANSWERED QUESTIONS

SCORING THE FREE-RESPONSE SECTION

For the free-response section, use this formula to calculate your raw score:

$$\underline{\hspace{1cm}} + \underline{\hspace{1cm}} + \underline{\hspace{1cm}} + \underline{\hspace{1cm}} + \underline{\hspace{1cm}} + \underline{\hspace{1cm}} = \underline{\hspace{1cm}}$$

problems one through six   raw score

The score for each problem should reflect how completely the question was answered, that is, the solution that was produced and the steps taken. You should gauge at what point a mistake was made, and determine whether any use of calculus or mathematics was incorrect.

Each problem is given a score of between 0 and 9 points. More points should be given for correct answers that include all work in the answer explanation, and fewer points should be given for incorrect answers and necessary work that was not written down. It would be helpful to have a teacher or an impartial person knowledgeable in calculus decide on how points should be awarded.

THE COMPOSITE SCORE

To obtain your composite score, use the following method:

$$1.200 \times \underline{\hspace{2cm}} = \underline{\hspace{2cm}} \text{ (weighted multiple-choice score)}$$

multiple-choice   round to the nearest whole number

raw score

NOW ADD:

$$\underline{\hspace{3cm}} + \underline{\hspace{3cm}} = \underline{\hspace{3cm}}$$

weighted multiple-   free-response   composite

choice raw score   raw score   score

Compare your score with this table to approximate your grade:

AP GRADE	COMPOSITE SCORE
5	78–102
4	64–77
3	45–63
2	30–44
1	0–29

The overall scores are interpreted as follows: 5–extremely well qualified; 4–well qualified; 3–qualified; 2–possibly qualified; and 1–no recommendation. Most colleges will grant students who earn a 3 or above either college credit or advanced placement. Check with your school guidance office about specific school requirements.

CONTACTING THE AP PROGRAM

For registration bulletins or more information about the Calculus AB exam, contact:

AP Services
P.O. Box 6671
Princeton, NJ 08541-6671
Phone: (609) 771-7300
Website: www.collegeboard.org/ap

Advanced Placement Examination in Calculus AB

REVIEW

Chapter 1

Elementary Functions: Algebraic, Exponential, Logarithmic, and Trigonometric

A. Properties of Functions

Definition: A function is a correspondence between two sets—the domain and the range—such that for each value in the domain there corresponds exactly one value in the range.

A function has three distinct features:

a) the set x which is the domain,

b) the set y which is the co-domain or range,

c) a functional rule, f, that assigns only one element $y \in Y$ to each $x \in X$. We write $y = f(x)$ to denote the functional value y at x.

Consider Figure 1. The "machine" f transforms the domain X, element by element, into the co-domain Y.

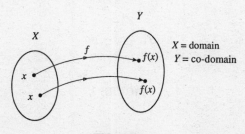

FIGURE 1

Parametric Equations

If we have an equation $y = f(x)$, and the explicit functional form contains an arbitrary constant called a parameter, then it is called a parametric equation. A function with a parameter represents not one but a family of curves.

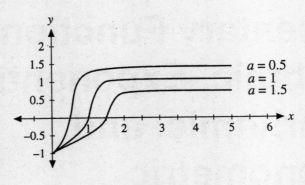

$$y = \frac{x^2 - a^2}{x^2 + a^2}, \ a \text{ is the parameter}$$

FIGURE 2

Often the equation for a curve is given as two functions of a parameter t, such as

$$X = x(t) \text{ and } Y = y(t).$$

Corresponding values of x and y are calculated by solving for t and substituting.

Vectors

A vector (AB) is denoted $\overrightarrow{AB}$, where B represents the head and A represents the tail. This is illustrated in Figure 3.

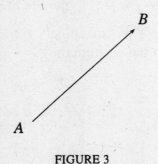

FIGURE 3

The length of a line segment is the magnitude of a vector. If the magnitude and direction of two vectors are the same, then they are equal.

Vectors which can be translated from one position to another without any change in their magnitude or direction are called free vectors.

The unit vector is a vector with a length (magnitude) of one.

The zero vector has a magnitude of zero.

The unit vector, $\vec{i}$, is a vector with magnitude of one in the directions of the x–axis.

The unit vector $\vec{j}$ is a vector with magnitude of one in the direction of the y–axis.

When two vectors are added together, the resultant force of the two vectors produce the same effect as the two combined forces. This is illustrated in Figure 4.

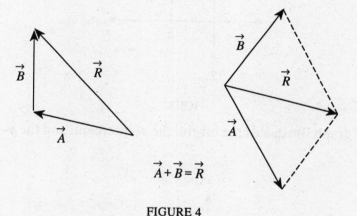

$$\vec{A} + \vec{B} = \vec{R}$$

FIGURE 4

In these diagrams, the vector $\vec{R}$ is called the resultant vector.

Combination of Functions

Let f and g represent functions, then

a)   the sum $(f + g)\,(x) = f(x) + g(x)$,

b)   the difference $(f - g)\,(x) = f(x) - g(x)$,

c)   the product $(fg)\,(x) = f(x)\,g(x)$,

d)   the quotient $\left(\dfrac{f}{g}\right)(x) = \dfrac{f(x)}{g(x)}$, $g(x) \neq 0$,

e)   the composition function $(g \circ f)(x) = g(f(x))$ where $f(x)$ must be in the domain of g.

Graphs of a Function

If (x, y) is a point or ordered pair on the coordinate plane R then x is the first coordinate and y is the second coordinate.

To locate an ordered pair on the coordinate plane simply measure the distance of x units along the x–axis, then measure vertically (parallel to the y–axis) y units.

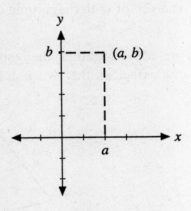

FIGURE 5

This graph illustrates the origin, the x–intercept, and the y–intercept.

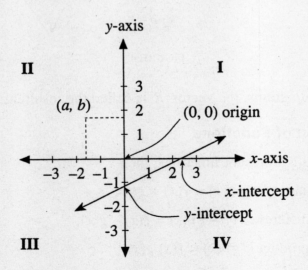

I, II, III, IV are called quadrants in the COORDINATE PLANE.
(a, b) is an ordered pair with x–coordinate a and y–coordinate b.
FIGURE 6 – Cartesian Coordinate System

The following three graphs illustrate symmetry.

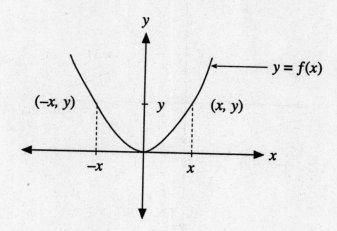

a) Symmetric about the y-axis

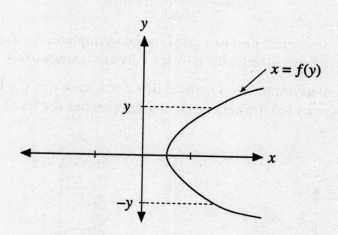

b) Symmetric about the x-axis
Note: This is not a function of x.

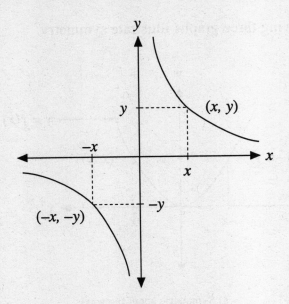

c) Symmetric about the origin.
FIGURE 7

Another important part of a graph is the asymptote. An asymptote is a line which will never be touched by the curve as it tends toward infinity.

A vertical asymptote is a vertical line $x = a$, such that the functional value $|f(x)|$ grows indefinitely large as x approaches the fixed value a.

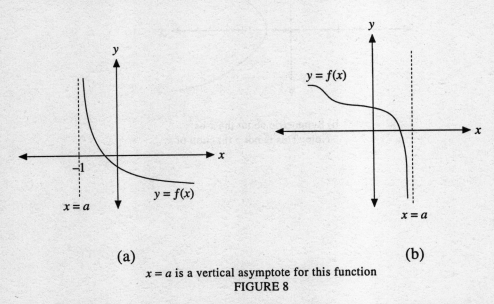

(a)   (b)

$x = a$ is a vertical asymptote for this function
FIGURE 8

The following steps encapsulate the procedure for drawing a graph:

a)   Determine the domain and range of the function.

b)   Find the intercepts of the graph and plot them.

c)   Determine the symmetries of the graph.

d)   Locate the vertical asymptotes and plot a few points on the graph near each asymptote.

e)   Plot additional points as needed.

Polar Coordinates

Polar coordinates is a method of representing points in a plane by the use of ordered pairs.

The polar coordinate system consists of an origin (pole), a polar axis and a ray of specific angle.

The polar axis is a line that originates at the origin and extends indefinitely in any given direction.

The position of any point in the plane is determined by its distance from the origin and by the angle that the line makes with the polar axis.

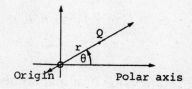

FIGURE 9

The coordinates of the polar coordinate system are (r, θ).

The angle (θ) is positive if it is generated by a counterclockwise rotation of the polar axis, and is negative if it is generated by a clockwise rotation.

The graph of an equation in polar coordinates is a set of all points, each of which has at least one pair of polar coordinates, (r, θ), which satisfies the given equation.

To plot a graph:

1.   Construct a table of values θ and r.

2.   Plot these points.

3.   Sketch the curve.

Inverse of a Function

Assuming that f is a one-to-one function with domain X and range Y, then a function g having domain Y and range X is called the inverse function of f if:

$$f(g(y)) = y \text{ for every } y \in Y \text{ and}$$

$$g(f(x)) = x \text{ for every } x \in X.$$

The inverse of the function f is denoted f^{-1}.

To find the inverse function f^{-1}, you must solve the equation $y = f(x)$ for x in terms of y.

Be careful: This solution must be a function.

Even and Odd Functions

A function is even if

$$f(-x) = f(x) \quad \text{or} \quad f(x) + f(-x) = 2f(x).$$

A function is said to be odd if

$$f(-x) = -f(x) \quad \text{or} \quad f(x) + f(-x) = 0.$$

Absolute Value

Definition: The absolute value of a real number x is defined as

$$|x| = \begin{cases} x & \text{if } x \geq 0 \\ -x & \text{if } x < 0 \end{cases}$$

For real numbers a and b:

a) $|a| = |-a|$

b) $|ab| = |a| \cdot |b|$

c) $-|a| \leq a \leq |a|$

d) $ab \leq |a| \, |b|$

e) $|a + b|^2 = (a + b)^2$

Periodicity

A function f with domain X is periodic if there exists a positive real number p such that $f(x + p) = f(x)$ for all $x \in X$.

The smallest number p with this property is called the period of f.

Over any interval of length p, the behavior of a periodic function can be completely described.

Zeroes of a Function

To locate an ordered pair on the coordinate plane simply measure the distance of x units along the x-axis, then measure vertically (parallel to the y-axis) y units.

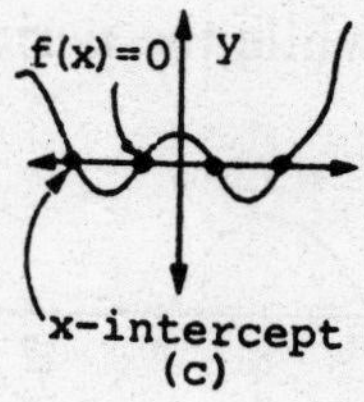

Zeroes of a function
FIGURE 10

B. Properties of Particular Functions

In order to graph a trigonometric function, it is necessary to identify the amplitude and the period of the function.

For example, to graph a function of the form

$$y = a \sin (bx + c)$$

$$a = \text{amplitude and } \frac{2\pi}{b} = \text{period.}$$

Let us graph the function $y = 2 \sin(2x + \frac{\pi}{4})$. Amplitude $= 2$, period $= \frac{2\pi}{2} = \pi$, phase $\angle = \frac{\pi}{8}$.

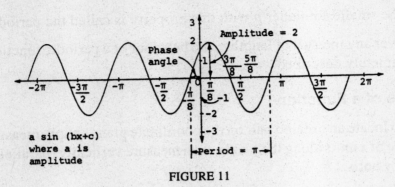

FIGURE 11

The following graphs represent the functions $y = \sin x$ and $y = \cos x$. The amplitude of each is one, while the period of each is 2π.

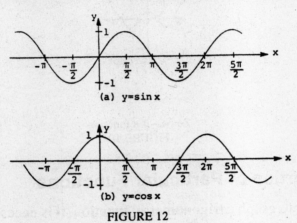

FIGURE 12

Identities and Formulas for Trigonometric Functions

Provided the denominators are not zero, the following relationships exist:

$$\sin t = \frac{1}{\csc t} \qquad\qquad \tan t = \frac{\sin t}{\cos t}$$

$$\cos t = \frac{1}{\sec t} \qquad\qquad \cot t = \frac{\cos t}{\sin t}$$

$$\tan t = \frac{1}{\cot t}$$

If PQR is an angle t and P has coordinates (x, y) on the unit circle, then by joining PR we get angle $PRQ = 90°$ and then we can define all the trigonometric functions in the following way:

sine of t, $\sin t = y$

cosine of t, $\cos t = x$

tangent of t, $\tan t = \dfrac{y}{x}$, $x \neq 0$

cotangent of t, $\tan t = \dfrac{x}{y}$, $y \neq 0$

secant of t, $\sec t = \dfrac{1}{x}$, $x \neq 0$

cosecant of t, $\csc t = \dfrac{1}{y}$, $y \neq 0$.

$\cos^2 x + \sin^2 x = 1$

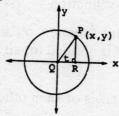

FIGURE 13

Therefore,

$\sec^2 = 1 + \tan^2\theta$, $\csc^2\theta = 1 + \cot^2\theta$

$\sin(A + B) = \sin A \cos B + \cos A \sin B$

$\sin(A - B) = \sin A \cos B - \cos A \sin B$

$\cos(A + B) = \cos A \cos B - \sin A \sin B$

$\cos(A - B) = \cos A \cos B + \sin A \sin B$

$\sin^2\theta = \dfrac{1 - \cos 2\theta}{2}$

$\cos^2\theta = \dfrac{1 + \cos 2\theta}{2}$

Sine law: $\dfrac{a}{\sin\theta} = \dfrac{b}{\sin\phi} = \dfrac{c}{\sin\psi}$

Cosine law: $a^2 = b^2 + c^2 - 2bc \cos\theta$

$$b^2 = c^2 + a^2 - 2ca \cos \phi$$

$$c^2 = a^2 + b^2 - 2ab \cos \psi$$

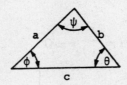

FIGURE 14

Exponential and Logarithmic Functions

If f is a nonconstant function that is continuous and satisfies the functional equation $f(x + y) = f(x) \cdot f(y)$, then $f(x) = a^x$ for some constant a. That is, f is an exponential function.

Consider the exponential function a^x, $a > 0$ and the logarithmic function $\log_a x$, $a > 0$. Then a^x is defined for all $x \in R$, and $\log_a x$ is defined only for positive $x \in R$.

These functions are inverses of each other,

$$a^{\log_a x} = x; \ \log_a(a^y) = y.$$

Let a^x, $a > 0$ be an exponential function. Then for any real numbers x and y

a) $a^x \times a^y = a^{x+y}$

b) $(a^x)^y = a^{xy}$

Let $\log_a x$, $a > 0$ be a logarithmic function. Then for any positive real numbers x and y

a) $\log_a(xy) = \log_a(x) + \log_a(y)$

b) $\log_a(x^y) = y \log_a(x)$

C. Limits

The following are important properties of limits: Consider

$$\lim_{x \to a} f(x) = L \text{ and } \lim_{x \to a} g(x) = K, \text{ then}$$

A)   Uniqueness—If $\lim_{x \to a} f(x)$ exists then it is unique.

B) $\lim\limits_{x \to a} [f(x) + g(x)] = \lim\limits_{x \to a} f(x) + \lim\limits_{x \to a} g(x) = L + K$

C) $\lim\limits_{x \to a} [f(x) - g(x)] = \lim\limits_{x \to a} f(x) - \lim\limits_{x \to a} g(x) = L - K$

D) $\lim\limits_{x \to a} [f(x) \times g(X)] = \lim\limits_{x \to a} f(x) \times \lim\limits_{x \to a} g(x) = L \times K$

E) $\lim\limits_{x \to a} \dfrac{f(x)}{g(x)} = \dfrac{\lim\limits_{x \to a} f(x)}{\lim\limits_{x \to a} g(x)} = \dfrac{L}{K}$ provided $K \neq 0$

Special Limits

A) $\lim\limits_{x \to 0} \dfrac{\sin x}{x} = 1$,

B) $\lim\limits_{x \to \infty} \left(1 + \dfrac{1}{n}\right)^n = e$,

Some nonexistent limits which are frequently encountered are:

A) $\lim\limits_{x \to 0} \dfrac{1}{x^2}$, as x approaches zero, x^2 gets very small and also becomes zero, therefore, $\dfrac{1}{0}$ is not defined and the limit does not exist.

B) $\lim\limits_{x \to 0} \dfrac{|x|}{x}$ does not exist.

Continuity

A function f is continuous at a point a if

$$\lim\limits_{x \to a} f(x) = f(a).$$

This implies that three conditions are satisfied:

A) $f(a)$ exists, that is, f is defined at a.

B) $\lim\limits_{x \to a} f(x)$ exists, and

C)   the two numbers are equal.

15

To test continuity at a point $x = a$ we test whether

$$\lim_{x \to a^+} M(x) = \lim_{x \to a^-} M(x) = M(a)$$

Theorems on Continuity

A) A function defined in a closed interval $[a, b]$ is continuous in $[a, b]$ if and only if it is continuous in the open interval (a, b), as well as continuous from the right at "a" and from the left at "b."

B) If f and g are continuous functions at a, then so are the functions $f + g$, $f - g$, fg, and $\dfrac{f}{g}$ where $g(a) \neq 0$.

C) If $\lim\limits_{x \to a} g(x) = b$ and f is continuous at b, $\lim\limits_{x \to a} f(g(x)) = f(b) = f[\lim\limits_{x \to a} g(x)]$.

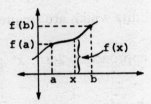

FIGURE 15

D) If g is continuous at a and f is continuous at $b = g(a)$, then

$$\lim_{x \to a} f(g(x)) = f[\lim_{x \to a} g(x)] = f(g(a)).$$

E) Intermediate Value Theorem. If f is continuous on a closed interval $[a, b]$ and if $f(a) \neq f(b)$, then f takes on every value between $f(a)$ and $f(b)$ in the interval $[a, b]$.

Chapter 2

Differential Calculus

A. The Derivative

The Definition and Δ-Method

The derivative of a function expresses its rate of change with respect to an independent variable. The derivative is also the slope of the tangent line to the curve.

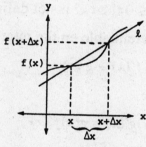

FIGURE 16

Consider the graph of the function f in Figure 16. Choosing a point x and a point $x + \Delta x$ (where Δx denotes a small distance on the x-axis) we can obtain both $f(x)$ and $f(x + \Delta x)$. Drawing a tangent line, l, of the curve through the points $f(x)$ and $f(x + \Delta x)$, we can measure the rate of change of this line. As we let the distance, Δx, approach zero, then

$$\lim_{\Delta x \to 0} \frac{f(x + \Delta x) - f(x)}{\Delta x}$$

becomes the instantaneous rate of change of the function or the derivative.

We denote the derivative of the function f to be f'. So we have

$$f'(x) = \lim_{\Delta x \to 0} \frac{f(x + \Delta x) - f(x)}{\Delta x}$$

If $y = f(x)$, some common notations for the derivative are

$$y' = f'(x)$$

$$\frac{dy}{dx} = f'(x)$$

$$D_x y = f'(x) \quad \text{or} \quad Df = f'$$

Rules for Finding Derivatives

General Rule:

A) If f is a constant function, $f(x) = c$, then $f'(x) = 0$.

B) If $f(x) = x$, then $f'(x) = 1$.

C) If f is differentiable, then $(cf(x))' = cf'(x)$

D) Power Rule:

If $f(x) = x^n$, $n \in Z$, then

$f'(x) = nx^{n-1}$; if $n \leq 0$ then x^n is not defined at $x = 0$.

E) If f and g are differentiable on the interval (a, b) then:

a) $(f + g)'(x) = f'(x) + g'(x)$

b) Product Rule:

$$(fg)'(x) = f(x)g'(x) = g(x)f'(x)$$

Example:

Find $f'(x)$ if $f(x) = (x^3 + 1)(2x^2 + 8x - 5)$.

$$f'(x) = (x^3 + 1)(4x + 8) + (2x^2 + 8x - 5)(3x^2)$$

$$= 4x^4 + 8x^3 + 4x + 8 + 6x^4 + 24x^3 - 15x^2$$

$$= 10x^4 + 32x^3 - 15x^2 + 4x + 8$$

c) Quotient Rule:

$$\left(\frac{f'}{g}\right)(x) = \frac{g(x)f'(x) - f(x)g'(x)}{[g(x)]^2}$$

Example:

Find $f'(x)$ if $f(x) = \dfrac{3x^2 - x + 2}{4x^2 + 5}$

$$f'(x) = \frac{-(3x^2 - x + 2)(8x) + (4x^2 + 5)(6x - 1)}{(4x^2 + 5)^2}$$

$$= \frac{-(24x^3 - 8x^2 + 16x) + (24x^3 - 4x^2 + 30x - 5)}{(4x^2 + 5)^2}$$

$$= \frac{4x^2 + 14x - 5}{(4x^2 + 5)^2}$$

F) If $f(x) = x^{\frac{m}{n}}$, then

$$f'(x) = \frac{m}{n} x^{\frac{m}{n} - 1}$$

where $m, n \in Z$ and $n \neq 0$.

G) Polynomials.

If $f(x) = (a_0 + a_1 x + a_2 x^2 + \ldots + a_x x^n)$ then

$f'(x) = a_1 + 2a_2 x + 3a_3 x^2 + \ldots + na_n x^{n-1}$.

This employs the power rule and rules concerning constants.

The Chain Rule

Chain Rule: Let $f(u)$ be a composite function, where $u = g(x)$. Then $f'(u) = f'(u)\, g'(x)$ or if $y = f(u)$ and $u = g(x)$ then $D_x y = (D_u y)\,(D_x u) = f'(u)g'(x)$.

Example:

Find the derivative of: $y = (2x^3 - 5x^2 + 4)^5$.

$$Dx = \frac{d}{dx}.$$

This problem can be solved by simply applying the theorem for $d(u^n)$. However, to illustrate the use of the chain rule, make the following substitutions:

$$y = u^5 \quad \text{where} \quad u = 2x^3 - 5x^2 + 4$$

Therefore, by the chain rule,

$$D_x y = D_u y \times D_x u = 5u^4 \, (6x^2 - 10x)$$

$$= 5 \, (2x^3 - 5x^2 + 4)^4 \, (6x^2 - 10x).$$

Implicit Differentiation

An implicit function of x and y is a function in which one of the variables is not directly expressed in terms of the other. If these variables are not easily or practically separable, we can still differentiate the expression.

Apply the normal rules of differentiation such as the product rule, the power rule, etc. Remember also the chain rule which states

$$\frac{du}{dx} \times \frac{dx}{dt} = \frac{du}{dt} \ .$$

Once the rules have been properly applied we will be left with, as in the example of x and y, some factors of $\dfrac{dy}{dx}$.

We can then algebraically solve for the derivative $\dfrac{dy}{dx}$ and obtain the desired result.

Example:

Find y' in terms of x and y, using implicit differentiation, where

$$y' = \frac{dy}{dx},$$

in the expression:

$$y^3 + 3xy + x^3 - 5 = 0.$$

The derivative of y^3 is $3y^2 y'$. The term $3xy$ must be treated as a product. The derivative of $3xy$ is $3xy' + 3y$. The derivative of x^3 is $3x^2$. The derivative of -5 is 0. Therefore,

$$3y^2 y' + 3xy' + 3y + 3x^2 = 0.$$

We can now solve for y':

$$y' = -\frac{y + x^2}{y^2 + x}.$$

Trigonometric Differentiation

The three most basic trigonometric derivatives are:

$$\frac{d}{dx}(\sin x) = \cos x,$$

$$\frac{d}{dx}(\cos x) = -\sin x,$$

$$\frac{d}{dx}(\tan x) = \sec^2 x.$$

Given any basic trigonometric function, it can be differentiated by applying these basics in combination with the general rules for differentiating algebraic expressions.

The following will be most useful if committed to memory:

$$D_x \sin u = \cos u \, D_x u$$
$$D_x \cos u = -\sin u \, D_x u$$
$$D_x \tan u = \sec^2 u \, D_x u$$
$$D_x \sec u = \tan u \sec u \, D_x u$$
$$D_x \cot u = -\csc^2 u \, D_x u$$
$$D_x \csc u = -\csc u \cot u \, D_x u$$

Inverse Trigonometric Differentiation

Inverse trigonometric functions may be sometimes handled by inverting the expression and applying rules for the direct trigonometric functions.

For example, $y = \sin^{-1} x$

$$D_x y = D_x \sin^{-1} x = \frac{1}{\cos y} = \frac{1}{\sqrt{1 - x^2}}, \ |x| < 1.$$

Here are the derivatives for the inverse trigonometric functions which can be found in a manner similar to the above function:

$$D_x \sin^{-1} u = \frac{1}{\sqrt{1-u^2}} \, D_x u, \qquad |u| < 1$$

$$D_x \cos^{-1} u = \frac{-1}{\sqrt{1-u^2}} \, D_x u, \qquad |u| < 1$$

$$D_x \tan^{-1} u = \frac{1}{1+u^2} \, D_x u, \qquad \text{where } u = f(x) \text{ differentiable}$$

$$D_x \sec^{-1} u = \frac{1}{|u|\sqrt{u^2-1}} \, D_x u, \qquad u = f(x), \, |f(x)| > 1$$

$$D_x \cot^{-1} u = \frac{-1}{1+u^2} \, D_x u, \qquad u = f(x) \text{ differentiable}$$

$$D_x \csc^{-1} u = \frac{-1}{|u|\sqrt{u^2-1}} \, D_x u, \qquad u = f(x), \, |f(x)| > 1$$

High Order Derivatives

The derivative of any function is also a legitimate function which we can differentiate. The second derivative can be obtained by:

$$\frac{d}{dx}\left[\frac{d}{dx}u\right] = \frac{d^2}{dx^2}u = u'' = D^2 u,$$

where $u = g(x)$ is differentiable.

The general formula for higher orders and the nth derivative of u is,

$$\underbrace{\frac{d}{dx}\frac{d}{dx}\cdots\frac{d}{dx}}_{n \text{ times}} u = \frac{d^{(n)}}{dx^{(n)}}u = u^{(n)} = D_x^{(n)} u \,.$$

The rules for first order derivatives apply at each stage of higher order differentiation (e.g., sums, products, chain rule).

A function which satisfies the condition that its nth derivative is zero, is the general polynomial

$$p_{n-1}(x) = a_{n-1}x^{n-1} + a_{n-2}x^{n-2} + \dots + a_0.$$

Derivatives of Vector Functions

A) Continuity

Let $f(x)$ be a function defined for all values of x near $t = t_0$ as well as at $t = t_0$. Then the function $f(x)$ is said to be continuous at t_0 if

$$\lim_{t \to t_0} f(t) = f(t_0)$$

if and only if for all $\varepsilon > 0$, there exists a $\delta > 0$, such that $|f(t) - f(t_0)| < \varepsilon$, if $|t - t_0| < \delta$.

B) Derivative

The derivative of the vector valued function $V(t)$ with respect to $t \in R$ is defined as the limit

$$\frac{dV(t)}{dt} = \lim_{\Delta t \to 0} \frac{V(t + \Delta t) - V(t)}{\Delta t}$$

If a vector is expressed in terms of its components along the fixed coordinate axes,

$$V = V_1(t)i + V_2(t)j + V_3(t)k,$$

there follows

$$\frac{dV(t)}{dt} = \frac{dV_1}{dt}i + \frac{dV_2}{dt}j + \frac{dV_3}{dt}k.$$

For the derivative of a product involving two or more vectors the following formulae are used:

$$\frac{d}{dt}(A \cdot B) = A \cdot \frac{dB}{dt} + \frac{dA}{dt} \cdot B$$

$$\frac{d}{dt}(A \times B) = A \times \frac{dB}{dt} + \frac{dA}{dt} \times B$$

$$\frac{d}{dt}(A \cdot B \times C) = \frac{dA}{dt} \cdot (B \times C) + A \cdot \left(\frac{dB}{dt} \times C\right) + A \cdot \left(\frac{dC}{dt} \times B\right).$$

Parametric Formula for $\dfrac{dy}{dx}$

According to the chain rule,

$$\frac{dy}{dt} = \frac{dy}{dx} \cdot \frac{dx}{dt} \ .$$

Since $\dfrac{dx}{dt} \neq 0$, we can divide through $\dfrac{dx}{dt}$ to solve for $\dfrac{dy}{dx}$. We then obtain the equation

$$\frac{dy}{dx} = \frac{dy}{dt} \div \frac{dx}{dt} \ .$$

Example:

Find $\dfrac{dy}{dx}$ from

$$y = x^3 - 3x^2 + 5x - 4,$$

where $x = t^2 + t$.

From these equations, we find

$$\frac{dy}{dx} = 3x^2 - 6x + 5$$

$$= 3(t^2 + t)^2 - 6(t^2 + t) + 5,$$

$$\frac{dx}{dt} = 2t + 1.$$

Since

$$\frac{dy}{dt} = \frac{dy}{dx} \cdot \frac{dx}{dt}$$

from the chain rule,

$$\frac{dy}{dt} = [3(t^2 + t)^2 - 6(t^2 + t) + 5] \, (2t + 1).$$

We can also first substitute the value of x in terms of t into the equation for y. We then have:

$$y = (t^2 + t)^3 - 3(t^2 + t)^2 + 5(t^2 + t) - 4 .$$

When we differentiate this with respect to t, we obtain:

$$\frac{dy}{dt} = 3(t^2 - t)^2 (2t + 1) - 6 (t^2 + t) (2t + 1) + 5(2t + 1)$$

$$= [3(t^2 + t)^2 - 6(t^2 + t) + 5] (2t + 1),$$

which agrees with the previous answer.

The first method using the chain rule, however, often results in the simpler solution when dealing with problems involving parametric equations.

Exponential and Logarithmic Differentiation

The exponential function e^x has the simplest of all derivatives. Its derivative is itself.

$$\frac{d}{dx} e^x = e^x \quad \text{and} \quad \frac{d}{dx} e^u = e^u \frac{du}{dx}$$

Since the natural logarithmic function is the inverse of $y = e^x$ and $\ln e = 1$, it follows that

$$\frac{d}{dx} \ln y = \frac{1}{y} \frac{dy}{dx} \quad \text{and} \quad \frac{d}{dx} \ln u = \frac{1}{u} \frac{du}{dx}$$

If x is any real number and a is any positive real number, then

$$a^x = e^{x \ln a}$$

From this definition we obtain the following:

a) $\quad \dfrac{d}{dx} a^x = a^x \ln a \quad \text{and} \quad \dfrac{d}{dx} a^u = a^u \ln a \, \dfrac{du}{dx}$

b) $\quad \dfrac{d}{dx} (\log_a x) = \dfrac{1}{x \ln a} \quad \text{and} \quad \dfrac{d}{dx} \log_a |u| = \dfrac{1}{u \ln a} \dfrac{du}{dx}$

Sometimes it is useful to take the logs of a function and then differentiate since the computation becomes easier (as in the case of a product).

Steps in Logarithmic Differentiation

1. $y = f(x)$ given

2. $\ln y = \ln f(x)$ take logs and simplify

3. $D_x(\ln y) = D_x(\ln f(x))$ differentiate implicitly

4. $\dfrac{1}{y} D_x y = D_x(\ln f(x))$

5. $D_x y = f(x) D_x(\ln f(x))$ multiply by $y = f(x)$

To complete the solution it is necessary to differentiate $\ln f(x)$. If $f(x) < 0$ for some x then step 2 is invalid and we should replace step 1 by $|y| = |f(x)|$, and then proceed.

Example:

$$y = (x + 5)(x^4 - 1)$$

$$\ln y = \ln [(x + 5)(x^4 - 1)] = \ln (x + 5) + \ln (x^4 + 1)$$

$$\frac{d}{dx} \ln y = \frac{d}{dx} \ln (x + 5) + \frac{d}{dx} \ln (x^4 + 1)$$

$$\frac{1}{y} \frac{dy}{dx} = \frac{1}{x+5} + \frac{4x^3}{x^4 + 1}$$

$$\frac{dy}{dx} = (x + 5)(x^4 + 1) \left[\frac{1}{x+5} + \frac{4x^3}{x^4 + 1} \right]$$

$$= (x^4 + 1) + 4x^3(x + 5)$$

This is the same result as obtained by using the product rule.

The Mean Value Theorem

If f is continuous on $[a, b]$ and has a derivative at every point in the interval (a, b), then there is at least one number c in (a, b) such that

$$f'(c) = \frac{f(b) - f(a)}{b - a}$$

Notice in Figure 17 that the secant has slope

$$\frac{f(b) - f(a)}{b - a}$$

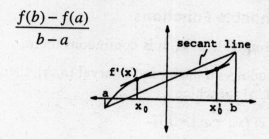

FIGURE 17

and $f'(x)$ has slope of the tangent to the point $(x, f(x))$. For some x_0 in (a, b) these slopes are equal.

Example:

If $f(x) = 3x^2 - x + 1$, find the point x_0 at which $f'(x)$ assumes its mean value in the interval $[2, 4]$.

Recall the mean value theorem. Given a function $f(x)$ which is continuous in $[a, b]$ and differentiable in (a, b), there exists a point x_0 where $a < x_0 < b$ such that:

$$\frac{f(b) - f(a)}{b - a} = f'(x_0),$$

where x_0 is the mean point in the interval.

In our problem, $3x^2 - x + 1$ is continuous, and the derivative exists in the interval $(2, 4)$. We have:

$$\frac{f(4) - f(2)}{4 - 2} = \frac{\left[3(4)^2 - 4 + 1\right] - \left[3(2)^2 - 2 + 1\right]}{4 - 2}$$

$$= f'(x_0),$$

or

$$\frac{45 - 11}{2} = 17 = f'(x_0) = 6x_0 - 1$$

$$6x_0 = 18$$

$$x_0 = 3 .$$

$x_0 = 3$ is the point where $f'(x)$ assumes its mean value.

Theorems of Differentiable Functions

A) If $f(x)$ is differentiable at x_0, it is continuous there.

B) If $f(x)$ is continuous on the closed interval $[a, b]$, then there is a point $x' \in [a, b]$ for which

$$f(x') < f(x) \ (x : x \in [a, b])$$

C) If $f(x)$ is continuous on the closed interval $[a, b]$, then there is a point x_0 in $[a, b]$ for which

$$f(x_0) \geq f(x) \ (x : x \in [a, b])$$

D) If $f(x)$ is an increasing function on an interval, then at each point x_0, where x is differentiable we have

$$f'(x_0) \geq 0$$

E) If $f(x)$ is strictly increasing on an interval, and suppose also that $f'(x_0) > 0$ for some x_0 in the interval, then the inverse function $f^{-1}(x)$ if it exists, is differentiable at the point $y_0 = f(x_0)$.

F) If $f(x)$ is differentiable on the interval $[a, b]$, and $g(x)$ is a differentiable function in the range of f, then the composed function $h = g \circ f \ (h(x) = g[f(x)])$ is also differentiable on $[a, b]$.

G) Suppose that $f(x)$, $g(x)$ are differentiable on the interval $[a, b]$ and that $f'(x) = g'(x)$ for all $x \in [a, b]$, then there is a constant c such that $f(x) = g(x) + C$.

H) Rolle's Theorem

   If $f(x)$ is continuous on $[a, b]$, differentiable on (a, b), and $f(a) = f(b) = 0$, then there is a point δ in (a, b) such that $f'(\delta) = 0$.

I) Mean Value Theorem

   a) f is continuous on $[a, b]$

   b) f is differentiable on (a, b) then there exists some point $\delta \in (a, b)$, such that

$$f'(\delta) = \frac{f(b) - f(a)}{b - a}.$$

L'Hôpital's Rule

An application of the Mean Value Theorem is in the evaluation of

$$\lim_{x \to a} \frac{f(x)}{g(x)} \text{ where } f(a) = 0 \text{ and } g(a) = 0.$$

L'Hôpital's Rule states that if the

$$\lim_{x \to a} \frac{f(x)}{g(x)}$$

is an indeterminate form (i.e., $\frac{0}{0}$ or $\frac{\infty}{\infty}$), then we can differentiate the numerator and the denominator separately and arrive at an expression that has the same limit as the original problem.

Thus,

$$\lim_{x \to a} \frac{f(x)}{g(x)} = \lim_{x \to a} \frac{f'(x)}{g'(x)}$$

In general, if $f(x)$ and $g(x)$ have properties

1) $f(a) = g(a) = 0$
2) $f^{(k)}(a) = g^{(k)}(a) = 0$ for $k = 1, 2, \ldots n$; but
3) $f^{(n + 1)}(a)$ or $g^{(n + 1)}(a)$ is not equal to zero, then

$$\lim_{x \to a} \frac{f(x)}{g(x)} = \lim_{x \to a} \frac{f^{(n+1)}(x)}{g^{(n+1)}(x)}$$

B. Application of the Derivative

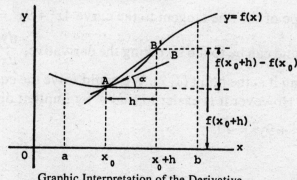

Graphic Interpretation of the Derivative
FIGURE 18

29

Graphically the derivative represents the slope of the tangent line *AB* to the function at the point $(x_0, f(x_0))$.

Tangents and Normals

Tangents

A line which is tangent to a curve at a point "*a*", must have the same slope as the curve. That is, the slope of the tangent is simply

$$m = \lim_{h \to 0} \frac{f(a+h) - f(a)}{h}$$

Therefore, if we find the derivative of a curve and evaluate for a specific point, we obtain the slope of the curve and the tangent line to the curve at that point.

A curve is said to have a vertical tangent at a point $(a, f(a))$ if f is continuous at a and

$$\lim_{x \to a} |f'(x)| = \infty .$$

Normals

A line normal to a curve at a point must have a slope perpendicular to the slope of the tangent line. If $f'(x) \neq 0$ then the equation for the normal line at a point (x_0, y_0) is

$$y - y_0 = \frac{-1}{f'(x_0)} (x - x_0).$$

Example:

Find the slope of the tangent line to the ellipse $4x^2 + 9y^2 = 40$ at the point $(1, 2)$.

The slope of the line tangent to the curve $4x^2 + 9y^2 = 40$ is the slope of the curve and can be found by taking the derivative, $\dfrac{dy}{dx}$ of the function and evaluating it at the point $(1, 2)$. We could solve the equation for y and then find y'. However it is easier to find y' by implicit differentiation. If

$$4x^2 + 9y^2 = 40,$$

then

$$8x + 18y(y') = 0.$$

$$18y(y') = -8x$$

$$y' = \frac{-8x}{18y} = \frac{-14x}{9y} \ .$$

At the point $(1, 2)$, $x = 1$ and $y = 2$. Therefore, substituting these points into $y' = \dfrac{4x}{9y}$, we obtain:

$$y' = \frac{-4(1)}{9(2)} = -\frac{2}{9}$$

The slope is $-\dfrac{2}{9}$.

Minimum and Maximum Values

If a function f is defined at an interval I, then

A) f is increasing on I if $f(x_1) < f(x_2)$ whenever x_1, x_2 are in I and $x_1 < x_2$.

B) f is decreasing on I if $f(x_1) > f(x_2)$ whenever $x_1 < x_2$ in I.

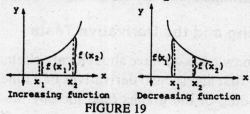

Increasing function   Decreasing function
FIGURE 19

C) f is constant if $f(x_1) = f(x_2)$ for every x_1, x_2 in I.

Suppose f is defined on an open interval I and C is a number in I then,

a) $f(c)$ is a local maximum value if $f(x) \leq f(c)$ for all X in I.

b) $f(c)$ is a local minimum value if $f(x) \geq f(c)$ for all x in I.

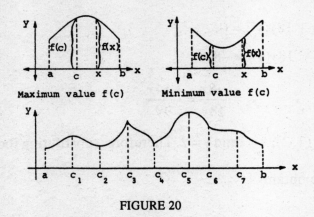

FIGURE 20

Solving Maxima and Minima Problems

Step 1. Determine which variable is to be maximized or minimized (i.e., the dependent variable y).

Step 2. Find the independent variable x.

Step 3. Write an equation involving x and y. All other variables can be eliminated by substitution.

Step 4. Differentiate with respect to the independent variable.

Step 5. Set the derivative equal to zero to obtain critical values.

Step 6. Determine maxima and minima.

Curve Sketching and the Derivative Tests

Using the knowledge we have about local extrema and the following properties of the first and second derivatives of a function, we can gain a better understanding of the graphs (and thereby the nature) of a given function.

A function is said to be smooth on an interval (a, b) if both f' and f'' exist for all $x \in (a, b)$.

The First Derivative Test

Suppose that c is a critical value of a function f, in an interval (a, b), then if f is continuous and differentiable we can say that,

A)   if $f'(x) > 0$ for all $a < x < c$ and $f'(x) < 0$ for all $c < x < b$, then $f(c)$ is a local maximum.

B)   if $f'(x) < 0$ for all $a < x < c$ and $f'(x) > 0$ for all $c < x < b$, then $f(c)$ is a local minimum.

C) if $f'(x) > 0$ or if $f'(x) < 0$ for all $x \in (a, b)$ then $f(c)$ is not a local extrema.

Concavity

If a function is differentiable on an open interval containing c, then the graph at this point is

A) concave upward (or convex) if $f''(c) > 0$;

B) concave downward if $f''(c) < 0$.

If a function is concave upward then f' is increasing as x increases. If the function is concave downward, f' is decreasing as x increases.

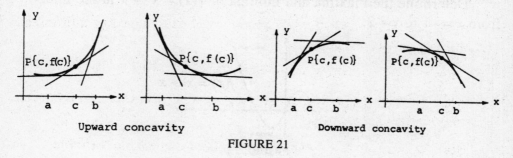

Upward concavity   Downward concavity

FIGURE 21

Points of Inflection

Points which satisfy $f'(x) = 0$ may be positions where concavity changes. These points are called the points of inflection. It is the point at which the curve crosses its tangent line.

Graphing a Function Using the Derivative Tests

The following steps will help us gain a rapid understanding of a function's behavior.

A) Look for some basic properties such as oddness, evenness, periodicity, boundedness, etc.

B) Locate all the zeroes by setting $f(x) = 0$.

C) Determine any singularities, $f(x) = \infty$.

D) Set $f'(x)$ equal to zero to find the critical values.

E) Find the points of inflection by setting $f''(x) = 0$.

F) Determine where the curve is concave, $f'' < 0$, and where it is convex, $f''(x) > 0$.

G) Determine the limiting properties and approximations for large and small |x|.

H) Prepare a table of values x, $f(x)$, $f'(x)$ which includes the critical values and the points of inflection.

I) Plot the points found in Step H and draw short tangent lines at each point.

J) Draw the curve making use of the knowledge of concavity and continuity.

Example:

Determine the maxima and minima of $f(x) = x^3 - x$ in the interval from $x = -1$ to $x = 2$.

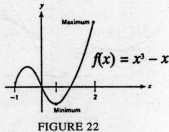

FIGURE 22

To determine the extreme points, we find $f'(x)$, equate it to 0, and solve for x to obtain the critical points. We have:

$$f'(x) = 3x^2 - 1 = 0. \qquad x^2 = \frac{1}{3}.$$

Therefore, critical values are $x = \pm \dfrac{1}{\sqrt{3}}$. Now

$$f\left(\frac{1}{\sqrt{3}}\right) = -\frac{2}{3\sqrt{3}} \quad \text{and} \quad f\left(-\frac{1}{\sqrt{3}}\right) = \frac{2}{3\sqrt{3}}.$$

Evaluating f at the end points of the interval we have $f(-1) = 0$ and $f(2) = 6$. Therefore, $x = 2$, an end point, is the maximum point for f, and $x = \dfrac{1}{\sqrt{3}}$ is the minimum point as can be seen in $[-1, 2]$ are 6 and $-\dfrac{2}{3\sqrt{3}}$.

The point $\left(-\dfrac{1}{\sqrt{3}}, \dfrac{2}{3\sqrt{3}}\right)$ is not an absolute maximum, but it is a relative maximum.

Rectilinear Motion

When an object moves along a straight line we call the motion rectilinear motion. Distance s, velocity v, and acceleration a, are the chief concerns of the study of motion.

Velocity is the proportion of distance over time.

$$v = \frac{s}{t}$$

Average velocity $= \dfrac{f(t_2) - f(t_1)}{t_2 - t_1}$

where t_1, t_2 are time instances and $f(t_2) - f(t_1)$ is the displacement of an object.

Instantaneous velocity at time t is defined as

$$v - D \, s(t) = \lim_{h \to 0} \frac{f(t+h) - f(t)}{h}$$

We usually write

$$v(t) = \frac{ds}{dt} \; .$$

Acceleration, the rate of change of velocity with respect to time is

$$a(t) = \frac{dv}{dt} \; .$$

It follows clearly that

$$a(t) = v'(t) = s''(t) \; .$$

When motion is due to gravitational effects, $g = 33.2$ ft/sec^2 or $g = 9.81$ m/sec^2 is usually substituted for acceleration.

Speed at time t is defined as $|v(t)|$. The speed indicates how fast an object is moving without specifying the direction of motion.

Example:

A particle moves in a straight line according to the law of motion:

$$s = t^3 - 4t^2 - 3t.$$

When the velocity of the particle is zero, what is its acceleration?

The velocity, v, can be found by differentiating this equation of motion with respect to t. Further differentiation gives the acceleration. Hence, the velocity, v, and acceleration, a, are:

$$v = \frac{ds}{dt} = 3t^2 - 8t - 3,$$

$$a = \frac{dv}{dt} = 6t - 8.$$

The velocity is zero when

$$3t^2 - 8t - 3 = (3 + 1)(t - 3) = 0,$$

from which

$$t = -\frac{1}{3} \text{ or } t = 3.$$

The corresponding values of the acceleration are

$$a = -10 \text{ for } t = -\frac{1}{3}, \quad \text{and}$$

$$a = +10 \text{ for } t = 3.$$

Rate of Change and Related Rates

Rate of Change

In the last section we saw how functions of time can be expressed as velocity and acceleration. In general, we can speak about the rate of change of any function with respect to an arbitrary parameter (such as time in the previous section).

For linear functions $f(x) = mx + b$, the rate of change is simply the slope m.

For nonlinear functions we define the

1) average rate of change between points c and d to be (see Figure 23)

$$\frac{f(d) - f(c)}{d - c}$$

2)   instantaneous rate of change of f at the point x to be

$$f'(x) = \lim_{h \to 0} \frac{f(x+h) - f(x)}{h}$$

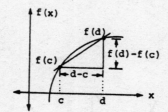

FIGURE 23

If the limit does not exist, then the rate of change of f at x is not defined.

The form, common to all related rate problems, is as follows:

A)   Two variables, x and y, are given. They are functions of time, but the explicit functions are not given.

B)   The variables, x and y, are related to each other by some equation such as $x^2 + y^3 - 2x - 7y^2 + 2 = 0$.

C)   An equation which involves the rate of change $\dfrac{dx}{dt}$ and $\dfrac{dy}{dt}$ is obtained by differentiating with respect to t and using the chain rule.

As an illustration, the previous equation leads to

$$2x\,\frac{dx}{dt} + 3y^2\,\frac{dy}{dt} - 2\,\frac{dx}{dt} - 14y\,\frac{dy}{dt} = 0$$

The derivatives $\dfrac{dx}{dt}$ and $\dfrac{dy}{dt}$ in this equation are called the related rates.

Example:

A point moves on the parabola $6y = x^2$ in such a way that when $x = 6$ the abscissa is increasing at the rate of 2 ft. per second. At what rate is the ordinate increasing at that instant? See Figure 24.

Since

$$6y = x^2,$$

$$6\frac{dy}{dt} = 2x\frac{dx}{dt}, \quad \text{or}$$

$$\frac{dy}{dt} = \frac{x}{3} \times \frac{dx}{dt}. \tag{1}$$

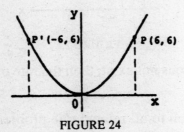

FIGURE 24

This means that, at any point on the parabola, the rate of change of ordinate = $(x/3)$ times the rate of change of abscissa. When $x = 6$, $\frac{dx}{dt} = 2$ ft. per second. Thus, substitution gives:

$$\frac{dy}{dt} = \frac{6}{3} \times 2 = 4 \text{ ft/sec.}$$

Chapter 3

Integral Calculus

A. Antiderivatives

Definition

If $F(x)$ is a function whose derivative $F'(x) = f(x)$, then $F(x)$ is called the antiderivative of $f(x)$.

Theorem:

If $F(x)$ and $G(x)$ are two antiderivatives of $f(x)$, then $F(x) = G(x) + c$, where c is a constant.

Power Rule for Antiderivatives

Let "a" be any real number, "r", any rational number not equal to -1, and "c" an arbitrary constant.

$$\text{If } f(x) = ax^r, \text{ then } F(x) = \frac{1}{r+1}x^{r+1} + c.$$

Theorem:

An antiderivative of a sum is the sum of the antiderivatives.

$$\frac{d}{dx}(F_1 + F_2) = \frac{d}{dx}(F_1) + \frac{d}{dx}(F_2) = f_1 + f_2$$

B. Application of Antiderivatives $y = y_0 e^{Kt}$: The Law of Exponential Change.

Example:

In the course of any given year, the number y of cases of a disease is reduced by 10%. If there are 10,000 cases, today, about how many years will it take to reduce the number of cases to less than 1,000?

$$y = y_0 e^{Kt}$$

$y_0 = 10,000$, so $y = 10,000e^{Kt}$. When $t = 1$, there are 10% fewer cases or 9,000 cases remaining so

$$9,000 = 10,000\, e^K$$

$$e^K = 0.9 \quad \text{therefore,} \quad K = \ln 0.9$$

Then $\quad 1,000 = 10,000e^{(\ln 0.9)t} \Rightarrow$

$$0.1 = e^{(\ln 0.9)t} \Rightarrow \ln 0.1 = \ln 0.9t$$

So $\quad\quad t = \dfrac{\ln 0.1}{\ln 0.9} \approx 21.9 \text{ years}$

Another application of the antiderivative involves its use with velocity. The following problem illustrates this.

Example:

A body falls under the influence of gravity (gx 32 ft./sec^2) so that its speed is $v = 32t$. Determine the distance it falls in 3 sec. Let $x = $ distance.

$$v = f(t) = 32t$$

The velocity is dependent on time because of the following general relationship:

$$v = gt + v_i$$

where v increases indefinitely as time goes on — neglecting air resistance and some other factors. The initial velocity v_i is zero in this case because the body starts from rest.

Assuming the distance covered is dx in time t, we can represent the velocity in a differential form:

$$\frac{dx}{dt} = v = 32t.$$

Integrating to find the relationship between x and t yields:

$$\int dx = \int 32t \, dt \, .$$

$$x = \frac{32t^2}{2} + C \, .$$

$x = 0$ when $t = 0$. Therefore,

$$0 = 16(0)^2 + C, C = 0.$$

$$x = 16t^2.$$

The distance the body falls from the reference point,

$$x = 16t^2 = 16(3)^2 = 144 \text{ ft.}$$

C. Techniques of Integration

Table of Integrals

$$\int \alpha \, dx = \alpha x + C.$$

$$\int x^n dx = \frac{1}{n+1} x^{n+1} + C, n \neq 1.$$

$$\int \frac{dx}{x} = \ln |x| + C.$$

$$\int e^x dx = e^x + C.$$

$$\int p^x dx = \frac{p^x}{\ln p} + C.$$

$$\int \ln x \, dx = x \ln x - x + C.$$

$$\int \cos x \, dx = \sin x + C.$$

$$\int \sin x \, dx = -\cos x + C.$$

$$\int \sec^2 x \, dx = \tan x + C.$$

$$\int \sec x \, \tan x \, dx = \sec x + C.$$

$$\int \tan x \, dx = \ln |\sec x| + C.$$

$$\int \cot x \, dx = \ln |\sin x| + C.$$

$$\int \sec x \, dx = \ln |\sec x + \tan x| + C.$$

$$\int \csc x \, dx = \ln |\csc x - \cot x| + C.$$

When integrating trigonometric functions, the power rule is often involved. Before applying the fundamental integration formulas, it also may be necessary to simplify the function. For that purpose, the common trigonometric identities are most often applicable as, for example, the half-angle formulas and the double-angle formulas. Again, no general rule can be given for finding the solutions. It takes a combination of experience and trial-and-error to learn what to substitute to arrive at the best solution method.

Example:

Integrate:

$$\int \cos x \, e^{2 \sin x} dx.$$

This problem is best solved by the method of substitution. We let $u = 2 \sin x$. Then $du = 2 \cos x \, dx$. Substituting, we obtain:

$$\int \cos x \, e^{2\sin x} dx = \frac{1}{2} \int e^{2\sin x} \, (2 \cos x \, dx)$$

$$= \frac{1}{2} \int e^u du = \frac{1}{2} e^u + C$$

$$= \frac{1}{2} \int e^{2\sin x} + C.$$

Integration by Parts

Differential of a production is represented by the formula

$$d(uv) = u \, dv + v \, du.$$

Integration of both sides of this equation gives

$$uv = \int u \, dv + \int v \, du \qquad (1)$$

$$\int u \, dv = uv - \int v \, du \qquad (2)$$

Equation (2) is the formula for integration by parts.

Example:

Evaluate $\int x \ln x \, dx$

Let

$$u = \ln x \qquad\qquad dv = xdx$$

$$du = \frac{1}{x}dx \qquad\qquad v = \frac{1}{2}x^2$$

Thus,

$$\int x \ln x \, dx = \frac{1}{2}x^2 \ln x - \int \frac{1}{2}x^2 \; \frac{1}{x}dx$$

$$= \frac{1}{2}x^2 \ln x - \frac{1}{2}\int x \, dx$$

$$= \frac{1}{2}x^2 \ln x - \frac{1}{4}x^2 + c$$

Integration by parts may be used to evaluate definite integrals. The formula is:

$$\int_a^b u \, dv = [uv]_a^b - \int_a^b v \, du$$

Example:

Integrate: $\int x \cdot \cos x \cdot dx$.

In this case we use integration by parts, the rule for which states:

$$\int u \, dv = uv - \int v \, du.$$

Let $u = x$ and $dv = \cos x \, dx$. Then $du = dx$ and

$$v = \int \cos x \cdot dx = \sin x.$$

$$\int u \cdot dv = uv - \int v \cdot du$$

becomes $\int x \cdot \cos x \cdot dx = x \cdot \sin x - \int \sin x \cdot dx.$

To integrate $\int \sin x \, dx$ we use the formula, $\int \sin u \, du = -\cos u + C.$ This gives:

$$\int x \cdot \cos x \cdot dx = x \sin x - (-\cos x) + C$$

$$= x \sin x + \cos x + C.$$

Trigonometric Substitution

If the integral contains expressions of the form

$$\sqrt{a^2 - x^2}, \quad \sqrt{a^2 + x^2} \quad \text{or} \quad \sqrt{x^2 - a^2},$$

where $a > 0$, it is possible to transform the integral into another form by means of trigonometric substitution.

General Rules for Trigonometric Substitutions

1. Make appropriate substitutions.

2. Sketch a right triangle.

3. Label the sides of the triangle by using the substituted information.

4. The length of the third side is obtained by use of the Pythagorean Theorem.

5. Utilize sketch, in order to make further substitutions.

   A. If the integral contains the expression of the form $\sqrt{a^2 - x^2}$, make the substitution $x = a \sin \theta$.

   $$\sqrt{a^2 - x^2} = \sqrt{a^2 - a^2 \sin^2 \theta} = \sqrt{a^2 - (1 - \sin^2 \theta)}$$

   $$= \sqrt{a^2 \cos^2 \theta} = a \cos \theta.$$

   In trigonometric substitution the range of θ is restricted.

   For example, in the sine substitution the range of $\theta = -\dfrac{\pi}{2} \leq$

$\theta \le \dfrac{\pi}{2}$. The sketch of this substitution is shown in Figure 25.

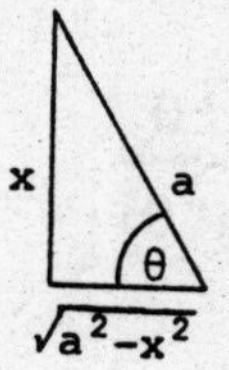

$x = a \sin \theta$, thus $\sin \theta = \dfrac{x}{a}$

FIGURE 25

B. If the integral contains the expression of the form $\sqrt{x^2 - a^2}$, make the substitution $x = a \sec \theta$. The sketch is shown in Figure 26.

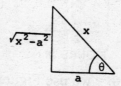

$x = a \sec \theta$
FIGURE 26

C. If the integral contains the expression of the form $\sqrt{a^2 + x^2}$, make the substitution $x = a \tan \theta$. The sketch is shown in Figure 27.

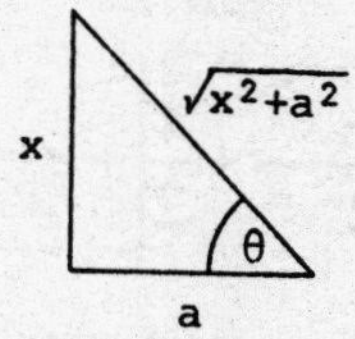

$x = a \tan \theta$
FIGURE 27

Example:

Evaluate $\displaystyle\int \dfrac{dx}{\sqrt{4 + x^2}}$

Let $x = 2 \tan \theta;$ $dx = 2 \sec^2 \theta \, d\theta$

Thus, $$\int \frac{dx}{\sqrt{4+x^2}} = \int \frac{2\sec^2\theta\, d\theta}{\sqrt{4+(2\tan\theta)^2}}$$

$$= \int \frac{2\sec^2\theta\, d\theta}{\sqrt{4(1+\tan^2\theta)}}$$

$$= \int \frac{2\sec^2\theta\, d\theta}{2\sqrt{\sec^2\theta}}$$

$$= \int \sec\theta\, d\theta$$

$$= \ln|\sec\theta + \tan\theta| + c.$$

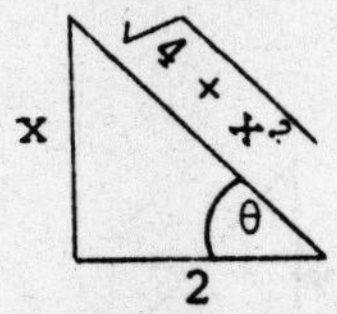

FIGURE 28

To convert from θ back to x we use Figure 28 to find:

$$\sec\theta = \frac{\sqrt{4+x^2}}{2} \quad \text{and} \quad \tan\theta = \frac{x}{2}.$$

Therefore,

$$\int \frac{dx}{\sqrt{4+x^2}} = \ln\left|\frac{\sqrt{4+x^2}}{2} + \frac{x}{2}\right| + c.$$

Summary of Trigonometric Substitutions

Given Expression	Trigonmetric Substitution
$\sqrt{x^2 - a^2}$	$x = a\sec\theta$
$\sqrt{x^2 + a^2}$	$x = a\tan\theta$
$\sqrt{a^2 - x^2}$	$x = a\sin\theta$

D. The Definite Integral

Area

To find the area under a graph of a function f from a to b, we divide the interval $[a, b]$ into n subintervals, all having the same length $\dfrac{b-a}{n}$. This is illustrated in the following figure.

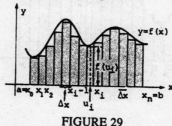

FIGURE 29

Since f is continuous on each subinterval, f takes on a minimum value at some number u_i in each subinterval.

We can construct a rectangle with one side of length $[x_{i-1}, x_i]$, and the other side of length equal to the minimum distance $f(u_i)$ from the x-axis to the graph of f.

The area of this rectangle is $f(u_i) \Delta x$. The boundary of the region formed by the sum of these rectangles is called the inscribed rectangular polygon.

The area (A) under the graph of f from a to b is

$$A = \lim_{x \to 0} \sum_{i=1}^{n} f(u_i)\Delta x \ .$$

The area A under the graph may also be obtained by means of circumscribed rectangular polygons.

In the case of the circumscribed rectangular polygons the maximum value of f on the interval $[x_{i-1}, x_i]$, v_i, is used.

Note that the area obtained using circumscribed rectangular polygons should always be larger than that obtained using inscribed rectangular polygons.

Definition of Definite Integral

Definition:

Let f be a function that is defined on a closed interval $[a, b]$. A Riemann Sum of f for P is any expression R_p of the form,

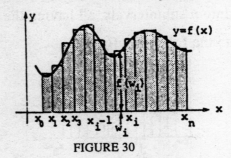

FIGURE 30

$$R_p = \sum_{i=1}^{n} f(w_i)\Delta x_i,$$

where w_i is some number in $[x_{i-1}, x_i]$, for $i = 1, 2, ..., n$.

Definition:

Let f be a function that is defined on a closed interval $[a, b]$. The definite integral of f from a to b, denoted by

$$\int_a^b f(x)\, dx$$

is given by

$$\int_a^b f(x)\, dx = \lim_{P \to 0} \sum_i f(w_i)\Delta x_i,$$

provided the limit exists.

Theorem:

If f is continuous on $[a, b]$, then f is integrable on $[a, b]$.

Theorem:

If $f(a)$ exists, then

$$\int_a^a f(x)\, dx = 0.$$

Properties of the Definite Integral

A) If f is integrable on $[a, b]$ and k is any real number, then kf is integrable on $[a, b]$ and

$$\int_a^b kf(x)\, dx = k \int_a^b f(x)\, dx\,.$$

B) If f and g are integrable on $[a, b]$, then $f + g$ is integrable on $[a, b]$ and

$$\int_a^b [f(x) + g(x)]\, dx = \int_a^b f(x)\, dx + \int_a^b g(x)\, dx.$$

C) If $a < c < b$ and f is integrable on both $[a, c]$ and $[c, b]$ then f is integrable on $[a, b]$ and

$$\int_a^b f(x)\, dx = \int_a^c f(x)\, dx + \int_c^b f(x)\, dx.$$

D) If f is integrable on a closed interval and if a, b, and c are any three numbers on the interval, then

$$\int_a^b f(x)\, dx = \int_a^c f(x)\, dx + \int_c^b f(x)\, dx.$$

E) If f is integrable on $[a, b]$ and if $f(x) \geq 0$ for all x in $[a, b]$, then

$$\int_a^b f(x)\, dx \geq 0.$$

The Fundamental Theorem of Calculus

The fundamental theorem of calculus establishes the relationship between the indefinite integrals and differentiation by use of the mean value theorem.

Mean Value Theorem for Integrals

If f is continuous on a closed interval $[a, b]$, then there is some number P in the open interval (a, b) such that

$$\int_a^b f(x)\, dx = f(P)\, (b - a)$$

To find $f(P)$ we divide both sides of the equation by $(b - a)$ obtaining

$$f(P) = \frac{1}{b-a} \int_a^b f(x)\, dx.$$

Definition of the Fundamental Theorem

Suppose f is continuous on a closed interval $[a, b]$, then

a) If the function G is defined by:

$$G(x) = \int_a^x f(t)\, dt,$$

for all x in $[a, b]$, then G is an antiderivative of f on $[a, b]$.

b) If F is any antiderivative of f, then

$$\int_a^b f(x)\, dx = F(b) - F(a)$$

E. Applications of the Integral

Area

If f and g are two continuous functions on the closed interval $[a, b]$, then the area of the region bounded by the graphs of these two functions and the ordinates $x = a$ and $x = b$ is

$$A = \int_a^b [f(x) - g(x)]\, dx\,.$$

where $\quad f(x) \geq 0 \quad$ and $\quad f(x) \geq g(x)$

$\qquad a \leq x \leq b$

This formula applies whether the curves are above or below the x-axis.

The area below $f(x)$ and above the x-axis is represented by

$$\int_a^b f(x)$$

The area between $g(x)$ and the x-axis is represented by $\int g(x)$.

Example:

Find the area of the region bounded by the curves

$$y = x^2 \quad \text{and} \quad y = \sqrt{x}\,.$$

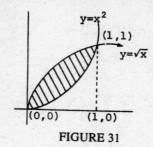

FIGURE 31

$$\text{Area} = A = \int_0^1 \left(\sqrt{x} - x^2\right) dx$$

$$= \int_0^1 \sqrt{x}\, dx = \int_0^1 x^2\, dx$$

$$= \left[\frac{2}{3}x^{\frac{3}{2}} - \frac{1}{3}x^3\right]_0^1 = \left[\frac{2}{3} - \frac{1}{3}\right] = \frac{1}{3}$$

Volume of a Solid of Revolution

If a region is revolved about a line, a solid called a solid of revolution is formed. The solid is generated by the region. The axis of revolution is the line about which the revolution takes place.

There are several methods by which we may obtain the volume of a solid of revolution. We shall now discuss three such methods.

Disk Method

The volume of a solid generated by the revolution of a region about the x-axis is given by the formula

$$V = \pi \int_a^b [f(x)]^2\, dx,$$

provided that f is a continuous, nonnegative function on the interval $[a, b]$.

Shell Method

This method applies to cylindrical shells exemplified by

FIGURE 32

The volume of a cylindrical shell is

$$V = \pi r_2^2 h - \pi r_1^2 h$$

$$= \pi (r_2 + r_1)(r_2 - r_1) h$$

$$= 2 \pi \left(\frac{r_2 + r_1}{2} \right)(r_2 - r_1) h$$

where r_1 = inner radius

   r_2 = outer radius

   h = height

Let $r = \dfrac{r_2 + r_1}{2}$ and $\Delta r = r_2 - r_1$, then the volume of the shell becomes

$$V = 2\pi r h \Delta r$$

The thickness of the shell is represented by Δr and the average radius of the shell by r.

Thus,

$$V = 2\pi \int_a^b x f(x)\, dx$$

is the volume of a solid generated by revolving a region about the y-axis. This is illustrated by Figure 33.

FIGURE 33

Parallel Cross Sections

A cross section of a solid is a region formed by the intersection of a solid by a plane. This is illustrated by Figure 34.

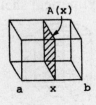

FIGURE 34

If x is a continuous function on the interval $[a, b]$, then the volume of the cross sectional area $A(x)$ is

$$V = \int_a^b A(x)\ dx.$$

Area of Surface of Revolution

A surface of revolution is generated when a plane is revolved about a line.

If f' and g' are two continuous functions on the interval $[a, b]$ where $g(t) = 0$, $x = f(t)$, and $y = g(t)$ then, the surface area of a plane revolved about the x-axis is given by the formula

$$S = \int_a^b 2\pi g(t)\ \sqrt{[f'(t)]^2 + [g'(t)]^2}\ dt$$

Since $x = f(t)$ and $y = g(t)$,

$$S = \int_a^b 2\pi y\ \sqrt{\left(\frac{dx}{dt}\right)^2 + \left(\frac{dy}{dt}\right)^2}\ dt$$

If the plane is revolved about the y-axis, then the surface area is

$$S = \int_a^b 2\pi x\ \sqrt{\left(\frac{dx}{dt}\right)^2 + \left(\frac{dy}{dt}\right)^2}\ dt$$

These formulas can be simplified to give the following:

$$S = 2\pi y \int_a^b ds$$

for revolution about the x-axis, and

$$S = 2\pi x \int_a^b ds$$

for revolution about the y-axis.

In the above equations, ds is given as $ds = \sqrt{1 + f'(x)^2}\ dx$.

Advanced Placement Examination in Calculus AB

EXAM I

ADVANCED PLACEMENT
CALCULUS AB
EXAM I

SECTION I

PART A

Time: 55 minutes
28 questions

DIRECTIONS: Each of the following problems is followed by five choices. Solve each problem, select the best choice, and blacken the correct space on your answer sheet. Calculators may not be used for this section of the exam.

NOTE: Unless otherwise specified, the domain of function f is assumed to be the set of all real numbers x for which $f(x)$ is a real number.

1. $\int_{-2}^{-1} \sqrt{2}\, x^{-2} dx$ is approximately

   (A) −0.707

   (B) 0.619

   (C) 2.475

   (D) −2.475

   (E) 0.707

2. If $f(x) = \pi^2$, then $f'(1) =$

   (A) 2π

   (B) 0

   (C) π

   (D) 1

   (E) π^2

3. If $y = \dfrac{1}{3\sqrt{e^x}}$, then $y'(1)$ is approximately

   (A) 0.239   (D) –0.088

   (B) 2.150   (E) 0.171

   (C) –0.239

4. $\displaystyle \lim_{h \to 0} \frac{\sin(\pi + h) - \sin \pi}{h}$

   (A) 1   (D) $+ \infty$

   (B) 0   (E) $- \infty$

   (C) –1

5. The slope of the line tangent to the curve $y^3 + x^2y^2 - 3x^3 = 9$ at $(1, 2)$ is approximately

   (A) 0.0625   (D) –2.29

   (B) 3.2   (E) –3.2

   (C) –11.45

6. If $f'(x) = \sin x$ and $f(\pi) = 3$, then $f(x) =$

   (A) $\cos x + 4$ (D) $\cos x + 3$

   (B) $-\cos x + 2$ (E) $-\cos x - 2$

   (C) $-\cos x + 4$

7. The position of a particle moving along a straight line at any time t is given by $s(t) = 2t^3 - 4t^2 + 2t - 1$. What is the acceleration of the particle when $t = 2$?

   (A) 32   (D) 8

   (B) 16   (E) 0

   (C) 4

8. If $f[g(x)] = \sec(x^3 + 4)$, $f(x) = \sec x^3$, and $g(x)$ is <u>not</u> an integer multiple of $\dfrac{\pi}{2}$, then $g(x) =$

    (A) $\sqrt[3]{x+4}$

    (B) $\sqrt[3]{x-4}$

    (C) $\sqrt[3]{x^3+4}$

    (D) $\sqrt[3]{x} - 4$

    (E) $\sqrt[3]{x} + 4$

9. The horizontal asymptotes of $f(x) = \dfrac{1 - |x|}{x}$ are given by

    (A) $y = 1$

    (B) $y = -1$

    (C) $x = 0,\, x = 1,\, x = -1$

    (D) $y = 0$

    (E) $y = 1,\, y = -1$

10. The acceleration of a particle moving on a line is $a = t^{-\frac{1}{2}} + 3t^{\frac{1}{2}}$. If the particle was at rest at $t = 0$, then what was its velocity at $t = 9.61$?

    (A) 65.782

    (B) 68.782

    (C) -1

    (D) 1

    (E) 45.782

11. The domain of the function defined by $f(x) = \ln(x^2 - x - 6)$ is the set of all real numbers x such that

    (A) $x > 0$

    (B) $-2 \le x \le 3$

    (C) $-2 \le x$ or $x \ge 3$

    (D) $-2 < x < 3$

    (E) $-2 > x$ or $x > 3$

12. $\int_1^{\sqrt{5}} \frac{\ln(x^2)}{x}\,dx$ is approximately

(A) 1.296

(D) 0.648

(B) 0.420

(E) 0.805

(C) 1

13. If $y = \arccos(\cos^4 x - \sin^4 x)$, then $y'' =$

(A) 2

(D) $-2(\sin x + \cos x)$

(B) 0

(E) -1

(C) $-2(\cos x - \sin x)$

14. If $\dfrac{f(x_1)}{f(x_2)} = f\left(\dfrac{x_1}{x_2}\right)$ for all real numbers x_1 and x_2, (except those for which $x_2 \neq 0$ and $f(x_2) \neq 0$), which of the following could define f?

(A) $f(x) = \dfrac{1}{x}$

(D) $f(x) = \ln x$

(B) $f(x) = x^2 + 3$

(E) $f(x) = e^x$

(C) $f(x) = x + 1$

15. $\dfrac{\ln(x^3 e^x)}{x} =$

(A) $\dfrac{3(\ln x + e^x)}{x}$

(D) $\dfrac{3\ln x + x}{x}$

(B) $\ln(x^3 e^x - x)$

(E) $\dfrac{3\ln x}{x}$

(C) $\ln x^2 + 1$

16. $\lim\limits_{x \to 1} \dfrac{\dfrac{1}{x+1} - \dfrac{1}{2}}{x-1} =$

(A) $-\dfrac{1}{4}$

(D) 0

(B) -1

(E) does not exist

(C) $\dfrac{1}{4}$

17. If $\dfrac{r^2}{r-1} \geq r$, then

(A) $r \geq 0$

(D) $r \leq 0$ or $r \geq 1$

(B) $r \leq 0$

(E) $0 \leq r < 1$

(C) $r \leq 0$ or $r > 1$

18. If $f'(c) = 0$ for $f(x) = 3x^2 - 12x + 9$, where $0 \leq x \leq 4$, then $c =$

(A) 2

(D) 1

(B) 3

(E) $\dfrac{1}{3}$

(C) 0

19. $\lim\limits_{x \to 9} \dfrac{x-9}{3-\sqrt{x}} =$

(A) 6

(D) -12

(B) -6

(E) $+\infty$

(C) 0

20. $\int \left(x - \frac{1}{x}\right)^2 dx =$

(A) $\frac{1}{3}\left(x - \frac{1}{x}\right)^3 + C$

(D) $\frac{1}{3}x^3 - 2x - \frac{1}{x} + C$

(B) $\frac{1}{3}\left(x - \frac{1}{x}\right)^3 \left(1 + \frac{1}{x^2}\right) + C$

(E) $\frac{1}{3}(1 - \ln x)^3 + C$

(C) $\frac{1}{3}x^3 - 2x - \frac{1}{x^2} + C$

21. If $e^{g(x)} = \frac{x^x}{x^2 - 1}$, then $g(x) =$

(A) $x \ln x - 2x$

(D) $\frac{x \ln x}{\ln(x^2 - 1)}$

(B) $\frac{\ln x}{2}$

(E) $x \ln x - \ln (x^2 - 1)$

(C) $(x - 2) \ln x$

22. If $h(x) = \frac{x^2 + 1}{x^2}$ where $x > 1$, then $h^{-1} (x) =$

(A) $\frac{1}{\sqrt{x - 1}}$

(D) $\frac{1}{\sqrt{x - 1} + 1}$

(B) $\sqrt{\frac{x}{1 + 2x}}$

(E) $\frac{1}{-\sqrt{x - 1}}$

(C) $\frac{-1}{\sqrt{x}}$

23. If $f(x) = \begin{cases} \dfrac{2x-6}{x-3} & x \neq 3 \\ 5 & x = 3 \end{cases}$, then $\lim\limits_{x \to 3} f(x) =$

    (A) 5

    (B) 1

    (C) 2

    (D) 6

    (E) 0

24. If $f(x) = \dfrac{\sqrt{x+2}}{x+2}$ and $g(x) = \dfrac{1}{x} - 2$, then $f[g(x)] =$

    (A) $\dfrac{\sqrt{\dfrac{1}{x} - 2}}{\dfrac{1}{x} - 2}$

    (B) $\sqrt{\dfrac{1-2x}{x}}$

    (C) $\dfrac{\sqrt{\dfrac{1}{x-2} + 2}}{\dfrac{1}{x-2} + 2}$

    (D) $\sqrt{x}$

    (E) $\dfrac{\sqrt{x}}{x}$

25. If $\tan x = 2$, then $\sin 2x =$

    (A) $\dfrac{2}{5}$

    (B) $\dfrac{4\sqrt{5}}{5}$

    (C) $\dfrac{4}{5}$

    (D) $\dfrac{4}{3}$

    (E) $\dfrac{2}{3}$

26. Let $f(x) = x^3$. Find the value of x_1 that satisfies the Mean Value Theorem on the closed interval $[1, 3]$.

    (A) 1.414   (D) 2.000

    (B) 1.732   (E) 2.082

    (C) 2.351

27. At what value of x does $f(x) = \dfrac{x^3}{3} - x^2 - 3x + 5$ have a relative minimum?

    (A) -1 only   (D) 3 only

    (B) 0 only   (E) -1 and 3

    (C) $+1$ only

28. Properties of the definite integral are:

    I. $\displaystyle\int_a^b cf(x)\, dx = c\int_a^b f(x)\, dx$

    II. $\displaystyle\int_a^b f(x)\, dx = -\int_b^a f(x)\, dx$

    III. $\displaystyle\int_b^a [f(x) \cdot g(x)]\, dx = \int_a^b f(x)\, dx \cdot \int_a^b g(x)\, dx$

    (A) I only   (D) I, II, and III

    (B) II only   (E) I and II only

    (C) III only

PART B

Time: 50 minutes

17 questions

DIRECTIONS: Calculators may be used for this section of the test. Each of the following problems is followed by five choices. Solve each problem, select the best choice, and blacken the correct space on your answer sheet.

NOTES:

1. Unless otherwise specified, answers can be given in unsimplified form.

2. The domain of function f is assumed to be the set of all real numbers x for which $f(x)$ is a real number.

---

29. If $f(x) = \log_b x$, then $f(bx) =$

    (A) $bf(x)$

    (B) $f(b)\, f(x)$

    (C) $1 + f(x)$

    (D) $x\, f(b)$

    (E) $f(x)$

30. If $f(x) = \begin{cases} x+1 & x \le 1 \\ 3+ax^2 & x > 1 \end{cases}$, then $f(x)$ is continuous for all x if $a = ?$

    (A) 1

    (B) -1

    (C) $\dfrac{1}{2}$

    (D) 0

    (E) -2

31. If $g(x) = \dfrac{-x - f(x)}{f(x)}$, $f(1) = 4$ and $f'(1) = 2$, then $g'(1) =$

    (A) $-\dfrac{1}{2}$

    (B) $\dfrac{11}{8}$

    (C) $\dfrac{3}{16}$

    (D) $\dfrac{1}{8}$

    (E) $-\dfrac{1}{8}$

32. The domain of $f(x) = \sqrt{4 - x^2}$ is

    (A) $-2 \le x \le 2$

    (B) $-2 \le x$ or $x \ge 2$

    (C) $-2 < x$ or $x > 2$

    (D) $-2 < x < 2$

    (E) $x \ge 2$

33. $\displaystyle\int \dfrac{x + e^x}{xe^x}\, dx =$

    (A) $-e^{-x} - \dfrac{1}{x^2} + C$

    (B) $e^{-x} - \ln |x| + C$

    (C) $-e^{-x} + \ln x + C$

    (D) $-\dfrac{1}{e^{2x}} + \ln |x| + C$

    (E) $e^{-x} - \dfrac{1}{x^2} + C$

34. The area enclosed by the graphs of $y = x^2$ and $y = 2x + 3$ is

    (A) $\dfrac{38}{3}$

    (B) $\dfrac{40}{3}$

    (C) $\dfrac{34}{3}$

    (D) $\dfrac{16}{3}$

    (E) $\dfrac{32}{3}$

35. The volume of revolution formed by rotating the region bounded by $y = x^3$, $y = x$, $x = 0$ and $x = 1$ about the x–axis is represented by

(A) $\pi \int_0^1 (x^3 - x)^2 \, dx$

(D) $\pi \int_0^1 (x^2 - x^6) \, dx$

(B) $\pi \int_0^1 (x^6 - x^2) \, dx$

(E) $2\pi \int_0^1 (x^6 - x^2) \, dx$

(C) $2\pi \int_0^1 (x^2 - x^6) \, dx$

36. The vertical asymptote and horizontal asymptote for $f(x) = \dfrac{\sqrt{x}}{x+4}$ are

(A) $x = -4$, $y = 0$

(B) no vertical asymptote, $y = 0$

(C) no vertical or horizontal asymptote

(D) $x = -4$, no horizontal asymptote

(E) $x = -4$, $y = 1$

37. If $f(x) = x^3 - x$, then

(A) $\dfrac{\sqrt{3}}{3} = x$ is a local maximum of f

(B) $\dfrac{\sqrt{3}}{3} = x$ is a local minimum of f

(C) $\sqrt{3} = x$ is a local maximum of f

(D) $\sqrt{3} = x$ is a local minimum of f

(E) $-\sqrt{3} = x$ is a local minimum of f

38. If $\int_a^b f(x)\, dx = 0$, then necessarily

    (A) $f(x) = 0$ (D) $f(-x) = -f(x)$

    (B) $a = b$ (E) None of these

    (C) $f(x) = 0$ or $a = b$

39. $\int_0^2 x^2$ is

    (A) 3.27   (D) 3.02

    (B) 2.83   (E) 1.98

    (C) 4.21

40. The position of a particle moving along a straight line at any time t is given by $S(t) = 2t^3 - 4t^2 + 2t - 1$. The least velocity during the time interval $[0, 2]$ is

    (A) 4.25   (D) −1.5

    (B) 0.5   (E) 3

    (C) −0.67

41. The acceleration of a particle moving on a line is

    $$a(t) = t^{-\frac{1}{2}} + 3t^{\frac{1}{2}}.$$

    Starting from rest, the distance traveled by the particle from $t = 0$ to $t = 3.61$ is approximately

    (A) 632.15   (D) 300.1

    (B) 65.78   (E) 28.95

    (C) 20.21

42. Let $f(x) = 3x^2 - 12x + 7$. If $f(x) = 0$, then x equals

    (A) 1 and 2

    (B) −2.28 and 1

    (C) 3 and 2.5

    (D) 0.71 and 3.28

    (E) 1 and −6

43. Let $f(x) = x^3 - x$. If $f'(-x) = -f'(x)$, find x.

    (A) −1 and 1

    (B) 0 only

    (C) All x

    (D) ± 0.58

    (E) None of these

44. At each point (x, y) on a curve, the slope of the curve is $3x^2 (y - 6)$. If the curve contains the point $(0, 7)$, then its equation is:

    (A) $y = 6e^{x^3}$

    (B) $y = x^3 + 7$

    (C) $y = 6e^{x^3} + 7$

    (D) $y^2 = x^3 + 6$

    (E) $y = e^{x^3} + 6$

45. The coefficient of x^3 in the Taylor series for $f(x) = \ln x$ about $x = 1$ is

    (A) $\dfrac{1}{6}$

    (B) $\dfrac{2}{3}$

    (C) $\dfrac{1}{2}$

    (D) $\dfrac{1}{3}$

    (E) $\dfrac{1}{4}$

SECTION II

Time: 1 hour and 30 minutes
6 problems

DIRECTIONS: Show all your work. Grading is based on the methods used to solve the problem as well as the accuracy of your final answers. Please make sure all procedures are clearly shown. For some problems or parts of problems it will be necessary to use a calculator.

NOTES:
1. Unless otherwise specified, answers can be given in unsimplified form.

2. The domain of function f is assumed to be the set of all real numbers x for which $f(x)$ is a real number.

1. Let f be the function given by $f(x) = 1 + \dfrac{1}{x} + \dfrac{1}{x^2}$.

   (A) Find the x and y intercepts.

   (B) Write an equation for each vertical and each horizontal asymptote for the graph of f.

   (C) Find the intervals on which f is increasing and decreasing.

   (D) Find the maximum and minimum value of f.

2. (A) Find the slope of the line $2x + y - 7 = 0$.

   (B) Find the slope of the tangent line to the semicircle

   $$x^2 + y^2 = 5, \, y \geq 0.$$

   (C) Find the point on this semicircle having the tangent that is perpendicular to the line $2x + y - 7 = 0$ in part (A).

   (D) Find the intercepts of the tangent line in part (C).

3. (A) Let f have the properties described below

$$f''(x) \text{—} \text{—} \text{—} \text{—} \begin{array}{c}\text{Not}\\\text{Defined}\end{array} \text{—} \text{—} \text{—} 0 \text{—} \text{—} \text{—} \text{—} \text{—} \text{—}$$

$$f'(x) \text{—} \text{—} \text{—} \text{—} \begin{array}{c}\text{Not}\\\text{Defined}\end{array} + \quad + \quad + \quad 0 \text{—} \text{—} \text{—} \text{—} \text{—} \text{—}$$

$$\begin{array}{ccc} & 3 & & 5 & & x \end{array}$$

x	0	2	3	4	5	6
$f(x)$	-25	-100	-200	-75	0	-10

$$\lim_{x \to -\infty} f(x) = 0$$

   (A) Find the intervals where f is concave down.

   (B) Find the equation of each vertical tangent line.

   (C) Find each point of inflection of f.

   (D) Sketch the graph of f.

4. Let the graph of $s(t)$, the position function (in feet) of a moving particle, be as given below. Let t be time measured in seconds.

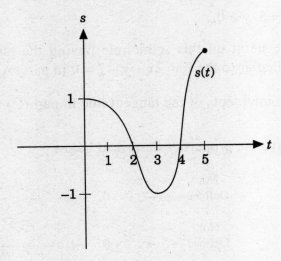

The concavity changes at $t = 2$ and $t = 4$.

(A) Find the values of t for which the particle is moving to the right and when it is moving to the left (i.e., when velocity is positive or negative, respectively).

(B) Find the values of t for which the acceleration is positive and for which it is negative.

(C) Find the values of t for which the particle is speeding up (i.e., when $|v|$ is increasing).

5. Function $f(x) = 2x^2 + x^3$.

(A) Find the local maximum of $f(x)$.

(B) Find the local minimum of $f(x)$.

(C) Evaluate $\int_{-2}^{1} f(x)dx$.

6. A flood light is on the ground 45 meters from a building. A thief 2 meters tall runs from the floodlight directly towards the building at 6 meters/sec. How rapidly is the length of his shadow on the building changing when he is 15 meters from the building?

FIGURE

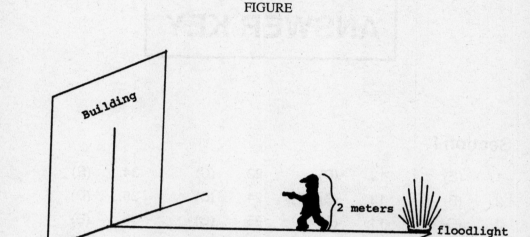

ADVANCED PLACEMENT CALCULUS AB EXAM I

ANSWER KEY

Section I

1.	(E)	12.	(D)	23.	(C)	34.	(E)
2.	(B)	13.	(B)	24.	(D)	35.	(D)
3.	(C)	14.	(A)	25.	(C)	36.	(B)
4.	(C)	15.	(D)	26.	(E)	37.	(B)
5.	(A)	16.	(A)	27.	(D)	38.	(E)
6.	(B)	17.	(C)	28.	(E)	39.	(B)
7.	(B)	18.	(A)	29.	(C)	40.	(C)
8.	(C)	19.	(B)	30.	(B)	41.	(A)
9.	(E)	20.	(D)	31.	(E)	42.	(D)
10.	(A)	21.	(E)	32.	(A)	43.	(E)
11.	(E)	22.	(A)	33.	(C)	44.	(E)
						45.	(D)

Section II

See Detailed Explanations of Answers.

ADVANCED PLACEMENT
CALCULUS AB
EXAM I

DETAILED EXPLANATIONS
OF ANSWERS

$$\boxed{\textbf{SECTION I}}$$

1. **(E)**

$\int_{-2}^{-1} \sqrt{2}\, x^{-2} dx = \sqrt{2} \int_{-2}^{-1} x^{-2} dx$. Since $\int \frac{1}{x^2} dx = -\frac{1}{x}$, we have

$$\sqrt{2}\left[-x^{-1}\right]_{-2}^{-1} = \sqrt{2}\left\{-\left[\frac{1}{(-1)} - \frac{1}{(-2)}\right]\right\}$$

$$= \sqrt{2}\left\{1 - \frac{1}{2}\right\}$$

$$= \frac{\sqrt{2}}{2}$$

$$\approx 0.707\ldots$$

2. **(B)**

$f(x) = \pi^2$. The value of $f(x)$ is constant, therefore its derivative is zero.

3. **(C)**

$$y = (e^x)^{-\frac{1}{3}} = e^{-\frac{x}{3}}$$

$$\therefore \ y' = e^{-\frac{x}{3}}\left(-\frac{1}{3}\right)$$

$$= -\frac{1}{3}e^{-\frac{x}{3}}$$

$$y'(1) = -\frac{1}{3e^{\frac{1}{3}}}$$

Since $3e^{\frac{1}{3}} = (27e)^{\frac{1}{3}} \approx (73)^{\frac{1}{3}} \approx 4, \ \ y'(1)$ must be near $-\frac{1}{4}$.

4. **(C)**

$$\lim_{h\to 0}\frac{\sin(\pi + h) - \sin \pi}{h}$$

This expression is the definition of the derivative of the function sin x, when the derivative is evaluated at $x = \pi$. Since $\dfrac{d(\sin x)}{dx} = \cos x$, and $\cos \pi = -1$, the answer is (C).

5. **(A)**

$$\frac{d}{dx}(y^3 + x^2 y^2 - 3x^3) = \frac{d}{dx}(9)$$

$$3y^2 y' + 2xy^2 + 2yy'x^2 - 9x^2 = 0$$

<u>Note</u>: the product rule must be used when differentiating $x^2 y^2$. Factor y' from the first and third terms.

$$y'(3y^2 + 2yx^2) = 9x^2 - 2xy^2$$

$$y' = \frac{9x^2 - 2xy^2}{3y^2 + 2x^2 y}$$

$\dfrac{dy}{dx}$ at $(1, 2)$ is $\dfrac{9(1)^2 - 2(1)(2)^2}{3(2)^2 + 2(1)^2(2)} = \dfrac{1}{16} = 0.0625$

6. **(B)**

$f(x) = \displaystyle\int f'(x)dx = \int \sin x\, dx = -\cos x + C.$

Since $f(\pi) = 3$ and $\cos \pi = -1$, $C = 2$

Therefore, $f(x) = -\cos x + 2$.

7. **(B)**

$a(t) = s''(t) = \dfrac{d}{dt}(6t^2 - 8t + 2) = 12t - 8$

$a''(2) = 24 - 8 = 16$

8. **(C)**

Let $y = g(x)$, then $f[g(x)] = f(y) = \sec y^3$.

Since $f[g(x)] = \sec(x^3 + 4)$ then $\sec(y^3) = \sec(x^3 + 4)$

$$y^3 = x^3 + 4$$

$$y = g(x) = \sqrt[3]{x^3 + 4}$$

9. **(E)**

For large positive values of x, the function $f(x)$ behaves as

$\displaystyle\lim_{x \to +\infty} \dfrac{1 - |x|}{x} = \lim_{x \to +\infty} \dfrac{1 - x}{x}$

$\qquad = \displaystyle\lim_{x \to +\infty} \dfrac{1}{x} - 1 = -1$

Likewise, as $x \to -\infty$,

$\displaystyle\lim_{x \to -\infty} \dfrac{1 - |x|}{x} = \lim_{x \to -\infty} \dfrac{1 + x}{x}$

$\qquad = \displaystyle\lim_{x \to -\infty} \dfrac{1}{x} + 1 = 1$

The horizontal asymptotes are $y = -1$ and $y = 1$.

10. **(A)**

$$\text{velocity} = \int_0^{9.61} \left(t^{-\frac{1}{2}} + 3t^{\frac{1}{2}} \right) dt$$

$$= \left(2t^{\frac{1}{2}} + 2t^{\frac{3}{2}} \right) \Bigg|_0^{9.61}$$

$$= 2(3.1 - 0) + 2(3.1^3 - 0)$$

$$= 65.782$$

11. **(E)**

The domain is all reals such that $x^2 - x - 6 > 0$

    or $(x - 3)(x + 2) > 0$

    or $x < -2$ or $x > 3$.

12. **(D)**

Since $\ln(x^2) = 2 \ln x$, we have

$$\int_1^{\sqrt{5}} \frac{\ln(x^2)}{x} dx = 2 \int_1^{\sqrt{5}} \frac{\ln x}{x} dx.$$

This integral can be evaluated by using the substitution $u = \ln x$. The integrand becomes u, with $du = \dfrac{dx}{x}$, and the limits of integration change to

$$u(1) = \ln 1 = 0$$

$$u(\sqrt{5}) = \ln(\sqrt{5}) = 0.805. \text{ (You need a calculator here.)}$$

We get

$$\int_0^{0.805} u\, du = u^2 \Big|_0^{0.805}$$

$$= (0.805)^2 - 0 = 0.648$$

13. **(B)**

$y = \arccos(\cos^4 x - \sin^4 x)$

$= \arccos[(\cos^2 x + \sin^2 x)(\cos^2 x - \sin^2 x)]$

$= \arccos[(1)(\cos 2x)]$

$= \arccos[\cos 2x]$

$= 2x + 2\pi m$

$\quad -2x + 2\pi m$

$y' = \pm 2,\ y'' = 0$

14. **(A)**

$$\frac{f(x_1)}{f(x_2)} = \frac{\dfrac{1}{x_1}}{\dfrac{1}{x_2}} = \frac{x_2}{x_1}$$

Likewise $f\left(\dfrac{x_1}{x_2}\right) = \dfrac{1}{\left(\dfrac{x_1}{x_2}\right)} = \dfrac{x_2}{x_1}$.

15. **(D)**

$$\frac{\ln(x^3 e^x)}{x} = \frac{\ln x^3 + \ln e^x}{x} = \frac{3\ln x + x}{x}$$

16. **(A)**

$$\lim_{x \to 1} \frac{\dfrac{1}{x+1} - \dfrac{1}{2}}{x-1}$$

Obtain a common denominator in the main numerator.

$$\lim_{x \to 1} \frac{\dfrac{2-(x+1)}{2(x+1)}}{x-1} = \lim_{x \to 1} \frac{1-x}{2(x+1)(x-1)}$$

$$= \lim_{x \to 1} \frac{-1}{2(x+1)}$$

$$= \frac{-1}{2(1+1)} = -\frac{1}{4}$$

Note: $\dfrac{1-x}{x-1} = -1$ for $x \neq 1$

17. **(C)**

$\dfrac{r^2}{r-1} \geq r$ is equivalent to

$\dfrac{r^2}{(r-1)} - r \geq 0$. The lefthand side can be rewritten as

$$\frac{r^2 - r(r-1)}{r-1} = \frac{r}{(r-1)} = \frac{r(r-1)}{(r-1)^2}$$

Express r with a denominator of $r - 1$.

Thus the original problem is the same as $\left\{ \dfrac{r(r-1)}{(r-1)^2} \right\} \geq 0$

Then $r = 0$ when the numerator and denominator are both positive or both negative.

Three cases:

1. $\{ \ \} = 0$. Then $r = 0$ or $r = 1$. However, the lefthand side is undefined for $r = 1$, therefore $r = 0$.

2. r and $r - 1$ are both positive, therefore $r > 1$.

3. r and $r - 1$ are both negative, therefore $r < 0$, therefore $\{ \ \} \geq 0$ for $r \leq 0$ or $r > 1$.

18. **(A)**

$$f'(x) = 6x - 12$$

$$f'(c) = 0$$

$$6c - 12 = 0$$

$$c = 2$$

19. **(B)**

$$\lim_{x \to 9} \frac{x-9}{3-\sqrt{x}}$$

Rationalize the denominator by multiplying by $\dfrac{3+\sqrt{x}}{3+\sqrt{x}}$

$$= \lim_{x \to 9} \frac{(x-9)(3+\sqrt{x})}{(3-\sqrt{x})(3+\sqrt{x})}$$

$$= \lim_{x \to 9} \frac{(x-9)(3+\sqrt{x})}{9-x}$$

$$\text{Note: } \frac{x-9}{9-x} = -1 \text{ for } x \neq 9$$

$$= \lim_{x \to 9} -\left(3+\sqrt{x}\right)$$

$$= -6$$

20. **(D)**

$$\int \left(x - \frac{1}{x}\right)^2 dx = \int \left(x^2 - 2x\frac{1}{x} + \frac{1}{x^2}\, dx\right)$$

$$\int \left(x^2 - 2 + x^{-2}\right) dx = \frac{1}{3}x^3 - 2x - \frac{1}{x} + C$$

21. **(E)**

$$e^{g(x)} = \frac{x^x}{x^2 - 1} \text{ Take the natural logarithm of both sides.}$$

$$\ln e^{g(x)} = \ln\left(\frac{x^x}{x^2 - 1}\right)$$

$$g(x) = \ln x^x - \ln\left(x^2 - 1\right)$$

$$= x \ln x - \ln\left(x^2 - 1\right)$$

22. **(A)**

Suppose $y = h(x)$. If we can solve for x as a function of y, i.e., find $x = g(y)$, then the function $g(x)$ is the inverse function of h, that is $g = h^{-1}$.

Starting with $y = \dfrac{x^2 + 1}{x^2} = 1 + \dfrac{1}{x^2}$, we have $x^2 = \dfrac{1}{y-1}$. Since $x > 1$, we take

the positive square root to get $x = \dfrac{1}{\sqrt{y-1}}$, therefore, $x - g(y) = \dfrac{1}{\sqrt{y-1}}$.

Finally, $h^{-1}(x) = g(x) = \dfrac{1}{\sqrt{x-1}}$.

23. **(C)**

$$\lim_{x \to 3} f(x) = \lim_{x \to 3} \frac{2x - 6}{x - 3} = \lim_{x \to 3} \frac{2(x - 3)}{x - 3} = 2$$

24. **(D)**

$$f[g(x)] = f\left(\frac{1}{x} - 2\right) = \frac{\sqrt{\left(\frac{1}{x} - 2\right) + 2}}{\left(\frac{1}{x} - 2\right) + 2}$$

$$= \frac{\sqrt{\frac{1}{x}}}{\frac{1}{x}} = \frac{\frac{1}{\sqrt{x}}}{\frac{1}{x}} = \frac{1}{\sqrt{x}} \times \frac{x}{1}$$

Rationalize the denominator

$$= \frac{x}{\sqrt{x}} \times \frac{\sqrt{x}}{\sqrt{x}}$$

$$= \sqrt{x}$$

25. **(C)**

If $\tan x = 2 = \frac{2}{1}$, we have the following diagram. The hypotenuse is $C = \sqrt{1^2 + 2^2} = \sqrt{5}$.

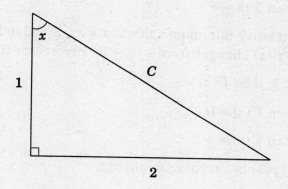

$$\sin 2x = 2 \sin x \cos x$$

$$= 2 \left(\frac{2}{\sqrt{5}} \right) \left(\frac{1}{\sqrt{5}} \right)$$

$$= \frac{4}{5}$$

26. **(E)**

$f(x) = x^3$ $\qquad$ $f(b) = f(3) = 27$

$f'(x_1) = 3x_1{}^2$ $\qquad$ $f(a) = f(1) = 1$

$f(b) - f(a) = (b - a) f'(x_1)$

$27 - 1 = (3 - 1)(3x_1{}^2)$

$x = \sqrt{\dfrac{13}{3}} = 2.082$

27. **(D)**

$f'(x) = x^2 - 2x - 3 = (x + 1)(x - 3)$

$(x + 1)(x - 3) = 0 \Rightarrow x = -1$ and 3 are critical values.

The numbers -1 and 3 divide the x-axis into 3 intervals, from $-\infty$ to -1, -1 to 3, and 3 to $-\infty$.

$f(x)$ has a relative minimum value at $x = x_1$, if and only if $f'(x_1) = 0$ and the sign of $f'(x)$ changes from $-$ to $+$ as x increases through x_1.

If $-1 < x < 3$, then $f'(x) = -$

If $x = 3$, then $f'(x) = 0$

If $x > 3$, then $f'(x) = +$

Therefore, $f(3)$ is a relative minimum.

28. **(E)**

III is not a property of the definite integral. For example, let $f(x) = x$, $g(x) = \dfrac{1}{x}$. Then

$$\int_a^b f(x) \cdot g(x)\, dx = \int_a^b x \cdot \frac{1}{x}\, dx$$

$$= \int_a^b dx = b - a,$$

but

$$\int_a^b f(x)\, dx \cdot \int_a^b g(x)\, dx = \int_a^b x\, dx \cdot \int_a^b \frac{1}{x}\, dx$$

$$= \frac{x^2}{2}\Big|_a^b - \ln|x|\Big|_a^b$$

$$= \frac{b^2}{2} - \frac{a^2}{2} + \ln\left|\frac{b}{a}\right|$$

$$\neq b - a$$

29. **(C)**

$$f(bx) = \log_b(bx)$$

$$= \log_b b + \log_b x$$

$$= 1 + \log_b x$$

$$= 1 + f(x)$$

30. **(B)**

$f(x)$ is continuous for $x < 1$ and $x > 1$ because polynomials are continuous for all reals. We must determine "a" such that $f(x)$ is continuous at $x = 1$.

(i) $f(1) = 1 + 1 = 2$, thus $f(1)$ is defined.

(ii) $\lim_{x \to 1} f(x)$ exists if $\lim_{x \to 1^+} f(x) = \lim_{x \to 1^-} f(x)$

$$\lim_{x \to 1^+} f(x) = \lim_{x \to 1^+} \left(3 + ax^2\right) = 3 + a(1)^2 = 3 + a$$

$$\lim_{x \to 1^-} f(x) = \lim_{x \to 1^-} (x + 1) = 1 + 1 = 2$$

If $\lim_{x \to 1^+} f(x) = \lim_{x \to 1^-} f(x)$, then $3 + a = 2$

$$a = -1$$

Hence, $\lim_{x \to 1} f(x) = 2$ if $a = -1$.

(iii) Since $\lim\limits_{x\to 1} f(x) = f(1)$ the nf is continuous when $a = -1$

The graph of $f(x)$ with $a = -1$ is sketched below:

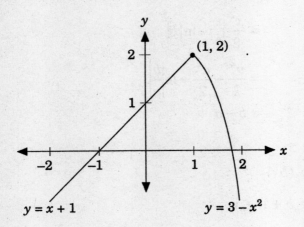

31. **(E)**

$$g(x) = -\frac{(x+f(x))}{f(x)} \qquad f(1) = 4,\ f'(1) = 2$$

$$g'(x) = -\left[\frac{(1+f'(x))f(x) - f'(x)(x+f(x))}{[f(x)]^2}\right]$$

$$g'(1) = -\left[\frac{(1+f'(1))f(1) - f'(1)(1+f(1))}{(f(1))^2}\right]$$

$$= -\left[\frac{(1+2)4 - 2(1+4)}{16}\right]$$

$$= -\left[\frac{12-10}{16}\right]$$

$$= -\frac{1}{8}$$

32. **(A)**

$$4 - x^2 \geq 0$$

$$(2 - x)(2 + x) \geq 0$$

Consider the following sign diagram:

x					-2			2			
$2 - x$	$+$	$+$	$+$	$+$	$+$	0	$-$	$-$	$-$
$2 + x$	$-$	$-$	0	$+$	$+$	$+$	$+$	$+$	$+$
$(2 - x)(2 + x)$	$-$	$-$	0	$+$	$+$	0	$-$	$-$	$-$

Since $(2 - x)(2 + x) \geq 0$ when $-2 \leq x \leq 2$, the domain is $-2 \leq x$

33. **(C)**

$$\int \frac{x + e^x}{xe^x}\, dx = \int \left(\frac{x}{xe^x} + \frac{e^x}{xe^x} \right) dx$$

$$= \int \left(e^{-x} + x^{-1} \right) dx$$

$$= -e^{-x} + \ln x + C$$

34. **(E)**

First determine where the graphs $y = x^2$ and $y = 2x + 3$ intersect.

$$x^2 = 2x + 3$$

$$x^2 - 2x - 3 = 0$$

$$(x - 3)(x + 1) = 0$$

$$x = 3, -1$$

$$A = \int_{-1}^{3} \left(2x + 3 - x^2\right) dx$$

$$= \int_{-1}^{3} \left\{(2x + 3) - x^2\right\} dx$$

$$= \left(x^2 + 3x - \frac{1}{3}x^3\right)\Big|_{-1}^{3}$$

$$= 3^2 - (-1)^2 + 3\big(3 - (-1)\big) - \frac{1}{3}\left(3^3 - (-1)^3\right)$$

$$= 9 - 1 + 3(4) - \frac{1}{3}(27 + 1)$$

$$= 20 - \frac{28}{3}$$

$$= \frac{32}{3}$$

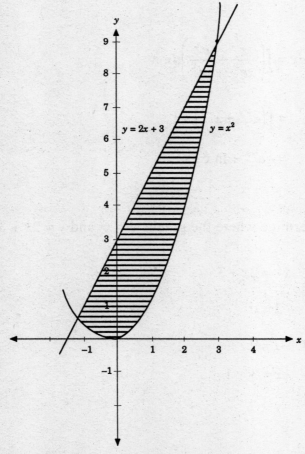

35. **(D)**

$\pi \int_0^1 x^2 dx$ represents the volume of the solid:

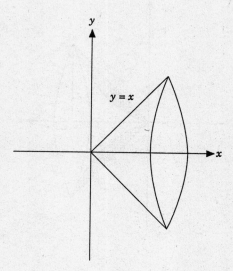

$\pi \int_0^1 x^6 dx$ represents the volume of the solid:

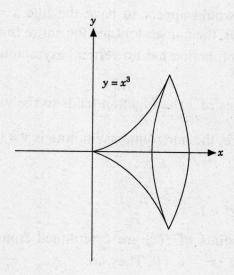

Subtracting

$$\pi \int_0^1 x^2 dx - \pi \int_0^1 x^6 dx$$

$\pi \int_0^1 \left(x^2 - x^6\right)dx$, we have the solid of revolution:

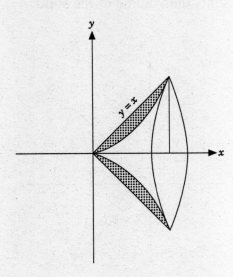

with $V = \pi \int_0^1 \left(x^2 - x^6\right)dx$

36. **(B)**

The function would appear to have the line $x = -4$ as a vertical asymptote. However, the numerator (and the entire function) are defined only for $x \geq 0$. This function has no vertical asymptote.

For large values of x the function tends to the value $y \approx \dfrac{\sqrt{x}}{x} \to 0$, as $x \to \infty$. Therefore, the horizontal asymptote is $y = 0$.

37. **(B)**

$$f'(x) = 3x^2 - 1.$$

The critical points of $f(x)$ are determined from the roots of this equation, i.e., from $3x^2 - 1 = 0$. They are:

$$x = \pm\frac{1}{\sqrt{3}} = \pm\frac{\sqrt{3}}{3}$$

The nature of each critical point is dictated by a higher order derivative:

$$f''(x) = 6x$$

Since $f''\left(\dfrac{\sqrt{3}}{3}\right) = 2\sqrt{3} > 0$, the point $x = \dfrac{\sqrt{3}}{3}$, $y = \dfrac{-2\sqrt{3}}{9}$ is a local minimum.

$f''\left(-\dfrac{\sqrt{3}}{3}\right) = -2\sqrt{3} < 0$, $-\dfrac{\sqrt{3}}{3} = x$ is a local maximum (not listed as an answer).

38. **(E)**

$\displaystyle\int_{-1}^{1} x^3 dx = 0$ but $x^3 \neq 0$ and $-1 \neq 1$; this eliminates answers (A), (B), and (C).

$\displaystyle\int_{0}^{\pi} \cos x \, dx = 0$, but $\cos x$ is not an odd function; this eliminates answer (D), and leaves only answer (E).

39. **(B)**

Use the calculator to solve the problem directly. For example,

fnInt $(X^\wedge x, x, 0, 2)$.

Pressing ENTER, gives 2.83.

40. **(C)**

The rate of movement of the particle is the velocity $s'(t)$. Use your graphic calculator to draw both $s(t)$ and $s'(t)$.

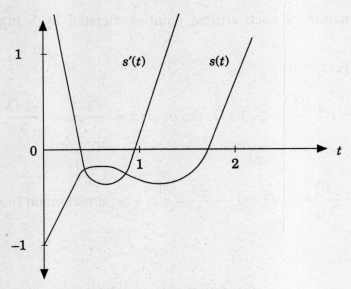

The velocity is given by $v(t) = 6t^2 - 8t + 2$.

The acceleration $a(t) = 12t - 8$ vanishes at $t = \dfrac{2}{3}$; at this time the velocity has reached its minimum. This occurs during the interval $[0,2]$.

Therefore, the minimum velocity of $v = -\dfrac{2}{3}$ occurs at $t = \dfrac{2}{3}$.

41. **(A)**

Since the particle starts from rest, the distance it travels can be found by integrating twice: first to find the velocity as a function of time, and then to find the distance as a function of time. We have:

$$a(t) = \frac{1}{\sqrt{t}} + 3\sqrt{t}.$$

Therefore, $v(t) = 2\sqrt{t} + 2t^{\frac{3}{2}}$ (since $v(0) = 0$)

and $d(t) = \dfrac{4}{3}t^{\frac{3}{2}} + \dfrac{4}{5}t^{\frac{5}{2}}$

Distance travelled is $d(3.61) - d(0) = 28.95 - 0 = 28.95$

42. **(D)**

    Use the quadratic formula:

    $$x = \frac{12 \pm \sqrt{144 - 84}}{6}$$

    $$= 2 \pm \sqrt{\frac{15}{3}}$$

    $$\approx 2 \pm \frac{4}{3}$$

    Therefore, roots near $\frac{2}{3}$ and $3\frac{1}{3}$.

43. **(E)**

    $f(x) = x^3 - x$

    $f'(x) = 3x^2 - 1$, an *even* function.

    $f'(x)$ can satisfy $f'(x) = -f'(-x)$, which is the defining characteristic of an *odd* function, at $x = 0$ but *only* if $f'(x) =$ passes through the origin. It does not. Therefore, the answer is (E).

44. **(E)**

    Solve the differential equation $\frac{dy}{dx} = 3x^2(y - 6)$

    Separate variables: $3x^2 dx = \frac{dy}{(y - 6)}$, and integrate

    $$3\int x^2 dx = \int \frac{dy}{(y - 6)}$$

    $$x^3 = \ln(y - 6) + C$$

    $$\ln(y - 6) = x^3 - C$$

    $$y - 6 = e^{x^3} - C$$

    $$y = e^{x^3 - C} + 6$$

Let $A = e^{-C}$, then $y = Ae^{x^3} + 6$

Substitute in $(0, 7)$: $7 = A + 6$

$A = 1 = e^{-C} \Rightarrow c = 0$

Therefore, $y = e^{x^3} + 6$.

45. **(D)**

The coefficients for the power series of $f(x)$ about $x = b$ are given by:

$$a_n = \frac{f^{(n)}}{n!}$$

$$f(x) = \ln x \qquad\qquad f(1) = 0$$

$$f'(x) = \frac{1}{x} \qquad\qquad f'(1) = 1$$

$$f''(x) = -\frac{1}{x^2} \qquad\qquad f''(1) = -1$$

$$f'''(x) = \frac{2}{x^3} \qquad\qquad f'''(1) = 2$$

$$a_3 = \frac{f'''(1)}{3!} = \frac{2}{3!} = \frac{1}{3}$$

SECTION II

1. **(A)**

If $x = 0$, $f(x)$ is undefined, so there is no y-intercept.

If $y = f(x) = 0$, then

$$0 = 1 + \frac{1}{x} + \frac{1}{x^2}$$

$$\Rightarrow 0 = \frac{x^2 + x + 1}{x^2}$$

$$\Rightarrow x^2 + x + 1 = 0$$

$$\Rightarrow x = \frac{-1 \pm \sqrt{1-4}}{2}$$

which gives non-real solutions, so there is no x-intercept.

(B)

$$y = \frac{x^2 + x + 1}{x^2}$$

As $x \to \pm\infty$, we see $f(x) \to 1$, so $y = 1$ is a horizontal asymptote. As $x \to 0$, the function tends to $y \approx \frac{1}{x^2}$, which has the vertical asymptote $x = 0$.

(C)

$$f'(x) = -\frac{1}{x^2} - \frac{2}{x^3}, f \text{ is increasing when}$$

$$f'(x) = -\frac{1}{x^2} - \frac{2}{x^3} > 0$$

$$\Rightarrow -x - 2 > 0 \text{ if } x > 0$$

$$\Rightarrow x < -2 \text{ if } x > 0; \text{ impossible.}$$

OR $-2 < x$ if $x < 0$, so $-2 < x < 0$ and the interval on which $f(x)$ increases is $(-2, 0)$

$f(x)$ is decreasing if $f'(x) = -\dfrac{1}{x^2} - \dfrac{2}{x^3} < 0$.

If $x > 0$, then $-\dfrac{1}{x^2} - \dfrac{2}{x^3} < 0$

$$\Rightarrow -x - 2 < 0 \Rightarrow -2 < x, \text{ and } x > 0$$

so one interval of decreasing $f(x)$ is $(0, \infty)$.

If $x < 0$, then $-\dfrac{1}{x^2} - \dfrac{2}{x^3} < 0$

$$\Rightarrow -x - 2 < 0 \Rightarrow -2 < x \text{ and } x > 0$$

so, another interval on which $f(x)$ is decreasing is $(-\infty, -2)$.

(D)

Since $y' = \dfrac{-(x+2)}{x^3}$ and $y'' = \dfrac{2(x+3)}{x^4}$

We see that $\left(-2, \dfrac{3}{4}\right)$ is a local minimum. In fact, it is *the* minimum of the function.

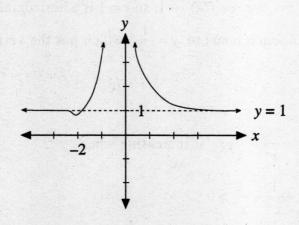

2. (A)

$2x + y - 7 = 0$, $y = 7 - 2x$, slope $= -2$

(B)

By implicit differentiation,

$2x + 2yy' = 0$

$$\Rightarrow y' = -\frac{2x}{2y} = -\frac{x}{y} = -\frac{x}{\sqrt{5 - x^2}}$$

(C)

The slope of the perpendicular must be the negative reciprocal of -2,

namely, $\frac{1}{2}$. Now,

$$-\frac{x}{y} = \frac{1}{2} \Rightarrow y = -2x.$$

Since, $x^2 + y^2 + 5$, we see $x^2 + (-2x)^2 = 5$

$\Rightarrow x^2 + 4x^2 = 5$, $5x^2 = 5$, $x = \pm 1$

If $x = 1$, $y = -2x = -2$

If $x = -1$, $y = -2x = 2$

Since $y \geq 0$ was specified, the point is $(-1, 2)$

(D)

The tangent line has equation

$$y - 2 = \frac{1}{2}(x + 1)$$

$$\Rightarrow y = \frac{x}{2} + \frac{5}{2}$$

When $x = 0$, $y = \frac{5}{2}$ so $\left(0, \frac{5}{2}\right)$ is the y-intercept.

When $y = 0$, $x = -5$ so $(-5, 0)$ is the x-intercept.

3.   (A)

$f(x)$ is concave down where $f''(x) < 0$ namely on the intervals $(-\infty, 3)$, $(3, 5)$ and $(5, \infty)$.

(B)

Vertical tangent at $x = 3$.

(C)

No inflection point exists because the concavity (sign of the second derivative) never changes.

(D)

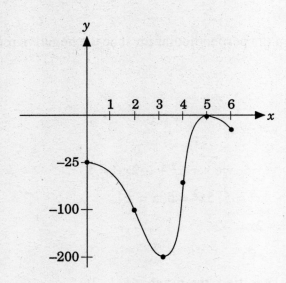

4.   (A)

$s(t)$ is increasing (particle is moving to the right) when $3 < t \le 5$.

The particle is moving to the left when $s(t)$ is decreasing, namely when $1 \le t < 3$.

(B)

The acceleration is positive when $s''(t) > 0$ which is when the graph is concave up. This occurs for $2 < t < 4$.

The acceleration is negative when the graph is concave down, namely when $0 \le t < 2$ or $4 < t < 5$.

(C)

The particle is speeding up when the velocity and acceleration are both positive or both negative. This occurs when $3 \le t < 4$ or $1 < t < 2$.

5. (A)

Draw the graph of $f(x)$.

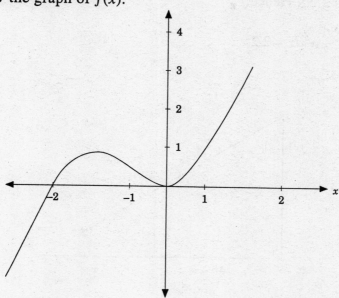

$y = 2x^2 + x^3$

$y' = 4x + 3x^2$

$y'' = 4 + 6x$

Roots of y' at $(x = 0, y = 0)$; $\left(x = -\dfrac{4}{3}, \ y = \dfrac{32}{27} \right)$

Use y'' to show that the point $(0,0)$ is local minimum while $\left(-\dfrac{4}{3}, \dfrac{32}{27} \right)$ is local maximum.

$f(x)$ has a local maximum in $-2 < t < -1$. By using viewing window $[-2, 0]$ $[0, 2]$, the value of this maximum can be found to be 1.19 at $x = -1.35$.

(B)

In the graph, it can be easily seen that $f(x)$ has a local minimum at $x = 0$; its value equals 0.

(C)

By using your calculator, $\displaystyle\int_{-2}^{1} f(x)$ can easily be solved by

$$fnInt\ (2x\verb|^|2 + x\verb|^|3, x, -2, 1)$$

which gives 2.25. Hence,

$$\int_{-2}^{1} 2x^2 + x^3\,dx = 2.25$$

6.

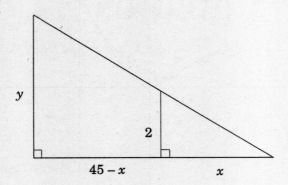

Let y = length of shadow

x = distance thief has run

The distance between the thief and the wall is $45 - x$. When the thief

is 15 meters from the wall, $x = 30$. We know $\dfrac{dx}{dt} = 6m/sec$. We want to find

$\dfrac{dy}{dt}$.

By similar triangles,

$$\frac{y}{2} = \frac{45}{x} \Rightarrow y = \frac{90}{x}, \ \text{so} \frac{dy}{dx} = -\frac{90}{x^2}$$

By the chain rule,

$$\frac{dy}{dt} = \frac{dy}{dx}\frac{dx}{dt}. \ \ \text{At } x = 30, \ \frac{dy}{dt} = -\frac{90}{30^2} \times 6$$

$$= -\frac{540}{900} = -\frac{3}{5} \ \text{m/sec.}$$

Advanced Placement Examination in Calculus AB

EXAM II

ADVANCED PLACEMENT CALCULUS AB EXAM II

SECTION I

PART A

Time: 55 minutes
28 questions

DIRECTIONS: Each of the following problems is followed by five choices. Solve each problem, select the best choice, and blacken the correct space on your answer sheet. Calculators may not be used for this section of the exam.

NOTE: Unless otherwise specified, the domain of function f is assumed to be the set of all real numbers x for which $f(x)$ is a real number.

---

1. $\int_1^2 \frac{x^3 + 1}{x^2} \, dx =$

   (A) 0

   (B) $\frac{3}{2}$

   (C) 2

   (D) 1

   (E) 3

2. If $f(x) = \sqrt{1 - x^2}$, which of the following is NOT true?

   (A) Domain of $f = [-1, 1]$

   (B) $[f(x)]^2 + x^2 = 1$

(C) Range of f is $[0, 1]$

(D) $f(x) = f(-x)$

(E) The line $y = 1$ intersects the graph of f at two points.

3. $\lim\limits_{x \to \infty} \left(1 + \dfrac{1}{n}\right)^{n+2} =$

(A) e^2 (D) e

(B) $e + 2$ (E) $e + e^2$

(C) $2e$

4. $\lim\limits_{x \to 0} \dfrac{\cos^2 x - 1}{2x \sin x} =$

(A) -1 (D) $\dfrac{1}{2}$

(B) $-\dfrac{1}{2}$ (E) 0

(C) 1

5. If $y = \dfrac{1}{\sqrt{2x+3}}$, then $y'(0)$ is approximately

(A) 0.193 (D) 5.196

(B) -0.096 (E) -140.296

(C) -0.193

6. If $f(x) = |x|$, then

(A) Domain of $f' =$ Domain of f.

(B) $f'(x) = \dfrac{|x|}{x}$ for every real number x.

(C) $(f'(x)) (f(x)) = f(x)$ for every real number x.

(D) Range of f' is the set $\{-1, 1\}$.

(E) The graph of f' is

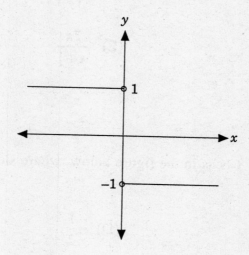

7. $\int_0^1 (2x + 1)^{-3}\, dx$ is approximately

(A) 0.888

(B) −1.111

(C) −0.277

(D) −1.500

(E) 0.222

8. If $f(x + c) = f(x) \cdot f(c)$ for every real number x and c and $f(0) \neq 1$, then $f(0) =$

(A) 1

(B) 0

(C) 0 and 1

(D) −1

(E) $\sqrt{2}$

9. If $y = \dfrac{x-1}{x+1}$, then $\dfrac{dy}{dx} =$

    (A) $\dfrac{2x}{(x+1)^2}$

    (B) $\dfrac{2}{x+1}$

    (C) $\dfrac{2}{(x+1)^2}$

    (D) $-\dfrac{2}{(x+1)^2}$

    (E) $\dfrac{2x}{x+1}$

10. If the graph of f is as in the figure below, where slope of $L_1 = 2$, then $f'(x_0)$ is

    (A) $\dfrac{1}{2}$

    (B) -2

    (C) 2

    (D) $-\dfrac{1}{2}$

    (E) 0

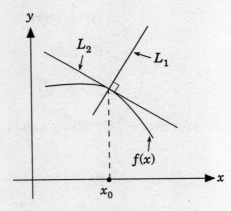

11. If $f(x) = \dfrac{1}{x-2}$ and $\displaystyle\lim_{x \to (-k+1)} f(x)$ does not exist, then $k =$

    (A) 2

    (B) 3

    (C) 1

    (D) -2

    (E) -1

12. If $f(x) = \dfrac{1}{10 - \sqrt{x^2 + 64}}$ is not continuous at c, then $c =$

    (A) 6

    (B) –6

    (C) ±6

    (D) ±4

    (E) 5

13. If $f(x) = \dfrac{1}{x-2}$, $(fg)'(1) = 6$, and $g'(1) = -1$, then $g(1) =$

    (A) –5

    (B) 5

    (C) –7

    (D) 7

    (E) 8

14. If $f'(x) = \dfrac{(x^4 + 5x + 1)(12x) - (6x^2 - 1)(4x^3 + 5)}{(x^4 + 5x + 1)^2}$ and $f(0) = 2$, then $f(1)$ is approximately

    (A) 0.102

    (B) 0.714

    (C) 3.714

    (D) 3.102

    (E) 0.857

15. $\displaystyle\int_0^1 (\sec^2 x - \tan^2 x)\, dx =$

    (A) 3

    (B) 5

    (C) 2

    (D) 4

    (E) 1

16. Suppose $2 \le f(x) \le (1-x)^2 + 2$ for all $x \ne 1$ and that $f(1)$ is undefined. What is $\lim_{x \to 1} f(x)$?

(A) 3

(D) $\dfrac{5}{2}$

(B) 2

(E) 1

(C) 4

17. If f is differentiable at 0, and $g(x) = [f(x)]^2$, $f(0) = f'(0) = -1$, then $g'(0) =$

(A) -2

(D) 4

(B) -1

(E) 2

(C) 1

18. $\dfrac{dy}{dx} = x \cot(3x^2)$, then $y =$

(A) $\ln |\sin 3x^2| + c$

(D) $\dfrac{1}{6} \ln |\sin 3x^2| + c$

(B) $6 \ln |\sin 3x^2| + c$

(E) $\ln c |\sin 3x^2|$

(C) $6 \ln c |\sin 3x^2|$

19. If the k-th derivative of $(3x - 2)^3$ identically is zero, then k is necessarily

(A) 4

(D) 2

(B) 3

(E) 5

(C) ≥ 4

20. If $\arctan (x) = \ln (y^2)$, then, in terms of x and y, $\dfrac{dy}{dx} =$

(A) $\dfrac{1}{1-x^2}$

(D) $\dfrac{y}{1+x^2}$

(B) $\dfrac{-1}{1-x^2}$

(E) $\dfrac{y}{2(1+x^2)}$

(C) $\dfrac{y}{1-x^2}$

21. The volume $V(\text{in}^3)$ of unmelted ice remaining from a melting ice cube after t seconds is $V = 2{,}000 - 40t + 0.2t^2$. How fast is the volume changing when $t = 40$ seconds?

(A) -26 in^3/sec

(D) 0 in^3/sec

(B) 24 in^3/sec

(E) -24 in^3/sec

(C) 120 in^3/sec

22. If $\displaystyle\int_a^b f(x)\,dx = 8$, $a = 2$, f is continuous, and the average value of f on $[a, b]$ is 4, then $b =$

(A) 0

(D) 3

(B) 2

(E) 5

(C) 4

23. If $0 \le x \le 1$, then $\dfrac{d}{dx}\displaystyle\int_x^0 \dfrac{dt}{2+t} =$

(A) $\dfrac{1}{x+2}$

(D) $\ln |2 + x| + c$

(B) $-\dfrac{1}{x+2}$

(E) $-\ln |2 + x| + c$

(C) $\ln |2 + x|$

24. $\lim\limits_{x \to -1} \dfrac{x + x^2}{x^2 - 1} =$

   (A) $-\dfrac{1}{2}$

   (B) 1

   (C) -1

   (D) $\dfrac{1}{2}$

   (E) Does not exist

25. For $x \neq 0$, $\lim\limits_{h \to 0} \dfrac{1}{h}\left(\dfrac{1}{x+h} - \dfrac{1}{x}\right) =$

   (A) $\dfrac{1}{x^2}$

   (B) $-\dfrac{2}{x}$

   (C) $-\dfrac{1}{x^2}$

   (D) $-\dfrac{2}{x^2}$

   (E) 0

26. If $2x^3 + 3xy + e^y = 6$, what is y' when $x = 0$?

   (A) -0.896

   (B) 0.896

   (C) 1.792

   (D) -1.792

   (E) 0

27. The area between the line $y = x$ and the curve $y = \dfrac{1}{2}x^2$ is

   (A) 1

   (B) $\dfrac{1}{2}$

   (C) $\dfrac{2}{3}$

   (D) $\dfrac{3}{2}$

   (E) 2

28. An ellipse with semiaxes a and b has area πab. If the area is 9π (held constant), how fast is b increasing when $a = 1$ and a is decreasing at $\frac{1}{2}$ units/minute?

(A) $4\frac{1}{2}$ units/minute

(D) 3 units/minute

(B) $\frac{2}{9}$ units/minute

(E) Cannot tell

(C) 3π units/minute

PART B

Time: 50 minutes
17 questions

DIRECTIONS: Calculators may be used for this section of the test. Each of the following problems is followed by five choices. Solve each problem, select the best choice, and blacken the correct space on your answer sheet.

NOTES:
1. Unless otherwise specified, answers can be given in unsimplified form.

2. The domain of function f is assumed to be the set of all real numbers x for which $f(x)$ is a real number.

29. Let $f(x) = 2\sqrt{x}$. If $f(c) = f'(c)$, then c equals

(A) 0

(D) 0.5

(B) 0.82

(E) 2.1

(C) 1.2

30. A particle moves along the x–axis. Its velocity is given by

$$V(t) = \begin{cases} t^2 & \text{for } 0 \le t \le 2 \\ t+2 & \text{for } t > 2 \end{cases}$$

If it starts at the origin, its position after 4 seconds is $x =$

(A) $37\dfrac{1}{3}$

(D) $\dfrac{8}{3}$

(B) $12\dfrac{2}{3}$

(E) 6

(C) 10

31. If $f'(x) = g'(x)$, $f'(x)$ and $g'(x)$ are continuous in $[-1, 1]$, and $f(0) - g(0) = 2$, then

   (A) $f(x) - g(x) = -2$

   (B) $\int_{-1}^{1} (f(x) - g(x))\, dx = 4$

   (C) $\int_{-1}^{1} (f(x) - g(x)) = 0$

   (D) The graphs of $f(x)$ and $g(x)$ intersect in $[-1, 1]$.

   (E) $\int_{-1}^{1} (g(x) - f(x))\, dx = 4$

32. An antiderivative of $\dfrac{x}{\sqrt{16 + x^2}}$ is

   (A) $x\sqrt{16 + x^2}$ (D) $\sqrt{16 + x^2}$

   (B) $x\,(16 + x^2)$ (E) $\left(\dfrac{1}{2} \ln \left|16 + x^2\right| \right)(\ln x)$

   (C) $\ln \left|16 + x^2\right|$

33. $\lim\limits_{x \to \infty} \dfrac{(1 - 2x^2)^3}{(x^2 + 1)^3}$

   (A) 8   (D) ∞

   (B) 1   (E) -8

   (C) 0

34. The function f defined by $f(x) = x + \dfrac{1}{x}$ has relative minimum at $x =$

    (A) -1

    (B) $-\dfrac{1}{2}$

    (C) 0

    (D) 1

    (E) $\dfrac{1}{2}$

35. The area of a region bounded by the parabola $8 + 2x - x^2$ and the x–axis is:

    (A) $41\dfrac{1}{3}$

    (B) 36

    (C) 20

    (D) $9\dfrac{1}{3}$

    (E) 24

36. $\displaystyle\int_{-1}^{1} |x^2 - 1| \, dx =$

    (A) $\dfrac{4}{3}$

    (B) 0

    (C) $-\dfrac{4}{3}$

    (D) $\dfrac{2}{3}$

    (E) $\dfrac{5}{3}$

37. Let $f(x) = x^3 - 2x$. The relationship between its local minimum and local maximum is

    (A) $f_{min} = 2f_{max}$

    (B) $f_{min} = f_{max}$

    (C) $f_{min} = -f_{max}$

    (D) $f_{min} = 1.5 f_{max}$

    (E) $f_{min} = \sqrt{f_{max}}$

38. Which of the following functions is not symmetric with respect to the origin?

    (A) $\tan x$

    (B) $\dfrac{1}{x}$

    (C) $\cot x$

    (D) $\sin x$

    (E) $\cos x$

39. Estimate the largest value of $|y'(x)|$ for $y = \sqrt{1-x}$ inside $0 \le x \le 0.8$.

    (A) -1.12

    (B) 5.00

    (C) 0

    (D) 3

    (E) 2

40. If $f(x) = x^{\frac{1}{2}} \ln x$, then $f'(2)$ equals

    (A) -0.75

    (B) 0.95

    (C) 0.25

    (D) 0

    (E) 0.75

41. Which of the following statements is/are true?

    I.   If f is continuous everywhere, then f is differentiable everywhere.

    II. If f is differentiable everywhere, then f is continuous everywhere.

    III. If f is continuous and $f(x) \ge 2$ for every x in $[3, 7]$, then $\int_{3}^{7} f(x)\, dx > 8$.

    (A) I only

    (B) II only

    (C) III only

    (D) I and III only

    (E) II and III only

42. Let $g(x)$ be the inverse of $f(x)$, i.e., $f(g(x)) = x = g(f(x))$. If $f'(x) = g'(x)$, then $f'(1)$ is necessarily

    (A) 1

    (B) –1

    (C) 0

    (D) ±1

    (E) $\dfrac{1}{2}$

43. Which of the following is NOT true about $y = \cos(-x + \pi)$?

    (A) y has the same period as $\cos(x - \pi)$.

    (B) y has the same period as $\tan(2 - \dfrac{x}{2})$.

    (C) y has only one inflection point in $(-\pi, \pi)$.

    (D) $\dfrac{d^2 y}{dx^2} + y = 0$.

    (E) y has minimum at $x = 0$.

44. $\lim\limits_{x \to 0} \dfrac{\sin 2x - 2x}{x^3} =$

    (A) Does not exist

    (B) 1

    (C) $-\dfrac{4}{3}$

    (D) ∞

    (E) $-\infty$

45. If a is a constant, then $\displaystyle\int_0^\infty x e^{ax}\, dx$

    (A) always diverges

    (B) always converges

    (C) converges if $a > 0$

    (D) converges if $a < 0$

    (E) None of these

SECTION II

Time: 1 hour and 30 minutes
6 problems

DIRECTIONS: Show all your work. Grading is based on the methods used to solve the problem as well as the accuracy of your final answers. Please make sure all procedures are clearly shown. For some problems or parts of problems it will be necessary to use a calculator.

NOTES:

1. Unless otherwise specified, answers can be given in unsimplified form.

2. The domain of function f is assumed to be the set of all real numbers x for which $f(x)$ is a real number.

---

1. Show that, if f is continuous and $0 \le f(x) \le 1$ for every x in $[0, 1]$, then there exists at least one point c such that $f(c) = c$. (Hint: Apply the intermediate value theorem to $g(x) = x - f(x)$, or try to answer it by sketching graphs which represent the possible cases of the graph of f.)

2. Let $f(x) = \ln (x^2 - x - 6)$

   (A) The domain of $f(x)$ is $x < b$ or $x > a$. Find a and b.

   (B) Find $f(5)$.

   (C) Find $f'(-3)$.

3. If $f(x) = \dfrac{1-x^2}{x^2+1}$, then

    (A) Find the domain of f.

    (B) Find $\lim\limits_{x \to \infty} f(x)$ and $\lim\limits_{x \to -\infty} f(x)$.

    (C) Find the intervals where f increases and where it decreases. Justify your answer.

    (D) Find the equation of the tangent line that is parallel to the x-axis.

4. A conical silver cup 8 inches across the top and 12 inches deep is leaking water at the rate of 2 inches^3 per minute. (Figure below.) At what rate is the water level dropping:

    (A) when the water is 6 inches deep?

    (B) when the cup is half full?

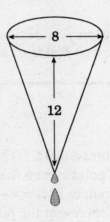

5. $y = f(x)$ is a function where f' and f'' exist and have the following characteristics:

x	$x < -2$	$x = -2$	$-2 < x < 0$	$0 < x < 2$	$x = 2$	$x > 2$
$f'(x)$	+	0	−	−	0	+
$f''(x)$	−	−	−	+	+	+

If $f(-2) = 8$, $f(0) = 4$ and $f(2) = 0$, then

    (A) Find all inflection points of $-2f$

    (B) Find all relative minimum and relative maximum values of $-2f$

    (C) Discuss the concavity of $-2f$

    (D) Sketch the graph of $-2f$.

6.   (A) At what values of x do $y = x$ and $y = x^3$ intersect?

    (B) Find the area of the region bounded by $y = x$ and $y = x^3$

    (C) Find the volume obtained by rotating the region in (B) about the x-axis.

ADVANCED PLACEMENT CALCULUS AB EXAM II

ANSWER KEY

Section I

1.	(C)	12.	(C)	23.	(B)	34.	(D)
2.	(E)	13.	(A)	24.	(D)	35.	(B)
3.	(D)	14.	(C)	25.	(C)	36.	(A)
4.	(B)	15.	(E)	26.	(B)	37.	(C)
5.	(C)	16.	(B)	27.	(C)	38.	(E)
6.	(D)	17.	(E)	28.	(A)	39.	(A)
7.	(E)	18.	(D)	29.	(D)	40.	(B)
8.	(B)	19.	(C)	30.	(B)	41.	(B)
9.	(C)	20.	(E)	31.	(B)	42.	(D)
10.	(D)	21.	(E)	32.	(D)	43.	(C)
11.	(E)	22.	(C)	33.	(E)	44.	(C)
						45.	(D)

Section II

See Detailed Explanations of Answers.

ADVANCED PLACEMENT
CALCULUS AB
EXAM II

DETAILED EXPLANATIONS
OF ANSWERS

$$\boxed{\textbf{SECTION I}}$$

1. **(C)**

$$\frac{x^3+1}{x^2} = \frac{x^3}{x^2} + \frac{1}{x^2}$$

$$= x + \frac{1}{x^2}$$

Therefore,

$$\int_1^2 \frac{x^3+1}{x^2}\,dx = \int_1^2 \left(x + x^{-2}\right) dx$$

$$= \left(\frac{x^2}{2} - \frac{1}{x}\right)\Big|_1^2$$

$$= \left(2 - \frac{1}{2}\right) - \left(\frac{1}{2} - 1\right)$$

$$= 2$$

Remark: Use parentheses as on the previous page to avoid computational errors like: $2 - \dfrac{1}{2} - \dfrac{1}{2} - 1 = 0$.

2. **(E)**

(i) $y = \sqrt{1 - x^2}$ is defined $\Leftrightarrow 1 - x^2 \geq 1$

$$\Leftrightarrow x^2 \leq 1$$

$$\Leftrightarrow |x| \leq 1$$

Therefore, domain = $[-1, 1]$

(ii) $y \geq 0$ for every x in $[-1, 1]$ and its graph is as follows:

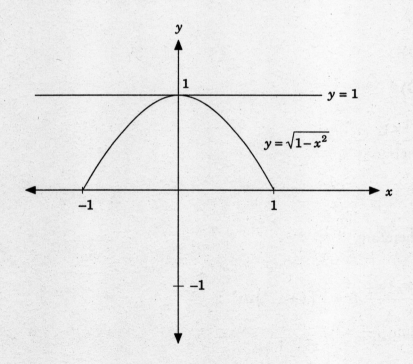

Moreover, its range is $[0, 1]$.

Finally, $f(x)$ is 1 only when $x = 0$. Hence, (E) is not true.

3. **(D)**

$$\left(1+\frac{1}{n}\right)^{n+2} = \left(1+\frac{1}{n}\right)^n\left(1+\frac{1}{n}\right)^2 \qquad \text{(i)}$$

Therefore,

$$\lim_{n\to\infty}\left(1+\frac{1}{n}\right)^{n+2} = \lim_{n\to\infty}\left(1+\frac{1}{n}\right)^n \times \lim_{n\to\infty}\left(1+\frac{1}{n}\right)^2, \quad \text{from (i).}$$

$$= (e) \times (1)^2$$

$$= e$$

Note: $\left(1+\frac{1}{n}\right)^{n+2} \neq \left(\left(1+\frac{1}{n}\right)^n\right)^2$ and therefore, e^2 is incorrect.

4. **(B)**

$$\cos^2 x - 1 = -(1 - \cos^2 x) \qquad \text{(i)}$$

$$= -\sin^2 x$$

Therefore, $\displaystyle\lim_{x\to 0}\frac{\cos^2 x - 1}{2x\sin x}$ becomes, using substitution (i)

$$\lim_{x\to 0}\frac{-\sin^2 x}{2x\sin x} = \lim_{x\to 0}\left(-\frac{1}{2}\right)\frac{\sin x}{x}$$

$$= -\frac{1}{2},$$

since $\displaystyle\lim_{x\to 0}\frac{\sin x}{x} = 1$.

You can also use L'Hôpital's rule.

Also see from (i) above that $\cos^2 x - 1 \neq \sin^2 x$. Thus $\dfrac{1}{2}$ is not the limit.

5. **(C)**

$$y = \frac{1}{\sqrt{2x+3}} = (2x+3)^{-\frac{1}{2}}$$

Using chain rule,

$$\frac{dy}{dx} = \left[-\frac{1}{2}(2x+3)^{-\frac{1}{2}-1} \right] \times \left[\frac{d}{dx}(2x+3) \right]$$

$$= \left[-\frac{1}{2}(2x+3)^{-\frac{3}{2}} \right] \times 2$$

$$= -\frac{1}{(2x+3)^{\frac{3}{2}}}$$

So, $y^1(0) = \dfrac{1}{\sqrt{(0+3)^3}} = -\dfrac{1}{\sqrt{27}} \approx -0.193$

6. **(D)**

$$|x| = \begin{cases} x & \text{for } x > 0 \\ -x & \text{for } x < 0 \end{cases}$$

$$\Rightarrow f'(x) = \begin{cases} 1 & \text{for } x > 0 \\ -1 & \text{for } x < 0 \end{cases}$$

But f is not differentiable at 0.

As a result, Domain of $f' = \{x \in R \mid x \neq 0\}$, while Domain of $f = R$. Consequently, A, B, and C are false. Moreover, the graph of f' is:

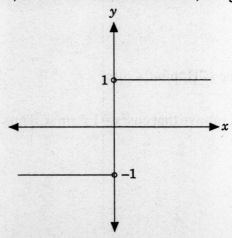

7. **(E)**

Let $u = 2x + 1$. Then, $du = 2dx$, i.e., $dx = \dfrac{du}{2}$. Also, when $x = 0$, $u = 1$ and when $x = 1$, $u = 3$. The original integral becomes

$$\frac{1}{2}\int_1^3 u^{-3}\, du = \frac{1}{2}\left[-\frac{1}{2}u^{-2}\right]\Big|_1^3$$

$$= -\frac{1}{4}\left[\frac{1}{9} - 1\right]$$

$$= \frac{1}{4}\times\frac{8}{9}$$

$$= \frac{2}{9}$$

$$\approx 0.222\ldots$$

8. **(B)**

Let $x = c = 0$

Then $f(0 + 0) = f(0) \times f(0)$, i.e., $f(0) = [f(0)]^2$

There are two possibilities:

(i) $f(0) = 0$

(ii) $f(0) = 1$

We are given that case (ii) is not allowed. Therefore, $f(0) = 0$.

9. **(C)**

$$y = \frac{x-1}{x+1}$$

$$\Rightarrow \frac{dy}{dx} = \frac{1\times(x+1) - (x-1)\times 1}{(x+1)^2}$$

$$= \frac{x+1-x+1}{(x+1)^2}$$

$$= \frac{2}{(x+1)^2}.$$

Unlike the product rule, we do not add $(1)(x+1)$ and $(1)(x-1)$. If you add them you will get $\frac{2x}{(x+1)^2}$, which is incorrect.

10. **(D)**

Referring to the graph in the problem:

Let slope of $L_1 = m_1$

Let slope of $L_2 = m_2$

We know that $m_1 \, m_2 = -1$, since the slopes of two, non-vertical, perpendicular lines are negative reciprocals of each other.

$$\Leftrightarrow m_2 = -\frac{1}{2}$$

Since L_2 is tangent to the graph of f at x_0, we have

$$f'(x_0) = -\frac{1}{2}$$

11. **(E)**

$\frac{1}{x-2}$ has no limit only at $x = 2$; see the graph below.

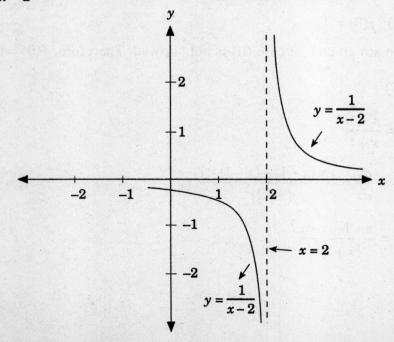

Therefore, $-k + 1 = 2$

$\Leftrightarrow k - 1 = -2$, by multiplying both sides by (-1)

$\Leftrightarrow k = -1$, adding 1 to both sides.

12. **(C)**

The expression $\sqrt{x^2 + 64}$ is defined for all x.

The quotient $\dfrac{1}{10 - \sqrt{x^2 + 64}}$ is not continuous at those values of x for which the denominator vanishes, i.e., where

$10 = \sqrt{x^2 + 64}$.

This occurs when

$x^2 = 36$, that is, when

$x = \pm 6$.

13. **(A)**

$(fg)'(1) = f'(1)g(1) + f(1)g'(1)$
by the product rule(*)

$f(1) = \dfrac{1}{1-2} = -1$ (i)

$f'(x) = -\dfrac{1}{(x-2)^2}$

Therefore, $f'(1) = -\dfrac{1}{(1-2)^2} = -1$ (ii)

$g'(1) = -1$ (iii)

$(fg)'(1) = 6$ (iv)

Now substitute (i) – (iv) in (*) above:

$6 = (-1)g(1) + (-1)(-1)$

$\Leftrightarrow g(1) = -5$

14. **(C)**

From the quotient rule the given expression is the derivative of

$$f(x) = \frac{6x^2 - 1}{x^4 + 5x + 1} + c$$

Since $f(0) = 2$, $c = 3$.

So, $f(x) = \frac{6x^2 - 1}{x^4 + 5x + 1} + 3$.

And $f(1) = \frac{6(1)^2 - 1}{(1)^4 + 5(1) + 1} + 3$

$$= \frac{5}{7} + 3$$

$$= 3\frac{5}{7}$$

$$f(1) = 3\frac{5}{7} \approx 3.714$$

15. **(E)**

By trigonometric identity:

$$\sec^2 x = 1 + \tan^2 x$$

$$\Rightarrow \sec^2 x - \tan^2 x = 1$$

$$\Rightarrow \int_0^1 \left(\sec^2 x - \tan^2 x \right) dx$$

$$= \int_0^1 1 \times dx$$

$$= 1.$$

<u>Remark</u>: Whenever expressions like $\sec^2 x - \tan^2 x$, $\cos^2 x - 1$, $\sin^2 x$, etc. appear in a problem, it is worth trying trigonometric identities first.

16. **(B)**

$\lim\limits_{x \to 1} 2 = 2$, and

$\lim\limits_{x \to 1} (1 - x)^2 + 2 = 2$

Therefore, $2 \le \lim\limits_{x \to 1} f(x) \le 2$, from the figure.

$\Leftrightarrow \lim\limits_{x \to 1} f(x) = 2$.

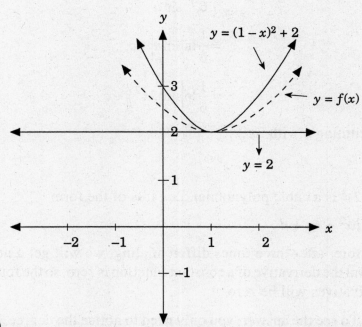

17. **(E)**

$g(x) = [f(x)]^2$

$\Rightarrow g'(x) = 2 \times [f(x)] \times f'(x)$

Therefore, $g'(0) = 2 \times f(0) \times f'(0)$

$= 2 \times (-1)(-1)$

$= 2$

A common arithmetic error is: $2 (-1) (-1) = -2$.

18. **(D)**

By the method of substitution:

Let $u = 3x^2$

$$\Rightarrow \frac{du}{dx} = 6x$$

$$\Leftrightarrow dx = \frac{du}{6}, \text{ after cross multiplication and division.}$$

Therefore, $\int x \cot\left(3x^2\right) dx = \frac{1}{6} \int \cot u \, du$

$$= \frac{1}{6} \int \frac{\cos u}{\sin u} \, du$$

$$= \frac{1}{6} \ln|\sin u| + c$$

$$= \frac{1}{6} \ln\left|\sin\left(3x^2\right)\right| + c,$$

(substituting u with $3x^2$) .

19. **(C)**

$(3x - 2)^3$ is a cubic polynomial, i.e., it is of the form

$ax^3 + bx^2 + cx + d$.

Therefore, after three times differentiating, we will get a non-zero constant. But the derivative of a constant function is zero, so the fourth and higher derivatives will be zero.

Note: To see the answer, you only need to notice the degree. You do not have to do the actual computation.

20. **(E)**

$$\frac{d}{dx}\left(\arctan(x)\right) = \frac{d}{dy}\left(\ln\left(y^2\right)\right) \times \frac{dy}{dx}$$

$$\frac{1}{1+x^2} = \frac{2y}{y^2} \times \frac{dy}{dx}$$

$$\frac{y}{2\left(1+x^2\right)} = \frac{dy}{dx}$$

21. **(E)**

$$\frac{dV}{dt} = -40 + 2(0.2)t$$

$$= -40 + 0.4t$$

Therefore, $\frac{dV}{dt}(40) = -40 + (0.4)(40)$

$$= -24 \text{ in}^2/\text{sec}.$$

You should not change it to positive. It is negative, because V is a decreasing function.

22. **(C)**

Average value of f in

$$[a, b] = \frac{1}{b-a} \int_a^b f(x)\,dx$$

$$\Leftrightarrow 4 = \frac{1}{b-2} \times 8$$

substituting the given values

$$\Leftrightarrow 4(b-2) = 8$$

$$\Leftrightarrow b = 4.$$

23. **(B)**

$$\frac{d}{dx} \int_a^x f(t)\,dt = f(x) \text{ whenever } f \text{ is continuous in } [a, b].$$

Since $\dfrac{d}{dx} \displaystyle\int_x^0 \frac{dt}{2+t} = \frac{d}{dx}\left(-\int_0^x \frac{dt}{2+t}\right)$

$$= -\frac{d}{dx}\left(\int_0^x \frac{dt}{2+t}\right),$$

we get $\dfrac{d}{dx} \displaystyle\int_x^0 \frac{dt}{2+t} = -\frac{1}{2+x}$, since $\dfrac{1}{2+t}$ is continuous in $[0, 1]$.

24. **(D)**

$$\frac{x+x^2}{x^2-1} = \frac{x(1+x)}{(x-1)(x+1)}$$

$$= \frac{x}{x-1}, \text{ for } x \neq 1.$$

Therefore, $\lim\limits_{x\to-1}\dfrac{x+x^2}{x^2-1} = \lim\limits_{x\to-1}\dfrac{x}{x-1}$

$$= \frac{-1}{-1-1}$$

$$= \frac{1}{2}$$

<u>Remark</u>: The limit at $x = -1$ exists though the function is not defined there.

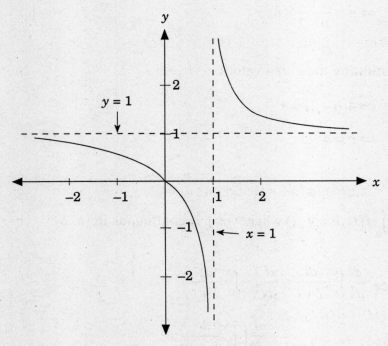

25. **(C)**

$$\frac{1}{h}\left(\frac{1}{x+h}-\frac{1}{x}\right)=\frac{1}{h}\frac{\left(x-(x+h)\right)}{(x+h)x}, \quad \text{for } x\neq 0.$$

$$=\frac{1}{h}\frac{(-h)}{(x+h)x}$$

$$=-\frac{1}{(x+h)x} \qquad\qquad\qquad (i)$$

Thus, $\displaystyle\lim_{h\to 0}\frac{1}{h}\left(\frac{1}{x+h}-\frac{1}{x}\right)=\lim_{h\to 0}\left(\frac{-1}{x+h}\right)\left(\frac{1}{x}\right)$ from (i) above.

$$=-\frac{1}{x}\times\frac{1}{x}$$

$$=-\frac{1}{x^2}$$

Or, simply, if you observe, the limit desired is

$$\frac{d}{dx}\left(\frac{1}{x}\right)=-\frac{1}{x^2}$$

26. **(B)**

Using implicit differentiation

$$6x^2+3xy'+3y+e^y y'=0, \text{ so}$$

$$y'=-\frac{6x^2+3y}{3x+e^y}$$

$y(0) = \ln 6$, hence

$$y'(0)=\frac{-3\ln 6}{6}=-\frac{1}{2}\ln 6 = 0.896$$

27. **(C)**

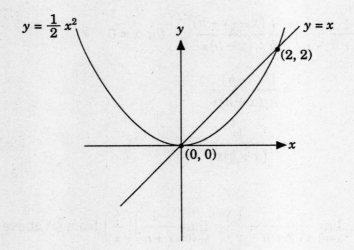

The curve is below the line, so

$$\text{Area} = \int_0^2 \left(x - \frac{1}{2}x^2 \right) dx = \left(\frac{x^2}{2} - \frac{x^3}{6} \right)\Big|_0^2 = 2 - \frac{8}{6} = \frac{2}{3}.$$

28. **(A)**

The area of an ellipse $= \pi ab$, so $\pi ab = 9\pi$, $b = \dfrac{9}{a}$.

Thus, $\dfrac{db}{dt} = \dfrac{-9}{a^2} \dfrac{da}{dt} = -9\left(-\dfrac{1}{2} \right) = 4\dfrac{1}{2}$.

29. **(D)**

Solve

$$2\sqrt{c} = \frac{1}{\sqrt{c}}$$

$$2c = 1$$

$$c = \frac{1}{2}$$

30. **(B)**

$$x(4) - x(0) = \int_0^4 V(t)\, dt$$

$$= \int_0^2 t^2\, dt + \int_2^4 (t+2)\, dt$$

$$= \frac{t^3}{3}\Big|_{t=0}^{t=2} + \left(\frac{t^2}{2} + 2t\right)\Big|_{t=2}^{t=4}$$

$$= \left(\frac{8}{3} - 0\right) + \left(\frac{16}{2} + 8\right) - \left(\frac{4}{2} + 4\right)$$

$$= 12\frac{2}{3}$$

Hence, $x(4) = 12\frac{2}{3} + x(0)$

$$= 12\frac{2}{3} + 0$$

since it started at the origin.

31. **(B)**

$$f'(x) = g'(x)$$

$$\Leftrightarrow f'(x) - g'(x) = 0$$

$$\Leftrightarrow \frac{d}{dx}(f(x) - g(x)) = 0$$

$\Leftrightarrow f(x) - g(x)$ is a constant, since the only function whose derivative is zero on an interval is a constant function.

But, $f(0) - g(0) = 2$. Thus, $f(x) - g(x) = 2$ throughout $[-1, 1]$.

Hence, $\int_{-1}^{1} [f(x) - g(x)]\, dx = \int_{-1}^{1} 2\, dx$

$$= 2x\Big|_{-1}^{1}$$

$$= 2 - (-2)$$

$$= 4$$

32. **(D)**

Let $u = 16 + x^2$

$du = 2x \, dx$

then

$$\int \frac{x}{\sqrt{16+x^2}} \, dx = \int \frac{x}{2x\sqrt{u}} \, du$$

$$= \frac{1}{2} \int \frac{du}{\sqrt{u}}$$

$$= \frac{1}{2} \int u^{\frac{-1}{2}} \, du$$

$$= \frac{1}{2} \times \frac{u^{\frac{1}{2}}}{\frac{1}{2}} + C$$

$$= u^{\frac{1}{2}} + C$$

$$= \sqrt{16+x^2} + C$$

Letting $C = 0$, we see that $\sqrt{16+x^2}$ is an antiderivative.

33. **(E)**

$$\lim_{x\to\infty} \frac{\left(1-2x^2\right)^3}{\left(x^2+1\right)^3} = \left(\lim_{x\to\infty} \frac{\left(1-2x^2\right)}{\left(x^2+1\right)}\right)^3$$

$$= \left(\lim_{x\to\infty} \frac{-2x^2+1}{x^2+1}\right)^3$$

$$= \left(\lim_{x\to\infty} \frac{-2+\dfrac{1}{x^2}}{1+\dfrac{1}{x^2}}\right)^3$$

$$= (-2)^3$$

$$= -8$$

34. **(D)**

$$f'(x) = 1 - \frac{1}{x^2} \qquad\qquad\qquad \text{(i)}$$

$$\Leftrightarrow f'(x) = \frac{x^2-1}{x^2}$$

Therefore, $f'(x) = 0 \Leftrightarrow x = \pm 1$.

$$f''(x) = \frac{d}{dx}\left(1-x^{-2}\right) \text{ differentiating (i) above.}$$

$$= \frac{2}{x^3}$$

$$\Rightarrow f''(1) = 2 > 0 \text{ and } f''(-1) = -2 < 0.$$

Hence, f has relative min. at $x = 1$.

35. **(B)**

$$8 + 2x - x^2 = 0$$

$$\Leftrightarrow -(x^2 - 2x - 8) = 0$$

$\Leftrightarrow x = 4$ or $x = -2$

The graph of $y = 8 + 2x - x^2$ from $(-2, 4)$ is

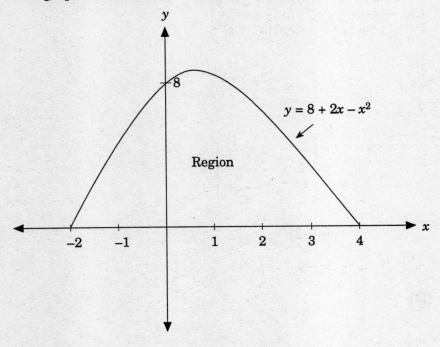

Now, area of region $= \displaystyle\int_{-2}^{4} \left(8 + 2x - x^2\right) dx$

$$= \left(8x + x^2 - \frac{x^3}{3}\right)\Bigg|_{x=-2}^{x=4}$$

$$= \left(32 + 16 - \frac{64}{3}\right) - \left(-16 + 4 - \frac{(-2)^3}{3}\right)$$

$$= 64 - \frac{84}{3}$$

$$= 36$$

<u>Remark:</u> You have to be careful in handling $\dfrac{-(-2)^3}{3}$ in the second set of parentheses: $(-2)^3 = -8$

$$\Rightarrow \frac{-(-2)^3}{3} = \frac{-(-8)}{3}$$

$$= \frac{8}{3}$$

If you make the error $\dfrac{-(-2)^3}{3} = \dfrac{-8}{3}$, you will get:

$32 + 16 - \dfrac{64}{3} + 16 - 4 + 41\dfrac{1}{3}$, which is incorrect.

36. **(A)**

When x ranges from -1 to 1 the values of $x^2 - 1$ are negative (except at the endpoints, when this function vanishes).

Consequently, $|x^2 - 1| = -(x^2 - 1)$

$$= 1 - x^2$$

for $-1 \le x \le 1$.

Thus, $\displaystyle\int_{-1}^{1} \left|\left(x^2 - 1\right)\right| dx = \int_{-1}^{1} \left(1 - x^2\right) dx$

$$= \left(x - \dfrac{x^3}{3}\right)\Big|_{-1}^{1}$$

$$= \dfrac{4}{3}$$

You have to take the same precaution as in problem 35.

37. **(C)**

Draw the graph of $f(x)$.

Since $f(x)$ is an odd function of x, the answer must be (C).

38. **(E)**

A function is symmetric with respect to the origin if and only if $f(-x) = -f(x)$ for every real number x. You can also simply answer the question by looking at the graphs. As you will see below, for the first four graphs the reflection through the origin of a point $(x, f(x))$ is the point $(-x, f(-x))$:

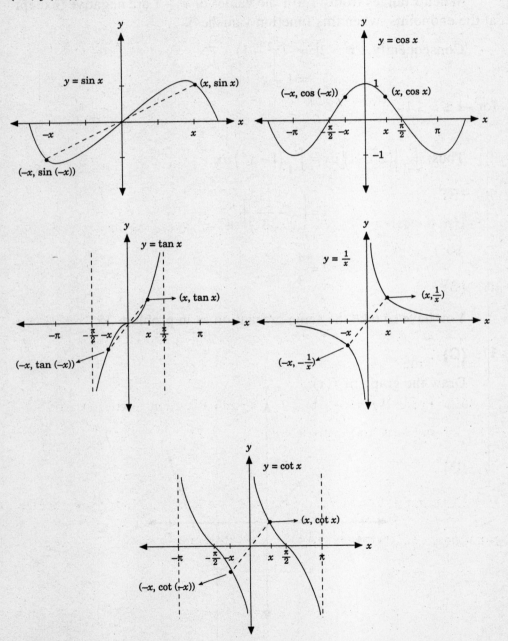

39. **(A)**

We have $y' = \dfrac{-1}{2\sqrt{1-x}}$.

This is clearly a strictly decreasing function as x ranges from 0 to 0.8. Its longest magnitude is then at the endpoint $x = 0.8$ when

$$|y'| = \frac{1}{2\sqrt{0.2}}$$

$$= \frac{1}{\sqrt{0.8}}$$

$$\cong \frac{1}{0.9}$$

$y'(0.8) = -1.118.$

40. **(B)**

Use the calculator directly to find (2). For example,

der 1 (x^ 0.5 ln x, x, 2) gives 0.95.

41. **(B)**

I.   False: $f(x) = |x|$ is continuous at $x = 0$, but is not differentiable at $x = 0$.

II. True.

III. False: If $f(x) = 2$, then $\int_{3}^{7} f(x)\, dx = 8$, which means integral does not have to be greater than 8.

42. **(D)**

Consider $f(x) = x^2$ and $g(x) = \sqrt{x}$. Clearly, f and g are inverse functions, i.e., $f(g(x)) = g(f(x)) = x$. However, $g'(x) \neq \dfrac{1}{f'(x)}$.

43. **(C)**

period of $\tan\left(2-\dfrac{x}{2}\right) = \pi \div \dfrac{1}{2} = 2\pi$

period of $\cos(x-\pi) = $ period of $\cos(-x+\pi) = 2\pi$.

$\dfrac{d}{dx}(\cos(-x+\pi)) = (-1)(-\sin(-x+\pi))$, by the chain rule.

$$= \sin(-x+\pi).$$

$$\Rightarrow \dfrac{d^2}{dx^2}(\cos(-x+\pi)) = \dfrac{d}{dx}\sin(-x+\pi)$$

$$= \cos(-x+\pi), \text{ by the chain rule.}$$

Therefore, $\dfrac{d^2}{dx^2} + y = \cos(-x+\pi) + (-1)\cos(-x+\pi) = 0$.

Moreover, if $f(x) = \cos(-x+\pi)$, then

$$f''(x) = -\cos(-x+\pi).$$

Therefore, $f''\left(-\dfrac{\pi}{2}\right) = -\cos\left(-\left(-\dfrac{\pi}{2}\right)+\pi\right)$

$$= -\cos\dfrac{3\pi}{2}$$

$$= 0$$

Also, $f''\left(\dfrac{\pi}{2}\right) = -\cos\left(-\dfrac{\pi}{2}\right)+\pi$

$$= -\cos\dfrac{3\pi}{2}$$

$$= 0$$

Hence, it will have more than one inflection point.

44. **(C)**

Indeterminate form $\dfrac{0}{0}$, so by L'Hôpital's rule:

$$\lim_{x \to 0} \frac{\sin 2x - 2x}{x^3} = \lim_{x \to 0} \frac{2\cos 2x - 2}{3x^2} = \frac{0}{0}$$

Apply L'Hôpital again:

$$\lim_{x \to 0} \frac{-4\sin 2x}{6x} = \lim_{x \to 0} \frac{-8\cos 2x}{6} = -\frac{4}{3}$$

45. **(D)**

Integrating by parts,

$$\int_0^\infty x e^{ax} dx = \lim_{b \to \infty} \left\{ \frac{x e^{ax}}{a} \Big|_0^b - \int_0^b \frac{1}{a} e^{ax} dx \right\}$$

$$= \lim_{b \to \infty} \left(\frac{b e^{ab}}{a} - \frac{e^{ab}}{a^2} + \frac{1}{a^2} \right).$$

In order to have $e^{ab} \to 0$ as $b \to \infty$ we must have $a < 0$.

SECTION II

1. (A)

Let $g(x) = x - f(x)$. Since $0 \le f(x) \le 1$ for $0 \le x \le 1$ we know that $g(0) \le 0$ and that $g(1) \ge 0$.

Three cases:

1. If $g(0) = 0$ then $f(0) = 0$

2. If $g(1) = 0$ then $f(1) = 1$, ... otherwise:

3. For this case, the continuous function assumes positive and negative values for certain values of its domain. By the I.V. Theorem, they must exist some value c of the domain such that $g(c) = 0$ in which case $c = f(c)$.

Alternatively, the graph of f should take one of the following forms:

If f does not start at the origin, then its graph will be like those in (A), (C) or (F). If f does not touch the point $(1,1)$, then its graph will resemble (B), (C), or (D); otherwise it will be like (E). In either case the graph of $y = f(x)$ will intersect the graph of $y = x$ at some $x = c$.

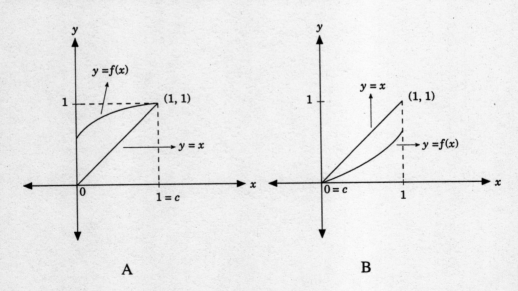

A   B

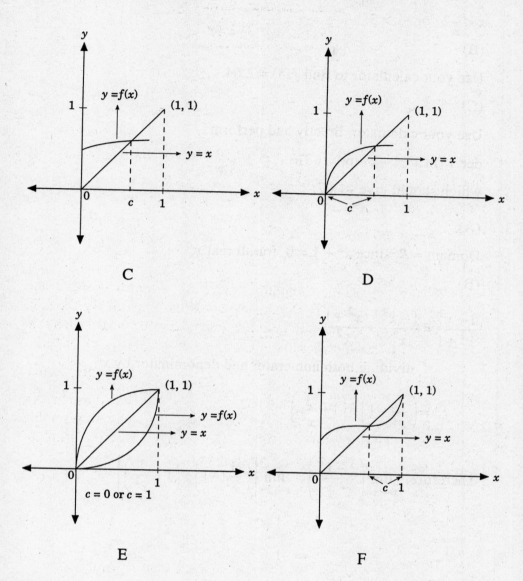

C

D

E

F

2. (A)

Since the argument of the function ln ( ) must be positive, we have

$0 < (x^2 - x - 6)$

or

$0 < (x - 3)(x + 2)$

Therefore,

$x < -2$ or $x > 3$.

(B)

Use your calculator to find $f(5) = 2.64$.

(C)

Use your calculator directly and perform

der 1 (ln $x^\wedge 2 - x - 6$, x, -3),

which should give -1.67.

3. (A)

Domain $= R$, since $x^2 + 1 \neq 0$, for all real x.

(B)

$$\frac{1-x^2}{x^2+1} = \frac{1-x^2}{x^2} \div \frac{x^2+1}{x^2}$$

dividing both numerator and denominator by x^2

$$= \left(\frac{1}{x^2} - 1\right) \div \left(1 + \frac{1}{x^2}\right)$$

Therefore, $\lim\limits_{x \to \pm\infty} \left(\frac{1-x^2}{x^2+1}\right) = \lim\limits_{x \to \pm\infty} \left[\left(\frac{1}{x^2} - 1\right) \div \left(1 + \frac{1}{x^2}\right)\right]$

$$= -1 \div 1$$

$$= -1$$

(C)

We can tell when the function is increasing or decreasing by investigating the sign of $f'(x)$.

$$f'(x) = -\frac{4x}{\left(x^2+1\right)^2}, \text{ by the quotient rule} \qquad \text{(i)}$$

Also, $(x^2 + 1)^2 > 0$, for any x,

$-4x > 0$, when $x < 0$,

$-4x < 0$, when $x > 0$.

Hence, $-\dfrac{4x}{\left(x^2+1\right)^2} > 0$, when $x < 0$, and

$-\dfrac{4x}{\left(x^2+1\right)^2} < 0$, when $x > 0$.

Therefore, $f'(x) > 0$ when $x < 0$, and

$f'(x) < 0$ when $x > 0$.

(D)

The tangent line is parallel to the x-axis so its slope is zero. It is seen that $f'(x)$ vanishes for $x = 0$.

Since $f(0) = 1$, the point of tangency is $(0, 1)$ and the equation of the tangent line is $y = 1$.

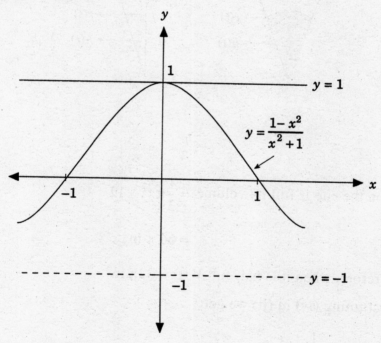

4. (A)

Since $V = \dfrac{\pi}{3}r^2h$ of $r = \dfrac{h}{3}$, we have $V = \dfrac{\pi}{27}h^3$.

Therefore, $\dfrac{dV}{V} = 3\dfrac{dh}{h}$ and so

$$\dfrac{dV}{dt} = 3 \times \dfrac{V}{h} \times \dfrac{dh}{dt}.$$

When $h = 6$, $V = 8\pi$. Since $\dfrac{dV}{dt} = 2$, we get

$$\dfrac{dh}{dt} = \dfrac{1}{2\pi} \text{ inches/min.}$$

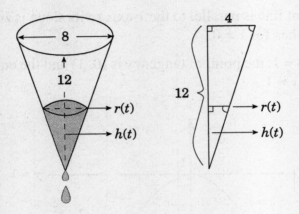

(B)

When the cup is full its volume $= \dfrac{1}{3}\pi 4^2 \times 12$

$$= 64\ \pi\ \text{in}^3$$

Therefore, when it is half full $V(t) = 32\pi\ \text{in}^3$.　　　　　(iv)

Substituting (iv) in (ii) we get:

$$32\pi = \dfrac{1}{27}\pi h^3$$

$$\Leftrightarrow h = 6\sqrt[3]{4}\ .$$　　　　　(v)

Finally using (i), (iii) and (v):

$$\frac{dh}{dt} = \frac{18}{\pi\left(6\sqrt[3]{4}\right)^2} \text{ inches/min.}$$

$$= \frac{1}{2\pi\sqrt[3]{4^2}} \text{ inches/min.}$$

$$= \frac{\sqrt[3]{4}}{8\pi} \text{ inches/min.}$$

5. (A)

$$\frac{d^2}{dx^2}(-2f) = -2f''.$$

From the chart, $-2f'' > 0$ in $(-\infty, 0)$, and

$$-2f'' < 0 \quad \text{in} \quad (0, \infty).$$

Therefore, $-2f$ has inflection point at $x = 0$.

(B)

(i) $\frac{d}{dx}(-2f) = -2f' < 0$ in $(-\infty, -2)$ from the chart.

$$-2f' > 0 \text{ in } (-2, 0) \text{ from the chart.}$$

$\Rightarrow -2f$ has relative min. at $x = -2$.

(ii)   By similar argument as in (i), $-2f$ has relative max at $x = 2$ and equals 0.

(C)

Again from the table, $-2f'' > 0$ in $(-\infty, 0)$, and

$$-2f'' < 0 \quad \text{in} \quad (0, \infty).$$

So, it is concave upward in $(-\infty, 0)$ and concave downward in $(0, \infty)$.

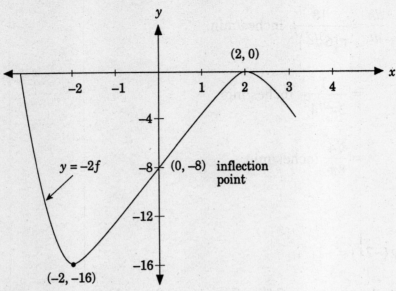

6. (A)

y = x and y = x³ intersect

$\Leftrightarrow x = x^3$

$\Leftrightarrow x - x^3 = 0$

$\Leftrightarrow x(1 - x^2) = 0$

$\Leftrightarrow x = -1, x = 0, x = 1.$

(B)

Determine which lies above the other:

x	x		x^3
$-\dfrac{1}{2}$	$-\dfrac{1}{2}$	$<$	$-\dfrac{1}{8}$
$\dfrac{1}{2}$	$\dfrac{1}{2}$	$>$	$\dfrac{1}{8}$

Therefore, $y = x^3$ lies above $y = x$ in $(-1, 0)$ and $y = x$ lies above $y = x^3$ in $(0, 1)$.

$$\text{Area} = \int_{-1}^{0} \left(x^3 - x\right) dx + \int_{0}^{1} \left(x - x^3\right) dx$$

$$= 2\int_{0}^{1} \left(x - x^3\right) dx$$

$$= 2\left(\frac{x^2}{2} - \frac{x^4}{4}\right)\Big|_{0}^{1}$$

$$= \frac{1}{2}$$

(C)

$$\text{Volume} = \int_{-1}^{0} \pi\left(x^2 - x^6\right) dx + \pi\int_{0}^{1} \left(x^2 - x^6\right) dx,$$

since $x^2 > x^6$ in $(-1, 0)$; look at the figure.

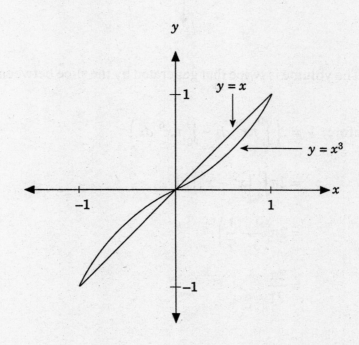

Remark: Do not write $\int_{-1}^{0} \left(x - x^3\right) dx$, since area is non-negative.

Also, do not write $\int_{-1}^{0} \left(x^6 - x^2 \right) dx$ since volume is non-negative.

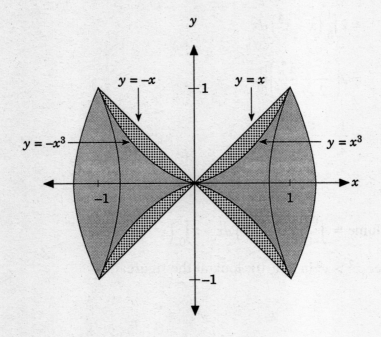

(C) The volume is twice that generated by the slice between 0 and 1.

Therefore, $V = 2\left(\int_{1}^{0} \pi x^2 \, dx - \int_{0}^{1} \pi x^6 \, dx \right)$

$$= 2\pi \int_{0}^{1} \left(x^2 - x^6 \right) dx$$

$$= 2\pi \left(\frac{1}{3} - \frac{1}{7} \right)$$

$$= \frac{8\pi}{21}$$

Advanced Placement Examination in Calculus AB

EXAM III

ADVANCED PLACEMENT
CALCULUS AB
EXAM III

SECTION I

PART A

Time: 55 minutes
28 questions

DIRECTIONS: Each of the following problems is followed by five choices. Solve each problem, select the best choice, and blacken the correct space on your answer sheet. Calculators may not be used for this section of the exam.

NOTE: Unless otherwise specified, the domain of function f is assumed to be the set of all real numbers x for which $f(x)$ is a real number.

1. For what value of x will the tangent lines to $y_1 = \ln x$ and $y_2 = 2x^2$ be parallel?

   (A) 0

   (B) $\dfrac{1}{4}$

   (C) $\dfrac{1}{2}$

   (D) 1

   (E) 2

2. If $f(x) = 2^{x^3+1}$, then $f'(1)$ is approximately

   (A) 2.000

   (B) 4.000

   (C) 6.000

   (D) 2.773

   (E) 8.318

3. Let $f'(x) = \sin(\pi x)$ and $f(0) = 0$. Then $f(1) = $?

(A) $-\dfrac{1}{\pi}$ (D) $\dfrac{2}{\pi}$

(B) $\dfrac{1}{\pi}$ (E) None of these

(C) $-\dfrac{2}{\pi}$

4. Let the velocity at a time t of a point moving on a line be defined by $V(t) = 2^t \ln 2$ cm/sec. How many centimeters did the point travel from $t = 0$ sec. to $t = 2$ sec.?

(A) 8.882   (D) 8.121

(B) 9.882   (E) 10.003

(C) 4.104

5. Find the slope of the tangent line to the graph of $y = \dfrac{5}{4 + x^3}$ when $x = 1$.

(A) 8.047   (D) 1.000

(B) –0.600   (E) None of the above

(C) –0.200

6. Let $f(x) = e^{bx}$, $g(x) = e^{ax}$ and find the value of b such that

$$D_x\left(\frac{f(x)}{g(x)}\right) = \frac{f'(x)}{g'(x)}$$

(A) $\dfrac{a^2}{a^2 - 1}$ (D) $\dfrac{a-1}{a^2}$

(B) $\dfrac{a^2}{a+1}$ (E) $\dfrac{a^2}{a-1}$

(C) $\dfrac{a+1}{a^2}$

7. Suppose $x^2 - xy + y^2 = 3$. Find $\dfrac{dy}{dx}$ at the point (a, b).

    (A) $\dfrac{a-2b}{2a-b}$

    (D) $\dfrac{b-2a}{2b+a}$

    (B) $\dfrac{b-2a}{2b-a}$

    (E) $\dfrac{b+2a}{2b+a}$

    (C) $\dfrac{a-2b}{2a+b}$

8. $\lim\limits_{h \to 0} \dfrac{e^{x+h} - e^x}{h}$ equals

    (A) 0

    (D) $-\infty$

    (B) 1

    (E) None of these

    (C) $+\infty$

9. $\displaystyle\int_{-2}^{-1} x^{-4}\, dx = $?

    (A) $\dfrac{7}{2}$

    (D) $\dfrac{31}{160}$

    (B) $\dfrac{31}{8}$

    (E) None of these

    (C) $\dfrac{7}{24}$

10. If $f'(x) = \dfrac{x^2}{2}$ where $f(0) = 0$ then $3f(4) =$

    (A) 0

    (B) 3

    (C) 12

    (D) 24

    (E) 32

11. $\displaystyle\lim_{x \to +\infty}\left(\dfrac{1}{x} - \dfrac{x}{x-1}\right) = ?$

    (A) −1

    (B) 0

    (C) 1

    (D) 2

    (E) None of these

12. Let $R = \displaystyle\int_0^a \cos(x^2)\,dx$ and $S = \displaystyle\int_0^a \tan x\,dx$.

    Find $\displaystyle\int_{-a}^{a}\left[\cos(x^2) + \tan x\right]dx$.

    (A) $2R$

    (B) $2S$

    (C) $R + 2S$

    (D) $S + 2R$

    (E) $2R + 2S$

13. If $\sin y = \cos x$, then find $\dfrac{dy}{dx}$ at the point $\left(\dfrac{\pi}{2},\ \pi\right)$.

    (A) −1

    (B) 0

    (C) 1

    (D) $\dfrac{\pi}{2}$

    (E) None of these

14. For which of the following intervals is the graph of
$y = x^4 - 2x^3 - 12x^2$ concave down?

(A) $(-2, 1)$

(D) $(-\infty, -1)$

(B) $(-1, 2)$

(E) $(-1, +\infty)$

(C) $(-1, -2)$

15. $\int_1^e x \ln x \, dx = ?$

(A) e

(D) $\dfrac{e-1}{2}$

(B) $\dfrac{e^2-1}{2}$

(E) None of these

(C) $\dfrac{e^2+1}{4}$

16. If $f'(x) = 2(3x + 5)^4$, then the fifth derivative of $f(x)$ at

$x = -\dfrac{5}{3}$ is

(A) 0

(D) 3,888

(B) 144

(E) None of these

(C) 1,296

17. Let $f'(x) = \dfrac{x}{\sqrt{x^2 - 8}}$. Which of the following interval notations represents the most inclusive domain for f?

(A) $\left(2\sqrt{2}, -2\sqrt{2}\right)$

(B) $\left[2\sqrt{2}, -2\sqrt{2}\right]$

(C) $\left(-\infty, +\infty\right)$

(D) $\left(-\infty, -2\sqrt{2}\,\right] \cup \left[\,2\sqrt{2}, +\infty\right)$

(E) $\left(-\infty, -2\sqrt{2}\right) \cup \left(2\sqrt{2}, +\infty\right)$

18. If $f(x) = \ln x$, then $f\left(\dfrac{3}{2}\right) =$

(A) $\dfrac{\ln 3}{\ln 2}$

(D) $\displaystyle\int_2^3 \ln t\, dt$

(B) $\ln 2 - \ln \dfrac{1}{2}$

(E) $\displaystyle\int_2^3 \dfrac{1}{t}\, dt$

(C) $\displaystyle\int_{\ln 2}^{\ln 3} e^t\, dt$

19. If $y = \dfrac{3}{\sin x + \cos x}$ then $\dfrac{dy}{dx} =$

(A) $3\sin x - 3\cos x$

(D) $\dfrac{-3}{(\sin x + \cos x)^2}$

(B) $\dfrac{6\sin x}{1 + 2\sin x \cos x}$

(E) $\dfrac{3(\sin x - \cos x)}{1 + 2\sin x \cos x}$

(C) $\dfrac{3}{\cos x - \sin x}$

20. $\int_{-2}^{-1} \left| x^{-3} \right| dx =$

    (A) $\dfrac{3}{8}$

    (B) $\dfrac{5}{8}$

    (C) $\dfrac{15}{4}$

    (D) $\dfrac{15}{64}$

    (E) None of these

21. $\displaystyle \lim_{x \to 0} \dfrac{\dfrac{3}{x^2}}{\dfrac{2}{x^2} + \dfrac{105}{x}} =$

    (A) 0

    (B) 1

    (C) $\dfrac{3}{2}$

    (D) $\dfrac{3}{107}$

    (E) None of these

22. The graph of f is shown in the figure. Which of the following could be the graph of $\int f(x)\, dx$?

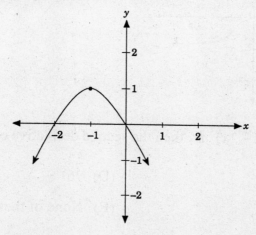

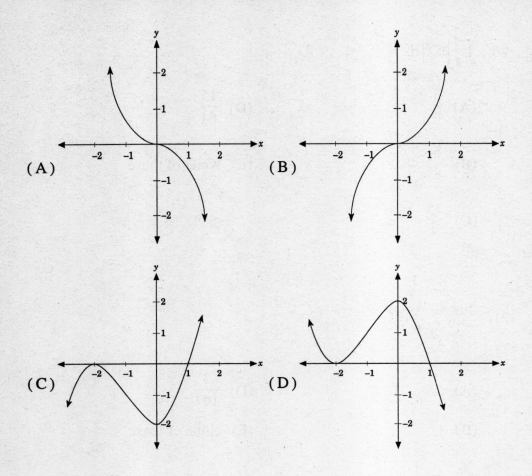

(A)

(B)

(C)

(D)

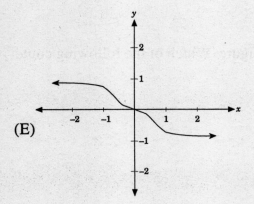

(E)

23. If $f(x) = \int (1-2x)^3 \, dx$, then the second derivative of $f(x)$ at $x = \dfrac{1}{2}$ is

(A) −48

(D) 96

(B) −12

(E) None of these

(C) 0

24. Let $F(x) = \int_1^x f(t)\, dt$, and use the graph given of $f(t)$ to find $F'(1) =$

(A) 0

(D) $\dfrac{1}{2}$

(B) 1

(E) None of these

(C) 2

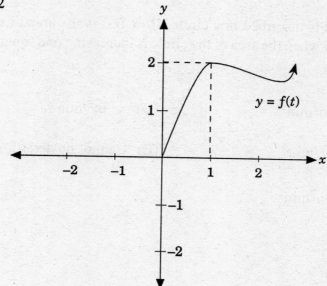

25. $\int x^{-1}\, dx =$

(A) $\dfrac{x^{-2}}{-2} + C$

(D) $-x + c$

(B) $x + C$

(E) None of these

(C) Undefined

26. $\int_0^4 \dfrac{dx}{(x-1)^{2/3}} =$ approximately

(A) 1.327

(D) 4.326

(B) 7.326

(E) None of the above

(C) 3

27. How many relative or absolute maxima does $x - \cos x$ have on the interval $(-2\pi, 2\pi)$?

(A) 1

(D) 4

(B) 2

(E) 5

(C) 3

28. A square is inscribed in a circle. How fast is the area of the square changing when the area of the circle is increasing one square inch per minute?

(A) $\dfrac{1}{2}$ in²min

(D) $\dfrac{\pi}{2}$ in²/min

(B) 1 in²/min

(E) Cannot be determined

(C) $\dfrac{2}{\pi}$ in²min

PART B

Time: 50 minutes

17 questions

DIRECTIONS: Calculators may be used for this section of the test. Each of the following problems is followed by five choices. Solve each problem, select the best choice, and blacken the correct space on your answer sheet.

NOTES:

1. Unless otherwise specified, answers can be given in unsimplified form.

2. The domain of function f is assumed to be the set of all real numbers x for which $f(x)$ is a real number.

---

29. The area that is enclosed by $y = x^3 + x^2$ and $y = 6x$ for $x \geq 0$ is

(A) $\dfrac{29}{12}$

(D) 6

(B) 3

(E) $\dfrac{32}{3}$

(C) $\dfrac{16}{3}$

30. $\displaystyle\lim_{x \to 0} \frac{\arctan x}{\tan x}$ equals

(A) 0

(D) $-\infty$

(B) 1

(E) None of these

(C) $+\infty$

31. Find the area in the first quadrant that is enclosed by $y = \sin 3x$ and the x–axis from $x = 0$ to the first x–intercept on the positive x–axis.

(A) $\dfrac{1}{3}$

(D) 2

(B) $\dfrac{2}{3}$

(E) 6

(C) 1

32. A particle moves along a straight line. Its velocity is

$$V(t) = \begin{cases} t^2 & \text{for } 0 \le t \le 2 \\ t+2 & \text{for } t \ge 2 \end{cases}$$

The distance travelled by the particle in the interval $1 \le t \le 3$ is

(A) 3

(D) 5

(B) 7.1

(E) 6.8

(C) 4.3

33. Let $f(x) = x + \dfrac{1}{x^{1.6}}$. Then, $\displaystyle\int_{0.1}^{2} f(x)$ equals

(A) 3.64

(D) 5.1

(B) 4.99

(E) 11.2

(C) 7.53

34. $\displaystyle\lim_{x \to -4^+} \dfrac{4x - 6}{2x^2 + 5x - 12}$ equals

(A) 0

(D) $-\infty$

(B) 1

(E) None of these

(C) $+-\infty$

35. Let $g(x) = e^{-x^2}$ and determine which one of the following statements is true.

   (A) g is a decreasing function.

   (B) g is an odd function.

   (C) g is symmetric with respect to the x–axis.

   (D) $(0.5, e^{-0.25})$ is a point of inflection.

   (E) None of these.

36. The graph shown represents $y = f(x)$. Which one of the following is NOT true?

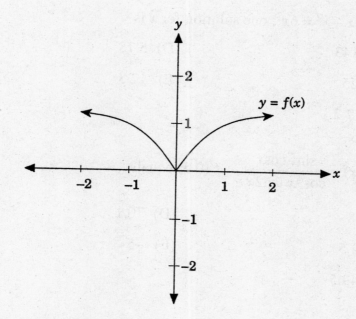

   (A) f is continuous on $(-2, 2)$.

   (B) $\lim\limits_{x \to 0} f(x) = f(0)$.

   (C) f is differentiable on $(-2, 2)$.

   (D) $\lim\limits_{x \to 0^-} f(x) = f(0)$.

   (E) $f'(x) < 0$ for $x < 0$

37. Which one of the following is NOT an antiderivative of sec x?

    (A) $\ln|\sec x + \tan x| + C$

    (B) $-\ln|\sec x - \tan x| + C$

    (C) $\ln\left|\dfrac{1 - \sin x}{\cos x}\right| + C$

    (D) $\ln\left|\dfrac{1 + \sin x}{\cos x}\right|$

    (E) $\ln\left|\dfrac{\cos x}{1 - \sin x}\right|$

38. If $8 + 2x - x^2 = 6x^3$, one solution for x is

    (A) 1.143   (D) 5.78

    (B) 2.25   (E) 12.3

    (C) −17.2

39. Let $f(x) = \dfrac{\sin x \, \cos x}{\cos 9x \, \tan 2x}$. $f'(0.5)$ equals

    (A) 3.8   (D) 70.1

    (B) −2.5   (E) −5

    (C) −49.5

40. Let $f(x) = \dfrac{x}{\sqrt{4 - x^2}}$. The minimum of $f'(x)$ is

    (A) 0.5   (D) −0.5

    (B) 1   (E) 2

    (C) −1

41. Suppose $f(x)$ is a continuous function on $[1, 2]$ and $f(1) = 2$, $f(1.5)$ $= 0.5$, and $f(2) = -3$. Which of the following is FALSE?

    (A) The maximum value of f in $[1, 2]$ is 2.

    (B) $f(c) = 0$ for some real value of c.

    (C) $\lim\limits_{x \to 2^-} f(x) = -3$

    (D) $|f(2)| - |f(1)| \le |f(2) - f(1)|$

    (E) $\lim\limits_{x \to \frac{5}{4}} f(x) = f\left(\frac{5}{4}\right)$

42. Find the value of c such that the area between the line $y = c$ and the parabola $y = x^2$ is $\dfrac{1}{48}$.

    (A) $\dfrac{1}{512}$

    (B) $\dfrac{1}{64}$

    (C) $\dfrac{1}{32}$

    (D) $\dfrac{1}{16}$

    (E) None of these

43. Let f', g' be differentiable functions that are derivatives of f and g, respectively. If $f'(x) \le g'(x)$ for all real x, which of the following must be true (if $b > a$)?

    I. $\lim\limits_{x \to a} f'(x) \le \lim\limits_{x \to a} g'(x)$

    II. $\int_a^b f'(x)\,dx \le \int_a^b g'(x)\,dx$

    III. $f(x) \le g(x)$, for all real x

    IV. $\int_a^b f(x)\,dx \le \int_a^b g(x)\,dx$

(A) I only

(D) I, II, and III

(B) II only

(E) I, II, III, and IV

(C) I and II only

44. The volume generated by revolving $y = x^3 (-1 \le x \le 1)$ around the y-axis is

(A) π

(D) $\dfrac{2\pi}{5}$

(B) 2π

(E) $\dfrac{4\pi}{5}$

(C) $\dfrac{6\pi}{5}$

45. The curves $y = \dfrac{x^2}{2}$ and $y = 1 - \dfrac{x^2}{2}$ intersect in the first quadrant. The angle at which they intersect is

(A) 30°

(D) 90°

(B) 45°

(E) 0°

(C) 60°

SECTION II

Time: 1 hour and 30 minutes
6 problems

DIRECTIONS: Show all your work. Grading is based on the methods used to solve the problem as well as the accuracy of your final answers. Please make sure all procedures are clearly shown. For some problems or parts of problems it will be necessary to use a calculator.

NOTES:

1. Unless otherwise specified, answers can be given in unsimplified form.

2. The domain of function f is assumed to be the set of all real numbers x for which $f(x)$ is a real number.

---

1. Let f be the function defined by $f(x) = \dfrac{x}{(x-1)^2}$

   (A) Sketch the graph of $y = f(x)$. Be sure to label all relative extrema, points of inflection, and asymptotes.

   (B) Use interval notation to indicate where the function is increasing, decreasing, concave up, and concave down.

   (C) State the domain and range of the function and indicate why the function does not have an inverse over its domain.

(D) Write the equation (in standard form) for the tangent line to $y = f(x)$ that passes through a point of inflection.

2. Let $f(x) = \dfrac{3}{2 + 105x}$

    (A) Find $f'(0)$

    (B) What happens to the graph of $f(x)$ versus x near $x = -0.019$? Explain.

    (C) Find $\displaystyle\int_0^2 f(x)\, dx$.

3. Let the growth rate (in grams/sec) of a plant culture be directly proportional to the weight (in grams) of the plant culture present at the same instant.

    (A) Write a formula for the rate of growth of the plant culture in terms of the current weight of the plant culture.

    (B) Solve the differential equation in part (A) to find the weight of the plant culture X as a function of time.

    (C) If the weight of the culture at the beginning of the experiment $(t = 0)$ is 10 grams, and the weight after one second $(t = 1)$ is 100 grams, find the weight of the culture after 0.5 seconds.

    (D) Find the difference between the instantaneous rate of growth when t is one second and the average rate of growth for the first second.

4. Let $y = \cos(2x^2)$ for x in the interval $[0, c]$ where c is the first positive x–intercept.

    (A) Find the volume of the region between $y = f(x)$ and $y = 0$ in the interval $[0, c]$, rotating about the y–axis.

    (B) Find the average value of $y = f'(x)$ over the given interval.

(C) Write (DO NOT EVALUATE) the definite integral expression for the volume of the region between $y = 1$ and $y = f(x)$ on the given interval, rotating about the x–axis.

5. Assume the volume V of a cube is increasing at a constant rate of 3 cm^3 per second. Let t_0 be the instant when the rate of change of the volume (cm^3/sec) is numerically equal to the rate of change of the surface area (cm^2/sec) for the cube. Assume $V = 0$ when $t = 0$.

   (A) Find the value(s) of t_0.

   (B) Find the rate of change of the length of a side when $t = t_0$.

   (C) Find the rate of change of the surface area when $t = t_0$.

6. The vertical speed of a glider (ft/min) is indicated by the following graph.

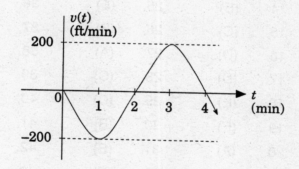

   (A) Let $t \in [0,4]$ and sketch the graph of $y(t)$, where y is the altitude in feet and t is the time in minutes. Assume $y(0) = 627$ ft $\approx$ $\left(500 + \dfrac{400}{\pi}\right)$ ft.

   (B) For what value(s) of t will the glider be at a minimum altitude for Let $t \in [0,4]$?

   (C) For what value(s) of t will the glider be at a maximum altitude for Let $t \in [0, 4]$?

   (D) For what value(s) of t is the graph of $y = f(t)$ concave up?

ADVANCED PLACEMENT CALCULUS AB EXAM III

ANSWER KEY

Section I

1.	(C)	12.	(A)	23.	(C)	34.	(C)
2.	(E)	13.	(C)	24.	(C)	35.	(E)
3.	(D)	14.	(B)	25.	(E)	36.	(C)
4.	(A)	15.	(C)	26.	(B)	37.	(C)
5.	(B)	16.	(D)	27.	(A)	38.	(A)
6.	(E)	17.	(D)	28.	(C)	39.	(C)
7.	(B)	18.	(E)	29.	(C)	40.	(A)
8.	(E)	19.	(E)	30.	(B)	41.	(A)
9.	(C)	20.	(A)	31.	(B)	42.	(D)
10.	(E)	21.	(C)	32.	(E)	43.	(C)
11.	(A)	22.	(D)	33.	(C)	44.	(C)
						45.	(D)

Section II

See Detailed Explanations of Answers.

ADVANCED PLACEMENT
CALCULUS AB
EXAM III

DETAILED EXPLANATIONS
OF ANSWERS

SECTION I

1. **(C)**

    $y_1 = \ln x$ and $y_2 = 2x^2$, with $y_1 = \dfrac{1}{x}$ and $y_2 = 4x$

    Set the derivatives equal and get

    $\dfrac{1}{4} = 4x$, or

    $\dfrac{1}{4} = x^2$. This has the solutions $x = \pm\dfrac{1}{2}$

    Since $y = \ln x$ is not defined for $x = -\dfrac{1}{2}$, the solution is $x = \dfrac{1}{2}$.

2. **(E)**

    $f(x) = 2^{x^3+1}$ then $f'(x) = 2^{x^3+1} (\ln 2) D(x^3 + 1)$

    If

    $\qquad = 2^{x^3+1} (\ln 2)(3x^2)$

So $f'(1) = 2^2(\ln 2)(3)$

$\qquad = 12\ln 2$

$\qquad \approx 8.318$

3. **(D)**

$y = f(x) = \displaystyle\int \sin(\pi x)\, dx$

$\quad = -\dfrac{1}{\pi}\cos(\pi x) + C$

Since $y = 0$ when $x = 0$:

$\quad 0 = -\dfrac{1}{\pi}\cos 0 + C, \quad \text{so} \quad C = \dfrac{1}{\pi} \quad \text{and}$

$f(x) = -\dfrac{1}{\pi}\cos(\pi x) + \dfrac{1}{\pi}.$

Therefore, $f(1) = -\dfrac{1}{\pi}\cos\pi + \dfrac{1}{\pi}$

$\qquad\qquad\quad = -\dfrac{1}{\pi}(-1) + \dfrac{1}{\pi}$

$\qquad\qquad\quad = \dfrac{2}{\pi}$

4. **(A)**

$V(t) = 2^t \ln 2, \quad \text{so} \quad s(t) = 2^t + c.$

We can set $c = 0$ since it is subtracted out.

$\quad s(0) = 2^0 = 1$

$s(2.5) = 2^{2.5}$

$\qquad \cong 5.657$

Distance $= s(2.5) - s(0)$

$\qquad\qquad = (9.882 + c) - (1 + c)$

= 8.882 cm.

Distance traveled = 4.657 cm.

5. **(B)**

$y' = 5 \times (-1)(4 + x^3)^{-2}(3x^2)$. When $x = 1$ this becomes

$= -5(5)^{-2}(3)$

$= -\dfrac{15}{25}$

$= -\dfrac{3}{5}$

Therefore, $y'(1) = -0.600$

6. **(E)**

$D_x\left(\dfrac{f(x)}{g(x)}\right) = \dfrac{e^{ax}be^{bx} - e^{bx}ae^{ax}}{e^{2ax}}$

$= \dfrac{(b - a)e^{bx}}{e^{ax}}$

$\dfrac{f'(x)}{g'(x)} = \dfrac{be^{bx}}{ae^{ax}}$

Now equate the two to get

$\dfrac{b}{a} = b - a$ or $b = ab - a^2 \Rightarrow$

$a^2 = ab - b \Rightarrow a^2 = b(a - 1)$

Therefore, $\dfrac{a^2}{a - 1} = b$

7. **(B)**

    Differentiate $x^2 - xy + y^2 = 3$ implicitly to get

    $2x - (xy' + y) + 2yy' = 0.$

    Now solve for y':

    $2x - xy' - y + 2yy' = 0$

    $y'(2y - x) = y - 2x$

    $y' = \dfrac{y - 2x}{2y - x} \cdot$

    Let $x = a$, $y = b$ to get $y' = \dfrac{b - 2a}{2b - a}.$

8. **(E)**

    $\displaystyle \lim_{h \to 0} \frac{e^{x+h} - e^x}{h}$ equals the derivative of e^x by using the definition of
    the derivative

    $\displaystyle f'(x) = \lim_{h \to 0} \frac{f(x+h) - f(x)}{h}$

    $= e^x \quad \text{for} \quad f(x) = e^x$

9. **(C)**

    $\displaystyle \int_{-2}^{-1} x^{-4} dx = \frac{x^{-3}}{-3} \bigg|_{-2}^{-1}$

    $\displaystyle = -\frac{1}{3}\left(\frac{1}{-1} - \frac{1}{-8}\right)$

    $\displaystyle = -\frac{1}{3}\left(-\frac{7}{8}\right)$

    $\displaystyle = \frac{7}{24}$

10. **(E)**

$$f(x) = \int \frac{x^2}{2}\, dx$$

$$= \frac{x^3}{6} + C$$

Let $x = 0$; $\quad f(0) = \frac{1}{6}(0)^3 + C \qquad 0 = C$

$$f(x) = \frac{1}{6}x^3$$

$$3f(4) = 3 \times \frac{1}{6} \times (4)^3$$

$$= 32$$

11. **(A)**

$$\lim_{x \to +\infty}\left(\frac{1}{x} - \frac{x}{x-1}\right) = \lim_{x \to +\infty} \frac{x - 1 - x^2}{x(x-1)}$$

$$= \lim_{x \to +\infty} \frac{-x^2 + x - 1}{x^2 - x}$$

$$= \lim_{x \to +\infty} \frac{-1 + \dfrac{1}{x} - \dfrac{1}{x^2}}{1 - \dfrac{1}{x}}$$

$$= -1$$

12. **(A)**

$\cos(x^2)$ is an even function and $\tan x$ is an odd function so

$$\int_{-a}^{a} \cos(x^2)\, dx = 2R; \quad \int_{-a}^{0} \tan x\, dx = -\int_{0}^{a} \tan x\, dx$$

Then $\displaystyle\int_{-a}^{a}\left[\cos\left(x^2\right)+\tan x\right]dx = 2R+0$

$$= 2R$$

13. **(C)**

Differentiate $\sin y = \cos x$ implicitly.

$$\frac{dy}{dx}\cos y = -\sin x, \quad \frac{dy}{dx} = -\frac{\sin x}{\cos y}.$$

At $\left(\dfrac{\pi}{2},\ \pi\right)$, $\quad \dfrac{dy}{dx} = -\dfrac{\sin\left(\dfrac{\pi}{2}\right)}{\cos(\pi)}$

$$= \frac{-1}{-1}$$

$$= 1$$

14. **(B)**

$$y = x^4 - 2x^3 - 12x^2$$

$$y' = 4x^3 - 6x^2 - 24x$$

$$y'' = 12x^2 - 12x - 24$$

$$= 12(x-2)(x+1)$$

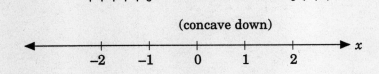

$$+ + + + + 0 - - - - - - - - - - - - 0 + + +$$

(concave down)

15. **(C)**

Use integration by parts with

$u = \ln x$	$du = \dfrac{1}{x}\,dx$
$dv = x$	$v = \dfrac{x^2}{2}$

$$\int_1^e x \ln x\, dx = \frac{x^2}{2}\ln x - \int_1^e \frac{x}{2}\,dx$$

$$= \left(\frac{x^2}{2}\ln x - \frac{x^2}{4}\right)\Big|_1^e$$

$$= \frac{e^2 + 1}{4}$$

16. **(D)**

If $f'(x) = 2\,(3x + 5)^4;$ $\qquad f''(x) = 24\,(3x + 5)^3$

$f'''(x) = 216\,(3x + 5)^2\,;$ $\qquad f^{(4)}(x) = 1{,}296\,(3x + 5)$

$f^{(5)}(x) = 3{,}888$ so $f\left(-\dfrac{5}{3}\right) = 3{,}888$

17. **(D)**

$$f'(x) = \frac{x}{\sqrt{x^2 - 8}} \quad \text{then} \quad f(x) = \int x\left(x^2 - 8\right)^{-\frac{1}{2}} dx$$

Let $u = x^2 - 8$ and $du = 2x\, dx$, so

$$f(x) = \frac{1}{2}\int u^{-\frac{1}{2}}\, du$$

$$= \frac{1}{2}\times 2u^{\frac{1}{2}} + C$$

$$= \sqrt{x^2 - 8} + C.$$

We must have $|x^2 - 8| \geq 0$ in order for f to be real-valued so

$$(x + 2\sqrt{2})(x - 2\sqrt{2}) \geq 1$$

$$+ + + + + 0 - - - - - - - - 0 + + + + +$$

$x \leq -2 \cap \sqrt{2}$ or $x \geq 2\sqrt{2}x$

which is written in interval notation as

$$(-\infty, -2\sqrt{2}\,] \cup [\,2\sqrt{2}, +\infty)$$

18. **(E)**

Recall that $\ln x = \int_1^x \dfrac{1}{t}\, dt$, and that $\ln \dfrac{a}{b} = \ln a - \ln b$

We have: $\ln \dfrac{3}{2} = \ln 3 - \ln 2$

$$= \int_1^3 \frac{1}{t}\, dt - \int_1^2 \frac{1}{t}\, dt$$

$$= \int_2^3 \frac{1}{t}\, dt$$

19. **(E)**

$$y = \frac{3}{\sin x + \cos x} = \frac{3}{u} \quad \text{where } u = \sin x + \cos x$$

So $\dfrac{dy}{dx} = 3(-1)u^{-1-1}\dfrac{du}{dx}$ using the derivative of a power and chain rule theorems.

Thus, $\dfrac{dy}{dx} = \dfrac{-3}{(\sin x + \cos x)^2}(\cos x - \sin x)$

$$= \dfrac{3(\sin x - \cos x)}{\sin^2 x + 2\sin x \cos x + \cos^2 x}$$

$$\dfrac{dy}{dx} = \dfrac{3(\sin x - \cos x)}{1 + 2\sin x \cos x},$$

using the identity $\sin^2 x + \cos^2 x = 1$

20. **(A)**

Note $|n| = \begin{cases} n & \text{if } n \geq 0 \\ -n & \text{if } n < 0 \end{cases}$

so $|x^{-3}| = -x^{-3}$ for x in $[-2, -1]$

Now $\displaystyle\int_{-2}^{-1} |x^{-3}|\, dx = \int_{-2}^{-1} -x^{-3}\, dx$

$$= -\left(\dfrac{x^{-3+1}}{-3+1}\right)\Big|_{-2}^{-1}$$

$$= \dfrac{x^{-2}}{2}\Big|_{-2}^{-1}$$

$$= \dfrac{1}{2}\left[\dfrac{1}{(-1)^2} - \dfrac{1}{(-2)^2}\right]$$

$$= \dfrac{1}{2}\left[1 - \dfrac{1}{4}\right]$$

$$= \dfrac{1}{2}\left(\dfrac{3}{4}\right)$$

$$= \dfrac{3}{8}$$

21. **(C)**

$$\lim_{x \to 0} \frac{\dfrac{3}{x^2}}{\dfrac{2}{x^2} + \dfrac{105}{x}} \boxed{\dfrac{x^2}{x^2}} = \lim_{x \to 0} \frac{3}{2 + 105x}$$

$$= \frac{3}{2 + 0}$$

$$= \frac{3}{2}$$

22. **(D)**

Consider $\dfrac{d}{dx} \displaystyle\int f(x)\, dx = f(x)$. So the following graph is the graph of

the derivative of $\displaystyle\int f(x)\, dx$. Note the graph of the derivative indicates:

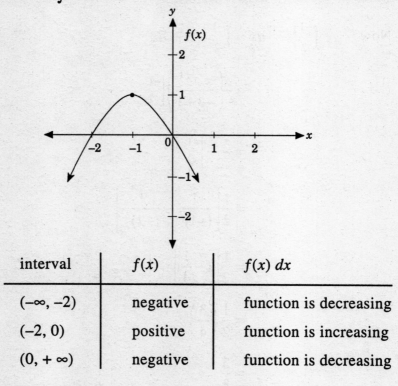

interval	$f(x)$	$f(x)\, dx$
$(-\infty, -2)$	negative	function is decreasing
$(-2, 0)$	positive	function is increasing
$(0, +\infty)$	negative	function is decreasing

Therefore the graph of the function has a relative minimum when $x = -2$ and a relative maximum when $x = 0$. Choice (D) is the only choice with correct locations of the relative minimum and relative maximum. Since $\int f(x)\,dx = F(x) + C$ for any real number C, the graph would be adjusted up if $C > 0$ and down if $C < 0$.

23. **(C)**

If $\quad f(x) = \int (1 - 2x)^3\,dx$

then $\quad f'(x) = (1 - 2x)^3$

since $\quad \dfrac{d}{dx}\int f(x)\,dx = f(x)$ by definition.

$$f''(x) = 3(1 - 2x)^2(-2)$$

$$= -6(1 - 2x)^2$$

$$f''\!\left(\frac{1}{2}\right) = -6\left(1 - 2\left(\frac{1}{2}\right)\right)^2$$

$$= 0$$

24. **(C)**

$F(x) = \int_1^x f(t)\,dt$; the graph of $f(t)$ is as shown.

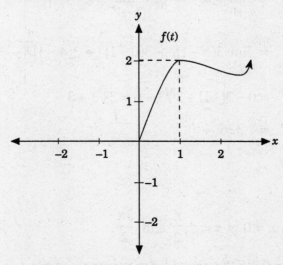

Now $F'(x) = f(x)$ using the Fundamental Theorem of Calculus.

So, $F'(1) = f(1) = 2$, using the graph of f.

25. **(E)**

$$\int x^{-1}\,dx = \int \frac{1}{x}\,dx$$

$$= \ln x + C \quad \text{since} \quad \frac{d}{dx}(\ln x + C)$$

$$= \frac{1}{x}$$

26. **(B)**

Since the function $f(x) = \dfrac{1}{(x-1)^{2/3}}$ becomes infinite at $x = 1$, which lies between the limits of integration, we must split the integral into two parts and take limits.

$$\int_0^4 \frac{dx}{(x-1)^{2/3}} = \lim_{a\to 1^-} \int_0^a \frac{dx}{(x-1)^{2/3}} + \lim_{b\to 1^+} \int_b^4 \frac{dx}{(x-1)^{2/3}}$$

$$= \lim_{a\to 1^-} 3(x-1)^{\frac{1}{3}}\Big|_0^a + \lim_{b\to 1^+} 3(x-1)^{\frac{1}{3}}\Big|_b^4$$

$$= \lim_{a\to 1^-} 3(a-1)^{\frac{1}{3}} - 3(0-1)^{\frac{1}{3}} + 3(4-1)^{\frac{1}{3}} - \lim_{b\to 1^+} 3(b-1)^{\frac{1}{3}}$$

$$= 0 - 3(-1) + 3\sqrt[3]{3} - 0 = 3\sqrt[3]{3} + 3$$

$$= 7.326$$

27. **(A)**

$y' = 1 + \sin x = 0$ at $x = -\dfrac{\pi}{2}$ and $\dfrac{3\pi}{2}$.

$y'' = \cos x = 0$, so the second derivative test fails.

However, notice that $y'(x) \geq 0$ for all x, so y is monotone increasing. Thus, the only max is at 2π.

28. **(C)**

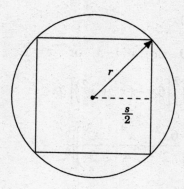

The side of the square, s, is $\sqrt{2}r$. The areas are $A = \pi r^2$ and $A_s = 2r^2$. Thus, $\dfrac{d}{dt}(A_s) = 4r\dfrac{dr}{dt}$. Since

$$\frac{d}{dt}(A_0) = 1 = 2\pi r\frac{dr}{dt}, \quad \frac{dr}{dt} = \frac{1}{2\pi r}.$$

So, $\dfrac{d}{dt}(A_s) = 4r; \quad \dfrac{1}{2\pi r} = \dfrac{2}{\pi}.$

29. **(C)**

Solve the equations simultaneously to find the points of intersection.

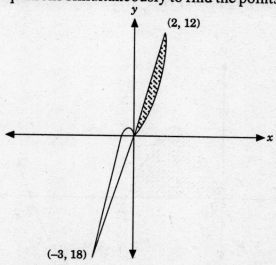

$$x^3 + x^2 = 6x$$

$$x^3 + x^2 - 6x = 0$$

$$x(x+3)(x-2) = 0$$

$$x = 0 \quad \text{or} \quad x = -3 \quad \text{or} \quad x = 2$$

$$A = \int_0^2 \left[6x - \left(x^3 + x^2 \right) \right] dx$$

$$= \left(\frac{6x^2}{2} - \frac{x^4}{4} - \frac{x^3}{3} \right) \Big|_0^2$$

$$= \frac{16}{3}$$

30. **(B)**

$$\lim_{x \to 0} \frac{\arctan x}{\tan x} = \lim_{x \to 0} \frac{\dfrac{1}{1+x^2}}{\sec^2 x} \text{ , using L'Hôpital's Rule,}$$

$$= \frac{1}{1}$$

$$= 1$$

31. **(B)**

The period of $y = \sin (ax)$ is $\dfrac{2\pi}{a}$.

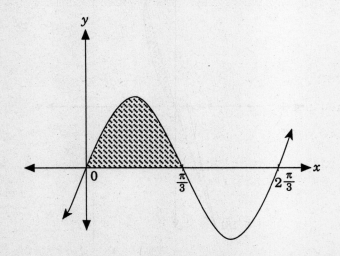

$$\int_0^{\frac{\pi}{3}} \sin(3x)\, dx = \frac{1}{3}\int_0^\pi \sin u\, du \text{ where } u = 3x$$

$$A = \frac{1}{3}(-\cos u)\Big|_0^\pi$$

$$= \frac{1}{3}\big[-(-1)-(-1)\big]$$

$$= \frac{2}{3}$$

32. **(E)**

The graph of $V(t)$ is

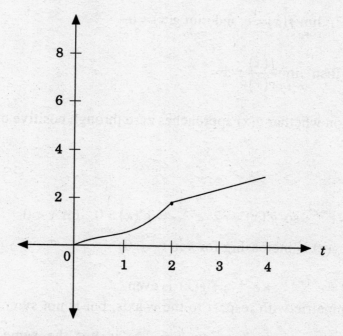

The distance travelled between $t = 1$ and $t = 2$ is

$fnInt(x\text{^}2, x, 1, 2) = 2.3$.

The distance travelled between $t = 2$ and $t = 3$ is

$fnInt(x + 2, x, 2, 3) = 4.5$.

Hence, from $t = 1$ to $t = 3$, the particle travelled $2.3 + 4.5 = 6.8$.

33. **(C)**

Use your calculator to solve this problem:

$$fnInt\left(x + \frac{1}{x^\wedge 1.6}, \; x, \; 0.1, \; 2\right), \text{ which should give 7.53.}$$

34. **(C)**

$$\lim_{x \to -4^+} \frac{4x - 6}{2x^2 + 5x - 12} = \lim_{x \to -4^+} \frac{2(2x - 3)}{(2x - 3)(x + 4)}$$

$$= \lim_{x \to -4^+} \frac{2}{x + 4}$$

$$= +\infty$$

Note: If $\lim\limits_{x \to a} f(x) = c$ and $\lim\limits_{x \to a} g(x) = 0$,

then $\lim\limits_{x \to a} \dfrac{f(x)}{g(x)} = \pm\infty$

depending on whether $g(x)$ approaches zero through positive or negative values of x.

35. **(E)**

$$g(x) = e^{-x^2} \text{ so } g'(x) = -2xe^{-x^2} \Rightarrow g'(x) > 0 \quad \text{for } x < 0$$

Thus, $g(x)$ is increasing for x in $(-\infty, 0)$

$$g(-x) = e^{-(-x)^2} = e^{-x^2} \Rightarrow g(x) \text{ is even.}$$

$g(x)$ is symmetric with respect to the y–axis, but is not symmetric with respect to the x–axis because $y = e^{-x^2}$ is not the same graph as $-y = e^{-x^2}$. $g''(x) = 2e^{-x^2}(2x^2 - 1)$ so points of inflection occur when

$2x^2 - 1 = 0 \Rightarrow x = \sqrt{\dfrac{1}{2}}$. Therefore, answers (A)–(D) are not true.

36. **(C)**

The left-hand derivative at $x = 0$ is negative and the right-hand derivative at $x = 0$ is positive, so the function is not differentiable at $x = 0$. Therefore, f is not differentiable on the entire interval $(-2, 2)$.

37. **(C)**

Let $u = \sec x + \tan x$ and $du = (\sec x \tan x + \sec^2 x)\, dx$

So, $\displaystyle\int \frac{1}{u}\, du = \int \frac{(\sec x + \tan x)\sec x}{(\tan x + \sec x)}\, dx$

$$= \int \sec x\, dx$$

But $\displaystyle\int \frac{1}{u}\, du = \ln|u| + C$

$$= \ln|\sec x + \tan x| + C$$

which is (A)

(B) follows since

$$-\ln|\sec x - \tan x| = \ln\left|\frac{1}{\sec x - \tan x}\right|$$

$$= \ln|\sec x + \tan x|$$

(D) is correct because

$$\sec x + \tan x = \frac{1}{\cos x} + \frac{\sin x}{\cos x}$$

$$= \frac{1 + \sin x}{\cos x}$$

(E) is correct because

$$\frac{1 + \sin x}{\cos x} = \frac{\cos x}{1 - \sin x}$$

38. **(A)**

Let $f(x) = 8 + 2x - x^2$ and $g(x) = 6x^3$. Draw the graph of $f(x)$ and $g(x)$.

$(6x^3 + x^2 - 2x - 8)$ changes sign between $x = 1$ and $x = 2$; one of the roots lies there.

Let $x = 1 + \varepsilon$ (with $x^2 \cong 1 + 2\varepsilon$, $x^3 \cong 1 + 3\varepsilon$). We find that $\varepsilon \approx \dfrac{1}{6}$. Therefore, the root lies near $x = 1.16$.

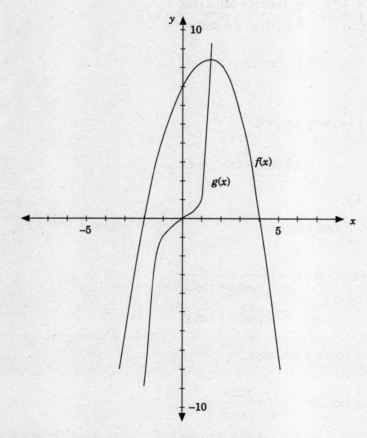

One solution is between 1 and 2 on the x–axis. Reset window to $[1, 2] \times [8, 10]$. This solution can be found to be 1.143.

39. **(C)**

Use your calculator to solve this problem. For example,

$$\text{der } 1\!\left(\frac{\sin x \cos x}{\cos 9x \tan 2x}, \ x, \ 0.5\right) \cdot -49.5 \text{ will be given as the answer.}$$

40. **(A)**

Draw the graphs of $f(x)$ and $f'(x)$.

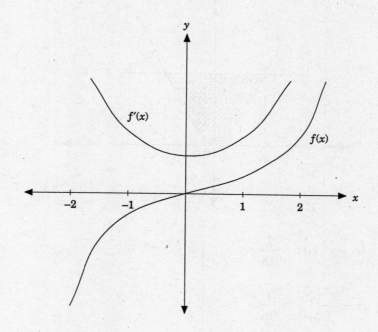

$f'(x) = \dfrac{4}{\left(4-x^2\right)^{\frac{3}{2}}}$. Minimum of f' at $x = 0$ when $f' = \dfrac{4}{4^{\frac{3}{2}}}$

$$= \frac{1}{2}.$$

Obviously, the minimum occurs at $x = 0$. Set the window to $[-2, 2] \times [-1, 1]$ and trace the x variable to $x = 0$. The minimum is $f'(0) = 0.5$.

41. **(A)**

(A) is false. There is not enough information to tell where the maximum is.

(B) is true because of the intermediate value theorem.

(C) is true because of the definition of continuity on $[a, b]$.

(D) is true for any a, b as a consequence of the triangle inequality, i.e., $|a| - |b| \le |a - b|$.

(E) is true because of the definition of continuity.

42. **(D)**

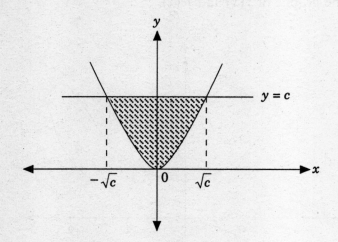

$$2\int_0^{\sqrt{c}} \left(c - x^2\right) dx = \frac{1}{48}$$

$$cx - \frac{x^3}{3}\bigg|_0^{\sqrt{c}} = \frac{1}{96}$$

$$\Rightarrow \frac{2}{3}c^{\frac{3}{2}} = \frac{1}{96}$$

$$\Rightarrow \left(c^{\frac{3}{2}}\right)^{\frac{2}{3}} = \left(\frac{1}{64}\right)^{\frac{2}{3}}$$

So, $c = \dfrac{1}{16}$.

43. **(C)**

III and IV can be shown false by taking

$$f(x) = x^2 + 1$$

$$g(x) = x^2.$$

(I) is true because differentiable functions (in case f' and g') are necessarily continuous; the limit follows from this property. (II) is one of the elementary properties of integrals.

44. **(C)**

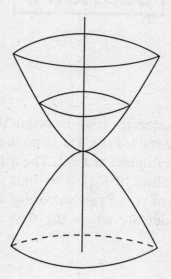

$V = 2 \times$ top half

$$= 2\int_0^1 \pi x^2 dy = 2\pi \int_0^1 y^{\frac{2}{3}} dy = \frac{6\pi}{5} y^{\frac{5}{3}} \Big|_0^1$$

$$= \frac{6\pi}{5}$$

45. **(D)**

Setting $\dfrac{x^2}{2} = 1 - \dfrac{x^2}{2}$, $x = 1$ so $y = \dfrac{1}{2}$

$y_1' = x = 1$, $y_2' = -x = -1$

so $\theta = 45° - (-45°) = 90°$.

SECTION II

1. (A)

Note that the only intercept is at the origin $(0, 0)$ since 0 is the only number to make the numerator zero. The denominator is zero when $x = 1$, so sketch in a vertical asymptote at $x = 1$. The limit of $f(x)$ as $x \to +\infty$ is zero through positive values of $f(x)$. The limit $f(x)$ as $x \to +\infty$ is zero through negative values of $f(x)$. Sketch a portion of the graph as indicated in figure (1a). Next calculate where the first and second derivatives change sign.

$$f'(x) = \frac{\left[(x-1)^2 \times 1\right] - \left[x(2)(x-1)\right]}{(x-1)^2}$$

$$= \frac{-x-1}{(x-1)^3}$$

$$= \frac{1+x}{(1-x)^3}$$

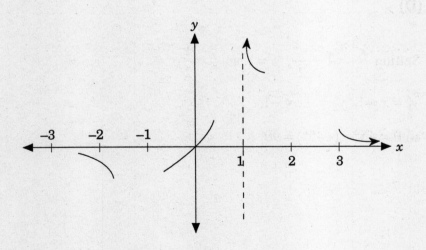

(using the quotient rule for derivatives)

$(-x-1)$ $+ + + + + + + 0 - - - - - - - - - - - - - - - -$ numerator

$(x-1)^3$ $- - - - - - - - - - - - - - - - 0 + + + + + + + +$ denominator

decreasing   increasing   decreasing

$$\longleftarrow \underset{-3}{|} \quad \underset{-2}{|} \quad \underset{-1}{\times} \quad \underset{0}{|} \quad \underset{1}{\times} \quad \underset{2}{|} \quad \underset{3}{|} \longrightarrow t$$

Interval	f' numerator	f' denominator	$f'(x)$	Behavior of f
$(-\infty, -1)$	positive	negative	negative	decreasing
$(-1, 1)$	negative	negative	positive	increasing
$(1, +\infty)$	negative	positive	negative	decreasing

$$f''(x) = \frac{(x-1)^3(-1) - (-x-1)3(x-1)^2}{(x-1)^4}$$

$$= \frac{2x+4}{(x-1)^4}$$

$(2x+4)$ $- - - 0 +$ numerator

$(x-1)^4$ $+ + + + + + + + + + + + + + + + + 0 + + + + + + + +$ denominator

concave down   concave up   concave down

$$\longleftarrow \underset{-3}{|} \quad \underset{-2}{\times} \quad \underset{-1}{|} \quad \underset{0}{|} \quad \underset{1}{\times} \quad \underset{2}{|} \quad \underset{3}{|} \longrightarrow t$$

Using the first derivative test, we see that $f'(x) = 0$ when

$$0 = \frac{-x-1}{(x-1)^3} \Rightarrow 0 = -x - 1 \Rightarrow x = -1$$

is a critical point. Taking the second derivative, we have

$$f''(x) = \frac{-(x-1)^3 - (-x-1)3(x-1)^2}{(x-1)^6}$$

$$= \frac{(x-1)^2(-x+1+3x+2)}{(x-1)^6}$$

$$= \frac{2x+4}{(x-1)^4}.$$

At $x = -1$,

$$f''(x) = \frac{2(-1)+4}{(-2)^4}$$

$$= \frac{2}{16} > 0.$$

So, $(-1, f(-1))$ is a relative minimum. To find inflection points, we set $f''(x) = 0$.

$$0 = \frac{2x+4}{(x-1)^4}$$

$$\Rightarrow 2x + 4 = 0$$

$$\Rightarrow x = -2.$$

So, $(-1, f(-1))$ is a point of inflection.

The completed sketch of the graph is as follows:

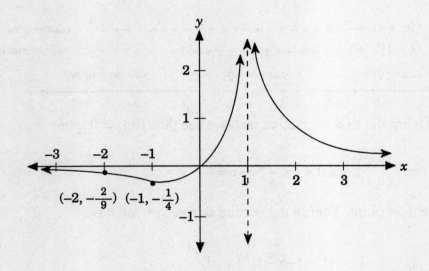

(B)

f is increasing on $(-1, 1)$ and decreasing on $(-\infty, -1)$ and $(1, \infty)$. f is concave down on $(-\infty, -2)$ and concave up on the intervals $(-2, 1)$ and $(1, +\infty)$. See part (A) for appropriate work.

(C)

The domain of f is all reals except $x = 1$. The range of f is all reals greater than or equal to $-\dfrac{1}{4}$. The function f does not have an inverse over the domain of f because f is not a one-to-one function. For example, $f\left(-\dfrac{1}{2}\right) = f(-2) = -\dfrac{2}{9}$, so two different values of x can go to the same value of $y = f(x)$.

(D)

Use the point-slope form for the equation of a line:

$$y - y_1 = m(x - x_1), \quad \text{where} \quad x_1 = -2 \quad \text{and} \quad x_2 = -\frac{2}{9}$$

and
$$m = f'(-2)$$

$$= \frac{2-1}{(-3)^3}$$

$$y = -\left(-\frac{2}{9}\right)$$

$$= -\frac{1}{27}(x - (-2))$$

or $\quad x + 27y + 8 = 0$

2. (A)

Using the first derivative formation,

$$\text{der } 1\left(\frac{3}{2 + 105x}, \ x, \ 0\right)$$

$f(0) = -78.75$ can be found.

(B)

Draw the graph of $f(x)$ for $-1 < x < 1$.

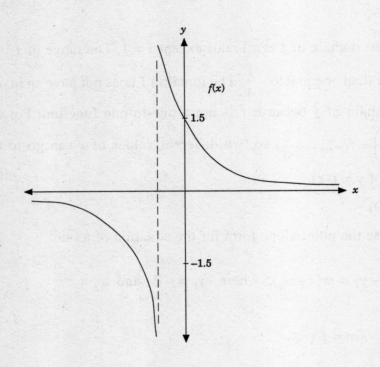

$f(x)$ is defined for $x_o = \dfrac{-2}{105} \approx -0.019$

As x approaches x_0 from the left, $f(x) \to -\infty$

As x approaches x_0 from the right, $f(x) \to +\infty$

(C)

Using the calculator to $\displaystyle\int_0^2 f(x)$ by

$$fnInt\left(\frac{3}{2+105x},\ x,\ 0,\ 2\right)$$

you get

$$\int_0^2 f(x)\, dx = 0.1332$$

3. (A)

Let t = time in seconds for plant growth.

x = weight (in grams) of plant culture X at time t.

$$\frac{dx}{dt} = k\, x$$

────── weight of the culture

───── constant of variation

───── instantaneous rate of change

(B)

The solution for the differential equation $f'(t) = k\, f(t)$ is $f(t) = A\, e^{kt}$, so let $x = f(t)$ and then $x = A\, e^{kt}$ where $A = x_0$ is the initial value of x.

(C)

For $x = f(t) = A\, e^{kt}$, let $t = 0$ and then $10 = f(0) = A\, e^0$; so $A = 10$. Let $t = 1$ and then $100 = f(1) = 10e^k$.

Dividing by 10 gives $10 = e^{\,k}$, so $k = \ln 10$. This means $x = f(t) = 10\, e^{\,t\, \ln 10} = 10\, e^{\ln 10t} = 10(10^t) = 10^{t+1}$.

If $x = 0.5$ then $f(.5) = 10^{1.5} = 10\sqrt{10}$ grams.

$x = x_0 e^{kt}$ with $x_0 = 10$.

Since $100 = 10 \times e^k$ we have $e^k = 10$.

Therefore, $x\!\left(\dfrac{1}{2}\right) = 10e^{\,k\frac{1}{2}}$

$$= 10(10)^{\frac{1}{2}}$$

$$= 10\sqrt{10}$$

(D)

The instantaneous rate of growth is $f'(t) = D_t (10^{t+1})$.

Now $f'(t) = 10^{t+1} \ln 10$, so $f'(1) = 100 \ln 10$ gm/sec.

Average rate of growth $\qquad \dfrac{f(1) - f(0)}{1-0} = 100 - 10 = 90$ gm/sec.

Therefore, $f'(1) -$ Ave. rate $= (100 \ln 10 - 90)$ gm/sec.

4. **(A)**

c is such that $2c^2 = \dfrac{\pi}{2}$, i.e., $c = \dfrac{\sqrt{\pi}}{2}$

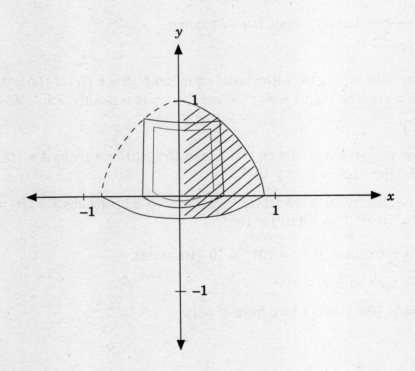

Using the method of shells, the volume $= 2\pi \displaystyle\int_a^b x\, f(x)\, dx$.

Volume $= 2\pi \displaystyle\int_0^{\sqrt{\frac{\pi}{4}}} x \cos(2x^2)\, dx = 2\pi \int_0^{\frac{\pi}{2}} \frac{1}{4} \cos(u)\, du$

where we have set $u = 2x^2$ so, $du = 4x\, dx$

$$\text{Volume} = \frac{\pi}{2}\sin u \Big|_0^{\frac{\pi}{2}}$$

$$= \frac{\pi}{2}$$

(B)

$$\langle f' \rangle = \frac{1}{c-0} \int_0^c \frac{dy}{dx}\, dx$$

$$= \frac{1}{c} u \Big|_0^c$$

$$= -\frac{1}{c} \times 1$$

$$= -\frac{2}{\sqrt{\pi}}$$

(C)

Using the method of cylindrical washers, the volume is

$$\pi \int_a^b \left\{ [f(x)]^2 - [g(x)]^2 \right\} dx \Rightarrow \pi \int_0^{\sqrt{\frac{\pi}{4}}} \left[1^2 - \left(\cos\left(2x^2\right) \right)^2 \right] dx$$

$$= \pi \int_0^{\sqrt{\frac{\pi}{4}}} \sin^2\left(2x^2\right) dx$$

5. (A)

$$V'(t) = V(t)$$

$$= \int V'(t)\, dt$$

$$= \int 3\, dt$$

$$= 3t + C$$

Since $\dfrac{dV}{dt} = k$, a constant, and $V(0) = 0$, we must have $V = kt$. Here, $k = 3$ cc/sec.

Length of a side: $L(t) = V^{\frac{1}{3}} = (kt)^{\frac{1}{3}}$

Surface area: $S(t) = 6 \times L^2 = 6(kt)^{\frac{2}{3}}$

Since $V(0) = 0$, $V(t) = 3t$ so $t_0 = \dfrac{1}{3} V(t_0)$.

Therefore, $\quad \dfrac{dV}{dt} = k$

$$\frac{ds}{dt} = \frac{4k}{(kt)^{\frac{1}{3}}}$$

$$\frac{dL}{dt} = \frac{k}{3(kt)^{\frac{2}{3}}}$$

At t_0, we have $k = \dfrac{4k}{\left(kt_0\right)^{\frac{1}{3}}}$

or, $kt_0 = 64$. Therefore, $t_0 = \dfrac{64}{k} = \dfrac{64}{3} = 21\dfrac{1}{3}$ seconds.

(B)

$$\frac{dL}{dt} = \frac{k}{3(kt)^{\frac{2}{3}}} \quad \text{at } t = t_0; \ kt_0 = 64. \text{ Therefore,}$$

$$\frac{dL}{dt} = \frac{3}{3(64)^{\frac{2}{3}}}$$

$$= \frac{1}{16} \text{ cm/se}$$

(C)

$$\frac{ds}{dt} = \frac{4k}{(kt)^{\frac{1}{3}}} \quad \text{at } t_0; \ kt_0 = 64. \text{ Therefore,}$$

$$\frac{ds}{dt} = 3 \text{cm}^2/\text{sec.}$$

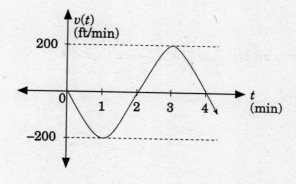

6. (A)

Integration of the speed with respect to the time shows that $y(t) = $ constant $+ \dfrac{400}{\pi}\cos\left(\dfrac{2\pi t}{4}\right)$. The initial condition $y(0) \approx 500 + \dfrac{400}{\pi}$ leads to $y(t)$

$= 500 + \dfrac{400}{\pi}\cos\left(\dfrac{2\pi t}{4}\right)$.

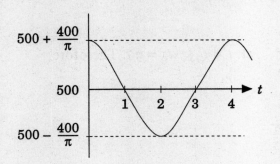

(B)

Minimum altitude when $\dfrac{2\pi t}{4} = \pi \Rightarrow t = 2$ min.

(C)

Maximum altitude when $\dfrac{2\pi t}{4} = 0$ or $2\pi \Rightarrow t = 0$ or 4 min.

(D)

$y(t)$ is concave up for $\dfrac{\pi}{2} < \dfrac{2\pi t}{4} < \dfrac{3\pi}{2} \Rightarrow 1 < t < 3$

Advanced Placement Examination in Calculus AB

EXAM IV

Exam IV is also on CD-ROM in our special interactive AP Calculus AB Test*ware*®. It is highly recommended that you first take this exam on computer. You will then have the additional study features and benefits of enforced timed conditions, individual diagnostic analysis, and instant scoring. See page xiv for guidance on how to get the most out of our AP Calculus AB book and software.

ADVANCED PLACEMENT
CALCULUS AB
EXAM IV

SECTION I

PART A

Time: 55 minutes
28 questions

DIRECTIONS: Each of the following problems is followed by five choices. Solve each problem, select the best choice, and blacken the correct space on your answer sheet. Calculators may not be used for this section of the exam.

NOTE: Unless otherwise specified, the domain of function f is assumed to be the set of all real numbers x for which $f(x)$ is a real number.

---

1. Which of the following represents a function?

   (A) $x^2 + y^2 = 1$ (C) $x^2 - y = 0$

   (B) $y^2 = x$ (D) $y = \pm\sqrt{1 - x^2}$

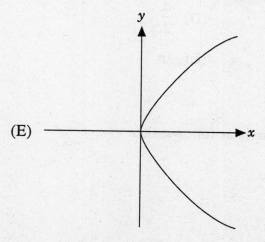

   (E)

2. If $f(x) = x - 2$ and $g(x) = |x|$, then

   (A) $(g \circ f)(3) + f(3) = 0$

   (B) $(g \circ f)(1) + f(1) = 0$

   (C) $\dfrac{(g \circ f)(0)}{f(0)} = -1$

   (D) $\dfrac{(g \circ f)(0)}{f(0)} = 1$

   (E) $2(g \circ f)(x) \neq f(x)$ for every x

3. If $\dfrac{x^2}{1 - x^2}$, then

   (A) Domain of $f = R\backslash\{1\}$

   (B) f is an odd function

   (C) The line $y = -1$ is a horizontal asymptote

   (D) $x = -1$ is the only vertical asymptote

   (E) f is never zero

4. If $f(x) = a \sin (bx + c)$ and $f'(x) = 2a \cos (bx + c)$, then the period of f is

   (A) π (D) $\dfrac{\pi}{2}$

   (B) 4π (E) 3π

   (C) 2π

5. If the graph of f is as shown as follows, then

   $$\lim_{x \to 3}\left([f(x)]^2 + 2f(x) + 1\right) =$$

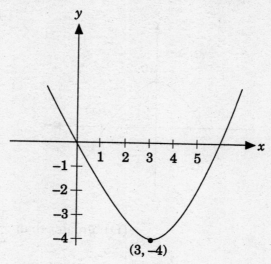

(3, −4)

(A) 8   (D) 9

(B) 10   (E) 25

(C) 11

6. If $y(x) = e^{3x} - \tan 3x - 1$,

   find $\lim\limits_{x \to 0} \dfrac{y(x)}{x^2}$.

   (A) 1   (D) ∞

   (B) −1   (E) $\dfrac{9}{2}$

   (C) Does not exist

7. Which of the following has a real root?

   (A) $x^3 - x + 5 = 0$ (D) $(x - 1)^2 + 3 = 0$

   (B) $x^2 + 1 = 0$ (E) $x^2 + 5 = 0$

   (C) $(x + 1)^2 + 1 = 0$

8. The graph of $f(x)$ is as shown below. If the graph of $-f(x) + c$, c a constant, does not intersect the x-axis, then c must be

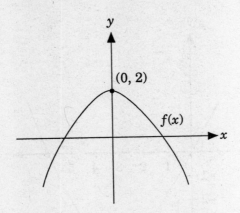

(A) 2

(D) greater than $\dfrac{3}{2}$

(B) greater than 1

(E) less than 2

(C) greater than 2

9. If f has a derivative at $x = 2$ and $g(x) = (x - 2)^2 f(x)$, then

(A) $g'(2)$ does not exist

(D) $g'(2) < 0$

(B) $g'(2) = 0$

(E) $g'(2) > 0$

(C) $g'(2)$ cannot be determined

10. If $f(x) = \sqrt{x + 2}$, then

$$\lim_{h \to 0} \frac{f(2 + h) - f(2)}{h} =$$

(A) 4

(D) $\dfrac{1}{4}$

(B) 0

(E) 1

(C) $\dfrac{1}{2}$

11. Given $f(x) = 2x^2 - 3x + 5$ and $g(x) = x^2 + 2x + 4$,

    if $f'(a) = g'(a)$ then $a =$

    (A) 2

    (D) $\dfrac{2}{5}$

    (B) $\dfrac{5}{6}$

    (E) $\dfrac{5}{2}$

    (C) $-\dfrac{2}{5}$

12. If $y = A \sin x + B \cos x$, then

    (A) $y + \dfrac{d^2y}{dx^2} = 0$

    (D) $y + \dfrac{d^2y}{dx^2} < 0$

    (B) $y + \dfrac{d^2y}{dx^2} \neq 0$

    (E) $-y + \dfrac{d^2y}{dx^2} = 0$

    (C) $y + \dfrac{d^2y}{dx^2} > 0$

13. Let $f(x) = \dfrac{2}{3}x^{\frac{3}{2}}$ and suppose that the line $y = 2.5x$ is parallel to the tangent of $f(x)$ at x_0. x_0 must approximately equal

    (A) −6.25

    (D) 0.71

    (B) 4.00

    (E) 12.50

    (C) 6.25

14. The value of $\dfrac{dy}{dx}$ when $x = 1$ and $y = -1$ given that

    $4x^2 + 2xy - xy^3 = 0$ is

    (A) 7   (D) 11

    (B) 5   (E) 6

    (C) 9

15. The domain of $y = \sqrt{(x-1)(x-2)}$ is

    (A) $|x| < 2$ (D) $(-\infty, 1] \cup [2, \infty)$

    (B) $(1, 2)$ (E) $[1, 2]$

    (C) $|x| > 1$

16. If the graph of $f(x)$ is as shown below, then

    (A) Domain of $\dfrac{1}{f'(x)} = (1, 4)$

    (B) Domain of $\dfrac{1}{f'(x)} = [1, 4]$

    (C) $f'(x) > 0$ on $(1, 4)$

    (D) $f'(x) < 0$ on $(1, 4)$

    (E) $f'(x_0) = 0$ at some point in $(1, 4)$

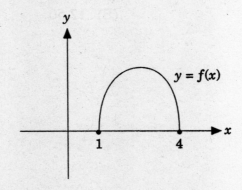

17. If $\dfrac{dy}{dx} = 3\cos^2 x - 3\sin^2 x$, then $y =$

(A) $\sin(2x) + C$

(D) $\dfrac{3}{2}\cos(2x) + C$

(B) $3\sin(2x) + C$

(E) $\dfrac{2}{3}\sin(2x) + C$

(C) $\dfrac{3}{2}\sin(2x) + C$

18. $\lim\limits_{x\to 0}\dfrac{x - \tan x}{x - \sin x} =$

(A) -2

(D) $-\dfrac{1}{2}$

(B) 2

(E) Does not exist

(C) 0

19. If $\lim\limits_{n\to\infty}\dfrac{6n^2}{200 - 4n + kn^2} = \dfrac{1}{2}$, then $k =$

(A) 3

(D) 8

(B) 6

(E) 2

(C) 12

20. If $\lim\limits_{n\to\infty}\left(1 + \dfrac{1}{n}\right)^{kn} = \dfrac{1}{e^2}$, then $k =$

(A) 1

(D) $-\dfrac{1}{e}$

(B) -2

(E) $\dfrac{1}{e}$

(C) $\dfrac{1}{2}$

21. If $y = -\dfrac{1}{\sqrt{x^2+1}}$, then $\dfrac{dy}{dx} =$

   (A) $\dfrac{x}{\left(x^2+1\right)^{\frac{1}{2}}}$

   (B) $-\dfrac{x}{\left(x^2+1\right)^{\frac{1}{2}}}$

   (C) $-\dfrac{x}{\left(x^2+1\right)^{\frac{3}{2}}}$

   (D) $\dfrac{x}{\left(x^2+1\right)^{\frac{3}{2}}}$

   (E) $\dfrac{x}{x^2+1}$

22. If $y = \ln\left[(x+1)\,(x+2)\right]$, then $\dfrac{dy}{dx} =$

   (A) $\dfrac{1}{x+1} + (x+2)$

   (B) $\dfrac{1}{(x+2)} + (x+1)$

   (C) $\dfrac{1}{(x+1)\,(x+2)}$

   (D) $\dfrac{x+1}{x+2}$

   (E) $\dfrac{1}{x+1} + \dfrac{1}{x+2}$

23. If $f(x) = ae^{kx}$ and $\dfrac{f'(x)}{f(x)} = -\dfrac{5}{2}$ then $k =$

   (A) -5

   (B) $-\dfrac{5}{2}$

   (C) $-\dfrac{2}{5}$

   (D) $\dfrac{5}{2}$

   (E) $\dfrac{2}{5}$

24. The rate of change of the area of an equilateral triangle with respect to its side S at $S = 2$ is

    (A) 0.43

    (D) 7.00

    (B) 1.73

    (E) 0.50

    (C) 0.87

25. If $f(x) = e^{\frac{x^3}{3} - x}$, then $f(x)$

    (A) increases in the interval $(-1, 1)$

    (B) decreases for $|x| > 1$

    (C) increases in the interval $(-1, 1)$ and decreases in the intervals $(-\infty, -1) \cup (1, \infty)$

    (D) increases in the intervals $(-\infty, -1) \cup (1, \infty)$ and decreases in the interval $(-1, 1)$

    (E) increases in the interval $(-\infty, \infty)$

26. $\int_1^2 \frac{x^2 + 1}{x^3 + 3x + 1} dx =$

    (A) 0.231

    (D) 0.535

    (B) 0.406

    (E) 1.609

    (C) 0.366

27.

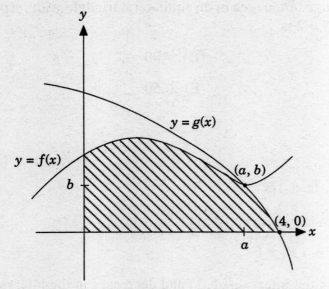

The curves $y = f(x)$ and $y = g(x)$ shown in the figure above intersect at the point (a, b). The area of the shaded region, bounded by these curves and the coordinate axes, is given by

(A) $\int_0^a (f(x) - g(x))\, dx$

(B) $\int_0^a (g(x) - f(x))\, dx$

(C) $\int_0^a f(x)\, dx - \int_a^4 g(x)\, dx$

(D) $\int_0^a f(x)\, dx + \int_a^4 g(x)\, dx$

(E) $\int_0^4 g(x)\, dx - \int_0^a f(x)\, dx$

28. Let $f(x) = \sqrt{x-1}$ for $x \geq 1$. What are the possible x-values, usually denoted by c in the statement of the Mean Value Theorem, at which f' attains its mean value over the interval $1 \leq x \leq 5$?

(A) 1

(D) 1 and 2

(B) 2

(E) 1 and 4

(C) 4

PART B

Time: 50 minutes
17 questions

DIRECTIONS: Calculators may be used for this section of the test. Each of the following problems is followed by five choices. Solve each problem, select the best choice, and blacken the correct space on your answer sheet.

NOTES:
1. Unless otherwise specified, answers can be given in unsimplified form.

2. The domain of function f is assumed to be the set of all real numbers x for which $f(x)$ is a real number.

29. If $f(x) = x - \dfrac{1}{x}$, which of the following is <u>NOT</u> true?

(A) $f\left(\dfrac{1}{x}\right) = -f(x)$ (D) $f(-x) = -f(x)$

(B) $f\left(\dfrac{1}{x}\right) = f(-x)$ (E) None of these

(C) $f(x) = f(-x)$

30. If x and y are two positive numbers such that $x + y = 20$ and xy is as large as possible then

(A) $x = 12$ and $y = 8$ (D) $x = 20$ and $y = 0$

(B) $x = 10$ and $y = 10$ (E) $x = 8$ and $y = 12$

(C) $x = 5$ and $y = 15$

31. If the rate of change of $f(x)$ at $x = x_0$ is twice the rate of change of $f(x)$ at $x = 4$, and $f(x) = 2\sqrt{x}$ then x_0 is

(A) 8

(D) 16

(B) 1

(E) 4

(C) 2

32. The area enclosed by $f(x) = x^3 + x^2$ and $g(x) = \ln(x + 1)$ for $x > 0$ is

(A) 0.0513

(D) 2.89

(B) 0.01

(E) 7.8

(C) 2.5

33. The area in the first quadrant that is enclosed by $y = \sin 3x \cos x$ and the x-axis from $x = 0$ to the first x-intercept on the positive side is

(A) 1

(D) 2.5

(B) 0.56

(E) 1.5

(C) 0.78

34. If the graph of f is as shown below, then the graph of

$y = 2 + f(x)$

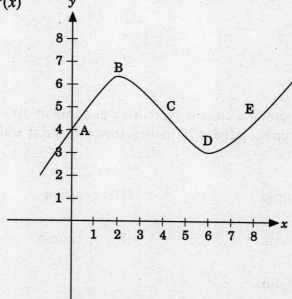

(A) is concave downward in the interval (2, 6)

(B) is concave upward in the interval (0, 8)

(C) has an inflection point at $x = 5$

(D) is concave downward in the interval (0, 3)

(E) is concave downward in the interval (0, 8)

35. If $f(x) = g(x) - \dfrac{1}{g(x)}$, $g(0) = 3$ and $g'(0) = 2$, then $f'(0)$ is approximately

(A) 1.778

(D) 2.222

(B) 2.333

(E) 1.222

(C) 3.222

36. If the acceleration (ft/sec^2) of a moving body is $\sqrt{4t+1}$ and the velocity at $t = 0$, $v(0) = -4\dfrac{1}{3}$, then the distance travelled between time $t = 0$ and $t = 2$ is

(A) $\dfrac{119}{30}$

(D) $\dfrac{149}{30}$

(B) $-\dfrac{119}{30}$

(E) -4

(C) $-\dfrac{149}{30}$

37. If the volume of a cube is increasing at a rate of 300 in^3/min at the instant when the edge is 20 inches, then the rate at which the edge is changing is

(A) $\dfrac{1}{4}$ in/min

(D) 1 in/min

(B) $\dfrac{1}{2}$ in/min

(E) $\dfrac{3}{4}$ in/min

(C) $\dfrac{1}{3}$ in/min

38. $6\int_{-1}^{1} \dfrac{x^3 + 1}{x + 1} \, dx =$

   (A) 4   (D) 8

   (B) 2   (E) 16

   (C) 12

39. If $f(x) = x^3 - 2x$, then f has

   (A) a relative Max. at $x = \sqrt{\dfrac{2}{3}}$ and a relative Min. at $x = -\sqrt{\dfrac{2}{3}}$

   (B) an absolute Max. at $x = -\sqrt{\dfrac{2}{3}}$

   (C) a relative Min. at $x = \sqrt{\dfrac{2}{3}}$ and a relative Max. at $x = -\sqrt{\dfrac{2}{3}}$

   (D) an absolute Min. at $x = \sqrt{\dfrac{2}{3}}$

   (E) a relative Min. at $x = -\sqrt{\dfrac{2}{3}}$ and a relative Max. at $x = \sqrt{\dfrac{2}{3}}$

40. If $f(x) = 256x^{-\frac{1}{2}} + 64x^{\frac{1}{2}} + 3x^{\frac{2}{3}}$, then $f'(64)$ equals

   (A) 4.25   (D) 10.25

   (B) 8.75   (E) 5.78

   (C) 0.75

41. The smallest value of $y = x^2(1 - x^{-1})$ is

   (A) 0   (D) -1

   (B) -0.25   (E) 1

   (C) 0.25

42. Given the following graph of the continuous function $f(x)$,

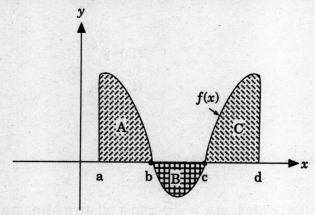

with: area of region $A = 3$

area of region $B = 1\dfrac{1}{2}$

area of region $C = 2$, then $\displaystyle\int_a^d f(x)\,dx =$

(A) $\dfrac{5}{2}$ (D) 5

(B) $\dfrac{7}{2}$ (E) $\dfrac{2}{5}$

(C) $\dfrac{13}{2}$

43. $\displaystyle\int x\cos(4x)\,dx =$

(A) $\dfrac{1}{4}\sin(4x) + C$

(B) $\dfrac{x}{4}\sin(4x) + C$

(C) $\dfrac{x}{4}\sin(4x) + \dfrac{1}{16}\cos(4x) + C$

(D) $\dfrac{x}{4}\sin(4x)-\dfrac{1}{16}\cos(4x)+C$

(E) $\dfrac{x}{4}-\dfrac{1}{16}\cos(4x)+C$

44. If $x=t^3-3t$ and $y=\left(t^2+1\right)^2$, then at $t=2$, $\dfrac{dy}{dx}$ is

   (A) 40   (D) $\dfrac{9}{40}$

   (B) 9   (E) 0

   (C) $\dfrac{40}{9}$

45. An equation of the line normal to the graph of $y=x^4-3x^2+1$ at the point where $x=1$ is

   (A) $2x-y+3=0$ (D) $x-2y-3=0$

   (B) $x-2y+3=0$ (E) $x-2y=0$

   (C) $2x-y-3=0$

SECTION II

Time: 1 hour and 30 minutes
6 problems

DIRECTIONS: Show all your work. Grading is based on the methods used to solve the problem as well as the accuracy of your final answers. Please make sure all procedures are clearly shown. For some problems or parts of problems it will be necessary to use a calculator.

NOTES:
1. Unless otherwise specified, answers can be given in unsimplified form.

2. The domain of function f is assumed to be the set of all real numbers x for which $f(x)$ is a real number.

1. If $f(x) = \dfrac{1}{2} + \dfrac{1}{2} \cos(2x)$, $0 \le x \le \pi$, then

   (A) find $\lim\limits_{x \to \frac{\pi}{4}} f(x)$

   (B) find the average value of f on $[0, \pi]$.

   (C) show that $|\, f(b) - f(a)\,| \le |\, b - a\,|$ for any $a < b$.

2. Given $f(x) = 2x^2 - 2x + 5$ and $g(x) = x^2 + 2x + 4$

   (A) Find the values of x where $f(x) = g(x)$.

   (B) If $f'(a) = g'(a)$, find a.

   (C) Use the results from (A) to find $\int_a^b (g(x) - f(x))$, where a and b are where $f(x) = g(x)$.

3. Let f be an even function which has a derivative at every value of x in its domain. If $f(2) = 1$ and $f'(2) = 5$, then

   (A) Find $f'(-2)$ and $f'(0)$.

   (B) Let L_1 and L_2 be the tangents to the graph of f at $x = 2$ and $x = -2$, respectively. Find the coordinates of the point p at which L_1 and L_2 intersect.

4. The graphs of f, g, and h are as given below:

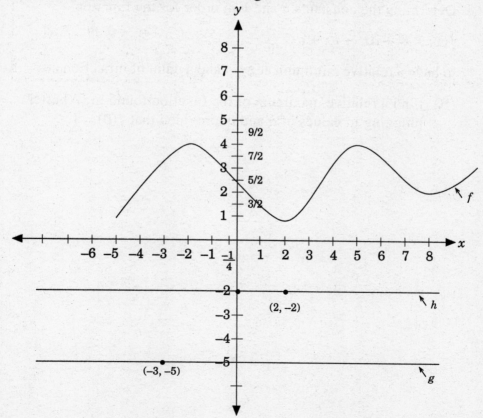

(A) Where is $(h - g)f$ concave upward and where is it concave downward?

(B) Sketch $(h - g)f$.

5. (A) At which point(s), if any, do $y = \sin x$ and $y = \cos x$ intersect in the interval $\left[0, \dfrac{\pi}{2}\right]$.

(B) Find the area of the region between $y = \sin x$, and

$y = \cos x$, from $x = 0$ to $x = \dfrac{\pi}{2}$.

(C) Set up an integral for the volume obtained by rotating the region in (b) about the x-axis.

6. (A)

Determine the constants a and b in order for the function

$f(x) = x^3 + ax^2 + bx + c$

to have a relative minimum at $x = 4$ and a point of inflection at $x = 1$.

(B) Find a relative maximum of the function found in (A) after plugging in values of a and b, provided that $f(0) = 1$.

ADVANCED PLACEMENT CALCULUS AB EXAM IV

ANSWER KEY

Section I

1.	(C)	12.	(A)	23.	(B)	34.	(D)
2.	(C)	13.	(C)	24.	(B)	35.	(D)
3.	(C)	14.	(A)	25.	(D)	36.	(C)
4.	(A)	15.	(D)	26.	(C)	37.	(A)
5.	(D)	16.	(E)	27.	(D)	38.	(E)
6.	(E)	17.	(C)	28.	(B)	39.	(C)
7.	(A)	18.	(A)	29.	(C)	40.	(A)
8.	(C)	19.	(C)	30.	(B)	41.	(B)
9.	(B)	20.	(B)	31.	(B)	42.	(B)
10.	(D)	21.	(D)	32.	(A)	43.	(C)
11.	(E)	22.	(E)	33.	(B)	44.	(C)
						45.	(D)

Section II

See Detailed Explanations of Answers.

ADVANCED PLACEMENT
CALCULUS AB
EXAM IV

DETAILED EXPLANATIONS
OF ANSWERS

SECTION I

1. **(C)**

$$x^2 - y = 0 \Leftrightarrow y = x^2$$

is represented by the parabola shown below, and no vertical line intersects the graph in more than one point, so $y = x^2$ is a function.

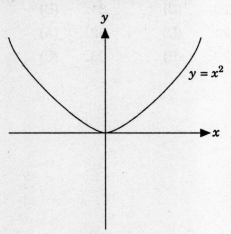

The graph of $y = y = \pm\sqrt{1 - x^2}$ is also the circle as shown above.

The graph of $y^2 = x$ is the one shown in choice (E).

In (A), (B), (D), and (E) there is a line parallel to the y-axis (a vertical line) that cuts the graph of the given relations more than once. Hence they do not represent functions.

The graph of $x^2 + y^2 = 1$ is the circle:

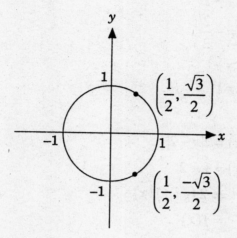

2.   **(C)**

$$(g \circ f)(x) = g(f(x))$$
$$= g(x-2)$$
$$= |x-2|$$

Therefore,

(i) $(g \circ f)(3) + f(3) = |3-2| + (3-2)$
$$= 1+1$$
$$= 2$$
$$\neq 0.$$

(ii) $(g \circ f)(1) - f(1) = |1-2| - (1-2)$
$$= |-1| - (-1)$$
$$= 1+1$$
$$= 2$$
$$\neq 0$$

(iii) $\dfrac{(g \circ f)(0)}{f(0)} = \dfrac{|0-2|}{0-2}$

$= \dfrac{|-2|}{-2}$

$= -\dfrac{2}{2}$

$= -1$

$\neq 1$

(iv) $2(g \circ f)(x) = 2|x-2|$

$f(x) = x - 2$

$\Rightarrow 2(g \circ f)(x)$

$= f(x)$

for $x = 2$, since both are zero at $x = 2$.

Hence, only (C) is true.

3.   **(C)**

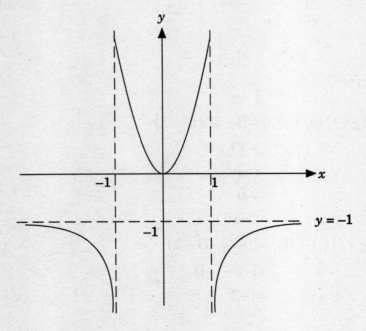

$$f(x) = \frac{x^2}{1-x^2} = -1 + \frac{1}{1-x^2}.$$

The graph of f shows that (D) and (E) are false and (C) is true. Also, since the graph is symmetric with respect to the y-axis, it shows that f is an even function, so (B) is false. Domain $f = R \setminus \{-1, 1\}$, so (A) is false.

4. **(A)**

$f(x) = a \sin (bx + c)$

$\Rightarrow f'(x) = ab \cos (bx + c)$ by the chain rule, and

$f'(x) = 2a \cos (bx + c)$ from what is given,

$\Rightarrow b = 2$.

Hence, $f(x) = a \sin (2x + c)$ and the period $= \dfrac{2\pi}{2} = \pi$.

5. **(D)**

From the graph,

$\displaystyle\lim_{x \to 3} f(x) = -4$

Therefore, $\displaystyle\lim_{x \to 3}\left([f(x)]^2 + 2f(x) + 1\right) = (-4)^2 + 2(-4) + 1$

$$= 9$$

6. **(E)**

Using Taylor's expansion, we have:

$$e^{3x} \approx 1 + 3x + \frac{(3x)^2}{2!} + 0(x^3)$$

$$\tan 3x \approx 3x + 0(x^3)$$

$$\lim_{x \to 0} \frac{y(x)}{x^2} = \frac{9}{2!}$$

$$= \frac{9}{2}.$$

<u>Note</u>: The sine or cosine of any angle is always between -1 and 1. Therefore, even though $\dfrac{1}{x}$ gets larger and larger as $x \to 0$ $\sin\left(\dfrac{1}{x}\right)$ and $\cos\left(\dfrac{1}{x}\right)$ are confined to lie between -1 and 1.

7. **(A)**

Let $f(x) = x^3 - x + 5$

It is possible to find two values of x at which f has different signs, say at $x = -2$ and $x = 0$:

$$f(-2) = (-2)^3 - (-2) + 5$$
$$= -8 + 2 + 5$$
$$= -1 < 0 \qquad \text{and}$$

$$f(0) = 5 > 0$$

Therefore, by the Intermediate Value Theorem, $x^3 - x + 5 = 0$ has a real root between $x = -2$ and $x = 0$.

All of the other choices have imaginary roots only, as they are of the form $= y^2 = -c,\ c > 0$

For example, in (D) $(x - 1)^2 + 3 = 0 \Rightarrow (x - 1)^2 = -3$

and only an imaginary number can have a square which is a negative number.

8. **(C)**

I.

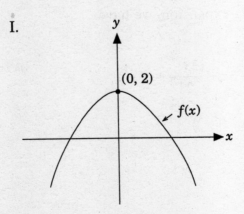

II.

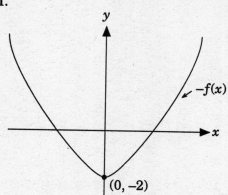

III.

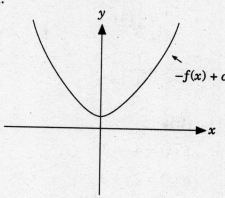

We see that in order for the graph of $f(x)$ to not intersect the x-axis, $-f(x) + c$ must lie completely above the axis. Since the lowest point on the graph $-f(x)$ is the point $(0, -2)$, this point must be raised (along with the rest of the graph) to above the x-axis. This can be accomplished by adding $c > 2$.

9. **(B)**

$g'(x) = 2 (x - 2) f(x) + (x - 2)^2 f'(x)$, by the product rule.

$\Rightarrow g'(2) = 2(0) f(2) + (2 - 2)^2 f'(2)$

$\qquad = 0 + 0 = 0.$

10. **(D)**

$\lim_{h \to 0} \dfrac{f(2 + h) - f(2)}{h} = f'(2)$, by the definition of derivative.

But $f'(x) = \dfrac{d}{dx}\left((x + 2)^{\frac{1}{2}} \right)$

$\qquad = \dfrac{1}{2}(x + 2)^{-\frac{1}{2}},$

by the power rule and chain rule,

$\Rightarrow f'(2) = \dfrac{1}{2}(2 + 2)^{-\frac{1}{2}}$

235

$$= \frac{1}{2}(4)^{-\frac{1}{2}}$$

$$= \frac{1}{4}$$

11. **(E)**

$$f'(x) = 4x - 3$$

$$g'(x) = 2x + 2$$

Therefore, $f'(a) = g'(a)$

$$\Rightarrow 4a - 3 = 2a + 2$$

$$\Rightarrow 2a = 5$$

$$\Rightarrow a = \frac{5}{2}$$

12. **(A)**

$$y = A \sin x + B \cos x$$

$$\Rightarrow \frac{dy}{dx} = A \cos x - B \sin x$$

$$\Rightarrow \frac{d^2y}{dx^2} = \frac{d}{dx}(A \cos x - B \sin x)$$

$$= -A \sin x - B \cos x$$

$$= -(A \sin x + B \cos x)$$

$$= -y$$

Therefore, $y + \dfrac{d^2y}{dx^2} = y - y = 0$

13. **(C)**

$$f'(x) = \frac{dy}{dx}$$

$$= \left(\frac{3}{2}\right)\left(\frac{2}{3}\right)x^{\frac{3}{2}-1}$$

$$= x^{\frac{1}{2}}$$

by the power rule for differentiation.

$\Rightarrow f'(x_0)$ must equal the slope of the line $y = 2.5x$

$\Rightarrow f'(x_0) = 2.5$

$\Rightarrow x_0^{\frac{1}{2}} = 2.5$

$\Rightarrow x_0 = 6.25$

14. **(A)**

By implicit differentiation,

$$8x + 2x\frac{dy}{dx} + 2y - y^3 - 3xy^2\frac{dy}{dx} = 0$$

$$\Leftrightarrow (3xy^2 - 2x)\frac{dy}{dx} = 8x + 2y - y^3,$$

after moving the terms containing $\frac{dy}{dx}$ to one side,

$$\Rightarrow \frac{dy}{dx} = \frac{8x + 2y - y^3}{3xy^2 - 2x}.$$

Therefore, when $x = 1$ and $y = -1$,

$$\frac{dy}{dx} = \frac{8 - 2 - (-1)^3}{3 \times 1(-1)^2 - 2 \times 1}$$

$$= \frac{8 - 2 + 1}{1}$$

$$= 7.$$

15. **(D)**

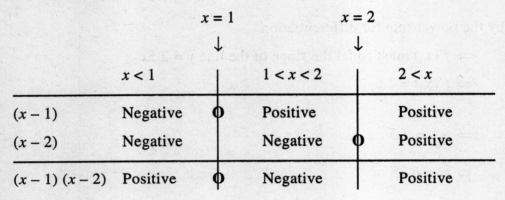

As the chart shows, when $1 < x < 2$, $(x - 1)(x - 2) < 0$

$\Rightarrow y = \sqrt{(x-1)(x-2)}$ is undefined. Otherwise, y is defined.

16. **(E)**

Since $f(1) = 0$ and $f(4) = 0$, by the mean value theorem (or by Rolle's theorem), there is an $x_0 \in (1, 4)$, such that

$$f'(x_0) = \frac{f(4) - f(1)}{4 - 1} = 0$$

17. **(C)**

$$\frac{dy}{dx} = 3\cos^2 x - 3\sin^2 x$$

$$= 3(\cos^2 x - \sin^2 x)$$

$$= 3\cos(2x),$$

since $\cos(2x) = \cos^2 x - \sin^2 x$

$$\Rightarrow y = \int 3\cos(2x)\, dx$$

By the method of substitution, if we let

$$2x = u$$

$$\Rightarrow 2dx = du$$

$$\Rightarrow dx = \frac{du}{2}$$

$$\Rightarrow \int 3\cos(2x)\, dx = 3\int \cos u \left(\frac{du}{2}\right)$$

$$= \frac{3}{2}\sin u + c, \quad \text{where} \quad u = 2x$$

$$= \frac{3}{2}\sin(2x) + c.$$

18. **(A)**

$\dfrac{x - \tan x}{x - \sin x}$ is an indeterminate form of the type $\dfrac{0}{0}$.

Also: $\dfrac{(x - \tan x)'}{(x - \sin x)'} = \dfrac{1 - \sec^2 x}{1 - \cos x}$ which is again of the $\dfrac{0}{0}$ type.

Therefore, $\dfrac{\left(1 - \sec^2 x\right)'}{(1 - \cos x)'} = -\dfrac{2(\sec x)(\sec x)(\tan x)}{\sin x}$, by chain rule

$$= -\frac{2\left(\dfrac{1}{\cos x}\right) \times \dfrac{1}{\cos x} \times \dfrac{\sin x}{\cos x}}{\sin x}$$

$$= -\frac{2}{\cos^3 x}.$$

Moreover, $\lim\limits_{x \to 0} -\dfrac{2}{\cos^3 x} = -2$, since $\lim\limits_{x \to 0} \cos x = 1$.

Hence, by L'Hôpital's rule

$$\lim_{x \to 0} \frac{x - \tan x}{x - \sin x} = \lim_{x \to 0} \frac{1 - \sec^2 x}{1 - \cos x}$$

$$= \lim_{x \to 0} -\frac{2}{\cos^3 x}$$

$$= -2$$

19. **(C)**

$$\lim_{n \to \infty} \frac{6n^2}{200 - 4n + kn^2} = \lim_{n \to \infty} \frac{\dfrac{6n^2}{n^2}}{\dfrac{200}{n^2} - \dfrac{4}{n} + k},$$

by dividing both the numerator and the denominator by n^2.

Therefore,

$$\lim_{n \to \infty} \frac{6n^2}{200 - 4n + kn^2} = \lim_{n \to \infty} \frac{6}{\dfrac{200}{n^2} - \dfrac{4}{n} + k}$$

$$= \frac{6}{k}, \quad \text{since} \quad \frac{200}{n^2} \to 0 \quad \text{and} \quad \frac{4}{n} \to 0.$$

From what is given, $\dfrac{6}{k} = \dfrac{1}{2}$

$$\Rightarrow k = 12$$

20. **(B)**

$$\lim_{n\to\infty}\left(1+\frac{1}{n}\right)^{kn} = \lim_{n\to\infty}\left[\left(1+\frac{1}{n}\right)^n\right]^k$$

$$= \left[\lim_{n\to\infty}\left(1+\frac{1}{n}\right)^n\right]^k, \text{ by property of limit of powers}$$

$$= e^k, \text{ since } \lim_{n\to\infty}\left(1+\frac{1}{n}\right)^n = e.$$

But we are given that

$$\lim_{n\to\infty}\left(1+\frac{1}{n}\right)^{kn} = \frac{1}{e^2}$$

$$= e^{-2}$$

$$\Rightarrow e^k = e^{-2}$$

$$\Rightarrow k = -2$$

21. **(D)**

$$y = -\frac{1}{\sqrt{x^2+1}}$$

$$= -\left(x^2+1\right)^{-\frac{1}{2}}$$

$$\Rightarrow \frac{dy}{dx} = (-1)\left(-\frac{1}{2}\right)\left(x^2+1\right)^{-\frac{3}{2}}(2x), \text{ by the chain rule,}$$

$$= \frac{x}{\left(x^2+1\right)^{\frac{3}{2}}}$$

22. **(E)**

$$\frac{dy}{dx} = \frac{1}{(x+1)(x+2)}\left[\frac{d}{dx}\left((x+1)(x+2)\right)\right],$$

by the chain rule

$$= \frac{1}{(x+1)(x+2)}\left((x+2)+(x+1)\right),$$

by the product rule

$$= \frac{1}{x+1} + \frac{1}{x+2}.$$

Alternatively, we can use the fact that $\ln(ab) = \ln(a) + \ln(b)$, so that

$$y = \ln\left[(x+1)(x+2)\right]$$

$$= \ln(x+1) + \ln(x+2)$$

$$\Rightarrow \frac{dy}{dx} = \frac{1}{x+1} + \frac{1}{x+2}.$$

23. **(B)**

$$f'(x) = kae^{kx}$$

$$\Rightarrow \frac{f'(x)}{f(x)} = \frac{kae^{kx}}{ae^{kx}}$$

$$= k$$

$$\Rightarrow k = -\frac{5}{2}$$

24. **(B)**

$$\frac{\text{height}}{s} = \sin 60°$$

$$\Leftrightarrow \text{height} = s(\sin 60°)$$

$$= s\frac{\sqrt{3}}{3}$$

$$\Rightarrow \text{Area} = \frac{1}{2}h(S)$$

$$= \left(\frac{1}{2}\right)\frac{\sqrt{3}(s)(s)}{2}, \quad \text{substituting for } h$$

$$= \frac{\sqrt{3}s^2}{4}$$

$$\Rightarrow s\frac{dA}{ds} = \frac{\sqrt{3}S}{2}$$

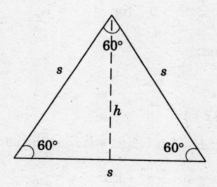

Therefore, when $s = 2$, $\dfrac{dA}{ds} = \dfrac{2\sqrt{3}}{2}$

$$= \sqrt{3}$$

$$\approx 1.73$$

25. **(D)**

$$f(x) = e^{\frac{x^3}{3} - x}$$

$$\Rightarrow f'(x) = (x^2 - 1)e^{\frac{x^3}{3} - x}, \text{ by the chain rule.}$$

We see $f(x) = e^{\frac{x^3}{3} - x} > 0$ for every real number x, and

$$x^2 - 1 = (x+1)(x-1)$$

$$\Rightarrow x^2 - 1 < 0 \quad \text{when} \quad x \in (-1, 1) \quad \text{and}$$

$$x^2 - 1 > 0 \quad \text{when} \quad |x| > 1.$$

Hence,

$$f'(x) = (x^2 - 1) \, e^{\frac{x^3}{3} - x} < 0 \quad \text{for} \quad x \in (-1, 1) \quad \text{and}$$

$$f'(x) = (x^2 - 1) \, e^{\frac{x^3}{3} - x} > 0 \quad \text{for} \quad |x| > 1.$$

(D) is the answer.

26. **(C)**

Let $u = x^3 + 3x + 1$

Then $du = 3x^2 dx + 3 dx = 3(x^2 + 1)dx$ so the integrand is:

$$\frac{x^2 + 1}{x^3 + 3x + 1} dx = \frac{1}{3} \times \frac{3(x^2 + 1)dx}{x^3 + 3x + 1} = \frac{1}{3} \times \frac{du}{u}$$

Also, if $x = 1$ then $u = (1)^3 + 3(1) + 1 = 5$,

and, if $x = 2$ then $u = (2)^3 + 3(2) + 1 = 15$.

$$\int_1^2 \frac{x^2 + 1}{x^3 + 3x + 1} dx = \int_5^{15} \frac{1}{3} \times \frac{du}{u}$$

$$= \frac{1}{3} \ln |u| \Big\|_5^{15}$$

$$= \frac{1}{3} \ln 15 - \frac{1}{3} \ln 5$$

$$= \frac{1}{3} (\ln 15 - \ln 5)$$

$$= \frac{1}{3} \left(\ln \frac{15}{5} \right)$$

$$= \frac{1}{3} \ln 3 = 0.366$$

27.   **(D)**

The area of a region bounded above by the graph of a function and below by the x-axis is the integral of the function. Since the given region is bounded above by two functions, its area is the sum of the integrals of the two functions.

Let A_1 be the area of the region bounded by f, and let A_2 be the area of the region bounded by g:

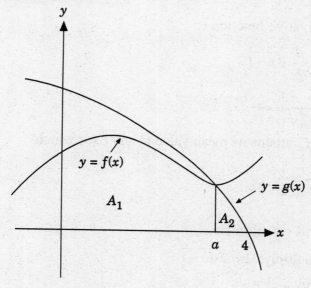

The total area is their sum:

$A = A_1 + A_2$

$$= \int_0^a f(x)dx + \int_a^4 g(x)dx$$

28.   **(B)**

The Mean Value Theorem states that the equation

$$f'(c) = \frac{f(b) - f(a)}{b - a}$$

holds for some c between a and b. Here $a = 1$ and $b = 5$ are given and

$f(x) = \sqrt{x - 1}$. The right-hand side of the equation is:

$$\frac{f(b) - f(a)}{b - a} = \frac{f(5) - f(1)}{5 - 1}$$

$$= \frac{\sqrt{5 - 1} - \sqrt{1 - 1}}{4}$$

$$= \frac{\sqrt{4} - \sqrt{0}}{4} = \frac{2 - 0}{4}$$

$$= \frac{1}{2}$$

This is the mean value of the derivative function f' over the interval $1 \le x \le 5$.

The derivative function is:

$$f'(x) = \frac{d}{dx} \sqrt{x - 1}$$

$$= \frac{1}{2\sqrt{x - 1}}$$

Hence f' attains its mean value at any c for which

$$\frac{1}{2\sqrt{c - 1}} = \frac{1}{2}$$

Solve this equation for c:

Cross multiply: $2 = 2\sqrt{c - 1}$

Divide by 2: $1 = \sqrt{c - 1}$

Square both sides: $1 = c - 1$

Add 1 to both sides: $c = 2$

29. (C)

$$f(x) = x - \frac{1}{x}$$

$$\Rightarrow f\left(\frac{1}{x}\right) = \frac{1}{x} - \frac{1}{\frac{1}{x}}$$

$$= \frac{1}{x} - x$$

$$= -\left(x - \frac{1}{x}\right) \qquad \text{factoring out } -1.$$

$$= -f(x), \qquad \text{so (A) is true.}$$

$$f\left(\frac{1}{x}\right) = -f(x) = -x + \frac{1}{x}$$

$$= -x - \frac{1}{-x} = f(-x), \qquad \text{so (B) is true.}$$

$$f(-x) = (-x) - \frac{1}{(-x)}$$

$$= -x + \frac{1}{x}$$

$$= -\left(x - \frac{1}{x}\right)$$

$$= -f(x), \qquad \text{so (C) is false.}$$

30. **(B)**

$$x + y = 20$$

$$\Rightarrow y = 20 - x$$

$$\Rightarrow xy = x(20 - x)$$

$$= 20x - x^2$$

Now let $f(x) = 20x - x^2$

$$\Rightarrow f'(x) = 20 - 2x$$

$$\Rightarrow f'(x) = -2(x - 10)$$

$$f'(x) = 0 \Rightarrow 0 = -2(x - 10)$$

$$\Rightarrow x = 10$$

We see that $f''(x) = -2 < 0$, so we have a maximum at the critical point $x = 10$. Since $x + y = 20$, we see $y = 10$.

31. **(B)**

$$f(x) = 2\sqrt{x}$$

$$= 2x^{\frac{1}{2}}$$

$$\Rightarrow f'(x) = (2)\left(\frac{1}{2}\right)x^{\frac{1}{2}-1}$$

$$= \frac{1}{\sqrt{x}}$$

We are given that $f'(x_0) = 2f'(4)$

$$\Rightarrow \frac{1}{\sqrt{x_0}} = 2\frac{1}{\sqrt{4}}$$

$$\Rightarrow \frac{1}{\sqrt{x_0}} = 1$$

$$\Rightarrow x_0 = 1$$

32. **(A)**

Draw the graphs of $f(x)$ and $g(x)$.

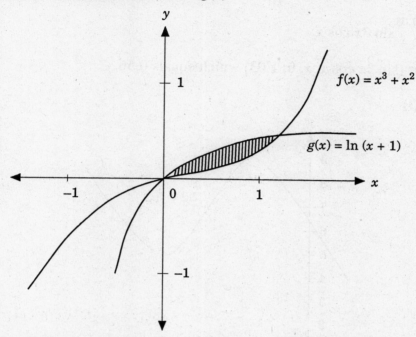

Reset viewing window to [0, 1] • [0, 1] and trace to the intersection point of $f(x)$ and $g(x)$, which should turn out to be $x = 0.5238$, $y = 0.418$.

The area enclosed is the integral $\int_0^{0.5238} \ln(x + 1) - (x^3 + x^2)$, using your calculator, which can easily be computed. The number is 0.0513.

33. **(B)**

Draw the graphs of $y = \sin 3x \cos x$.

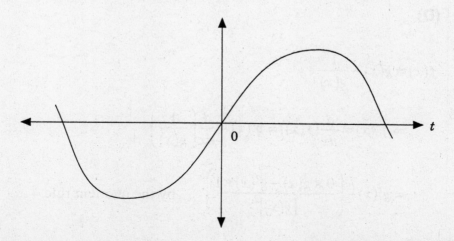

Tracing the first value of x when $y = 0$ gives the x-intercept 1.03.

Then the area is the integral

$$\int_0^{1.03} \sin 3x \cos x$$

or *fnInt* ($\sin 3x \cos x$, x, 0, 1.03) which equals 0.56.

34. **(D)**

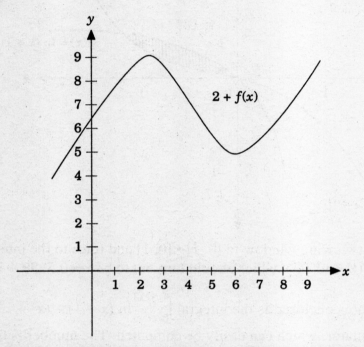

As you can see from the graph on the previous page, lifting the graph vertically upwards or downwards does not change the nature of the concavity of the inflection points.

35. **(D)**

$$f(x) = g(x) - \frac{1}{g(x)}$$

$$\Rightarrow f'(x) = \frac{d}{dx}(f(x)) = g'(x) - \frac{d}{dx}\left(\frac{1}{g(x)}\right)$$

$$= g'(x) - \left(\frac{0 \times g(x) - g'(x) \times 1}{\left[g(x)\right]^2}\right), \qquad \text{by the quotient rule.}$$

$$= g'(x) - \left(-\frac{g'(x)}{[g(x)]^2} \right)$$

$$= g'(x) + \frac{g'(x)}{[g(x)]^2}$$

As a result, $f'(0) = g'(0) + \dfrac{g'(0)}{[g(0)]^2}$

$$= 2 + \frac{2}{9}$$

$$= \frac{20}{9}$$

$$\approx 2.222$$

Calculator: $20 \div 9 = \approx 2.222$

36. **(C)**

Let $s(t) = $ distance travelled in time t.

$$\Rightarrow \text{ acceleration} = \frac{d^2 s}{dt^2} = (4t+1)^{\frac{1}{2}} \quad \text{and}$$

$$v(t) = \frac{ds}{dt} = \int a(t)\,dt$$

$$= \int_0^t (4t+1)^{\frac{1}{2}}\,dt$$

$$= \frac{1}{4} \times \frac{2}{3} \times (4t+1)^{\frac{3}{2}} \Big|_0^t$$

$$v(t) - v(0) = \frac{1}{6}\left((4t+1)^{\frac{3}{2}} - 1 \right)$$

$$\Rightarrow v(t) = \frac{1}{6}\left((4t+1)^{\frac{3}{2}} - 1 \right) - \frac{13}{3}$$

or $v(t) = v(t) = \frac{1}{6}(4t+1)^{\frac{3}{2}} - \frac{9}{2}$.

Integrating this yields:

$$\Rightarrow s(t) = \frac{1}{60}(4t+1)^{\frac{5}{2}} - \frac{9}{2}t + C$$

$$\Rightarrow s(2) - s(0) = \left(\frac{1}{60}(9)^{\frac{5}{2}} - 9 + C\right) - \left(\frac{1}{60} + C\right)$$

$$= \frac{3^5}{60} - 9 - \frac{1}{60}$$

$$= \frac{243}{60} - 9 - \frac{1}{60}$$

$$= 4 + \frac{2}{60} - 9$$

$$= -\frac{149}{30}$$

37. **(A)**

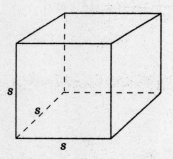

Let the edge of the cube at time t be $S(t)$.

$$\Rightarrow V = S^3$$

$$\Rightarrow \frac{dV}{dt} = 3[S]^2 \frac{dS}{dt}, \text{ by the chain rule.}$$

But we are given that $\frac{dV}{dt}$ 300 in^3/ min.

So, $300 \text{ in}^3/\text{min.} = 3S^2 \dfrac{dS}{dt}$

$$\Rightarrow \frac{dS}{dt} = \frac{300}{3S^2} \text{ in}^3/\text{min.}$$

Therefore, when the edge is 20 inches long,

$$\frac{dS}{dt} = \frac{300 \text{ in}^3/\text{min.}}{(3)(20)(20) \text{ in}^2}$$

$$= \frac{1}{4} \text{ in/min.}$$

38. **(E)**

Using your calculator,

$$fnInt\left(\frac{6(x^{\wedge}3+1)}{x+1}, \ x, \ -1, \ 1\right),$$

which gives 16.

39. **(C)**

$f(x) = x^3 - 2x$

$\Rightarrow f'(x) = 3x^2 - 2$

Therefore, $f'(x) = 0$

$$\Rightarrow 3x^2 - 2 = 0$$

$$\Rightarrow x = \pm\sqrt{\frac{2}{3}}$$

Also, $f''(x) = 6x$

$$\Rightarrow f''\left(\sqrt{\frac{2}{3}}\right) = 6\sqrt{\frac{2}{3}} > 0$$

and $f''\left(-\sqrt{\dfrac{2}{3}}\right) = -6\sqrt{\dfrac{2}{3}} < 0$.

Hence, f has a relative Max. at $x = -\sqrt{\dfrac{2}{3}}$ and a relative Min. at $x = \sqrt{\dfrac{2}{3}}$ by the second derivative test.

40. **(A)**

You can directly solve this problem by using the calculator. For example,

$$\text{der } 1\left(256x\wedge(-0.5) + 64x\wedge 0.5 + 3x\wedge\left(\dfrac{2}{3}\right),\ x,\ 64\right)$$

should get 4.25.

41. **(B)**

Draw the graph of $y = x^2(1 - x^{-1})$.

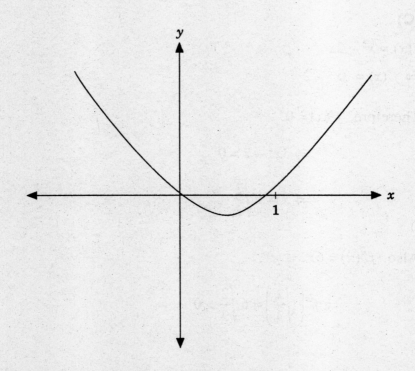

Set the viewing window to [0, 1] • [−1, 1]. By tracing y to the lowest value, you can get $y = -0.25$.

42. **(B)**

$$\int_a^b f(x)\,dx = \int_a^b f(x)\,dx + \int_b^c f(x)\,dx + \int_c^d f(x)\,dx.$$

Since $f(x)$ is non-negative in $[a, b]$ and $[c, d]$ the integral of $f(x)$ in $[a, b]$ and $[c, d]$ corresponds with the areas of regions A and C, respectively.

Since $f(x)$ is ≤ 0 in $[b, c]$, the integral is actually the negative of the area of region B.

Hence, $\int_a^d f(x)\,dx = 3 - \left(1\dfrac{1}{2}\right) + 2$

$$= 3\dfrac{1}{2}$$

$$= \dfrac{7}{2}$$

43. **(C)**

Use integration by parts:

Let $u = x$ and $dv = \cos(4x)\,dx$

$\Rightarrow du = dx$ and $v = \dfrac{1}{4}\sin(4x)$

$\Rightarrow \displaystyle\int x\cos(4x)\,dx = \dfrac{x}{4}\sin(4x) - \int \dfrac{1}{4}\sin(4x)\,dx$

$$= \dfrac{x}{4}\sin(4x) + \dfrac{1}{16}\cos(4x) + c.$$

44. **(C)**

First find the derivatives of the two functions and evaluate them at $t = 2$:

$$x = t^3 - 3t \implies \frac{dx}{dt} = 3t^2 - 3$$

$$\implies \frac{dx}{dt}\Big|_{t=2} = 3(2)^2 - 3 = 9$$

$$y = (t^2 + 1)^2 \implies \frac{dy}{dt} = 2(t^2 + 1) \cdot 2t$$

$$\implies \frac{dy}{dt}\Big|_{t=2} = 2((2)^2 + 1) \cdot 2(2) = 40$$

Then use the fact that

$$\frac{dy}{dx} = \frac{\left(\dfrac{dy}{dt}\right)}{\left(\dfrac{dx}{dt}\right)}:$$

$$\frac{dy}{dx}\Big|_{t=2} = \frac{\dfrac{dy}{dt}\Big|_{t=2}}{\dfrac{dx}{dt}\Big|_{t=2}} = \frac{40}{9}$$

45.   **(D)**

The normal line is the line that is perpendicular to the curve at the given point. Its equation is $y = y_0 + m(x - x_0)$ where (x_0, y_0) is the given point and m is the slope. At the point where $x = 1$,

$$y = x^4 - 3x^2 + 1$$

$$= (1)^4 - 3(1)^2 + 1$$

$$= -1$$

Thus, $(x_0, y_0) = (1, -1)$. The slope m of the normal line is the negative reciprocal of the slope of the tangent line, which is the value of the derivative at the given point;

$$\text{i.e.,} \quad m = \frac{-1}{\dfrac{dy}{dx}\Big|_{x=1}}$$

Since $\dfrac{dy}{dx} = \dfrac{d}{dx}\left(x^4 - 3x^2 + 1\right)$

$= 4x^3 - 6x,$

$m = \dfrac{-1}{\left(4x^3 - 6x\right)\big|_{x=1}}$

$= \dfrac{-1}{(4-6)}$

$= \dfrac{-1}{-2}$

$= \dfrac{1}{2}$

Thus, the equation of the normal line is:

$y = y_0 + m(x - x_0)$

$y = -1 + \dfrac{1}{2}(x - 1)$

$2y = -2 + (x - 1)$

$2y = x - 3$

$x - 2y - 3 = 0$

SECTION II

1. **(A)**

$$\lim_{x \to \frac{\pi}{4}} \left(\frac{1}{2} + \frac{1}{2}\cos(2x) \right) = \lim_{x \to \frac{\pi}{4}} \frac{1}{2} + \lim_{x \to \frac{\pi}{4}} \frac{1}{2}\cos(2x), \text{ by addition rule.}$$

$$= \frac{1}{2} + \frac{1}{2} \lim_{x \to \frac{\pi}{4}} \cos(2x),$$

since $\lim_{x \to a} c\, f(x) = c \lim_{x \to a} f(x)$

$$= \frac{1}{2} + \frac{1}{2} \times \cos\left(2 \times \frac{\pi}{4} \right), \text{ since } \cos x \text{ is a continuous function.}$$

$$= \frac{1}{2} + \frac{1}{2}\cos\frac{\pi}{2}$$

$$= \frac{1}{2} + \frac{1}{2} \times 0, \text{ since } \cos\frac{\pi}{2} = 0,$$

$$= \frac{1}{2}$$

(B)

$$\text{Average value} = \frac{1}{\pi - 0} \int_0^\pi \left(\frac{1}{2} + \frac{1}{2}\cos(2x) \right) dx$$

$$= \frac{1}{\pi} \left(\int_0^\pi \frac{1}{2}\, dx + \frac{1}{2} \int_0^\pi \cos(2x)\, dx \right)$$

$$= \frac{1}{\pi} \left(\frac{1}{2} \times \pi + \frac{1}{2} \times \frac{1}{2}\sin(2x) \Big|_0^\pi \right)$$

$$= \frac{1}{\pi} \left(\frac{\pi}{2} + \frac{1}{4}(\sin 2\pi - \sin 0) \right)$$

$$= \frac{1}{2},$$

since $\sin 2\pi = \sin 0 = 0$

(C)

First, $f(b) = \dfrac{1}{2} + \dfrac{1}{2}\cos (2b)$

and $f(a) = \dfrac{1}{2} + \dfrac{1}{2}\cos (2a).$

$$\Rightarrow f(b) - f(a) = \frac{1}{2}(\cos (2b) - \cos (2a)).$$

By the Mean Value Theorem,

$$f(b) - f(a) = (b - a) f'(c) \text{ for some } a < c < b.$$

But, $f'(c) = -\sin (2c)$,

since $f'(x) = \dfrac{1}{2} \times 2(-\sin 2x)$, by the chain rule.

$$\Rightarrow | f(b) - f(a)| = |-\sin(2c)| \, |b - a|$$
$$\Rightarrow | f(b) - f(a)| \le | b - a|, \text{ since } |-\sin (2c)| \le 1.$$

2. (A)

Use a viewing window of $[-5, 5] \bullet [-5, 40]$ and draw the graphs of $f(x)$ and $g(x)$.

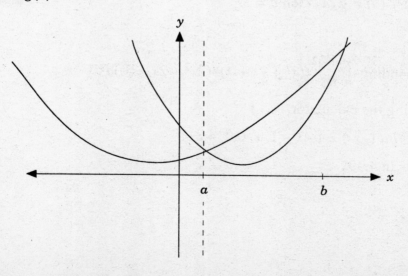

By tracing on the graphs to the integrational points, you can find points $a = 0.268\ldots$ and $b = 3.732\ldots \left(2 \pm \sqrt{3}\right)$

(B)

Draw the graphs of $f'(x)$ and $g'(x)$.

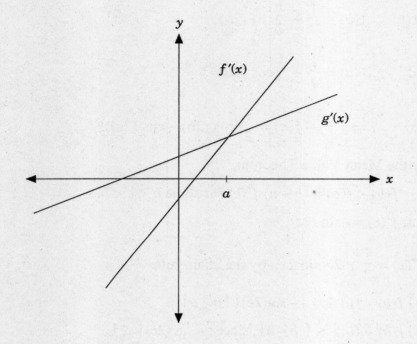

$f'(x) = 4x - 2$

$g'(x) = 2x + 2$

if $f'(a) = g'(a)$ then $a = 2$.

(C)

Finding $\displaystyle\int_{0.268}^{0.3732} ((x^2 + 2x + 4) - (2x^2 - 2x + 5))dx$

by using the calculator.

fnInt $(-x \wedge 2 + 4x - 1, x, 0.2, 4.81)$

results in 4.49.

3. (A)

    (i)

    f is an even function

    $\Rightarrow f(x) = f(-x)$ for every x

    $\Rightarrow f'(x) = -f'(-x)$, by chain rule

Therefore, $f'(-x) = -f'(x)$

    $\Rightarrow f'(2) = -f'(-2)$

    $\Rightarrow f'(-2) = -f'(2)$

    $\Rightarrow f'(-2) = -5$, since $f'(2) = 5$.

    (ii)

    $f'(x) = -f'(-x)$

    $\Rightarrow f'(0) = -f'(-0)$

    $\Rightarrow f'(0) = -f'(0)$

    $\Rightarrow f'(0) + f'(0) = 0$, adding $f'(0)$ to both sides.

    $\Rightarrow 2f'(0) = 0$

    $\Rightarrow f'(0) = 0$, multiplying both sides by $\dfrac{1}{2}$.

    (B)

    Slope of $L_1 = f'(2) = 5$

    Slope of $L_2 = f'(-2) = -5$

    Moreover, L_1 passes through $(2, 1)$ and L_2 passes through $(-2, 1)$, since $f(2) = f(-2) = 1$, because f is an even function.

    Therefore, the point slope form of the equation of

    L_1 is $y - 1 = 5(x - 2)$ and that of

    L_2 is $y - 1 = -5(x + 2)$.

    $\Rightarrow y = 5(x - 2) + 1$

and $y = -5(x + 2) + 1$

    Solving these two equations simultaneously, we have:

$5(x-2) + 1 = -5(x+2) + 1$

$\Rightarrow 5(x-2) + 5(x+2) = 0$

$\Rightarrow 10x = 0$

$\Rightarrow x = 0$

$\Rightarrow y = 5(x-2) + 1$

$\qquad = 5(0-2) + 1$

$\qquad = 5(-2) + 1$

$\qquad = -10 + 1$

$\Rightarrow y = -9$

So, $P = (0, -9)$

4.   (A)

h is the constant function $h(x) = -2$.

By similar reasoning, $g(x) = -5$.

$\qquad \Rightarrow h(x) - g(x) = -2 - (-5) = 3$, a positive constant.

Therefore, $(h-g)f = 3f$.

Since $\dfrac{d}{dx}(3f) = 3f'$ and $\dfrac{d^2}{dx^2}f = 3f''$, then $3f$, like f, is concave upward in the intervals

$$\left(-\frac{1}{4}, \ 3\right) \cup (6, \ 9);$$

and $3f$ is concave downward in the intervals

$$\left(-5, \ -\frac{1}{4}\right) \cup (3, \ 6).$$

(B)

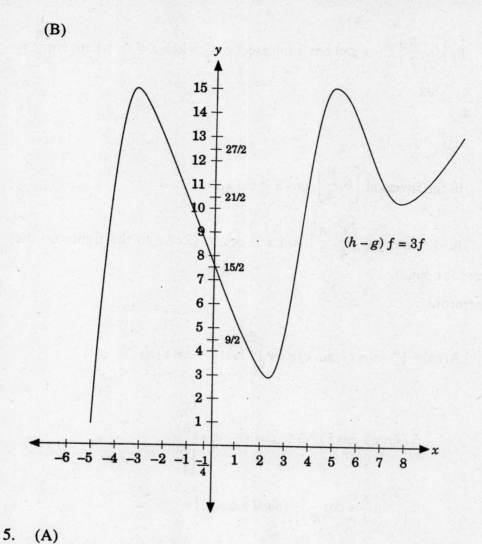

$(h - g) f = 3f$

5. **(A)**

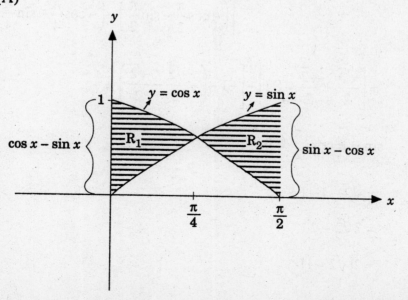

In $\left[0, \dfrac{\pi}{2}\right]$ sin x and cos x intersect only when $x = \dfrac{\pi}{4}$ where $\sin \dfrac{\pi}{4} =$

$\cos \dfrac{\pi}{4} = \dfrac{\sqrt{2}}{2}$.

(B)

In the inverval $\left[0, \dfrac{\pi}{4}\right]$, cos $x \geq$ sin x.

In the interval $\left[\dfrac{\pi}{4}, \dfrac{\pi}{2}\right]$, sin $x \geq$ cos x. (Refer to the figure on the previous page).

Therefore,

$$\text{Area} = \int_0^{\frac{\pi}{4}} (\cos x - \sin x)\,dx + \int_{\frac{\pi}{4}}^{\frac{\pi}{2}} (\sin x - \cos x)\,dx$$

$$= (\sin x + \cos x)\Big|_0^{\frac{\pi}{4}} + (-\cos x - \sin x)\Big|_{\frac{\pi}{4}}^{\frac{\pi}{2}}$$

$$= \left[\left(\sin\frac{\pi}{4} + \cos\frac{\pi}{4}\right) - (\sin 0 + \cos 0)\right] +$$

$$\left[\left(-\cos\frac{\pi}{2} - \sin\frac{\pi}{2}\right) - \left(-\cos\frac{\pi}{4} - \sin\frac{\pi}{4}\right)\right]$$

$$= \left[\frac{\sqrt{2}}{2} + \frac{\sqrt{2}}{2} - (1)\right] + \left[-1 - \left(-\frac{\sqrt{2}}{2} - \frac{\sqrt{2}}{2}\right)\right],$$

since $\quad \sin 0 = \cos\dfrac{\pi}{2} = 0.$

$$= \sqrt{2} - 1 - 1 + \sqrt{2}$$

$$= 2\sqrt{2} - 2$$

$$= 2\left(\sqrt{2} - 1\right)$$

(C)

To find volume, we note that in R_1 $\sin x \leq \cos x$ (Refer to figure above).

$$\Rightarrow dV = \pi(\cos^2 x - \sin^2 x) \, dx$$

In R_2 $\sin x \geq \cos x$

$$\Rightarrow dV = \pi(\sin^2 x - \cos^2 x) \, dx$$

Therefore,

$$\text{volume} = \int_0^{\frac{\pi}{4}} \pi\left(\cos^2 x - \sin^2 x\right) dx + \int_{\frac{\pi}{4}}^{\frac{\pi}{2}} \pi\left(\sin^2 x - \cos^2 x\right) dx$$

$$= 2\pi \int_0^{\frac{\pi}{4}} \cos 2x \, dx$$

$$= \pi$$

6.   (A)

$$f'(x) = 3x^2 + 2ax + b.$$

Since f has a relative minimum at $x = 4$, then

$$f'(4) = 3(4)^2 + 2a\,(4) + b = 0$$

$$\Rightarrow 48 + 8a + b = 0 \tag{1}$$

(must also check that $f''(4) > 0$, which it is)

Since f has an inflection point at $x = 1$

$$\Rightarrow f''(1) = 0 \quad \text{but} \quad f''(x) = 6x + 2a$$

$$f''(1) = 0 \Rightarrow 6 + 2a = 0$$

$$\Rightarrow a = -3 \tag{2}$$

We substitute equation (2) into equation (1) to find b:

$$48 + 8(-3) + b = 0$$

$$24 + b = 0$$

$$b = -24.$$

(B)

When we plug $a = -3$ and $b = -24$ into

$$f(x) = x^3 + ax^2 + bx + c \quad \text{we get}$$

$$f(x) = x^3 + 3x^2 + 24x + c$$

But, $f(0) = 1$

$$\Rightarrow 1 = f(0) = 0^3 - 3(0)^2 - 24(0) + c = c$$

Hence, $\quad f(x) = x^3 - 3x^2 - 24x + 1$

$$\Rightarrow f'(x) = 3x^2 - 6x - 24$$

So, $\qquad f'(x) = 0$

$$\Rightarrow 3x^2 - 6x - 24 = 0$$

$$\Rightarrow x^2 - 2x - 8 = 0 \quad \text{(multiplying both sides by } \frac{1}{3}\text{)}$$

$$\Rightarrow (x - 4)(x + 2) = 0$$

$$\Rightarrow x = 4 \text{ or } x = -2$$

Moreover, $f''(x) = 6x - 6$

Plugging in the critical points $x = 4$, $x = -2$, we see that

$$\Rightarrow f''(4) = 18 > 0 \text{ and } f''(-2) = -18 < 0$$

Hence, f has a relative Max. at $x = -2$ and a relative Min. at $x = 4$.

So, the relative Maximum of f is

$$f(-2) = -8 - 12 + 48 + 1$$

$$= 29.$$

Advanced Placement Examination in Calculus AB

EXAM V

Exam V is also on CD-ROM in our special interactive AP Calculus AB Test*ware*®. It is highly recommended that you first take this exam on computer. You will then have the additional study features and benefits of enforced timed conditions, individual diagnostic analysis, and instant scoring. See page xiv for guidance on how to get the most out of our AP Calculus AB book and software.

ADVANCED PLACEMENT
CALCULUS AB
EXAM V

SECTION I

PART A

Time: 55 minutes
28 questions

DIRECTIONS: Each of the following problems is followed by five choices. Solve each problem, select the best choice, and blacken the correct space on your answer sheet. Calculators may not be used for this section of the exam.

NOTE: Unless otherwise specified, the domain of function f is assumed to be the set of all real numbers x for which $f(x)$ is a real number.

1. If $3x^2 - x^2y^3 + 4y = 12$ determines a differentiable function such that $y = f(x)$, then $\dfrac{dy}{dx} =$

(A) $\dfrac{-3x + 2xy^3}{2}$

(D) $\dfrac{-6x + 2xy^3 + 3x^2y^2}{4}$

(B) $\dfrac{-6x + 2xy^3}{-3x^2y^2 + 4}$

(E) $\dfrac{-6x + 2xy^3}{3x^2y^2 + 4}$

(C) $\dfrac{-3x + 2xy^3 + 6}{2}$

2. $\int_1^4 \dfrac{5x^2 - x}{2\sqrt{x}} \, dx =$

(A) 29

(D) $\dfrac{311}{12}$

(B) $\dfrac{113}{6}$

(E) $\dfrac{100}{3}$

(C) $\dfrac{86}{3}$

3. The area in the first quadrant that is enclosed by the graphs of $x = y^3$ and $x = 4y$ is

(A) 4

(D) 1

(B) 8

(E) 0

(C) –4

4. For what value of c is $f(x) = \begin{cases} 3x^2 + 2, & x \ge -1 \\ -cx + 5, & x < -1 \end{cases}$ continuous?

(A) 3

(D) None

(B) –3

(E) 0

(C) 6

5. $\displaystyle\lim_{x \to \infty} \sqrt[3]{\dfrac{8 + x^2}{x(x+1)}} =$

(A) 0

(D) 1

(B) 2

(E) Does not exist

(C) $\sqrt[3]{9}$

6. If $y = \tan(\text{arcsec } x)$, then $\dfrac{dy}{dx} =$

(A) $\sqrt{x^2 - 1}$

(D) $\dfrac{x}{\sqrt{x^2 - 1}}$

(B) $\dfrac{x}{\sqrt{1 + x^2}}$

(E) $\dfrac{x}{\sqrt{1 - x^2}}$

(C) $\dfrac{\sqrt{x^2 - 1}}{x}$

7. Let $f(x) = 2x^5 - x^3 + x^2 + 2$ and $g(x) = f^{-1}(x)$. If $f(1) = 4$ then $g'(4) =$

(A) 9

(D) $\dfrac{1}{2,002}$

(B) $\dfrac{1}{9}$

(E) $\dfrac{1}{2,376}$

(C) $\dfrac{1}{4}$

8. $\displaystyle\lim_{x \to 0^-} (1 - x)^{\frac{2}{x}} =$

(A) e^{-2}

(D) e^2

(B) -2

(E) Does not exist

(C) 2

9. If $f(x) = |x|$ for all real numbers x, then $f'(x)$ is a real number for

(A) $x < 0$ only

(D) $x \neq 0$ only

(B) $x > 0$ only

(E) All real numbers x

(C) $x = 0$ only

10. Note that $\sin\dfrac{\pi}{2} \neq \sin\left(\dfrac{\pi}{2}\right)^{\circ}$ since $\sin\dfrac{\pi}{2} = 1$ and $\sin\left(\dfrac{\pi}{2}\right)^{\circ} = \sin(1.578)^{\circ}$

$\cong 0.03$. Find $\dfrac{d}{dx}\sin(x^{\circ})$ when x° is measured in degrees, and x in radians.

(A) $\cos(x^{\circ})$

(D) $\dfrac{\pi}{180}\cos(x^{\circ})$

(B) $\dfrac{\pi}{2}\cos(x^{\circ})$

(E) $\dfrac{\pi}{180}\cos x$

(C) $\cos\left(\dfrac{\pi x}{180}\right)$

11. $\displaystyle\int \dfrac{\log\left(x^3 \times 10^x\right)}{x}\,dx =$

(Note: log stands for $\log_{10}$ and ln stands for $\log_e$)

(A) $\dfrac{3\ln 10}{2}(\log x)^2 + x + C$

(B) $\dfrac{3}{2\ln 10}(\ln x)^2 + x + C$

(C) $\dfrac{6\log x}{\ln 10} + x + C$

(D) $\dfrac{3(\log x)^2}{\ln 10} + x + C$

(E) $3\ln 10(\ln x^2) + x + C$

12. $f(x) = 2x^3 - 9x^2 + 12x - 3$ is decreasing for

   (A) $x < 2$

   (D) $1 < x$

   (B) all values of x

   (E) $1 < x < 2$

   (C) $x < 1$ and $x > 2$

13. The equation of the horizontal asymptote of $f(x) = \dfrac{|x|}{|x|+x}$ is:

   (A) $y = \dfrac{1}{2}$

   (D) $y = -1$

   (B) $y = 0$

   (E) $x = 0$

   (C) $y = 1$

14. Find the point on the parabola $y = x^2$ which is closest to the point $(6, 3)$.

   (A) $(1\dfrac{1}{2}, \ 2\dfrac{1}{4})$

   (D) $(3, 9)$

   (B) $(2\dfrac{1}{2}, \ 6\dfrac{1}{4})$

   (E) $(1\dfrac{3}{4}, \ 3\dfrac{1}{16})$

   (C) $(2, 4)$

15. $\lim\limits_{x \to -1} \dfrac{\sqrt{x^2+3}-2}{x+1} =$

   (A) 0

   (D) 2

   (B) -2

   (E) Does not exist

   (C) $-\dfrac{1}{2}$

16. The area bounded by the parabola $y^2 = 2x - 2$ and the line $y = x - 5$ is

    (A) 22

    (D) $\dfrac{52}{3}$

    (B) 18

    (E) $\dfrac{26}{3}$

    (C) $\dfrac{14}{3}$

17. Population growth in a certain bacteria colony is best described by the equation $y = t^2 e^{3t^2 + \sqrt{t}}$, where t is in hours. The rate of growth of the colony at $t = 1$ is

    (A) 464.084

    (D) 300.290

    (B) 245.692

    (E) 545.982

    (C) 409.486

18. $\displaystyle \int \frac{e^{2x}}{e^x - 3} \, dx =$

    (A) $\left(e^x + 3\right) + 3\ln\left|e^x + 3\right| + C$

    (B) $e^x - 3\ln\left|e^x - 3\right| + C$

    (C) $\left(e^x - 3\right) + 3\ln\left|e^x - 3\right| + C$

    (D) $\left(e^x - 3\right) - \dfrac{3}{\left(e^x - 3\right)^2} + C$

    (E) $\left(e^x - 3\right) + \dfrac{3}{\left(e^x - 3\right)^2} + C$

19. If $xy - x = 2y - 5$, then which of the following must be true?

    I.   The relation is a function of x.

    II. The domain is $\{x \mid x \neq 2\}$.

    III. The range is all reals.

    (A) I only

    (B) II only

    (C) I and II only

    (D) I and III only

    (E) I, II, and III

20. If $h(x) = \sqrt{x^2 - 4}$, $x \leq -2$, then $h^{-1}(x) =$

    (A) $\sqrt{x^2 + 4}$

    (B) $-\sqrt{x^2 + 4}$

    (C) $-\sqrt{x + 4}$

    (D) $\sqrt{x + 4}$

    (E) $-\sqrt{x^2 - 4}$

21. Which of the following is the graph of $y = 1 + 2^{x+3}$?

    (A)

(B)

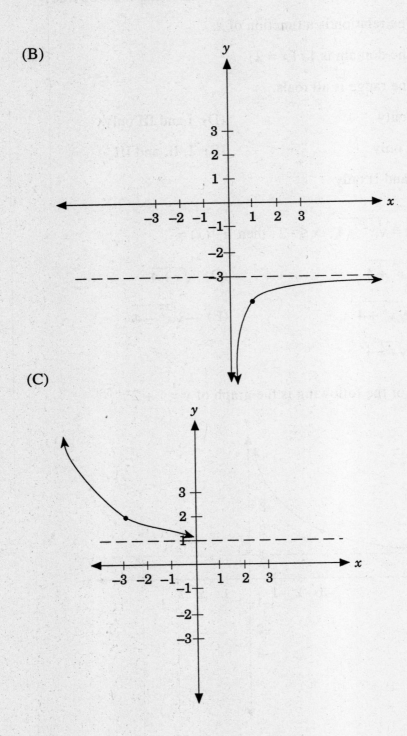

(C)

(D)

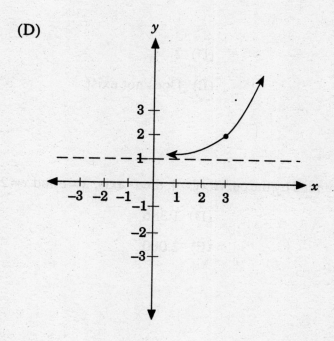

(E)

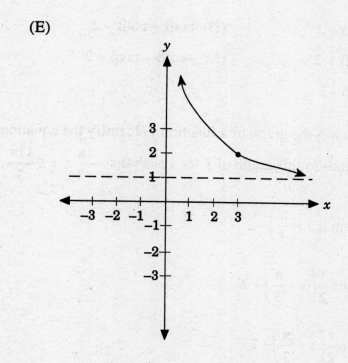

22. $\displaystyle\lim_{x\to 0}\frac{\sin 2x}{x\cos x}=$

(A) 0

(D) 2

(B) 1

(E) Does not exist

(C) $\dfrac{1}{2}$

23. Find the area bounded by the curve $xy=4$, the x–axis, $x=e$ and $x=2e$.

(A) 4.000

(D) 1.386

(B) 0.693

(E) 2.000

(C) 2.773

24. $\dfrac{\cos 2\beta-\sin 2\beta}{\sin\beta\cos\beta}=$

(A) $\cot\beta-\tan\beta-2$

(D) $\tan\beta+\cot\beta-2$

(B) $\cot\beta+\tan\beta+2$

(E) $-\cot\beta-\tan\beta-2$

(C) $\tan\beta-\cot\beta-2$

25. The figure shown is the graph of a function f. Identify the equation which corresponds to this graph of f for x such that $-\dfrac{\pi}{3}\le x\le\dfrac{11\pi}{3}$.

(A) $f(x)=-3\sin 2\left(x-\dfrac{\pi}{3}\right)-2$

(B) $f(x)=-3\sin\dfrac{1}{2}\left(x-\dfrac{\pi}{3}\right)+2$

(C) $f(x)=3\sin\dfrac{1}{2}\left(x+\dfrac{\pi}{3}\right)-2$

(D) $f(x) = -3\sin\frac{1}{2}\left(x + \frac{\pi}{3}\right) - 2$

(E) $f(x) = 3\sin\frac{1}{2}\left(x - \frac{\pi}{3}\right) - 2$

26. Data suggests that between the hours of 1:00 P.M. and 3:00 P.M. on Sunday, the speed of traffic along a street is approximately $S(t) = 3t^2 + 10t$ miles per hour, where t is the number of hours past noon. Compute the average speed of the traffic between the hours of 1:00 P.M. and 3:00 P.M.

(A) 70

(D) 44

(B) 66

(E) 22

(C) 33

27. The solution of the equation $(x+1)\dfrac{dy}{dx} = x\left(y^2 + 1\right)$ is

(A) $\ln|y + 1| = \tan^{-1}x + C$

(B) $\ln|y + 1| = x - \tan^{-1}x + C$

(C) $\tan^{-1}y = \ln|x + 1| + C$

(D) $\tan^{-1}y = x - \ln|x + 1| + C$

(E) None of the above

28. What are all the values of x for which the series

$$1 + \frac{x^2}{2!} + \frac{x^4}{4!} \cdots + \frac{x^{2n}}{(2n)!} + \ldots \text{ converges?}$$

(A) $-1 \leq x \leq 1$ (D) $-1 < x < 1$

(B) $0 \leq x \leq 1$ (E) All values of x

(C) $0 < x < 2$

PART B

Time: 50 minutes

17 questions

DIRECTIONS: Calculators may be used for this section of the test. Each of the following problems is followed by five choices. Solve each problem, select the best choice, and blacken the correct space on your answer sheet.

NOTES:

1. Unless otherwise specified, answers can be given in unsimplified form.

2. The domain of function f is assumed to be the set of all real numbers x for which $f(x)$ is a real number.

---

29. If $y = \dfrac{2(x-1)^2}{x^2}$, then which of the following must be true?

    I.   The range is $\{y \mid y \geq 0\}$.

    II. The y–intercept is 1.

    III. The horizontal asymptote is $y = 2$.

    (A) I only   (D) I and II only

    (B) II only   (E) I and III only

    (C) III only

30. If $g(x + 3) = x^2 + 2$, then $g(x)$ equals

    (A) $\sqrt{x-3}$ (D) $\sqrt{x-3} + 2$

    (B) $(x-3)^2 + 2$ (E) $\sqrt{x-3} - 2$

    (C) $(x-3)^2 - 2$

31. The slope of the tangent line to the graph $y = \dfrac{x^2}{\sqrt[3]{3x^2 + 1}}$ at $x = 1$ is approximately

    (A) 0.945

    (D) 1.191

    (B) 2.381

    (E) 1.575

    (C) 1.890

32. If x and y are functions of t which satisfy the relation $x^4 + xy + y^4 = 1$, then $\dfrac{dy}{dt} =$

    (A) $\left(\dfrac{4x + y}{x + 4y^3}\right)\dfrac{dx}{dt}$

    (D) $-\left(\dfrac{4x^3 + y}{x + 4y}\right)\dfrac{dx}{dt}$

    (B) $-\left(\dfrac{4x^3 + y}{x + 4y^3}\right)\dfrac{dx}{dt}$

    (E) $\left(-\dfrac{4x^3 + y}{x + 4y^3}\right)\dfrac{dx}{dt}$

    (C) $-\left(\dfrac{x + 4y^3}{4x^3 + y}\right)\dfrac{dx}{dt}$

33. If $g(u) = \sqrt{u^3 + 2}$, $f(1) = 2$ and $f'(1) = -5$, then $\dfrac{d}{dx}\big(g(f(x))\big)$ at $x = 1$ is approximately

    (A) 9.487

    (D) −9.487

    (B) 18.974

    (E) 4.330

    (C) −4.330

34. If $y = \dfrac{1}{\sin\left(t + \sqrt{t}\right)}$, then $y'(1)$, in radians, is approximately

    (A) −0.002   (D) 410.267

    (B) −1,641.070   (E) −0.070

    (C) 0.755

35. Find $\int \arctan x \, dx$ using integration by parts.

    (A) $\arctan x + \ln(1 + x^2) + C$

    (B) $x \arctan x + C$

    (C) $\dfrac{1}{\left(1 + x^2\right)} + C$

    (D) $x \arctan x - \dfrac{1}{2}\ln(1 + x^2) + C$

    (E) $\ln(1 + x^2) + x \arctan x + C$

36. If $y = -\ln\left|\dfrac{1 + \sqrt{1 - x^2}}{x}\right|$ then $\dfrac{dy}{dx} =$

    (A) $\dfrac{1}{x\sqrt{1 - x^2}}$ (D) $\dfrac{1}{\sqrt{1 - x^2}}$

    (B) $\dfrac{1}{x} - \dfrac{1}{\sqrt{1 - x^2}}$ (E) $\dfrac{x}{\sqrt{1 - x^2}}$

    (C) $\dfrac{x + 1}{x\sqrt{1 - x^2}}$

37. Let $F = \dfrac{6000k}{k\sin\theta + \cos\theta}$ where k is a constant. For which value of

θ is $\dfrac{dF}{d\theta} = 0$ for $\dfrac{-\pi}{2} < \theta < \dfrac{\pi}{2}$?

(A) $\theta = \arctan\dfrac{1}{k}$ (D) $\theta = \arctan k$

(B) $\theta = 0$ (E) $\theta = \operatorname{arccot} k$

(C) $\theta = \dfrac{\pi}{2}$

38. If $f(x) = \dfrac{1}{\sin(x + \sqrt{x})}$, calculate $\int_0^1 f(x)$.

(A) 2.57   (D) 98.10

(B) 10.26   (E) 1.65

(C) –3.10

39. $f(x) = \left(x^2 - 3\right)^{\frac{2}{3}}$ is increasing for which values of x?

(A) $-\sqrt{3} \le x \le \sqrt{3}$

(B) $x \le -\sqrt{3}$ or $x > \sqrt{3}$

(C) $-3 \le x \le 3$

(D) $-\sqrt{3} < x < 0$ or $x > \sqrt{3}$

(E) $f(x)$ is never increasing.

40. If $y = \tan(\arccos x)$ then $\dfrac{dy}{dx} =$

   (A) $\dfrac{-1}{x^2\sqrt{1-x^2}}$

   (D) $\dfrac{1}{x\sqrt{1-x^2}}$

   (B) $\dfrac{1}{x^2\sqrt{1-x^2}}$

   (E) $\dfrac{-1}{x^2\sqrt{x^2-1}}$

   (C) $\dfrac{-1}{x\sqrt{1-x^2}}$

41. Which of the following statements is true?

   (A) $\log_{\frac{1}{2}} 2 < \log_{\frac{1}{\sqrt{2}}} 2$

   (B) $\log_3 (2+4) = \log_3 2 + \log_3 3$

   (C) $\log_{10} 2 > \log_{10} 4$

   (D) $\log_{\frac{1}{5}} (5\sqrt{5}) = \dfrac{2}{3}$

   (E) $\log_{\frac{1}{2}} 2 - \log_{\frac{1}{2}} 4 = \log_{\frac{1}{2}} 2$

42. Let $f(x) = (x^2 - 3)^2$. The local minimum of $f'(x)$ is

   (A) 7.99

   (D) −7.99

   (B) 5.80

   (E) 6.28

   (C) 3.25

43. $f(x) = \dfrac{x^2}{e^x}$.

$\displaystyle\int_0^5 \dfrac{x^2}{e^x}$ is

(A) 2.25

(D) 1.75

(B) 1.30

(E) 12.50

(C) 7.10

44. The equation of the line tangent to the curve $x(t) = t^2$, $y(t) = t^3 - 1$ at the point (4, 7) is

(A) $x - 3y = -5$

(D) $4x + 7y = 12$

(B) $3x - y = 5$

(E) $x^2 + y^3 = 1$

(C) $4x - 7y = 0$

45. $\displaystyle\int \dfrac{1}{(x+3)(x+4)}\,dx =$

(A) $\ln\dfrac{|x+3|}{|x+4|} + C$

(B) $\ln\dfrac{|x+4|}{|x+3|} + C$

(C) $\ln\dfrac{|x-4|}{|x-3|} + C$

(D) $(\ln|x+3|)(\ln|x+4|) + C$

(E) $\ln|(x+3)(x+4)| + C$

SECTION II

Time: 1 hour and 30 minutes
6 problems

DIRECTIONS: Show all your work. Grading is based on the methods used to solve the problem as well as the accuracy of your final answers. Please make sure all procedures are clearly shown. For some problems or parts of problems it will be necessary to use a calculator.

NOTES:

1. Unless otherwise specified, answers can be given in unsimplified form.

2. The domain of function f is assumed to be the set of all real numbers x for which $f(x)$ is a real number.

---

1. Let f be the function given by $f(x) = \dfrac{x^2 - 4}{1 - x^2}$.

   (A) Find the domain of f.

   (B) Find the range of f.

   (C) Find the equations for each vertical and each horizontal asymptote.

   (D) Find the critical points.

2. At a child's party, there is a contest to see which child can run the fastest from a point 20 feet from a fence, to the fence, and then to a point 30 feet from the fence as in the figure shown. Find the point on the fence to where the children should run in order to minimize the distance by using the following:

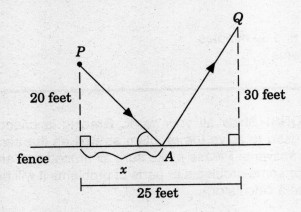

(A) Express $\overline{PA}$ and $\overline{QA}$ in terms of x.

(B) Find x.

3. The current I in a circuit is given by $I(t) = 20 \sin(311t) + 40 \cos(311t)$. Let $\cos\theta = \dfrac{1}{\sqrt{5}}$ and $\sin\theta = \dfrac{2}{\sqrt{5}}$.

(A) Verify, by use of the sum formula for the sine function, that
$I(t) = 20\sqrt{5} \sin(311t + \theta)$.

(B) Determine the peak current (the maximum value of I) by the second derivative test.

4. Use the information below to answer the following questions about $y = f(x)$:

$$\lim_{x \to 2^-} f(x) = -\infty, \qquad \lim_{x \to 2^+} f(x) = \infty, \qquad \lim_{x \to -1^-} f(x) = \infty$$

$$\lim_{x \to -1^+} f(x) = -\infty, \qquad \lim_{x \to \infty} f(x) = 0, \qquad \lim_{x \to -\infty} f(x) = 0$$

Interval	$(-\infty, -4)$	$(-4, 0)$	$(0, \infty)$
sign of $f'(x)$	$-$	$+$	$-$

$$f(-4) = -\frac{2}{3}, \quad f(0) = -6, \quad f(-2) = 0$$

$f(2)$ and $f(-1)$ are undefined.

(A) Find the intervals where f is increasing and where f is decreasing.

(B) Find the equation for each horizontal and each vertical asymptote.

(C) Find the local maximum and minimum values of f.

(D) Sketch f. Label asymptotes, local extrema, and intercepts.

5. Let $f(x) = \frac{2}{3} x^{\frac{3}{2}}$ and suppose that the line $y = cx + d$ is tangent to $f(x)$ at x_0.

(A) If $x_0 = 2$, find c and d.

(B) If $c = 1$, find x_0 and d.

(C) Find $\int_0^3 \frac{2}{3} x^{\frac{3}{2}} dx$.

6. A projectile is fired directly upward from the ground with an initial velocity of 112 feet/second, and its distance above the ground after t seconds is $s(t) = 112t - 16t^2$ feet.

(A) What are the velocity and acceleration of the projectile at $t = 3$ seconds?

(B) At what time does the projectile reach its maximum height?

(C) What is the velocity at the moment of impact?

(D) The projectile travels (up and back) 392 feet. A bug traverses the

arc of the curve $y = \dfrac{\sqrt{\left(x^2 - 2\right)^3}}{3}$ from $x = 1$ foot to $x = 10$ feet.

Which distance is longer, the path of the projectile or the path traversed by the bug?

ADVANCED PLACEMENT CALCULUS AB EXAM V

ANSWER KEY

Section I

1.	(B)	12.	(E)	23.	(C)	34.	(C)
2.	(C)	13.	(A)	24.	(A)	35.	(D)
3.	(A)	14.	(C)	25.	(D)	36.	(A)
4.	(E)	15.	(C)	26.	(C)	37.	(D)
5.	(D)	16.	(B)	27.	(D)	38.	(E)
6.	(D)	17.	(A)	28.	(E)	39.	(D)
7.	(B)	18.	(C)	29.	(E)	40.	(A)
8.	(A)	19.	(C)	30.	(B)	41.	(B)
9.	(D)	20.	(B)	31.	(A)	42.	(A)
10.	(D)	21.	(A)	32.	(B)	43.	(D)
11.	(A)	22.	(D)	33.	(D)	44.	(B)
						45.	(A)

Section II

See Detailed Explanations of Answers.

ADVANCED PLACEMENT
CALCULUS AB
EXAM V

DETAILED EXPLANATIONS
OF ANSWERS

SECTION I

1. **(B)**

$$\frac{d}{dx}\left(3x^2 - x^2y^3 + 4y\right) = \frac{d}{dx}(12)$$

$$6x - 2xy^3 - x^2 3y^2 y' + 4y' = 0$$

$$6x - 2xy^3 + y'\left(-3x^2y^2 + 4\right) = 0$$

$$y'\left(-3x^2y^2 + 4\right) = -6x + 2xy^3$$

$$y' = \frac{-6x + 2xy^3}{-3x^2y^2 + 4}$$

$$\frac{dy}{dx} = \frac{-6x + 2xy^3}{-3x^2y^2 + 4}$$

2. **(C)**

$$\int_1^4 \frac{5x^2 - x}{2\sqrt{x}}\, dx = \int_1^4 \frac{5x^2 - x}{2x^{\frac{1}{2}}}\, dx$$

$$= \int_1^4 \left(\frac{5x^{\frac{3}{2}}}{2} - \frac{x^{\frac{1}{2}}}{2} \right) dx$$

$$= \left(x^{\frac{5}{2}} - \frac{1}{3} x^{\frac{3}{2}} \right) \Big|_1^4$$

$$= \left(2^5 - 1^5 \right) - \frac{1}{3}\left(2^3 - 1^3 \right)$$

$$= (31) - \frac{7}{3}$$

$$= \frac{86}{3}$$

3. **(A)**

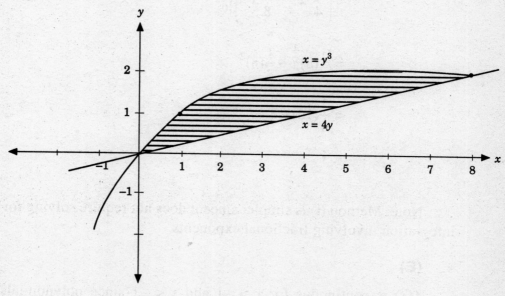

(i) $A = \int_0^2 \left(4y - y^3\right) dy$

$= \left(2y^2 - \dfrac{y^4}{4}\right)\Big|_0^2$

$= 2(2)^2 - \dfrac{1}{4}(2)^4$

$= 8 - 4$

$= 4$

or (ii) $A = \int_0^8 \left(\sqrt[3]{x} - \dfrac{x}{4}\right) dx$

$= \int_0^8 \left(x^{\frac{1}{3}} - \dfrac{1}{4}x\right) dx$

$= \left(\dfrac{3}{4}\, x^{\frac{4}{3}} - \dfrac{1}{8}x^2\right)\Big|_0^8$

$= \dfrac{3}{4}(8)^{\frac{4}{3}} - \dfrac{1}{8}(8)^2$

$= \dfrac{3}{4}(16) - 8$

$= 4$

<u>Note</u>: Method (i) is simpler since it does not require solving for y or integration involving fractional exponents.

4. **(E)**

$f(x)$ is continuous for $x > -1$ and $x < -1$ since polynomials are continuous for all reals.

For $x = -1$, $3x^2 + 2 = 5$.

For $c = 0$,

$$\lim_{x \to -1^-} (-cx + 5) = \lim_{x \to -1^-} (5) = 5$$

Therefore, if $c = 0$ then for all values of x_0 we have

$$\lim_{x \to x_0} f(x) = f(x_0)$$

The graph of $f(x)$ with $c = 0$ is sketched below:

$$f(x) = \begin{cases} 3x^2 + 2 & x \geq -1 \\ 5 & x < -1 \end{cases}$$

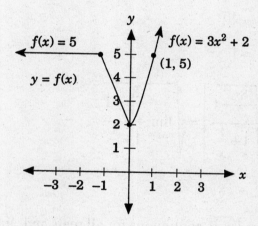

5. **(D)**

$$\lim_{x \to \infty} \sqrt[3]{\frac{8 + x^2}{x(x + 1)}} = \lim_{x \to \infty} \sqrt[3]{\frac{8 + x^2}{x^2 + x}}$$

$$= \lim_{x \to \infty} \sqrt[3]{\frac{(8 + x^2)\dfrac{1}{x^2}}{(x^2 + x)\dfrac{1}{x^2}}}$$

$$= \lim_{x \to \infty} \sqrt[3]{\frac{\left(\dfrac{8}{x^2}\right) + 1}{1 + \dfrac{1}{x}}}$$

$$= 3\sqrt{\lim_{x \to \infty} \frac{\left(\dfrac{8}{x^2}\right)+1}{1+\dfrac{1}{x}}}$$

$$= 3\sqrt{\frac{\lim\left(\dfrac{8}{x^2}\right)+\lim(1)}{\lim(1)+\lim\left(\dfrac{1}{x}\right)}}$$

$$= 3\sqrt{\frac{0+1}{1+0}}$$

$$= \sqrt[3]{1}$$

$$= 1$$

Note: $\displaystyle \lim_{x \to \infty}\left[3\sqrt{\frac{\dfrac{8}{x^2}+1}{1+\dfrac{1}{x}}}\right] = 3\sqrt{\lim_{x \to \infty}\frac{\dfrac{8}{x^2}+1}{1+\dfrac{1}{x}}}$

because $f(x) = \sqrt[3]{x}$ is continuous for all reals and $\displaystyle \lim_{x \to \infty}\frac{\dfrac{8}{x^2}+1}{1+\dfrac{1}{x}}$ exists.

6. **(D)**

Let $\theta = \text{arcsec } x$.

By the identity $\tan^2\theta + 1 = \sec^2\theta$, we have

$\tan^2(\text{arcsec } x) + 1 = \sec^2(\text{arcsec } x)$

$$\Rightarrow y^2 + 1 = x^2$$

$$\Rightarrow y = \pm\sqrt{x^2 - 1}$$

Hence, $y = \pm\left(x^2 - 1\right)^{\frac{1}{2}}$

therefore, $y' = \dfrac{\pm x}{\sqrt{x^2 - 1}}$.

7. **(B)**

Since $g(x) = f^{-1}(x)$ then $f(g(x)) = x$

Differentiating both sides with respect to x gives:

$$\frac{d}{dx}f(g(x)) = \frac{d}{dx}(x)$$

Using the chain rule, we obtain $f'(g(x)) \times g'(x) = 1$

Hence, $g'(x) = \dfrac{1}{f'(g(x))}$.

Since $f(1) = 4$ and $g(4) = 1$

therefore, $g'(4) = \dfrac{1}{f'(g(4))}$

$$= \frac{1}{f'(1)}$$

Since $f'(x) = 10x^4 - 3x^2 + 2x$

$$f'(1) = 10 - 3 + 2$$

$$= 9$$

therefore, $g'(4) = \dfrac{1}{9}$

8. **(A)**

$$\lim_{x \to 0^-} (1-x)^{\frac{2}{x}}$$

Let $\quad y = (1-x)^{\frac{2}{x}}$

$$\ln y = \ln(1-x)^{\frac{2}{x}}$$

$$= \frac{2}{x}\ln(1-x)$$

$$= \frac{2\ln(1-x)}{x}$$

By L'Hôpital's Rule, $\displaystyle \lim_{x \to 0^-} \ln y = \lim_{x \to 0^-} \frac{2\ln(1-x)}{x}$

$$= \lim_{x \to 0^-} \frac{2\left(\dfrac{1}{1-x}\right)(-1)}{1}$$

$$= \lim_{x \to 0^-} -\frac{2}{1-x}$$

$$= -2$$

Therefore, $\displaystyle \lim_{x \to 0^-} \ln y = -2$

$$\lim_{x \to 0^-} (1-x)^{\frac{2}{x}} = \lim_{x \to 0^-} y$$

$$= \lim_{x \to 0^-} e^{\ln y}$$

$$= e^{\lim_{x \to 0^-} \ln y}$$

$$= e^{-2}$$

9. **(D)**

We know that $f(x) = |x| = \begin{cases} x & \text{if} \quad x \ge 0 \\ -x & \text{if} \quad x < 0 \end{cases}$

Hence, $f'(x) = \begin{cases} 1 & \text{if} \quad x > 0 \\ -1 & \text{if} \quad x < 0 \end{cases} = \dfrac{x}{|x|}$, for $x \ne 0$

Therefore, $f'(x)$ is a real number for all $x \ne 0$.

10. **(D)**

Since (degrees) $= \left(\dfrac{\text{degrees}}{\text{radians}}\right)$ (radians), or $x° = \dfrac{360}{2\pi} x$, we have

$$\frac{d}{dx}\sin(x^\circ) = \frac{d}{dx}\sin\left(\frac{180}{\pi}x\right)$$

$$= \frac{180}{\pi}\cos\left(\frac{180}{\pi}x\right)$$

$$= \frac{180}{\pi}\cos(x^\circ)$$

11. **(B)**

$$\int \frac{\log\left(x^3 \times 10^x\right)}{x}\,dx = \int \frac{\log x^3 + \log 10^x}{x}\,dx$$

$$= \int \frac{3\log x + x}{x}\,dx$$

$$= \int \left(\frac{3\log x}{x} + 1\right)dx$$

$$= \int \left(1 + A\frac{\ln x}{x}\right)dx \quad \text{where} \quad A = \frac{3}{\ln 10}$$

$$= x + \frac{A}{2}(\ln x)^2 + C$$

$$= x + \frac{3}{2\ln 10}(\ln x)^2 + C$$

12. **(E)**

We see that

$$f'(x) = 6x^2 - 18x + 12 = 6(x - 1)(x - 2)$$

$$f'(x) > 0 \text{ for } x > 2 \text{ or } x < 1$$

$$f'(x) < 0 \text{ for } 1 < x < 2$$

13. **(A)**

$$\lim_{x \to +\infty} \frac{|x|}{|x+1|+x} = \lim_{x \to +\infty} \frac{x}{x+1+x}$$

$$= \lim_{x \to +\infty} \left(\frac{x}{2x+1}\right)\left(\frac{\frac{1}{x}}{\frac{1}{x}}\right)$$

$$= \lim_{x \to +\infty} \frac{1}{2+\frac{1}{x}}$$

$$= \frac{1}{2}$$

$$\lim_{x \to -\infty} \frac{|x|}{|x+1|+x} = \lim_{x \to -\infty} \frac{-x}{-(x+1)+x}]$$

$$= \lim_{x \to -\infty} \frac{-x}{-1}$$

$$= \lim_{x \to -\infty} x$$

$$= -\infty$$

Thus $y = \dfrac{1}{2}$ is a horizontal asymptote.

14. **(C)**

We want to minimize the distance $D = \sqrt{(x-6)^2 + (y-3)^2}$ from a point (x, y) to the point $(6, 3)$ subject to $y = x^2$.

We can do this more easily if we square both sides to remove the square root sign.

We have $D^2 = (x-6)^2 + (y-3)^2$

We can now replace y with x^2 since the point is on the parabola $y = x^2$.

We expand to get: $D^2 = (x-6)^2 + (x^2-3)^2$

$$= x^2 - 12x + 36 + x^4 - 6x^2 + 9$$

$$= x^4 - 5x^2 - 12x + 45.$$

We now take the derivative and set it equal to zero:

$$4x^3 - 10x - 12 = 0$$

Dividing by 2 gives $0 = 2x^3 - 5x - 6$

$$0 = (x-2)(2x^2 + 4x + 3)$$

The roots of $2x^2 + 4x + 3 = 0$ are

$$x = \frac{-4 \pm \sqrt{16-24}}{4},$$

which are not real numbers.

So $x = 2$ and $y = x^2 = 4$. The point on the parabola is then $(2, 4)$.

15. **(C)**

Apply L'Hôpital's rule.

$$\lim_{x \to -1} \frac{\sqrt{x^2+3} - 2}{x+1} = \lim_{x \to -1} \frac{\frac{1}{2}(x^2+3)^{-\frac{1}{2}}(2x)}{1}$$

$$= \lim_{x \to -1} \frac{x}{\sqrt{x^2+3}}$$

$$= -\frac{1}{\sqrt{4}}$$

$$= -\frac{1}{2}$$

16. **(B)**

$$y^2 = 2x - 2 \qquad y = x - 5$$

To find the points of intersection, replace y with $x - 5$ in $y^2 = 2x - 2$

$$(x-5)^2 = 2x - 2$$

$$x^2 - 10x + 25 = 2x - 2$$

$$x^2 - 12x + 27 = 0$$

$$(x-9)(x-3) = 0$$

$$x = 9 \Rightarrow y = 9 - 5 = 4, \qquad (x, \ y) = (9, \ 4)$$

$$x = 3 \Rightarrow y = 3 - 5 = -2, \qquad (x, \ y) = (3, \ -2)$$

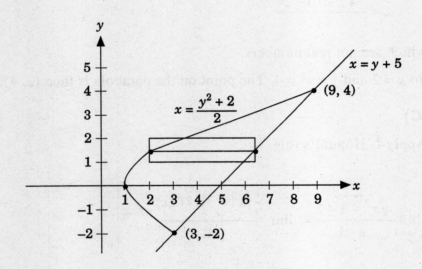

$$A = \int_{-2}^{4} \left[(y+5) - \left(\frac{y^2 + 2}{2} \right) \right] dy$$

$$= \frac{1}{2} \int_{-2}^{4} \left(2y + 10 - y^2 - 2 \right) dy$$

$$= \frac{1}{2} \int_{-2}^{4} \left(-y^2 + 2y + 8 \right) dy$$

$$= \frac{1}{2}\left[-\frac{y^3}{3} + y^2 + 8y \right]\Big|_{-2}^{4}$$

$$= \frac{1}{2}\left[-\frac{1}{3}(64+8) + (16-4) + 8(4+2) \right]$$

$$= \frac{1}{2}\left[-\frac{72}{3} + 12 + 48 \right]$$

$$= \frac{1}{2}[36]$$

$$= 18$$

17. **(A)**

$$y = t^2 e^{3t^2 + \sqrt{t}} = t^2(e^{3t^2 + t^{\frac{1}{2}}})$$

$$y' = 2t(e^{3t^2 + t^{\frac{1}{2}}}) + (e^{3t^2 + t^{\frac{1}{2}}})(6t + \frac{1}{2}t^{-\frac{1}{2}})t^2$$

$$y'(1) = 2(1)(e^{3+1}) + e^{3+1}(6 + \frac{1}{2}(1)) \times 1$$

$$= 2e^4 + 6.5e^4$$

$$= 8.5e^4$$

$$\approx 464.084$$

18. **(C)**

$$\int \frac{e^{2x}}{e^x - 3} \, dx$$

Let $u = e^x - 3 \Rightarrow u + 3 = e^x$

$$du = e^x \, dx$$

$$\int \frac{e^x(e^x dx)}{e^x - 3} = \int \frac{(u+3)}{u}\, du$$

$$= \int \left(1 + \frac{3}{u}\right) du$$

$$= u + 3\ln|u| + C$$

$$= \left(e^x - 3\right) + 3\ln\left|e^x - 3\right| + C$$

19. **(C)**

$$xy - x = 2y - 5$$

$$xy - 2y = x - 5$$

$$y(x - 2) = x - 5$$

$$y = \frac{x-5}{x-2}.$$

y is a function of x with domain $\{x \mid x \neq 2\}$.

To determine the range we solve for x

$$x = \frac{2y - 5}{y - 1}$$

$$= 2 - \frac{3}{y - 1}$$

y can assume all values except $y = 1$.

Hence, only I and II are true.

20. **(B)**

$$y = h(x) = \sqrt{x^2 - 4}$$

Solving for x we get $x = \pm\sqrt{y^2 + 4}$.

Since $x \le -2$ we take $x = h^{-1}(y) = -\sqrt{y^2 + 4}$.

Therefore, $h^{-1}(x) = -\sqrt{x^2 + 4}$

21. **(A)**

$$y = 1 + 2^{x+3}$$

$$y' = 2^{x+3} \ln 2$$

Since $y' > 0$, y is always increasing. Graphs (A), (B), and (D) are increasing. The ordered pair $(-3, 2)$ is a point on the graph, and (A) is the only one of these graphs which includes $(-3, 2)$.

22. **(D)**

$$\lim_{x \to 0} \frac{\sin 2x}{x \cos x} = \lim_{x \to 0} \frac{2 \sin x \cos x}{x \cos x}$$

$$= 2 \lim_{x \to 0} \frac{\sin x}{x}.$$

Apply L'Hôpital's rule:

$$= 2 \lim_{x \to 0} \frac{\cos x}{1}$$

$$= 2(1)$$

$$= 2$$

Note: $\lim\limits_{x \to 0} \dfrac{\sin x}{x} = 1$ is also a well–known theorem.

23. **(C)**

We write $xy = 4$ as $y = \dfrac{4}{x}$. We want to find the area between $y = \dfrac{4}{x}$ and $y = 0$ (the x-axis), with $x = e$ and $x = 2e$ as the limits of integration.

Hence,

$$A = \int_e^{2e} \left(\frac{4}{x} - 0 \right) dx$$

$$= 4 \int_e^{2e} \frac{dx}{x}$$

$$= 4 \ln x \Big|_e^{2e}$$

$$= 4(\ln 2e - \ln e)$$

$$= 4 \ln \frac{2e}{e}$$

$$= 4 \ln 2$$

$$= 2.77259\ldots$$

24. **(A)**

$$\frac{\cos 2\beta - \sin 2\beta}{\sin \beta \cos \beta} = \frac{\left(\cos^2 \beta - \sin^2 \beta \right) - (2 \sin \beta \cos \beta)}{\sin \beta \cos \beta}$$

$$= \frac{\cos^2 \beta}{\sin \beta \cos \beta} - \frac{\sin^2 \beta}{\sin \beta \cos \beta} - \frac{2 \sin \beta \cos \beta}{\sin \beta \cos \beta}$$

$$= \frac{\cos \beta}{\sin \beta} - \frac{\sin \beta}{\cos \beta} - 2$$

$$= \cot \beta - \tan \beta - 2$$

25. **(D)**

The graph has the form $A + B \sin k (x - x_0)$.

The average value of y is -2, therefore, $A = -2$.

The lows are confined to $-5 \le y \le 1$, therefore, $|B| = 3$. However, the phase dictates that $B = -3$.

The period is $\dfrac{11\pi}{3} - \left(-\dfrac{\pi}{3}\right) = 4\pi$, therefore, $2\pi k = 4\pi$, or $k = \dfrac{1}{2}$.

Finally, $-\dfrac{\pi}{3} - x_0 = 0$, therefore, $x_0 = -\dfrac{\pi}{3}$ (using the left-most point).

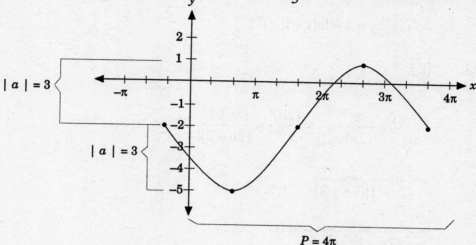

26. **(C)**

Average Speed $= \dfrac{1}{3-1} \int_1^3 \left(3t^2 + 10t\right) dt = \dfrac{1}{2}\left(t^3 + 5t^2\right)\Big|_1^3$

$= \dfrac{1}{2}(27 + 45 - 1 - 5) = \dfrac{1}{2}(66) = 33$ mph

27. **(D)**

Change the equation to differential form, then separate the variables and integrate.

$(x+1)dy = x\left(y^2 + 1\right)dx$

$\displaystyle\int \dfrac{dy}{y^2 + 1} = \int \dfrac{xdx}{x+1}$

Let $u = x + 1$, $du = dx$

Then $\displaystyle\int \dfrac{xdx}{x+1} = \int \dfrac{u-1}{u}\,du = \int \left(1 - \dfrac{1}{u}\right)du$

$= u - \ln|u| + C'$

$$= (x+1) - \ln|x+1| + C'$$

$$= x - \ln|x+1| + C$$

$$\Rightarrow \tan^{-1} y = x - \ln|x+1| + C$$

28.   **(E)**

$$\frac{u_n + 1}{u_n} = \frac{x^{2n+2}}{(2n+2)!} \times \frac{(2n)!}{x^{2n}} = \frac{(2n)! \, x^2}{(2n+2)!}$$

$$= \frac{x^2}{(2n+1)(2n+2)}$$

$$\lim_{n \to \infty} \frac{x^2}{(2n+1)(2n+2)} = 0$$

Hence the series converges for all values of x.

29.   **(E)**

$$y = \frac{2(x-1)^2}{x^2}$$

(i)   The function is positive and continuous for all values of $x \neq 0$. Since $\lim\limits_{x \to 0^+} f(x) \to +\infty$ and $f(1) = 0$, the range is $0 \leq y$.

(ii)   At $x = 0$, y is undefined, hence there is no y-intercept.

Note: $x = 1$ is an x-intercept.

(iii) $\lim\limits_{x \to \pm\infty} \dfrac{2(x-1)^2}{x^2} = \lim\limits_{x \to \pm\infty} \dfrac{2 \times 2(x-1)}{2x}$, applying L'Hôpital's rule,

$$= 2 \lim_{x \to \pm\infty} \frac{1}{1}$$

$$= 2$$

Therefore, $y = 2$ is a horizontal asymptote. Only I and III are true.

30. **(B)**

$g(u + 3) = u^2 + 2$

Let $x = u + 3$, i.e., $u = x - 3$

Therefore, $g(x) = (x - 3)^2 + 2$

31. **(A)**

$$y = \frac{x^2}{\sqrt[3]{3x^2 + 1}}$$

$$= \frac{x^2}{(3x^2 + 1)^{\frac{1}{3}}}$$

$$y' = \frac{2x(3x^2 + 1)^{\frac{1}{3}} - \frac{1}{3}(3x^2 + 1)^{-\frac{2}{3}}(6x)x^2}{(3x^2 + 1)^{\frac{2}{3}}}$$

$$= \frac{2x(3x^2 + 1)^{\frac{1}{3}} - (3x^2 + 1)^{-\frac{2}{3}}2x^3}{(3x^2 + 1)^{\frac{2}{3}}}$$

$$y'(1) = \frac{2(3 + 1)^{\frac{1}{3}} - (3 + 1)^{-\frac{2}{3}}(2)}{(3 + 1)^{\frac{2}{3}}}$$

$$= \frac{2(4)^{\frac{1}{3}} - 2(4)^{-\frac{2}{3}}}{4^{\frac{2}{3}}} \times \frac{4^{\frac{2}{3}}}{4^{\frac{2}{3}}}$$

$$= \frac{2(4) - 2}{(4)^{\frac{4}{3}}}$$

$$= \frac{6}{4(4)^{\frac{1}{3}}}$$

$$= \frac{3}{2\sqrt[3]{4}} \times \frac{\sqrt[3]{2}}{\sqrt[3]{2}}$$

$$= \frac{3\sqrt[3]{2}}{2\sqrt[3]{8}}$$

$$= \frac{3\sqrt[3]{2}}{4}$$

Therefore, the slope of the tangent line at $x = 1$ is $\dfrac{3\sqrt[3]{2}}{4}$.

Calculator: $2\sqrt[3]{x} \times .75 \approx 0.945$

32. **(B)**

$$x^4 + xy + y^4 = 1.$$

Differentiate both sides with respect to t.

$$\frac{d}{dt}\left(x^4 + xy + y^4\right) = \frac{d}{dt}(1)$$

$$4x^3 \frac{dx}{dt} + \frac{dx}{dt} \times y + \frac{dy}{dt} \times x + 4y^3 \frac{dy}{dt} = 0$$

$$\frac{dy}{dt}\left(x + 4y^3\right) = -(4x^3 + y)\frac{dx}{dt}$$

$$\frac{dy}{dt} = -\left(\frac{4x^3 + y}{x + 4y^3}\right)\frac{dx}{dt}.$$

33. **(D)**

$g(u) = \sqrt{u^3 + 2}$,

$g'(u) = \dfrac{1}{2}(u^3 + 2)^{-\frac{1}{2}} 3u^2$

$\dfrac{d}{dx}(g(f(x))) = g'(f(x))f'(x)$

At $x = 1$ $= g'(f(1))f'(1)$

$= g'(2)(-5)$

$= \dfrac{1}{2}(2^3 + 2)^{-\frac{1}{2}} 3(2^2)(-5)$

$= \dfrac{1}{2\sqrt{10}} 12\,(-5)$

$= -\dfrac{30}{\sqrt{10}} \times \dfrac{\sqrt{10}}{\sqrt{10}}$

$= -\dfrac{30\sqrt{10}}{10}$

$= -3\sqrt{10}$

≈ -9.487

Calculator: $+/- \; 3x \; 10\sqrt{x} \approx -9.487$

34. **(C)**

$y = \dfrac{1}{\sin(t + \sqrt{t})}$

$= \left(\sin\left(t + t^{\frac{1}{2}} \right) \right)^{-1}$

$$y' = -1\left(\sin\left(t + t^{\frac{1}{2}}\right)\right)^{-2} \cos\left(t + t^{\frac{1}{2}}\right)\left(1 + \frac{1}{2}t^{-\frac{1}{2}}\right)$$

Therefore, $y'(1) = -1(\sin 2)^{-2} \cos 2\left(1 + \frac{1}{2}\right)$

$$= -\frac{3}{2}\frac{\cos 2}{\sin^2 2} \approx 0.755$$

Calculator: $2 \cos + (2 \sin x^2) = x +/- 1.5 \approx .755$

35. **(D)**

Let $u = \arctan x$, $dv = dx$. Then $du = \dfrac{1}{1 + x^2}\,dx$ and $v = x$, so integration by parts gives:

$$\int \arctan x\,dx = x\arctan x - \int \frac{x}{1 + x^2}\,dx$$

Now let $z = 1 + x^2$, $dz = 2x\,dx$.

Then $\displaystyle\int \frac{x}{1 + x^2}\,dx = \frac{1}{2}\int \frac{dz}{z}$

$$= \frac{1}{2}\ln z + C$$

$$= \frac{1}{2}\ln\left(1 + x^2\right) + C.$$

So, $\displaystyle\int \arctan x\,dx = x\arctan x - \frac{1}{2}\ln\left(1 + x^2\right) + C.$

36. **(A)**

$$y = -\ln\left|\frac{1 + \sqrt{1 - x^2}}{x}\right| = \ln\left|\frac{x}{1 + \sqrt{1 - x^2}}\right|$$

$$= \ln|x - 1\,\ln|1 + \sqrt{1 - x^2}\,|$$

$$\frac{dy}{dx} = \frac{1}{x} - \frac{1}{1 + \sqrt{1 - x^2}} \frac{1}{2} \left(1 - x^2\right)^{-\frac{1}{2}} (-2x)$$

$$= \frac{1}{x} + \frac{1}{\left(1 + \sqrt{1 - x^2}\right)} \frac{x}{\left(\sqrt{1 - x^2}\right)}$$

$$= \frac{\left(1 + \sqrt{1 - x^2}\right)\sqrt{1 - x^2} + x^2}{x\left(1 + \sqrt{1 - x^2}\right)\left(\sqrt{1 - x^2}\right)}$$

$$= \frac{\sqrt{1 - x^2} + \left(1 - x^2\right) + x^2}{x\left(1 + \sqrt{1 - x^2}\right)\left(\sqrt{1 - x^2}\right)}$$

$$= \frac{1 + \sqrt{1 - x^2}}{x\left(1 + \sqrt{1 - x^2}\right)\left(\sqrt{1 - x^2}\right)}$$

$$= \frac{1}{x\sqrt{1 - x^2}}$$

37. **(D)**

$$F = \frac{6,000k}{k\sin\theta + \cos\theta}$$

$$= 6,000k(k\sin\theta + \cos\theta)^{-1}$$

$$\frac{dF}{d\theta} = -6,000k(k\sin\theta + \cos\theta)^{-2}(k\cos\theta - \sin\theta)$$

$$= -\frac{6,000k(k\cos\theta - \sin\theta)}{(k\sin\theta + \cos\theta)^2}$$

$$\frac{dF}{d\theta} = 0 \Rightarrow k\cos\theta - \sin\theta = 0 \Rightarrow k = \tan\theta$$

Hence, $\theta = \arctan k$.

38. **(B)**

This problem can be solved directly by using your calculator. For example,

$$fnInt\left(\frac{1}{\sin(x+\sqrt{x})}, \ x, \ 0, \ 1\right)$$

gives 1.65.

39. **(D)**

$$f(x) = \left(x^2 - 3\right)^{\frac{2}{3}}$$

$$f'(x) = \frac{2}{3}\left(x^2 - 3\right)^{-\frac{1}{3}} 2x$$

$$= \frac{4x}{3}\left(x^2 - 3\right)^{-\frac{1}{3}}$$

$f'(x) > 0$ for

  (i) $x > 0$ and $x^2 - 3 > 0$ or

  (ii) $x < 0$ and $x^2 - 3 < 0$

  (i) $\{x > 0\}$ and $\{x^2 - 3 > 0\} \Rightarrow$

        $\{x > 0\}$ and $\{x < -\sqrt{3}\}$ or $\{x > \sqrt{3}\}$ so $\{x > \sqrt{3}\}$

  (ii) $\{x < 0\}$ and $\{x^2 - 3 < 0\} \Rightarrow$

              $\{x < 0\}$ and $\{x^2 < 3\}$

        $\{x > 0\}$ and $\{-\sqrt{3} < x < \sqrt{3}\} \Rightarrow$

              $\{-\sqrt{3} < x < 0\}$

Thus $f(x) = \left(x^2 - 3\right)^{\frac{2}{3}}$ is increasing for x such that

$-\sqrt{3} < x < 0$ or $x > \sqrt{3}$

40. **(A)**

$y = \tan u$ with $u = \cos^{-1} x$

therefore, $\dfrac{dy}{dx} = \dfrac{dy}{du}\dfrac{du}{dx}$

$$= (\sec^2 u)\left(\dfrac{-1}{\sqrt{1-x^2}}\right)$$

$$= \dfrac{1}{\cos^2 u}\dfrac{-1}{\sqrt{1-x^2}}$$

$$= \dfrac{-1}{x^2\sqrt{1-x^2}}$$

41. **(B)**

(A)　$\log_{\frac{1}{2}} 2 = -1$

$\log_{\frac{1}{\sqrt{2}}} 2 = -2$

(B)　$\log_3(2+4) = \log_3 6$

$$= \log_3(2 \times 3)$$

$$= \log_3 2 + \log_3 3$$

True

(C)　$\log_{10} 4 = \log_{10} 2^2$

$$= 2\log_{10} 2$$

(D) $\log_{\frac{1}{5}}\left(5\sqrt{5}\right) = \log_{\frac{1}{5}}\left(5^{\frac{3}{2}}\right)$

$$= \log_{\frac{1}{5}}\left[\left(\frac{1}{5}\right)^{-\frac{3}{2}}\right]$$

$$= -\frac{3}{2}$$

(E) $\log_{\frac{1}{2}} 2 - \log_{\frac{1}{2}} 4 = \log_{\frac{1}{2}}\left(\frac{2}{4}\right)$

$$= \log_{\frac{1}{2}}\left(\frac{1}{2}\right) = 1$$

But $\log_{\frac{1}{2}} 2 = -1$

42. **(A)**

$$f(x) = (x^2 - 3)^2$$

$$y = f'(x) = 4x^2 - 12x$$

$$y' = 12(x^2 - 1)$$

$$y'' = 24x$$

$y' = 0$ at $x = 1$. Using y'', we see that the Max. is at $x = -1$.

Therefore, $f'(-1) = 8$ is the Max.

43. **(D)**

    You can solve this problem by using your calculator. For example,

    $$fnInt\left(\frac{x^2}{e^x}, \ x, \ 0, \ 5\right)$$

    which would give 1.75.

44. **(B)**

    Since the curve passes through (4, 7) only when $t = 2$,
    there is only one tangent line at (4, 7).

    $x(t) = t^2$ $\qquad\qquad$ $y(t) = t^3 - 1$
    $x'(t) = 2t$ $\qquad\qquad$ $y'(t) = 3t^2$
    $x'(2) = 4$ $\qquad\qquad$ $y'(2) = 12$

    The slope of the tangent line is

    $$m = \frac{y'(2)}{x'(2)} = \frac{12}{4} \Rightarrow \frac{y-7}{x-4} = \frac{12}{4}, \text{ so}$$

    $$y - 7 = 3x - 12 \Rightarrow 3x - y = 5.$$

    Another way to solve this is to see that

    $$y = t^3 - 1 = \left(t^2\right)^{\frac{3}{2}} - 1 = x^{\frac{3}{2}} - 1, \text{ so } y' = \frac{3}{2}x^{\frac{1}{2}}$$

    and at the point (4, 7), we have $y' = \frac{3}{2}(4)^{\frac{1}{2}} = 3$, so

    $$y - 7 = 3(x - 4) \Rightarrow y = 3x - 5, \text{ or}$$

    $$3x - y = 5.$$

45. **(A)**

Use partial fractions:

Let $\dfrac{1}{(x+3)(x+4)} = \dfrac{A}{(x+3)} + \dfrac{B}{(x+4)}$

$1 = A(x+4) + B(x+3)$

$1 = (A+B)x + (4A+3B)$

$0 = A+B$

$1 = 4A+3B$

$\Rightarrow A = 1 \text{ and } B = -1$

SECTION II

1. **(A)**

Domain $(f) = \{x \mid x \neq \pm 1\}$ because $f(x)$ is undefined when the denominator $1 - x^2 = 0$

$$\Rightarrow x^2 = 0$$

$$\Rightarrow x = \pm 1.$$

(B)

Range $(f) = $ Domain (f^{-1}). To find $f^{-1}(x)$, interchange x and y, then solve for y. We have:

$$x = \frac{y^2 - 4}{1 - y^2}$$

$$x(1 - y^2) = y^2 - 4$$

$$x - xy^2 = y^2 - 4$$

$$x + 4 = y^2 + xy^2$$

$$= y^2(1 + x)$$

$$\frac{x + 4}{1 + x} = y^2$$

$$\pm\sqrt{\frac{x + 4}{x + 1}} = y$$

$$= f^{-1}(x).$$

Domain $f^{-1} = \{x \mid x \neq -1\}$, so Range $(f) = \{y \mid y \neq -1\}$.

(C)

We have vertical asymptotes where $f(x)$ is undefined, at $x = 1$ and $x = -1$.

We have horizontal asymptotes at $y = \lim\limits_{x \to \pm\infty} f(x)$

We see $\lim\limits_{x \to \pm\infty} f(x) = \lim\limits_{x \to \pm\infty} \dfrac{x^2 - 4}{1 - x^2}$

$$= \lim_{x \to \pm\infty} \frac{1 - \dfrac{4}{x^2}}{\left(\dfrac{1}{x^2}\right) - 1}$$

$$= -\frac{1}{1}$$

$$= -1,$$

so $y = -1$ is the only horizontal asymptote.

(D)

The critical points occur where $f'(x) = 0$.

$$f'(x) = \frac{\left(1 - x^2\right)(2x) - \left(x^2 - 4\right)(-2x)}{\left(1 - x^2\right)^2}$$

The numerator must be zero, so we have

$$2x - 2x^3 + 2x^3 - 8x = 0$$

$$-6x = 0$$

$$x = 0$$

is the only critical point.

Note: $f'(x) = 0$ is undefined at $x = \pm 1$, but $x = \pm 1$ is not in the domain of f.

2. (A)

$\overline{PA}^2 = 20^2 + x^2$ by the Pythagorean theorem.

$\overline{PA} = \sqrt{400 + x^2}$

Similarly, $\overline{QA} = \sqrt{30^2 + (25 - x)^2}$

$$= \sqrt{900 + 625 - 50x + x^2}$$

$$= \sqrt{1,525 - 50x + x^2}$$

(B)

We want to find x which minimizes $\overline{PA} + \overline{QA}$.

Let $f(x) = \overline{PA} + \overline{QA}$

$$= \sqrt{400 + x^2} + \sqrt{1,525 - 50x + x^2}$$

Then $f'(x) = \dfrac{1}{2}(400 + x^2)^{-\frac{1}{2}} 2x + \dfrac{1}{2}(1,525 - 50x + x^2)^{-\frac{1}{2}}(-50 + 2x)$

$$= \dfrac{x}{\sqrt{400 + x^2}} + \dfrac{x - 25}{\sqrt{1,525 - 50x + x^2}}$$

$$= \dfrac{x}{\sqrt{400 + x^2}} + \dfrac{x - 25}{\sqrt{900 + (25 - x)^2}}$$

To minimize, we set $f'(x) = 0$ and solve for x.

$$0 = \dfrac{x}{\sqrt{400 + x^2}} + \dfrac{x - 25}{\sqrt{900 + (25 - x)^2}}.$$

Finding a common denominator:

$$0 = \dfrac{x\sqrt{900 + (25 - x)^2} + (x - 25)\sqrt{400 + x^2}}{\sqrt{400 + x^2}\sqrt{900 + (25 - x)^2}}$$

The numerator must be zero, so we have

$$0 = x\sqrt{900 + (25 - x)^2} + (x - 25)\sqrt{400 + x^2} \text{, or}$$

$$x\sqrt{900+(25-x)^2} = (25-x)\sqrt{400+x^2}$$

$$\frac{x}{25-x} = \frac{\sqrt{400+x^2}}{\sqrt{900+(25-x)^2}}$$

(assuming $x \neq 25$).

Squaring both sides, we have

$$\frac{x^2}{625-50x+x^2} = \frac{400+x^2}{900+(25-x)^2}$$

and cross–multiplying gives

$$900x^2 + 625x^2 - 50x^3 + x^4$$

$$= 250{,}000 - 20{,}000x + 1{,}025x^2 - 50x^3 + x^4$$

$$\Rightarrow 500x^2 + 20{,}000x - 250{,}000 = 0$$

$$\Rightarrow x^2 + 40x - 500 = 0$$

$$(x+50)(x-10) = 0$$

Therefore, $x = 10, -50$.

We know x is a distance, so it cannot be negative. Hence $x = 10$.

An alternate way to solve the problem is to see that the distance is minimized if the incident angles are equal.

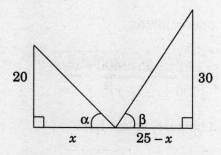

If $\alpha = \beta$, then $\cot \alpha = \cot \beta$

$$\frac{x}{20} = \frac{25 - x}{30}$$

$$30x = 500 - 20x$$

$$50x = 500$$

$$x = 10$$

3. (A)

The sine of a sum of two angles is given by $\sin (a + b) = \sin a \cos b + \sin b \cos a$.

So,

$$20\sqrt{5} \sin(311t + \theta) = 20\sqrt{5} \left[\sin(311t)\cos\theta + \sin\theta\cos(311t)\right]$$

$$= 20\sqrt{5} \left(\frac{\sin(311t)}{\sqrt{5}} + \frac{2\cos(311t)}{\sqrt{5}}\right)$$

$$= 20\sin(311t) + 40\cos(311t) = I(t).$$

(B)

$$I(t) = 20\sqrt{5}\sin(311t + \theta)$$

$$I'(t) = 20\sqrt{5}(311)\cos(311t + \theta) = 0$$

$$\Rightarrow \cos(311t + \theta) = 0$$

$$\Rightarrow 311t + \theta = \frac{\pi}{2} + \pi k,$$

for some integer k.

$$\Rightarrow t = \frac{\dfrac{\pi}{2} - \pi k - \theta}{311}$$

$$\Rightarrow t = \frac{\pi}{622} - \frac{\pi k}{311} - \frac{\theta}{311}$$

Now $I''(t) = -20\sqrt{5}(311)^2 \sin(311t + \theta)$

So $I''\left(\dfrac{\pi}{622} - \dfrac{\pi k}{311} - \dfrac{\theta}{311}\right)$

$$= -20\sqrt{5}(311)^2 \sin\left(\frac{\pi}{2} - \pi k - \theta + \theta\right)$$

$$= -20\sqrt{5}(311)^2 \sin\left(\frac{\pi}{2} - \pi k\right)$$

$$= -20\sqrt{5}(311)^2 \left[\sin\left(\frac{\pi}{2}\right)\cos(-\pi k) + \sin(-\pi k)\cos\left(\frac{\pi}{2}\right)\right]$$

$$= -20\sqrt{5}(311)^2 [1 + 0]$$

$$= -20\sqrt{5}(311)^2 < 0,$$

So we have a maximum by the second derivative test. The maximum value of $I(t)$ occurs at

$$t = \frac{\pi}{622} - \frac{\pi k}{311} - \frac{\theta}{311}$$

and this maximum value is

$$I\left(\frac{\pi}{622} - \frac{\pi k}{311} - \frac{\theta}{311}\right)$$

$$= 20\sqrt{5}\sin\left(\frac{\pi}{2} - \pi k - \theta + \theta\right)$$

$$= 20\sqrt{5}\sin\left(\frac{\pi}{2} - \pi k\right)$$

$$= 20\sqrt{5}\left[\sin\left(\frac{\pi}{2}\right)\cos(-\pi k) + \sin(-\pi k)\cos\left(\frac{\pi}{2}\right)\right]$$

$$= 20\sqrt{5}.$$

4.   (A)

f is increasing when $f'(x) > 0$. By the chart, we see this occurs between $x = -4$ and $x = 0$, so f is increasing on the interval $[-4, 0]$.

f is decreasing when $f'(x) < 0$ which occurs on the intervals $(-\infty, -4]$ and $[0, \infty)$.

(B)

Vertical asymptotes occur where the function tends to ∞. Here $f(x)$ is undefined at $x = -1$, 2, and

$$\lim_{x\to2^+} f(x) = \infty, \quad \lim_{x\to2^-} f(x) = -\infty,$$

$$\lim_{x\to-1^+} f(x) = -\infty, \quad \text{and} \quad \lim_{x\to-1^-} f(x) = \infty,$$

So, $x = -1$ and $x = 2$ are vertical asymptotes.

Since $\lim_{x\to\pm\infty} f(x) = 0$, we have $y = 0$ as a horizontal asymptote.

(C)

$f(-4) = -\dfrac{2}{3}$ is a local minimum, since $f'(x) < 0$ for $x < -4$ and $f'(x) > 0$ for $x > -4$.

$f(0) = -6$ is a local maximum, since $f'(x) < 0$ for $x < 0$ and $f'(x) < 0$ for $x > 0$.

(D)

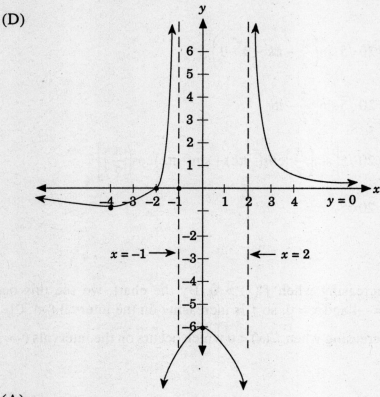

$x = -1 \longrightarrow$ $\longleftarrow x = 2$

5. (A)

At the point of tangency, x_0,

$$\frac{2}{3}x_0^{\frac{3}{2}} = cx_0 + d \quad \text{and} \quad x_0^{\frac{1}{2}} = c$$

If $x_0 = 2$, then $c = \sqrt{2}$ and $d = \dfrac{2\sqrt{2}}{3}$

(B)

If $c = 1$, then $x_0 = 1$ if $d = -\dfrac{1}{3}$

(C)

$$\int_0^3 \frac{2}{3}x^{\frac{3}{2}}\, dx = \frac{2}{3} \times \frac{2}{5} \times x^{\frac{5}{2}}\Big|_0^3$$

$$= \frac{4}{15} \times 3 \times 3 \times \sqrt{3}$$

$$= \frac{12\sqrt{3}}{5}$$

6. **(A)**

Velocity $= v(t) = s'(t) = 112 - 32t$, so $v(3) = 112 - 96 = 16$ ft/sec.

Acceleration $= a(t) = v'(t) = s''(t) = -32$, so $a(3) = -32$ ft/sec.

(B)

Maximum height occurs when $v(t) = 0$.

$$112 - 32t = 0$$

$$\Rightarrow 112 = 32t$$

$$\Rightarrow t = \frac{112}{32} = \frac{7}{2} \text{ seconds.}$$

Alternately, $s(t) = 0$ when

$$112t - 16t^2 = 0$$

$$\Rightarrow 112t = 32t$$

$$\Rightarrow t = \frac{112}{32} = \frac{7}{2} \text{ seconds.}$$

(C)

The time of impact occurs when $s(t) = 0$ for the second time.

$$0 = 112t - 16t^2 = (112 - 16t)t$$

therefore, $t = \dfrac{112}{16} = 7$ sec.

The velocity at $t = 7$ is $v(7) = s'(7) = 112 - 32(7) = -112$ ft/sec.

(D)

Arc length $= \displaystyle\int_1^{10} \sqrt{1 + (y')^2} \, dx$ for the path of the bug.

$$y = \frac{1}{3}(x^2 - 2)^{\frac{3}{2}}$$

$$y' = \frac{1}{3} \times \frac{3}{2}(x^2 - 2)^{\frac{1}{2}} \, 2x$$

$$= x\sqrt{x^2 - 2}$$

$$(y')^2 = x^2(x^2 - 2)$$

$$= x^4 - 2x^2$$

$$\text{Arc length} = \int_1^{10} \sqrt{1 + x^4 - 2x^2} \, dx$$

$$= \int_1^{10} \sqrt{(x^2 - 1)^2} \, dx$$

$$= \int_1^{10} (x^2 - 1) \, dx$$

$$= \left(\frac{x^3}{3} - x \right) \Big|_1^{10}$$

$$= \frac{1,000}{3} - 10 - \frac{1}{3} + 1$$

$$= 324 \ \text{feet.}$$

The path of the projectile = 392 feet, which is longer than the path of the bug.

Advanced Placement Examination in Calculus AB

EXAM VI

Exam VI is also on CD-ROM in our special interactive AP Calculus AB Test*ware*®. It is highly recommended that you first take this exam on computer. You will then have the additional study features and benefits of enforced timed conditions, individual diagnostic analysis, and instant scoring. See page xiv for guidance on how to get the most out of our AP Calculus AB book and software.

ADVANCED PLACEMENT
CALCULUS AB
EXAM VI

SECTION I

PART A

Time: 55 minutes
28 questions

DIRECTIONS: Each of the following problems is followed by five choices. Solve each problem, select the best choice, and blacken the correct space on your answer sheet. Calculators may not be used for this section of the exam.

NOTE: Unless otherwise specified, the domain of function f is assumed to be the set of all real numbers x for which $f(x)$ is a real number.

1. If $x < 0$ and $f(x) = |x|$ then $f(f(x))$ is equal to:

   (A) x

   (B) $-x$

   (C) $\dfrac{1}{x}$

   (D) $\dfrac{1}{-x}$

   (E) undefined

2. Which one of the following functions satisfies the condition that

   $\displaystyle\int_{-a}^{a} f(x)\, dx = 0$ for any number a?

   (A) $f(x) = x^3 - x^2 + x$

(B) $f(x) = \dfrac{x^4 + x^3}{x}$

(C) $f(x) = x^4 - x^2$

(D) $f(x) = (x + 1)^3 - (3x^2 + 1)$

(E) None of these

3. Find the area enclosed between the graphs of $x + 2 = y^2$ and $y = x$.

(A) $\dfrac{9}{2}$ (D) $\dfrac{26}{6}$

(B) $\dfrac{7}{2}$ (E) None of these

(C) $\dfrac{19}{2}$

4. Let $(-2, g(-2))$ be a relative maximum for $g(x) = 2x^3 + hx^2 + kx - 6$. Use the fact that $\left(-\dfrac{1}{2},\ g\left(-\dfrac{1}{2}\right)\right)$ is an inflection point to find the value of $(h - k)$.

(A) 9 (B) –9

(C) 15 (D) –15

(E) 24

5. $\displaystyle \lim_{x \to 0} \dfrac{\sin x}{|x|} =$

(A) –1 (D) $\dfrac{1}{2}$

(B) 0 (E) None of these

(C) 1

6. Find the instantaneous rate of change of the area of a circle with respect to the circumference C.

    (A) C

    (D) $\dfrac{C}{2\pi}$

    (B) $\dfrac{C}{2}$

    (E) π

    (C) $\dfrac{C}{\pi}$

7. $\lim\limits_{x \to 1} \dfrac{2x-2}{x^3 + 2x^2 - x - 2} =$

    (A) 0

    (D) $+\infty$

    (B) $\dfrac{1}{3}$

    (E) $-\infty$

    (C) $\dfrac{2}{3}$

8. Determine which of the following is/are (an) asymptote(s) for the graph of $y = \dfrac{e^x}{x}$:

    I. $x = 0$

    II. $y = 0$

    III. $y = x$

    (A) I only

    (D) I and II

    (B) II only

    (E) II and III

    (C) III only

9. Let $F(x)$ be an antiderivative of $f(x)$. Suppose $F(x)$ is defined by

$$F(x) = \begin{cases} |x| & \text{if } x < 0 \\ -\sin x & \text{if } x \geq 0 \end{cases}$$

Evaluate $[f(b) - f(a)]$ for $a = -\dfrac{\pi}{2}$ and $b = \dfrac{\pi}{2}$.

(A) −1

(D) $\dfrac{\pi + 1}{2}$

(B) 0

(E) $\dfrac{\pi + 1}{-2}$

(C) 1

10. Let $g(x) = f'(x)$ where $f(x) = \cos(\arcsin x)$. Which one of the following statements is <u>FALSE</u> concerning $g(x)$?

(A) The domain of g is $[-1, 1]$.

(B) The range of g is $(-\infty, +\infty)$.

(C) g is a decreasing function.

(D) g is concave down for $x > 0$.

(E) $(0, 0)$ is a point of inflection for $y = g(x)$.

11. Let $f(x) = \sqrt{2 - x}$. Then $\lim\limits_{x \to 2^-} f'(x) =$

(A) 0

(D) $+\infty$

(B) 1

(E) $-\infty$

(C) −1

12. Let $f(x) = \dfrac{\dfrac{1}{x} - x}{\dfrac{1}{x} + x}$. Then $f'(2.5)$ is approximately:

(A) −0.190

(D) 1.005

(B) 0

(E) None of these

(C) 0.190

13. Let $R = \displaystyle\int_{\frac{1}{\sqrt{2}}}^{1} \dfrac{2x}{\sqrt{1-x^4}}\, dx$ and find the interval that contains R.

(A) $(-\infty, 0.5]$

(D) $(1.5, 2]$

(B) $(0.5, 1]$

(E) $(2, +\infty)$

(C) $(1, 1.5]$

14. Suppose a particle moves on a straight line with a position function of $s(t) = 3t^3 - 11t^2 + 8t$. In what interval of time is the particle moving to the left on the line?

(A) $(-\infty, 0)$

(D) $\left(\dfrac{4}{9}, 2\right)$

(B) $(0, 1)$

(E) $(2, +\infty)$

(C) $\left(1, \dfrac{8}{3}\right)$

15. Let $f'(x) = (x + 2)^3 (3 - 2x)^5 (2x - 1)^{-3} (3x - 4)^{-2}$.

Find $f'(1)$.

(A) −270

(D) 135

(B) −243

(E) None of these

(C) 54

16. $\int \left(\csc^2 x\right) 2^{\cot x}\, dx =$

(A) $\dfrac{2^{\cot x}}{\cot x (\ln 2)} + C$

(B) $\dfrac{2 \csc^2 x}{(\ln 2) \cot x} + C$

(C) $\dfrac{-2^{\cot x}}{\ln 2} + C$

(D) $\dfrac{2^{\cot x} \csc^2 x}{\cot x (\ln 2)} + C$

(E) $\dfrac{1}{\cot x (\ln 2)} + C$

17. Let $f(x) = x^2 + 1$ and $g(x) = \dfrac{1}{x-2}$. Which one of the following statements is FALSE?

(A) $g(f(x))$ is continuous at $x = 2$.

(B) $f(g(x))$ is continuous at $x = 1$.

(C) $g(f(x))$ has two points of discontinuity.

(D) $\lim\limits_{n \to \infty} f(g(x)) = 1$

(E) $D_x\left[g(f(2))\right] = -4$

18. Assume $g(x)$ is a continuous function for which:

$g'(x) > 0$ and $g''(x) > 0$ for $x < a$

$g'(x) > 0$ and $g''(x) < 0$ for $x > a$

$g'(x)$ and $g''(x)$ are undefined for $x = 1$

Which of the following statements is true about the point $(a, g(a))$?

(A) It is a relative minimum.

(B) It is a relative maximum.

(C) It is a point of inflection.

(D) $y = g(a)$ is an asymptote.

(E) None of these.

19. Use $f(x) = \begin{cases} 2 - x^2 & \text{for } x \geq 0 \\ 2 + x & \text{for } x < 0 \end{cases}$ and find

$$\lim_{h \to 0} \frac{f(x+h) - f(x)}{h}$$

(A) 0   (D) 2

(B) 1   (E) None of these

(C) -1

20. $\lim\limits_{n \to \infty}\left[1 - n\left(\sin\frac{1}{n}\right)^2\right] =$

(A) 0   (D) ∞

(B) -1 (E) None of the above

(C) 1

21. Let the velocity at time t of a point moving on a line be defined by $v(t)$ $= 2^t \ln 2$ (cm/sec). How many centimeters did the point travel between $t = 0$ and $t = 2$ sec?

(A) 3   (D) $4 \ln 2$

(B) 4   (E) $\frac{5}{2} \ln 2$

(C) $\frac{2}{3} \ln 2$

22. Find the equation of the tangent line to the graph of $y = \dfrac{\ln x}{e^x}$ using $(1, 0)$ as the coordinates of the point of tangency.

    (A) $x - ey - 1 = 0$

    (B) $x + ey - 1 = 0$

    (C) $x - y - 1 = 0$

    (D) $x + y - 1 = 0$

    (E) None of these

23. Find the average value for $y = \dfrac{e^{\sqrt{x}}}{\sqrt{x}}$ in the interval $[1, 4]$.

    (A) 3.114   (D) 103.760

    (B) 34.587   (E) 0.778

    (C) 9.324

24. $\lim\limits_{x \to a} \dfrac{\sqrt[3]{x} - \sqrt[3]{a}}{x - a} =$

    (A) 0   (D) $\dfrac{\sqrt[3]{a}}{3a}$

    (B) $2\sqrt[3]{a}$ (E) None of these

    (C) $\dfrac{3}{2}\sqrt[3]{a^2}$

25. $\lim\limits_{x \to \infty} \dfrac{(\ln x)^2}{x} =$

    (A) ∞ (D) 2

    (B) 1   (E) 0

    (C) $\ln 2$

26. At what value does $f(x) = 4x^5 + 15x^4 + 20x^3 + 10x^2$ have a relative maximum ?

(A) −2

(D) 1

(B) −1

(E) 2

(C) 0

27. The length of the arc given by
$x = 4\cos^3 t$
$y = 4\sin^3 t$

$0 \le t \le \dfrac{\pi}{2}$ is:

(A) $\dfrac{\pi}{2}$

(D) 3

(B) $\dfrac{3\pi}{2}$

(E) 6

(C) 3π

28. Point A moves to the right along the positive x-axis at 7 units per second while point B moves upward along the negative y-axis at 2 units per second. At what rate is the distance between A and B changing when A is at $(8, 0)$ and B is at $(0, -6)$?

(A) $\dfrac{32}{5}$

(D) $-\dfrac{22}{5}$

(B) 5

(E) $-\dfrac{32}{5}$

(C) $\dfrac{22}{5}$

PART B

Time: 50 minutes
   17 questions

DIRECTIONS: Calculators may be used for this section of the test. Each of the following problems is followed by five choices. Solve each problem, select the best choice, and blacken the correct space on your answer sheet.

NOTES:
1. Unless otherwise specified, answers can be given in unsimplified form.

2. The domain of function f is assumed to be the set of all real numbers x for which $f(x)$ is a real number.

---

29. Let $f(x) = \sin |x|$ and determine which one of the following statements is <u>TRUE</u>:

    (A) $f(x) \geq 0$

    (B) f is an odd function

    (C) $\int_{-\frac{\pi}{4}}^{\frac{\pi}{4}} f(x)\, dx = 0$

    (D) f is symmetric with respect to the line $x = 0$

    (E) f is differentiable at $x = 0$

30. Let $h(x) = \dfrac{f(g(x)) - g(f(x))}{f(x)}$ where $f(x) = x - 1$ and $g(x) = x^2$ and x is any real number. What is the range of h?

    (A) All reals

(B) All reals except 1

(C) Positive reals

(D) Negative reals

(E) None of these

31. Find the volume of the solid of revolution generated when the region enclosed by the graphs of $x = y^2$ and $x = 2y$ is revolved about the y-axis.

(A) 4.189

(D) 4.114

(B) 8.378

(E) −1.269

(C) 13.404

32. Let $f(x) = \sin^2 x \cos^2 2x.$ $\int_0^2 f(x)$ equals

(A) 0.715

(D) 0.015

(B) 1.211

(E) 4.782

(C) 3.121

33. $f(x) = \dfrac{2x}{\sqrt{1 - x^4}}$. The minimum of $f'(x)$ is:

(A) 1

(D) 2

(B) 0

(E) 3

(C) −1

34. Let $f(x) = -x + x \ln x$ and calculate $D_x\left[f^{-1}(0)\right]$.

(A) 0

(D) e^{-1}

(B) 1

(E) None of these

(C) e

35. Let $y = u^5$, $\dfrac{du}{dx} = 2$, $\dfrac{d^2u}{dx^2} = -3$, and $\dfrac{d^3u}{dx^3} = 5$.

    Find the value of $\dfrac{d^3y}{dx^3}$ at $u = 1$.

    (A) −20   (D) 145

    (B) −35   (E) None of these

    (C) 25

36. Let f be differentiable for all reals with critical values at $x = 6$ and
    $x = -12$. For what values of x will $f'\left(\dfrac{x}{3}\right) = 0$?

    (A) 0 and −2   (D) 6 and −12

    (B) 2 and −4   (E) 18 and −36

    (C) −2 and 4

37. Suppose a particle moves on a straight line with a position fraction
    of $s(t) = 3t^3 - 11t^2 + 8t$. The highest velocity with which the particle
    moves in the negative direction is

    (A) −5.4   (D) −4

    (B) 0   (E) 2

    (C) 2.5

38. $\dfrac{\int_0^1 x\,e^x\,dx}{\int_0^1 e^{-x}\,dx} =$

   (A) $\dfrac{e}{e-1}$

   (D) $\dfrac{e^2}{e-1}$

   (B) $\dfrac{e^2+1}{4}$

   (E) None of these

   (C) $\dfrac{1}{2}$

39. Let $f(x) = \ln(\ln x)$ and find the domain of $f(x)$ in interval notation.

   (A) $(0, +\infty)$

   (D) $[1, +\infty)$

   (B) $[0, +\infty)$

   (E) None of these

   (C) $(1, +\infty)$

40. Let f be a continuous, one-to-one function such that

   $$f(1) = e^{-1}, \quad f^{-1}(1) = 0 \quad \text{and} \quad f'(1) = -2e^{-1}.$$

   Which of the following statements are true?

   I. f is decreasing

   II. f^{-1} is decreasing and one-to-one

   III. $D_x\left[f^{-1}\left(e^{-1}\right)\right] = -\dfrac{e}{2}$.

   (A) I and II

   (D) I, II, and III

   (B) I and III

   (E) None of these

   (C) II and III

41. $\int_0^2 x^x$ is

    (A) 3.27   (D) 1.98

    (B) 2.83   (E) 3.02

    (C) 4.21

42. Let $\alpha = \angle BAC$ in $\triangle ABC$ with $\overline{AB} = c$ and $\overline{AC} = b$, where b and c are constants and $c > b$. Side $\overline{BC}$ changes length as the measure of α changes. Find the instantaneous rate of change of the area of $\triangle ABC$ when $\alpha = \dfrac{\pi}{3}$. Assume the instantaneous rate of change of α is 2.

    (A) $cb\sqrt{2}$ (D) $\dfrac{cb}{\sqrt{2}}$

    (B) $cb\sqrt{3}$ (E) $\dfrac{cb}{2}$

    (C) $\dfrac{cb\sqrt{3}}{2}$

43. $f(x) = \dfrac{e^{\sqrt{x}}}{\sqrt{x}}$. $f'(c) = 0$. Then c equals

    (A) 3   (D) 2

    (B) 0   (E) 7

    (C) 1

44. As a particle moves along the line $y = 2x + 7$, its minimum distance from the origin is:

(A) $\dfrac{7}{5}$

(D) $\dfrac{\sqrt{5}}{7}$

(B) $\dfrac{7}{5}\sqrt{5}$

(E) $\dfrac{7}{3}\sqrt{5}$

(C) $\dfrac{14}{5}$

45. The base of a solid is the region enclosed by the graph of $x = 1 - y^2$ and the y-axis. If all plane cross sections perpendicular to the x-axis are semicircles with diameters parallel to the x-axis, then the volume is:

(A) $\dfrac{\pi}{8}$

(D) $\dfrac{3\pi}{4}$

(B) $\dfrac{\pi}{4}$

(E) $\dfrac{3\pi}{2}$

(C) $\dfrac{\pi}{2}$

SECTION II

Time: 1 hour and 30 minutes
6 problems

DIRECTIONS: Show all your work. Grading is based on the methods used to solve the problem as well as the accuracy of your final answers. Please make sure all procedures are clearly shown. For some problems or parts of problems it will be necessary to use a calculator.

NOTES:

1.   Unless otherwise specified, answers can be given in unsimplified form.

2.   The domain of function f is assumed to be the set of all real numbers x for which $f(x)$ is a real number.

1.   Let $f(x) = \dfrac{x^2 - 2x + 1}{2 + x - x^2}$ for x in $(-\infty, +\infty)$.

(A) Find the critical values of f.

(B) Sketch the graph of f; label local extrema and asymptotes.

(C) f has one point of inflection at $(p, f(p))$. Find two consecutive integers n and $n + 1$ such that $n < p < n + 1$.

2. Population growth in a certain bacteria colony is best described by the equation

$$y = t^2 e^{3t^2 t \sqrt{t}}$$

(A) Find the rate of growth at $t = 1$.

(B) Find the lowest rate for $t > 0$.

(C) Find the highest rate for $t > 0$.

3. Let $f(x) = (e^{-\cos x}) \sin x$.

(A) Find $f'(x)$.

(B) Find $f''(x)$.

(C) Use parts (A) and (B), together with symmetry and axes intercepts, to sketch the graph of $y = f(x)$. Make sure your graph depicts the correct concavity.

(D) Evaluate $\int_0^a f(x)\, dx$ where a is the first point of inflection of $f(x)$ in the interval $(0, \pi)$.

4. Find a third degree polynomial function given the following information:

(i) The axes intercepts are $(1, 0)$ and $(0, 12)$.

(ii) Relative maximum at $x = -\dfrac{2}{3}$.

(iii) Point of inflection at $x = \dfrac{5}{3}$.

(A) For what values of x is the function positive?

(B) For what values of x is the derivative of the function positive?

(C) Find the interval(s) in which the function is concave down.

5. Make a rain gutter from a long strip of sheet metal of width w inches using the following prescribed methods. In each case, find the dimension across the top to maximize the amount of rainwater the gutter can handle.

   (A) Bend the metal in the middle to form a V–shaped (isosceles Δ) rain gutter. Find the value of x that maximizes the amount of water the gutter can handle by maximizing the cross–sectional area of the gutter.

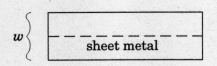

   (B) Bend the metal in two places to form an isosceles trapezoid as follows:

   Find the value of x that will maximize the amount of water the gutter can handle by maximizing the cross–sectional area of the gutter.

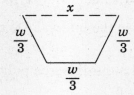

6. Let $f(x)$ be continuous on $[-a, a]$ where $a > 0$, $f(a) = 2$, and $f'(a) = 1$.

   (A) Find an equation for the tangent line to $y = f(x)$ at the point $(a, f(a))$.

   (B) Suppose $f(x)$ is an odd function, i.e., $f(-x) = -f(x)$, and $F(x)$ is an antiderivative for f. Find $F(a) - F(-a)$. Be sure to show work to justify your conclusions.

   (C) If the graph of $f(x)$ lies below the tangent line to $y = f(x)$ at $(a, f(a))$ for all x in $[-a, a]$, then find the area between $y = f(x)$ and the tangent line from $x = -a$ to $x = a$ as a function of a.

ADVANCED PLACEMENT CALCULUS AB EXAM VI

ANSWER KEY

Section I

1.	(B)	12.	(A)	23.	(A)	34.	(B)
2.	(D)	13.	(C)	24.	(D)	35.	(D)
3.	(A)	14.	(D)	25.	(E)	36.	(E)
4.	(C)	15.	(B)	26.	(B)	37.	(A)
5.	(E)	16.	(C)	27.	(E)	38.	(A)
6.	(D)	17.	(E)	28.	(C)	39.	(C)
7.	(B)	18.	(C)	29.	(D)	40.	(D)
8.	(D)	19.	(E)	30.	(E)	41.	(B)
9.	(C)	20.	(C)	31.	(C)	42.	(E)
10.	(A)	21.	(A)	32.	(A)	43.	(C)
11.	(E)	22.	(A)	33.	(D)	44.	(B)
						45.	(B)

Section II

See Detailed Explanations of Answers.

ADVANCED PLACEMENT
CALCULUS AB
EXAM VI

DETAILED EXPLANATIONS
OF ANSWERS

SECTION I

1. **(B)**

$$f(f(x)) = ||x||$$

$$= |x|$$

$$= -x \qquad \text{since } x < 0.$$

2. **(D)**

An odd function will satisfy this condition. None of the functions are odd except

$$f(x) = (x+1)^3 - (3x^2 + 1)$$

$$= (x^3 + 3x^2 + 3x + 1) - (3x^2 + 1)$$

$$= x^3 + 3x$$

$$= -f(-x).$$

Since $f(x)$ is odd, $\int_{-a}^{a} f(x)\, dx = 0$

3. **(A)**

The two curves intersect at $(-1, -1)$ and $(2, 2)$. Therefore,

$$\text{Area} = \int_{-1}^{2} \left[y - \left(y^2 - 2 \right) \right] dy = \left(\frac{y^2}{2} - \frac{y^3}{3} + 2y \right) \Big|_{-1}^{2}$$

$$= \frac{9}{2}.$$

4. **(C)**

$$g(x) = 2x^3 + hx^2 + kx - 6$$

so $\quad g'(x) = 6x^2 + 2hx + k \quad$ and

$$g''(x) = 12x + 2h$$

$$g'(-2) = 0 \Rightarrow$$

$$0 = 24 - 4h + k$$

$$g''\left(-\frac{1}{2}\right) = 0 \Rightarrow$$

$$0 = -6 + 2h \quad \text{so } 3 = h$$

Now $\quad k = -12 \quad$ and $\quad h - k = 3 - (-12) = 15$

5. **(E)**

If $x > 0$, $\quad \lim_{x \to 0} \dfrac{\sin x}{|x|} = \lim_{x \to 0} \dfrac{\sin x}{x}$

$$= 1$$

If $x < 0$, $\quad \lim_{x \to 0} \dfrac{\sin x}{|x|} = \lim_{x \to 0} \dfrac{\sin x}{-x}$

$$= -1$$

So, $\quad \lim_{x \to 0} \dfrac{\sin x}{|x|} \quad$ does not exist.

6. **(D)**

$A = \pi r^2$ and

$C = 2\pi r$

$$\Rightarrow \frac{C}{2\pi} = r$$

$$A = \pi \left(\frac{C}{2\pi} \right)^2 = \frac{C^2}{4\pi}$$

so, $\dfrac{dA}{dC} = \dfrac{2C}{4\pi}$

$$= \frac{C}{2\pi}$$

7. **(B)**

$$\lim_{x \to 1} \frac{2x - 2}{x^3 + 2x^2 - x - 2} = \lim_{x \to 1} \frac{2(x-1)}{(x-1)(x+1)(x+2)}$$

$$= \lim_{x \to 1} \frac{2}{(x+1)(x+2)}$$

$$= \frac{1}{3}$$

8. **(D)**

$f(x) = \dfrac{e^x}{x} \Rightarrow f$ becomes infinite at $x = 0$, so we have a vertical asymptote at $x = 0$.

Also, $\lim\limits_{x \to -\infty} f(x) = 0$, so there is a horizontal asymptote at $y = 0$.

We see that $\lim\limits_{x \to +\infty} f(x) = +\infty$ so there are no other asymptotes.

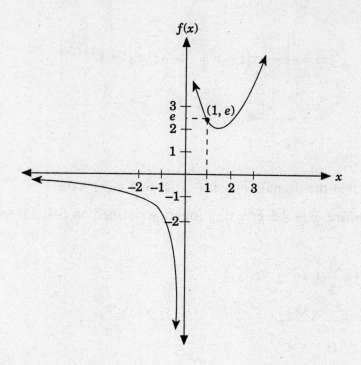

9. **(C)**

$$F(x) = \begin{cases} |x| & \text{if } x < 0 \\ -\sin x & \text{if } x \geq 0 \end{cases}$$

$$f(x) = F'(x) = \begin{cases} -1 & \text{if } x < 0 \\ -\cos x & \text{if } x \geq 0 \end{cases}$$

$$f\left(\frac{\pi}{2}\right) - f\left(-\frac{\pi}{2}\right) = -\cos\frac{\pi}{2} - (-1)$$

$$= 1$$

10. **(A)**

$f(x) = \cos(\arcsin x)$ so

$$g(x) = f'(x) = -\sin(\arcsin x)\frac{1}{\sqrt{1-x^2}}$$

$$= \frac{-x}{\sqrt{1-x^2}}$$

Now $g'(x) = -\left[-\dfrac{1}{2}x\left(1-x^2\right)^{-\frac{3}{2}}(-2x)+\left(1-x^2\right)^{-\frac{1}{2}}\right]$

$$= \dfrac{-1}{\left(1-x^2\right)^{\frac{3}{2}}}$$

Note that the domain of g is $(-1, 1)$ and $g'(x) < 0$.

Therefore, g is a decreasing function defined on $(-1, 1)$

$g''(x) = \dfrac{3}{2}(1-x^2)^{-\frac{5}{2}}(-2x)$

$$= \dfrac{-3x}{(1+x^2)^{\frac{5}{2}}}$$

$\Rightarrow g''(0) = 0,$

so, 0 is an inflection point.

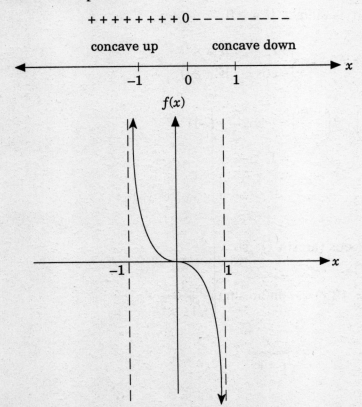

$f(x)$

11. **(E)**

If $f(x) = \sqrt{2-x}$ then $f'(x) = \dfrac{-1}{2\sqrt{2-x}}$.

Let $x = 2 - \varepsilon$ with $\varepsilon > 0$. Then

$$\lim_{x \to 2^-} f'(x) = \lim_{\varepsilon \to 0^+} -\frac{1}{2} \times \frac{1}{\sqrt{\varepsilon}}$$

$$\to -\infty$$

12. **(A)**

$$f(x) = \frac{1-x^2}{1+x^2}$$

$$f'(x) = \frac{(1+x^2)(-2x) - (1-x^2)(2x)}{(1+x^2)^2}$$

$$= \frac{-4x}{(1+x^2)^2}$$

$$f'(2.5) = \frac{-4(2.5)}{(1+(2.5)^2)^2}$$

$$\approx \frac{-10}{52.563}$$

$$\approx -0.190$$

13. **(C)**

$R = \displaystyle\int_{\frac{1}{\sqrt{2}}}^{1} \frac{2x}{\sqrt{1-x^4}}\, dx.$ Let $u = x^2$ and $du = 2x\, dx$

$$R = \int_{\frac{1}{\sqrt{2}}}^{1} \frac{du}{\sqrt{1-u^2}}\, dx = \arcsin u \Big|_{\frac{1}{\sqrt{2}}}^{1}$$

$$= \frac{3\pi}{6} - \frac{\pi}{6}$$

$$= \frac{\pi}{3}$$

$$\approx 1.05 \in (1, \ 1.5]$$

14. **(D)**

The particle is moving to the left when $v(t) < 0$

$$v(t) = s'(t) = 9t^2 - 22t + 8$$

$$= (9t - 4)(t - 2)$$

$$+ + + + + + + + + + 0 - - - - - - 0 + + + + + + +$$

right   left   right

The particle is moving to the left in $\left(\dfrac{4}{9}, \ 2 \right)$

15. **(B)**

Let $f(x) = (x+2)^3 (3-2x)^5 (2x-1)^{-3} (3x-4)^{-2}$

$\ln y = 3\ln(x+2) + 5\ln(3-2x) - 3\ln(2x-1) - 2\ln(3x-4)$

$$\frac{1}{y} y' = \frac{3}{x+2} + \frac{5(-2)}{3-2x} + \frac{-3(2)}{2x-1} + \frac{-2(3)}{3x-4}$$

Therefore, $f'(1) = f(1) \left[\dfrac{3}{3} + \dfrac{-10}{1} + \dfrac{-6}{1} + \dfrac{-6}{-1} \right]$

$$= (3^3)(1^5)(1)^{-3}(-1)^{-2}(-9)$$

$$= 27 \times (-9)$$

$$= -243$$

16. **(C)**

$\int (\csc^2 x)\, 2^{\cot x}\, dx$. Let $u = \cot x$ and $du = -\csc^2 x\, dx$

$$-\int 2^u\, du = \frac{-2^u}{\ln 2} + C$$

$$= \frac{-2^{\cot x}}{\ln 2} + C$$

17. **(E)**

Let $f(x) = x^2 + 1$ and $g(x) = \dfrac{1}{x-2}$.

$$f(g(x)) = f\left(\frac{1}{x-2}\right) = \left(\frac{1}{x-2}\right)^2 + 1,$$

which is continuous at $x = 1$

$$\lim_{x \to \infty} f(g(x)) = \lim_{x \to \infty} \left[\left(\frac{1}{x-2}\right)^2 + 1\right]$$

$$= 0^2 + 1$$

$$= 1$$

$$g(f(x)) = g\left(x^2 + 1\right) = \frac{1}{x^2 - 1},$$

which is continuous at $x = 2$ and discontinuous at $x = 1$ and -1.

But $D_x\big[g(f(x))\big] = -1(x^2 - 1)^{-2}(2x)$,

and $D_x\big[g(f(2))\big] = -1(2^2 - 1)^{-2}(2)(2)$

$$= -\frac{4}{9}, \quad \text{not} \ -4.$$

18. **(C)**

Since $g''(x)$ exists in a deleted neighborhood of $x = a$ (although not for $x = a$), and since $g''(x)$ changes sign upon passing through $x = a$, we can conclude that $g(x)$ has a point of inflection at $x = a$.

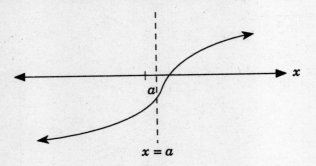

19. **(E)**

As $h \to 0$ through positive values of h, we have $\displaystyle\lim_{h \to 0^+} \frac{f(\ ) - f(\ )}{h} = 0$.

However, as $h \to 0$ through negative values, we have $\displaystyle\lim_{h \to 0^-} \frac{f(\ ) - f(\ )}{h} = 1$. The discrepancy means that the limit does not exist for $h \to 0$.

20. **(C)**

$$\lim_{n \to \infty}\left[1 - n\left(\sin\frac{1}{n}\right)^2 \right] = 1 - \lim_{n \to \infty} n\left(\sin\frac{1}{n}\right)^2.$$

Let $x = \dfrac{1}{n}$.

Then as $n \to \infty$, we see $x \to 0$.

So, $\lim\limits_{n\to\infty}\left[1-n\left(\sin\dfrac{1}{n}\right)^2\right]=1-\lim\limits_{x\to0}\dfrac{(\sin x)^2}{x}$

$$=1-\lim\limits_{x\to0}\left[\left(\dfrac{\sin x}{x}\right)(\sin x)\right]$$

$$=1-\left(\lim\limits_{x\to0}\dfrac{\sin x}{x}\right)\left(\lim\limits_{x\to0}\sin x\right)$$

$$=1-(1\times0)$$

$$=1-0$$

$$=1.$$

21. **(A)**

The position of the point at time t is given by

$s(t)=\displaystyle\int 2^t\ln 2\,dt=2^t+C$

$s(0)=1+C$

$s(2)=2^2+C$

distance traveled $=s(2)-s(0)=3$

22. **(A)**

$y=e^{-x}\ln x$

Therefore, $\quad y'=-e^{-x}\ln x+e^{-x}\times\dfrac{1}{x}$

$\qquad\qquad y'(1)=e^{-1}$

Therefore, the tangent line is $(y-0)=\dfrac{1}{e}(x-1)$ or $x-ey-1=0$

23. **(A)**

Find the average value for $y = \dfrac{e^{\sqrt{x}}}{\sqrt{x}}$ in the interval [1, 4].

Let $u = \sqrt{x}$, so $du = \dfrac{dx}{2\sqrt{x}}$

Average value $= \dfrac{1}{4-1}\displaystyle\int_1^4 \dfrac{e^{\sqrt{x}}}{\sqrt{x}}\,dx$

$= \dfrac{2}{3}\displaystyle\int_1^2 e^u\,du$

$= \dfrac{2e}{3}(e-1)$

≈ 3.114

24. **(D)**

$\displaystyle\lim_{x \to a} \dfrac{\sqrt[3]{x} - \sqrt[3]{a}}{x - a} = \dfrac{\frac{1}{3}x^{-\frac{2}{3}}}{1}\Bigg|_{x=a}$

$= \dfrac{1}{3}a^{-\frac{2}{3}}$

$= \dfrac{1}{3} \times \dfrac{\sqrt[3]{a}}{a}$

25. **(E)**

$\displaystyle\lim_{x \to \infty} \dfrac{(\ln x)^2}{x} = \dfrac{\infty}{\infty}$, an indeterminate form.

By L'Hôpital's rule, we have $\lim\limits_{x\to\infty} \dfrac{(\ln x)^2}{x} = \lim\limits_{x\to\infty} \dfrac{2(\ln x)x^{-1}}{1}$

$$= \lim\limits_{x\to\infty} \frac{2\ln x}{x}$$

$$= \frac{\infty}{\infty},$$

still indeterminate.

Applying L'Hôpital's rule again, we have $\lim\limits_{x\to\infty} \dfrac{\frac{2}{x}}{1} = \lim\limits_{x\to\infty} \dfrac{2}{x}$

$$= 0.$$

26.   **(B)**

The relative maximum occurs at a critical point. Since the function is a polynomial, its critical points are those points where its derivative is zero.

The derivative is: $f'(x) = 20x^4 + 60x^3 + 60x^2 + 20x$

Factor: $f'(x) = 20x(x^3 + 3x^2 + 3x + 1)$

$$= 20x(x+1)^3$$

This is zero at: $x = 0$ and $x = -1$

Use the First Derivative Test to see which of these is a relative maximum. Check $f'(x)$ at sample points in each of the intervals bounded by the critical points:

-2 is in $(-\infty, -1)$: $f'(-2) = 40 > 0$,
so $f(x)$ is increasing on $(-\infty, -1)$;

$-\dfrac{1}{2}$ is in $(-1, 0)$: $f'\left(-\dfrac{1}{2}\right) = -\dfrac{5}{4} < 0$,

so $f(x)$ is decreasing on $(-1, 0)$;

1 is in $(0, \infty)$: $f'(1) = 160 > 0$
so $f(x)$ is increasing on $(0, \infty)$.

Thus f has a relative maximum at $x = -1$ because $f(x)$ is increasing on $(-\infty, -1)$ and decreasing on $(-1, 0)$.

27.   **(E)**
The arc length formula is:

$$L = \int_0^{\frac{\pi}{2}} \sqrt{\left(\frac{dx}{dt}\right)^2 + \left(\frac{dy}{dt}\right)^2} \, dt$$

Here:

$$\frac{dx}{dt} = \left(12\cos^2 t\right)(-\sin t)$$

$$\frac{dy}{dt} = \left(12\sin^2 t\right)(\cos t)$$

so:

$$\left(\frac{dx}{dt}\right)^2 = 144\sin^2 t \, \cos^4 t$$

$$\left(\frac{dy}{dt}\right)^2 = 144\sin^4 t \, \cos^2 t$$

so:

$$\left(\frac{dx}{dt}\right)^2 + \left(\frac{dy}{dt}\right)^2 = 144\sin^2 \cos^4 t + 144\sin^4 t \, \cos^2 t$$

$$= \left(144\sin^2 \cos^2 t\right)\left(\cos^2 t + \sin^2 t\right)$$

$$= \left(144\sin^2 t \, \cos^2 t\right)(1)$$

so:

$$\sqrt{\left(\frac{dx}{dt}\right)^2 + \left(\frac{dy}{dt}\right)^2} = 12\sin t \, \cos t$$

Thus:

$$L = \int_0^{\frac{\pi}{2}} 12\sin t \, \cos t \, dt$$

$$= 6\sin^2 t \Big|_0^{\frac{\pi}{2}}$$

$$= 6(1)^2 - 6(0)^2$$

$$= 6$$

28.   **(C)**

Let: $x = |OA|$

$\quad\quad\, y = |OB|$

$\quad\quad\, z = |AB|$

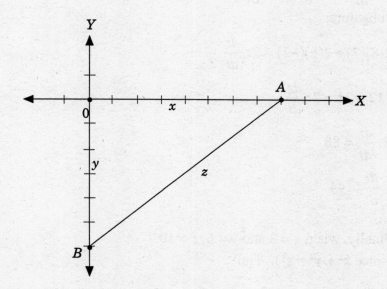

Then x, y, and z are functions of time t, and by the Pythagorean Theorem: $x^2 + y^2 = z^2$

The rates of change of x, y, and z are their derivatives with respect to t:

$$\frac{dx}{dt} = 7$$

$$\frac{dy}{dt} = -2$$

$$\frac{dz}{dt} = ?$$

(Note that $\frac{dy}{dt}$ is negative because the distance $y = |OB|$ is decreasing.)

To find $\frac{dz}{dt}$, differentiate the Pythagorean equation with respect to t:

$$x^2 + y^2 = z^2$$

$$\frac{d}{dt}\left(x^2 + y^2\right) = \frac{d}{dt}\left(z^2\right)$$

$$2x\frac{dx}{dt} + 2y\frac{dy}{dt} = 2z\frac{dz}{dt}$$

Substitute:

$$2(8)(7) + 2(6)(-2) = 2z\frac{dz}{dt}$$

$$112 - 24 = 2z\frac{dz}{dt}$$

$$2z\frac{dz}{dt} = 88$$

$$z\frac{dz}{dt} = 44$$

Finally, when $x = 8$ and $y = 6$, $z = 10$
(since $x^2 + y^2 = z^2$). Thus:

$$10\frac{dz}{dt} = 44$$

$$\frac{dz}{dt} = \frac{44}{10} = \frac{22}{5}$$

29. **(D)**

$$f(x) = \sin|x|$$

$f(x) < 0$ for x in $\left(\dfrac{\pi}{2}, \pi\right)$ and f is even, not odd.

$$\int_{-\frac{\pi}{4}}^{\frac{\pi}{4}} f(x)\, dx = 2\int_{0}^{\frac{\pi}{4}} f(x)\, dx \neq 0$$

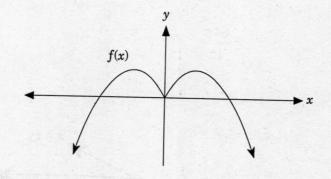

f is symmetric with respect to $x = 0$ since f is even. f is not differentiable at $x = 0$ because the right-hand and left-hand derivatives are $+1$ and -1, respectively.

30. **(E)**

$$h(x) = \frac{f(g(x)) - g(f(x))}{f(x)}$$

$$= \frac{(x^2 - 1) - (x - 1)^2}{x - 1}$$

$$= \frac{(x + 1)(x - 1) - (x - 1)(x - 1)}{(x - 1)}$$

$$= \frac{(x - 1)[(x + 1) - (x - 1)]}{(x - 1)}$$

$$= [x + 1 - x + 1]$$

$$= 2.$$

Since h is a constant function, the range of h is $\{2\}$.

31. **(C)**

The two curves intersect at $(0, 0)$ and $(4, 2)$. Using washers, the volume is

$$\pi\int_0^2 \left[(2y)^2 - (y^2)^2\right] dy = \pi\int_0^2 (4y^2 - y^4)\, dy$$

$$= \pi\left(\frac{4y^3}{3} - \frac{y^5}{5}\right)\Big|_0^2$$

$$= \frac{64\pi}{15}$$

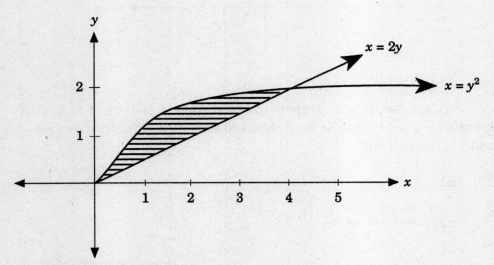

Using shells, the volume is

$$2\pi\int_0^4 x\left(x^{\frac{1}{2}} - \frac{1}{2}x\right) dx = 2\pi\int_0^4 \left(x^{\frac{3}{2}} - \frac{1}{2}x^2\right) dx$$

$$= \frac{64\pi}{15}$$

Calculator: $64 \times \pi \div 15 = \approx 13.404$

32. **(A)**

This is a direct calculator problem. For example,

fnInt $((\sin x \cos 2x)^\wedge 2, x, 0, 2)$ can easily give the answer 0.715.

33. **(B)**

Draw the graph $f'(x)$

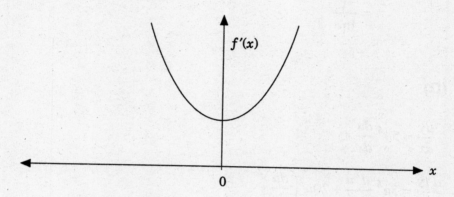

$$f'(x) = 2\frac{\left(1+x^4\right)}{\left(1-x^4\right)^{\frac{3}{2}}}$$

The minimum is clearly at $x = 0$, where $f'(0) = 2$.

Obviously, a minimum exists at $x = 0$. By tracing on the graph to $x = 0$, you find $f'_{min}(x) = 2$.

34. **(B)**

$f(x) = -x + x \ln x$ and $f(e) = -e + e = 0$ so $e = f^{-1}(0)$

Also, $f'(x) = -1 + \dfrac{x}{x} + \ln x = \ln x$.

$$D_x(f^{-1}(x)) = \frac{1}{f'(f^{-1}(x))}$$

$$D_x(f^{-1}(0)) = \frac{1}{f'(f^{-1}(0))}$$

$$= \frac{1}{f'(e)}$$

$$= \frac{1}{\ln e}$$

$$= 1$$

35. **(D)**

$$\frac{dy}{dx} = 5u^4 \frac{du}{dx}$$

$$\frac{d^2 y}{dx^2} = 5u^4 \frac{d^2 u}{dx^2} + 20u^3 \left(\frac{du}{dx}\right)^2$$

$$\frac{d^3 y}{dx^3} = 5u^4 \frac{d^3 u}{dx^3} + 20u^3 \frac{du}{dx} \times \frac{d^2 u}{dx^2} + 20u^3 \times 2 \times$$

$$\left(\frac{du}{dx}\right) \times \frac{d^2 u}{dx^2} + 60u^2 \times \frac{du}{dx} \times \left(\frac{du}{dx}\right)^2$$

$$\frac{d^3 y}{dx^3} = 5(1)5 + 20(1)(2)(-3) + 20(1)^3(2)(2)(-3) + 60(1)^2 2(2)^2$$

$$= 25 - 120 - 240 + 480$$

$$= 145$$

36. **(E)**

$f'(6) = 0$ and $f'(-12) = 0$

$f'\left(\dfrac{x}{3}\right) = 0$ when $\dfrac{x}{3} = 6$ or $\dfrac{x}{3} = -12$

so $x = 18$ or $x = -36$

37. **(A)**

Draw the graphs of $s(t)$ and $s'(t)$.

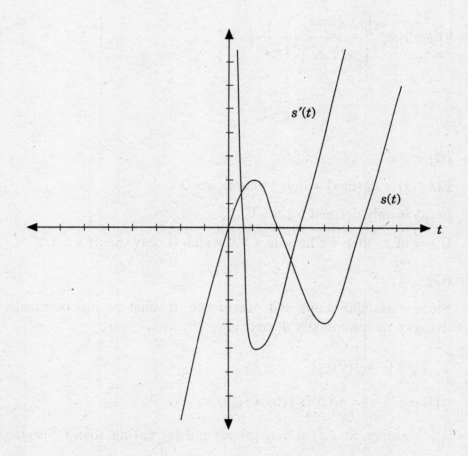

By tracing the most negative $s'(t)$, you get -5.4 at $t = 1.27$.

38. **(A)**

$$\int_0^1 x\, e^x\, dx = x\, e^x \Big|_0^1 - \int_0^1 e^x\, dx = 1$$

$$\int_0^1 e^{-x}\, dx = -e^{-x} \Big|_0^1$$

$$= -e^{-1} + e^0$$

$$= 1 - e^{-1}$$

Therefore, $\dfrac{\displaystyle\int_0^1 x\, e^x\, dx}{\displaystyle\int_0^1 e^{-x}\, dx} = \dfrac{1}{1 - e^{-1}}$

$$= \frac{e}{e - 1}$$

39. **(C)**

Let $f(x) = \ln (\ln x) = \ln u$ where $u > 0$.

$\ln (u)$ is only defined for $u > 0$.

If $u = \ln x$, then we have $\ln x > 0$ which is only true if $x > 1$.

40. **(D)**

Since f is continuous and one-to-one, it must be monotonically increasing or monotonically decreasing.

$$f^{-1}(1) = 0 \Rightarrow f(0) = 1$$

$$f(1) = e^{-1} < 1 = f(0) \Rightarrow f(0) > f(1),$$

so f is decreasing. Since f is one–to–one and decreasing, then f^{-1} is also.

$$D_x(f^{-1}(x)) = \frac{1}{f'(f^{-1}(x))}, \quad \text{so}$$

$$D_x(f^{-1}(e^{-1})) = \frac{1}{f'(f^{-1}(e^{-1}))}$$

$$= \frac{1}{f'(1)}$$

$$= \frac{1}{-2e^{-1}}$$

$$= -\frac{1}{2}e$$

41. **(B)**

Use the calculator for solving the problem directly. For example,

fnInt $(x\hat{\ }x, x, 0, 2)$,

pressing ENTER gives 2.83.

42. **(E)**

$$\frac{h}{b} = \sin\alpha \quad \text{so} \quad h = b\sin\alpha$$

$$A = \frac{1}{2}(\text{base} \times \text{height})$$

$$= \frac{1}{2}cb\sin\alpha$$

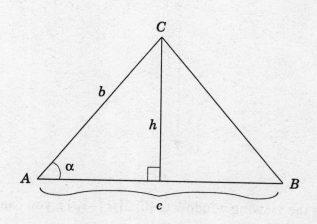

$$\frac{dA}{dt} = \frac{1}{2}cb\cos\alpha\left(\frac{d\alpha}{dt}\right) \Rightarrow \quad \text{at} \quad x = \frac{\pi}{3}$$

$$= \frac{1}{2}cb\cos\left(\frac{\pi}{3}\right)(2)$$

$$= \frac{cb}{2}$$

43. **(C)**

Draw the graphs $f(x)$ and $f'(x)$.

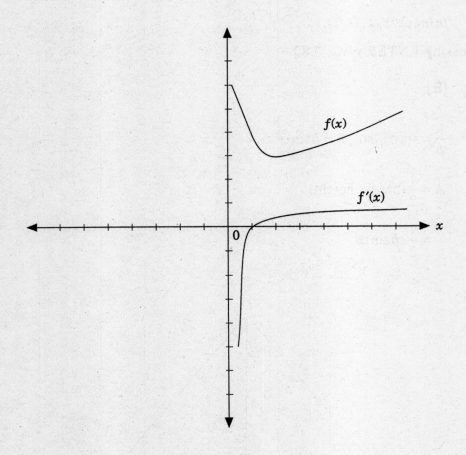

Resetting the viewing window to $[0, 2] \times [-1, 1]$, you can easily find that $c = 1$.

$$f'(x) = \frac{e^{\sqrt{x}}}{2x^{\frac{3}{2}}}\left(\sqrt{x}-1\right)$$

$f'(x) = 0$ when $\sqrt{x} = 1$, i.e, when $x = 1$.

44. **(B)**

The distance from a point $P(x, y)$ to the origin $(0, 0)$ is given by:

$$D = \sqrt{x^2 + y^2}$$

This is minimal where $u = D^2 = x^2 + y^2$ is minimal. If $P(x, y)$ is on the given line, then its coordinates x and y satisfy the equation $y = 2x + 7$. Substituting, we have:

$$u = x^2 + y^2$$
$$= x^2 + (2x + 7)^2$$

This function is minimal where its derivative is zero:

$$0 = \frac{du}{dx} = 2x + 2(2x+7) \cdot 2$$
$$= 10x + 28$$

i.e. $x = -\dfrac{28}{10} = -\dfrac{14}{5}$

and $y = 2x + 7 = 2\left(-\dfrac{14}{5}\right) + 7 = \dfrac{7}{5}$

Here: $D = \sqrt{u} = \sqrt{x^2 + y^2}$

$$= \sqrt{\left(-\frac{14}{5}\right)^2 + \left(\frac{7}{5}\right)^2}$$

$$= \frac{7}{5}\sqrt{5}$$

45.　**(B)**

The area of each semicircular cross section is

$$A_x = \frac{1}{2}\left(\pi y^2\right) = \frac{\pi}{2}y^2$$

where x is the point on the x-axis locating the cross section and y is the radius of the cross section:

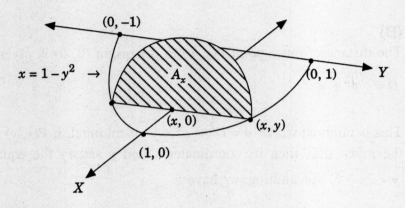

Then the total volume is

$$V = \int_0^1 A_x\,dx$$

$$= \int_0^1 \frac{\pi}{2}y^2\,dx$$

$$= \int_0^1 \frac{\pi}{2}(1-x)\,dx,\text{ since }y^2 = 1-x$$

$$= \frac{\pi}{2}\left[x - \frac{1}{2}x^2\right]_0^1$$

$$= \frac{\pi}{2}\left[\left((1) - \frac{1}{2}(1)^2\right) - \left((0) - \frac{1}{2}(0)^2\right)\right]$$

$$= \frac{\pi}{2}\left[\frac{1}{2}\right]$$

$$= \frac{\pi}{4}$$

SECTION II

1. **(A)**

$$f'(x) = \frac{(-x^2 + x + 2)(2x - 2) - (x^2 - 2x + 1)(-2x + 1)}{(x-2)^2(x+1)^2}$$

$$= \frac{(x-1)\left[-2x^2 + 2x + 4 + 2x^2 - 3x + 1\right]}{(x-2)^2(x+1)^2}$$

$$= \frac{(x-1)(-x+5)}{(x-2)^2(x+1)^2}$$

The critical values are $x = 5, 2, -1$, and 1, since $f'(x)$ at these points is either zero or undefined.

(B)

$$f(x) = \frac{(x-1)^2}{(2-x)(x+1)}$$

```
+ + + + + + + + + + + + + + + + + 0 - - -    (2 - x)
- - - - - 0 + + + + + + + + + + + + + +    (x + 1)
```

$$f'(x) = \frac{(x-1)(-x+5)}{(x-2)^2(x+1)^2}$$

```
(x - 1)    - - - - - - - - 0 + + + + + + + + + + + + + + + + + + + + +

(-x + 5)   + + + + + + + + + + + + + + + + + + + + + + + + + + + 0 - - -
```

decreasing   increasing   decreasing

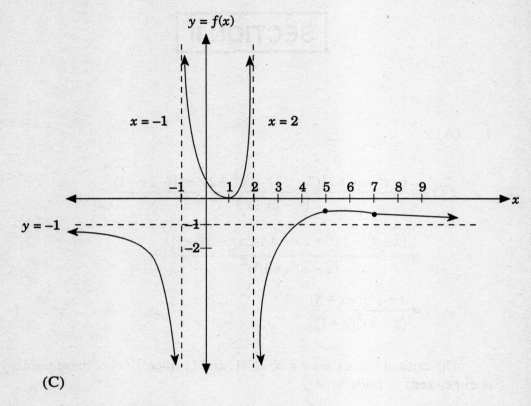

(C)

$$f''(x) = \frac{\left[(x-2)^2(x+1)^2\right]D_x\left[(x-1)(-x+5)\right]-\left[(x-1)(-x+5)\right]D_x\left[(x-2)^2(x+1)^2\right]}{(x-2)^4(x+1)^4}$$

$$f''(x) = \frac{2\left[(x-2)(x+1)(-x+3)+(x-1)(x-5)(2x-1)\right]}{(x-2)^3(x+1)^3}$$

$$f''(x) = \frac{2(x^3-9x^2+15x-11)}{(x-2)^3(x+1)^3}$$

The second derivative is zero between 7 and 8 so there is a point of inflection between $n = 7$ and $n + 1 = 8$.

$$f''(7) = \frac{2(7^3-9(7^2)+15(7)-11)}{(7-2)^3(7+1)^3}$$

$$= \frac{2(-4)}{5^3 8^3} < 0$$

and $f''(8) = \dfrac{2(8^3 - 9(8^2) + 15(8) - 11)}{(8-2)^3(8+1)^3}$

$= \dfrac{2(45)}{6^3 9^3} > 0,$

so, $f''(x) = 0$ between $x = 7$ and $x = 8$, indicating an inflection point.

2. **(A)**

$$y = t^2 \exp\!\left(3t^{3.5}\right)$$

$$y' = \left(2t + 10.5t^{4.5}\right)\exp\!\left(3t^{3.5}\right)$$

$$y'(1) = 12.5e^3$$

$$\approx 211$$

(B)

It can be seen from the graph as $t \to 0$, $y' \to 0$. Zero is the limit of y' as $t \to 0$, however, the value is never actually assumed by y' since t never reaches $t = 0$.

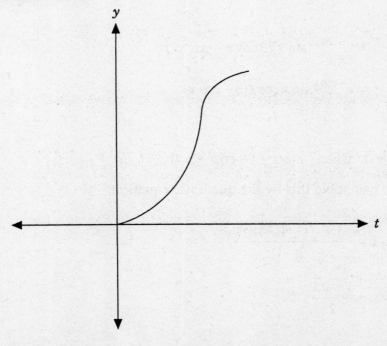

(C)

Obviously, as $t \to \infty$, $y' \to \infty$.

3. (A)

$$f'(x) = \left(e^{-\cos x}\right)(\cos x)) + \sin x \left(e^{-\cos x}\right)\sin x$$

$$= e^{-\cos x}\left[\cos x + \sin^2 x\right]$$

$$= e^{-\cos x}\left[\cos x + (1 - \cos^2 x)\right]$$

(B)

$$f'(x) = e^{-\cos x}\left[-\sin x + 2\cos x + 3x\cos x + \sin^3 x\right]$$

$$= e^{-\cos x}\left[-\sin x + 3\sin x \cos x + \sin^3 x\right]$$

$$= e^{-\cos x}(\sin x)\left(3\cos x + \sin^2 x - 1\right)$$

$$= e^{-\cos x}(\sin x)\left(3\cos x - \left(1 - \sin^2 x\right)\right)$$

$$= e^{-\cos x}(\sin x)\left(3\cos x - \cos^2 x\right)$$

$$= e^{-\cos x}\sin x \cos x(3 - \cos x)$$

(C)

$y' = 0$ when $\cos x + 1 - \cos^2 x = 0$.

We can solve this by the quadratic equation:

$$\cos x = -\frac{1 \pm \sqrt{1 - 4(-1)(1)}}{2(-1)}$$

$$= \frac{1 - \sqrt{5}}{2}.$$

Note that $\cos x = \dfrac{1+\sqrt{5}}{2}$ is not possible because $\dfrac{1+\sqrt{5}}{2} > 1$ and $\cos x$ is always ≤ 1.

So, $x = \arccos\left(\dfrac{1-\sqrt{5}}{2}\right) + 2k\pi \leftarrow$ Location of relative extrema for any integer k.

Let $y'' = 0$ to find points of inflection.

$y'' = 0$ when $\sin x = 0$ or $\cos x = 0$ ($3 - \cos x = 0$ is impossible, as is $e^{-\cos x} = 0$).

$\Rightarrow x = k\pi$ or $x = \dfrac{\pi}{2} + k\pi$ are where the points of inflection are found, for any integer k.

The function crosses the x-axis when $f(x) = e^{-\cos x} (\sin x) = 0$, i.e., when $\sin x = 0$, namely $x = k\pi$, $k =$ any integer.

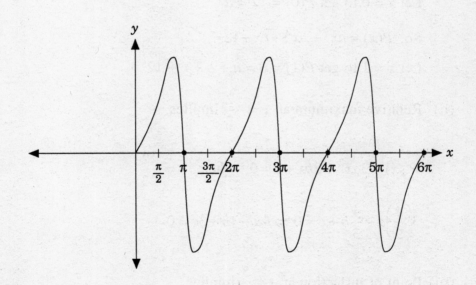

(D)

$$\int_0^{\frac{\pi}{2}} e^{-\cos x} \sin x \, dx = \int_{-1}^0 e^u du \quad \text{where} \quad u = -\cos x, \quad du = \sin x \, dx$$

$$= e^u \Big|_{-1}^0$$

$$= e^0 - e^{-1}$$

$$= 1 - \frac{1}{e}$$

4. (A)

Start with a general third degree polynomial of the form

$$P(x) = ax^3 + bx^2 + cx + d$$

(i)   The intercepts are $(1, 0)$ and $(0, 12)$.

Let $x = 0$ to get $P(0) = 12 = d$

So, $P(x) = ax^3 + bx^2 + cx + 12$

Let $x = 1$ to get $P(1) = 0 = a + b + c + 12$

(ii) Relative maximum at $x = -\dfrac{2}{3}$ implies

$$P'(x) = 3ax^2 + 2bx + c = 0 \quad \text{when} \quad x = -\frac{2}{3}$$

$$3\left(\frac{4}{9}\right)a - \frac{4}{3}b + c = 0 \Rightarrow 4a - 4b + 3c = 0$$

(iii) Point of inflection at $x = \dfrac{5}{3}$ implies

$$P''(x) = 6ax + 2b = 0 \quad \text{when} \quad x = \frac{5}{3}$$

$$6\left(\frac{5}{3}\right)a + 2b = 0 \Rightarrow 5a + b = 0$$

Now solve the equations above simultaneously.

$a + b + c = -12$

$4a - 4b + 3c = 0$

$5a + b = 0$

$\Rightarrow 5a = -b$

$a - 5a + c = -12$

$\Rightarrow -4a + c = -12$

$4a + 4(5a) + 3c = 0$

$\Rightarrow 24a + 3c = 0 \Rightarrow 8a + c = 0$

$12a = 12, \quad a = 1, \quad b = -5, \quad c = -12 + 4a = -8.$

The simultaneous solution is $a = 1, b = -5, c = -8$

so, $P(x) = x^3 - 5x^2 - 8x + 12$

$= (x - 1)(x - 6)(x + 2)$

(A)

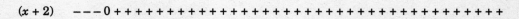

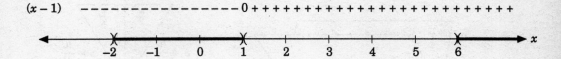

The polynomial is positive for $-2 < x < 1$ or $x > 6$.

(B)

$P'(x) = 3x^2 - 10x - 8$

$= (3x + 2)(x - 4)$

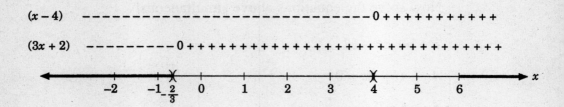

The derivative is positive for $x < -\dfrac{2}{3}$ or $x > 4$.

(C)

$P''(x) = 6x - 10 = 2(3x - 5)$. When $P''(x) < 0$, the function is concave down.

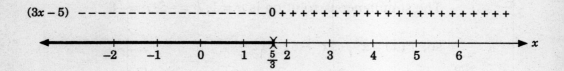

The function is concave down for $x < \dfrac{5}{3}$.

5. (A)

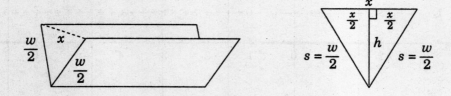

If $s = \dfrac{w}{2}$ then $h^2 = s^2 - \left(\dfrac{x}{2}\right)^2$ for $x \in [0, 2s]$, by the Pythagorean theorem. So the cross-sectional area is

$$A = \frac{1}{2}bh = \frac{1}{2}x\sqrt{s^2 - \frac{x^2}{4}}, \quad \text{so} \quad A^2 = \frac{x^2 s^2}{4} - \frac{x^4}{16},$$

which is an easier function to work with.

The maximum value of a continuous function in a closed interval occurs at the end points or at a critical value. So evaluate the function at 0, $2s$, and any critical values.

To find the critical values, we differentiate A^2 with respect to x:

$$2AA' = \frac{s^2}{4} 2x - \frac{4x^3}{16} = \frac{x}{4}(2s^2 - x^2)$$

Set $A' = 0$ to find critical value(s). If $A' = 0$ then $x = 0$ or $2s^2 - x^2 = 0$. $x = 0$ makes no constructive sense, so $x = s\sqrt{2}$.

Evaluate A at the endpoints and critical point to get:

x	A
0	0
$2s$	0
$s\sqrt{2}$	$\dfrac{s^2}{2}$

The maximum amount of water is handled when

$$x = s\sqrt{2} = \frac{w\sqrt{2}}{2}$$

(B)

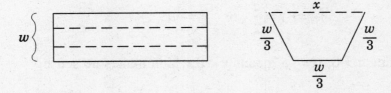

If $a = \dfrac{w}{3}$ then $h^2 = a^2 - y^2$ for $y \in [0, a]$, by the Pythagorean theorem.

$$A = \frac{1}{2}h(2y + 2a) = \frac{2}{2}\sqrt{a^2 - y^2}\,(y + a)$$

$$= (y + a)\sqrt{a^2 - y^2}\,.$$

Taking the derivative of A with respect to y, we have

$$A' = (y + a)\frac{1}{2}(a^2 - y^2)^{-\frac{1}{2}}(-2y) + \sqrt{a^2 - y^2}$$

$$= (a^2 - y^2)^{-\frac{1}{2}}\left[-y^2 - ay + a^2 - y^2\right]$$

$$= \frac{(-2y^2 - ay + a^2)}{\sqrt{a^2 - y^2}}$$

The maximum value of a continuous function in a closed interval occurs at a critical value or its endpoints. So evaluate the function at 0 and a and any critical values. We find critical values as follows:

If $A' = 0$ then $-2y^2 - ay + a^2 = 0$

$$(-2y + a)(y + a) = 0$$

$$\Rightarrow y = \frac{a}{2} \quad \text{or} \quad y = -a\,.$$

Since $a > 0$, $y = -a$ means $y < 0$ which makes no sense.

So $y = \frac{a}{2}$ is a critical value. We then have:

y	A
0	a^2
a	0
$\dfrac{a}{2}$	$\dfrac{3a^2\sqrt{3}}{4} > a^2$

So the maximum amount of water is handled when $y = \dfrac{a}{2}$, which

means $x = a + 2y = a + a = 2a = \dfrac{2w}{3}$.

6.   (A)

$y - y_1 = m(x - x_1)$ so

$y - 2 = 1(x - a)$

$y = x - a + 2$

(B)

The integral of an odd function over an interval symmetric about the origin (say, from $x = -a$ to $x = a$) must vanish.

We start with:

$$\int_{-a}^{a} f(a) - f(-a) = \int_{-a}^{a} f(x)\,dx$$

as given, and then split integral into two parts whose values add up to zero.

$$\int_{-a}^{a} f(x)\,dx = \int_{-a}^{0} f(x)\,dx + \int_{0}^{a} f(x)\,dx$$

We must rewrite the first integral on the right. We use the change of variable $u = -x$

$x = -u$ therefore $dx \rightarrow -du$

$x = 0 \rightarrow u = 0$

$x = -a \rightarrow u = a$

$f(x) \rightarrow f(-u) = -f(a)$

The integral becomes

$$-\int_{-a}^{0} f(-x)\, dx \Rightarrow \int_{-a}^{0} -f(u)\,(-du)$$

$$= \int_{a}^{0} f(u)\,(du)$$

$$= \int_{0}^{a} f(u)\,(du)$$

or, equivalently, $-\int_{0}^{a} f(x)\, dx$. Hence, we see that

$$\int_{-a}^{a} f(x)\, dx = 0$$

(C)

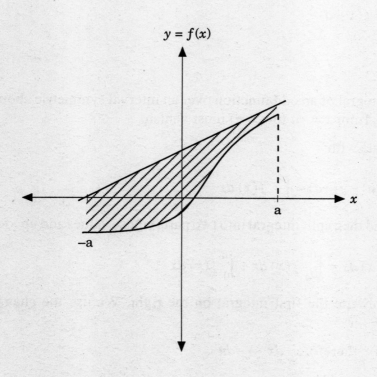

$$A = \int_{-a}^{a} \left[(x - a + 2) - f(x) \right] dx$$

$$= \left[\frac{x^2}{2} + (2 - a) - F(x) \right] \Big|_{-a}^{a}$$

$$= \left[\frac{a^2}{2} + (2 - a)a - F(a) \right] - \left[\frac{a^2}{2} + (2 - a)(-a) - F(a) \right]$$

$$= 2a(2 - a) - F(a) + F(-a)$$

$$= 2a(2 - a)$$

since $F(-a) = F(a)$

Advanced Placement Examination in Calculus AB

ANSWER SHEETS

AP Calculus AB
Test 1

1. Ⓐ Ⓑ Ⓒ Ⓓ Ⓔ
2. Ⓐ Ⓑ Ⓒ Ⓓ Ⓔ
3. Ⓐ Ⓑ Ⓒ Ⓓ Ⓔ
4. Ⓐ Ⓑ Ⓒ Ⓓ Ⓔ
5. Ⓐ Ⓑ Ⓒ Ⓓ Ⓔ
6. Ⓐ Ⓑ Ⓒ Ⓓ Ⓔ
7. Ⓐ Ⓑ Ⓒ Ⓓ Ⓔ
8. Ⓐ Ⓑ Ⓒ Ⓓ Ⓔ
9. Ⓐ Ⓑ Ⓒ Ⓓ Ⓔ
10. Ⓐ Ⓑ Ⓒ Ⓓ Ⓔ
11. Ⓐ Ⓑ Ⓒ Ⓓ Ⓔ
12. Ⓐ Ⓑ Ⓒ Ⓓ Ⓔ
13. Ⓐ Ⓑ Ⓒ Ⓓ Ⓔ
14. Ⓐ Ⓑ Ⓒ Ⓓ Ⓔ
15. Ⓐ Ⓑ Ⓒ Ⓓ Ⓔ
16. Ⓐ Ⓑ Ⓒ Ⓓ Ⓔ
17. Ⓐ Ⓑ Ⓒ Ⓓ Ⓔ
18. Ⓐ Ⓑ Ⓒ Ⓓ Ⓔ
19. Ⓐ Ⓑ Ⓒ Ⓓ Ⓔ
20. Ⓐ Ⓑ Ⓒ Ⓓ Ⓔ
21. Ⓐ Ⓑ Ⓒ Ⓓ Ⓔ
22. Ⓐ Ⓑ Ⓒ Ⓓ Ⓔ
23. Ⓐ Ⓑ Ⓒ Ⓓ Ⓔ

24. Ⓐ Ⓑ Ⓒ Ⓓ Ⓔ
25. Ⓐ Ⓑ Ⓒ Ⓓ Ⓔ
26. Ⓐ Ⓑ Ⓒ Ⓓ Ⓔ
27. Ⓐ Ⓑ Ⓒ Ⓓ Ⓔ
28. Ⓐ Ⓑ Ⓒ Ⓓ Ⓔ
29. Ⓐ Ⓑ Ⓒ Ⓓ Ⓔ
30. Ⓐ Ⓑ Ⓒ Ⓓ Ⓔ
31. Ⓐ Ⓑ Ⓒ Ⓓ Ⓔ
32. Ⓐ Ⓑ Ⓒ Ⓓ Ⓔ
33. Ⓐ Ⓑ Ⓒ Ⓓ Ⓔ
34. Ⓐ Ⓑ Ⓒ Ⓓ Ⓔ
35. Ⓐ Ⓑ Ⓒ Ⓓ Ⓔ
36. Ⓐ Ⓑ Ⓒ Ⓓ Ⓔ
37. Ⓐ Ⓑ Ⓒ Ⓓ Ⓔ
38. Ⓐ Ⓑ Ⓒ Ⓓ Ⓔ
39. Ⓐ Ⓑ Ⓒ Ⓓ Ⓔ
40. Ⓐ Ⓑ Ⓒ Ⓓ Ⓔ
41. Ⓐ Ⓑ Ⓒ Ⓓ Ⓔ
42. Ⓐ Ⓑ Ⓒ Ⓓ Ⓔ
43. Ⓐ Ⓑ Ⓒ Ⓓ Ⓔ
44. Ⓐ Ⓑ Ⓒ Ⓓ Ⓔ
45. Ⓐ Ⓑ Ⓒ Ⓓ Ⓔ

AP Calculus AB
Test 2

1. Ⓐ Ⓑ Ⓒ Ⓓ Ⓔ
2. Ⓐ Ⓑ Ⓒ Ⓓ Ⓔ
3. Ⓐ Ⓑ Ⓒ Ⓓ Ⓔ
4. Ⓐ Ⓑ Ⓒ Ⓓ Ⓔ
5. Ⓐ Ⓑ Ⓒ Ⓓ Ⓔ
6. Ⓐ Ⓑ Ⓒ Ⓓ Ⓔ
7. Ⓐ Ⓑ Ⓒ Ⓓ Ⓔ
8. Ⓐ Ⓑ Ⓒ Ⓓ Ⓔ
9. Ⓐ Ⓑ Ⓒ Ⓓ Ⓔ
10. Ⓐ Ⓑ Ⓒ Ⓓ Ⓔ
11. Ⓐ Ⓑ Ⓒ Ⓓ Ⓔ
12. Ⓐ Ⓑ Ⓒ Ⓓ Ⓔ
13. Ⓐ Ⓑ Ⓒ Ⓓ Ⓔ
14. Ⓐ Ⓑ Ⓒ Ⓓ Ⓔ
15. Ⓐ Ⓑ Ⓒ Ⓓ Ⓔ
16. Ⓐ Ⓑ Ⓒ Ⓓ Ⓔ
17. Ⓐ Ⓑ Ⓒ Ⓓ Ⓔ
18. Ⓐ Ⓑ Ⓒ Ⓓ Ⓔ
19. Ⓐ Ⓑ Ⓒ Ⓓ Ⓔ
20. Ⓐ Ⓑ Ⓒ Ⓓ Ⓔ
21. Ⓐ Ⓑ Ⓒ Ⓓ Ⓔ
22. Ⓐ Ⓑ Ⓒ Ⓓ Ⓔ
23. Ⓐ Ⓑ Ⓒ Ⓓ Ⓔ

24. Ⓐ Ⓑ Ⓒ Ⓓ Ⓔ
25. Ⓐ Ⓑ Ⓒ Ⓓ Ⓔ
26. Ⓐ Ⓑ Ⓒ Ⓓ Ⓔ
27. Ⓐ Ⓑ Ⓒ Ⓓ Ⓔ
28. Ⓐ Ⓑ Ⓒ Ⓓ Ⓔ
29. Ⓐ Ⓑ Ⓒ Ⓓ Ⓔ
30. Ⓐ Ⓑ Ⓒ Ⓓ Ⓔ
31. Ⓐ Ⓑ Ⓒ Ⓓ Ⓔ
32. Ⓐ Ⓑ Ⓒ Ⓓ Ⓔ
33. Ⓐ Ⓑ Ⓒ Ⓓ Ⓔ
34. Ⓐ Ⓑ Ⓒ Ⓓ Ⓔ
35. Ⓐ Ⓑ Ⓒ Ⓓ Ⓔ
36. Ⓐ Ⓑ Ⓒ Ⓓ Ⓔ
37. Ⓐ Ⓑ Ⓒ Ⓓ Ⓔ
38. Ⓐ Ⓑ Ⓒ Ⓓ Ⓔ
39. Ⓐ Ⓑ Ⓒ Ⓓ Ⓔ
40. Ⓐ Ⓑ Ⓒ Ⓓ Ⓔ
41. Ⓐ Ⓑ Ⓒ Ⓓ Ⓔ
42. Ⓐ Ⓑ Ⓒ Ⓓ Ⓔ
43. Ⓐ Ⓑ Ⓒ Ⓓ Ⓔ
44. Ⓐ Ⓑ Ⓒ Ⓓ Ⓔ
45. Ⓐ Ⓑ Ⓒ Ⓓ Ⓔ

AP Calculus AB
Test 3

1. Ⓐ Ⓑ Ⓒ Ⓓ Ⓔ
2. Ⓐ Ⓑ Ⓒ Ⓓ Ⓔ
3. Ⓐ Ⓑ Ⓒ Ⓓ Ⓔ
4. Ⓐ Ⓑ Ⓒ Ⓓ Ⓔ
5. Ⓐ Ⓑ Ⓒ Ⓓ Ⓔ
6. Ⓐ Ⓑ Ⓒ Ⓓ Ⓔ
7. Ⓐ Ⓑ Ⓒ Ⓓ Ⓔ
8. Ⓐ Ⓑ Ⓒ Ⓓ Ⓔ
9. Ⓐ Ⓑ Ⓒ Ⓓ Ⓔ
10. Ⓐ Ⓑ Ⓒ Ⓓ Ⓔ
11. Ⓐ Ⓑ Ⓒ Ⓓ Ⓔ
12. Ⓐ Ⓑ Ⓒ Ⓓ Ⓔ
13. Ⓐ Ⓑ Ⓒ Ⓓ Ⓔ
14. Ⓐ Ⓑ Ⓒ Ⓓ Ⓔ
15. Ⓐ Ⓑ Ⓒ Ⓓ Ⓔ
16. Ⓐ Ⓑ Ⓒ Ⓓ Ⓔ
17. Ⓐ Ⓑ Ⓒ Ⓓ Ⓔ
18. Ⓐ Ⓑ Ⓒ Ⓓ Ⓔ
19. Ⓐ Ⓑ Ⓒ Ⓓ Ⓔ
20. Ⓐ Ⓑ Ⓒ Ⓓ Ⓔ
21. Ⓐ Ⓑ Ⓒ Ⓓ Ⓔ
22. Ⓐ Ⓑ Ⓒ Ⓓ Ⓔ
23. Ⓐ Ⓑ Ⓒ Ⓓ Ⓔ

24. Ⓐ Ⓑ Ⓒ Ⓓ Ⓔ
25. Ⓐ Ⓑ Ⓒ Ⓓ Ⓔ
26. Ⓐ Ⓑ Ⓒ Ⓓ Ⓔ
27. Ⓐ Ⓑ Ⓒ Ⓓ Ⓔ
28. Ⓐ Ⓑ Ⓒ Ⓓ Ⓔ
29. Ⓐ Ⓑ Ⓒ Ⓓ Ⓔ
30. Ⓐ Ⓑ Ⓒ Ⓓ Ⓔ
31. Ⓐ Ⓑ Ⓒ Ⓓ Ⓔ
32. Ⓐ Ⓑ Ⓒ Ⓓ Ⓔ
33. Ⓐ Ⓑ Ⓒ Ⓓ Ⓔ
34. Ⓐ Ⓑ Ⓒ Ⓓ Ⓔ
35. Ⓐ Ⓑ Ⓒ Ⓓ Ⓔ
36. Ⓐ Ⓑ Ⓒ Ⓓ Ⓔ
37. Ⓐ Ⓑ Ⓒ Ⓓ Ⓔ
38. Ⓐ Ⓑ Ⓒ Ⓓ Ⓔ
39. Ⓐ Ⓑ Ⓒ Ⓓ Ⓔ
40. Ⓐ Ⓑ Ⓒ Ⓓ Ⓔ
41. Ⓐ Ⓑ Ⓒ Ⓓ Ⓔ
42. Ⓐ Ⓑ Ⓒ Ⓓ Ⓔ
43. Ⓐ Ⓑ Ⓒ Ⓓ Ⓔ
44. Ⓐ Ⓑ Ⓒ Ⓓ Ⓔ
45. Ⓐ Ⓑ Ⓒ Ⓓ Ⓔ

AP Calculus AB
Test 4

1. Ⓐ Ⓑ Ⓒ Ⓓ Ⓔ
2. Ⓐ Ⓑ Ⓒ Ⓓ Ⓔ
3. Ⓐ Ⓑ Ⓒ Ⓓ Ⓔ
4. Ⓐ Ⓑ Ⓒ Ⓓ Ⓔ
5. Ⓐ Ⓑ Ⓒ Ⓓ Ⓔ
6. Ⓐ Ⓑ Ⓒ Ⓓ Ⓔ
7. Ⓐ Ⓑ Ⓒ Ⓓ Ⓔ
8. Ⓐ Ⓑ Ⓒ Ⓓ Ⓔ
9. Ⓐ Ⓑ Ⓒ Ⓓ Ⓔ
10. Ⓐ Ⓑ Ⓒ Ⓓ Ⓔ
11. Ⓐ Ⓑ Ⓒ Ⓓ Ⓔ
12. Ⓐ Ⓑ Ⓒ Ⓓ Ⓔ
13. Ⓐ Ⓑ Ⓒ Ⓓ Ⓔ
14. Ⓐ Ⓑ Ⓒ Ⓓ Ⓔ
15. Ⓐ Ⓑ Ⓒ Ⓓ Ⓔ
16. Ⓐ Ⓑ Ⓒ Ⓓ Ⓔ
17. Ⓐ Ⓑ Ⓒ Ⓓ Ⓔ
18. Ⓐ Ⓑ Ⓒ Ⓓ Ⓔ
19. Ⓐ Ⓑ Ⓒ Ⓓ Ⓔ
20. Ⓐ Ⓑ Ⓒ Ⓓ Ⓔ
21. Ⓐ Ⓑ Ⓒ Ⓓ Ⓔ
22. Ⓐ Ⓑ Ⓒ Ⓓ Ⓔ
23. Ⓐ Ⓑ Ⓒ Ⓓ Ⓔ

24. Ⓐ Ⓑ Ⓒ Ⓓ Ⓔ
25. Ⓐ Ⓑ Ⓒ Ⓓ Ⓔ
26. Ⓐ Ⓑ Ⓒ Ⓓ Ⓔ
27. Ⓐ Ⓑ Ⓒ Ⓓ Ⓔ
28. Ⓐ Ⓑ Ⓒ Ⓓ Ⓔ
29. Ⓐ Ⓑ Ⓒ Ⓓ Ⓔ
30. Ⓐ Ⓑ Ⓒ Ⓓ Ⓔ
31. Ⓐ Ⓑ Ⓒ Ⓓ Ⓔ
32. Ⓐ Ⓑ Ⓒ Ⓓ Ⓔ
33. Ⓐ Ⓑ Ⓒ Ⓓ Ⓔ
34. Ⓐ Ⓑ Ⓒ Ⓓ Ⓔ
35. Ⓐ Ⓑ Ⓒ Ⓓ Ⓔ
36. Ⓐ Ⓑ Ⓒ Ⓓ Ⓔ
37. Ⓐ Ⓑ Ⓒ Ⓓ Ⓔ
38. Ⓐ Ⓑ Ⓒ Ⓓ Ⓔ
39. Ⓐ Ⓑ Ⓒ Ⓓ Ⓔ
40. Ⓐ Ⓑ Ⓒ Ⓓ Ⓔ
41. Ⓐ Ⓑ Ⓒ Ⓓ Ⓔ
42. Ⓐ Ⓑ Ⓒ Ⓓ Ⓔ
43. Ⓐ Ⓑ Ⓒ Ⓓ Ⓔ
44. Ⓐ Ⓑ Ⓒ Ⓓ Ⓔ
45. Ⓐ Ⓑ Ⓒ Ⓓ Ⓔ

AP Calculus AB
Test 5

1. Ⓐ Ⓑ Ⓒ Ⓓ Ⓔ
2. Ⓐ Ⓑ Ⓒ Ⓓ Ⓔ
3. Ⓐ Ⓑ Ⓒ Ⓓ Ⓔ
4. Ⓐ Ⓑ Ⓒ Ⓓ Ⓔ
5. Ⓐ Ⓑ Ⓒ Ⓓ Ⓔ
6. Ⓐ Ⓑ Ⓒ Ⓓ Ⓔ
7. Ⓐ Ⓑ Ⓒ Ⓓ Ⓔ
8. Ⓐ Ⓑ Ⓒ Ⓓ Ⓔ
9. Ⓐ Ⓑ Ⓒ Ⓓ Ⓔ
10. Ⓐ Ⓑ Ⓒ Ⓓ Ⓔ
11. Ⓐ Ⓑ Ⓒ Ⓓ Ⓔ
12. Ⓐ Ⓑ Ⓒ Ⓓ Ⓔ
13. Ⓐ Ⓑ Ⓒ Ⓓ Ⓔ
14. Ⓐ Ⓑ Ⓒ Ⓓ Ⓔ
15. Ⓐ Ⓑ Ⓒ Ⓓ Ⓔ
16. Ⓐ Ⓑ Ⓒ Ⓓ Ⓔ
17. Ⓐ Ⓑ Ⓒ Ⓓ Ⓔ
18. Ⓐ Ⓑ Ⓒ Ⓓ Ⓔ
19. Ⓐ Ⓑ Ⓒ Ⓓ Ⓔ
20. Ⓐ Ⓑ Ⓒ Ⓓ Ⓔ
21. Ⓐ Ⓑ Ⓒ Ⓓ Ⓔ
22. Ⓐ Ⓑ Ⓒ Ⓓ Ⓔ
23. Ⓐ Ⓑ Ⓒ Ⓓ Ⓔ

24. Ⓐ Ⓑ Ⓒ Ⓓ Ⓔ
25. Ⓐ Ⓑ Ⓒ Ⓓ Ⓔ
26. Ⓐ Ⓑ Ⓒ Ⓓ Ⓔ
27. Ⓐ Ⓑ Ⓒ Ⓓ Ⓔ
28. Ⓐ Ⓑ Ⓒ Ⓓ Ⓔ
29. Ⓐ Ⓑ Ⓒ Ⓓ Ⓔ
30. Ⓐ Ⓑ Ⓒ Ⓓ Ⓔ
31. Ⓐ Ⓑ Ⓒ Ⓓ Ⓔ
32. Ⓐ Ⓑ Ⓒ Ⓓ Ⓔ
33. Ⓐ Ⓑ Ⓒ Ⓓ Ⓔ
34. Ⓐ Ⓑ Ⓒ Ⓓ Ⓔ
35. Ⓐ Ⓑ Ⓒ Ⓓ Ⓔ
36. Ⓐ Ⓑ Ⓒ Ⓓ Ⓔ
37. Ⓐ Ⓑ Ⓒ Ⓓ Ⓔ
38. Ⓐ Ⓑ Ⓒ Ⓓ Ⓔ
39. Ⓐ Ⓑ Ⓒ Ⓓ Ⓔ
40. Ⓐ Ⓑ Ⓒ Ⓓ Ⓔ
41. Ⓐ Ⓑ Ⓒ Ⓓ Ⓔ
42. Ⓐ Ⓑ Ⓒ Ⓓ Ⓔ
43. Ⓐ Ⓑ Ⓒ Ⓓ Ⓔ
44. Ⓐ Ⓑ Ⓒ Ⓓ Ⓔ
45. Ⓐ Ⓑ Ⓒ Ⓓ Ⓔ

AP Calculus AB
Test 6

1. Ⓐ Ⓑ Ⓒ Ⓓ Ⓔ
2. Ⓐ Ⓑ Ⓒ Ⓓ Ⓔ
3. Ⓐ Ⓑ Ⓒ Ⓓ Ⓔ
4. Ⓐ Ⓑ Ⓒ Ⓓ Ⓔ
5. Ⓐ Ⓑ Ⓒ Ⓓ Ⓔ
6. Ⓐ Ⓑ Ⓒ Ⓓ Ⓔ
7. Ⓐ Ⓑ Ⓒ Ⓓ Ⓔ
8. Ⓐ Ⓑ Ⓒ Ⓓ Ⓔ
9. Ⓐ Ⓑ Ⓒ Ⓓ Ⓔ
10. Ⓐ Ⓑ Ⓒ Ⓓ Ⓔ
11. Ⓐ Ⓑ Ⓒ Ⓓ Ⓔ
12. Ⓐ Ⓑ Ⓒ Ⓓ Ⓔ
13. Ⓐ Ⓑ Ⓒ Ⓓ Ⓔ
14. Ⓐ Ⓑ Ⓒ Ⓓ Ⓔ
15. Ⓐ Ⓑ Ⓒ Ⓓ Ⓔ
16. Ⓐ Ⓑ Ⓒ Ⓓ Ⓔ
17. Ⓐ Ⓑ Ⓒ Ⓓ Ⓔ
18. Ⓐ Ⓑ Ⓒ Ⓓ Ⓔ
19. Ⓐ Ⓑ Ⓒ Ⓓ Ⓔ
20. Ⓐ Ⓑ Ⓒ Ⓓ Ⓔ
21. Ⓐ Ⓑ Ⓒ Ⓓ Ⓔ
22. Ⓐ Ⓑ Ⓒ Ⓓ Ⓔ
23. Ⓐ Ⓑ Ⓒ Ⓓ Ⓔ

24. Ⓐ Ⓑ Ⓒ Ⓓ Ⓔ
25. Ⓐ Ⓑ Ⓒ Ⓓ Ⓔ
26. Ⓐ Ⓑ Ⓒ Ⓓ Ⓔ
27. Ⓐ Ⓑ Ⓒ Ⓓ Ⓔ
28. Ⓐ Ⓑ Ⓒ Ⓓ Ⓔ
29. Ⓐ Ⓑ Ⓒ Ⓓ Ⓔ
30. Ⓐ Ⓑ Ⓒ Ⓓ Ⓔ
31. Ⓐ Ⓑ Ⓒ Ⓓ Ⓔ
32. Ⓐ Ⓑ Ⓒ Ⓓ Ⓔ
33. Ⓐ Ⓑ Ⓒ Ⓓ Ⓔ
34. Ⓐ Ⓑ Ⓒ Ⓓ Ⓔ
35. Ⓐ Ⓑ Ⓒ Ⓓ Ⓔ
36. Ⓐ Ⓑ Ⓒ Ⓓ Ⓔ
37. Ⓐ Ⓑ Ⓒ Ⓓ Ⓔ
38. Ⓐ Ⓑ Ⓒ Ⓓ Ⓔ
39. Ⓐ Ⓑ Ⓒ Ⓓ Ⓔ
40. Ⓐ Ⓑ Ⓒ Ⓓ Ⓔ
41. Ⓐ Ⓑ Ⓒ Ⓓ Ⓔ
42. Ⓐ Ⓑ Ⓒ Ⓓ Ⓔ
43. Ⓐ Ⓑ Ⓒ Ⓓ Ⓔ
44. Ⓐ Ⓑ Ⓒ Ⓓ Ⓔ
45. Ⓐ Ⓑ Ⓒ Ⓓ Ⓔ

INSTALLING REA'S SOFTWARE

System Requirements.

Macintosh: Any Macintosh with a 68020 or higher processor or Power Macintosh, 4 MB of RAM memory minimum, System 7.1 or later. At least 5 MB of hard disk space available.

Windows: Any PC with 4 MB of RAM memory minimum, Windows 3.1x, Windows 95, or Windows 98. At least 5 MB of hard disk space available.

MACINTOSH INSTALLATION

1. Insert the AP Calculus AB TEST*ware*® CD into the CD-ROM drive.

2. Double-click on the REA AP Calculus AB Installer icon. The installer will automatically place the program into a folder entitled "REA AP Calculus AB". If the name and location are suitable, click the Install button. If you want to change this, type over the existing information, and then click Install.

3. Start REA AP Calculus AB TEST*ware*® by double-clicking on its icon.

WINDOWS INSTALLATION

1. Insert the AP Calculus AB TEST*ware*® CD into the CD-ROM drive.

2. From the Start Menu, choose the Run command. When the Run dialog box appears, type d:\setup (where d is the letter of your CD-ROM drive) at the prompt and click OK.

3. The installation process will begin. A dialog box proposing the directory "REA_CALC" will appear. If the name and location are suitable, click OK. If you wish to specify a different name or location, type it in and click OK.

4. Start REA AP Calculus AB TEST*ware*® by double-clicking on its icon.

TECHNICAL SUPPORT

REA TEST*ware*® is backed by toll-free customer / technical support. For problems with **installation or operation of your software**, contact Chariot Software Group. Any problems with the book should be directed to Research & Education Association.

Chariot Software Group
Phone: 1-800-242-7468 (Pacific Time)
FAX: 1-800-800-4540
America On-line: Chariot TS
Internet: csg.support@chariot.com

USING YOUR INTERACTIVE TEST*ware*®

REA's AP Calculus AB TEST*ware*® is **EASY** to **LEARN AND USE**. To achieve maximum benefits, we recommend that you take a few minutes to go through the on-screen tutorial on your computer. The "screen buttons" are also explained here to familiarize you with the program.

Program Help and Test Directions

To get help at any time during the test, choose the **Program Help** button which reviews basic functions of the program. The **Test Directions** button allows you to review the specific exam directions during any part of the test.

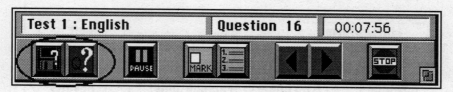

Stop Test

At any time during the test or when you are finished taking the test, click on the **Stop** button. The program will forward you to the following screen.

This screen allows you to go to the next test section, suspend or quit the test, or it can return you to the last question accessed prior to clicking the **Stop** button.

Arrow Buttons

When an answer is selected, click on the Right Arrow button or press the Return key to proceed to the next question.

Mark Questions

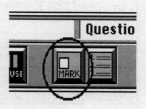

If you are unsure about an answer to a particular question, the program allows you to mark it for later review. Flag the question by clicking on the **Mark** button.

Table of Contents

To review all marked questions, review answer choices, or skip to any question within a test section, click on the **Table of Contents** button.

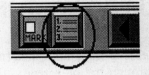

Results

Review and analyze your performance on the test by clicking on the **Results** button.

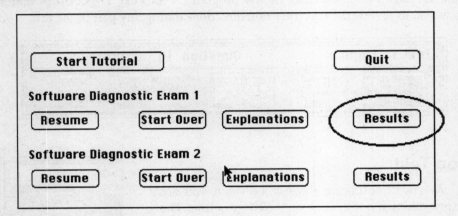

Explanations

In Explanations mode, click on the **Explanation** button to pop up a detailed explanation to any question. At the end of every explanation is a page reference to the appropriate review section in the book.

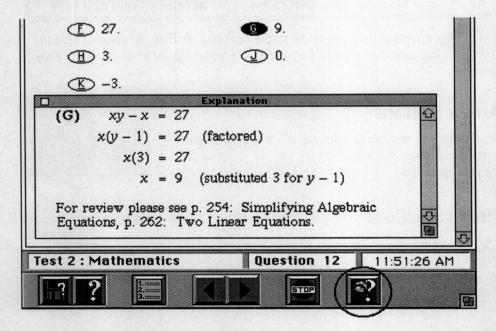

The
Secret Life
of School
Supplies

The Secret Life of School Supplies

Vicki Cobb

Illustrated by Bill Morrison

J. B. LIPPINCOTT   NEW YORK

The author gratefully acknowledges the assistance of the following people: Kathy Dinan, the New Rochelle Wildcliff Museum's papermaker; Dan Lent of the Technological Association of the Pulp and Paper Industry; Greg Neff of Binney & Smith; Reese Schmidt of Shaeffer Eaton; Shirley Heimbuch of the Bic Pen Co.; Peter Columbus of Borden's Chemical Co. A special thanks to Judith Fried for all her research leg work.

Library of Congress Cataloging in Publication Data
Cobb, Vicki.
   The secret life of school supplies.

   SUMMARY: Discusses the scientific and technological principals involved in the manufacture of such school supplies as paper, ink, pencils, chalk, glue and erasers.
   Includes experiments and formulas for making your own supplies.
   I. Paper—Juvenile literature.   II. Ink—Juvenile literature.   III. Writing—Materials and instruments—Juvenile literature.   IV. Adhesive—Juvenile literature.   [1. Paper   2. Ink.   3. Writing—Materials and instruments.   4. Adhesives]   I. Morrison, Bill, 1935-   ill.   II. Title.
TS1230.C6   670   81-47108
ISBN 0-397-31924-X   AACR2
ISBN 0-397-31925-8 (lib. bdg.)

2   3   4   5   6   7   8   9   10

First Edition

For Theo whose love of pen and ink is no secret

Contents

The Secret Life of School Supplies

1 We Thought You'd Never Ask

If your school supplies could talk and tell you the stories of how they came to be, you would be surprised. Paper, pencils, pens, and paste didn't just appear, ready-made, on your desk as they exist today. Each represents a long history of human successes and failures, discoveries and inventions, based on the best scientific and technological knowledge available. In their own way, your seemingly simple school supplies represent some of the greatest technological achievements the world has ever known. Think of what life would be like without paper, or ink, or pencils. Each is so unique that there is no good substitute for it. Yet they are so commonplace, inexpensive, and good at their jobs that most of us simply take them for granted. It's our guess that you would be amazed at how much you *don't* know about these ordinary objects of daily life. It's not that their science and technology is classified information. It's just that people never stop to ask.

In this book we do ask the questions. What are the unique scientific properties that enable each kind of school supply to do its job? How can you create your own at home? What are the basic principles of science behind each object? These questions and more are asked in each chapter. You can discover the answers yourself by doing your own experiments and getting involved with your school supplies in ways you never dreamed possible.

One of the secrets in the life story of school supplies is the excitement of discovery experienced long ago by some scientist or inventor, whose name may be lost to history. Now you, too, can experience the same thrill of looking at the familiar in a new light. You, too, can find yourself shaking your head in amazement, as they must have, exclaiming to yourself, "I never thought of it that way!" School supplies, for all their ordinariness, are,

after all, products of human creativity. People dreamed them up, made them, refined them, and looked to nature as their source and inspiration in the process. The essence of such discovery is hard to talk about. It is yours, however, through this book.

Here's how to use this book: You can, first of all, simply read it as you might read any book of non-fiction. We've included a great deal of background on the history of technology behind modern products, always stressing the principles without getting bogged down in details. Second, you can use this book as a laboratory manual. We've given lots of procedures for experiments. These procedures work. We've checked them all out in our home laboratory. But you may think of another way to do them. Don't let us stop you! No book has *ever* been the final word to any creative experimenter. Perhaps you will make discoveries no one else has made. Trust your own hunches. Follow up your own results. Think of this book as a beginning.

Your school supplies can be the start of a scientific adventure! Discover their secret life.

2 Paper

The paper this book is printed on, the paper you write on, and just about all the paper you use in your daily life is a modern invention, about one hundred years old. Paper, as you know it, is inexpensive and plentiful. It's used for a lot more than written communication and record keeping. You'll find it as the main packaging material of most of the products you buy. You dry your hands on it, blow your nose in it, eat off it, drink out of it, carry groceries in it, wrap garbage in it, and you'll find it in the construction of furniture and houses. It has even been known to show up as clothing.

Paper has not always been so commonplace. Paper in abundance was made possible by two ground-breaking steps in manufacturing. First, there was the invention of a paper-making machine, the Fourdrinier, around 1803, which replaced the slow process of making paper by hand, sheet by sheet. Instead of producing individual sheets, the Fourdrinier produces a huge roll of a seemingly endless sheet. Second, in the 1850s, a process for using wood as the raw material for paper was developed. Early paper had been made mostly from rags and other fibrous materials that were not as easy to harvest or as plentiful as wood. These two advances in technology led to the tremendous growth of the paper industry as the production of paper from wood gradually took over. But paper is not a new idea. In fact, modern paper was invented almost two thousand years ago.

The invention of modern paper is credited to Ts'ai Lun, a Chinese nobleman, who lived about 100 A.D. He made paper from bamboo and mulberry stalks. His paper was a big improvement over the writing material available at that time, which had been invented about 2000 B.C. That was a mat made from an Egyptian reed called *papyrus* from which we get the word "paper." Papyrus was so thick that writings were stored as rolled-up scrolls. Ts'ai Lun's paper was thin enough to make a pile of pages. Thus books were now possible.

All paper has one idea in common. Here's how you can see it: Tear a sheet of paper. Stroke the torn edge several times between your thumb and forefinger. Look closely at the torn edge. (A magnifying glass helps.) You'll see a fringe of tiny, threadlike fibers. Paper is a mat of millions of such tiny fibers pressed together. Tear different kinds of paper you have around the house: paper napkins, stationery, newsprint, tissues, etc. In some paper the fibers are closely knit, some paper is loosely woven, some paper has a filler between the fibers, some is coated, some has a textured design. But all of the paper has those tiny threads sticking out of the torn edge.

You can begin your lab work on school supplies by investigating paper. The experiments in this chapter will show you the principles of paper making, as well as the properties of paper and how to test some of these properties.

☆ Recycled Paper: Forming the Matted Sheet

During manufacturing, a sheet of paper starts out being about 99 percent water and 1 percent fiber and ends up being about 90 percent fiber and 10 percent water. To see how this happens we're giving directions for making recycled paper. As we mentioned earlier, the actual making of a sheet of paper was one of the two major problems in paper manufacturing. The other was finding a source of fibers. We've divided the two problems here as well. First, we'll give you directions so you can see what paper fibers look like before they become paper. A mixture of paper fibers in water is called a *slurry*. By making paper from paper, you can see what a good paper-making slurry should look like. Then you will be better prepared to know what to look for when you experiment with other fibers.

Materials and Equipment
- 20 sheets of bathroom tissue
- mixing bowl
- eggbeater or blender
- about 2 cups of water
- ½ cup liquid laundry starch
- 2″ square wire screening
- rolling pin
- blotting paper, pieces of an old army blanket, or newspaper
- iron

We selected bathroom tissue as the raw material for recycled paper because it is made to disintegrate easily in water. Most other papers have sizing added that fills up space between fibers and gives them "wet strength."

Procedure
Tear the tissue into small pieces. Put them in the blender or a bowl with the water. Blend or beat the mixture until it is cloudy and smooth with no big pieces. Notice the size of the fibers in the slurry. They are almost too small to see with the naked eye. Pour your slurry into the mixing bowl and add the liquid laundry starch. Stir in additional water if necessary to make a depth of three or four inches.

The actual making of a sheet of paper involves catching a thin, even layer of fibers on a wire screen. Handmade or "laid" paper is made in a mold with a wire screen bottom and a flat open frame, called a *deckle,* that fits over the screen. The deckle traps the slurry in a rectangular shape. After the water drains off, the deckle is removed. In handmade papers the deckle produces a tapered, ragged, "deckle" edge that stationers find attractive. You can find stationery that has an artificially produced deckle edge on machine-made paper. You don't need a deckle to make paper if you're not fussy about having a straight edge.

You can use wire screening that is used for windows or you can use an even finer screening. The smaller the holes in the screen, the smoother your finished sheet will be. We used screening from a "spatter shield." This is a gadget found in houseware departments that you use to cover frying pans so that the grease won't spatter out of the pan.

Stir the slurry with your hand so that the fibers are evenly distributed. Quickly dip the wire screen into the mixture at an angle. Remove the screen horizontally so that you catch a web of slurry on the screen. It may take some practice to get an even layer of fiber on the screen. Place the screen, fiber side up, on some blotting paper, old blanket, or newspaper. Cover it with another piece of blotting material. Roll it hard with a rolling pin. Turn the whole thing over and gently remove the wire screen. Your sheet of newly formed paper will stick to the blotter. You can let it dry, or you can iron it dry between blotters with a warm iron.

Observations and Suggestions
Compare your recycled paper with the original tissue. Which is more tightly woven or "denser"? What role does sizing play in making paper more or less dense? Hold the point of a felt-

tipped pen straight down on the original tissue and your recycled paper. On which does the ink spread faster? What effect does the density of paper and sizing have on the absorption of ink? Pull apart each kind of paper. Which is stronger? Paper makers call this difference "tensile strength." Which paper products must have high tensile strength? Which ones should have low tensile strength?

Try making other kinds of recycled paper. Use blotting paper, art paper, and typing paper as your source of fibers. Compare your results for absorption, density, and tensile strength.

The Fourdrinier operates on the same principle as handmade paper. It is basically a long belt or wire screen that moves like a tractor tread. The slurry is poured on like a waterfall at one end. As the screen moves, it also vibrates from side to side, shaking the water through the holes in the screen. The wet paper is pressed through rollers and dried as it comes off the other end of the wire screen. The Fourdrinier makes it possible to manufacture all kinds of paper in giant rolls that is later cut into sheets or otherwise processed.

☆ Lint Paper and Other Fibers

The invention of the Fourdrinier did not solve one of the paper maker's biggest headaches. In fact, the ability to make paper faster made an old problem worse. Paper manufacturers needed to find a larger and larger supply of fibers.

The natural material of paper-making fibers is cellulose, present in all plants. Cellulose makes the walls of plant cells rigid. Cellulose fibers form the threads running down a stalk of celery.

Theoretically, any plant can be a source of cellulose fibers. But, of course, some plants are better than others. Ts'ai Lun took bamboo and mulberry bark, chopped it up, put it in water, and beat it to a pulp with some kind of wooden club. Throughout history there have been all kinds of inventions for getting the cellulose fibers out of plants and rags. People have used mallets and mortars and pestles. They've wet down rags and allowed them to mildew or rot, thus breaking down the fibers. Rotten rags were later boiled in ashes to produce even finer fibers. Then they were washed to clean away the rot and dirt. Although this method created minute fibers that produced a very smooth sheet of paper, it was not useful for later manufacturers because it was wasteful. At least one third of the rags were destroyed in the process.

Early paper mills used human muscle power on all kinds of milling devices to grind fibers to a pulp. In the nineteenth century, a beater invented in Holland, fittingly called the Hollander beater, was the most widely used machine for producing paper pulp from rags.

The fiber problem was solved when people figured out how to get fibers from wood. The inspiration for using wood to make paper is credited to an eighteenth-century Frenchman named Réné Antoine de Reaumur. The source of his inspiration was the wasp. De Reaumur noticed that wasps built their football-shaped nests from wood scrapings combined with their saliva. It took another hundred years, however, before human beings could duplicate the wasps' process. Wood fibers are held together naturally with a strong cementlike substance called *lignin.* Wood couldn't be used as a source of fibers until there was a process for separating the fibers from the lignin on a large scale.

Today the pulp-making process is both mechanical and chemi-

cal. Wood is mechanically broken down by chopping and grinding. Then it is cooked with strong chemicals that dissolve the lignin. The pulp is then washed and bleached depending on its intended use. The higher the quality of paper, the more the pulp is treated to remove traces of lignin. Newsprint is the most inexpensive paper white enough for printing. It still contains a great deal of lignin, which causes newspaper to yellow with age.

The next experiments will give you an idea of the size of the problem pulp makers overcame for producing the tiny fibers needed for good paper.

Rag Paper

Materials and Equipment
- a strip of linen handkerchief
- scissors
- paper-making equipment: bowl, laundry starch, wire screen, rolling pin, blotting material, eggbeater

Procedure
Cut up a strip of rag into the smallest threads you can make. You can further break down the fibers by boiling them and beating them. To do it right takes several hours. *Don't* put the threads in a blender as you may burn out the motor. When the fibers are ready, make a slurry and make paper as you did in the last experiment.

Observations and Suggestions
Rag paper has been known to last as long as eight hundred years without falling apart. It does not need sizing to have tensile strength. The fibers knit together with a few horizontal forward-and-back and from side-to-side shakes of the screen as the water is draining off. The finest paper today is still made from rags and rag is often added to high quality paper for strength. Rag pickers throughout history collected rags from people for paper making. All kinds of rags have been used, including the wrappings from Egyptian mummies.

Lint Paper

Materials and Equipment
– lint from the dryer
– paper-making equipment (as in previous experiment)
– blender or food processor

Procedure
In our search for fibers we chopped up absorbent cotton and cheesecloth and found that neither produced the proper slurry. We boiled sawdust and produced one smelly failure. Then we

had the insight of using lint from the lint trap in a clothes dryer. "Eureka," we yelled, as the various colored fibers separated in a pot of water into a slightly clumpy slurry. A few turns of the blender refined the mixture. Our lint was multicolored because we got it from a commercial dryer many people had used. If you want to be a purist, clean out the lint trap and make your own white lint by drying a new white flannel garment or white towels. Adjust the amount of water you add to your slurry depending on how much lint you gather.

Observations and Suggestions
Experiment with different fibers. A blender or food processor is almost essential. Try marsh grass, dandelion fuzz, milkweed, corn silk, pineapple tops, cabbage, and celery. An expert in hand-made paper making told us that these fibers should work, although you may have to strengthen them with paper or rag fibers. She also told us that carrots don't work. Their fiber content is too low.

☆ Properties of Paper

How would you describe paper so that you can distinguish it from all other materials? The identifying characteristics of any material are its "properties." All materials have general properties, such as weight and volume. But it is the special properties that make one material different from all others. A good understanding of the special properties of a substance does more than identify it. It can also tell you how it may be used. All paper has certain properties in common. Differences in special properties determine whether finished paper will be used for printing, wrapping, or wiping up.

The next experiments demonstrate the basic properties of all paper.

Grain

Machine-made paper is formed on a moving screen. This motion affects the direction in which the fibers align. More fibers line up parallel to the direction of the screen's motion than at right angles to it. This produces a grain in the paper.

Paper folds more easily with the grain than against it. You can use this information to find the grain in any sheet of paper. Here's how: Take two identical sheets of paper. Bend one sheet along the long end without creasing it. Pinch it about one inch from the fold. Do the same thing with the other sheet in a direction perpendicular to the first bend. Bend it across its width. Compare the size and shape of the loops you form. The paper bent with the grain will have a much flatter and narrower loop than the paper folded against the grain.

Brightness

Brightness is the amount of light paper reflects. Among white papers, brightness is determined by several factors. These include how highly purified the fibers are (that is, how much lignin is still present), the kinds of fillers and sizing used, and how dense the paper is. Papers that are less dense, or porous, because of air pockets, are brighter than denser papers. Air pockets reflect high amounts of light.

You can tell the difference in brightness between many kinds of papers simply by looking at them. Newsprint is clearly not as bright as typing paper. However, we have designed a test that helps you see differences that can't be seen as easily when you hold one sample of white paper against another.

You will need a piece of black construction paper, scissors, and several different samples of white paper. Cut one-inch square windows in the black construction paper at least an inch and a half apart. Under bright illumination, put a different sample of white paper under each window. The contrast with the black frame makes it easy to see differences in brightness.

Most paper used for printing reflects between 60 and 90 percent of the light hitting its surface. When fluorescent dyes are added into coated papers, the brightness is almost 100 percent. The legibility of print depends on the contrast between the darkness of the ink and the brightness of the paper.

Opacity

The degree to which a sheet of paper will prevent you from seeing through it is its opacity. Printers call it the "show-through" of paper and, as you can imagine, it is of great importance to printers who want to print on both sides of a sheet of paper. Paper manufacturers increase the opacity of paper by adding special mineral fillers, such as clay and talc, to the pulp and by coating finished paper with dyes.

A simple way to compare the opacity of different papers is to place them over the black-and-white design on the next page. The design will show through some papers more than others. Another method of measuring opacity is to use your black win-

dows from the brightness experiment. Use two samples of each kind of paper. Put a sheet of white paper behind one sample and a sheet of black paper behind the other. The black border of the windows will exaggerate the loss of brightness. You can compare this loss of brightness as a measure of opacity.

Curl

Although paper seems pretty dry, all paper still contains a small amount of moisture. It will also absorb moisture from the air. Changes in moisture affect the size of paper; it swells. If more moisture and, therefore, more swelling occurs on one side of a sheet than on the other, the paper curls. In this experiment, the less dense the paper, the more it will curl, so curling is a measure of how tightly packed the paper fibers are.

Preheat the oven to 400° F.

Cut strips of different kinds of paper one inch wide by four inches across the grain. Dip each strip of paper in water and lay it flat across a cookie sheet. Smooth the strips with your fingers so they adhere to the cookie sheet. Heat the strips for fifteen minutes or until dry. We tested different kinds of paper and found that paper towels had the most curl, and blotting paper the least. It is also clear that blotting paper is much more dense than the toweling. Neither has any fillers to cut down on absorption.

Watermarks and Two-Sided Characteristics

When paper is still a newly formed wet film, traces of events that happen to it remain after the sheet is dried. You can see the results of these events in much the same way you can see a footprint in dried mud. If you hold a sheet of paper up to the light, you can just make out the series of parallel lines that were left there by the screen. The fibers are aligned slightly differently over the wires because the water didn't drain quite so fast under the wires as between them. Thus the direction of the fibers makes a pattern you can see. You can also see the marks the screen left behind in your handmade papers.

Watermarks are invisible designs made during manufacturing when the web passes over a raised design on the dandy roller, which is the first roller to pass over the newly formed paper. The paper becomes thinner, and more dense, and less opaque. Light passes more easily through a watermark than through the surrounding paper. Thus watermarks become visible when you hold paper up to the light or when you wet it. Stamp collectors look for watermarks on stamps by soaking them. You can make a watermark on ordinary writing paper. Soak a sheet of paper in water until it is completely wet. Smooth the wet sheet on a cookie sheet and place a dry sheet over it. Draw a design on the dry sheet with a pencil or ball-point pen. Be careful to press hard without tearing the paper. Remove the top sheet. You'll see the impression of your watermark on the wet sheet. The design will disappear when the paper is dry (unless you hold it up to the light), but it will be easily visible if you wet the paper again.

Paper is formed on a wire screen. Thus the underside will bear the marks of the screen, while the topside, which is pressed against felt during the drying process, will have a smoother finish. Fold over a sheet of paper and feel both sides at once with the tips of two fingers. The felt side is smoother than the wire side. If printers are only printing on one side of a sheet of paper, they prefer to print on the felt side because of its smoother finish.

Absorption

The rate at which paper absorbs water, that is, acts like a sponge, will determine its use. Paper that is used for blotters, or for toweling, must be very absorbent. Paper that will be used for ink should be less absorbent or the ink will spread when it comes in contact with the paper. Paper manufacturers change the absorption of paper by adding different fillers and sizers during manufacturing. One laid paper crafter we know dips her rag paper in a very dilute solution of animal hide glue to prepare it to receive ink.

You can compare the absorption rates of different papers in an experiment. Cut strips of different samples (with the grain) that are a half inch wide and five inches long. Put the ends in a glass of water that is filled to a depth of one inch. Fold the top ends over the rim of the glass to hold them in place. Let the experiment stand. See where the water climbs the fastest.

3 Ink

Where would civilization be today without ink? One thing is certain, historians would not be studying old manuscripts. Perhaps the single most important quality of ink is that it stays legible for centuries, thus preserving written records of past generations. Ink is as old as history. In fact, it's fair to say without ink there might not be any history.

Ink has a distinct identity that no one confuses with paint or dye. Ink is defined as a liquid for making marks on a surface that will retain those marks. It is not used normally to coat surfaces, as is paint, or to color materials, as is dye. Ink can be many different colors, although the most popular shades for writing inks are blue and black. It can be applied with different kinds of writing instruments (more on this in chapter 4) and printing presses. Most ink winds up on paper, although it can be used on other surfaces. You read it, write messages with it, mark your laundry with it, and sign your name to important documents with it. If it accidentally winds up in the wrong place, you may be faced with the challenge of stain removal. Often soap and water won't work and strong chemicals such as bleaches and acids, which will do the job, can also permanently destroy the surface of the stained material. Indelible and permanent inks have a way of living up to their reputation.

The earliest ink wasn't ink as we know it today. Historians think it was probably soot or charcoal left over from a fire. Scratches were made on stone or clay tablets and soot was rubbed into the scratches. When the surface was wiped clean, the dark material remained in the scratches. Not exactly an efficient way to dash off notes!

Writing ink and printing ink are different from each other. Printing ink is more like paint and has an oil base, while writing ink usually contains water. The experiments in this chapter are limited to writing inks, the kinds you're most likely to get your hands on. You'll be experimenting in creating your own inks and analyzing existing inks. Believe us, these experiments can make their mark!

☆ Permanent Ink

Ink is made up of three parts that vary according to the intended use. One part is the coloring agent, which can be a pigment or a dye (or both). A pigment is finely divided colored material that does not dissolve. Instead, it is held in suspension by the liquid of the ink, which is the second part and is called the *vehicle*. Pigments remain behind on the surface after the vehicle evaporates. Pigments adhere to the writing surface because of the third substance, called the *binder,* that's been added to the ink. A pigment does not sink beneath the surface of the paper. Dyes, on the other hand, do dissolve in the vehicle and will sink beneath the writing surface.

One of the earliest writing inks came from Arabia and contained powdered carbon as the pigment. The source of the carbon was probably charcoal. Honey served as both vehicle and binder.

The honey-soot mixture was dried into cakes to which water was added just before writing. Carbon is a permanent pigment and documents written with carbon ink remain as black as the day they were written. In the next experiment try making your own honey-soot ink.

Materials and Equipment
– sources of finely divided charcoal (see the procedure)
– plates
– toothpicks
– metal teaspoon
– hammer or rolling pin

Procedure
Make different kinds of honey-soot ink by using different sources of carbon. Mix the carbon on a plate with about a half teaspoon of honey. Stir with a toothpick and use the toothpick to write with. Here are some suggestions for obtaining finely divided carbon.

Get some charred wood from a fireplace, or some charcoal for barbecuing. Put it between several sheets of newspaper and pound it to a fine powder with a hammer or rolling pin.

One of the best pure carbon pigments is lampblack that forms when a fuel burns incompletely. You can collect your own lampblack. Since you will be using fire, CHECK WITH AN ADULT BEFORE YOU DO THIS! Light a large candle in a candleholder. Hold the bowl of the spoon over the flame. (Watch that the handle doesn't get too hot.) Lampblack will collect on the bowl of the spoon as an extremely finely divided powder. The spoon prevents the fuel (the wax of the candle) from burning completely and forming carbon dioxide, a colorless gas. The metal in the spoon removes heat from the burning reaction, thus making the burning incomplete. You've stopped a chemical reaction from going to completion. To make ink from the lampblack, put a few drops of honey in the bowl of the spoon and stir in the carbon with a toothpick.

Observations and Suggestions
Compare the inks made with different sources of carbon pigment. Which ink is the most effective? Which carbon is the blackest? Which is the most finely divided? How do these qualities affect the quality of ink? Put a drop of household bleach on your dried ink spot. Does the color fade? What does this tell you about the permanence of carbon pigment inks?

Try using other vehicles besides honey for your inks. Unflavored gelatin can also be used as a vehicle. Soften a package first, according to the directions. Dissolve it in a quarter cup boiling water. Add a few drops of this mixture to your charcoal sample. Compare this ink to ink made with honey. If you add carbon pigment to a few drops of white glue that you have diluted with a few drops of water, the mixture dries and looks very much like India ink.

Modern India ink is made with pure carbon black as a pigment. The vehicle is water. The binder is a chemical that only works in an alkaline (or basic) solution. A word here on alkalis: Alkalis or bases are solutions that affect the colors of certain dyes. They change the dye in litmus paper from pink to blue. They have a slippery feel. You wouldn't want to feel some strong bases, such as lye, that are dangerously corrosive. They are noted for the way they react with another group of solutions known as acids.

Soap, ammonia, and baking soda are common household alkalis. Vinegar, lemon juice, and cream of tartar are acids you
are likely to have at home. Acids and bases react to form a salt
and water.

The alkali that dissolves the binder in India ink is ammonia.
Ammonia in a solution escapes as a gas. Chemists call it a "fugitive" substance because it disappears into the air when the ink
dries. When you write with India ink both the water and the
fugitive ammonia evaporate, leaving behind a mark that is both
indelible and waterproof. India ink won't wash off. It will run
however, under the right conditions, as many a sorry artist has
discovered. If you paint over dried India ink with a basic liquid,
the binder dissolves and the ink runs. Acrylic paints are alkaline.
An artist who paints over an India ink drawing with acrylic
paints will ruin the drawing. What experiments do these facts
suggest to you?

☆ Iron Ink

The most popular writing ink of the eighteenth and nineteenth
centuries contained compounds of iron. Compounds are pure substances that form when simpler pure substances, elements, combine chemically. Water is a compound of hydrogen and oxygen.
Rust is a compound of iron and oxygen. Compounds are often
quite different in their properties from the elements that form
them. A chemist knows that a reaction has taken place when
the end product is different from the materials used at the start.
In the next experiment you will be making a chemical reaction
that produces the iron compounds of writing ink. There are two

ways you know that a chemical reaction is taking place. First, you will see a color change in the experimental solution. Chemists consider a color change as one indication of a chemical reaction. Second, you will see a "precipitate." A precipitate is the formation of tiny particles that do not dissolve in water. They make a clear solution look cloudy. In the reaction you see in this experiment, the cloudiness is as thick and as black as ink. And for several hundred years, it *was* ink.

Materials and Equipment
– a tea bag
– boiling water
– small jars with a cover
– three or four iron-sulfate tablets (sold in drugstores, inexpensively, as *ferrous sulfate,* for iron-deficiency anemia)

Procedure
First you have to remove the colored coating on the ferrous-sulfate tablets. Put three or four tablets in a jar and cover them with water. Stir. You'll see the coating dissolve. Pour off the water and rinse the tablets several times until there is no trace of the coating. The tablets that remain will be white. Add about two teaspoons of hot water and stir. The iron sulfate dissolves. The chalky deposit that remains on the bottom of the jar is a chemically inactive powder used to make the tablets. You can filter your solution, if you wish. Pour it through a funnel lined with coffee filter paper or paper toweling. This step is not necessary, however, as the chalky deposit will always settle on the bottom of the jar. Notice that the iron-sulfate solution is clear and colorless.

Your second solution for this experiment is the strongest tea you can make. Pour about a quarter cup of boiling water over a tea bag in a small jar. Let it brew for at least ten minutes. Remove the tea bag.

Mix the two solutions together. Before using as ink, let it stand overnight.

Observations and Suggestions

When the two solutions are mixed the reaction is immediate. The black precipitate that forms is called iron tannate. The iron in the iron-sulfate solution reacts with a weak acid in tea called tannic acid. A chemist would use the following words to describe the reaction:

Iron sulfate plus tannic acid react to yield iron tannate and sulfuric acid.

If you have heard that sulfuric acid is an especially dangerous substance, you are right. However, in this reaction the amount of sulfuric acid that forms is so small that there is absolutely no danger involved. BUT DON'T DRINK THIS INK!

Use a crow-quill pen and holder to write with your iron-tannate ink. Iron tannate darkens when it is exposed to the oxygen in the air, still another chemical reaction. See if your ink does this. Add a little honey as a binder. Small amounts of honey, corn syrup, or sugar have been added to ink through the ages to make it flow more easily. Gelatin was suggested as a binder for home-made India ink. You might want to experiment to see if it works here. We would guess that it won't. Tannic acid is used for tanning leather. It turns the gelatin in hides into a tough insoluble material. You might get another precipitate if there is still any tannic acid left in your ink. The binder that was used when iron ink was popular is a gum that is not now commercially available.

You can do other experiments using different sources of iron and tannic acid. Try making ink with metallic iron. Use steel wool that doesn't have soap in it. (This may be bought in a hardware store.) Pour strong tea over steel wool and let the mixture sit overnight before you try to write with it. If it looks rusty, you've got rust, or iron oxide, instead of iron tannate. Add a little vinegar to keep the rust from forming.

The best old writing ink contained another iron compound in addition to iron tannate. It was iron gallate, which formed when iron sulfate reacted with gallic acid. Gallic acid is not as readily available as tannic acid. But you may be able to get some if you live near oak trees. Gallic acid is found in oak "galls," which are small bumps found in oak leaves and twigs. Galls form around the eggs of an insect that bores into leaves and twigs to deposit them. The tree reacts to this invasion by forming a swelling as the plant tissues grow around the eggs. The best galls for the manufacturing of old iron ink came from the Middle East. But if you can find oak galls, try making your own gallic acid. Gather leaves and twigs containing the galls. Bruise them with a hammer. Put them in a stainless steel or enamel pot with water to cover. Simmer them, slightly covered, for two hours. Add water as needed to replace the water that evaporates. Separate the gallic-acid solution by straining. Mix a small amount with iron-sulfate solution and add a small amount to your iron-tannate tea. Another possible source of gallic acid is sumac. See if you can get the boiled water of sumac twigs to react with iron sulfate.

We read in one of our old source books about an ink that was made by boiling tea, iron sulfate, and pomegranate peels together.

We're not sure if the pomegranate peels are a source of dye or of gallic acid. Experiment and find out.

☆ Artificially Aging Ink

Careful consideration should be given to the kind of ink used for important documents. Unfortunately, this has not always been the case. Manuscripts written in unstable inks are affected over the years by light, oxygen, and moisture to the point where they are no longer legible. At first there is a discoloration of the pen tracks from black to brown, which slowly spread until the marks are a pale rusty brown. In fact, these marks *are* rust, which is a compound of iron and oxygen. After forty years, one of our sources claimed, all of the ink qualities may be destroyed.

You don't, however, have to wait forty years to see the aging process of iron ink. You can speed up the process to less than an hour.

Materials and Equipment
– large jar and lid (one that contained pickles or mayonnaise)
– household ammonia
– a strip of paper ½" wide x 3" long
– rubber band
– iron ink from the last experiment
– crow-quill pen or toothpick

Procedure
Pour just enough ammonia into the jar to cover the bottom. Screw on the lid so you don't have to smell the fumes.

Put a small dot of iron ink on the end of the strip of paper. Wait until it is completely dry. Fold the top end of the strip up. Hang it over the rim of the jar. The dot should be facing out so you can easily see it through the glass. Hold the strip in place with the rubber band and screw on the lid.

Observations and Suggestions
The spot of ink first turns dark. Then it starts becoming brown and thin so that you can see the paper through it. Eventually the spot becomes completely brown.

Most modern writing inks do not contain iron compounds as pigments. They are mixtures of both pigments and dyes, some of which are affected by an alkaline environment. The ammonia-filled jar is a good place to see just which inks will change due to the alkali. Cut strips of paper. Put a spot of ink at the end of each strip and label the source of the ink at the other end. Fold the paper over the top and hang in place over the rim of the jar. You'll find that some inks change dramatically due to the ammonia. However, when these strips are removed and exposed to air, the original color returns due to the fugitive nature of the ammonia. It evaporates and leaves the ink the way it was originally.

☆ Bleaching and Light Fastness

Many pigments and dyes used in modern inks are affected by light. In time they fade. In the next experiment you compare the light fastness of different inks with their reaction to chemical bleaching.

Materials and Equipment
- different samples of writing inks: felt-tip pens, markers, ball points, etc.
- pencil
- ruler
- paper
- black construction paper
- paper clips
- household bleach
- glass pan

Procedure

Use the ruler and pencil to draw a straight line lengthwise down the center of a sheet of paper. Draw rectangular samples of different inks so that the line passes through the middle of each rectangle. Label each sample so you know where it came from. Cover half of the samples with a sheet of black construction paper lined up against the pencil line. Hold the black paper in place with paper clips. Place in a sunny spot or under a fluorescent light. This part of the experiment is the slow part. It may take a month or more to get results.

Now for the fast part. Make quarter-inch dots of different inks about an inch apart along the edge of a sheet of paper. Label each sample with a pencil. Pour some bleach into a shallow pan to a depth of about one inch. Dip the ink spots in the bleach.

Observations and Suggestions

Some inks will be unaffected, some inks will be slightly faded, and some inks will leave no visible traces.

Inks that contain pigments may be unaffected by bleach. India ink will not be affected. Ball-point ink is a combination of metallic dyes that are not as susceptible to bleach as are the dyes you'll find in markers.

Keep a record of the behavior of different ink samples in bleach and compare them with the samples exposed to light. Lift the black paper and compare both sides of the colored rectangle to see fading. How does light fastness compare to chemical bleaching?

☆ Paper Chromatography Analysis

Most commercial inks are mixtures of dyes and pigments. The vehicle for most of them is water. For these reasons, commercial inks can be analyzed by one of the modern chemist's most useful procedures, namely, paper chromatography.

Chromatography means "writing with color," and it separates mixtures of colored chemicals into their separate components.

Materials and Equipment
- coffee filter paper (or white paper toweling)
- scissors
- pencil
- ruler
- tall jars (such as olive jars or pickle jars)
- cellophane tape
- samples of different inks
- water

Procedure
Cut strips of filter paper a little bit longer than the depth of the jar. They should be about an inch and a half wide. You will be

hanging them over some tape stretched across the top of the jar in such a way that the bottom of the strip almost touches the bottom of the jar.

Draw a horizontal pencil line one inch from the bottom of the strip. Make a quarter-inch spot of ink on the line. Touch the ink samples to the paper on the line and the ink will spread in a circle. Allow it to dry and touch it again. You want to get an intense but small spot of ink on the filter paper. Allow it to dry thoroughly. (If you wish, you can use a hair dryer to blow it dry.) Be sure and label the top of the strip with the type of ink sample.

Put water in the bottom of the jar to a depth of about a half inch. Hang each strip over some tape stretched across the top of the jar. The bottom of the strip should rest freely in the water, but the spot should be above the water level. The filter paper acts like a wick and the water line will move up the paper.

Observations and Suggestions

The water moves up the paper, against gravity, by capillary action. This is the same principle that makes the water level in a straw higher than the water level outside the straw (more on capillarity in the next chapter). Water is both attracted to the paper and to itself, thus the filter paper acts as a wick drawing water up its surface. Water soluble dyes will be carried along the surface of the filter paper by the moving water. Different dyes, however, will travel at different rates with the moving water. Thus they will be separated into separate bands.

If an ink spot does not move, you can conclude that the coloring agent is an insoluble pigment. Ball-point-pen ink is only moderately soluble in water. It is soluble in nail-polish remover. (See

p. 42.) The coloring matter is very highly concentrated metallic dyes that will not move as well in paper chromatography with a water solvent as the more soluble dyes found in felt-tip pens, markers, and fountain-pen inks.

4 Writing Instruments

Want to make a note of something or send someone a letter? No problem. All you have to do is grab a piece of paper and a pencil or pen. It's as easy as ABC. You do it without any special training (other than having learned how to write.)

It wasn't always so easy. Here's what a person had to go through back in the Middle Ages just to write a few words. First the writing surface had to be prepared to receive the ink. One of the earliest writing materials was a very thin, specially prepared sheep or goat skin known as "vellum." The vellum was made by a process of scraping, pressing, and drying. Just before it was to be written on, it was "pounced," which means it was rubbed with pumice, a very fine abrasive. The pumice made the vellum smooth and got rid of any excess grease that prevented the ink from sticking. When paper started replacing vellum, pouncing with powdered resin kept the ink from sinking into the paper too deeply. As writing paper improved, the pounce pot was filled with a kind of chalk powder that was sprinkled on wet ink to

keep it from smudging until it dried. Blotting paper eventually replaced any form of pouncing. So much for preparing the writing surface.

The job that required the most craft and skill was preparing the pen. Early pens were made from goose and duck feathers. In fact, the word "pen" comes from the Latin "penna," meaning feather. In order to prepare a pen, a special knife, fittingly called a *penknife,* was essential. The penknife was first sharpened on an oil stone. Then it was used in a series of steps to carve the tubular end of a goose feather or quill into the shape of a nib. Once all these tasks were accomplished, all you needed was a full ink pot and you were ready to write. For hundreds of years, writing was the job of professionals called *scribes* or *scriveners.* Putting words down on vellum or paper was a highly skilled and time-consuming task.

Today the art of carving nib is all but lost, although penknives are still around as small-bladed knives that serve many uses.

You have a choice of writing with wet or dry writing instruments and in a variety of colors. You can pick a felt-tip pen, ball-point pen, fountain pen, pencil, or crayon to jot your written words.

In this chapter writing instruments are the inspiration for exploring the scientific principles behind these devices.

☆ Instruments for the Ink Pot

The problem solved by a pen is the delivery of a colored liquid to a surface in the form of a line that curves and twists. There are any number of devices that can put ink on paper as wavy lines, but they all have their limitations. Do an experiment to see for yourself.

Materials and Equipment
- ink (or food coloring)
- paper
- scissors
- ruler
- toothpick
- nail
- drinking straw (plastic or paper)
- pen nib in pen holder

Procedure
Dip the toothpick in the ink and draw a straight line from right to left on the piece of paper. When your hand reaches near the edge of the paper, lift it up and start another line at the left-hand side of the paper. Repeat until you run out of ink. Follow

the same procedure using the nail. Cut the straw at an angle and use it as if it were a pen to repeat the procedure. Then use the pen nib in the pen holder.

Now, holding each item as if it were a pen, make continuous curling loops. Try to make the loops as uniform as possible. Use a freshly cut straw, not the straw you used to make the straight line.

Measure the length of the lines you drew. Count the number of loops you made before you ran out of ink.

Observations and Suggestions

Which writing instrument drew the longest line? Which was least effective? What were some of the problems of trying to draw loops with each instrument? What advantage did the straw have over the toothpick and nail? What was its biggest disadvantage?

☆ The Capillarity Equation

You would not be able to put ink on paper for the purpose of writing without a little help from Mother Nature. This help comes in the force of attraction between the liquid ink and the surface of the pen and the liquid ink and the surface of the paper. The force of attraction between a liquid and a surface that allows the liquid to wet the surface is called *capillarity*. Do the following experiment to see capillarity in action.

Materials and Equipment

−3 or 4 plastic straws of different diameters (we used one 2mm in diameter, 3mm, and 7mm)

– a metric ruler showing millimeters
– blotting paper or an absorbent paper napkin
– cotton swabs (optional)
– pencil
– at least one brand of ink
– small glass of water

Procedure
This procedure involves some fairly precise measurement. It may take several trials before you get consistent results.

Dip the straw with the smallest diameter several inches into the water. Slowly remove the straw and hold it up to the light. You will see that some water remains in the end of the straw that will not drip out. The force holding the water in the tube and that which enables it to creep up the tube is capillarity. It is equal to gravity for the weight of liquid in the straw.

Do the same with the two other straws. In each case water remains behind but the height of the water in the tube changes. You will see that the smaller the diameter of the tube, the longer the length of water held by capillarity.

The question this experiment answers is: How does the diameter of a straw affect the volume of liquid held by capillarity? With a pencil, write the diameter of each straw about two inches apart on your blotting paper. Dip the narrowest straw in water. Hold it up to the light to make sure that you have trapped the liquid in the end of the straw. Carefully blot the outside of the straw of excess water with a cotton swab. Now, holding the straw vertically, put the wet end on the blotting paper above the label for that straw's diameter. The water is now more attracted to the paper than it is attracted to the straw and it wets the paper, spreading into a circular blot. The force that allows it to spread on the paper is capillarity in action again. Hold the straw in place, gently lifting it and touching it to the paper in the same spot until all the water is out of the straw and the blot doesn't get any larger. Outline the blot in pencil. Repeat the procedure with straws of other diameters. Make sure that the blot is made only by liquid inside the straw and that each straw is holding its maximum amount by capillarity. You may have to gently wipe the outside of the wet end with a swab and do several trials for each diameter.

Measure the diameters of the blots. Repeat the procedures using different inks.

Observations and Suggestions

Amazing but true, all the blots for any particular liquid will be the same diameter! The narrow straw holds exactly as much liquid by capillarity as the wide straw. Capillarity depends on the nature of the liquid and the degree to which it wets the plastic wall of the straw. Thus all plastic straws will attract the same volume of water regardless of diameter. You will see a difference between water and ink. And if you get really proficient you may be able to measure differences between inks with this procedure.

You can get waxed-paper drinking straws. Compare capillarity of a waxed-paper straw to one of plastic with the same diameter.

☆ The Design of the Nib

By the beginning of the nineteenth century, handwriting was no longer a specialty practiced only by professional scribes. It was a basic skill taught to schoolchildren. The quill pen, which was the most common early writing instrument, had one very important disadvantage: It wore out too quickly. The penknife was kept handy to recarve a worn nib. Although metal nibs made from gold and silver had been around since the sixteenth century, steel nibs that did not wear out so quickly were not generally available until 1829, when they were first manufactured in Birmingham, England. Fifty years later, the steel nib had almost completely replaced the quill. You can easily buy steel nibs of the classic "crow-quill" shape in stationery and art stores. You can also buy nibs with other shapes that draw different kinds of lines.

The slit in a crow-quill nib is there to give the steel flexibility. When you write you press with different amounts of force. If you try to write with a nail or knitting needle dipped in ink, you can see how hard it is to get the ink to flow evenly as you change pressure on the tip. Experiment with different crow-quill nibs. Feel how hard you have to press to get the slit to separate enough to form two lines. Some crow quills have a tiny ball at the end. This allows the pen to move more smoothly over the paper without scratching. Try writing your name with different kinds of nibs. Some will feel more comfortable for your handwriting than others. The design of nibs changed over the years as the style of writing changed.

The hole in the nib acts as a reservoir for ink. Capillarity and surface tension keep the ink in the hole. You can compare the amount of ink different styles of nibs will hold by dipping each once and drawing lines on blotting paper until you run out of ink. Measure the length of the lines. Fill in a hole with a dab of rubber cement. Measure the difference in the amount of ink the nib now holds.

☆ Fountain Pens

The inconvenience of interrupting one's thoughts while writing in order to renew your supply of ink presented an irresistible challenge. A number of inventors thought up solutions to the problem of supplying a nib with a large reservoir of ink.

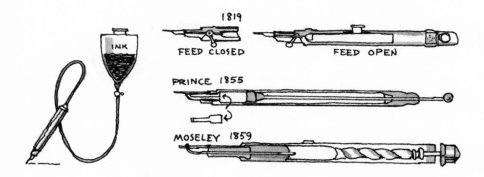

There is still room for creativity. Try your hand at building a better fountain pen!

☆ Ball-Point Pens

The basic principle of a ball-point pen is the delivery of ink to paper by a tiny ball rotating in a socket connected to an ink supply.

Take apart a ball-point pen to see how it works. We used a Bic pen. The job is messy so do it on some newspaper. To remove the ink tube and ball point from the clear plasic barrel of the pen, gently twist the tip. It easily comes out of the barrel. Now remove the ink tube from the tip by gently pulling it apart. Let the ink run into a bottle cap. Blow it out from the clear end. Notice how thick it is. The consistency of the ball-point-pen ink is one of the secrets to its operation. How does ball-point ink compare to writing ink?

Use a magnifying glass to inspect the ball. You can remove the metal tip from its plastic case by holding the plastic casing with one pair of pliers and pulling on the metal tip with another. Clean your fingers with nail-polish remover. Do a paper chromatograph of ball-point ink to analyze the pigments. Put a spot about one inch from the bottom of a strip of coffee filter paper. Let the spot dry. Use the same procedure you used for chromatography on p. 31, only use nail-polish remover instead of water.

Ball-point ink is delivered to paper by a tiny ball that is 0.7 to 1.0 mm in diameter. Since the amount of ink that covers the ball is so small, ball-point ink contains very concentrated pigments in order to make the line as dark as ordinary writing ink. The amount of ink in a ball-point refill will draw a continuous line 1500 to 2000 yards long. (A football field is 100 yards long.) The same amount of writing ink will draw a line between 80 and 100 yards long.

Although capillarity is important in feeding the ink to the ball through a small tube, gravity is also an important force that affects the ball-point pen. See how long a line you can draw writing upside down, before the ink no longer feeds the ball. Compare lengths of lines made by different brands of ball points to see if there is any difference.

The continuous feeding of ink to the ball depends on a vacuum seal between the ball and the ink. If you write upside down long enough, you can introduce an air bubble behind the ball, breaking the seal. If that happens, the pen is useless for all practical purposes. It will no longer write right side up. For this reason it is not a good idea to keep ball-point pens upside down in your pocket. If your body heat warms up the ink, air can leak out the back of the tube. Your pen has "exploded" in your pocket. Messy business indeed!

☆ Chalk

A hundred years ago chalk would be the most familiar writing instrument for children entering school. They learned to form letters with a slate and "slate pencil," which was chalk in a special holder. The slate was a small blackboard they could hold in their hands to practice writing. It was too difficult to master the technique of pen and ink at the same time as learning handwriting. Pen and ink were used by older students. Chalk is, of course, still used in schools today. No one has found a cheaper way to put words on a large surface that everyone in a class

can see—words that can be easily erased, so that new words can be displayed.

Chalk has two properties that serve its purpose as a writing instrument. First, it is white, so it can easily be seen in contrast to a black slate surface or the more common modern green chalkboard. Second, it is an extremely soft mineral. It can be rubbed on a surface to form a streak, and the powder of the streak can be easily rubbed off.

Hardness is a property that is measured by mineralogists. They define hardness as "the resistance offered by a smooth surface to a scratch made by a point or edge." A diamond is the hardest substance on earth. It can scratch all other minerals and nothing can make a mark on it except another diamond. Several minerals have been selected as examples of increasing hardness on a scale of one to ten. The softest mineral is talc. Here are some standards for you to rank the hardness of substances you are likely to have around your home:

No. 1—the softest of minerals leave flakes on the fingers. They have a soft, greasy feel. Examples include talc and graphite. (We'll be discussing the graphite in pencils in the next experiment.)

No. 2—this group can be scratched with your fingernail.

No. 3—can be cut by a knife and scratched by a copper penny but cannot be scratched by your fingernail.

No. 4—can be scratched by a knife and can be cut with difficulty.

No. 5—can be scratched with a knife with difficulty. They can't be cut.

No. 6—cannot be scratched with a knife but can be scratched by a harder substance.

No. 7—will scratch glass but cannot be scratched by a file. Most minerals used as gem stones are in this group or harder. A diamond is a No. 10.

Chalk is ranked as a No. 2. It can be scratched with your fingernail but it does not have a greasy feel to it. You can use the hardness tests to rank objects you have around the house, including ice, plastic, nails, glass, and different metals.

The Acid Test

There are two kinds of chalk commercially available. One is simply labeled "white chalk" and the other has the label "anti-dust." They are different chemicals. Do a simple chemical experiment to check out the difference.

Materials and Equipment
– white chalk
– anti-dust chalk
– white vinegar
– two small glasses
– waxed paper
– hammer

Procedure
Break off a small piece of one chalk sample. Put it in a piece of waxed paper and fold the piece over several times. Hammer the chalk into a powder. Put the powder in a glass and add a small amount of vinegar. Repeat the procedure with the other chalk sample.

Observations and Suggestions

You will notice tiny bubbles rising from the anti-dust chalk. These are bubbles of carbon-dioxide gas that are released in a chemical reaction with acid. Anti-dust chalk is made from limestone. Its chemical name is calcium carbonate and it is known as the mineral *calcite.* Limestone is formed over millions of years from the shells of sea animals that sank to the bottom of the ocean. Limestone is also known as "chalk" to the mineralogists. It has a hardness of 3, which is too hard to leave a streak on a blackboard. Anti-dust chalk is manufactured to get around this problem. It is finely powdered limestone mixed with a clay binder. The claylike mixture is forced through a small hole or die, like toothpaste, to form sticks. These are then hardened in an oven.

The other sample of white chalk may have a few carbon-dioxide bubbles rising from its surface due to some carbonate impurities, but there are strikingly fewer bubbles if any. Ordinary white chalk is not limestone or "chalk" but a soft mineral called *gypsum.* Gypsum contains no carbonate; it is chemically known as calcium sulfate. Gypsum has a hardness of 2. The next experiment explores a peculiar property of gypsum. You will make your own "chalk."

Anytime you get bubbles coming off a mineral when you put it in acid, like vinegar, you know you have carbonate present. Put seashells and eggshells in vinegar to check for the presence of carbonate.

Make Your Own Chalk

You can make your own white chalk and anti-dust chalk.

Materials and Equipment
- plaster of Paris
- waxed paper
- 3 eggshells
- hammer
- flour
- water
- measuring spoons
- paper cups for mixing

Procedure

To make ordinary chalk use plaster of Paris, which may be bought at a hardware store. Plaster of Paris is calcium sulfate made from mined gypsum that has been very carefully dried. Gypsum contains water in the structure of its crystals. When it is heated in a very carefully controlled way, at about 250° F, half of this water is driven off and you have the fine, white powder of plaster of Paris. When water is added, the gypsum is restored to its original state. We tried to make plaster of Paris from commercial white chalk by heating it in our oven at 250° F, but we were not successful. Perhaps you can have better luck. However, you can easily see how the water returns plaster of Paris to its crystallized state of gypsum, as well as seeing how it functions as a writing instrument.

Mix two tablespoons of plaster of Paris in a paper cup with two tablespoons of water. The consistency will be that of sour cream. Fold a one-foot-long piece of waxed paper in half. Pour the liquid plaster in a narrow line down the center of the waxed paper. Roll the paper around the liquid plaster to form a tube. You have made a mold for the plaster. It takes twenty minutes for the plaster to set. Feel the plaster as it sets. It will feel warm. Heat is given off as the water is incorporated into the gypsum crystals. Unwrap your "chalk" after a half-hour. Let it dry for three days before writing with it.

Eggshells provide the "lime" for your anti-dust chalk. Remove the membrane inside each of three eggshells. Put the broken shells in the center of a large piece of waxed paper. Fold the paper over and over around the shells. Hammer the shells to produce a fine powder. You may have to change waxed paper a few times before you get the fine powder you want.

Make a flour-water paste as a binder for your eggshells. Mix one tablespoon of flour with one tablespoon of very hot water. Add the powdered eggshells. Shape the mixture into a stick and roll it up in a new piece of waxed paper. Let it dry for three days.

Observations and Suggestions
Check out your "chalks" on a flower pot. Compare them with commercially prepared chalk. Can they all be scratched with your fingernail? Do they all leave a streak on the flower pot? Do they all erase when you rub the streak with a cloth?

☆ Pencils

Pencils are not a new idea. They've been around since the time of Queen Elizabeth I when huge deposits of the soft, black mineral graphite were discovered in Cumberland, England. It was very obvious that the black streak a chunk of graphite left behind when it was rubbed against a hard surface made it quite suitable as a writing instrument. Its main advantage was that it was dry. This was especially useful for surveyors who had to make notes outside and found the quill and ink very inconvenient in working situations. The problems with graphite were that it was extremely fragile and crumbled easily and that it made the writer's hands dirty. These difficulties were solved with the invention of holders made from a variety of materials, including precious metals and wood. Pencils in Elizabethan days were quite expensive.

The modern wood pencil was created by Joseph Dixon, born in Massachusetts in 1799. When he was thirteen years old he made his first pencil in his mother's kitchen. His sea-going father would return from voyages with graphite in the hull of his ship, which was used simply as a ballast, or weight, when there was no cargo to transport. This graphite was later dumped overboard to make room for shipments for export. Joseph Dixon got some of this excess graphite, pounded it into powder, mixed it with clay, and rolled it into long strips that he baked in his mother's oven to make the "lead" for his pencil. This dried the "lead"

and made it firm. He then put a strip of "lead" between two grooved sticks of cedar and glued them together to make a sandwich. He chose cedar because it is soft, can be easily sharpened, and is relatively free of knots. All you had to do was sharpen the pencil with a knife and it was ready to write.

Dixon later invented machines to mass produce his pencil, but the public was not ready for his newfangled writing instrument and he lost money on it. Finally, during the Civil War, more than forty years after he took his first rolled "lead" out of his mother's oven, the pencil was accepted. It seemed that soldiers on the battlefield needed a writing instrument that was dry, easy to carry, and ready to write at a moment's notice. The pencil did the job. By 1869, four years after the war had ended and three years after Dixon had died, Dixon's company was producing 86,000 pencils a day that sold for only a nickel a piece.

Pencil "lead" is not lead, a metallic element, but another element, namely carbon. Pure carbon is found in nature as crystals, as well as in non-crystalline forms such as coal. Crystals are a regular arrangement of atoms or molecules of a pure substance that have a distinct geometric shape. Carbon is an unusual element in many ways. But one unusual aspect of carbon is the difference between its two crystalline forms, graphite and diamond. In graphite crystals, carbon atoms are arranged in flat, six-atom rings that fit together like bathroom tiles. These rings form flat sheets piled on top on one another. The attraction between sheets of graphite crystals is extremely weak, so they easily slide past one another. Graphite is, therefore, very flaky and one of the softest substances on earth. The other crystalline form of carbon, the diamond, is at the opposite end of the hardness scale. It is the hardest substance on earth. The carbon atoms in diamonds are strongly held in a boxlike arrangement that gives the regular shape to a rough diamond crystal. The very strong attraction between all the carbon atoms in this three-dimensional arrangement is the cause of a diamond's extreme hardness.

The hardness of pencils is due to the addition of clay to powdered graphite in the manufacturing process. Clay is a binder for the graphite. The amount of clay is varied to make pencils of different hardness. Do the next experiment to compare pencils of different hardness.

Materials and Equipment
– pencils of a range of hardness (we used Mongols #1, #2, and #3)
– pencil sharpener
– paper
– metric ruler showing millimeters

Procedure
Sharpen all your pencils to points that are all the same length. Measure the length of exposed "lead" with the ruler to be sure they are all the same length.

Holding the pencil perpendicular to the paper, make twenty lines across the page. Repeat the process with each pencil. Measure the length of the worn-down lead tips.

Observations and Suggestions
The lower the number of a pencil, the softer the "lead." We found that our #1 pencil was more worn down than the #2 and #3. When we looked at the tips of the worn pencils, we could see

that the softest pencil had a tip with the widest diameter, the hardest pencil had the smallest diameter, and the pencil in the middle number was worn a medium amount.

Soft pencils make the darkest marks and are most easily smudged. Hard pencils make grayer marks and are harder to smudge.

The slippery nature of graphite makes it very useful as a lubricant especially for small, hard-to-reach places like locks. We read that you can use a pencil to get a metal zipper to work more smoothly. Rub a pencil against the teeth of a zipper and see if this is so.

☆ Crayons and Carbon Paper

Crayons are dry writing instruments in which pigments are evenly distributed throughout a wax vehicle. There are a variety of waxes found in plants and animals and they are also produced synthetically. Waxes are related to fats but they are harder and less greasy. They melt at higher temperatures than most common fats but their melting point is much lower than the temperature at which water boils. The wax in crayons melts at about 129° F. When waxes are melted and when they are rubbed, the molecules line up in a regular way, which makes a waxy surface shiny. The wax in crayons is also somewhat sticky and will adhere to various surfaces, smooth as well as rough. Crayonlike pencils are used in laboratories for marking glassware and china where ink and pencil won't adhere.

The pigments in crayons are added to the melted wax during the manufacturing process. Similar pigments are added to color candles except that the pigments are far more concentrated in crayons. Compare crayon marks on paper with marks made by a colored candle, to see the difference. We were told that the colors in crayons are largely synthetic because they have to be non-toxic. As a result, there is a tremendous difference in light fastness among the pigments in a box of crayons. Do an experiment to check this out.

Materials and Equipment
- a box of sixteen crayons
- white paper
- black construction paper
- tape

Procedure
With each color in the box of crayons, make a band across a sheet of white paper. Cover half of the bands with a sheet of black construction paper. Tape the half-covered sheet of bands to a sunny window. Check for fading every week. Keep a record of which colors fade fastest.

Observations and Suggestions
It has been said that the greens and browns are more light fast than the violets and magentas. See if your results confirm this.

Carbon paper is made from a wax-base containing black or blue pigment that is "ironed" onto paper during manufacturing to form a film. The pigment is undoubtedly a carbon black which is very light fast. You might want to use the procedure above to check this out.

If you look at a sheet of carbon paper you'll see that it has the shiny look of wax laid down by heat. Smell it. Compare the smell to unscented candles and crayons. You can make your own carbon paper by laying down a color with crayon. Pressure with a pencil or ball point on the reverse side transfers the wax to another sheet of paper. If any of these experiments inspire you to try and melt wax, DON'T DO IT OVER A FLAME! You can easily melt crayon shavings in an aluminum foil pan over a light bulb. See if you can figure out how to make carbon paper from crayons.

5 Adhesives

Every time you seal an envelope, put pictures in an album, attach a label, leave a note on the door, or permanently stick one piece of paper to another you use an adhesive. Adhesives are substances that hold materials together by surface attachment. Four kinds of adhesives you can get at the stationery store are: pastes, glues, gums, and pressure-sensitive tapes and labels. Although there are differences in the properties of each kind of adhesive, all of them share one common property—namely, all adhesives come in very close contact with the surface of the material, or substrate, with which they form a bond. And by close, we mean close. In order for an adhesive bond to form, the molecules of the adhesive must physically penetrate, actually hook into, the surface molecules of the substrate. Thus many adhesives start out wet and then harden into a strong film that holds the surfaces together.

Most of the adhesives used on paper have a water base. Paper is a porous substrate that allows for the evaporation of water.

The bond forms during the process of evaporation. Most pastes and glues are made up of molecules that are long chains of repeating units of groups of atoms. Such molecules are called *polymers*. When the adhesive is wet, the polymers actually hook into the surface of the substrate. As the adhesive dries and sets, the molecules of the adhesive cross link into each other, forming a film that sticks to itself. Adhesives that work on porous surfaces may not work on non-porous surfaces such as plastic. The force with which a substance sticks to itself is called *cohesion*. Naturally, adhesives must have cohesive as well as adhesive strength. Otherwise, the bond will separate easily.

The properties of different adhesives, the types of substrates they cling to, the strength of the bonds they form, and the cost of production determine what they are useful for. In this chapter we explore how to make your own paste and glue, how to measure the bond strength of adhesives, and how to compare the rates of set of different adhesives. For the inquiring mind adhesives is something to get stuck on!

☆ A Formula for Paste

The main ingredients of paste are starch and water. Starch is found in many plants but its main commercial sources are seeds such as wheat, rice, and corn, and tubers (storage roots) such as potatoes and arrowroot. Although these sources contain some impurities, the commercial manufacturing processes produce a fairly uniform product of powdered starch granules. Starch is a good adhesive because it is a natural polymer. Starch molecules are long chains of sugar molecules linked together. You can learn some of the peculiar properties of starch by making paste.

Materials and Equipment
– 1 tablespoon flour
– 4 tablespoons water
– 1 teaspoon sugar
– wooden spoon
– small frying pan
– paper cup
– plastic wrap

Procedure
Mix the flour, water, and sugar in the frying pan. Gently heat the mixture, stirring constantly. When it thickens, remove it from the heat. Store it in a paper cup covered with plastic wrap.

Observations and Suggestions
Notice that the starch does not dissolve in cold water. It forms a suspension. When starch is heated, the starch granules swell, forming a mass called a *gel*. Different starches form gels with different properties. Make pastes substituting corn starch, potato

starch, and rice starch (from health-food stores) for flour. Some of the pastes you make may only be useful as an adhesive while the mixture is warm.

The sugar you add in this formula is what professional chemists call a *plasticizer;* that is, it gives a flexibility to the material, making the dried film less likely to crack. Make paste with and without sugar. Spread equal amounts of both pastes on a non-porous surface like the plastic cover of a tennis-ball or coffee can. See which film cracks more.

Thin pastes contain molecules that are shorter than starch molecules but are not broken down completely into sugar molecules. This intermediate size is called a *dextrin.* Many syrups contain dextrins. See if you can concoct a thin paste using dextrins along with starches.

Homemade pastes are very perishable. You'll only be able to keep them for a few days before molds start to grow. However, moldy paste can be a beginning of a whole new set of experiments, so let them grow if you're interested.

A chemical test for starch is the appearance of a blue-black color when you put a drop of iodine on it. Test your homemade pastes for starch. Use iodine from the medicine chest. Then test commercial pastes. Are they made with starch?

☆ A Formula for Milk Glue

The white color of milk is due to a soluble group of milk proteins called *casein.* Many proteins are also polymers that have adhesive strength and casein is one of them. However, it must be treated in order to get it in a state in which it can act as glue.

Materials and Equipment
- ½ cup skim milk (you can use fresh fat-free milk, or powdered
  milk to which you have added water)
- 1 teaspoon vinegar
- small frying pan
- spoon
- strainer
- small saucer
- 1 teaspoon baking soda
- 1 tablespoon warm water
- fork

Procedure
Put the milk in the frying pan with the vinegar. Stir constantly
as you heat gently. The acid in the vinegar makes the casein
clump together into a solid mass. This process is similar to the
coagulation of an egg when you scramble it. It is a permanent
change and the casein will never again be the way it was in
its natural state. You have made the soluble casein insoluble,
and you have also taken the first step in cheese making, creating
curds and whey. The coagulated casein is the curd and the yellow-
ish liquid is the whey.

Separate the curds and whey with the strainer. Put the curds
on a small saucer, add the warm water, and mash in the baking
soda with a fork. Force the mixture through the strainer and
store it for a day in a paper cup covered with plastic wrap.

Observations and Suggestions
When you coagulate the casein by adding acid you produce an
insoluble form of the casein. Casein cannot act as a glue in this

condition, so you have to treat it to make it soluble again. You do this by neutralizing the acid by adding a base. Baking soda (sodium bicarbonate) is an alkali in solution. The bubbles that form when you add baking soda and water to the acid-casein curd is carbon dioxide. The process of getting the casein back into a soluble form takes time, so your casein glue will not be ready for at least twenty-four hours. When it is ready to use, it is a smooth milky-white and creamy liquid.

Note: White glues are not casein glues. They are made from a synthetic polymer that is suspended in water. Their bond is stronger and more flexible than casein glue.

☆ A Formula for Gum

The glue that is used for gummed labels comes from the bones and hides of animals. It can be laid down on one surface and dried, ready to stick to another surface when moistened. The ability to become sticky when wet and nonsticky when dry in a reversible way is the reason this adhesive is used on envelopes, stamps, and labels.

Materials and Equipment
- 1 packet unflavored gelatin
- 1 tablespoon cold water
- 1 tablespoon boiling water
- ½ teaspoon corn syrup
- small bowl
- spoon
- clean paint brush
- pieces of paper, clippings, etc.

Procedure

Sprinkle the package of gelatin over one tablespoon of cold water. It will swell and soften in about ten minutes. When it is soft add the 3 tablespoons of boiling water and the corn syrup. Stir until it is dissolved.

Paint the mixture on the pieces of paper. Let dry. To use as an adhesive, moisten the dried surfaces and stick them on other pieces of paper.

Observations and Suggestions

Gelatin is a protein manufactured by heating animal connective tissue, such as skin, tendons, and ligaments, with acid. It will not dissolve in cold water but will swell as it absorbs it or when in contact with it. It will dissolve in hot water, and when a gelatin solution cools, it traps the water in its structure, giving it a semi-solid structure. Your gelatin adhesive will gel when cooled, but you can turn it back into a liquid by heating it again over hot water.

The old-fashioned animal-hide glue is a poor grade of gelatin made by cooking bones and hides in acid. It is then dried and ground, and sold in a powdered form. One of our source books said that you could tell a good grade of such animal glue from a poor one by the amount of water it absorbed. The more water the glue absorbed, the higher the quality of the glue (and the more refined the gelatin in it). Animal-hide glues have to be heated to be usable and applied while still warm. They harden to form an extremely strong bond and are used for wood furniture.

See if you can improve the adhesive qualities of your gelatin glue by adding a teaspoon of vinegar (an acid) and heating it for a few minutes. Be careful not to let the water evaporate completely. Add water as needed to keep the level the same. Compare the strength of the bonds using the tests discussed later on in this chapter.

☆ Viscosity Test

One of the important properties of an adhesive is the easy way in which it flows over a surface. Some adhesives flow more easily than others. The resistance to flowing is called *viscosity*. Molasses has high viscosity; water has low viscosity. In the laboratory viscosity is measured by having the liquid flow through a narrow straw. Here's how you can do your own viscosity test.

Materials and Equipment
- an assortment of liquid glues and other liquids, such as syrup, water, and molasses
- pencil
- ruler

– long plastic straws
– tissues
– newspaper
– clock with second hand (optional)

Procedure
This is a messy experiment so work on newspapers. We used plastic drinking straws that were ten inches long. Although the fluid is contained in the straw and very little of its surface is exposed to the air, the setting time for the moving end will affect your results—so you have to work very quickly.

Prepare a straw for each glue sample you intend to test. Make a pencil mark on each straw that is one inch from an end. Mark off half-inch intervals down the rest of the straw. Dip a straw into an adhesive liquid to the one-inch mark. Hold it there until the slow-moving stuff has time to reach the mark. Remove the straw, holding it horizontally, and wipe off the outside with a tissue. By holding it up to the light you should be able to see if the proper amount of adhesive is inside. Lay the straw down while you put another adhesive in another marked straw.

Since the adhesives will set, compare only two at a time. Put both straws in a vertical position with the adhesive at the top. Hold them while you observe the fluid move down the straw. Some fluids are more viscous (will flow more slowly) than others. See if you can rank them. If you want to be especially accurate, time the rate of flow in half inches per second.

Observations and Suggestions
Since most liquid adhesives are fairly viscous we suggest that you hold the straw in a vertical position. If you want to use this technique to compare viscosities of other kinds of fluids including

water, you will have to hold the straws at a much smaller angle. Viscosity is important in water-base adhesives. If it is too high it won't penetrate or wet the substrate sufficiently to form a strong bond. If it is too runny the film will be too thin to form a bond.

Here's a peculiar phenomenon related to viscosity that affects commercial library paste. Commercial library paste is so thick that it doesn't flow at all. It has been treated with chemicals in order to prevent it from getting moldy, and these have had a strange effect on its viscosity. Commercial library paste is like quicksand. Both are what is called *thixotropic,* which means these are fluids that flow more easily if you beat them. Quicksand seems as if it can support your weight. You step on it and begin sinking. Most people get into a panic and start thrashing about trying to get out. This is the worst thing you can do. Your mechanical motion decreases the viscosity even more rapidly and you sink faster. You should move as little as possible while you wait for help.

Try beating some commercial library paste. You can work a small amount on a plate with a spatula. The agitation breaks down the interlocking molecular structure and the paste becomes runny. If you allow it to rest (without drying out) it will become firm again. Pour it into a container that can be covered while you wait for it to get thick again.

☆ Testing Bond Strength

How strong does an adhesive bond have to be? Obviously it must be strong enough to do the job. The adhesive bond holding two pieces of paper together does not have to be as strong as a bond attaching a leg to a table. Adhesive bonds can be measured by adding weights until the bond breaks. In these tests, however, you use your own strength to get a general feel of how much force it takes to break an adhesive bond.

There are three kinds of bond failures. When you do the following tests, look closely at the broken bond to determine the kind of failure that has occurred. Adhesive failure occurs when the adhesive just doesn't work. The bond never actually forms. If you use Elmer's Glue to adhere wood to metal you will have adhesive failure.

Substrate failure is easy to see because the surface of the substrate has been torn. This bond doesn't separate at the place where the adhesive meets the surface. The paper fibers are ripped off the surface. Most of the bonds you'll be testing with paper adhesives break due to substrate failure.

Finally, there's the cohesive failure of the adhesive. The separation occurs right in the middle of the adhesive film. Sometimes you'll see this when you lick a gummed envelope and it doesn't seal properly. Wallpaper paste is manufactured to have cohesive failure. You can tear wallpaper off a wall without taking any of the wall surface or leaving behind pieces of wallpaper.

Materials and Equipment
– an assortment of pastes, glues, and tapes
– scissors
– manila folders 9″ deep
– ruler
– pencil

Procedure
To test tensile strength cut quarter-inch strips down the nine-inch side of a manila folder through both sides. The bottom of

a manila folder has one crease and one or two pre-fold marks that are designed to easily crease when the file folder is thick with papers. Fold your strip on the pre-fold mark closest to the existing crease. You now have a long, skinny strip with a square U in the middle. Do the same thing with another strip. Put a glue or paste sample on the small surface between the creases. Stick it to the same area on the other strip. Be sure to label the glue used for each bond. Allow the bond to dry thoroughly before you try testing it.

Pull back the strips so that you are pulling against the bond. Hold two strips in each hand and pull until you break the bond. Some glues will make a stronger bond than others. You should be able to feel the difference.

Tensile strength is the force needed to break a bond by pulling in a direction at right angles to the bond.

To test shear strength cut a one-inch strip along both sides of the fold of the nine-inch side. Cut out the folded part, making two strips. Cut off about an inch and a half of one strip. You now have two long strips and one short one.

Fasten the short strip to a longer one with one of your pastes or glues. Make an overlap of one-eighth inch. Write the name of the glue you used next to the bond. Join the other long strip to the short one with a different adhesive. Again, keep the overlap the same. Allow both bonds to dry thoroughly.

Shear strength is the force needed to break a bond by pulling along the bond. Grasp the two free long ends in each hand and pull. The weaker adhesive bond will break first.

Peel strength is measured by peeling the top piece off the bottom. Use it to compare the bond strength of adhesive tapes. To test peel strength put various samples of different pressure-sensitive tapes and labels on some colored paper. Pull the piece of tape or label off by folding one end backwards against the surface and pulling with the back end touching the surface. You can see the peel strength of the adhesive by the amount of paper fiber that comes off with it. Colored paper has more visible fibers, that's why we suggest using it for this test.

Observations and Suggestions

Pressure-sensitive tapes are made with an adhesive called an *elastomer.* Elastomers are large molecules having rubberlike properties. You can see some of these properties with rubber cement. Put a blob of rubber cement on a non-porous surface, such as the plastic top of a coffee can. Allow it to dry. The dried blob will ball up when you remove it. It can be stretched but will return to its original shape when you let go. A film of elastomers on tape or pressure-sensitive labels is very sticky and forms a weak but permanent bond.

☆ The Blush Test

There are a number of white glues that dry to form transparent films. Some of these white glues are water resistant. There is a simple test you can do that will show which of these dried films are, in fact, water resistant.

Put a thick film of each sample on a non-porous surface such as the metal top of a jar or the plastic cover of a coffee can. Label them so you know which is which. Allow the films to dry completely. Put a drop of water in the middle of each sample of dried film. If the film is not water resistant, it will become white again. Scientists call the appearance of a white area on exposure to water "blushing."

You now have a way of knowing what glue to use if you want to make a paper cup.

☆ A Test for the Rate of Set

How long does it take for a liquid adhesive to get sticky? The length of time is called the rate of set and, you guessed it, rate of set is another one of those properties that varies among adhesives. Here's how you can have a rate-of-set race.

Materials and Equipment
– at least two different brands of paper paste or glue
– sheets of white paper
– tissues
– a spatula or knife

Procedure
Fold one sheet of paper one inch along the shorter side. This will be your top sheet and the fold makes a tab you can grab onto.

Now, working quickly, lay an application of each adhesive in rows parallel to the long side of another sheet of paper. The rows should be about two inches apart. Draw one row into a thin film by passing the spatula along it. Wipe the spatula clean and quickly draw it down the other adhesive. Cover both films with the tabbed sheet.

Hold the tab of the top sheet of paper and slowly peel it back. Setting time is defined as the time it takes to see paper fibers being torn as you pull the sheets apart.

Observations and Suggestions

The setting time for an adhesive depends on the job to be done. If the substrates are porous, you don't want the adhesive to set before it has a chance to penetrate the surface.

Setting time for any particular water-base adhesive varies depending on temperature, humidity, and the thickness of the film.

6 Rubber

Rubber, one of the truly important materials of modern life, got its name because of its usefulness as an eraser. Back in 1770 rubber was little more than a fascinating oddity that engaged the attention of scientists in America and Europe. One of them, Sir Joseph Priestley, an Englishman famous for his discovery of oxygen, was fooling around with this strange material. He discovered that it could be used for rubbing out pencil marks. The English at first called it "India-rubber" because it came from the New World and because it rubbed out pencil marks. Rubber had been brought back to Europe by Columbus who had found West Indian natives playing games with rubber balls. Rubber was the dried sap from certain trees found in the West Indies and South America. The label "India" was given to many discoveries in the New World, including the islands of the Caribbean, under the mistaken notion that Columbus had arrived in India by traveling west.

The Mayan Indians of South America also knew about rubber. They made cuts in the bark of rubber trees and collected the sticky milky-white sap that oozed out. This sap could be dried, molded, and hardened over a fire. The Mayans used it to coat woven fabric that was then fashioned into waterproof shoes. They poured the liquid sap over clay pots to form a film. When the film had dried and hardened, they removed it from the mold and used the containers as rubber bottles for carrying liquids. And like the West Indians, the Mayans also made balls of dried sap that had the incredible ability to bounce high into the air after striking the ground.

Natural rubber was brought back to Europe where it stimulated the imagination of many inventors who tried to make a variety of objects from it. In 1823, one inventor, a Scotsman named Charles Macintosh, figured out how to dissolve rubber in a solvent. The dissolved rubber was used to coat fabric that Macintosh made into rainwear called mackintoshes. Unfortunately the mackintosh exhibited the same serious limitations of natural rubber discovered by other experimenters. Rubber was susceptible to temperature changes. It became soft and sticky in hot weather and stiff and brittle in cold. Despite the interest of inventors who made all kinds of rubber objects from tubing to mail sacks to tablecloths, the goods "spoiled" during the warm weather, falling apart into a sticky mess, and these hopefuls often suffered financial losses.

If only rubber could be made stable to temperature changes, full advantage could be taken of its other remarkable properties! This was the challenge that obsessed the American inventor Charles Goodyear. Goodyear ran his family into debt, and even spent time in jail for not paying his bills, all because he spent most of his time experimenting with rubber, always hoping his discoveries would pay off. Finally, in 1839, Goodyear made the discovery that eliminated the problems of natural rubber and made it stable to temperature extremes. Like many great discoveries, Goodyear's was a lucky accident coming unexpectedly after years of hardship and failure. The legend of his day of discovery may not be completely true, but it makes a good story.

Apparently Goodyear had promised his wife that he would stop doing his experiments. He had mixed many chemicals with rubber in an effort to find some ingredient that would make it stable and all he had found were two—magnesium and nitric acid—that produced even a small change for the better. The trouble was that the changes these chemicals produced only affected the surface of rubber so their use was limited. Not experimenting was one thing to promise. Not thinking about rubber was another. Goodyear dreamed up some new ideas for experiments and one day, in February of 1830, when his wife was out of the house, he broke his word and started a few experiments. In one of them, he mixed rubber with sulfur. Much to his dismay, his wife returned sooner than expected, and Goodyear accidentally spilled his experiment on the stove. When he recovered his baked experiments, the piece that had contained sulfur was no longer sticky, but firm and dry. The change was permanent, yet the material still had the bounce of natural rubber.

The process invented by Goodyear, heating raw rubber with sulfur, is called *vulcanization* (after Vulcan, the Roman god of fire). Because of vulcanization, rubber became practical for all kinds of products from tires to footwear to gloves to rubber bands. Today there are more than 50,000 separate applications for this unusual material.

Rubber is still used, of course, for the purpose for which it was named, rubbing out pencil marks. It is also found among your school supplies in the form of an adhesive and as elastic bands. In this chapter you'll explore some of its remarkable properties. They're bound to stretch your imagination!

☆ Natural Rubber

The sap that comes from a rubber tree is called *latex*. Rubber particles are suspended in water making the sap milky white and sticky. It is collected by making a small incision along the bark of a rubber tree (known among botanists as *Hevea brasiliensis*) that is just deep enough to reach the layer inside the bark where the sap flows but is not deep enough to cut through this layer. Cutting through would eventually kill the tree. A small catch cup is hung at the end of the cut, and the latex oozes out and runs down the cut to be collected at the end of the day. One mature healthy rubber tree produces about twelve pounds of rubber a year.

You can collect latex from dandelion and milkweed stems. Or if you live near the desert, you can get it from stubby guayule bushes. Cut the stems and gently press the milky latex out the cut end. It is easier to get latex out of milkweed than dandelions. Try and collect about a teaspoonful. You can get the latex to clump together, or coagulate, into rubber in two ways. One is to let it dry in the air. This produces something very similar to crepe rubber. The other method is to dissolve it in about half a glass of water. Pour in vinegar, stirring constantly with a spoon. Vinegar is an acid that coagulates the rubber. Acid treatment of latex is another method used for preparing crude rubber. Remove the ball from the spoon, squeeze out the water, and let it dry for several days.

Check out the effects of temperature extremes on your raw rubber. Put it in a small piece of aluminum foil on top of a lit light bulb and put another piece in the freezer overnight. What effect does this treatment have on it? Squeeze it between your fingers to feel the difference.

You can recover natural crepe rubber from rubber cement. Rubber cement is made by milling (mechanically rolling and kneading) many tiny pieces of crepe rubber. The milling makes the rubber as flexible as possible. The milled rubber is then mixed with highly flammable solvents. WHEN YOU USE RUBBER CEMENT, DO IT IN A WELL-VENTILATED AREA AND BE SURE THAT THERE IS SOME ADULT SUPERVISION AT THE TIME YOU USE IT. DON'T PUT A MATCH OR ANY OTHER FLAME ANYWHERE NEAR RUBBER CEMENT.

Materials and Equipment
– rubber cement
– scissors
– a small plate
– cotton fabric (optional)

Procedure
Spread about two tablespoons of rubber cement in a smooth layer on the plate. Put it in a well-ventilated spot to dry. It will take at least an hour to become completely dry. When it is dry, peel it off the plate. The rubber will stick to itself and you can roll it into a small ball. Let the ball dry, or "cure," for several days.

Observations and Suggestions
The milky-white rubber cement becomes the natural straw color of crepe rubber. The rubber ball shows many of the properties of natural rubber. If you hold it between your fingers for a while, it will become stickier due to the heat of your hand. If you squeeze it, it will spring back to its original shape. This property is called *resiliency,* and it is one of the most valuable properties of rubber. Resiliency gives rubber its bounce. Drop your little crepe rubber ball on the floor. It will bounce quite high.

Let your ball dry, or cure, for several days. Save it for the next experiment.

Try painting rubber cement on fabric. Put a piece of rubber-coated cloth in the freezer overnight. Does it get stiff? What happens when you try to wrinkle it?

☆ Erasability

Compare the erasability of different kinds of rubber.

Materials and Equipment
– an assortment of erasers, including Art Gum, pencil and ink erasers, and some old erasers
– rubber bands
– balloons
– ball of rubber cement
– any other rubber objects you may find around the house
– paper
– pencil

Procedure
Make pencil marks on a sheet of paper. Try and keep them uniform as to darkness. Try erasing the marks with the various rubber erasers and other objects.

Observations and Suggestions
What happens to the surface of the rubber when you rub it against the paper? Can you rub out pencil marks with any kind of rubber? Rubber both picks up as well as cuts the carbon marks of pencil. Most erasers also contain finely ground pumice, a kind

of volcanic rock, that increases the roughness of the eraser. This roughness is called an *abrasive,* which actually cuts the paper fibers at the surface. Ink erasers contain more abrasives than pencil erasers. Look closely at the surface of the paper with a magnifying glass to see how the abrasives in an eraser work.

☆ The Chemistry of Rubber

Rubber is a compound made up of elements. Do two experiments that reveal which elements are present.

Materials and Equipment
– samples of rubber—a piece of rubber band, erasers
– a small metal dish or jar cover
– matches
– aluminum foil
– silver polish
– flat silver surface (small silver tray; a quarter dated before 1964)

Procedure
Rubber burns. This means that it is made up of elements that will combine with oxygen in the air. Most flammable substances are made up of two elements, hydrogen and carbon, that combine with oxygen to give off carbon dioxide and water along with the heat and light energy of a flame. CHECK WITH AN ADULT BEFORE YOU USE MATCHES! Do this experiment outside or in a well-ventilated spot. Put a sample of rubber in a metal dish. Prop it up with a small piece of aluminum foil so that the air can circulate freely around it. Light it with a match. Hold a piece of aluminum foil about five inches above the flame to catch the sooty material

that comes off.

Here's the set-up for the second experiment. Follow the directions on the silver-polish container and polish a silver surface. Almost any silver or silver-plated object will do as long as it has a flat area. Put your rubber objects on the freshly polished surface. Paint one small area with rubber cement. Leave it undisturbed for two days. Then look under the rubber objects for tarnish.

Observations and Suggestions

Some rubber burns quietly. But we had a rubber band that crackled and sparked as it burned. These are tiny explosions as the hydrogen in the rubber burns. The carbon is released as sooty black smoke. You can collect it. It is the same carbon black as the kind you collected over a candle in chapter 3. The smell of burning rubber is due to some of the chemicals added during manufacturing. Rubber manufacturers add chemicals to slow down the aging of rubber, and it is probably these chemicals that give off the characteristic bitter smell of burned rubber.

Rubber that has been vulcanized contains sulfur. The second experiment is a test for sulfur. Silver tarnish is a black compound called silver sulfide. All that is needed is contact between the silver and the rubber for the sulfide to form. Under which objects did tarnish form? What happened underneath the rubber cement? How can you explain your findings?

☆ The Elastic Nature of Rubber

Rubber can take more of a beating than any other substance on earth. You can stretch it, squeeze it, twist it, and bend it, and it will spring back to its original shape . . . usually. And you can repeat the beating and we guarantee you will get tired before the rubber does. The ability to retain its original shape in spite of stress is called resiliency, or *elasticity*. Other materials such as metal and glass are also elastic. They, too, can take certain kinds of stress and return to their original shape—but only within their elastic limits. If you bend a steel rod too far, it will stay permanently bent. Glass is even more limited, and as soon as the stress exceeds its elastic limits, it breaks.

Robert Hooke (1635–1703), an English physicist, is known for the discovery of a law that defines elasticity. Rediscover Hooke's Law in the next experiment.

Materials and Equipment
– wooden ruler
– small brad or nail
– hammer
– thin rubber band
– wire hangers
– pencil and paper

Procedure
Hammer the nail into the ruler at the end of the one-inch line. Hang the rubber band on the nail. Being careful not to stretch the rubber band, measure its length. Write down your measurement. (Remember you must subtract the number one from your reading as you are starting at the one-inch mark.) Now hang one wire hanger on the rubber band. Again record its length. Make sure that the hanger is clear of the ruler and that you are not allowing the ruler to support any of the hanger's weight. Add another hanger and record the length of the rubber band.

Add a third and fourth hanger, recording the length of the rubber band. Repeat your measurements as you remove hangers one by one.

Observations and Suggestions

How much did the rubber band stretch with each hanger? Here's what we got:

		Amount of Stretch
rubber band alone	$1\frac{14}{16}''$	—
one hanger	$2\frac{3}{16}''$	$\frac{5}{16}''$
two hangers	$2\frac{7}{16}''$	$\frac{4}{16}''$
three hangers	$2\frac{11}{16}''$	$\frac{4}{16}''$
four hangers	$2\frac{15}{16}''$	$\frac{4}{16}''$

Our measurements show that for each hanger, the rubber band stretched between four- and five-sixteenths of an inch. Although there is a little difference in the measurements, they are more alike than they are different. Our results show Hooke's Law, which states that within the elastic limits of an elastic body, equal forces will stretch it equal amounts. We may assume that all the wire hangers weigh the same. Therefore, they will each stretch the rubber band (or elastic body) equal amounts.

Hooke's Law applies to any elastic body, including springs. It is the principle behind the spring balance in the grocery store and the mainspring in watches.

☆ Artificially Aging Rubber

The elastic nature of rubber is built into the rubber molecules. Rubber molecules are long chains of carbon and hydrogen atoms that are folded like an accordion. When you stretch the rubber, the molecules are stretched, only to return to their linked position when the force is removed. The longer the chains of rubber molecules, the more elastic the rubber is. If the chains are shortened, resiliency is lost. Rubber molecules can be shortened mechanically. Stretch and release a rubber band enough times and eventually the rubber will become "fatigued" and lose its resiliency. That is, it won't have quite as much snap to it. Of course, it takes a lot of stretching and releasing to reach this point. Manufacturers have machines that stretch and release rubber products to measure the amount of stretch they can take before losing resiliency.

Rubber molecules are also shortened with time. The aging of rubber occurs because oxygen combines slowly with rubber molecules. Where ever an oxygen molecule joins a rubber molecule the chain is broken. Chemicals are added to slow down this aging process during the manufacturing of rubber. Nevertheless, in time all rubber ages. You can do an experiment to speed up the process.

Materials and Equipment
– three identical, fairly wide rubber bands

– aluminum foil
– small pan or heatproof bowl about 6″ in diameter
– ruler

Procedure

Preheat your oven to 350° F. Wrap the outside of your pan with aluminum foil. This is to protect the pan in case the rubber melts. Stretch one rubber band around the foil-covered pan. Put another rubber band on a piece of aluminum foil. Put the two rubber bands in the oven for ten minutes.

Observations and Suggestions

Measure the length of the unheated rubber band. Stretch it several times. Does it remain the same size? Measure the length of the unstretched but heated rubber band. Stretch it and release it several times. Does it remain the same size? Measure the length of the rubber band that was stretched and heated. Does it have its former elasticity? Stretch it and release it several times. Does it return to the length it was when you first measured it?

How hard do you have to stretch each band to reach the elastic limit where it will break? How does heat affect the resiliency of rubber bands? In which case do you think that the rubber molecules were shortened the most?

VICKI COBB attended the University of Wisconsin on a Ford Foundation Early Admissions Scholarship, then continued her education at Barnard College, where she received her B.A. degree, and at Columbia University Teachers College, where she was awarded an M.A. degree.

After an early career as a science teacher, Ms. Cobb turned to writing. In addition to film strips and other educational aids, she has written scripts for network television and was the creator and principal personality of "the Science Game," an educational television series. Ms. Cobb, the author of many highly acclaimed books, is now devoting herself to full-time writing of science books for children.

BILL MORRISON has written and illustrated many books and stories for children. He is a member of the Society of Illustrators in New York, from whom he has received several awards in their National Exhibitions.

Mr. Morrison lives with his wife and children in Massachusetts, which he might also be found digging for artifacts as he enjoys his hobby, archeology.

Understanding Foreign Policy

UNDERSTANDING FOREIGN POLICY

MARTIN C. NEEDLER
University of Michigan

Holt, Rinehart and Winston, Inc.

NEW YORK   CHICAGO   SAN FRANCISCO   TORONTO   LONDON

Preface

This book grew out of the author's experiences in lecturing to student and lay audiences on the subject of American foreign policy. He was repeatedly struck in such encounters by the eagerness, earnestness, and good will with which Americans address themselves to foreign policy questions, characteristics that seem to him to deserve more than the baffled frustration that confrontation with the uncertainties of national policy in a complex world typically engenders.

Accordingly, this book has been written on the basis of two principles. One is to interpret broadly the area to be covered; the author has thus chosen, where it seemed appropriate, to violate academic boundary conventions and discuss regional organizations, Marxist ideology, American domestic politics, international relations theory, and any other topic that promised to be able to advance the cause of understanding. The other principle has been to structure the material so as to facilitate ready understanding. This has entailed an emphasis on continuing patterns and explanatory theory, as well as the maintenance of standards of concision that have sought economy without superficiality. The book's success in meeting the objectives set for it will doubtless be adjudged less than perfect; it is only to be expected that intentions should outpace performance in such an enterprise.

Understanding Foreign Policy is thus designed to serve the interested layman as well as the undergraduate as a general introduction to the field with which it deals. Used as a text in a college course, it might usefully be supplemented by one of the several collections of readings available.

Every attempt has been made to maintain balance and perspective in the point of view from which the book is written. At the same time, the author does have a point of view and tries to eschew the wishy-washy "on the one hand . . . , but on the other hand" with which writers of textbooks try to avoid controversy. It is hoped that this presentation of the material from a single consistent viewpoint will gain in intelligibility anything it may lose in acceptability.

Any merit that the book can claim lies primarily in the way in which the material is presented and, especially, interpreted; only in dealing with two or three subjects on which the secondary writings are thin, as in the discussion of Cuba, does the book reflect the author's own research in original sources. Its purpose, however, is to contribute not so much to knowledge as to understanding.

It is impossible to keep a true accounting of one's intellectual debts. There can be no doubt, however, of the author's liability to those of his teachers at Harvard whose courses impinged on the areas discussed in this book—David Bell, McGeorge Bundy, Rupert Emerson, J. Kenneth Galbraith, Barbara Ward, and especially Samuel P. Huntington. Special thanks are owed to his present colleagues, Inis L. Claude, Jr., and Harold K. Jacobson, for their comments on portions of the manuscript. Of course, the author bears sole responsibility for the book's present content. Secretarial assistance was provided by Elaine Wender, Nadine Phillips, and Susan Lawther.

Martin C. Needler

Ann Arbor, Michigan
August 1965

Contents

vii

I

The Foundations
of Foreign Policy

I

The National Interest— In Principle and Practice

Few things are as personal or individualized as one's approach to the problems of foreign policy. As in other areas of politics, the observer all too commonly projects his hopes and fears into his perception of reality so that nothing is rarer than a dispassionate appraisal of a foreign affairs problem.

In this book I shall be trying to take a realistic point of view, using "realism," that over-used and much abused word, as a mean term between optimism and pessimism, between idealism and cynicism. I shall be viewing the world neither as perfectible nor as degenerate; I shall be treating policy neither as an impotent struggle against implacable forces, nor as a ready and easy way of achieving miracles, but as a means of effecting limited but valuable changes in the external situation. This, after all, is the attitude most of us take in our own lives, and there is no reason to suppose that the same point of view will not prove equally serviceable in one's approach to foreign policy.

The book's concern with foreign policy will be both empirical and normative, that is, concerned both with what policy is and with what it should be. Clearly these are two different enterprises, the one descriptive, the other prescriptive; the one a statement of what policy has been, the

3

other a set of recommendations to future policy makers as to what it ought to be. While these are in principle two separate enterprises, they are nevertheless related in significant ways. First, a set of conclusions as to what foreign policy should be provides a basis on which to evaluate and criticize the policies of the past and of the present. Second, a solid understanding of what policy has been historically, and especially the fate with which past policies have met, will suggest to the would-be policy maker what alternative paths are available, and will give him a sense of the limits of the possible. In other words, knowledge of the history of policy is necessary as a basis for comprehending the probable consequences of various policy alternatives, thus making possible responsible policy making.

THE CONCEPT OF NATIONAL INTEREST

The most logical starting point for our inquiry is probably to ask: What is the purpose of foreign policy? What should the United States government try to accomplish as it acts in relation to other states? Perhaps it is neglect of this basic question that gives rise to so much of the existing disagreement on substantive questions of foreign policy.

There appears to be something of a consensus among those professionally involved in the formulation and observation of foreign policy that its core purpose, at the minimum, is the protection and promotion of "national interests." At a later point in the discussion we will investigate in detail the meaning of the concept of national interests. Before going into this problem, however, and without for the moment separating its descriptive and normative aspects, let us first ask whether this is all that states do or should do. Or are there goals above and beyond the pursuit of national interest that enter or should enter into a state's foreign policy?

A very widely accepted view is that the goals of a state's foreign policy should be limited to the pursuit of its self-interest and, indeed, are so limited, except for occasional "mistakes." If this is so, if all states single-mindedly pursue their self-interest, then foreign policy problems are concerned with how to secure the maximum advantage for oneself, now or in the future. The capacity to attain the realization of interests in the future is national power. Proceeding from this point of view, if a problem arises in which the state's immediate self-interest is not apparent, then its interest becomes that of the maximization of power, thus bettering the chances of its future realization of self-interested goals. Because this is the case, Hans J. Morgenthau has described this approach, with which he identifies himself, as the principle that states pursue (and should pursue) their "interest defined as power."

This view has of course a respectable intellectual lineage, being found in more general form in the writings of philosophers and amateur psychologists, Nietzsche and Hobbes for example, who have postulated the general rule that all men pursue power. This principle has of course a substantial empirical basis and can, in fact, be extended to cover the behavior of animals other than man; the barnyard "pecking order" is well known, and experiments with mice and other animals have indicated the existence of an urge to dominate independent of the more well-known biological drives.

The drive for power that so many observers perceive in the world of international relations, however, need not be based on the presumption of a general instinctual law of human behavior, but may instead be of a secondary nature, deriving logically from the principle of pursuit of self-interest. If power is defined in the most general way to mean the ability to make others do what one wants, it would thus include not only force in a military sense but also economic pressure, psychological influence, and so on; then clearly "power" is indeed needed to pursue any ends that may be postulated, and the pursuit of power becomes a necessary preliminary to the pursuit of any other goal of policy.

It should be noted that one may profess the most noble goals imaginable but the realistic attempt to attain them can only proceed by means of the techniques of power. Thus in the middle of the nineteenth century, Great Britain pursued a policy of putting an end to the slave trade. She did this not by praying or by passing resolutions, however, but by sending gunboats and troops to Africa.

The school of thought described above, then, finds in the pursuit of power the key to a general description of interstate behavior. But it provides more than a description: It furnishes at the same time a tool of analysis. If one wishes to understand why certain actions were taken, he looks not to the justifications officially announced, but to the imperatives of state behavior as logic teaches him they must be: to the principle of pursuit of power. Finally this mode of approach provides a normative basis on which one can evaluate any existing policy—does it effectively pursue interest defined as power?

THE CONCEPT OF NATIONAL INTEREST AS THE PURSUIT OF POWER: ITS STRENGTHS

In attempting to assess the merits of the principles of this school of thought in its three-fold function, first, as description, second, as analytic tool, and third, as basis for policy recommendations, it is necessary to acknowledge its usefulness before proceeding to point out its limitations. As a tool of analysis, it enables the observer to bypass the phase of investigating in detail the specific motives of all those involved in policy decisions. It directs one's attention away from the plausible but false justifications that states are wont to present to the public; the apothegm that language was given to man to disguise his thoughts is after all especially true of the diplomat, proverbially an honest man sent abroad to lie for his country.

Finally, this approach enables one to discern what might otherwise be missed: the continuities in a nation's foreign policy that are its abiding features despite changes in individual officeholders, despite changes in the party in control of the governmental apparatus, despite changes in the dominant ideology. On this point, Morgenthau has written:

> It is this assumption of the universality of the national interest in time and space which enables us to understand the foreign policies of Demosthenes and Caesar, of Kautilya and Henry the Eighth, of the statesmen of contemporary Russia and China. Regardless of all the differences in personality, social environment, convictions, and preferences, their thinking was predetermined and their actions could take place only within a narrow range, when they were faced with the task of protecting and promoting the rational core of the national interest.[1]

And a leading disciple of Morgenthau, Kenneth W. Thompson, has written, "Regardless of the party in power or the leaders and their private or public philosophies, British and American and French and Russian foreign policies display unities that transcend individual beliefs or ideologies."[2]

Morgenthau has taken this point so far as to criticize, in a letter to the New York *Times,* the view that American foreign policy is handicapped by its lack of information about the elements that enter into the making of Communist Chinese foreign policy, arguing, in effect, that one could tell what China's foreign policy was going to be without such detailed knowledge.

The great merit of the principle that states pursue power "as a general description" of the world of international politics is that it provides a starting point for a theory of international relations. No general theory is possible without a general statement of principles of behavior, which the interest-as-power hypothesis provides.

---

[1] Hans Morgenthau, *Dilemmas of Politics.* Chicago: University of Chicago Press, 1958, p. 67.

[2] Roy Macridis and Kenneth Thompson, eds., *Foreign Policy in World Politics,* 2d ed. Englewood Cliffs, N.J.: Prentice-Hall, 1962, p. 2.

"As a general policy recommendation" for the United States the great merit of the hypothesis is that it avoids the self-righteousness and sentimentalism that have been the traditional weaknesses of U.S. foreign policy. This was, for example, the way in which a similar approach was used by Alexander Hamilton to argue against the view that the United States should adopt a policy of friendliness towards France in gratitude for the aid that France had given to the independence movement.

> Between individuals, occasion is not unfrequently given for the exercise of gratitude. Instances of conferring benefits from kind and benevolent dispositions or feelings toward the person benefited, without any other interest on the part of the person who renders the service, than the pleasure of doing a good action, occur every day among individuals. But among nations they perhaps never occur. It may be affirmed as a general principle, that the predominant motive of good offices from one nation to another, is the interest or advantage of the nation which performs them.
>
> Indeed, the rule of morality in this respect is not precisely the same between nations as between individuals. The duty of making its own welfare the guide of its actions, is much stronger upon the former than upon the latter; in proportion to the greater magnitude and importance of national compared with individual happiness, and to the greater permanency of the effects of national than of individual conduct. Existing millions, and for the most part future generations, are concerned in the present measures of a government; while the consequences of the private actions of an individual ordinarily terminate with himself, or are circumscribed within a narrow compass.
>
> Whence it follows that an individual may, on numerous occasions, meritoriously indulge the emotions of generosity and benevolence, not only without an eye to, but even at the expense of, his own interest. But a government can rarely, if at all, be justifiable in pursuing a similar course; and, if it does so, ought to confine itself within much stricter bounds.[3]

THE CONCEPT OF NATIONAL INTEREST AS THE PURSUIT OF POWER: ITS WEAKNESSES

Although the approach to foreign policy that regards the pursuit of interest-as-power as its key *motif* must be credited with several distinctive merits, it also displays certain characteristic disadvantages. To begin

---

[3] From the *Gazette of the United States*, 1793. Reprinted in Robert A. Goldwin, ed., *Readings in American Foreign Policy*. New York: Oxford University Press, 1959, p. 614.

with, as a tool of analysis it has two principal weaknesses. First, it leads the observer to interpret reality on the premise that states have always behaved rationally. It is clearly true, however, that on many occasions states have been induced to embark on one course of policy or another irrationally. That is, irrationality exists in policy-making processes and has to be taken into account.

Second, the approach described exaggerates the admittedly very real continuities in national foreign policy. That is, although many of the elements of foreign policy do indeed remain constant despite changes in an administration's leaders, parties, and ideologies, nevertheless changes in personnel and ideas do quite regularly bring about significant modifications in policy. To argue otherwise leads one to absurd conclusions. To take an obvious case, it seems indubitable that Hitler's coming to power in Germany changed the direction of German foreign policy, and not merely in questions of detail.

A prime example of the misleading effect which the power-as-interest principle can have as a tool of analysis can be seen in the support given by James Reston of the New York *Times* to General Eisenhower in the election of 1952. Reston argued that American foreign policy was set by certain abiding features of America's international situation and by her permanent national interests, and that therefore there was no basis on which to choose between Eisenhower and Stevenson on the substance of the policies they would follow, but only on the amount of support that each could secure from the American people for the identical policies that each necessarily would pursue. On this basis Reston supported Eisenhower, although he was subsequently to regret his decision, to criticize Eisenhower's policies, and to support Stevenson in 1956.

"As a guide to general recommendations on policy," that is, as a general normative principle, the doctrine that the United States should pursue its interests defined in terms of power clearly leaves much to be desired. It seems to the present writer that it is perfectly open to a rational and informed student of foreign policy to reject courses of action that would result in an increase in national power and, therefore, in the more likely attainment of future national goals, on the grounds that they conflict with other value preferences that he has. To argue otherwise would lead to the justification of any act committed in the name of national interest. Of course individuals will vary in their views on this point, and in the last analysis it becomes a question of conscience; nevertheless one would surely seem justified in thinking he was behaving rationally and within his rights as a citizen, or even as an officeholder, if he refused to sanction say, the torture of prisoners to extract information, or the unleashing of a surprise attack on an innocent civilian population, whether this would result in an augmentation of the sum total of national power or not. In other words, there are values other than national interest by which one is entitled to judge actions.

On this point we now have the testimony of Robert Kennedy that in the Cuban "missile crisis" of October 1962 President Kennedy chose to impose a blockade on Cuba to induce the Russians to withdraw their missiles from the island, rather than to bomb the missile bases—although the latter would have been a more direct and more certain method of achieving the same end—because he did not wish to cause the loss of life that a bombing raid would entail.[4]

"As a general description of the world of international relations," finally, the approach of the interest-as-power school seems at first glance patently false. Quite obviously states do not always behave so as to maximize their power and to attain their self-interests. If they did, it would make no sense for Morgenthau and his followers to make policy recommendations, as I. L. Claude and others have pointed out. Quite clearly, if states always and inevitably do something, there is no point in trying to persuade them not to do something else.

However, it seems to this writer that the principle that states pursue power and ultimately self-interest, while certainly not 100 percent accurate, is not bad as a first approximation to a general descriptive theory of foreign policy. As a shorthand description of how the world of international relations operates, it seems to correspond closely enough to reality to be usable, but only if taken in a statistical rather than an absolute sense. That is, while all states do not always pursue power, most of them do most of the time. Descriptions of human behavior are useful if they are merely more true than false; and this one, while lacking the absolute validity which its proponents tend to claim, has still a rather high degree of verisimilitude. Despite the defects of the principle, therefore, it can provide a convenient starting point, and will do as a first approximation, in both its descriptive and its normative aspects. It can thus be regarded as of equivalent status to the statement, "Cars travel on the right-hand side of the road, therefore I had better drive on the right-hand side." That is, its factual element is not invariably true, nor is its normative element invariably good advice; nevertheless it is true and valid enough of the time to serve as a rough-and-ready general description and a pretty good rule of thumb. It is similar to the rules of good play in a game. Not everyone follows them, and competent players may, on occasion, be able to do better by disregarding them; but because most players tend to follow them, they provide a better basis for predicting the actions of players than anything else, and at the same time they provide a handy guide for play.

---

[4] New York *Times*, October 13, 1964.

To complete the analogy one should add that the players have no choice what game to play. That has already been decided. In other words, it is not possible unilaterally to reject the game as organized and substitute another one for it; one has only the choice of playing well or badly.

THE NATIONAL INTEREST

Let us then proceed on the premise that pursuit of national interest provides at least the everyday working principle of United States foreign policy—the automatic pilot that can be relied on for the routine cruising duties. If one removes the parentheses around the term, "national interest," and tries to translate this principle into operational terms as a guide for the making of foreign policy, however, then the problem is seen to become one of infinite complexity. An acute student and practitioner of United States foreign policy, Charles Burton Marshall, has written:

> The question in the arena of responsibility in handling an issue involving foreign policy alone is not whether, but how, to serve the national interest. That involves the question of what is the national interest in a particular situation. The question of serving the national interest is always a subtle and complex one in real situations.
>
> I am sure all of the following things are clearly in our national interest: To avoid war; to preserve our institutions; to have strong allies; to avoid inflation; to have a prosperous civilian economy; to find common grounds on which to stand with the various nations which have newly come to responsibility; to preserve our access to strategic waterways and vital raw materials; and to protect the property and safety of our nationals abroad. I could extend this list by dozens of items.
>
> Now any matter of foreign policy pertaining only to the realization of one of those items would not present an issue at all. No one would have to work his brains over time on it. No series of exhaustive meetings would have to be held. No protracted debate about the nuances and contradictions would be necessary. In such an instance the policy decision would crystallize spontaneously.
>
> In any practical question presenting a real issue the national interest has several aspects. Indeed, there are many national interests, not just one. The difficulties arise in the conflict of one interest with another; for example, in the clash of the interest in peace with the interest in preserving national institutions, in the clash of the interest in having a strong defense with the interest in having a strong civilian economy, or in the clash of the interest in preserving access to a waterway with the interest in eliciting the adherence of another country to one's cause.[5]

---

5 U.S. Department of State Bulletin, May 5, 1952. Reprinted in Goldwin, pp. 665–666.

The truth of this point, that clashes exist between goals each of which is clearly in the national interest, can readily be seen if one considers briefly three of the most basic aims of a state's policy: protecting its citizens abroad, promoting its trade, and maintaining its national security. It is clearly one of the minimum functions of the state to protect the rights of its citizens residing abroad. This is certainly maximized by the securing of extraterritoriality, the principle that one's citizens abroad are not subject to the courts of the states in which they are resident, but can only be tried by the judicial machinery of the home country. It has been demonstrably the case, however, that the securing of extraterritoriality has been a cause of great friction between the state of residence and the state of citizenship. In part because of this, the United States asks only for limited extraterritorial rights for members of its armed forces stationed abroad. In other words, because of the generalized national security interest in minimizing friction with foreign states, there has been a sacrifice of the goal of protecting citizens abroad.[6]

It is also clearly in the national interest to promote the country's trade. However, there exists a whole network of restrictions on trade—for example, a ban on the sale of strategic materials to unfriendly states—that illustrate how this basic principle too has been limited in the interest of national security.

One might say that within the constellation of national interests, the principle of national security has overriding priority. Yet this still may not help in clarifying policy goals in concrete situations; Arnold Wolfers has written perceptively of the ambiguities inherent in the concept of national security itself.[7] It may plainly seem to conduce to a higher level of national security for the United States to accumulate formidable weapons, for example. Yet if such behavior creates the belief in other states that its intentions are aggressive, one result may be that an armed coalition forms against the United States, whose security is on balance lessened rather than augmented.

Because the principle of national security seems of such preeminence among the multitude of goals that have a claim to be considered by policy makers, a powerful tendency exists for attempts to be made to justify every proposal on national security grounds, thus thoroughly confusing the issue. The recurrent discussion of whether limitations on oil imports are in the interest of national security or not can serve as an example. Those who wish to limit the importation of foreign oil argue that large oil imports create a dependence on foreign sources of supply

---

[6] The sacrifice has actually been more apparent than real, since foreign courts that have tried United States citizens in recent years have almost invariably been more lenient with them than United States courts would have been.

[7] " 'National Security' as an Ambiguous Symbol," *Political Science Quarterly*, December 1952.

that might suddenly be cut off in time of emergency, and that, therefore, a policy of heavy importation might result in an atrophy of the domestic oil industry that would then be unable to take up the slack if a discontinuance of foreign supply should occur. Those who oppose restrictions on the import of foreign oil, however, argue that the maximum possible importation of foreign oil means that oil reserves within the continental United States will be conserved, and thus instead of being exhausted will remain available if a sudden interruption of foreign supply should take place as a result of an international emergency. In this case, after one is argued to numbness by the partisans of each view, one realizes that what lies at the root of the position taken by each of the contending sides is simple economic interest. It is the oil producers not associated with foreign companies who campaign for the limitation of foreign oil imports, which threaten their position in the domestic market, and it is the consumers of oil, especially in the New England area, where oil is the principal fuel used for heating, who favor foreign oil imports, since the imported oil can normally be sold for less. In this case the argument of national security is merely being used as a more or less insincere justification for a position based ultimately on other considerations. Discoveries of this type led the historian, Charles A. Beard, to write that he was unable to discover any such thing as a common national interest over and above the special interests of specific segments of the population. Surely this view goes too far, however. There is plainly a general national security interest in the avoidance of military defeat and conquest; there is a national security interest in an avoidance of a dependence on a foreign state so complete that it would make blackmail regularly possible. Nevertheless it is certainly the case that every special economic interest that attempts to impose itself on the public purse first dons the garments of national need.

THE NATIONAL INTEREST IN PERSPECTIVE

A range of difficulties thus remains even if one grants that "national interests" must have primacy in determining foreign policy. One must sort out the authentic national interests from the spurious; this requires not only an eye that can see through the self-righteousness of the special pleading of pressure groups, but ultimately also a personal judgment into which one's own value preferences must enter. One has then to harmonize conflicts among various national interests, each of them genuine. And one has finally to face the conflict between short-range and long-range interests. How much should one discount a policy that aims at some unquestionable national good if its realization is far off in the future and its attainment therefore problematical?

This last difficulty arises out of the fact that decisions between policy alternatives are made in a context of factual uncertainty—that is, the choice of any policy involves a series of predictions as to its effect, predictions that must necessarily be imprecise and contain a large component of guesswork.

One is thus forced to conclude that the making of foreign policy does not involve the single-minded pursuit of some goal that has been given absolute priority over all others, but involves instead the attempt to seek an over-all maximum of various objectives. Consequently, there will enter into the process not only variations in the assessments of the probable outcome of alternative policies by different individuals, but also conflicts among individuals over the relative weight to be attached to the different objectives, since more than one such objective must be regarded as valid. Clearly, therefore, individual preferences as to values, as to "ideals," will enter into this process by the back door.

It remains to add to this formulation that the process of policy making is not a question of balancing cut-and-dried alternatives, but that the alternatives themselves have to be thought up, and that thus creativity must play a large role. The greatest statesmen have been, perhaps, not only those whose instincts in balancing off various interests and aspirations most represented what was best in national attitudes and values, but those whose vision extended to the creation of new roads for policy to take, and indeed to the perception of national interests previously only dimly comprehended.

THE NATIONAL INTEREST IN PRACTICE

In order to relate the theoretical considerations discussed above to the concrete problems of American foreign policy, it is necessary to survey the development of that policy down to the present era.

During the first years of the republic, the leading themes of foreign policy were not unlike those which are apparent in the early years of other states, both in the past and today. They followed logically on the movement for independence itself, the principal theme being the attempt to define the national domain in relation to the country's neighbors, together with a suspicion of the intentions of the former colonial power. There was little reluctance during this period to think in terms of armed force to attain national ends; after all, independence itself had been won by fighting, the profession of arms was familiar to many citizens of the republic, the country's political leaders had distinguished themselves on the field of combat, and continual warfare was in any case made necessary by the hostility of Indian tribes on the frontier. The sentiment of hostility towards the former colonial power, Great Britain, together with feelings of gratitude towards France for her help during the war for independence, inspired a wave of public support for intervention on the side of France in the Revolutionary and Napoleonic wars between France and Great Britain. This wave was, however, ridden out by Presidents Washington and Adams; Washington's policy was summarized as that of isolation from the quarrels of Europe and the avoidance of "entangling alliances"; Adams went further and attempted to prohibit propaganda for French revolutionary ideology by means of the Alien and Sedition Acts.

The two motivating forces of early foreign policy—an eighteenth-century version of anticolonialism, and territorial expansion—coalesced in the War of 1812, which had as one of its chief underlying motives the desire to annex Canada to the United States. Hostility to Great Britain diminished steadily over the succeeding years, but generalized anti-colonial feeling continued strong, and, augmented by concern for the national security, led in 1823 to the proclamation of the Monroe Doctrine, which bade the powers of Europe to keep "hands off" the Western Hemisphere.

The drive to secure the definitive establishment of the national boundaries, and incidentally to include within them as much territory as possible, became meanwhile the dominant theme of foreign policy. Jefferson had already bought a large tract of land from Napoleon which the history books record as the Louisiana Purchase. Settlers and troops carried forward the effective occupation of new territory taken from the Indians. The boundary line with Canada in the Pacific Northwest was defined and a "national liberation movement," not unlike those supported today by the Soviets, secured the independence of Texas from Mexico—the Anglo-Saxon rebels in the new republic later successfully petitioning for admission to the Union as a state. A successful war with Mexico, whose immediate cause was Mexican opposition to the annexation of Texas and difficulties over the definition of the Texas-Mexico boundary, but whose principal motive on the United States side was the acquisition of more territory, especially California, carried the process further. Hawaii, later to be "liberated" from a native monarch, also became first a republic and then a state in the Union.

With the final definition of the continental boundaries of the United States, America turned inward to attend to the political problems that eventuated in the Civil War, and then to the economic problems of postwar reconstruction and development. However, in 1898 the path of expansion was resumed with the Spanish-American War, and it looked as though the United States would join the powers of Europe in a full-fledged imperialism that would not only expand into territorially contiguous areas but would cross salt water as well.

This did indeed begin to occur. As a result of the war, Cuba was temporarily occupied, and the Philippine Islands, Guam, and Puerto Rico became United States territories.[8] Theodore Roosevelt followed McKinley's lead and the United States came by 1920 to own and operate an interocean canal through the middle of a Republic of Panama that United States warships had helped bring into existence, and to be exercising an effective protectorate not only over Cuba, but also over Haiti, the Dominican Republic, and Nicaragua, each of which was at one time occupied by United States Marines.

With 1920 came isolationism and a retrenchment on United States commitments abroad. After 1917, however, the United States had in any case outgrown her policy of local preponderance in North America and the Caribbean and was impelled to play the role of great power to which her wealth and size entitled her. And yet the America which has been called to act on a world stage has always done so reluctantly, has always looked back to the earlier policy of local preponderance as the "natural" one, has always as it were tempered her internationalism with her isolationism.

It should not be thought, however, that the policy of local preponderance was itself clear-cut and uncomplicated, at least as far as the basic motives underlying it were concerned. It has been fashionable for some time to explain the imperialism of the period in straightforward economic terms, as a search for captive markets and resources, and there is little doubt that such motives played a leading role. However, it seems clear, to this writer at least, that the motives that prompted Theodore Roosevelt to inaugurate the Marine occupations in the Caribbean, for example, or to agitate for war with Spain in the years before he came to the presidency, were of another sort.

Roosevelt was concerned rather with national security, in the sense of the maintenance of international order in the area, both for its own sake and to deny European powers an occasion to intervene in the Western Hemisphere. What probably motivated him even more was the desire that the United States should cut a heroic figure in the world and should take its rightful place in the ranks of the great powers.

There seems no reason, on the other hand, to doubt Woodrow Wilson's professions that his own interventions in Latin America were designed to teach the Latin Americans the virtues of democracy and constitutional processes—not an unexpected aim, perhaps, for a former professor of political science.

---

[8] The Filipinos were given their independence in 1946; they continue to be friendly to Americans, on both personal and interstate levels. The Stars and Stripes still fly over Guam and Puerto Rico.

Throughout the period before World War I there was criticism of the path of action on which the country had embarked. And yet the country had scarcely begun to develop a conception of national purpose that could inform her policy and be commensurate with her interests and capabilities. The justifications of policy—and not only those packaged for foreign consumption but those the American people gave to itself—tended to be a hodgepodge of national security, economic, and idealistic motives. A startling demonstration of this is provided in President McKinley's much-quoted explanation of why he had decided to annex the Philippine Islands.

> I walked the floor of the White House night after night until midnight," he said, "and I am not ashamed to tell you, gentlemen, that I went down on my knees and prayed Almighty God for light and guidance more than one night. And one night late it came to me this way—I don't know how it was, but it came: (1) That we could not give them back to Spain—that would be cowardly and dishonorable; (2) that we could not turn them over to France (*sic*) or Germany—our commercial rivals in the Orient—that would be bad business and discreditable; (3) that we could not leave them to themselves—they were unfit for self-government—and they would soon have anarchy and misrule over there worse than Spain's was; and (4) that there was nothing left for us to do but to take them all, and to educate the Filipinos, and uplift and civilize and Christianize them, and by God's grace do the very best we could by them, as our fellowmen for whom Christ also died. And then I went to bed, and to sleep, and slept soundly. . . .[9]

There had always been a strain of criticism of United States expansionism that based itself on idealistic grounds in arguing against aggression and self-aggrandizement by force of arms. Henry David Thoreau had spent time in the Concord jail rather than pay taxes to a government that was prosecuting an aggressive war against Mexico and returning fugitive slaves to their masters. Ex-President Grover Cleveland strongly opposed the Spanish-American War and the resultant annexation of territory. Indeed, as President, Cleveland had refused to consider the annexation of Hawaii and Santo Domingo,[10] which the governments of those territories had themselves requested.

---

[9] From Samuel Flagg Bemis, *A Diplomatic History of the United States,* 4th ed. New York: Holt, Rinehart and Winston, 1955, p. 472. The cynic will note that McKinley was speaking to a group of visiting clergymen, but there seems no reason to doubt the sincerity of a pious era. Curiously enough, it is likely that the proportion of Christians in the population of the Philippines, after 300 years of Spanish rule, was about the same, or perhaps slightly higher, than that in the United States at that time.

[10] That is, the Dominican Republic.

TABLE 1. Wars of the United States[a]

1775–1781	The American Revolution *v.* Great Britain
1798–1800	Naval war *v.* France over American shipping rights
1802–1805	The Tripolitan War *v.* the "Barbary pirates" of North Africa
1812–1814	The War of 1812 *v.* Great Britain
1846–1848	The Mexican War *v.* Mexico over territorial disputes
1861–1865	The Civil War
1898	The Spanish-American War *v.* Spain over treatment of Cuba
1899–1902	Anti-guerrilla warfare in the Philippines
1912–1933	Intermittent anti-guerrilla warfare in Haiti, the Dominican Republic and Nicaragua
1917–1918[b]	World War I *v.* Germany and Austria
1941–1945[b]	World War II *v.* Germany and Japan
1950–1953	The Korean war *v.* North Korea and China
1962[b]–	Anti-guerrilla warfare in South Vietnam

[a] Intermittent warfare against American Indian tribes is not included in the table.
[b] These wars were already in progress at the time the United States became involved.

Some observers, showing perhaps more patriotism than sense of proportion, have in fact chosen to treat the tradition of protest against expansion as the dominant one, and the actual movements of expansion themselves as "aberrations" of some kind.

After the United States had assumed its role of world power the local imperialism of the nineteenth and early twentieth centuries was indeed repudiated. During the 1920s and 1930s the Marine occupations in the Caribbean were liquidated; rights to intervene in Cuba under the so-called Platt Amendment were voluntarily relinquished; the Senate voted to compensate the Republic of Colombia for the loss of Panama, thus in effect acknowledging United States complicity in the secession of Panama from Colombia; the Philippines were scheduled for independence; and the United States subscribed to a new inter-American doctrine: that no state had the right to intervene in the affairs of another. One should, however, acknowledge that the dominant long-run tendency in the 100 years before American entry into the World War I had been one of steady acquisition of new territory by means both fair and foul.

But while some elements of United States foreign policy attracted criticism on the grounds that they betrayed American ideals, other elements were criticized as too idealistic in the sense that they ignored the realities of power. For example, Secretary of State John Hay had in 1899 enunciated the principle of American foreign policy known as the "Open Door" towards China, which stipulated that the citizens of all states should have equal rights and privileges in their commercial and other dealings in Chinese territory. Theodore Roosevelt had this to say about the Open Door policy:

> . . . I do not believe in our taking any position anywhere unless we can make good; and as regards Manchuria, if the Japanese choose to follow a course of conduct to which we are adverse, we cannot stop it unless we are prepared to go to war, and a successful war about Manchuria would require a fleet as good as that of England, plus an army as good as that of Germany. The Open Door policy in China was an excellent thing, and I hope it will be a good thing in the future, so far as it can be maintained by general diplomatic agreement; but, as has been proved by the whole history of Manchuria, alike under Russia and under Japan, the "Open Door" policy, as a matter of fact, completely disappears as soon as a powerful nation determines to disregard it, and is willing to run the risk of war rather than forego its intention.[11]

While these criticisms are mutually opposed, the one attacking alleged overidealism and lack of attention to power factors, the other criticizing alleged lack of idealism and hunger for power, they can be reconciled and presented as a single critique, as they have by some of the partisans of the "national interest-as-power" thesis discussed above. In following the argument, however, one should not forget the fact that it attempts to synthesize criticism derived from two quite opposed points of view.

THE KENNAN CRITIQUE OF "MORALISM-LEGALISM"

Probably the most potent critique of the leading features of American foreign policy since the Civil War is that of George F. Kennan, a skilled practitioner of the arts of diplomacy. The theme of Kennan's critique is that United States policy has been unrealistic, basing itself on legalistic formulas and moralistic feelings rather than on a hardheaded appreciation of the realities of power and interest. Thus Kennan argues that the war with Spain was unnecessary—McKinley allowed himself to be swept off his feet by public opinion aroused by the sinking of the "Maine" in Havana harbor and by emotional feelings of sympathy for the Cubans struggling for independence—and that a diplomatic settlement favorable to the United States could have been won from Spain without going to war.

Kennan regards the Open Door policy in China as meaningless or

---

[11] Quoted in George F. Kennan, *American Diplomacy, 1900–1950.* New York: New American Library (Mentor), 1952, p. 42.

worse. The United States did not have the military force available to back up the policy if it should be challenged, as in fact it later was by Russia. Moreover, when the Japanese approached the United States government with the proposal of combining forces to resist Russian encroachments, they were told that the use of force was not contemplated by the United States policy; this may well have contributed to the Japanese undervaluation of the willingness of the United States to use force, which was to have such a tragic *dénouement* in 1941.

Kennan criticizes in similar terms the United States decision to participate in World War I—not the decision itself, but the haphazard and ill-considered way in which it was made and carried into effect—and the policies that were followed during and after the war. He finds that no consideration was given to the essential requirements of national interest during the events prior to United States participation in the war; rather the United States under President Wilson blundered from one incident to another, allowing frictions with Germany to build up until war was drifted into.

Wilson's policies with respect to a postwar settlement he criticizes on other grounds. The creation of a series of independent states in east central Europe in line with Wilson's principles of democratic self-determination seems to Kennan a particular act of folly. These were, after all, small states overshadowed by their gigantic neighbors, Germany and the Soviet Union. The realist, thinking in terms of power, could only conclude that they were destined to become dominated by either Germany or Russia. And, in fact, that is what happened; first the Germans established their hegemony in the area, and then, after World War II, the Russians.

Finally, Kennan criticizes the policy of unconditional surrender followed by the Allies during World War II, arguing that the insistence on unconditional surrender stiffened the Germans' will to resist, since the Germans had no idea what the Allies intended to do with them in the event they would be victorious, and so imagined the worst. Moreover, this policy, which subordinated political considerations to military requirements, led United States policy makers to overlook the question of the postwar distribution of power, and consequently made possible the strong strategic position that the Russians assumed in eastern Europe at the end of the war.

ACHESON'S CRITIQUE OF DULLES

The deficiencies that Kennan believed he found in United States foreign policy are not necessarily of interest to the historian only but instead may be indicative of failings in the American approach to foreign policy that persist today. Thus, former Secretary of State Dean Acheson has criticized policies of his successor, John Foster Dulles,[12] in terms strikingly parallel to those used by Kennan. Thus Acheson criticized Dulles's anticolonialism in almost the same terms that Kennan used when speaking of Woodrow Wilson's policies towards eastern Europe: as a policy conceived on grounds of moralism that overlooked the realities of power; that many of the colonial countries, if given their independence, would not be able either to defend it or to use it wisely. Acheson also criticized Dulles's reliance on "declarations" and legal agreements just as Kennan criticized John Hay for his Open Door policy. That is, the declarations by themselves had no effect in the real world, and if not backed by military force were likely only to make the United States seem impotent and insincere. Dulles' brave words about "liberating" eastern Europe, for example, proved empty when the Hungarians did, in fact, revolt against Soviet dominance and were left to their fate by the United States. Finally one hears echoes of Kennan's criticisms of McKinley in Acheson's indictment of Dulles's weaknesses with relation to public opinion: for example, in his allowing Senator McCarthy to wreak havoc in the ranks of the professional foreign service with groundless charges of "softness on communism."

One need not subscribe to the entire catalogue of failings that appear in the indictments drawn by either Kennan or Acheson (the writer finds himself largely in agreement with Acheson, and agreeing more than disagreeing with Kennan) to acknowledge that emotionalism, moralism, crusading, the reliance on legal formulas, the reluctance to accept the realities of power, have traditionally marred United States foreign policy and are still with us today. Moreover, their persistence suggests that they stem from abiding characteristics of national life and not from the idiosyncrasies of individuals who have happened from time to time to guide American policy.

Let us then proceed to search for the underlying elements in American character, in American society, and in the American political system, to which can be attributed this apparent predisposition to deviate from a path of cautious realism in foreign policy.

SUGGESTED READINGS

Beard, Charles A., *The Idea of National Interest*. New York: Macmillan, 1934.

Bemis, Samuel Flagg, *A Diplomatic History of the United States,* 4th ed. New York: Holt, Rinehart and Winston, Inc., 1955.

---

[12] In his book, *Power and Diplomacy*. The general criticisms given are those of Mr. Acheson; the examples are supplied by the author.

Cook, Thomas I., and Malcolm Moos, *Power Through Purpose.* Baltimore: Johns Hopkins Press, 1954.

Council on Foreign Relations, *Basic Aims of United States Foreign Policy* (Senate Foreign Relations Committee Print, 86th Cong., 1st Sess., November 25, 1959). Washington, D.C.: Government Printing Office, 1959.

Kennan, George F., *American Diplomacy, 1900–1950.* New York: New American Library (Mentor), 1952.

Morgenthau, Hans J., *In Defense of the National Interest.* New York: Knopf, 1951.

——, *Politics Among Nations,* 3d ed. New York: Knopf, 1960.

Perkins, Dexter, *The American Approach to Foreign Policy,* rev. ed. Cambridge, Mass.: Harvard University Press, 1962.

Pratt, Julius W., *America's Colonial Experiment.* Englewood Cliffs, N.J.: Prentice-Hall, 1950.

Tannenbaum, Frank, *The American Tradition in Foreign Policy.* Norman, Okla.: University of Oklahoma Press, 1955.

Wolfers, Arnold, *Discord and Collaboration.* Baltimore: Johns Hopkins Press, 1962.

2

Foreign Policy in a Democratic Society

THE AMERICAN CHARACTER

It now seems generally accepted, and in the opinion of the present writer correctly so, that American society and the personality characteristics that it typically produces do not conduce to the development in national public opinion of that cautious realism most appropriate to the prosecution of a successful foreign policy. Before examining this contention in detail, however, one should point out several factors commonly overlooked in discussions of the problem.

First, many of the features described below as characteristic of American attitudes are in actuality not peculiarly American, but are common to all democratic states and indeed were already being stressed by Plato in his attack on democracy 2500 years ago. The special problems created for the successful conduct of foreign policy by the nature of a democratic state will be discussed later; one need merely note that they are shared by other western democracies, and are typical of the United States only to the extent that democratic ways are especially deeply ingrained in the American approach to problems of public policy.

Second, it cannot be assumed that the distinctive features of national character will embody themselves automatically in a state's foreign policy. Policy is made and executed, after all, by a specially selected elite not necessarily typical of the society as a whole, and it is shaped not only by the wishes of the national population, but also by the externally imposed necessities of the situation. It is thus not possible simply to deduce a nation's foreign policy from the leading features of the national temperament.

Third, one should bear in mind that what appear to be peculiarly American attitudes to foreign policy problems often may derive from the newness of America's present power position and the relative lack of an established national tradition in foreign policy, and consequently tend to resemble the attitudes of other newly powerful and often newly established states.

Finally, one should beware of making the usual assumption that the influence of national characteristics on foreign policy has been invariably on the debit side. Two features of the contemporary world that offer the greatest promise of the modification of international mores in a more civilized direction, the growth of international organizations, and the practice of developed countries of giving economic aid to the less developed, are in large part results of the application to the world scene of American generosity and the American mania for creating organizations.

It remains clear, nevertheless, that the type of temperament growing out of American society does not naturally contribute to the support of a realistic foreign policy. American society is competitive and optimistic, stresses private and material concerns, and is in continual flux. The attitudes that this society directly promotes are that improvement is possible and that satisfactory situations are attainable simply by the institution of appropriate mechanisms; that cheerfulness, generosity, and good will encourage similar attitudes on the part of others; and that states, like individuals, should be autonomous and self-reliant. Along with these attitudes, which flow directly from the nature of American reality, American society unintentionally develops personality patterns that produce other complementary attitudes. The preoccupation with private concerns fosters an often surprising ignorance about the world outside the national borders, while the highly competitive nature of American society fosters an insecurity that finds expression in emotional extremism. Thus, along with American generosity goes a fear of "being taken;" along with a need to be liked goes a reaction of bewilderment, frustration, and resentment if one's friendship is not reciprocated.[1]

THE VARIETY OF AMERICAN ATTITUDES

This is what one finds if he looks at "American character" as a single whole. But over and above those attitudes shared by the vast majority of Americans, it is clear that many of the diverse groups in the

---

[1] On this subject see Gabriel Almond, *The American People and Foreign Policy*, 2d ed. New York: Praeger, 1960, pp. 53–68.

population have their own distinctive attitudes and opinions that are of at least as much importance in encouraging deviations from the path of a realistic and pragmatic foreign policy as are the characteristics that can be ascribed to the entire national population.

One must first say that differences of approach to foreign policy exist between the two major parties, or rather between the factions within those parties. This is a fact about which too little has been said. In the desire to promote bipartisanship in foreign policy and to arrive at a definition of national interests that would be generally acceptable, writers of foreign policy have generally ignored the point that no conception of common national purpose (except one that is too nebulous to be of use) can be devised that would neutralize the very real differences in value assumptions that exist among different groups of Americans, that must enter into the very definition of national interest and cannot be argued or defined away. It is for this reason that statements as to what constitutes "the national interest" for purposes of policy making, such as those discussed in the previous chapter, must allow within themselves room for legitimate divergences of values.

One has thus to take into account, in searching for the "irrational" elements in American attitudes towards foreign policy, the specific points of view of the more extreme elements of the three broad political groupings into which Americans divide on ideological questions—Republicans, northern Democrats, and southern Democrats.

Among the extremely conservative elements of the Republican party, the tradition of isolationism, now somewhat modified and brought up to date, is not yet dead. The isolationist point of view, that the United States should have as little as possible to do with other countries and should even avoid becoming involved in international relations at all, has been fed by several streams of divergent social and economic origins. There is some truth in the view that isolationism stems from the geographic circumstances of the American Midwest, which is less concerned about what happens beyond the shores simply because it is further removed from those shores. It may well be, in addition, that the heavily German ancestry of the present-day midwesterners is of significance here, for involvement in international relations in either quarter of the first half of the twentieth century implied taking a position of hostility towards Germany.[2]

Economic factors surely have been of account here also. The desire for protection from foreign competition of midwestern manufacturing and agriculture, whose interests in this respect were opposed to those of eastern commercial and banking circles, have clearly contributed to an

---

[2] This point is stressed in Samuel Lubell, *The Future of American Politics*.

economic nationalism that undervalues contacts with other nations. One sees the economic bases of such a position clearly revealed in such events as the hearings of the Nye committee of the United States Senate, held during the 1920s to determine the causes of America's entry into World War I. The committee concluded that since the investors in the munitions industry were the only people who could presume to benefit directly from warfare, then the so-called merchants of death must somehow have been responsible for United States entry into the war. It is noteworthy that the committee was dominated by senators of western and midwestern agrarian background, Nye himself being from South Dakota. Of course the tradition of radical agrarian isolationism is a long one; the tension between Midwest and East probably has its origins in the archetypal clash of interest between farmer and banker.

Conservative Republican lack of support for a positive foreign policy may also be ascribed to the circumstance that it has been the Democratic party that has held national office during the war years of the twentieth century, and during the years of international tension that immediately preceded them.

This attitude stems additionally from the fact that an active foreign policy requires the spending of money—for military purposes, for foreign aid, and now for the support of the United Nations and other international organizations—and the Republican party remains in general averse to the spending of money; an entirely understandable attitude in view of the fact that, given the progressive income tax and the tendency of people with higher incomes to vote Republican, the average Republican pays more in taxes than the average Democrat.

An additional basis for conservative Republican mistrust of the actions necessary to the prosecution of an active foreign policy lies in the fact that several of our closest allies, and perhaps the preponderance of the so-called uncommitted countries, base their domestic policies on more-or-less Socialist premises to which the good Republican is instinctively hostile.

One has to acknowledge that factors stemming from individual psychology are also responsible for the attitudes towards foreign policy frequently assumed by the conservative-minded in both parties. It has been shown by Herbert McClosky[3] and others that those who are attracted to conservative political principles tend to be psychologically more insecure, more aggressive, less confident in human reason, less concerned about what happens to other people, more inclined to view situations as hopeless, more inclined to withdraw from awkward situa-

---

[3] In "Conservatism and Personality," *American Political Science Review,* March 1958.

tions than to attempt to master them. It is hardly to be expected that individuals with these characteristics will support policies of caution and patience, policies aimed at ameliorating long-range problems by careful negotiation, policies requiring compromise and military preparedness without aggressiveness—precisely those policies best adapted to promoting the whole range of values implicit in the concept of national interest.

Much of what has been said about conservative Republicans applies also to conservative southern Democrats. Added to these is a mistrust of policies of aid to the underdeveloped world and of support for the United Nations, since these involve assistance and accommodation to colored peoples. Southern Democrats do not always share the Republican antipathy to government spending, however, at least where this is devoted to military purposes. Many southern congressmen, typified by the Georgians, Senator Richard Russell and Representative Carl Vinson, who for many years presided over the armed services committees of Congress, have been very able students of military policy. A strong military tradition exists in the South, as opposed to the suspicion of the military commonly met with in the rest of the country, and a great many southerners enter career army service, thus identifying the section more strongly with defense needs.[4]

Reluctance to hew to paths of firmness and pragmatism in foreign policy can also be found among extreme "liberal" supporters of the Democratic party. Symmetrical with the mistrust for some of America's current allies felt among conservative ranks, one finds among ultraliberals a similar tendency to evaluate allies in terms of the form of their government and the domestic policies that they follow. Thus the Left is unhappy about cooperation with Fascist governments in Spain and Portugal, or with dictatorships in Latin America and Southeast Asia, regardless of any utility that such cooperation may have for immediate national interests. In addition, mistrust of Germany persists, and, specifically, hostility to German rearmament.

Frequently the liberal feels repugnance for the military effort as a whole, abhorring equally the obedience to authority necessary to military discipline and the violence implicit in the military mission itself. More likely than not, the ultraliberal suspects that the high level of military spending and perhaps even the Cold War itself stem less from national security needs than from the influence of business interests. A good illustration of this point of view can be found in *The Causes of World War Three* by C. Wright Mills, although one finds similar intonations elsewhere, for example in President Eisenhower's so-called Farewell Ad-

---

[4] This is discussed in Samuel P. Huntington, *The Soldier and the State,* 2d ed. New York: Random House, 1964, pp. 211–214.

dress. However, the liberal typically supports spending for foreign aid, conceiving this as analogous to domestic welfare spending, which he supports, although he is likely to incline to the rather naive belief that spending for foreign aid, by raising standards of living, will automatically eliminate the causes of war and of dictatorship. If the psychological needs of the conservative temperament incline the conservative to suspiciousness and emotional aggressiveness, the tendency of the liberal temperament is to meet problems with exaggerated gestures of friendliness and good will, and to make unnecessary concessions.

The reader may have been shocked to find the most dearly-held assumptions of his own thinking characterized here as emotional or unrealistic. The point is simply that the assumption of a position of realism in international relations means that one must make and support decisions that may not be emotionally the most appealing ones. It means that the head must take precedence over the heart; that in developing an apposite style of behavior in foreign policy questions, the United States, like the infant in Freudian theory, must pass from the pleasure principle to the reality principle.

POLICY AND PUBLICITY

If difficulties are presented to the rational conduct of foreign policy by the attitudinal characteristics that grow out of the nature of American society, it is equally true that comparable difficulties are created by the democratic nature of the American political system. The reader should understand what is meant here. The aim is not to suggest that, if the democratic system creates difficulties for foreign policy, then that system should be modified or abandoned. Certainly not, for every type of political system introduces its own characteristic biases into the conduct of policy. As will be seen below, dictatorial systems display their own characteristic defects. Nevertheless, democracies do exhibit typical weaknesses different from those common to nondemocratic systems, and it is well to take note of them.

A prime difficulty for the maker and executor of foreign policy in a democratic system is that a democracy thrives on, and indeed requires, maximum publicity for government actions. This is clearly necessary in the interest of developing an informed public, and in enabling the electorate to exercise its powers of choice wisely.[5] Publicity can, however, be one of the worst enemies of effective diplomacy.

The essence of successful diplomatic negotiation is compromise,

---

[5] On this point, see C. W. Cassinelli, *The Politics of Freedom: An Analysis of the Modern Democratic State*. Seattle: University of Washington Press, 1961, chapter 4.

compromise that allows a reasonable settlement of the issue in conflict in view of the interests of the parties concerned, and that leaves as little basis as possible for rancor and subsequent hostility to develop. But where negotiations are given full publicity, compromise becomes difficult to achieve. All too commonly a dispute over material interests becomes transmuted, during the process of preparing press releases, into one of ideological principle. While stating demands in concrete material terms makes it possible to reach a compromise by "splitting the difference," a dispute stated in terms of ideological principle either remains frozen at stalemate, without possibility of solution, or becomes part of a larger war of unconditional surrender.

But even where the dispute can be couched in material terms, the publicity natural to democracy also makes settlement difficult. It makes sense to enter a bargaining situation with a statement of one's maximum demands, so that in the process of compromise one ends up with something similar to what one was ready to settle for in the first place. If publicity is given to the original maximum demands, however, and popular expectations are built up around them, then a settlement for something less, even though it was what one really wanted in the first place, will appear to the public, and will be represented to the public by the opposition party, as a sell-out or a diplomatic defeat. Accordingly, pressures build up for maintaining the integrity of the original demands, negotiation becomes impossible, and no settlement is reached. Alternatively, popular pressure for some kind of settlement may be great, and as a result some formula of words may be agreed on which enables each side to represent the settlement to its own domestic opinion as a victory, but which means nothing, and which will only lead to future misunderstanding, recrimination, and mutual hostility.[6]

POLICY AND POLITICS

In a democracy it is impossible to insulate foreign policy from the pressures of domestic politics, despite widespread feeling that partisan politics should "stop at the water's edge." If this were simply a case of authentic disagreements over what policies best serve the national interest, no great harm would be done. All too often, however, "politics" in the sense of narrow considerations of personal and partisan advantage takes its toll of policy, which should ideally be framed only with a view to the national interest.

---

[6] This problem is discussed in Elmer Plischke, *Conduct of American Diplomacy*, 2d ed. Princeton, N.J.: D. Van Nostrand, 1961, chapter 2. It is also one of the themes of Sir Harold Nicolson's *The Evolution of Diplomatic Method*. New York: Macmillan, 1954.

The major political factors, narrowly defined, that characteristically impede the optimum formulation and execution of foreign policy in democracies are the following. First, there is a natural reluctance to take actions, however necessary, that will be unpopular with the electorate. Perhaps the classic case is that of Stanley Baldwin who, as he later confessed, led the British Conservative party to victory in the 1935 election on a platform opposing expenditures for rearmament, even though he was well aware that Germany under Hitler was staging an extensive rearmament program. Most politicians who have survived to the point of becoming the leaders of their states have allowed popular opinion to overrule their own better judgment at some time or other.

Second, the democratic chief executive is confronted with pressures from members of the legislature concerned with promoting special constituency interests, whose demands run counter to what the chief executive believes to be in the national interest. A typical case in the United States is that of a local industry wanting tariff protection when a tariff on the product in question might damage some other policy the executive is trying to pursue, by hurting the economy of a friendly foreign state, for example. This effect is most notable in democracies like the United States or France, which normally lack effective party discipline in the legislature.

Third, the executive is often induced to make personnel appointments, which he would not otherwise make, for "political" reasons. A striking case of this occurred during President Truman's term of office, when the late Senator William Langer, a powerful Republican who was then chairman of the Senate judiciary committee, discovered that there had never been an United States ambassador from North Dakota, his home state, whereupon he intimated to the President that no administration-sponsored legislation would clear the judiciary committee until a North Dakotan had been appointed ambassador.[7] President Truman hurriedly found a small and less important country whose friendship with the United States seemed unshakable, Nicaragua, and appointed as United States Ambassador Thomas Whelan, an active North Dakota Republican acceptable to Senator Langer. Ambassador Whelan subsequently served in Nicaragua for over ten years, a term whose length was without precedent in recent times. Opinions are mixed as to Whelan's performance as Ambassador; some conservatives have pointed with satisfaction to Whelan's close personal relations with the late Nicaraguan dictator, Anastasio Somoza, and his family (it is said that Whelan and

---

[7] Senator Langer's speech on this subject is preserved for posterity in the *Congressional Record* of December 8, 1950; cited in Roland Young, *The American Congress.* New York: Harper, 1958, p. 201.

Somoza used to play poker together regularly); but the majority of students of United States–Latin-American relations are of the opinion that Whelan damaged the reputation of the United States among the ordinary people of Nicaragua by the closeness of his association with the dictator.

There has however been a steady improvement in the quality of the appointments made to overseas posts as the importance of our overseas representation has increased with the growth of American influence, and the proportion of appointments made as a reward for political services has steadily declined. Nevertheless, they are still with us; the same Dwight D. Eisenhower who proclaimed during his election campaign that merit and merit alone would be his guide in making diplomatic appointments named as Ambassador to Cuba Earl E. T. Smith, whose meritorious service in the field of foreign relations to that date had consisted of a very capable performance as finance chairman for the Republican campaign in Florida in 1956. Despite Smith's mediocre record in Havana, President Kennedy also nominated Smith to an embassy, this time to Switzerland; his qualification for this appointment was presumably not his adeptness as a Republican fund-raiser, but his status as a personal friend and Palm Beach neighbor of the Kennedys.[8]

Even where personnel appointments are of the highest caliber, the rather frequent turnover in the personnel assigned to diplomatic and policy-making posts attendant on the quadrennial change in administrations has a certain disruptive influence. However, continual mobility into and out of jobs is characteristic of American society at large, and not only of government service.

POLICY AND DEMOCRATIC ATTITUDES

If the requirements of democracy are at times at odds with the requirements for the successful conduct of foreign policy insofar as publicity and the influence of domestic politics are concerned, difficulties are similarly created by the nature of democratic attitudes or ideological assumptions. One effect these attitudes give rise to is the widespread distrust of the professional diplomatist that exists in the United States. On this point George Kennan has the following to say:

> . . . To many Americans, the idea of residing permanently, as a profession, at the seats of other governments and of trying patiently to understand these governments and to mediate between their needs and ours, is repugnant. These people find such an occupation slightly unmanly. They question its necessity. They cannot under-

---

[8] Smith withdrew his name from consideration after opposition to his appointment developed in the Senate.

stand why anyone should want to do it. They suspect that it leads to a weakening of the attachment to traditional American values. They see in it a loss of true American innocence.[9]

The professional must, after all, act in ways that cause suspicions about his "Americanism" to arise in the breast of the more narrow-minded. He wears striped pants; he talks guardedly and acts with restraint even when dealing with the country's enemies; he speaks foreign languages. Clearly, mistrust of the professional diplomatist at this level is ridiculous. As a reaction to this mistrust, on the other hand, much of the writing on the subject implies that the professional foreign service officer is a superior being, untouched by human frailty, all-wise and all-knowing. This is by no means the case, and indeed there are pressures on the foreign service officer that incline him to lack of imagination and reluctance to take the initiative. Many excellent ambassadors of recent years have in fact been political appointees in the sense that they have come from outside the ranks of the professional foreign service. Under certain circumstances politicians and college professors can make very good ambassadors, provided they are chosen for their assignments on the basis of ability—the United States has been excellently served by such men as Chester Bowles in India, Edwin O. Reischauer in Japan, and Lincoln Gordon in Brazil, to name three "political" appointees of Kennedy. It would still be wrong to lose sight of the fact that the profession of diplomatist, like any other profession, requires skills that normally come with training and experience.

A disadvantage that democracies have that is not normally shared by dictatorships arises from the lack of an official doctrine to which national action is supposed to be subordinate. Because democracies regard differing views as legitimate, because there is no official set of values to which all are required to subscribe, there can hardly be a clear-cut set of priorities for national action in the field of foreign policy that would command general assent and serve as a continuing guide to policy making. Thus every decision must be worked out arduously from first principles; reaction time in coming up with a policy for meeting unprecedented situations is long, and democracies are notoriously slow to act. However, even where an established ideology is supposed to prevail, differences of approach to concrete policy problems still exist, as witnessed by the post-Stalin disputes between the Soviet Union and China and within the Soviet Union itself.

A more pervasive difficulty is that United States policy makers have not received during their political careers the training appropriate to

---

[9] From an address to the members of the Foreign Service Association, excerpted in the *Christian Science Monitor,* June 1961.

equip them for the world of international relations.[10] International politics entails the use of violence and threats in an environment where there is no agreement on basic procedures and values. In the domestic society of the United States, on the other hand, law and order are maintained, the decisions of courts are normally respected, and the will of arithmetical majorities prevails by common agreement. The politics of a dictatorship or of an unstable and revolutionary society trains one better to face the exigencies of international relations than the political life of a mature democracy. One meets much too often in the United States with the attempt to view international relations as though it were an extension of domestic politics, and accordingly to place too much stress on the decisions of international pseudo-parliamentary bodies, such as the United Nations General Assembly, or to lay more stress than circumstances warrant on the literal wording of treaties and the decisions of international tribunals, which are of limited significance.

POLICY AND DEMOCRATIC INSTITUTIONS

Finally, a set of difficulties arises from the nature of the institutions of the open society, its wide freedom of speech and of personal action. The open society speaks with many tongues, and the foreigner used to a less free environment may perhaps be pardoned for his bewilderment at the cacophony of voices, each of which purports to articulate American national policy. Many foreign rulers believe, or profess to believe, that editorial opinion in the American press is "inspired" by official sources and represents official points of view, as is commonly the case in other countries. Thus Fidel Castro intimated that he regarded as a sign of official United States hostility towards his government protests voiced in the American press against the haste and irregular procedures followed in the trials of Batista's secret police agents during his first months in power.

Probably more confusing than this is the presence of an enormous number of officeholders whose titles are not clearly understood abroad, each of whom has his own private foreign policy, about which he does not hesitate to make impressive pronouncements to the press. If someone with the impressive title of Senate majority leader or chairman of the House foreign affairs committee makes a speech on foreign policy, it seems reasonable, although it is incorrect, to suppose that his views reflect those of the administration. One presumes that by now most politically-conscious Americans have come to discount the Olympian pronouncements of most of the members of the Senate and to ignore as much as possible the "findings" of obscure congressional subcommittees; but one can hardly expect the foreigner to be equally sophisticated.

---

10 This applies with even greater force to political leaders in Great Britain.

Because of the open nature of American society, moreover, it is difficult to mature projects requiring secrecy; of course, surprise value is therefore lost. Andrew Berding, a former Assistant Secretary of State for Public Affairs, has written, only half in jest:

> I have long observed that the more highly classified a dispatch or paper may be, the greater are its chances of becoming public. The substance of a Top Secret dispatch might burst forth in forty-eight hours, that of a Secret paper in four days, that of a Confidential telegram in a week, that of an Official Use Only memorandum in a fortnight. And an unclassified paper might not become known at all. This is because the more highly classified matter, even though its circulation may be limited, attracts greater interest, weighs more on the minds of those involved, may call for quicker decision, and in general comports more activity, some of which seeps out into the open.[11]

Thus, for example, the supersecret American training of Cuban exiles for the April 1961 invasion of the island was well known about in informed circles beforehand and the location of the training bases was widely reported in the press.

Finally, one should acknowledge that because of the great freedom of action allowed individuals in a democracy it becomes more difficult than in a closed society to bring the totality of national power to bear on the resolution of a national security problem. Workers retain the right to strike, for example, even if their strike forces a postponement in the completion of a government missile program. The same missile program may go short of engineers because they have been hired away at higher salaries to help produce new color television sets. Of course, in emergencies democracies have shown themselves able to coordinate their resources more effectively for the support of national policy; nevertheless, in the "permanent emergency" in which American policy is likely to find itself for the foreseeable future, we have thus far largely contented ourselves with applying the rules appropriate to peacetime.

THE FOREIGN POLICY OF DEMOCRACIES AND DICTATORSHIPS

It is unfortunately the case that many of the superiorities that democracies enjoy over nondemocratic systems apply with much greater force to domestic than to foreign affairs; this is true, for example, of that prudential argument in favor of democracy, that as the person who wears the shoe is the best judge of whether it pinches, the electorate

---

[11] Andrew Berding, *Foreign Affairs and You!* New York: Doubleday, 1962, p. 161.

is the best judge of the value and efficacy of government policy, since it must bear the brunt of the effects of that policy.[12] The effects of a particular foreign policy can rarely be felt in pure form by the electorate, for the events that transpire in the international arena show the effects not only of one's own foreign policy but of the policies of a host of other states; moreover, the effect of a long-range policy, for example, the cultivation of good relations with a neighbor, is not likely to be appreciated within the short cycle of time for which a democratic government is elected, while one might say that the most important effects of a foreign policy are not what happens as a result of it but what it prevents from happening, and these effects, of course, are elusive.

One should not fall into the error of stressing only the disadvantages that democratic attitudes and modes of behavior have on the conduct of foreign policy, however. It should be noted with equal force that democracies have characteristic advantages in their ability to pursue rational foreign policies that are not shared by nondemocratic systems.

One has only to take a look at some of the colossal blunders made by dictatorships in foreign policy to appreciate the value of democratic controls. Consider, for example, Khrushchev's indictment of Stalin in his so-called secret speech to the Twentieth Party Congress; Khrushchev listed unnecessary errors by Stalin during World War II that cost the Soviet Union hundreds of thousands of lives.

When it was suggested to Stalin (by Mikoyan) that he might have been wrong about one such decision:

> You should have seen Stalin's fury! How could it be admitted that he, Stalin, had not been right! He is after all a "genius," and a genius cannot help but be right! Everyone can err, but Stalin considered that he never erred, that he was always right. He never acknowledged to anyone that he made any mistake, large or small, despite the fact that he made not a few mistakes in the matter of theory and in his practical activity. After the Party Congress we shall probably have to re-evaluate many wartime military operations and to present them in their true light.[13]

And Khrushchev went on to describe the evolution of the dictator's personality in terms that could apply to every tyrant from Agathocles to Macbeth to François Duvalier:

---

[12] This thesis is made much of in A. D. Lindsay's *The Modern Democratic State*. Of course, there are limitations to the extent to which this argument can be held to apply even to domestic affairs.

[13] Nikita S. Khrushchev, "The Crimes of the Stalin Era," published as a special edition of *The New Leader*, undated, p. 542.

We must state that, after the war, the situation became even more complicated. Stalin became even more capricious, irritable and brutal; in particular his suspicion grew. His persecution mania reached unbelievable dimensions. Many workers were becoming enemies before his very eyes. After the war, Stalin separated himself from the collective even more. Everything was decided by him alone, without any consideration for anyone or anything.[14]

Dictatorships are peculiarly dependent on the qualities of one man; yet the very nature of dictatorship tends to blur the perceptions of that man as to what is going on around him, because being dictator works changes in his psyche, and because his underlings are afraid to tell him the truth if doing so will imply that his policies have failed. As a result, despite their vast intelligence and espionage networks, dictators typically live in surprising ignorance of the actual state of affairs in the world outside their borders, and if they are apprised of the true situation, they frequently refuse to believe the evidence and even punish those who bring it. At the same time, subordinates are afraid to criticize plans matured by the dictator, no matter how unsound these may be; or they are bedazzled by the legend of infallibility built up around the dictator's person into surrendering their critical faculties altogether.

Moreover, the much-vaunted superiority of dictatorships in being able to mobilize national resources and devote them to the purposes of national policy reveals itself on closer examination to be in great part myth. Although a dictatorship does centralize vast authority to co-ordinate economic activities in the pursuit of a single goal, that very centralization leads to the development of bottlenecks, the unwillingness of subordinate officials to take necessary decisions, and a great loss of purposive direction caused by the alternation of subordinate officials between ruthless assertiveness, as they attempt to model themselves on the personal style of the dictator, and an extreme timidity stemming from fear of the severe penalties that can be applied in case of failure.

Democracies seem to share in some of these defects to the extent that they adopt authoritarian modes of behavior. Thus one sees in the failure of the British and French Suez expedition of 1956, and the closely comparable failure of the United States-sponsored exile invasion of Cuba in April 1961, many of the weaknesses of planning described above as characteristic of dictatorships; these were operations conceived and matured out of the arena of public discussion characteristic of democracy; discussion of both invasion attempts was restricted to a small group almost completely composed of people dependent on the chief of govern-

---

14 *Ibid.,* pp. 545–546.

ment for their appointment and future preferment; and the results were what could have been expected—intelligence estimates proved over-optimistic, and both expeditions resulted in failure because critical factors were overlooked in the planning. A significant contrast exists between the way in which the Cuban invasion was planned and the way in which the decision was reached not to intervene with air and sea forces equipped with nuclear weapons in the Indochinese war, six years before, after the French defeat at Dienbienphu. At that time, Secretary Dulles favored United States intervention but President Eisenhower first initiated wide consultations with congressional leaders and leaders of United States allies, consultations that uncovered major objections to the project. The contrast to the planning for the Cuban invasion is significant. In 1961 consultations with people outside the executive branch were minimal. Senator Fulbright, the chairman of the Senate foreign relations committee, was consulted, and he objected to the Cuban invasion, raising a series of very cogent arguments that were, however, overruled. There were apparently no consultations with our allies, except for the strongly anti-Castro government of Guatemala on whose soil invasion forces were being trained.

Similarly, there have been occasions in American history when that characteristic feature of dictatorships has appeared, the reluctance of foreign service officers to report developments abroad accurately because of fear that they will find themselves regarded as disloyal if their reports seem to deviate from the ideological line in the ascendant back home. This began to occur in the years of the middle 1950's during which Senator McCarthy succeeded in intimidating a great many members of the foreign service into refraining from a frank reporting of events, for fear that at some future date their reports would be pulled out of the files, and they would be summoned before a congressional subcommittee to be cross-examined about some uncheerful or defeatist implication in a word or phrase. Since the McCarthy era these fears have been dying down and members of the foreign service have in general returned to high standards of straightforwardness and factuality in their reporting and initiative in the performance of their other duties. The morale of the foreign service has risen markedly since the days when every impromptu accusation made by the late junior Senator from Wisconsin received front-page attention in every American newspaper.

LEADERSHIP AND PUBLIC OPINION

In discussing the problems that democratic public opinion creates for policy makers, public opinion was treated as a given to which the policy maker had to adjust. Of course, this is not wholly the case;

although in a democracy public opinion determines the general limits within which policy will be made, and excludes certain possible alternative lines of policy as unfeasible, political leadership in its turn helps shape public opinion within those limits. Theodore Roosevelt's comment on the presidency, that it was a "bully pulpit," is instructive. If he is able and willing to make use of the potentialities of his office, an American President has a great deal of influence in determining what public opinion will be. By his actions, by his example, by the themes he sounds in his speeches, a President can set the whole moral tone of his age.

And yet temptations for a President to make dishonest use of the resources of his office in the guidance of public opinion are strong. The requirement that will have become second nature to him by the time he reaches the presidency, that he always present his best face to the public, tempts a President to give plausible and popular, though false, accounts of why he is doing what he is, rather than to take the harder road and attempt to explain the actual motives of his policy and try to win support for it on that basis. At its best, responsible leadership of public opinion entails the ability to present a policy in simple and comprehensible terms, yet without falsifying it. The difficult art of the public explanation of policy reached perhaps its highest point with Franklin D. Roosevelt's characterization of the novel and complex idea of the Lend-Lease program: If my neighbor's house is burning down, I lend him my hose; I hope to get it back when he is finished if it's still usable, but I don't bargain with him about terms while his house is burning down.

Nevertheless, it remains true that after the responsible leader has done as much as possible to inform public opinion and to bring it along in support of his policies, he may still reach a point at which he undertakes a policy he knows to be unpopular, perhaps one that will cost him his political career, but which he believes to be right. There are many jocular definitions of the distinction between a statesman and a politician, such as "A statesman is a dead politician" or "A politician is a leader of your party, a statesman is a leader of my party." Perhaps as good a way as any of drawing the distinction is to say that in the last analysis a statesman is prepared to sacrifice his career in the public interest.[15]

One would hardly wish to rest a case for democratic government on the premise that its leaders always show this characteristic of statesmanship. Perhaps on the whole, therefore, the best argument is still that of James Fenimore Cooper, "We do not adopt the popular polity because it is perfect, but because it is less imperfect than any other."[16]

---

[15] This is the theme of President Kennedy's book, *Profiles in Courage.*

[16] *The American Democrat,* quoted in Bernard Crick, *The American Science of Politics.* Berkeley: University of California Press, 1959, p. 245.

SUGGESTED READINGS

Almond, Gabriel, *The American People and Foreign Policy*, 2d ed. New York: Praeger, 1960.

Berding, Andrew, *Foreign Affairs and You!* New York: Doubleday, 1962.

Brogan, Denis W., "The Illusion of American Omnipotence," *Harper's*, December 1952.

Lippmann, Walter, *Essays in The Public Philosophy*, Book I. New York: New American Library (Mentor), 1956.

Mills, C. Wright, *The Causes of World War III*. New York: Simon and Schuster, 1958.

Nicolson, Sir Harold, *The Evolution of Diplomatic Method*. New York: Macmillan, 1954.

Smith, M. Brewster, "Opinions, Personality, and Political Behavior," *Am. Pol. Sci. Rev.*, March 1958.

Westerfield, Bradford, *Foreign Policy and Party Politics: Pearl Harbor to Korea*. New Haven, Conn.: Yale University Press, 1955.

Wriston, Henry M., *Diplomacy in a Democracy*. New York: Harper & Row, 1956.

3

Machinery
for Policy Making

THE PROBLEM OF COMPLEXITY

When one looks at the agencies and institutions of government in the United States that are involved in the making and execution of foreign policy, two features immediately stand out: their number, and their independence of each other.

Although the President is, by tradition and by necessity, the leader in foreign policy formulation and execution, the Congress has an extensive and ramified role to play. This is so, of course, because much of the substance of foreign policy requires implementing legislation; it is true, too, because foreign policy, like other government functions, requires the expenditure of money, and it is the Congress that appropriates funds. In addition the Senate disposes of constitutional powers that create for it a distinctive position in the making of foreign policy: Its approval by a two-thirds vote is necessary for the conclusion of treaties; and its consent is necessary for the appointment of ambassadors and high-ranking officials. Moreover, the Constitution allots to the Congress the powers of declaring war and concluding peace.

Although in its formal actions each house of Congress acts as a unit, the recommendations on which the action of each house is based, and the important informal processes of consultation and the exercise of influence on the executive branch, are primarily a function of committees and key individuals. Normally, the legislative houses are inclined to follow the recommendations of the committee that has jurisdiction over the area of substantive policy in question. In actuality, however, a whole range of committees becomes involved in exercising the legislature's functions in the field of national security policy. The foreign affairs committee of the House of Representatives and the Senate foreign relations committee naturally take a leading role, especially the Senate committee. The armed services committees of each house are, of course, of crucial importance, since military policy is necessarily dependent on and intertwined with foreign policy. The judiciary committees have jurisdiction over questions concerning immigration and the rights of aliens, while the internal security subcommittee of the Senate judiciary committee often holds hearings on questions that are essentially in the field of foreign relations. The activities of other committees frequently take them into the area of foreign policy, as for example in the concern of the commerce and agriculture committees with foreign trade. In addition to these substantive-area committees, the government operations committees become involved in questions relating to the organization of the machinery of the foreign policy-making agencies within the executive branch; while for each area of substantive policy, there exists a corresponding subcommittee of the appropriations committees of each house, which have the task of passing upon the appropriation of funds for the staffing and execution of programs within the substantive area in question.

Several problems are posed by the sheer number of the legislative units that have a legitimate claim to hear and be heard in the formulation of foreign policy. The major problem of which one hears complaint is that policy-making officials must spend an inordinate amount of their time testifying before congressional committees, that is, appearing before them to make statements and answer questions. With very rare exceptions, congressional committees and subcommittees have resisted suggestions that hearings be held jointly, and a cabinet officer may find himself making the same statement before four different legislative committees. Moreover, the typical tendency is for committees to request the attendance of policy-making officials of the highest rank, and not to be satisfied with the appearance of officials of lesser standing, thus concentrating the burden of giving testimony on the leading officers of the executive branch.

Other effects of the large number of committees involved on the legislative side in the policy-making process are the difficulty of maintaining the confidentiality of information, as the possibility of "leaks" increases directly with the number of people privy to the information; and an increase in the number of people with important-sounding titles who are given to making authoritative-seeming pronouncements on delicate and complex questions much to the confusion of foreign opinion.

The congressional committee system has both its good and bad points. By allowing, and even demanding, that legislators specialize in one or two areas of public policy, it promotes the development of a laudable expertise, which makes the legislative process more informed and competent. At the same time, precisely because of the promotion of this expertise, taken together with the tendency of each house to defer to the opinion of its specialized committee, and the special position of power enjoyed by the committee chairmen, the entire fabric of American foreign policy must often be modified to accommodate the views, prejudices, or constituency interests of a single legislator strategically situated in the committee system. The point here is not that members of the legislature should be without influence on the making of foreign policy; as the people's representatives, they are certainly entitled to a large voice in the policy-making process. But the influence they wield should be that of the legislative body as a whole; instead of this, the system is organized so that when, by dint of the fortunate accidents of seniority, a legislator has advanced to a strategic chairmanship in the committee network, he is in effect empowered to dispose of the entire power of the legislature in the furtherance of ends that may not be generally shared by the country or even by the legislative body of which he is a member. The case of how the United States came to appoint its first ambassador from North Dakota has already been cited. One might also point to the instances in which the personal preferences of Harold Cooley, the chairman of the House agriculture committee, have determined from which states the United States would buy sugar and in what amounts, a question of economic life or death to a state that subsists primarily on the export of sugar, as some do; or the importance of the late Senator Robert Kerr of Kerr-McGee Oil Company and the state of Oklahoma in shaping our relations with Venezuela, as a by-product of his activities in defending the interests of independent domestic oil producers.

Of course, built into the separation of powers is the expectation that executive and legislative branches will each be jealous of the other's prerogatives, and by checking each other will insure that the constitutional system is kept in balance. This has proved to be in part the case, although the clash between the legislature and the executive branches is frequently secondary in American politics to the clash between the Democratic and Republican parties.

THE PROBLEM OF BIPARTISANSHIP

Running counter to the tendency towards conflict and the division of opinion characteristic of any democratic society stands the abiding expectation of the American public that all elements within the political system will rally round and stand united in the face of danger from abroad. This expectation finds expression in the adage already quoted, that "politics stops at the water's edge," and in the typical phenomenon that at times of international crisis leaders of the opposition party issue statements calling for all Americans to forget their partisan differences and support the President in the hour of the country's need.

In the attempt to translate this feeling of unity at a time of national crisis into a permanently operating feature of American political reality, the norm of bipartisanship in foreign policy has developed. Bipartisanship in foreign policy is of course a rather delicate plant to try to keep alive, set down as it is in the jungle of fierce partisanship; nevertheless, intermittent attempts are made to place policy on a bipartisan footing. One of the typical ways in which bipartisanship finds expression is the joint resolution of Congress, by which both houses of the legislature declare by substantial affirmative votes their support of some particular policy of the President. The use of the joint resolution is exemplified by the Vandenberg Resolution of 1948, which paved the way for American membership in NATO, or the 1959 resolution affirming support for the "Eisenhower Doctrine" in the Middle East. A bipartisan practice in continual use is the process of consultation, which has now come to be taken for granted, by which the President calls in key leaders, especially legislative leaders, of the opposition party to ask their opinion of major projected foreign policy moves.

Genuine bipartisanship in foreign policy has, however, remained largely an ideal rather than an operating reality, a principle honored more in the breach than in the observance. This is only to be expected, surely, given the realities of the political scene. How likely is it, after all, that officials of the administration will be genuinely interested in eliciting advice from members of the opposition party? A more plausible purpose for calling in opposition leaders is to demonstrate national solidarity behind a particular policy move in order to impress foreign states with the sincerity and conviction with which the whole nation supports it. The congressional joint resolution is an admirable technique for achieving this purpose. A motive present probably with equal or greater frequency is the desire on the part of the administration to insure against an attack being made on the policy in question on the floor of Congress or in the course of the next election campaign. If the opposition party should then launch its attack, administration spokesmen will be able to answer, "But it is your policy too; you agreed to it at the time."

Because of the awareness of the opposition party that this last motive may in fact be the dominant one, opposition leaders tend to show a great deal of uneasiness when approached to give the seal of bipartisan approval to a government policy. The suspicion is always present that the administration is simply trying to insure itself against legitimate criticism. That this fear is justified appears clearly when one considers some of the consultations that have taken place in recent years. After the massive failure of the exile invasion of Cuba in April of 1961, for example, President Kennedy hurriedly called in leading Republican spokesmen, including ex-President Eisenhower, in a rather desperate clutch at the straw of bipartisanship. Resentment at *ex post facto* consultation of this type is reflected in the unhappy comment of a Republican legislative leader, "We are in at the crash landings, but not at the takeoffs." Clearly, however, a genuine problem exists here: The President has the choice of going through the motions of nominal consultation with the opposition and then ignoring their advice, which leads to understandable resentment on their part; but he does not wish to go to the other extreme and allow opposition leaders to be able to veto policies of which they disapprove. Reaching a middle ground between these two extremes is a difficult and delicate proposition.

But even apart from this problem, the attempt to institute bipartisanship in foreign policy faces a great many difficulties. In the first place, under the American party system, members of the legislature do not follow party discipline, and therefore even if the party's major leaders should agree to support an administration in a given policy, this does not by any means commit all of the party's representatives in the Congress to go along. It is rare that a party leader will achieve such eminence that his colleagues will be content to follow his lead without question, as was often the case with Senator Vandenberg. A further difficulty is that in giving its endorsement to an administration policy the leaders of the opposition party can always insert explicit or implicit escape clauses.

In either case it is only too common that the bipartisan overlay given the policy has "worn off" by the time the next election comes around. And it is always possible to get around the accusation that one has violated a bipartisan agreement by protesting that one agreed to the policy in principle, but that the incompetent way in which it was carried out completely changed its nature.

The cynic might perhaps be excused for taking the view that the only way to keep a policy bipartisan is for it to be an unqualified success. It has in fact been the case that bipartisanship has lasted longest in the area in which American policy has had its strongest success, that is, in the reconstruction and defense of western Europe. Elsewhere in the world bipartisanship, if it ever existed, has rapidly ebbed away.

One might say that the concept of bipartisanship does not accurately capture the essence of the phenomenon. The problem that faces an administration is not strictly that of reconciling the opposition party with its conduct of foreign policy; it is actually more that of reconciling the conservative wing of the Republican party. This is as true for a Republican President as for a Democrat. President Eisenhower's congressional difficulties over the conduct of foreign policy were originated not by Democrats, of either the southern or the northern varieties, but by conservative members of his own party, such as Senators Knowland and McCarthy. Even though he was ostensibly Eisenhower's majority leader in the Senate, Senator Knowland doggedly went his own way on such questions as foreign aid and the use of military force in the Far East; and Senator McCarthy continued to make his allegations about the supposed control of American policy by a secret network of Communists in high government places after Eisenhower took office, as he had during the term of his predecessor.

This has necessarily been the case since it is the conservative midwestern and western ex-isolationist sector of the Republican party that represents the strongest strain of opposition both to the caution and realism that must characterize policy towards our enemies, and to the understanding and consciousness of common purpose that must characterize relations with our allies.

THE PRESIDENT'S ROLE

Although the participation of Congress in the making of foreign policy is an intrinsic part of the American system, the executive branch necessarily and inevitably takes primacy in this area. The conduct of foreign policy, after all, is a day-to-day operation requiring a continuity, secrecy, and promptness, which simply make it inappropriate as a subject of legislation. The Congress itself has recognized the necessity of executive primacy, and has reacted with resentment and frustration on occasions when a chief executive refused to take the lead in the making of foreign policy and instead deferred to Congress.

The President has ample powers under the Constitution to formulate and execute day-to-day policy, capped by his power as commander in chief of the armed forces. The powers of the presidency are so versatile in fact that Presidents have been able, in effect, to use them to exercise even those two supreme functions that the Constitution clearly reserves to the Congress: the approval of treaties, and the declaration of war. Although the Constitution clearly specifies that a treaty is not valid unless approved by a two-thirds vote of the Senate, a device has nevertheless evolved known as the executive agreement, under which Presidents make agreements with the chief executives of other states ostensibly on matters coming exclusively within the discharge of their functions as executive officers.

Power to make such agreements is clearly necessary in the day-today conduct of foreign relations, and is thus an indispensable aspect of the President's foreign policy role. At the same time the executive agreement power can infringe on the Senate's prerogative of passing on treaties, since no clear distinction between the matters properly dealt with by the one and those appropriately embodied in the other can be unequivocally made. Some executive agreements have been submitted to Congress for approval, some not, but in either case it is established that such agreements constitute valid law, binding individuals and overriding state laws that conflict with them.[1] It seems to be generally acknowledged, however, that executive agreements cannot be made that directly conflict with existing federal law.

Since the days when Thomas Jefferson ordered ships into action against the Barbary Coast pirates, Presidents have been using their powers as commanders in chief of the armed forces to send troops into battle, or to take other actions involving the use of armed force, without securing a congressional declaration of war beforehand, even though the ensuing military actions may appear equivalent in every respect to a war that had been formally declared by Congress as prescribed in the Constitution. A recent instance of a war fought without a congressional declaration on the basis of the President's use of his powers as commander in chief was the war in Korea, which lasted from 1950 to 1953.

Given the nature of armed conflict in the current era of world politics (which is considered in greater length in a later chapter), it may well be that the concept of a formal declaration of war is obsolete. Quite clearly, if a missile attack were launched on the United States by the Soviet Union in which intercontinental ballistic missiles were flying at supersonic speeds over the North Pole, it seems hardly likely that any American President would go through the prescribed form of having Congress convene and requesting it to declare war before launching American missiles in retaliation; while if ever such a war were begun by the United States—which one hopes could not happen—to request Congress to declare war would be equivalent to inciting the enemy to attack while the congressional debate was taking place. By the same token, more conventional uses of armed force are most likely to occur in limited and counterguerrilla actions around the periphery of the free world for which a formal declaration of war would be inappropriate.

The waging of military actions solely under presidential authority has not in fact taken away any power that Congress ever exercised against a President's expressed wish, however. That is, every congressional declaration of war has followed a presidential message requesting such a declaration, and Congress has never refused such a request.

---

[1] Nielson *v.* Johnson, 279 U.S. 47 (1929).

POLICY AND THE ORGANIZATION
OF THE EXECUTIVE

When one looks at the structure of that part of the executive branch that relates to the formulation and execution of national security policy, the picture presented is one of a diffusion of powers among a host of agencies, often related to each other only in a tenuous and even nominal fashion. Of course the President and his chief agent, the Secretary of State, have primacy in the field. Nevertheless, the presidency itself is complex; directly dependent on the President is the White House staff, which includes a variety of members with national security responsibilities—advisors, personal aides, special representatives and so on; and the executive office of the President, an administrative complex outside the cabinet departments. Within the executive office, the Bureau of the Budget has jurisdiction over budget and organizational questions and thus necessarily comes to make policy decisions, since questions of the budget are, at the same time, questions of the expansion or contraction of existing programs and the inauguration of new ones.

The State Department is itself organized into regional divisions, each of which has its own special outlook and interests. On this subject Andrew Berding has written:

> The regional bureaus of the Department are powerful organisms. They are jealous of their prerogatives in their own areas. They often fight battles to the expiring gasp to make prevail their points of view with regard to their areas. Understandably they are deeply concerned with our relations with the nations in their areas, they are daily involved in dozens of developments in their regions, they are exchanging hundreds of telegrams with embassies in their areas. Nevertheless a regional bureau is occasionally so embattled in maintaining a policy with regard to its area or a nation in its area that it fails to see that the policy can have adverse effects in other areas which perhaps outweigh the advantages in its own bailiwick.
>
> I once heard one of our most eminent foreign policy makers say, not for attribution, that a staff meeting of the Secretary of State resembled a king holding court of his feudal lords. Around the royal table sat the Prince of Europe, the Duke of Africa, the Baron of Latin America, the Lord of the Far East, and the Earl of the Near East and South Asia. Each believed he was sovereign in his own domain, with the right of life and death as far as his writ ran. Each thought the King existed only to register and proclaim the feudal lord's decrees. And far away from Washington was the Governor-General of the United Nations, so many thousands of miles away in fact that he could decide and act as he chose.[2]

---

2 Berding, pp. 33–34.

EXECUTIVE ORGANIZATION FOR FOREIGN RELATIONS

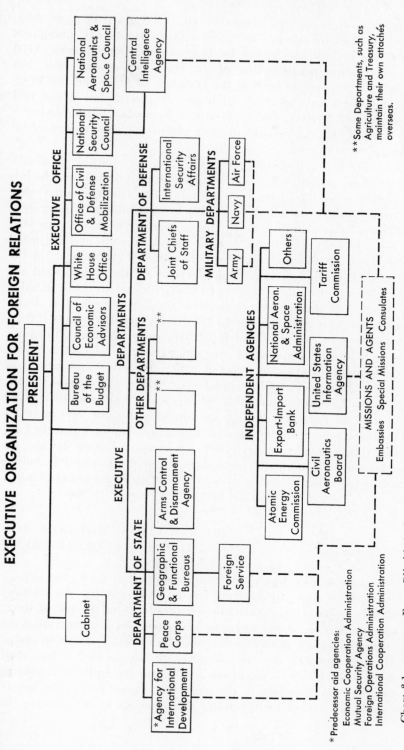

Chart 3.1. SOURCE: From Plischke's *Conduct of American Diplomacy*, 2nd ed. Copyright 1961, D. Van Nostrand Company, Inc., Princeton, N.J.

In addition to the divergences among the regional bureaus, some executive agencies are attached to the State Department in an ambiguous fashion; these include the Agency for International Development (AID) whose organization parallels that of the State Department itself, but whose head is responsible both to the Secretary of State and the President; the Peace Corps, similarly ambiguously placed, but whose first Director, Sargent Shriver, had as President Kennedy's brother-in-law a special relationship to him; and to some extent the new Arms Control and Disarmament Agency.

The Central Intelligence Agency (CIA), set up ostensibly to coordinate intelligence activities, that is, the collection of information, which is carried on by several agencies, both military and civilian, also has what might euphemistically be called "operating responsibilities." Under these miscellaneous responsibilities, the CIA is reputed to have attempted *coups d'état* in several countries—one, at least, successful—and organized invasions of two, Guatemala and Cuba. Because of the delicacy of the CIA's mission, its budget is not appropriated by the Congress in the normal fashion, but funds to support CIA activities are instead concealed under nondescript designations throughout the federal budget. Unfortunately, the necessary secrecy of the CIA's activities partly exempts it from the mechanisms of executive and legislative control necessary to assure both a high level of competence and the consistency of CIA activities with the general direction of national policy. Indeed, it has seemed at times as though the CIA had its own foreign policy. For example: President Kennedy had given orders that soldiers and officials who had served in the regime of Fulgencio Batista, the unsavory dictator who preceded Fidel Castro in power, be eliminated from the invasion force that the CIA organized during 1960 and early 1961; nevertheless, Castro was able to parade known *batistianos* who were captured at the Bay of Pigs before the Havana television cameras, much to the embarrassment of the United States.

ORGANIZATION AND CONTROL OF THE DEFENSE DEPARTMENT

Of course, a great many of the functions performed by the Department of Defense bear directly on foreign policy issues. An effective foreign policy must be supported by the possibility of the use of force; thus the capabilities of the forces in being will in part determine the types of foreign policy initiatives that the United States is able to undertake. It is unfortunately the case, moreover, that states tend to base their judgments of each other's intentions in part on the military capability that the other state possesses. At the same time, a good part of the negotiations undertaken with United States allies consists of determining the contours of joint defense policies and apportioning responsibilities under them.

Even more than other executive agencies, the Department of Defense and the structures of the armed forces over which it has jurisdiction constitute a colossally intricate set of mechanisms only with difficulty integrated with each other and only marginally responsive to attempts at control from the top. The difficulties that are always involved in imposing control over large bureaucratic organisms firmly set in their ways are especially acute in the case of the Defense Department. This is so not only because of the sheer size of the military juggernaut; it stems also from the overriding importance of the military function and the much greater respect accorded to high military officers than to public servants of equal rank in the civilian departments. These latter factors mean that Congress will often give a sympathetic hearing to a general or admiral who disagrees with the views of his civilian superiors; this encourages that recurring phenomenon of the American political scene, the sight of high military officials surreptitiously providing technical information to members of Congress opposed to the policies being followed by the civilian leaders of the administration. When this is taken together with the possibilities for avoiding carrying out unwelcome policies presented by the sheer vastness of the military bureaucracy, and the multiplicity of places available for the erection of roadblocks, one gains some sympathetic understanding of the complaint of President Franklin D. Roosevelt that the Navy was like a mattress; you could punch it and punch it, but no matter what you did it always remained the same.

The ambiguity in the subordination of military officers to civilian control is reflected in the organizational changes that have been made since the armed services were ostensibly "unified" in 1947. Although a single Department of Defense, having jurisdiction over the three individual services, was created at that time, each service retained its separate identity and, indeed, its separate civilian secretary; the Department of Defense became a kind of holding company tying together the three individual services at the top. Thus the aim of the proponents of unification—to limit interservice rivalry and overlapping responsibilities—has met with very little success. One can appreciate the difficulties involved in eliminating service chauvinism, supported and fostered as it is by considerable popular sentiment, and by those influential members of Congress who have "favorite" services they protect and defend, if one recalls that Dwight D. Eisenhower, a very popular President and a military hero, vowed before entering the presidency that one of the things he would accomplish before he left office was to put all members of the armed forces into a single uniform; of course, nothing ever came of the idea nor the concept of the military it represented.

The ambiguities of armed services unification and of civilian control of the military establishment are institutionalized in the ambiguous relationship among the Joint Chiefs of Staff—which consists of the military heads of each service and a chairman—the Secretary of Defense, and the President. The chiefs and their chairman are supposed to be subordinate to the Secretary of Defense, but nevertheless have access to the President to whom they can appeal against decisions of the secretary. At the same time, the military chief of each service is supposed to be subordinate to the civilian secretary of the service who is, in turn, subordinate to the defense secretary.

ORGANIZATIONAL COMPLEXITY IN PERSPECTIVE

Several historical and political factors are responsible for the intricacy and confusion of administrative relationships in the national security field. The augmentation of the international responsibilities of the United States came suddenly with the onset of World War II, and the performance of duties in the national security field became necessarily the task of all administrative agencies, whose functions had to be coordinated with a view to the successful prosecution of the war. It was not feasible to try to assign all such duties to the State Department. In addition many of the tasks that had to be performed in the national security area required military, commercial, or even agricultural skills traditionally found in departments of the government other than State. Moreover, these tendencies have persisted in the period of the Cold War, so that the State Department has lost the clear primacy it once had in the conduct of the nation's foreign policy.

An abiding tendency of United States administrative practice has in any case been to establish a new agency for the prosecution of each new program embarked upon by the government on the premise that existing agencies are too committed to the prosecution of existing programs, in their organization, skills, and emotional involvements to do justice to the new program. Administrative tidiness aside, there is much to be said for this point of view. A good example is that of the Peace Corps, set up on something of a crash basis with a director whose personal relationship to the late President blurred the lines of responsibility that appeared on the charts of organization. The striking success achieved in a short time by the Peace Corps was due largely to the dynamism given to it by this distinctive set of circumstances, which would surely have been lost if the organization and administration of the corps had proceeded at the usual pace through normal State Department channels.

Clearly, dangers exist in situations where responsibilities overlap. Different agencies may be pursuing policies in contradiction to each other, perhaps not even aware of the conflict. In any case obvious difficulties arise in the execution of a common policy requiring the participation of several different agencies, and thus a cumbersome process of coordination is necessary. Avoidance of responsibility becomes possible; delay becomes inevitable. The danger also exists that decisions of some importance may be lost track of and may be made at too low a level.

The best example of this latter practice comes not from a problem involving interagency coordination, however, but from the denial of visas to foreigners who come to the United States. The granting of visas is handled routinely by consular officials in the country from which the foreign visitor comes. On several occasions in the past, distinguished foreigners have been denied visas because some zealous junior consular official found what he thought was a pro-Communist association in the visitor's background even when on further inspection the presumed black mark turned out to be nothing of the sort. This type of thing has unnecessarily promoted anti-Americanism among some very influential individuals. Of course, the junior consular official is to blame only in part; equal responsibility is shared by the Department of State, whose attempt to secure immunity from attack from the late Senator Joseph R. Mc-Carthy meant adopting his standards in the department's security policies.

An equal danger is that of reconciling the divergent views of different agencies involved in the execution of a common policy by the conclusion of agreements among them that are only formulas of words liable to future misunderstandings and recriminations. Many examples of this are provided by the history of the attempts to define the roles of the three services with respect to the development of new weapons, such as missiles.

It should be noted that the problem of coordination arises "in the field," too, in the relations among the various government agencies at work in a given foreign country. Recent attempts to strengthen the position of the ambassador as the man responsible for all United States government activities in a country are to be welcomed; it remains open to question whether this authority can always be effectively asserted.

INTERAGENCY COORDINATION AT THE PRESIDENTIAL LEVEL

At the highest level attempts at coordination have taken various forms. One device has been the appointment of a special presidential assistant for national security affairs who has the job of coordinating the policies of the various departments with responsibilities in the national security field. The danger of the presidential assistant method of approach, however, is that the assistant tends to become either another important individual whose recommendations then have to be integrated with those of the departments by the President himself, as occurred to some extent in the case of McGeorge Bundy, President Kennedy's and President Johnson's assistant for national security affairs; or alternatively, that the presidential assistant attempts to take on the role of a substitute President, making top-level decisions that should only be made by the President himself, as was frequently the case in the area of domestic policy when Sherman Adams was President Eisenhower's "Chief of Staff." During President Eisenhower's term, Secretary of State Dulles was insistent that no presidential assistant be given responsibilities that challenged his primacy in the field of foreign policy; this position, together with policy disagreements between the two men, led to the resignation of Harold Stassen, Eisenhower's special assistant on disarmament questions.

By tradition and logic the Secretary of State heads the nation's foreign policy activities, under the President; and of course he plays the key role both in day-to-day administration and in the making of policy pronouncements. The importance of individual Secretaries of State varies, depending largely on their relations with the Presidents they serve, as Alexander DeConde and others have shown. However, no Secretary of State has the only voice a President listens to in foreign affairs: for considerations outside the area of his jurisdiction—budgetary and electoral ones, for example—necessarily weigh in the President's mind. For this reason, Presidents find it valuable to seek policy advice from White House assistants who have no "departmental" point of view.

The leading alternative to coordination by presidential assistant is coordination by committee, and two such major committees exist at the summit of policy making. Traditionally, use has, of course, been made of the President's cabinet, essentially a committee of coordination made up of the heads of executive departments. However, the make-up of the cabinet is inappropriate for it to serve as *the* committee of coordination in the field of national security policy. That is, various officeholders traditionally hold a seat in the cabinet whose participation in the making of foreign policy is hardly needed—the Postmaster General, for example. At the same time the participation of the holders of other offices whose positions have not entailed cabinet membership seems appropriate, such as the Directors of the Central Intelligence Agency and the U.S. Information Agency.[3]

In consideration of this problem the Congress established, under the terms of the National Security Act of 1947, a National Security Council composed of those officials, some of them cabinet members, others not, who held high positions in the national security field. The

---

3 This is the agency responsible for United States propaganda abroad.

National Security Council developed its own institutional apparatus, including a secretariat, as well as various techniques designed to see that its decisions are carried out by the appropriate agencies. The workings of the National Security Council have demonstrated the difficulties inherent in the coordination-by-committee approach, however, even after the question of the comprehensiveness of the group's membership had been resolved. One difficulty of the committee approach is that each member of the group bears responsibility for the operation of some great department of government, and, quite naturally, is prone to regard questions from the point of view of the defense of the interests of his department and the promotion of the programs in which it is concerned. One can thus often predict what the position of each individual will be on questions that arise. The Secretary of Defense will argue that the circumstances of the case, whatever it be, require an increase in the military budget that will enable him to accelerate the development and procurement of new weapons. The Secretary of the Treasury, seconded by the Director of the Budget Bureau, will point out that in view of the nation's financial situation a restriction of expenditures is needed. The Secretary of State will maintain that various delicate negotiations going forward require that action not be taken that would antagonize allies or the "uncommitted" states; and so on.

Given this circumstance, heads of departments and of agencies try to settle difficulties that arise without reference to other departments and try to avoid bringing them up in the Cabinet or in the National Security Council. On questions of such importance that the department cannot handle them by itself, the tendency is to go directly to the President, who is after all the one who would have to make the decision even if the issue were raised in a cabinet or National Security Council meeting.

It is understandable in view of these persistent features of the processes of interdepartmental coordination that the President tends to rely more on personal advisors attached to the White House staff who are free of departmental responsibilities, unprejudiced by department interests, and presumably able to regard issues from the point of view of the President himself. Similarly, the President may be tempted to rely on men who have his personal confidence and are free of departmental connections to bring him a fresh view of situations as roving ambassadors and personal confidants—the Colonel Houses and Harry Hopkinses who have appeared so frequently in American history and have been so resented by officeholders who feel themselves supplanted by the interloper. The pitfalls in this type of development are that the reliance that the President obviously places on his personal emissaries tends to undermine the morale of department officials, for example the ambassador who finds himself ignored by the President's dispatch of a roving representative to conduct negotiations over his head; and that in by-passing the departments in this way, the President's decisions may not be based on adequate background information, planning, and staff work generally.

Inevitably, one should note, regardless of the President's personal style in administrative organization, in the last analysis only he can make the definitive decision. The President is picked by the voters to make decisions on their behalf, after all; no matter how much help he may get from his aides, he will be held responsible for the big decisions, and it is only right that he should make them.

SUGGESTED READINGS

Dahl, Robert, *Congress and Foreign Policy,* rev. ed. New York: Norton, 1964.

De Conde, Alexander, *The American Secretary of State: An Interpretation.* New York: Praeger, 1962.

Graebner, Norman (ed.), *An Uncertain Tradition: American Secretaries of State in the Twentieth Century.* New York: McGraw-Hill, 1961.

Hulen, Bertram D., *Inside the Department of State.* New York: McGraw-Hill, 1939.

Huntington, Samuel P., *The Soldier and the State,* 2d ed. New York: Random House, Inc. (Vintage), 1964.

McCamy, James L., *The Administration of American Foreign Affairs.* New York: Knopf, 1952.

Plischke, Elmer, *The Conduct of American Diplomacy,* 2d ed. Princeton, N.J.: Van Nostrand, 1961.

Ransom, Harry Howe, *Central Intelligence and National Security.* Cambridge, Mass.: Harvard University Press, 1950.

Raymond, Jack, *Power at the Pentagon.* New York: Harper & Row, 1964.

Tully, Andrew, *CIA: The Inside Story.* New York: Morrow, 1962.

II

The Structure
of International Relations

4

The World of Sovereign States

Perhaps the most difficult task in the development of international relations theory is to determine the general nature of the goals that states set for themselves. The most comprehensive formulation, which has been discussed in a previous chapter, is that states typically pursue their national interests. This seems obviously true, so obviously indeed that it is of little value, since the term "national interests" is extremely broad and susceptible of any interpretation that one cares to give it. Even given its most general meaning, however, the statement that states pursue their national interests is not always correct. Statesmen and peoples may, and occasionally do, sacrifice marginal increments in the attainment of national interests to aspirations that stem from moral or ideological considerations rather than from strictly interested motives. In the actual positing of national goals, more importantly, clear analytic distinctions between objectives derived from considerations of interest and those stemming from ideological and emotional criteria normally are not made. Nevertheless, while certainly not invariably true, the rule of thumb that states pursue national interests is the closest approximation to a general description of state behavior that we have.

There is no reason to be shocked, as some people are, at the acknowledgment that this is the case. After all, statesmen, like other people, are hired to do a specific job, and that job is to serve the interests of the collectivity that they represent.

It is actually in the choice of means toward the achievement of some accepted goal that a greater degree of unpredictability and freedom of choice enters than in the selection of the goals themselves. That is, in any given situation a variety of methods of action, which may range from the use of force or the threat of force to economic pressures to promises of assistance, present themselves to the statesman in his dealings with representatives of other states. It may well be in this area of preferred means that states differ most from each other, rather than in the general character of the ends they pursue, although the latter is usually emphasized more heavily in the literature.

THE GENERAL CHARACTER OF INTERNATIONAL LAW: SOVEREIGNTY

International society, like all societies, functions more or less within a framework of a conventional set of procedures and customs, which is dignified by the name of "international law." International law does not, however, consist of a set of rules that one must not violate under pain of penalty; and it is not created by a legislature, nor enforced by a judicial and police system. One might say that acceptance of the obligations of international law is voluntary; there is no mechanism for their enforcement against the will of any state. This is another way of saying that no world government exists. The principle that states are bound to obey no superior authority, but themselves make the rules by which they live, is called the principle of sovereignty.

Sovereignty is the first premise of the system of international law that exists today; indeed it has been said[1] that the whole of international law is simply a series of deductions from the principle of sovereignty.

Although the concept of sovereignty is used today principally in the field of international relations, it was originally developed in relation to problems of domestic politics. The doctrine of sovereignty in its domestic application says that within any one territorial jurisdiction there can exist only one authoritative source of law. This sole authoritative source of law is then called the sovereign.

The doctrine of sovereignty is difficult to apply to the institutions of a modern constitutional state, with its bills of rights and its division of powers. Nevertheless, it retains meaning in the field of international relations. In international law the actual government of a state is sovereign within the jurisdiction of that state. That is, if a country is completely independent, its government is a sovereign authority not

---

1 By John Herz.

subject to control by any outside agency. Any multi-national enterprise must thus be based on the voluntary agreement of the states concerned.

Although the principle of sovereignty still provides the basis for international law, some theorists have questioned the realism of the principle as it applies to today's world. John Herz has argued, for example,[2] that the factual assumptions on which the doctrine of sovereignty is based no longer apply; that today the economic pressures that one state can use on another, the airplane that can fly over national boundaries, the radio waves that respect no frontiers, mean that no government, no matter how firmly entrenched, is in fact completely master of its own territory. Yet this has always been the case, after all; small states with large and powerful neighbors were never completely masters of their own destinies, regardless of how sovereign they were in international law. One has to remember that, in itself, lack of congruence with fact need not invalidate a legal concept; domestic systems of law abound in legal fictions.

It may well be, of course, that in years to come the legal concept of sovereignty will be modified and eventually transmuted into something else. The present world has witnessed numerous attempts at federation or confederation of states, and it may well be that new legal principles will evolve to replace the doctrine of sovereignty. The world has not always been organized into nation-states, and there is no basis for supposing that the present units of world politics must inevitably remain the same. Nevertheless, at the present time and for the foreseeable future, sovereignty remains the basic premise of the international legal system.

OBSERVANCE OF THE RULES
OF INTERNATIONAL LAW

Why should states assume binding obligations if they are subject to no superior authority? Why should states that are sovereign obey the precepts of international law?

Several sets of answers are possible here. Perhaps the most simple answer is that very often states do not in fact observe the rules of international law. For example, it had long been accepted that states have jurisdiction over the contiguous waters up to a distance of three miles off their shores. Recently, however, several states that derive appreciable income from fishing have attempted to reserve for their own boats rights to fish for twenty, 100, or even 200 miles from the shoreline. Attempts to enforce these new unilaterally established limits have led to clashes with the fishing fleets of larger states that found themselves excluded from waters they regarded as legitimately open to fishing. Thus, for example,

---

[2] In *International Politics in the Atomic Age*. New York: Columbia University Press, 1959.

in the last five years there has been a "codfish war" between Iceland and Great Britain, a "lobster war" between Brazil and France, and a "tuna war" between Ecuador and the United States. (These were of course not literal wars.) No clear settlement of the issue was reached in any of the cases. Ecuador, Peru, and Chile even concluded an agreement under which they pledged to support each other in the maintenance of a 200-mile-limit.

The rules of international law generally are observed, however, mainly because they carry advantages without putting very heavy demands on states. Often there is no reason why a state would choose not to obey a particular principle of international law. For example, it is an accepted practice that ships in distress signal their plight by flying their flags upside down. A ship in distress is under no compulsion to give this particular signal, of course, but obviously it is in her interest to do so. Many rules of international law are, similarly, of the nature of traffic regulations; even if there were no enforcement of the rule that cars travel to the right of the road, most drivers would follow the rule since it would be against one's own interest to violate it—one would simply run a greater risk of colliding with another automobile.

There is, however, a punishment for violating the rights of another state under international law; such an action entitles the other state to retaliate in like fashion. This is the negative half of the principle of reciprocity, which stipulates that one state should extend to another all the privileges it is granted by that state. Reciprocity deserves to be placed next to sovereignty among the most fundamental principles of international law.

An example of the reciprocity principle would be the standard practice in international relations for diplomats to receive various privileges in the country to which they are accredited, including immunity to prosecution under its laws. If the United States were to withdraw diplomatic privileges from the representatives of another state, that state would doubtless retaliate promptly by withdrawing the same privileges from American diplomats stationed there. This type of retaliation may seem childish and arbitrary in effect, but it is simply the way in which one state informs another that it intends to stand on its rights. Accordingly, states often follow principles of international law because they wish to have the same principles applied to themselves, a curious kind of applied Golden Rule.

A state may also act in accordance with principles of international law for propaganda and public relations purposes, either in the general sense that the state can then play the role of a peace-loving and law-abiding international citizen to foreign public opinion, or in the more specific sense that by living up to its obligations the state may preserve its international "credit rating," as it were. In part this may be a very literal credit rating; that is, a state that is financially hard-pressed may continue, nevertheless, to meet interest payments due to the foreign holders of government bonds in order to establish a reputation for faithful payment, which will stand it in good stead next time it wishes to float a bond issue. But it is true also in the general sense that a state that regularly violated treaty obligations would be likely to find after a time that other states were reluctant to conclude treaties with it.

Finally, it may be the case that a state, preferring a peaceful regulated world to one of violence and institutionalized blackmail, lives up to its obligations under international law because it genuinely wishes to strengthen the effect of law in international affairs. Great Britain and the United States are among the states that have appeared to act in this way on occasion, perhaps out of a sense of the responsibility that accompanies the possession of power.

THE CONTENT OF INTERNATIONAL LAW

If the binding character of international law is imprecise and variable, so also is its content. What provisions constitute the substance of international law? And how are they determined, in a world of sovereign states?

Partial answers to these questions are provided by Article 38 of the Statute of the International Court of Justice, which lists the criteria the Court is to apply in settling the disputes submitted to it. These are

a. International conventions, whether general or particular, establishing rules expressly recognized by the contesting states;
b. International custom as evidence of a general practice accepted as law;
c. The general principles of law recognized by civilized nations;
d. Subject to the provisions of Article 59,[a] judicial decisions and the teachings of the most highly qualified publicists of the various nations, as subsidiary means for the determination of rules of law.

Finally, the article reads that, if the parties agree, the Court may decide a case on the basis of general principles of equity.

One hardly needs to point out the vagueness of some of the standards to be applied. And of course the statute quoted refers only to cases which the parties have already agreed to submit to the International Court of Justice. In the normal course of events each state interprets the

---

[a] Article 59 stipulates that any decisions rendered by the Court are to be binding only with respect to the particular dispute at issue and the particular parties involved in the dispute.

precepts of international law for itself; not unexpectedly, wide differences of opinion emerge as to what constitutes the practice of "civilized nations," and how international conventions (that is, treaties) should be interpreted.

The point is simply that international law cannot serve to solve major substantive problems, and its existence, of course, in no way alters the structure of a world organized in a system of competing sovereignties. Nevertheless, it does add a measure of convenience and regularity to the relations among states. Moreover, it provides modes of adjusting minor differences between states that do not wish to resort to reciprocal threats for fear of prejudicing the good relations that exist between them.

One has to acknowledge the force of the argument that, at bottom, international law is the attempt to give legal sanction to the rule of the powerful and to the possessions of the rich; in this sense the Cynic, or for that matter the Marxist, theory of law as the will of the stronger or the will of the richer makes more sense as applied to international law than it does applied to domestic law.

The conservative bias of international law is clear. For example, the basic principle that the obligations of treaties are to be observed can be regarded as binding the future to the arrangements made by the past. "Have not" states or "angry young states," such as Hitler's Germany or Castro's Cuba, typically denounce treaties on the ground that they subordinate the requirements of justice to the maintenance of an unjust *status quo.*

The principle that obligations are enforced by retaliation of the state whose rights are violated likewise favors the strong state, for weaker states are less likely to be in a position from which they can effectively retaliate against states more powerful. The commonly accepted principle that compensation should be given for any property confiscated also works in the interest of those states whose citizens own property within the jurisdiction of other states. Insistence on the principle of compensation by the governments of the stronger and well-to-do states is, in fact, a recurrent cause of conflict between them and the governments of poorer countries.

To carry the argument further, the principle that there should be freedom of navigation on the high seas, that countries should not set aside parts of the water's surface for their exclusive use outside the traditional three-mile limit, clearly works in the interest of those powers that have strong navies and large fishing fleets and are able to take best advantage of the freedom that is nominally the right of all.

One of the principles that illustrates this aspect of international law most clearly is that which acknowledges the so-called "right of conquest." Under international law military victory creates a legitimate claim: quite literally, might makes right. In a sense the logic of this doctrine is unimpeachable. All legitimate titles to authority can be traced ultimately to success in battle; the claims of monarchs are founded almost always in the successful usurpation of the Crown by the original founder of the dynasty, those of republics in a successful act of rebellion against constituted authority. Viewed in this perspective, "the right of conquest" is a reasonable premise. Moreover, any system of law that pretends to effectiveness in the world of international relations must begin by accepting the reality that military victory is in fact unchallengeable; a system of law that failed to recognize this could not expect to have the slightest effect. In the field of international relations, then, the gulf between law and justice, at times a small one in systems of domestic law, is vast.

But international law is broad-minded; it must be if it is to comprehend the whole of international reality. Thus there are principles of international law that apply to the conduct of war, as well as those concerning the business of peacetime. Many people are inclined to scoff at the idea of common principles of international law applying to belligerents in a state of war with each other; and yet all wars are necessarily circumscribed within limits implicitly or explicitly adopted, providing they are not simply frenzies of massacre serving solely to gratify bloodlust—an extremely rare type of warfare, it should be noted. Even wars take place within a framework of common assumptions, and even between states at war, common interests exist—for example, the rights of neutrals or of prisoners of war. This is another way of saying that the modest prescriptions of international law remain relevant, regardless of changes in circumstances. Thus although international law as it stands at present cannot be regarded as preventing war or the development of enmities and clashes of interest, it may nevertheless serve to regularize and civilize the conduct of international relations—an achievement that should not lightly be dismissed.

THE TASKS OF DIPLOMACY TODAY

Within this quasi-legal framework, the conduct of relations among states goes forward. The management of inter-state relations constitutes diplomacy, which one could describe in general as the art of adjusting the varying and often clashing interests of states to the advantage of the state the diplomat represents, but also with a view to preserving amicable relations with other states where possible. In performing his function the diplomat engages in seeking common ground among the national interests of different states, in narrowing areas of disagreement among them, and in finding formulas that permit them to coexist. Of course, it may be necessary to imply that the state he represents will use force to effect a favorable settlement of an issue in dispute; but ideally, pressure of this nature is used with tact and discretion so that the other state is left an avenue to retreat from her position with grace, and without loss of face. In addition to these primary functions of diplomacy, the diplomat has representational, that is, ceremonial and social, duties; he also serves as a channel of communication, and in addition is charged with the general function of gathering information for the state that he represents in the country to which he is assigned.

The tasks of diplomacy have become monumental in our era. Ideally, diplomacy should have only a limited number of problems requiring attention, a great deal of time to work on them, and a certain freedom from the pressures of popular emotion that might impede their settlement on solely rational terms. But today an avalanche of international problems has descended, many of them, in effect, bearing deadlines, and many of them representing heavy emotional commitments. The world faces technical revolutions, a world population increasing at an extraordinary rate, demands for the independence of the non–self-governing territories whose justice is generally acknowledged, and a revolution, slowly gathering momentum, in the level of economic expectations of underprivileged peoples, who are no longer resigned to a miserable level of subsistence. It is thus not possible for diplomacy to conceive of its task as a simple maintenance of the *status quo,* even if this were permitted by one's conscience. The appropriate model that domestic politics affords to statesmen facing the problems of today's world is surely that of Great Britain or Sweden of the last 200 years, which have preserved a fabric of legality and domestic peace because the ruling and possessing classes were willing to accept change and meet justified demands; rather than, say, that of Germany or France of the same period, where traditional aristocracies attempted to maintain an unjust *status quo,* only to pay a heavy toll in revolutionary violence and civil war, while eventually losing all they had tried to defend and more.

If the world consisted only of states more or less satisfied with the *status quo,* then international relations would be a more peaceful business than in fact it is. It is so common as to be half-expected, however, that states develop ambitions to extend their domains or spheres of influence, either by the annexation of neighboring territories which contain peoples of similar ethnic origin, or by the domination of the surrounding geographic area, or in the unlimited fashion of "true" imperialism, by achieving a dominant position that logically stops at nothing short of world hegemony.

Naturally, other states normally prefer to retain their independence and national identities; they thus make preparations to defend themselves against any expansionist pretensions their neighbors may have, or may come to have. The aim is, of course, to deter potential or actual expansionism by making the costs of expansionist adventures prohibitively high, if not rendering them altogether impossible.

Clearly a greater deterrent to expansionist ambitions can be created if an ambitious state is presented not with a series of individual states each trying to defend itself in isolation but with an alliance of states prepared to unite their strength and act in concert against aggression. Where an alliance of defensive states is created that, by the aggregate amount of military power it has available, acts as a deterrent to aggression on the part of other states or combinations of states, one can say that a "balance of power" has been created.

COLLECTIVE SECURITY

If all the states in the international system have an interest in maintaining the *status quo,* or in preserving peace, they may take a step further in the direction of international organization and, rather than resting content with the system of contingent alliances and implicit understandings that constitute a balance of power, choose the more straightforward collective security agreement. Under a collective security system all states agree that they will come to the aid of any state that is attacked. It should be noted here that the commitment is not a limited one. The agreement will operate in the interest of any state that is attacked, and against any aggressor. It thus differs from the mutual defense alliance, with which it is often confused, in that the latter is a grouping of a limited number of states directed against possible attack from a particular state likely to become aggressive, or against a particular group of such states. Rival defensive alliances can and do exist. The NATO agreement is, strictly speaking, a mutual defense treaty, and not a collective security agreement.

The great strength of a collective security agreement, at least in principle, is that in allying the power of *all* states against *any* potential aggressor it creates a maximum of deterrent force committed to the maintenance of peace. In actuality, however, its very universality is its great weakness, since states are not equally hostile to all possible aggressors nor equally eager to defend all states that may possibly be attacked. This has been demonstrated by the history of collective security under the League of Nations and under the United Nations. The classic case of the failure of collective security under the League occurred when the League's members failed to come effectively to the aid of Ethiopia when attacked by Italy. Under the UN system collective security had an apparent success in the defense of South Korea against the aggression launched from North Korea. However, on examination it becomes clear that, if anything, the

South Korean case demonstrates the ultimate weakness of the collective security principle. Obviously, none of the Communist states that are members of the UN came to the aid of South Korea since they sympathized with, and indeed aided, the aggressor. By the same token, it is clear that if South Korea had invaded North Korea—a possibility that was not totally out of the question—the United States and its allies would not have come to the aid of North Korea, a Communist state, even though this is what obedience to the principle of collective security would have demanded.

SUGGESTED READINGS

Claude, Inis L., Jr., *Power and International Relations.* New York: Random House, Inc., 1963.

Herz, John, *International Politics in the Atomic Age.* New York: Columbia University Press, 1959.

Hobson, J. A., *Imperialism, A Study,* 2d ed. London: G. Allen, 1954.

Hoffmann, Stanley H. (ed.), *Contemporary Theory in International Relations.* Englewood Cliffs, N.J.: Prentice-Hall, 1960.

Kaplan, Morton, *System and Process in International Politics.* New York: Wiley, 1957.

Lenin, V. I., *Imperialism: The Highest Stage of Capitalism.* Moscow: Foreign Languages Publishing House, 1960.

Macridis, Roy (ed.), *Foreign Policy in World Politics,* 2d ed. Englewood Cliffs, N.J.: Prentice-Hall, 1962.

Morgenthau, Hans J., *Politics Among Nations,* 3d ed. New York: Knopf, 1960.

Rosecrance, Richard N., *Action and Reaction in World Politics.* Boston: Little, Brown, 1963.

Stoessinger, John, *The Might of Nations.* New York: Random House, Inc., 1963.

5

The United Nations

MEMBERSHIP AND FUNCTIONS

There are a variety of international organizations whose membership, in view of the purposes envisaged in their charters, should be open to all states. All of these organizations except one are, like the Universal Postal Union, for example, designed to accomplish some modest, technical, nonpolitical task. Only the UN itself is a body of potentially universal membership that discharges a multitude of functions, with political ones the most important. Neither the nature of its actual membership nor the character of the major political tasks the organization has set itself can be deduced unequivocally from the organization's charter, however; since the founding of the UN in San Francisco in 1945, both have changed greatly.

Let us then proceed to locate the position of the UN organization in the universe of possible organizations in terms of its place along the dimensions of membership and functions. In actuality these two dimensions are not completely independent of each other; as Professor Claude has remarked, one's conception of the appropriate criteria for membership in the international organization depends on what role one assumes it should play. This problem, of course, involves very real political questions, since the membership of the UN is, in fact, not universal, and at the time of writing some functioning governments are not members, nor are they likely to become members in the near future.

On the face of it, it does not appear to be easy to secure membership in the organization. The charter provides that a new member must secure affirmative votes from both of the organization's deliberative bodies. That is, a candidate must be recommended for membership by the Security Council; this requires the affirmative votes of nine out of the fifteen council members, and is subject to veto by the permanent members—the United States, the Soviet Union, Great Britain, France, and the Republic of China (Nationalist China). This recommendation is then voted upon by the General Assembly, where it needs the approval of two thirds of those voting yes or no. (Each member state of the UN has one vote in the General Assembly.)

This is the procedure required for the admission of a new member. The procedure to gain representation at the UN of the new *government* of a state already a member is simpler. Thus the Communist government of China at Peking, which is at present not represented, could have its emissary seated in the General Assembly as the rightful representative of that China, which already belongs to the UN by means of a vote of the assembly itself. The procedure by which a Communist Chinese representative could take over the seat of Nationalist China in the Security Council, on the other hand, cannot exactly be foreseen since the question might arise in several different forms, and the manner in which it was resolved would depend in part on the circumstances at the time. However in all probability the seating of a Chinese Communist in the Security Council would at some point require the affirmative vote of nine of the council members, and would be subject to veto by the permanent members. The problem of Chinese representation is the leading membership question that faces the organization at the time of writing, and it will be referred to throughout the discussion that follows, and also subsequently, in Chapter 11.

In discussing different theories of the functions that the UN organization can usefully perform, one can employ either of two different angles of vision. One can evaluate the UN either from the viewpoint of one's country's interests—in this case those of the United States—or from that of the interests of the UN itself—its need to survive and to strengthen itself. For Americans, as for citizens of many other countries, these two points of view can be integrated on the assumption that it is in the national interest of the United States that the UN survive and be strengthened; this is probably a view that most reasonable Americans take, although not all. Nevertheless, the double focus that exists relative to the problem should be borne in mind.

Most theories of the proper role of the UN seem to converge on one of three possible conceptions of the membership appropriate to the organization. These can be called theory *a:* that membership should be universal or as nearly universal as possible; theory *b:* that membership should go only to those states sincerely committed to the charter's prin-

TABLE 2. Members of the United Nations

Afghanistan	Dahomey	Kuwait	Rwanda
Albania	Denmark	Laos	Saudi Arabia
Algeria	Dominican	Lebanon	Senegal
Argentina	Republic	Liberia	Sierra Leone
Australia	Ecuador	Libya	Somalia
Austria	El Salvador	Luxembourg	South Africa
Belgium	Ethiopia	Madagascar	Spain
Bolivia	Finland	Malawi	Sudan
Brazil	France	Malaysia	Sweden
Bulgaria	Gabon	Mali	Syria
Burma	Ghana	Malta	Tanzania
Burundi	Greece	Mauritania	Thailand
Byelorussia	Guatemala	Mexico	Togo
Cambodia	Guinea	Mongolia	Trinidad and
Cameroon	Haiti	Morocco	Tobago
Canada	Honduras	Nepal	Tunisia
Central African	Hungary	Netherlands	Turkey
Republic	Iceland	New Zealand	Uganda
Ceylon	India	Nicaragua	Ukraine
Chad	Indonesia	Niger	USSR
Chile	Iran	Nigeria	United Arab
China (Nationalist)	Iraq	Norway	Republic
Colombia	Ireland	Pakistan	United Kingdom
Congo (Brazzaville)	Israel	Panama	United States
Congo (Leopoldville)	Italy	Paraguay	Upper Volta
Costa Rica	Ivory Coast	Peru	Uruguay
Cuba	Jamaica	Philippines	Venezuela
Cyprus	Japan	Poland	Yemen
Czechoslovakia	Jordan	Portugal	Yugoslavia
		Romania	

ciples of nonaggression and collective security; and theory *c:* that the organization's membership should consist especially, though not necessarily only, of the newer states, the smaller nonaligned or uncommitted states.

Other types of attitude towards the organization are apparently held by a few states, which if considered seriously would logically lead to rather novel and intriguing results. One such conception seems to animate French government policy under General de Gaulle, and also the policies of Portugal and the Union of South Africa. President de Gaulle appears to regard the UN organization as a cross that he must bear as penance for his sins. In this conception, being a member of the UN compels one to sit stoically while under verbal attack from delegates of insignificant and uncivilized states, harasses one into contributing funds for purposes of which one does not approve, coerces one into taking sides on issues in which one is not the least concerned, although by doing so one is forced to make enemies of the partisans of one viewpoint or the other. The appropriate membership theory would then be that membership in the organization should be forced on those states that one especially dislikes, or that have earned the enmity of the international community. However, this is a rather idiosyncratic view of the UN, a conception that no state has thus far seen fit to act on consistently.

Probably the theory of the UN's functions that is most consistent with the provisions of the charter is that the organization is to be a working alliance of like-minded states pursuing common purposes. Articles 3 to 6, the section of the charter which governs membership, clearly state this position. Membership is open to states signing the charter and "to all other peace-loving states which accept the obligations contained in the present Charter and, in the judgment of the Organization, are able and willing to carry out these obligations." Moreover, states may be suspended from membership or expelled from the organization altogether if they have "persistently violated the principles contained in the present Charter" (Article 6). The implication is that the organization is not supposed to include just anyone, but only those states that live up to its principles. If the organization is to be a working alliance, this approach makes a great deal of sense: It is difficult to work together with other states if you are pursuing goals different from and even opposed to theirs.

On the other hand, it is common for this quite reasonable conception to degenerate into a view of the UN as a sort of honor society to which only the pure in heart are admitted. The American press often takes this position, particularly in connection with the question of the admission of Communist China. Clearly this view pushes things too far. If only those states whose purposes are consonant with the categorical imperative of Immanuel Kant are admitted to membership, the membership roster is likely to be singularly blank, after all. Nevertheless, Article 4 does specify that members are to be "peace loving," and a good case can be made that the policies of Communist China are not in fact peace loving. A much greater degree of sophistication than this is possible, however. It is, after all, very rare that a state is not peace loving, in the sense that it desires war for its own sake. Perhaps this was the case with Hitler's Germany; perhaps not. Normally, any state would prefer to secure its objectives without the use of force if at all possible. At the same time most states are prepared to use force under certain circumstances if necessary. Thus the difference is not between states that are absolutely peace loving and those that are absolutely not; it is a difference between degrees of reluctance to fight—a difference which is surely significant, but which is not quite as straightforward as the charter appears to assume.

If one should adopt the conception of the UN as an alliance of like-minded states pursuing common goals, then the appropriate conclusion as to membership questions would be, presumably, that only democratic states contented with the *status quo* could be members. Clearly, Communist China would not qualify. At the same time Soviet Union might well have to be expelled, and the Republic of South Africa as well, together with a goodly number of other states that have shown themselves more eager for power than for peace—Sukarno's Indonesia, for example. United States officials, who have adopted this position in part, have thus been caught in a dilemma: They have urged the need for like-mindedness in answer to arguments that Communist China should be admitted, while at the same time arguing against it and preaching the advantages of universal membership when the question was one of, say, expelling the Soviet Union or the Republic of South Africa. Here, of course, one's political opinions readily become apparent, and the United States is far from being alone in her position of logical inconsistency—those urging the expulsion of South Africa are themselves usually to be found urging the admission of Communist China.

A rival conception of the UN's purposes to the foregoing is that the body should provide an arena in which disputes can be settled. If one adopts this conception of the UN organization, then far from wishing to confine membership to like-minded states, it should extend precisely to states that differ from one another, whose purposes conflict (and thus potentially to all states). Yet the UN is not adequate to the task of resolving disputes among major world powers, such as Cold War issues. It has been able to play a useful although minor role in helping to resolve disputes that have arisen among states not on opposite sides in the Cold War, as for example in the stationing of troops along the borders between Israel and her Arab neighbors, or in making the transfer of authority over West Irian (West New Guinea) between the Netherlands and Indonesia a peaceful one. But in any case, Articles 33 through 38 of the charter, which provide norms for peaceful settlement of disputes, envision the possibility that the organization may on request take a hand in the settlement of disputes to which a state that is not a member of the UN is a party; consequently, universal membership is not absolutely necessary to the organization's mission of peaceful settlement.

Other criteria for membership are suggested by consideration of other functions performed by the world body. One of the leading functions of the UN, for example, has been as a tool for facilitating diplomatic contacts. That is, the location at one point of representatives of so many different countries allows for spot checks of opinion on new proposals, and permits the ready coordination of the activities of groups of states that share common interests. The appropriate membership theory here would perhaps be that membership should extend to all states that engage in interstate relations.

The coverage that the world's press gives to debates in the General Assembly has some educational value for the world's populations. Stories from the UN have a good chance of making the first page of the news-paper, and can provide a measure of popular education in the issues of international relations. If the UN can be regarded as performing an educational function for the peoples of the world, it should equally be stressed that it has educational value for the delegates themselves. Ex-posure at close range to the continuing attempt to adjust national inter-ests and aspirations in the interest of world peace, to find formulas for the peaceful resolution of disputes, to bring pressure to bear on others, and have pressure brought to bear on oneself, constitutes something like an intensive short course in international politics. One can often observe something of a transition towards greater sophistication in delegates of newly independent states who first take their seats in the world organiza-tion under the impression that a positive contribution to the resolution of the world's problems consists in making fiery speeches on all topics, full of devotion to unimpeachable principles. As time goes on, the realities of power and interest are more appreciated. This educational process is of value not only as far as the delegate's own performance of his functions is concerned, and not only with respect to the part he plays by his reports and recommendations in shaping his nation's foreign policy— in the case of the smaller states, especially, this may be a considerable role—but also because UN delegates have gone on to become foreign ministers and even prime ministers or presidents of their states. If one were to consider this educational role as an important function of the UN organization, the corresponding membership theory would be that membership in the UN is most appropriate for the newly independent states that have not yet developed a tradition in national foreign policy.

Similar conclusions on the membership question are suggested by the fairly prevalent conception of the UN's function that debates can give voice to world opinion, thus inhibiting the less scrupulous acts of the great powers or their less defensible policies. This appears to have been the case, at least on occasion. The United States, for example, has steadily modified its position on the question of apartheid in South Africa, and the question of the treatment by Portugal of its African territories, be-cause of the need to take positions more acceptable to the independent African states. Seen in this perspective, then, the General Assembly serves as an agency through which the collective opinion of the smaller, espe-cially the non-European, states can be brought to bear.

Finally, the chief function of the UN could be regarded simply as to survive—that is, the organization can be conceived of as important less for what it is now than for what it may become. In this view the UN, as it continues to exist over the years, will be found useful for more and more duties and, like any successfully functioning institution, will grow steadily in influence, at some future date being able to play a more significant role in the cause of world peace than it does today.

There is even some evidence that this process is very gradually taking place. The UN has in fact been able to perform various roles, albeit minor ones, which no one else wanted or which no one else could fill. UN peacekeeping forces, for example, serve to watch over unsteady truces on the borders between Israel and the Arab states and between India and Pakistan. The UN has also been able to take part in the resolution of disputes that would otherwise have been complicated by problems of loss of face. The dispute between the Netherlands and Indonesia over control of West New Guinea is a case in point. By the spring of 1963, the dispute had already begun to give rise to abortive attempts at the violent settlement of the problem by the Indonesians, when the introduction of a UN presence made a peaceful solution possible. The Dutch for their part had no particular interest in maintaining sovereignty in West New Guinea; but they were committed to not turning over control of the territory to Indonesia. The self-evident solution that was developed was for the Dutch to hand over control to the UN, which then assumed responsibility for the subsequent transfer of power to the Indonesians.

The chief independent political role of the UN organization has indeed become the performance of these perhaps minor but nonetheless worthwhile political tasks, made possible by its position as a disinterested third party, in the resolution of questions that are not disputes between the allies of the Soviet Union or China on the one hand and those of the United States on the other.

This last conception of the appropriate function of the UN may be the key to the most reasonable approach that can be taken by the United States. Too many Americans tend to regard the UN as providing the solution to all the problems of international politics. And too many Americans, having learned that the UN can not in fact solve all the world's problems, or even its major ones, become disillusioned and regard the international organization as useless and a waste of money. But there is no justification for going to either extreme. The UN is a tool in the hands of the nations; it is a tool that has limited uses; it is not a multipurpose tool that can substitute for those two indispensable items, military power and resourceful statesmanship; in fact, like all tools the UN can be damaged, even irreparably, by being made to take on tasks beyond its capacity. Nevertheless it is useful, it comes in handy on many occasions, and it will doubtless find its uses in the future; it would make no sense to throw it away.

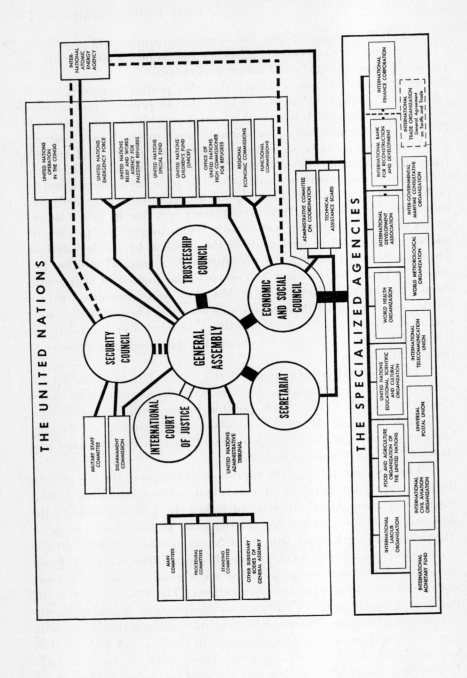

ORGANIZATION AND DEVELOPMENT

As is generally known, the principal political organs of the UN are the Security Council, the General Assembly, and the Secretary General's office. In the original conception of the UN embodied in the organization's charter, the Security Council was given primary authority to act in questions relating to the maintenance of international peace and security; under Article 12 of the charter, the General Assembly is not to make any recommendations with regard to a question that is before the Security Council. Moreover, the decisions of the Security Council carry a weight that those of the General Assembly do not have. The General Assembly has only the power to make "recommendations" to the membership.[1] Decisions of the Security Council, on the other hand, are intended to be legally binding on the membership—Article 25 stipulates that member nations agree to accept and carry out the provisions of Security Council resolutions.

In the early days of the UN organization, activity was centered in the Security Council, as seemed appropriate given the pre-eminent position allotted to the council by the charter. It was during these years that the problem of the big-power veto seemed to loom as the great obstacle to the effective functioning of the world organization. The veto power derives from the provisions of Article 27 of the charter, according to which a decision of the Security Council on other than procedural matters requires the affirmative vote of seven of the council members, including the votes of all five permanent members—the United States, the Soviet Union, Great Britain, France and the Republic of China.[2] If one of the permanent members votes negatively on a resolution, therefore, it cannot be carried.

The assumption underlying this set of voting arrangements was clearly that it would be possible for the five major World War II allies to work in harmony, at least on some questions, during the postwar period. At the same time, of course, provision of a big-power veto was simply a prudent safeguard to insure that the UN would not destroy itself by attempting to undertake a policy that ran counter to the wishes of one of the big powers, and which therefore, given the fragility of the organization, could not be enforced. Seen in this perspective the veto appears not as an imperfection in the UN structure, but rather as an expression of a realistic appreciation of the facts of national power without which the organization could hardly continue to function. It goes without saying,

---

[1] Decisions on "important matters" require a two-thirds vote of the assembly. Decisions on other questions are made by a majority of those present and voting (Article 18).

[2] That is, "Nationalist" China, the seat of whose government is at present on Formosa (or Taiwan).

moreover, that none of the major powers, and certainly neither the Soviet Union nor the United States, would have joined the organization if no veto had been provided for. The veto was included in the charter at the insistence of the United States negotiators just as much as of those of the Soviet Union.

The UN Charter provided originally for eleven members of the Security Council in all. In addition to the five permanent members, six nonpermanent members were to be elected by the General Assembly by a two-thirds vote, to serve two-year terms. In the early years of the world organization, before the influx of African and Asian states swelled the organization to over double its original size of fifty-one members, the nonpermanent members of the Security Council were elected to represent different blocs of member nations. Under this so-called gentlemen's agreement the nonpermanent seats were distributed in rough accordance with the numerical strength of various blocs, as follows: Latin America was assigned two seats, western Europe and eastern Europe (that is, the Soviet bloc) got one each, and one each went to the Middle East and to the states of the British Commonwealth. Observance of this formula avoided the necessity for pitched battles over the elections to fill Security Council seats as they became vacant.

Only a handful of new members were admitted to the organization during its first ten years of existence. As Cold War lines froze, the United States opposed Soviet-sponsored candidates for admission, and the Soviet Union returned the compliment. In late 1955, however, President Eisenhower and Secretary of State Dulles modified the United States' position and agreed to a "package deal" under which allies of both superpowers, together with several neutrals, were admitted to membership. Since that time the UN has lost its character as a more-or-less exclusive club, admission to membership in which was reserved principally for those states that had fought against the Axis Powers in World War II (or which had at least declared war—the pro-Axis government of Argentina underwent a "death-bed conversion," declaring war on Germany barely in time to be admitted to the San Francisco conference at which the organization was founded). Today membership in the UN has become almost universal, with only a handful of exceptions: those states that, like Liechtenstein or San Marino, are too small to shoulder the burdens of membership; the states divided by Cold War frontiers—the two Germanys, the two Koreas, the two Vietnams; Switzerland; and Communist China.

VOTING BLOCS IN TODAY'S UN

The increase in the membership of the organization has affected every aspect of its functioning. The gentleman's agreement on bloc representation in the Security Council, which had never gone completely unchallenged, finally broke down with the increase in the number of members from Africa and Asia. These areas had not been represented by earmarked seats under the gentlemen's agreement, with the exception of the Middle Eastern seat and, on occasion, the Commonwealth seat. As a result the tendency developed for elections to nonpermanent Security Council seats to be contested. Since a two-thirds majority was necessary for election, a common outcome was that of stalemate—the situation strongly resembling that of Democratic presidential nominating conventions before 1936, which also operated under a two-thirds rule—the result normally being that the Solomonian decision was taken to split the two-year term in two, one candidate agreeing to resign after one year of office and make way for the election of the other.

Of course, the groups of states enjoying virtually guaranteed representation under the gentlemen's agreement were reluctant to see it changed to reflect the geographic shifts in the organization's membership. The solution adopted was to expand the Security Council to fifteen members to allow for the informal earmarking of further seats for the African and Asian states.

With the changes in membership since 1956, the orientation of the General Assembly majority has changed also. In the original UN, after the Cold War had gotten under way, is was common for the United States to take initiatives in the Security Council that would be defeated only by dint of the Soviet Union's veto, while American resolutions would be able to command a reliable two-thirds majority in the General Assembly. During these years the UN deliberative bodies served mainly to register American propaganda victories and to portray the Soviet Union as an unreasoning obstacle to the achievement of any common purposes. The American majority in the General Assembly was in fact so reliable that it used to be referred to as the "automatic" majority. Out of the fifty to sixty member states the United States could regularly count on the support of the twenty Latin American countries and about fifteen states of western Europe and the "white" Commonwealth. Many of the African or Asian states that were original members of the organization were traditionally pro-American, like Liberia or the Philippines, or were linked to Britain by Commonwealth ties. Since the remaining "neutrals" often voted for American resolutions on their merits, it was not uncommon to find the Soviet Union voting alone with its bloc of half a dozen Eastern European dependencies.

Although the initial "package deal," which opened the doors to new members, involved chiefly European states, the new states admitted over the last decade have been mostly African and Asian, and increasingly prone to hold aloof from Cold War issues.

At present over half of the membership consists of African and Asian states. On issues involving racial discrimination or economic development these states normally vote together; but there is only one reliably solid voting bloc on every issue in the UN and that is the bloc of the Soviet satellites, now numbering ten states. There has been some marginal fluctuation in the Soviet bloc other than that caused by the admission of new members that have Communist governments: Yugoslavia dropped out after 1948, although it continues to vote with the Soviet Union more often than not; and Cuba acceded to the bloc's voting strength in 1961. Within the Afro-Asian membership, five or six distinct orientations are visible on Cold War issues, which translate themselves into habitual voting partnerships. In addition the different regional groupings caucus on the question of nominees to fill the organization's elective offices, such as the nonpermanent Security Council seats or the vice presidencies of the General Assembly (the General Assembly presidency is rotated as a matter of custom among the different non-Communist regional groupings). It is usual for the Latin American states to agree beforehand on the Latin American candidate for a vacant Security Council seat informally earmarked for Latin America.

The only "automatic majority" that can be said to exist in the General Assembly as constituted at present is thus an anticolonial majority. On anticolonial issues the votes of the African and Asian states combine with those of the Soviet bloc and those of many Latin American and Western alliance states to form a two-thirds majority of the assembly. In fact a modest or generally phrased anticolonial resolution can be carried by a virtually unanimous assembly, with perhaps Portugal and South Africa the only hold-outs. As the number of African and Asian members of the organization continues to increase, however, a tendency seems to be emerging for a new majority to be formed on questions of economic development and even on less controversial Cold War issues such as those dealing with some phases of arms control and disarmament.

CHANGES IN FUNCTIONING

As the UN evolved, the principal locus of activity of the world body has shifted. In the organization's early days the principal forum was, as the charter intended, the Security Council, which has primary responsibility for matters affecting international peace and security. As it became clear that the veto power incapacitated the Security Council from taking action on most issues that came before it, however, the tendency grew to ignore the council and to raise issues instead before the General Assembly. This tendency was formalized in the so-called Uniting for Peace resolution introduced by Secretary of State Acheson and passed by the General Assembly in 1950. Despite the seemingly clear statement of the charter that the General Assembly could not act on a matter that was before the Security Council, the Uniting for Peace resolution stipulated that when the Security Council was prevented from taking action on a matter affecting international peace and security by the use of the veto power, then the General Assembly could be called into session and assume jurisdiction over the question. The intention was to make possible collective security action, like that taken in Korea, against the Soviet Union or a Soviet satellite. One might say that here the General Assembly, like the generals of the aphorism, was fighting the last war.

In the Korean case itself the UN undertook to defend South Korea against the attack that had come from Communist North Korea, or rather to support and internationalize the action the United States had already unilaterally taken in assuming the defense of South Korea. The UN action in the Korean case was taken not by the General Assembly but by the Security Council, in the absence of the Soviet delegate, who had walked out in protest over the continuing presence of a Chinese Nationalist representative in the Chinese Security Council seat. Some commentators have speculated that Soviet absence from the Security Council at the time of the invasion of South Korea indicates that the Soviet Union was not party to the invasion, or that perhaps the North Koreans had "jumped the gun" and begun the invasion before the time for which it had been scheduled—since otherwise the Soviet Union's representative would have been in his seat to veto any Security Council action. However, the Soviet Union may have assumed that in the absence of its delegate the council could take no action; but the council's presiding officer ruled that the absence of the Soviet delegate did not constitute an implicit veto—and of course no one was there to object—although the Soviet Union has maintained ever since that the vote taken then was illegal.

Since that time, and especially since the membership agreement of 1955, the tendency has been for more and more issues to be taken up in the General Assembly and fewer in the Security Council. In fact, so many issues are raised before the assembly that it has run into severe scheduling and limitation-of-debate problems. Many commentators have indeed criticized the lengthy and wordy debates and the proliferation of resolutions.

One limitation on the scope of UN activity, which has, on the face of things, been particularly violated by the wide-ranging debates and the strongly anticolonial resolutions introduced in today's General Assembly is the provision of paragraph 7 of Article 2 of the charter that "nothing contained in the present Charter shall authorize the United Nations to intervene in matters which are essentially within the domestic jurisdiction of any state." This rule was often ignored in the past by the United States–led majority in passing resolutions condemning the Soviet

Union—for example, for maintaining "slave labor" camps. Now it is regularly violated, for example, on questions touching on racial inequality in the Republic of South Africa.

The loss of the pro-United States automatic majority was for some time not compensated for by the formation of another majority grouping on issues outside the framework of anticolonialism or racial equality, however, and thus on many issues no resolution at all could be passed, or at most one so watered down that it contained nothing but platitudinous righteousness.

Interestingly, a result of this vagueness and generality in General Assembly resolutions was to allow a new freedom of scope to the Secretary General. That is, the terms of a mandate given the Secretary General by the assembly were so vague as to be consistent with any line of policy he chose to pursue. This was clearly the case with regard to UN policy during the crises in the Congo during 1960–1963. As the UN assumed new responsibilities, which led it to take an active operating role, a great deal of discretion was necessarily entrusted to the administrative chief of operations. It was because of this expansion in the role of the Secretary General, of course, that Khrushchev broached his plan for a tripartite or "troika" Secretariat General with decisions to be taken jointly by representatives of the Western alliance, the Soviet bloc, and the uncommitted states. In the event that this proposal had been accepted the result would have been to create a veto power not only in the Security Council but in the administration of the organization as well.

As the General Assembly has come increasingly to be dominated by a small-power African and Asian majority that votes disarmament and economic development resolutions favored by neither the United States nor the Soviet Union, a "North-South" split has emerged comparable to that between East and West. If this trend should continue, the Security Council might reassume the prominence it has lost to the General Assembly.

During his second term of office, which was brought to an untimely end by his death in an airplane crash, Secretary General Hammarskjöld received considerable criticism, not only from Soviet bloc representatives, but from disinterested observers as well, for acting more and more in conjunction with the United States and its allies and playing less and less an impartial role. There is certainly some truth to this comment. The present writer is inclined to suggest, however, that evolution in this direction is only to be expected of any Secretary General. A similar comment might have been made about the first holder of the office, Trygve Lie, and it may yet come to be made of U Thant. That is, any Secretary General is likely to discover as time goes on that the United States and Britain alone of the great powers seem to have been interested in the fate of the organization for its own sake. All members continue to pursue their national interests, of course, but Britain and the United States have normally conceived of the preservation and promotion of the interests of the organization itself as necessarily in their own interest.

This has been demonstrated in several ways, one of which is the financing of the organization's activities. Some of the smaller states have been remiss in meeting their commitments to the organization's budget, while both the Soviet Union and France have refused to pay their assessments for the special expenditures made necessary by emergency operations outside the regular budget. Several states have systematically kept their payments into the organization's coffers only slightly less than two years in arrears to avoid falling afoul of Article 19 of the charter, which stipulates that a member-state shall lose its General Assembly vote if it becomes more than two years behind in its dues payments.[3] The United States has, of course, met its normal budgetary obligations and has in addition paid special assessments and bought bonds that the organization floated in order to meet the unscheduled expenses of its Congo operation. Congress has provided, however, that the United States will pay no more than one third of the UN's regular budget, which happens to represent roughly the United States' share of the world's total income. The American share of emergency operations budgets has gone slightly over this proportion.

Political opposition to the UN within the United States has in part centered on the magnitude of American financial contributions to the organization. It seems unquestionable, however, that those who object to United States membership in the UN on this score dislike the organization in principle. Some tendencies in domestic political opinion doubtless take an antagonistic attitude to the UN out of opposition to government in general, or perhaps to any American participation in international relations. But a host of other anxieties, mostly neurotic, cluster around American participation in the world organization, ranging from fear that the UN will intervene in domestic civil rights problems in order to give effect to UN principles of racial equality, to concern that staff members of the UN delegations of the Communist bloc nations engage in espionage activities. There is evidence for the latter suspicion, needless to say; but it seems unrealistic to assume that Soviet espionage activities in the United States would cease if the UN did not exist.

It is paradoxical that some American opposition to the UN organization has focused on the theme that the organization should be expelled

---

[3] The failure of the General Assembly to enforce the provisions of Article 19 during its 1964–1965 session has left the validity of the article in question, as well as perpetuating a chaotic situation in the organization's finances.

from United States territory, its headquarters now being in Manhattan. Ironically, it is also the Soviet wish, often expressed, that UN headquarters should be moved elsewhere, for the very good reason that the present situation creates a network of American influences on organization personnel who live in the area, send their children to American schools, and so on. Any American of intelligence can see that this is an arrangement of benefit to the United States, and not the converse.

SUGGESTED READINGS

Aspaturian, Vernon V., "The Metamorphosis of the United Nations," *Yale Rev.,* Summer 1957.

Bailey, Sydney D., *The General Assembly of the United Nations.* New York: Praeger, 1961.

Bloomfield, Lincoln P., *The United Nations and U.S. Foreign Policy.* Boston: Little, Brown, 1960.

Claude, Inis L., Jr. *Swords Into Plowshares,* 3d ed. New York: Random House, Inc., 1964.

Gardner, Richard N., *In Pursuit of World Order.* New York: Praeger, 1964.

Jackson, Elmore, "The Developing Role of The Secretary-General," *Intern. Org.,* Summer 1957.

Nicholas, H. G., *The United Nations as a Political Institution.* New York: Oxford University Press, 1959.

Singer, J. David, *Financing International Organization.* The Hague: M. Nijhoff, 1961.

6

Regional and Functional International Organizations

The political organs of the UN form only part of the total picture of international organization. A range of other agencies exists within the UN structure charged with the performance of economic, social, cultural, and technical tasks of various kinds; and in addition, international organizations exist outside the UN framework, many of them on a regional basis, to serve common purposes shared by a number of states.

The specialized agencies and "nonpolitical" organs of the UN act in a variety of capacities, on relatively small budgets, performing tasks that are in themselves clearly worthwhile. The Food and Agriculture Organization attempts to promote higher living standards through improved food production; the World Health Organization tries to raise levels of health and sanitation; UNICEF, the United Nations children's fund, seeks to foster the welfare of children not adequately nourished or protected.

While these tasks are valuable in themselves, it is often argued that the work of the specialized agencies can itself have a political "payoff" by helping to promote world peace. This argument takes several forms. One is that as these organizations continue to perform needed tasks, loyalties to them will form and a sense of world community will emerge that can serve as a basis for political unity. This is a sophisticated argument, and there may be truth to it; it offers a solution to the problem of war only in the very long run, however, and it is liable to the criticism that for this gradual process of accretion of loyalties to proceed uninterrupted and unimpaired, a short-run solution to the problem of avoiding war must first be devised and successfully applied: There will be no "long run" unless we successfully traverse the "short run."

Another school of thought holds that the improvement of standards of living helps to prevent war by removing what are thought to be its causes: hunger, ignorance, and disease. This thesis is not sustained by deeper examination, however. It is true that the hungry may begin riots, and that the miserable may follow demagogues who promise them a better life at the expense of other groups or peoples. Wars have typically been begun, however, not by countries that, being poor and miserable, covet their neighbors' possessions, but by states that are affluent and powerful enough to believe that their aggressions will be successful against weaker neighbors.[1] Some misapprehensions on this score have arisen because the UN was formed originally by states that fought against dictators who claimed that their wars were fought in order to meet the economic needs of their peoples. One of Hitler's themes was the need of the German people for *Lebensraum* or "living space" to be gained by the conquest of the under-populated territories to Germany's east. In reality, however, it is difficult to avoid the conclusion that the demand for *Lebensraum* was simply another excuse with which Hitler tried to legitimize his drive for power for power's sake. Similarly, Mussolini pleaded Italy's high rate of population increase as his justification for the invasion and conquest of Ethiopia. Needless to say, few Italians settled in Ethiopia after it had been conquered, for this claim, too, served only as a cloak for simple ambition.

It is true, moreover, that rather than the resolution of social and economic problems' making the resolution of political problems possible, very often solution of the political problems is a prerequisite to the successful tackling of an economic or social problem. One of the leading problems that the UN has faced, for example, has been the care of the Arab refugees from Palestine who left their homes during the Arab-Israeli war of 1948–1949 and who are living today in displaced persons' camps in the Gaza Strip. Here the world community is confronted with the social and economic needs of people living in the camps, which are in

---

[1] It remains possible that improvement in living standards may strengthen a nation so that it is more able to resist aggression; by the same token, however, it may be strengthened to the point where it is more able to divert resources to prepare for aggression. Some chauvinistic groups in the United States have even opposed the activities of the UN children's fund for this reason.

themselves severe, because the refugees are not self-supporting and must be taken care of through UN charity. Yet at the same time they constitute a political problem because their fate is an issue in dispute between the Arab states and Israel. The severity of the human problem involved in the refugee question should not be minimized. The refugees have lived in camps for fifteen years, and indeed a generation has been born and raised in the camps. Nevertheless this problem cannot be resolved by social and economic means; it is first and foremost a political question. The Arab states maintain that the only just solution to the problem is for the refugees to be restored to their erstwhile homes in Palestine. The Israelis are unwilling to receive more than a token number of the refugees back, and argue that they have become embittered and indoctrinated by Egyptian propaganda and would create an insurmountable security problem if they were to return to present-day Israel. A more reasonable solution, the Israelis argue, is to resettle the Arab refugees in the Arab countries of the Middle East where they would be among people who were similar in language, religion, and way of life. The United States has suggested that it would be willing to assume the major part of the cost of such a resettlement. The Arab states are, however, unwilling to accept resettlement, and argue that this solution begs the basic question of justice; it is also true that some of the Arab countries find themselves with a labor surplus in relation to their economic structures and present resources.

It is unhappily the case that this problem, like many others, is subject only to a political solution, not to social and economic amelioration.

One should add here that the world's economic and social problems are of such a magnitude that the resources available to agencies of the UN are quite inadequate for the tasks involved. The world organization has had great difficulty in meeting its own operating expenses, without adding to its expenses by supplying capital to develop the economies of the poorer nations. In actuality, UN economic operations are confined almost exclusively to technical assistance, whereas the underdeveloped countries need development capital in amounts that can only come from the developed states. The latter, however, wish any aid that they give to be used in ways over which they can exercise a measure of control, and which will conduce to their own economic or political advantage, if possible.

REGIONAL ORGANIZATION
IN THE WESTERN HEMISPHERE

International organization on a continuing basis is a distinctively

American idea—"American" in both the national and the hemispheric senses. The American states have long maintained permanent regional organizational ties, which date from 1826 when Simón Bolívar himself summoned the first inter-American conference to meet at Panama; but this and other early attempts at the formulation of a hemispheric organization proved abortive because of the isolationism of some of the American states and the disorder and civil and international wars of others.

After the American Civil War, regular congresses of the states of the hemisphere were held, but they were limited to the discussion of technical and juridical matters of little political significance. Following the so-called first Pan-American Conference in Washington in 1889, a continuing organizational nucleus was maintained in the United States capital.

In 1948 the inter-American system was given its current form, that of the Organization of American States, with the twenty Latin American states and the United States as members, Canada preferring to remain aloof from the organization.[2] OAS practices and bylaws have been taken since as the model for another regional organization that has been established, the Organization of African Unity. Although these two organizations define their membership ostensibly in geographic terms, a political criterion is also apparent: Cuba, after declaring herself a Communist state, was suspended from OAS membership; states on the continent of Africa but ruled by groups of white-settler origin, such as the Republic of South Africa, are not members of the African organization. Another quasi-regional organization, the Arab League, is openly an organization of states of common ethnic background rather than a strictly regional grouping.

The OAS is a multifunctional organization, whose purposes extend to the settlement of disputes among the membership, mutual defense against threats originating from outside the hemisphere, and any other matters of common interest. The mutual defense commitment of the members is embodied in the Rio Treaty of 1947, under which the member states agree to regard an attack on any one of them as an attack on all. This treaty served in some respects as a model for the NATO treaty of 1949.

Although the OAS has been moderately active in attempting to dampen down conflicts among the member states, particularly in the Central American and Caribbean area, it has been used chiefly as a vehicle for the United States to rally support from the other American states for United States policies. One might say with justice that the OAS serves

---

2 The former British West Indian dependencies of Jamaica and Trinidad and Tobago have also applied for membership.

primarily to legitimize and constitutionalize the authority that the United States necessarily wields in the hemisphere by virtue of its overwhelming military and economic power. Nevertheless, in attempting to secure support for its policies, the United States is necessarily obliged to make concessions to Latin American viewpoints.

The United States has not always made the best use of the OAS, however; it has sometimes forced through resolutions with the aid of the smaller states over opposition from the major Latin American powers, reaping only a harvest of bad will—as in the 1954 anti-Communist Declaration of Caracas. At other times it has acted without consulting the OAS allies when their support easily might have been secured. United States relations with the Latin American states are bound to be delicate, as the latter are only too conscious of their difficult position relative to the overwhelming preponderance of North American power in the hemisphere.

An interesting and incipiently supranational feature of the OAS structure is that the organization can take decisions by a two-thirds vote of the membership, rather than needing unanimity, although no member is obliged to lend its military forces to joint undertakings of which it does not approve.

Within the group of nations that comprises the Organization of American States, other forms of international organization are developing also. The Latin American Free Trade Association, for example, comprises most of the states of South America,[3] together with Mexico, in a grouping designed to increase trade by reducing tariffs among the members.

Among the five Central American states and Panama, similiarly, a common market is in process of creation. In addition, the Central American states have their own regional organization, known by its Spanish initials as ODECA. Many Central Americans hope to make ODECA the nucleus of a federal government for the whole Central American isthmus.

FEDERATION AND AUTONOMY

The Central American situation points up one of the leading tendencies of today's world. Although the movement towards national independence and sovereignty for non–self-governing states seems irresistible and the roster of the sovereign states of the world expands each

---

[3] The terms "South America" and "Latin America" are not interchangeable, although they are often used as though they were. "Latin America" comprises the countries of Latin culture in South America, together with those in Central America and the Caribbean, and Mexico.

year, superimposed on this movement is a tendency for states to join together in larger groupings that entail the surrender of at least a modicum of sovereignty. These two tendencies often complement each other: A colonial territory seems too small to make its own way in the world as an independent state and the colonial power attempts to federate a number of colonies within the region into a nation better able to face the burdens of sovereignty as a unit. At the same time racial and religious antagonisms and considerations of economic advantage often make it impossible to keep such federations together. Thus the federation that the British promoted in their West Indian territories broke up as the dominant groups in the mainland territories, British Honduras and British Guiana, and subsequently those in the largest island territory, Jamaica, reckoned the political and economic disadvantages of federation to outweigh its advantages. Similarly an African federation that the British promoted, the federation of Southern Rhodesia, Northern Rhodesia, and Nyasaland, broke up because of the white-supremacy policy followed by European-settler government of Southern Rhodesia. President Nasser's attempt to federate Egypt and Syria into the United Arab Republic likewise collapsed because of Syrian opposition to domination by the Egyptians and to President Nasser's economic policies.

Similarly, the Malaysian federation experienced difficulties that led in 1965 to the withdrawal from it of Singapore. These difficulties derived ultimately from fear on the part of the Malays that the ethnic Chinese, especially numerous in Singapore, would come to dominate the federation. Accordingly, it appears that attempts at federation are operations of great fragility and the outlook for new attempts of this type does not seem encouraging.

THE EUROPEAN INTEGRATION MOVEMENT

The most important attempt at regional integration is the European unification movement, which has developed in the years since World War II. The states involved are West Germany, France, Italy, and the Benelux countries: Belgium, the Netherlands, and Luxembourg. The European integration movement is especially interesting because it approaches regional federation in the manner prescribed by the functionalists, that is, instead of tackling the problem of sovereignty head-on, it has tried to sneak up on it from the rear, as it were, by creating common economic institutions among the participating states. These institutions will, it is hoped, serve as the basis for a community of interest, for the sake of whose preservation particles of sovereignty may progressively be sacrificed. Thus the common European institutions are, in the first instance, economic—the European Coal and Steel Community (ECSC or the Schuman Plan), the European Economic Community (EEC or the Common Market), and the European atomic energy authority (Euratom). Although there are economic advantages in each of these arrangements, the purposes they are designed to serve are primarily political.

The political goals that were to be achieved by European integration were principally two: First, the consolidation of a Europe that could maintain its independence from either the United States or the Soviet Union; and second, the avoidance of future conflicts among members of the European community, especially between France and Germany. The latter aim seems to have been the principal goal of the statesmen who were especially responsible for the initiation of the European movement. The names of four major political leaders should be enumerated: Winston Churchill, who urged Franco-German reconciliation and cooperation in the building of a United States of Europe at a speech at Zürich in September of 1946; Robert Schuman, the Alsatian who had been both a soldier in the German army during World War I and a Prime Minister of France after World War II, and who appropriately became the first president of the advisory European parliament in 1958; Jean Monnet, the distinguished French civil servant who was the principal practical worker in the cause of European integration and who became first president of the High Authority of the Coal and Steel Community; and Konrad Adenauer, the German Chancellor born in the Catholic Rhineland, near the French border, who has been a Francophile all his life, and who, in an unguarded moment, is reported to have said that he preferred a united Europe to a united Germany.

The leading aim of Europeans belonging to this school of thought was to tie Germany so close to France that it would not again be possible for the two states to go to war, as they have done three times in the last 100 years. Germany would be prevented not only from making war on France herself, but also from undertaking other possible military adventures in central and eastern Europe.

A straightforward mode of foreclosing the possibility of independent German military initiatives was contained in the project for a European community that never materialized—the European Defense Community (EDC), the treaty for which was ratified by the other European states, but defeated by the French National Assembly in 1955. EDC was a far-reaching project that would have created a common European army, with a single uniform and a single chain of command in which the national contingents from the different European states would be so intermingled that it would be impossible to unscramble a purely national army that might be used for aggressive purposes. The project foundered on French reluctance to see Germans rearmed on any terms and to see French soldiers commanded by German officers, and especially over unwillingness that France should lose the capacity to undertake independent military initiatives; in view of French military commitments, for example in the Algerian war that was going on at the time, this was not an unreasonable position. The basic purpose of EDC, to allow a rearmament of Germany under which German forces would be used only for the general European purpose of deterring Soviet attack, was partially achieved by the admission of West Germany to the NATO alliance. The West German forces that have since been raised have either been placed under integrated NATO command or have been devoted to border-patrol purposes compatible with NATO objectives.

It should be noted that the two more important European communities, the Coal and Steel Community and the Common Market, do serve important economic ends, as well as providing the basis for future political integration. The Common Market, in eliminating tariffs among "the Six" by a schedule of stages spread over several years, creates wide markets that provide incentives for greater production and make possible the more rational allocation of materials and labor.[4] At the same time, by opening the more backward industrial firms, especially in France, to the competition of the more modern, more efficient enterprises, especially in West Germany, it was hoped that economic stagnation would be averted—although French industry had actually begun to modernize before the Common Market went into effect, and something of a French "economic miracle" had begun, which was, in its way, perhaps as impressive as the better-known German "economic miracle."

Another goal, which was also of importance, especially to the Coal and Steel Community, was to avoid the heavy concentrations of political power that, it was believed, had previously followed concentrations of economic power—for example, in the great German firms or combinations such as the Krupp iron and steel interests, I. G. Farben, the chemical trust, and so on. In line with this intention, as well as with the economic goals of fostering heightened competition in the Common Market area, regulations, which were in some respects similar to the American antitrust laws, were adopted to prevent the formation of cartels, restrictive trade agreements, discriminatory pricing policies, and the like.

It has become clear, as the promoters of the European integration movement intended, that a high degree of economic integration necessarily implies a degree of political integration as well. Thus, for example, a coordination of social welfare policies has developed among the states of

---

[4] The Common Market was preceded by a customs union among Belgium, the Netherlands, and Luxembourg, which showed the advantages that such an arrangement could have.

the European communities, since French businesses could legitimately complain that they were not competing on an equal basis with German firms so long as they had to pay higher wages and fringe benefits and make heavier contributions to social insurance funds. If the Common Market continues to develop, similar coordination or equalization of national policies will have to take place in other fields, for example, in monetary policy. A high degree of mobility of labor from areas of labor surplus to those of labor shortage within the Common Market has already developed.

In these European communities, the framework exists for the evolution of a future political federation of the six member-states, should each of them be willing to accept evolution in that direction. For a time it seemed as though the dominant political forces in each of the six were content that this should be so, with the Christian Democratic parties especially taking a strong pro-integration position. However, the coming to power of General de Gaulle, who is determined to establish a powerful and autonomous French state, has made it seem likely that the movement towards political integration will sooner or later be arrested and perhaps even reversed. At least de Gaulle's attitude towards the European unification movement so far seems to be that he can live with European unification only so long as it means that the other states of the community are willing to follow the French lead, making the community simply a louder voice with which French policy can speak.

RELATIONS OF OTHER STATES
TO THE EUROPEAN INTEGRATION MOVEMENT

The attitude of states outside "the Six" to the movement for integration has been varied. The United States has long supported European integration on principle, believing that a stronger Europe means a strengthened free world. In fact part of the impulse toward European unification was given by American insistence after World War II that the European states cooperate in drawing up their plans for the utilization of Marshall Plan assistance. With respect to the economic effects of the Common Market arrangements, the United States has taken a similarly optimistic approach, espousing the view that a more prosperous Western Europe means a larger market for American goods.

Whether this is in fact the case or whether the Common Market instead imposes high tariffs on American goods and discourages their entry into the Common Market area is a matter for concern and for hard bargaining between the community and the United States. The 1957 Treaty of Rome that established the Common Market stipulated that the external tariff that would be common to the six member states as the final stage of economic integration was reached would be no higher than an average of the tariffs that the six states had maintained independently. It might still be the case, nevertheless, that it would do little good to the United States or to the trading partners of the community if, say, a low German tariff on an imported item were raised to the point at which that item could no longer be sold profitably in Germany, and this were compensated for by lowering a high French tariff, if a traditional market for the item in question had existed in Germany but had never existed in France.

Clearly, it is possible for the Common Market system to be compatible with two quite opposed attitudes towards trade with the states outside the Common Market. One is the attitude ascribed to Ludwig Erhard, long the West German Economics Minister, and subsequently Adenauer's replacement as Chancellor. Erhard took the view that the outside tariff wall of the EEC should be as low as possible in order that both members of the community and states outside it could benefit from the advantages of as wide a free trade as was economically logical. There were, on the other hand, economic interests within the community, especially in agriculture, that had only with great difficulty been persuaded to face the heightened competition that came from the reduction of tariff barriers with other Common Market states, and which were not prepared to deal with competition from agricultural producers outside the community, especially with the highly efficient agriculture of the United States. This "closed" attitude toward Common Market trading patterns fits in well with the politically restrictive concepts of General de Gaulle and also, to some extent, of the leaders of the political integration movement, who take the view that openness to the outside world dilutes the forces binding the European states together.

These issues came to a head when the question of the admission of Great Britain to the Common Market arose. After much agonized self-examination, the Conservative government of Britain decided in 1962 that the economic advantages of admission to the Common Market outweighed opposing considerations and undertook negotiations for British entry. Although willing to share in the economic arrangements of the European community, however, the British were considerably less than enthusiastic over the prospect of eventual submission to common political institutions. Accordingly, British entry into the community was regarded askance by Europeans who looked on the Common Market as simply the foundation of a subsequent political unity that Britain, with its outside commitments to members of the Commonwealth, and its close relations with the United States, could hardly be expected to enter; and also by the Gaullists, who were well aware that even though France might manage to dominate a Europe of "the Six," it could hardly hope to dominate an association in which Britain was also a member. Not wishing to reveal the pure nationalism with which he regarded the future of the European community, President de Gaulle at first tried to keep Britain out of the Common Market by setting extremely hard conditions for British entry. When it became apparent that the British were so eager to enter the community that they were making a sincere attempt to meet these conditions, de Gaulle finally "tipped his hand" and vetoed British entry outright. Despite subsequent attempts to soften the blow by holding out the possibility that Britain might be admitted at some future date, it seemed clear that so long as the Gaullist orientation dominated in France, Britain would have to create her own future independent of the European community.

Several other European states were in a similar position to Britain with relation to the Common Market—that is, they wished to share in the low-tariff economic arrangements, but for one reason or another could not become full members of the community and participate in the common political institutions that were envisaged. Together with six of these states, Britain organized the European Free Trade Association (EFTA, or the "Outer Seven"), a trading area of states having about half the population of the Common Market region, which agreed to lower their tariffs with respect to each other on a comparable schedule to the one the Common Market countries were following without, however, concerting on a common external tariff. This association was conceived before Britain contemplated applying for Common Market membership, and was designed to place its members in a strong position so that they could negotiate with the Common Market for concessions that would avoid their being placed outside the EEC's high-external-tariff wall. President Kennedy had similar goals in mind when he requested and secured from the Congress in 1963 extensive powers to engage in mutual tariff-cutting negotiations with the EEC.

Some of the members of the "Outer Seven" organization, such as Norway, Denmark, and Portugal, traded heavily with the British and could not afford to enter the Common Market if this meant a tariff wall would be interposed between them and Britain. If Britain were to be admitted to the Common Market, on the other hand, they might well follow. The other members of the EFTA—Sweden, Switzerland, and Austria—found themselves unable to join in the European communities since they maintained neutral foreign policies that would be compromised by participation in the common political institutions of the communities, all of whose member states were allied with the United States in NATO.

One of the objections raised by the French negotiators to British entry into the Common Market concerned Britain's special economic relations with members of the British Commonwealth,[5] who are given special advantages in British markets. The Commonwealth countries, for their part, objected strenuously to Britain's apparent willingness to discontinue these special arrangements as a condition of its entry into the Common Market. The high-cost butter and mutton exports of New Zealand were especially vulnerable. It is also true, however, that France had secured duty-free admission to the Common Market countries for products from the former French colonies—a concession that the French were unwilling to extend to former British colonies—and that these countries, most of them in Africa, produced tropical products that competed directly with those originating in former British Africa, and also in many of the Latin American states.[6] Needless to say, these latter two groups of countries were extremely unhappy about this set of arrangements, which put them at a competitive disadvantage in selling their products in Europe, and Kwame Nkrumah of Ghana, especially, was bitter in his denunciation of the Common Market scheme.

SUGGESTED READINGS

Beloff, Nora, *The General Says No*. Baltimore: Penguin, 1963.

Benoit, Emile, *Europe at Sixes and Sevens*. New York: Columbia University Press, 1962.

Berger, Morroe, *The Arab World Today*. New York: Doubleday, 1962.

Burke, Fred G., *Africa's Quest for Order*. Englewood Cliffs, N.J.: Prentice-Hall, 1964.

Claude, Inis L., Jr., "The OAS, The UN, and the United States," *Intern. Conciliation,* March 1964.

Deutsch, Karl, *et al., Political Community and the North Atlantic Area*. Princeton, N.J.: Princeton University Press, 1957.

Dreier, John C., *The OAS and the Hemisphere Crisis*. New York: Harper & Row, 1962.

Haines, Charles Grove (ed.), *European Integration*. Baltimore: Johns Hopkins Press, 1957.

Kitzinger, Uwe, *The Politics and Economics of European Integration: Britain, Europe, and the U.S.*, rev. ed. New York: Praeger, 1963.

Manger, William, *Pan America in Crisis*. Washington, D.C.: Public Affairs Press, 1961.

---

[5] The Commonwealth is a sort of alumni association of former British colonies tied together somewhat by sentimental and cultural links, but especially by the system of tariff preference referred to above.

[6] The United States has undertaken to defend the interests of Latin American exporters in its tariff negotiations with the Common Market authorities.

III

The Politics of Antagonism

7

Soviet Policy and the Origins of the Cold War

THE ORIGINS OF THE COLD WAR

The central fact about United States foreign policy at the present time is, of course, the existence of the Cold War with the Soviet Union. Despite the widespread tendency among third states to hold both of the super-powers responsible for the initiation of the Cold War, the record strongly suggests that its origin lies in the policy of self-aggrandizement and refusal to cooperate with the West assumed by the Soviet Union at the end of World War II.

One of the first clear indications of what was in store was that the Soviet Union maintained her armed forces at the levels they had reached during the war, despite the coming of peace; the armies of the Western countries were demobilized as quickly as possible. At the same time by "reinterpreting" or openly violating agreements made with the United States, Britain, and France towards the end of the war, the Soviet Union extended her control over the neighboring states of eastern Europe.

Adjustment to the realities of Cold War was at first difficult for the United States. Most American thinking about the postwar world assumed that the cooperation among the major powers forged during the war would continue, and it was hoped that the world could be policed by a United Nations Security Council in which the major powers each had a veto, that is, which assumed that the major powers would often be able to act unanimously. The last serious attempt by the United States to secure Soviet cooperation was made in the unprecedented gesture of statesmanship by which the United States in 1946 offered to strengthen the UN and avoid the development of an arms race by placing control of atomic energy, for the uses of war and peace alike, under UN control—the so-called Baruch or Acheson-Lilienthal plan. It should be recalled that at the time the United States was the only atomic power and was thus making clear that she had no intentions of attempting to dominate the world by force, nor any objectives that could not be secured by peaceful means.

Unhappily for the future course of international relations, the Soviet Union rejected the Baruch plan. One can perceive several possible motives for what appears at first glance an illogical Soviet act in view of the fact that the plan represented the relinquishment on the part of the United States of a decisive military advantage. The Soviet Union, it may be, did not trust the United States to comply with the terms of its own plan, but suspected that the UN supervisory agency set up by the plan would be used to see that the Soviet Union did not develop its own atomic weapons while overlooking weapons that the United States had illegally concealed. Some plausibility is lent to this suspicion, over and above its consonance with what is known of Stalin's behavior during that period, by the fact that at the time countries friendly to the United States were in an overwhelming majority in the UN General Assembly; of the fifty-one original members, twenty were in Latin America, another dozen were in western Europe, and several of the remainder were members of the British Commonwealth. It may have been true at the same time that Stalin assumed that while the United States was ahead in atomic energy development for the moment, a concentrated Russian effort would lead to Soviet superiority at some future date.

The evidences that the Soviet Union was adopting a posture of Cold War were slow in penetrating the consciousness of western populations; when in June of 1946 Winston Churchill made his famous speech at Fulton, Missouri, in which he said "an iron curtain has fallen over central Europe," reactions of surprise and indignation were common. The series of Russian actions by which the dominance of eastern Europe was achieved soon made the situation clear, however.

It was during this period also that the Soviet Union attempted to accomplish in the Middle Eastern countries bordering it what it had already accomplished in eastern Europe. Soviet troops remained in Iran after the date on which Stalin had pledged they would be withdrawn; at the same time, the Soviet Union demanded that the Turks give up territory on the Soviet-Turkish border and conclude agreements that would have made Turkey a military satellite of the Soviet Union. A puppet government was formed in the north of Iran, while guerrilla warfare was begun by Greek Communists in the north of Greece. The United States and Great Britain took a firm diplomatic stand on the Turkish and Iranian questions, backed by the implication that force would be used unless the Soviet Union ceased its provocative actions. Under this pressure the Russians did in fact withdraw troops from Iran, and desisted from making demands on the Turks. Moreover, with American aid the Greek government was eventually able to put down the Communist-sponsored uprising.

Communist efforts met with greater success elsewhere, however. In February of 1948 a successful *coup d'état* was engineered that brought a Communist government to power in Czechoslovakia. In retrospect, one can clearly see that it was the Czech *coup* that aroused the West into making strenuous and sustained efforts to combat Soviet expansionism. The *coup* itself was carried out in such a manner as to remove any lingering beliefs democrats may have had that it was possible to co-operate with Communists, the Czech Communists having used their strategic positions in a coalition cabinet to prepare the *coup* secretly. Moreover, the democratic parties were deterred from mounting armed resistance to the takeover by the threat that Soviet troops, who were stationed on the borders of the country, would then intervene, touching off bloodshed and civil war. The events in Czechoslovakia struck a particularly sensitive nerve in the Western countries, since it had been Hitler's actions in occupying parts of Czechoslovakia not inhabited by ethnic Germans, in violation of the Munich agreement of 1938, which had first made it plain without question that his expansionist intentions extended potentially to all of Europe and, indeed, the world; and by refusing to stand fast in defense of Czechoslovakia's national integrity at Munich, the French and British practitioners of the diplomacy of appeasement had merely whetted Hitler's appetite for aggression the more. But the same mistake was not to be made again. A month after the Czech *coup* Britain, France, Belgium, the Netherlands, and Luxembourg signed the Brussels Pact, pledging each country to the defense of the others, which became the forerunner of the North Atlantic Treaty Organization.

Capping off the series of events that inaugurated the Cold War, the Berlin blockade was launched by the Russians in June of 1948. West Berlin is an enclave in Communist-held territory, occupied by the Western powers but lying about a hundred miles behind the Iron Curtain. Land access to West Berlin from West Germany can thus be cut off by the Communist East German government and its Russian sponsors. In 1948 the Russians did cut off land traffic into Berlin from the west in the hope of inducing the Allies to give up their foothold in the divided city. In an imaginative and resourceful action President Truman inaugurated an airlift of supplies to West Berlin, which reached massive proportions as the city became completely supplied from the air. Confronted with American determination to stay in Berlin, the Soviet Union refrained from expanding the scope of the conflict, by not interfering with the radar guidance systems of the planes flying the airlift, for example, and eventually agreed to call off the blockade.

THE WESTERN REACTION

These evidences of hostile Soviet intentions led, of course, to a series of Western responses that culminated in April 1949 with the signing of the North Atlantic treaty. Under the NATO treaty the signatory states agree that an armed attack against any of them in Europe or North America will be considered an attack against all of them; the states who were party to the original agreement were the United States, Great Britain, France, Canada, Denmark, Italy, Iceland, Belgium, the Netherlands, Luxembourg, Norway, and Portugal, with Greece, Turkey, and West Germany joining in the agreement subsequently.

Signature of the North Atlantic Treaty had been preceded by other actions of the United States and her allies designed to insure the safety and well-being of the non-Communist world in the face of the menacing attitude assumed by the Soviet Union. One of the first steps on this path was the Marshall Plan. This statesman-like initiative, undertaken when George Marshall was Secretary of State and Dean Acheson Under-Secretary, represents in many ways a landmark in the history of international relations. The plan itself was a program of economic aid designed to make possible the economic reconstruction of war-devastated Europe. The initial offer, made by Marshall in a Harvard commencement address, was couched in terms that would make possible the participation of the Soviet Union and her eastern European satellites, and for a time it appeared that the Communist states would actually become partners to the plan; if this had happened, with the integration of the Soviet economy into that of the United States and its allies that this surely implied, future world developments might well have taken a very different path from the one actually followed. Of course, this raised prospects that the Soviet Union was not willing to contemplate, and the Communist line became one of bitter attack on the plan.

From the point of view of United States policy, the Marshall Plan was a master stroke. It represented that rare type of occasion in which the imperatives of national security, economic interest, and altruism converge. From a purely altruistic point of view the plan could, of course, be defended in that it alleviated the very real hardship that the states of western Europe were undergoing in the wake of the destruction and dislocation of World War II—and there is no doubt that many Americans supported it on this basis. From the point of view of United States economic interests, the Marshall Plan presented the opportunity of rebuilding the economies of our major trading partners so that they could again become large-scale customers for our goods, thus enabling the American economy to forge ahead and reach new heights. Looked at in terms of national security criteria, the return of the European states to economic well-being would make it possible for their economies to assume the burdens required by their sharing in the joint defense effort; at the same time the end of the unemployment and misery then so widespread would undercut the very substantial appeal that the national Communist parties then had. (In France and Italy the local Communist parties were able to capture about a third of the vote and might have been in a position to come to power by peaceful means if the economic distress had continued.)

The plan, institutionalized in the Organization for European Economic Cooperation, proved a striking success. The western European economies were rebuilt; the depression that many economists had predicted would engulf the United States after the end of the war was avoided;[1] it was possible to diminish American aid as our allies became self-supporting and became able to assume their responsibilities in the common defense; and the rise in the strength of the Communist parties was arrested, and a downturn in their popular support began.

It soon became apparent, of course, that economic reconstruction by itself was not enough. Early in 1947 the government of Great Britain made it clear that it would not be able financially to carry the burden of supporting the Greeks and Turks in their confrontation with Soviet strength, and the United States acted to move American power into the developing vacuum. In a speech to a joint session of Congress, President Truman urged the approach that came to be known as the Truman Doctrine; Congress responded affirmatively to his request for money for economic and military aid to the two threatened countries, and the United States thus embarked on the line of policy that has continued to the present day.

George F. Kennan, then chairman of the State Department's policy planning staff, wrote a famous article that appeared anonymously in the influential monthly journal, *Foreign Affairs,* in which he developed a rationale for the new policy, to which he gave the name of "containment." The containment doctrine was based on the premise that the Soviet Union would seek to expand the sphere of her influence wherever

---

[1] Other factors were also of significance here.

probing around her borders disclosed a weak spot to exist. It was to be the task of the United States, by creating "positions of strength" all along the periphery of the Communist bloc, to see that such weak spots did not in fact exist. If this steady frustration of Soviet expansionist tendencies were maintained, one might have grounds to hope that Soviet expansionism would eventually atrophy; but, in any case, the way to prevent Soviet expansion was to make it militarily infeasible.

Thus the basic guidelines of American foreign policy for the Cold War period were laid down. They entailed, and have continued to entail since that time, four principal elements. First, the United States has attempted, by the steady improvement of its forces and weapons, to maintain a military superiority that would deter the Soviet Union from armed adventures. Second, by concluding alliances with threatened states or by making unilateral declarations, the United States has sought to show the Soviet Union that expansion in specific directions would not be tolerated. Third, the United States, by giving economic aid to her allies and indeed to all states determined to defend their independence against Soviet threats, has attempted to contribute to their economic and military strength against both internal and external dangers. Finally, the United States has embarked on what might be called "political warfare" with the Soviet Union designed to make clear to individuals and national populations who are inclined to be wooed by Soviet claims of a superior social system and a Soviet dedication to peace the relative advantages of non-Communist forms of political and economic organization. Subsequent chapters will take up in turn the problems involved in the clash of ideologies, in the giving of military and economic aid, and in the arms race and other forms of military contest. First, however, national policy in the Communist world, and the assumptions underlying it, should be examined.

THE DETERMINANTS OF SOVIET POLICY

Elucidation of the causal factors that underlie Soviet foreign policy has always presented difficulties to Western observers and there has, accordingly, been considerable variation among the viewpoints of leading students of the subject. Quite clearly, for example, the Soviet Union has exerted pressure on neighboring countries and has attempted to expand the sphere of its influence and control. Yet there can be distinguished—among others—three different types of explanation for this behavior, each of them carrying different implications for the foreign policies of the Western states. One can take a viewpoint that stresses considerations of ideology, and say that Soviet expansionism derives from a Marxist fervor to overthrow capitalism everywhere. One can take a narrower view of

Soviet intentions, and argue that Russian foreign policy is determined primarily by considerations of security; this view holds that the Russians are afraid of another invasion from the West, such as has occurred perhaps half a dozen times in the last two centuries, and are concerned to establish their control over neighboring states so as to create forward defensive positions. Or one can adopt the intermediate point of view that stresses the simple elements of pursuit of power in Soviet policy, holding that the Soviet Union, behaving like other states that have the power and the opportunity, seizes its chances of aggrandizing itself where possible. This latter view emphasizes the features that Soviet foreign policy shares with all other states; the view that the leaders of the Soviet Union are bent on nothing less than world conquest stresses the specifically Communist nature of the Soviet state; the interpretation of Soviet policy holding that security considerations are paramount stresses its position in the long tradition of Russian foreign policy, including policy before the Bolshevik Revolution.

Abundant evidence exists to substantiate the arguments made by proponents of each of these points of view. The scholar inclined to stress security considerations, for example, readily explains the Soviet pressures on Turkey at the end of World War II in the light of the traditional pre–1917 Russian desire to wrest from Turkey control of the Straits of the Dardanelles, through which Russian shipping must pass from the Black Sea to the Mediterranean. Behind this foreign policy goal lies the traditional Russian desire to give her shipping access to "warm water" ports, since the ocean ports of the Soviet Union are blocked by ice a good part of the year. Soviet post-war activities in northern Iran can similarly be placed in the category of traditional Russian foreign policy aims, northern Iran having constituted a Russian buffer against the British march north from India before World War I; indeed, an agreement with Great Britain in 1905 assigned northern Iran to the Russian sphere of influence.

If one wishes to stress the ideological determinants of Soviet foreign policy and their tendency to make its goals nothing less than universal in scope, on the other hand, then ample material exists, especially in the statements of Soviet leaders. "We shall bury you" and "your grandchildren will live under socialism" are quotable favorites. Clearly, the exponent of this point of view would argue that concern with traditional requirements of Russian security would not explain Soviet activities in Yemen or Indonesia; while the fact that Soviet ideology aims its appeal at all men everywhere surely reveals the universal scope of Soviet aspirations, just as the Czar's use of pan-Slavism was indicative of the limitation of pre-revolutionary Russian aspirations to eastern Europe.

The interpretation of Soviet foreign policy as the actions of just another big state out to get what it can, can likewise be supported

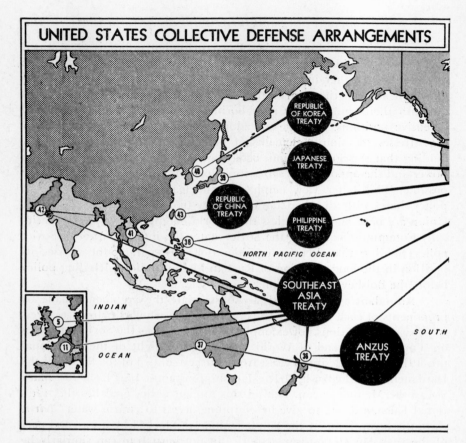

UNITED STATES COLLECTIVE DEFENSE ARRANGEMENTS

REPUBLIC OF KOREA TREATY

JAPANESE TREATY

REPUBLIC OF CHINA TREATY

PHILIPPINE TREATY

SOUTHEAST ASIA TREATY

ANZUS TREATY

NORTH PACIFIC OCEAN

INDIAN

OCEAN

SOUTH

ANZUS TREATY (3 NATIONS)
A treaty signed September 1, 1951, whereby each of the parties "recognizes that an armed attack in the Pacific Area on any of the Parties would be dangerous to its own peace and safety and declares that it would act to meet the common danger in accordance with its constitutional processes."
1 United States   36 New Zealand   37 Australia

JAPANESE TREATY (BILATERAL)
A treaty signed September 8, 1951, whereby Japan on a provisional basis requests, and the United States agrees, to "maintain certain of its armed forces in and about Japan . . . so as to deter armed attack upon Japan."
1 United States   39 Japan

PHILIPPINE TREATY (BILATERAL)
A treaty signed August 30, 1951, by which the parties recognize "that an armed attack in the Pacific on either of the Parties would be dangerous to its own peace and safety" and each party agrees that it will act "to meet the common

dangers in accordance with its constitutional processes."
1 United States   38 Philippines

REPUBLIC OF CHINA (Formosa) TREATY (BILATERAL)
A treaty signed December 2, 1954, whereby each of the parties "recognizes that an armed attack in the West Pacific Area directed against the territories of either of the Parties would be dangerous to its own peace and safety," and that each "would act to meet the common danger in accordance with its constitutional processes." The territory of the Republic of China is defined as "Taiwan (Formosa) and the Pescadores."
1 United States   43 Republic of China (Formosa)

REPUBLIC OF KOREA (South Korea) TREATY (BILATERAL)
A treaty signed October 1, 1953, whereby each party "recognizes that an armed attack in the Pacific Area on either of the Parties . . . would be dangerous to its own peace and safety" and that each Party "would act to meet the common

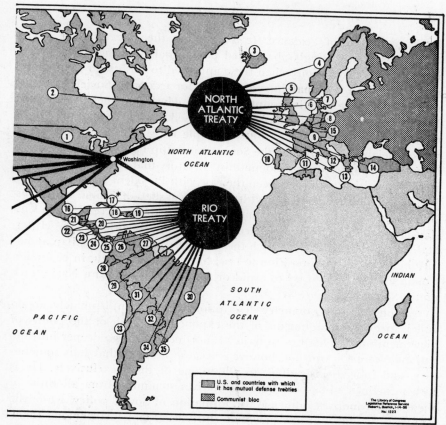

danger in accordance with its constitutional processes."

1 United States   40 Republic of Korea

SOUTHEAST ASIA TREATY (8 NATIONS)

A treaty signed September 8, 1954, whereby each party "recognizes that aggression by means of armed attack in the treaty area against any of the Parties . . . would endanger its own peace and safety" and each will "in that event act to meet the common danger in accordance with its constitutional processes."

1 United States   5 United Kingdom 11 France   36 New Zealand   37 Australia   38 Philippines   41 Thailand 42 Pakistan

NORTH ATLANTIC TREATY (15 NATIONS)

A treaty signed April 4, 1949, by which "the Parties agree that an armed attack against one or more of them in Europe or North America shall be considered an attack against them all; and . . . each of them . . . will assist the . . . attacked by taking forthwith, individually and in concert with the other Parties, such action

as it deems necessary including the use of armed force. . . ."

1 United States   2 Canada   3 Iceland 4 Norway   5 United Kingdom   6 Netherlands   7 Denmark   8 Belgium 9 Luxembourg   10 Portugal   11 France   12 Italy   13 Greece   14 Turkey   15 Federal Republic of Germany

RIO TREATY (21 NATIONS)

A treaty signed September 2, 1947, which provides that an armed attack against any American state "shall be considered as an attack against all the American States and . . . each one . . . undertakes to assist in meeting the attack. . . ."

1 United States   16 Mexico   *17 Cuba   18 Haiti   19 Dominican Republic   20 Honduras   21 Guatemala 22 El Salvador   23 Nicaragua   24 Costa Rica   25 Panama   26 Colombia   27 Venezuela   28 Ecuador   29 Peru   30 Brazil   31 Bolivia   32 Paraguay   33 Chile   34 Argentina   35 Uruguay

*Withdrawn, and displaced by OAS, 1964.

by a great deal of evidence. It is certainly the case that the Soviet Union has unhesitatingly abandoned policy goals seemingly dictated by ideological considerations when these appeared to clash with the requirements of Soviet national interest. Thus, for example, Soviet economic relations with the satellite countries, in the days when their domination by the Soviet Union was absolute, were based not on Communist ideals of equality or public welfare, but on simple Russian exploitation of her weaker neighbors. Similarly, the Soviet leadership has abandoned foreign Communist parties to non-Communist dictators that the Russian regime wished to cultivate; this has been the case with President Nasser of Egypt, just as it was thirty years ago with Chiang Kai-shek of China. No discussion of the abandonment of Communist ideals to the necessities of Russian national interests would be complete without mention of the Hitler-Stalin Pact of 1940, under which the Russian dictator executed an about-face in his policy of opposition to fascism, much to the chagrin of foreign Communist parties, to try to avoid or at least to postpone a Nazi attack on the Soviet Union.

None of these summary descriptions is able, unfortunately, to do full justice to the arguments of the exponents of each of the points of view mentioned. The present writer is not inclined to go deeper into the rationale of each position, however, because he feels that it is unnecessary, and indeed misleading, to adopt one of them exclusively. He is rather inclined to suspect that imperatives stemming from all three of these sets of motives influence the formation of Soviet policy, while the emphasis of policy at any one time shifts back and forth among them. There seems no reason to believe, moreover, that the bases of Soviet policy remain immutable; on the contrary, much evidence exists that the guidelines of policy change at different times and as different individuals achieve ascendancy within the structure of Soviet rule.

However, when Soviet policy comes to a crossroads, and a decision has to be made between alternative lines of action that stem from different conceptions of Soviet policy, the best predictor of Soviet policy seems to be that the Soviet Union acts like other powerful states in expanding where it can but in subordinating other goals to that of national security where necessary.

It is just as well that this should be so. For it is this fact that makes the containment policy reasonable and feasible. If the Soviet demand for world domination were unshakeable and insatiable no matter what obstacles presented themselves, then it is possible that the Soviet leadership would not be deterred by the threat of superior force, but might take rash and ill-considered actions that could plunge the world into another war. If, on the other hand, only limited and traditional security criteria were involved, it would be arguable that the West could purchase surcease from Soviet pressure by sacrificing to the Soviet Union the freedom of the states immediately surrounding her periphery. In other words, a policy of appeasement would then make sense. But this would carry with it two dangers; one, that each new belt of satellites would itself need to be protected by control over a further belt region, and thus a policy of steady expansionism could develop even out of the requirements of protection of the Soviet borders; but it would be equally possible that the appetite would come with eating, and a policy originally limited to border protection would become transformed into one of general expansionism if the addition of new territory were made that easy.

If Soviet policy can be understood simply as that opportunistic expansionism that has been present in the actions of other great powers, then what is the relevance of Communist ideology? Can it simply be ignored, as many have suggested, as having propaganda value, but of having no importance in the actual determination of the actions of the Soviet leaders?

PRINCIPLES OF CURRENT SOVIET FOREIGN POLICY

It is possible to discern in current Soviet foreign policy several guiding principles that are not quite the same as those that dominated Soviet policy in the early post-war years, nor are they the same as those principles that are urged by Communist China. They might be summarized as follows.

The first premise of Soviet policy is that the "socialist" camp is now strong enough to deter any Western attack. Thus, in all probability, a nuclear world war will not occur; the "imperialists," that is, the United States and its allies, realize that such an "all-out" war would bring general destruction and would thus be suicidal. It is, however, not completely impossible that such a war would occur, for it might be unleashed by the imperialists as an act of desperation when they come to realize that they are doomed to extinction. That is, nuclear war is possible, but only as an irrational act on the part of the West. It should be noted that Soviet leaders have acknowledged publicly that a general nuclear war might well mean the extinction of civilization; this was first said in public by Georgi Malenkov during his brief term as Premier. In this view, the Soviet Union itself would not begin such a war—there is no need for that since the cause of communism is advancing steadily and, indeed inevitably, without recourse to war.

This foreswearing of the possibility of general war means that the relations between the Soviet Union and the United States are conducted on the basis of "peaceful coexistence." While peaceful coexistence means that no general war will take place, however, it does not mean renunciation of "the class struggle." Ex-Premier Khrushchev made this clear on many occasions. That is, the Soviet leadership has no intention of giving up its goal of expanding the area in which Communist ways predominate. Different forms of military struggle are called for, however, as will be seen in a subsequent chapter. The period of peaceful coexistence is thus a period in which the balance of power is expected steadily to shift in favor of the Soviet bloc. Negotiations with the Western powers are certainly in order, but these can never be negotiations about the relinquishment of territory that has come into the Soviet camp. This also has been made clear in statements of Khrushchev and his successors. Negotiations may afford an opportunity for a breathing space, or they may determine the particular modes in which territory slipping from the West becomes Sovietized. This attitude has been sardonically characterized by Western observers as "what's mine is mine; what's yours is negotiable."

In its state relations with countries of the West, the theme of Soviet policy is to exploit the "contradictions" that, Marxist theory teaches the Soviet leaders, exist among Western states. On a political level the approach is to attempt to split the United States from its allies by making separate overtures to them and by attempting to accentuate the natural divergencies of interest that exist. Thus, for example, Soviet leadership long refrained from frontal attacks on President de Gaulle, hoping that his policy of strengthening France's autonomy would result in a weakening of France's NATO ties. This approach led to an embarrassing about-face on the part of the French Communist party, which had made a full-scale attack on one of de Gaulle's initiatives for the settlement of the Algerian question, only to change its view the following day after Khrushchev stated that de Gaulle's actions seemed to offer hope for the attainment of a just solution.

On the economic level the Soviet Union has attempted to exploit economic rivalries among the developed Western countries by dangling trade concessions before some of America's allies, particularly Great Britain, which, the Soviet leadership believes, is, as the second capitalist power, a natural rival of the United States. Indeed, this curious extension of Lenin's theory of imperialism has been carried to the point that Khrushchev on occasion hinted that he expected economic rivalries between the United States and Great Britain to be carried to the point of warfare—surely a clear indication of the limitations of the economic interpretation of history as a tool of analysis.

The line taken with respect to Communist party policy within the capitalist states is currently that "peaceful change to socialism" is possible. That is, the Soviet leadership now professes to believe that it is possible for Communist parties to come to power by legal and parliamentary means; these include the making of coalitions for tactical purposes with non-Communist parties, and, in the official formula, the means adopted must depend on the specific circumstances in each country.

In the colonial and ex-colonial areas the current line is to give support to the so-called national liberation movement. The Soviet Union and local Communist parties can support nationalist and anticolonial leaders even where these are non-Communist, even perhaps—up to a point—where they suppress the local Communist parties, as in the case of President Nasser. In the current era it is not necessary to insist that such states become Communist in order to merit Soviet support and assistance; if they are only detached from their Western connections this in itself weakens the imperialist camp and is to be accounted a gain.

As far as relations with other Communist states are concerned, the current Soviet position is that all members of the "Socialist camp" are equal, and all governing Communist parties are autonomous. However, the Communist party of the Soviet Union, as the senior ruling party, is the most experienced; it should show the way to the others, which, espousing principles of "proletarian internationalism," should voluntarily follow the Soviet lead.

So far as domestic politics in the satellites are concerned, the post-Stalin leadership of the Soviet party showed itself willing to tolerate quite a wide range of variation. It seems clear that today the limit to further evolution away from "Stalinism" is set by national leaders desirous of maintaining their own position, and not by the Russian leadership.

THE MOVEMENT AWAY FROM STALINISM

These then constitute the principal guidelines of current Soviet policies. Clearly, they add up to a considerable evolution away from the "hard" line followed in Stalin's day, although it is generally overlooked that some of the basic shifts in orientation actually took place during the last years of Stalin's life. Nevertheless, the dictator's successors have clearly been responsible for the development of Soviet policy to its present state.

The principal shifts of emphasis in policy since Stalin's day have occurred in the following respects. First of all, Stalin maintained tight control of the policies of the satellite countries. For pursuing policies that deviated from Russian guidelines no more than do those that almost all of the eastern European Communist states are at present following, Yugoslavia forfeited her good standing as a member of the bloc. What Marshal Tito and the other leaders of the Yugoslav party did was to take seriously the doctrine about the equality of Communist parties, and to react unfavorably to Soviet attempts at interference in domestic Yugoslav affairs. The evolution of the Soviet policy line towards the bloc countries since Stalin's death accordingly would have made it possible for Yugoslavia to be readmitted to the Communist commonwealth on the terms insisted on in the exchange of letters with Stalin in 1948; however, the Yugoslavs have become wary of the requirements of bloc unity, and have found in the period following the initial break with the Soviet Union that they can get along perfectly well, and, indeed, much better, on their own than as a member of the bloc. Further difficulty arose from the fact that Soviet attempts at rapprochement with Yugoslavia were regarded askance by leaders of those parties that remained loyal to a harder line more in keeping with Stalin's approach to inter-party relations, principally the Chinese Communists; this is no longer a factor, however, since attempts are no longer made by the Russians to placate the Chinese and those who think like them, where these involve substantial shifts of policy and not just the manipulation of verbal formulas.

This greater willingness to tolerate autonomy among the leadership of the satellite countries has gone in harness with a greater willingness to cooperate with non-Communist leaders, the so-called "bourgeois nationalists" in the ex-colonial countries. Almost to the end Stalin was reluctant to work with nationalist leaders like Nasser or Sukarno. The present leadership has carried along the change to a more cooperative attitude begun in the last year of Stalin's rule, even to the point of giving aid to the developing countries not under Communist rule, which would have been unthinkable fifteen years ago. The economic relations between Stalin's Russia and other states had always been based simply on the direct furtherance of Russian national interests; for example, trading arrangements were made with the eastern European satellites that were extremely disadvantageous to them, and actually represented what one might call "socialist exploitation." Because of this and other features of Soviet policy, there are anti-Soviet Marxists who regard the Soviet system as one of state capitalism, exhibiting the typical features of imperialist exploitation that Lenin attributed to capitalist states at a certain stage of their development.

As a consequence of the shift away from Stalinism, in the domestic sphere as well as in the foreign, fissures have developed within the Soviet bloc that have absorbed much of its strength and attention. However, one has to conclude that in some respects the shift has placed the Soviet Union in a stronger tactical position in the Cold War. Stalin was less inclined to embark on courses of action that entailed risks than the current Soviet leadership, for example; Khrushchev's "secret speech" at the Twentieth Party Congress pictures the late dictator as cautious to the point of fearfulness, beset by suspicions and indecisiveness. Khrushchev and his successors have seized opportunities that Stalin would have let go by. More important is the fact that the changes that have taken place in Soviet society since 1953 have given it a milder face and made the system more attractive to the non-Communist Left in Europe and Asia; the harsh excesses of policy in Stalin's day can plausibly be attributed to the personal faults of the dictator himself and made to seem less as inherent defects of the system. The results of this in more favorable attitudes towards the Soviet Union were clearly shown by the tenor of the discussion and resolutions of the October 1964 conference of nonaligned states that took place in Egypt. At the same time, of course, the change in policy has made it possible for non-Communist leaders in Asia, Africa, and Latin America to establish cooperative relations with the Soviet Union, since the Soviet leadership now regards the bourgeois nationalist leader as a "progressive" rather than as a "reactionary" force.

DOCTRINAL DIFFERENCES
BETWEEN RUSSIA AND CHINA

In these areas of policy the leadership of Communist China has tended to follow a more "Stalinist" position but has allied it to a more violent and revolutionary tactical line than the cautious Stalin followed. Various factors can be cited to account for this. In the first place the Chinese are in a more primitive stage of their revolution and have not reached the point of making the sophisticated adjustments to circumstances that have modified the single-minded revolutionary purity of the Russians. It may be, too, that the Chinese feel that as a large and powerful state in their own right, they would be demeaning themselves by following the Russian lead; moreover Mao Tse-tung seems to think that although he was junior to Stalin in his standing as a revolutionary, he personally should take preeminence over the present Russian leaders within the ranks of world Communist figures. In all probability, the Chinese stress on a harder, more "Left," more revolutionary, line corresponds more to the realities of Chinese experience in China itself, and it is also more appropriate to the tactical situation in the Asian countries with which China is more concerned, while a more restrained line seems to correspond more closely to tactical necessities in Europe, with which the Russians are more preoccupied.

One of the leading substantive differences between the outlooks of the Russian and Chinese Communists is over the question of the likelihood of general world war. It will be recalled that the Soviet Union officially takes the line that a nuclear war is unlikely to occur except as an act of desperation on the part of the imperialists; and that if it did occur it might mean the destruction of civilization. The Chinese position stresses the likelihood of such a war (although it is conceded that it may be possible to avoid it), and further, takes the view that if such a war should occur it would not entail the destruction of civilization, but only the destruction of capitalism. Moreover in the Chinese view, in such a war nuclear weapons by themselves would not prove a decisive factor. Here the Chinese position is surely influenced by the fact that China does not at the time of writing possess deliverable nuclear weapons, although it will doubtless come to possess them in time. The Chinese undervaluation of nuclear weapons is thus a normal reaction, probably a genuine one, and certainly the appropriate one in propaganda terms. China's great military strength lies, of course, in its enormous population, and accordingly its military doctrine stresses the importance of large land armies. If this line of analysis is correct, one can, therefore, anticipate a change in Chinese strategic doctrine as the Chinese come themselves to possess deliverable nuclear weapons, sometime in the coming decade.

The Chinese also differ strongly with the Russians over the question of cooperation with non-proletarian parties within the capitalist states. Here the Chinese have argued that "peaceful change to socialism" is a tactically unsound and, in any case, un-Marxist policy, and that Communist victory will come about only through proletarian revolution, in which the Communists rely on themselves alone, not on allies organized in a "popular front." There have been splits in several Communist parties over whether to follow the Russian or the Chinese line, with most of the parties, except those in countries bordering on China, taking the Russian view.

The Chinese reluctance to support use of only peaceful means and reluctance to cooperate with non-Communist elements extends also to the question of relations with bourgeois nationalists and neutralist leaders in the developing countries. This reached the extreme point in the case of India, of course. While the Soviet Union for its part was making every effort to cultivate India and Prime Minister Nehru, giving India great quantities of economic and military aid, the Chinese went so far as to invade border areas of the country over which they claimed jurisdiction. However, in this area of policy conflict as in the others, the conflict has been more apparent at the level of principle, and in practical matters neither side has been so extreme as its theoretical position would imply. Thus the Chinese have made many gestures of cooperation to non-Communist Asian and African nationalism, and were indeed even accused by Khrushchev of trying to form a non-white bloc.

On the question of the relations among states within "the socialist camp," the Chinese position is curiously paradoxical. On the one hand, the Chinese urge a return to Stalinism, to the hard line and tight control. In consonance with this approach, they denounce Yugoslav "revisionism," and the warmth of Russian relations with Yugoslavia during the period before the open break with the Chinese was in inverse proportion to the warmth of Russian relations with China; as the Russians attempted to conciliate the Yugoslavs, they alienated the Chinese, and vice versa. Nevertheless, seen from a non-Communist point of view, what the Chinese are doing is precisely what the Yugoslavs have done—that is, refused to take direction from Moscow. And the Chinese have been able to persevere in their independence for the same reason as the Yugoslavs; like the Yugoslavs, the Chinese made their own revolution, based firmly on the support of the peasants; the "revolution" was not made by a handful of armchair Marxists relying on the power of the Red Army, as was the case in almost all of the eastern European satellites.

Seen with hindsight, therefore, the break between the Soviet Union and Yugoslavia in 1948 no longer seems the isolated incident it appeared then, but the beginning of the evolution to a situation in which no single center dominates the Communist world to the complete elimination of autonomy elsewhere; this situation the Italian comrades have called "polycentrism." This is the kind of problem all empires are faced with, after all. Each country within the Soviet bloc has its own national interests, its own peculiar problems, its own national pride, and its own assertive leadership. Where a Red Army garrison is present, one swallows his national pride and follows the Soviet lead. But where the Red Army is absent and "proletarian internationalism" must depend on the bonds of ideological sympathy alone, there the will to autonomy has led each state to *de facto* independence of Moscow.

This occurred early not only in China and Yugoslavia but also in Albania. It is usually said that the Communist party has nowhere come to power in a free election. If one disregards the case of the tiny republic of San Marino, which was ephemerally ruled by an elected Communist government, the sole exception to the rule is provided by Albania. There a Communist government came to power not through peasant or proletarian revolution, as in China, Yugoslavia, Cuba, and Russia itself, not by Red Army invasion, as happened elsewhere, but by open election. After joining the Soviet bloc shortly after World War II ended, Albania had the status of a sort of subsatellite, being dependent on her large neighbor, Yugoslavia. The Albanians were never happy about this relationship of dependency, and when the Yugoslavs were put out of the bloc by Stalin, they took the lead in the bitterness of the vituperation they heaped on the head of Tito and his colleagues. Accordingly, Khrushchev's attempt to reach a rapprochement with Yugoslavia hit the Albanians very hard, and their opposition to the new Soviet line led them into outright defiance of the Soviet leadership. The break between the Soviet Union and Albania, which then became, in effect, dependent on the Chinese, reached extraordinary lengths. These actually included the executions of men that the Albanians charged were Soviet spies. Other noteworthy developments in the Soviet-Albanian "cold war" were the withdrawal of Soviet submarines from their base in Albania, and the defection of and granting of asylum to an Albanian diplomat stationed in Communist Czechoslovakia.

How should one interpret this divergence between Russian and Chinese policies from the viewpoint of the West? The dominant tendency has been to welcome the split, and to try to do nothing to narrow it on the premise that its existence weakens the Communist camp. However, as Alexander Eckstein pointed out some time ago, the existence of the split may well prove disadvantageous to the West in the long run. The difference of opinion is, after all, over the question of the most efficacious way of "burying" the West. Americans, nurtured on the doctrine of the benefits of competition, can perceive the dangers here; as in the competitive model of the economy, competition may lead to heightened efficiency and increased "production."

Khrushchev's introduction of missiles into Cuba may have been induced by a desire to meet the Chinese challenge. Since the resolution of the Cuban missile crisis, however, attempts to surpass the Chinese in militancy have dropped sharply, as shown by such indices as the frequency of challenges to Western authority in West Berlin. Nevertheless, the Soviet Union's tactical position has been strengthened by the split with the Chinse in the sense that the existence of a harder, more violent Chinese policy line makes that of the Soviet Union seem mild by comparison and thus creates a more favorable disposition towards the Soviet Union on the part of non-Communist leftists and neutralists.

It is now clear, however, that the split between Russia and China has gone beyond the stage of mere rivalry in the pursuit of common goals. The leaders of the Soviet Union are, in fact, caught in a dilemma that implies a fundamental reappraisal of national policy goals. So long as the Soviet Union was the unchallenged leader of the Communist bloc, ideological imperialism went hand-in-hand with national interest; but now that gains of the "Socialist camp" may accrue to the national account of the Chinese and not the Russians, a dilemma arises. The Chinese, after all, have national interests in conflict with those of Russia: there are disputes between the two over the demarcation of spheres of influence in Central Asia; China has been prepared to take military risks and accept propaganda losses in order to conquer lands to which ancient Chinese claims exist, like the borderlands of India, which are of no consequence to Russia; China wanted economic aid on a scale larger and on terms easier than the Russians were willing to provide; and the Chinese wished to possess their own atomic weapons, an aim in which the Russians, fearing to play the role of Frankenstein, refused to collaborate.

The Russians, accordingly, find themselves in the dilemma of having expansionist goals vis-à-vis the West, and *status quo* goals vis-à-vis China. Although it still seems premature to talk of a Russian-American alliance to contain the Chinese—the American contest with the Soviet Union proceeds with full force in many areas—reversals of alliance patterns, even of that scope, are not unknown to history.

SUGGESTED READINGS

Bell, Daniel, "Ten Theories in Search of Reality," *World Politics,* April 1958.

Dallin, Alexander, *The Soviet Union at the United Nations.* New York: Praeger, 1962.

Floyd, David, *Mao Against Khrushchev.* New York: Praeger, 1963.

Garthoff, Raymond, *Soviet Strategy in the Nuclear Age,* rev. ed. New York: Praeger, 1962.

Hsieh, Alice Langley, *Communist China's Strategy in the Nuclear Era.* Englewood Cliffs, N.J.: Prentice-Hall, 1962.

(George F. Kennan), "The Sources of Soviet Conduct," *Foreign Affairs,* July 1947.

Luard, Evan (ed.), *The Cold War: A Re-Appraisal.* New York: Praeger, 1964.

Seton-Watson, Hugh, *Neither War Nor Peace.* New York: Praeger, 1960.

Sokolovsky, Marshal V. D., *Military Strategy: Soviet Doctrine and Concepts.* New York: Praeger, 1963.

The Soviet-Yugoslav Dispute: Texts of the Published Correspondence. London: The Royal Institute of International Affairs, 1948.

Spanier, John, *American Foreign Policy Since World War II,* 2d ed. New York: Praeger, 1962.

Zagoria, Donald S., *The Sino-Soviet Conflict.* Princeton, N.J.: Princeton University Press, 1962.

8

Cold War:
The Ideological Dimension

In this chapter on ideology and propaganda, several distinct although related issues will be treated. After looking at the functions of ideology and doctrine in their relation to a nation's foreign policy efforts, the strengths and weaknesses of the ideological positions adopted by the two sides in the Cold War will be considered, followed by a discussion of propaganda techniques and their relative efficacy, and concluding with a look at the substance of some of the issues that have been raised in the course of the ideological battle.

THE FUNCTIONS OF IDEOLOGY

What functions does an explicit ideology perform in the making and execution of foreign policy? Here one should distinguish between ideology in its role as merely part of the content of propaganda, and ideology in its role as an actual determinant of a state's foreign policy.

The functions of ideology "as part of a state's propaganda effort" are three; not only does its intellectual power attract avowed converts abroad, but also diffusion of its basic ideas induces many who are not consciously committed to the ideology nevertheless to see things in a similar light; at the same time it creates a favorable impression of the nation's policy even among those who themselves reject its ideological premises by making it appear that acts of policy that are in actuality directed at furthering national interests are really high-minded gestures based on principle.

Of course an ideology may fulfill these functions either well or badly. To make a successful propaganda vehicle, an ideology must, to some extent at least, be consonant with actions actually taken; otherwise, it will only seem hypocritical. This has often been the fate of United States professions of an ideology of equality when contrasted with the well-known fact that Negro Americans, especially in the South, are not accorded equal treatment with whites. Frequently the American abroad finds this contrast thrown in his face and used, moreover, to cancel out any criticisms, however well-founded, of other ways of life, such as the Communist. "How can you talk about democracy when you discriminate against Negroes?" The story is told of an American visitor in Moscow who was being shown the subway by his Russian host. After admiring at length the subway's cleanliness and artistic decoration, he suddenly stopped and asked, puzzled, "But we have been here for twenty minutes; where are the trains?" Without hesitation the Russian rejoined, "Yes? And what about the Negroes in the South?"[1]

It was in awareness of this fact, that the plausibility of words is heightened by their consonance with actions, that Josef Goebbels, the Nazi propaganda specialist, used to speak of "propaganda of the deed."

A second criterion of the value of ideology as propaganda is its consonance with the needs of those at whom it is directed. It hardly strengthens the appeal of democracy if one makes much of the alleged fact that it is indissolubly connected with the Judeo-Christian tradition, as Secretary of State Dulles was fond of doing, if one's propaganda is directed primarily at Moslems, Hindus, and Buddhists, to say nothing of the large proportion of agnostics in the western European countries.

---

[1] Some time after he had first written the above, the author came across the following report in the New York *Times* of November 7, 1963, of an exchange between Khrushchev and a group of visiting American businessmen:

The angriest retort by Mr. Khrushchev came in response to a question about the Berlin wall.

"Is it necessary to build a Berlin wall and to shoot people down if they try to get over it?" asked Mr. Cook, the president of General Foods.

Mr. Khrushchev replied that a "state frontier is a state frontier" and that "every state" shot those who violated its borders. "You do this, we do this, and so does the German Democratic Republic (East Germany)," he asserted.

"Not to keep people in, we don't," Mr. Cook replied.

"In your country children are killed in a church for the sole reason that their color is different, that they are black instead of white," the Premier retorted. "So let's not argue on that point."

American overseas "information" campaigns are more sensitive to this point today, thank goodness, than they used to be.

The major "creative" function of ideology, as it informs the policy-making process—that is, as it is actually believed in by policy makers, not merely used by propagandists—is that it provides consistency and speed of reaction to national policy. Where one does not have a definite doctrinal position that implies a specific response to a new event, then much time is wasted in devising a policy specifically to meet that event; and since the policy has been adopted *ad hoc* it may work at cross-purposes with other policies adopted in similar piecemeal fashion to meet other contingencies. At the same time, a comprehensive ideology makes sense out of the events that occur and puts them in some type of evaluative context without which they are meaningless.

When, for example, a military *coup d'état* overthrows a civilian government, it strengthens United States policy if that sequence of events automatically has a certain value in relation to the goals the United States is trying to promote; otherwise, one runs the risk of hesitating and taking self-contradictory actions and letting opportunities go by, as has happened all too frequently.

Much of the ineffectiveness of United States policy in the past has stemmed from the lack of a clearly articulated doctrine relating the realities of international relations to the goals of United States policy. All too often, at a loss to know which path to follow with respect to a crisis in the internal politics of another country, the United States has fallen back on the one element of its foreign policy of which it is sure, that is, anti-communism, and it has supported the group or individual who looks, on the basis of some criterion or other—usually his own pronouncements—to be the most anti-Communist. He has all too often proved to be also the most incompetent, corrupt, cruel-hearted, and unpopular with his people, and the dirt has rubbed off on the American image. A long and depressing list of illustrations of this point could be cited.

The criteria of the adequacy of an ideology in its function "as a guide to policy making" are, first, that its principles be consonant with abiding national attitudes, that they be genuinely believed in. If this is not the case, then the "official" ideology will last no longer than the term of office of the administrator or political leader whose pet project it is, and it will fail to provide that consistency that is one of its chief reasons for being. This factor has unfortunately been lost sight of as many well-meaning publicists have tried to create a synthetic foreign policy doctrine for the United States without roots in the deepest national beliefs. Especially in a democratic society, where an official ideology cannot be decreed by the political leadership but must win adherence on the basis of its inherent attractiveness, any doctrine for American foreign policy must be essentially a codification and rationalization of existing American attitudes, not an "invented" substitute for them.

Further, one has to stipulate that the descriptive elements in an ideology that is to serve as a guide in foreign policymaking must correspond closely to the structure of reality itself. Clearly, a doctrine is useless that distorts the face of international reality. The Nazi ideology, for example, served Hitler well enough as a propaganda weapon during the period of his rise to power; however, it failed him badly as a guide in his foreign policy. For example, Hitler stated, and seemed to believe quite sincerely, that because of their lack of "racial purity," and the assumed prevalence of "Jewish financiers" in their public life, the fibre of British and French society had been so weakened that neither country would be able to offer him effective resistance.[2] It is now known how far from right these descriptive elements in his ideology were as applied to Britain.

THE CONTENT OF SOVIET IDEOLOGY

Because of the centrality of Marxism-Leninism to Soviet policy, and the permeation of Soviet pronouncements with terms derived from it, it is perhaps worthwhile to attempt a summarization of Marxism-Leninism's key principles.

1. The basis of Marxist historical analysis is "the dialectic." This is simply the principle, taken from Hegel, that history moves by opposites; any existing system of organization accumulates tensions and contradictions that grow to the point that the system is overwhelmed by them and becomes transformed into another system that is therefore in some sense its opposite.

2. The second basic principle of Marxist ideology is "materialism." Philosophical materialism asserts the primacy of material things; applied by Marx to human beings it signifies the view that what determines the style of human life is the way in which a man meets his primary need: to feed himself. This is seen as so basic to human existence that it dominates all aspects of social life. Thus the whole structure of human culture, moral, aesthetic, philosophical, and religious ideas, are considered to be dependent on the mode of production. In the Marxist formula the "superstructure" of a person's ideas is based on how he earns a living, that is, his relation to the means of production, that is, his economic class.

3. When these two principles are combined into "dialectical materialism," one has a complete theory of history. In the words of *The Communist Manifesto,* "the history of all hitherto existing society is the history of class struggles." In the current phase of history the struggle is between "bourgeoisie" and "proletariat," between those who own the means of production and those who own nothing but their labor.

---

[2] On this see, for one example, Hermann Rauschning, *The Voice of Destruction.* New York: Putnam, 1940, pp. 119–121.

The next series of Marxist principles has to do with the laws of capitalism and its economic processes.

4. The basis for Marx's analysis of capitalism is his "theory of labor value." For Marx as for many other thinkers, including St. Thomas Aquinas, the "value" of a product was determined by the labor that went into it; not only the labor immediately expended in its production, but also the labor expended to grow or mine the raw materials, and to fashion the tools or machinery involved. (Capitalist economics typically holds, in opposition to this theory, the theory of market value, according to which the "value" of a product depends on what someone is willing to pay for it, that is, upon the laws of supply and demand.)

5. From the principle of labor value follows the doctrine of "the exploitation of the worker" under capitalism. As everyone knows, it is the objective of the capitalist to make a profit, even over and above any salary he may pay himself for administrative tasks. This profit represents the difference between the price at which a product is sold and the sum total of the labor costs (including the costs of tools and materials) that went into its production. However, if the value of the product was created by the labor that went into it, and if labor is not compensated by the payment to it of all that value, but part is set aside for profit, then the margin of profit represents also the margin of exploitation, a portion of what was rightfully due to labor, but appropriated by the parasitic capitalist.

6. It is out of this very exploitation that "capitalist crises," that is, economic depressions, derive. Because of the margin between the price paid for a product and the wages paid to labor and because of the fact that the capitalist saves money, the total wages paid in the whole economy will be insufficient to buy all of the products produced by that economy at the prices set. Accordingly, a surplus of unbought commodities accumulates, and periodically the productive machinery is stopped until the backlog of commodities is consumed. This is in essence the Marxist theory of depressions under capitalism.

In dialectical fashion, however, capitalism prepares the ground for its own downfall. It brings workers together, organizes them, and gives them some education. At the same time, their misery steadily increases, and the crises of capitalism get worse and worse as the capitalist system itself grows.

7. This state of affairs continues until the proletarians, unable to bear the situation any longer, rise up in "revolution." The first form of social organization after the revolution is the dictatorship of the proletariat; that is, all forms of government are regarded by Marx as dictatorships of one class over another, and since the proletariat is now in control, a dictatorship of the proletariat results. However, the period of dictatorship of the proletariat lasts "only" as long as it takes to liquidate the survivals of the capitalist system.

8. With the complete liquidation of capitalist survivals, and after having gone through a necessary transitional period (in which, fifty years after the Bolshevik Revolution, the Soviet Union still officially considers itself to be) it proves possible to move into "the era of communism." In this idyllic period in which history reaches its culmination, class conflicts no longer exist because only a single class, or rather, ex-class, remains. Thus there is no exploitation and no need for an apparatus of government to supervise that exploitation; accordingly, "the state withers away." A stage

of economic abundance is reached (since there are no longer wasteful capitalist practices, depressions, and so on) in which there is no need for scarcity, oppression, or evil to exist.

Several adaptations were made in the Marxist scheme by Lenin, some of them actually going so far as implicitly to deny basic Marxist principles (this, of course, is not acknowledged by the official interpreters of Marxism-Leninism).

9. One of Lenin's major contributions (although it was only partly original) is the theory of "imperialism." According to Lenin, it is possible for capitalism to circumvent temporarily the problem of overproduction that leads to crises by the conquest of colonial territories that are used as captive markets for the production that would otherwise be in excess. The colonies also absorb surplus capital. In their imperialist stage of development, the capitalist societies compete for colonies until their colonial ambitions lead them into conflict. This was Lenin's interpretation of the origin of World War I.

At the same time, Lenin became skeptical that the proletariat, if left to its own devices, would spontaneously arise in revolution. In fact he took the view that, left to itself, the proletariat would achieve only what he called "trade union consciousness," that is, it would be content with attempting to secure higher wages and other concessions from the capitalist within the capitalist system without seeking to overthrow the system as such. The granting of these concessions by the capitalist would be facilitated by the availability of large profits from the exploitation of colonial areas. It would thus become possible to "bribe" sections of the working class and create a kind of labor aristocracy, content to share with the capitalists the ill-gotten gains of colonial exploitation. This is the category in which Marxist-Leninists place the leaders of non-Communist trade unions.

10. Lenin thus urged the view that for the revolution to come about it was necessary to create "a party of professional revolutionaries" who would form the "vanguard" of the proletariat and embody the revolutionary consciousness to which it could not aspire on its own. Because of the requirements of revolutionary activity in an inhospitable environment, the party had to operate secretly, and its members had to be disciplined to unquestioning obedience of the party leadership. This conception of party organization has left its impress on the Communist parties of today, even where they have come to power and need no longer function in the manner appropriate to a revolutionary party in the period before the seizure of power.

THE STRENGTHS AND WEAKNESSES OF SOVIET IDEOLOGY

Although Marxist-Leninist ideology contains many inaccurate descriptions of reality, it has nevertheless many points of strength in its function of guiding Soviet foreign policy. One of the ideology's great strengths is that it stresses the importance of conflict in the world—conflict within capitalist states, conflict among capitalist states, conflict between capitalist states and the Soviet Union. Accordingly, it prepares

Soviet leaders psychologically for participation in a world of sovereign states in which the law of life is conflict. And while providing the Marxist-Leninist with a rough description of the world on which he can rely, it allows for enough flexibility (too much, in fact, for it to be really "scientific") that the Soviet leaders are not necessarily bound in a strait jacket of inappropriate reactions to international events. Finally, it provides the people of the Soviet Union, as well as its leadership, with a conviction that their cause is righteous and will triumph eventually, and thus with a faith that sustains them through adversity.

In its propaganda functions, the strengths of Soviet ideology are even more apparent. It is a doctrine that is understandable on all intellectual levels, and can be made to appeal to anyone from the most humble sharecropper to the most sophisticated university professor. At the same time it is a plausible doctrine that draws strength from the fact that some of its basic principles correspond to well-known and easily observable phenomena, such as the existence in the same society of rich and poor. Moreover, the explicit value goals of the ideology have wide appeal: the ending of exploitation, the realization of human equality, the abolition of class distinctions.

Further, the concepts of superstructure, economic determinism, and the bribery of the labor aristocracy by the capitalist provide Marxism-Leninism with tools that can be used to "explain" absolutely anything that happens. Thus, if labor disorders take place, the working class is preparing to revolt; if no disorders take place, this constitutes clear evidence that working-class leadership has been bribed by the capitalists. If wages go down, this proves capitalist exploitation; if they are increased, it proves that the capitalists in their anxiety are trying to "buy off" the proletariat. If a colonial power refuses to relinquish control of its colony, this proves that it benefits from imperialist exploitation; if, on the other hand, it is willing to give the colony independence, this shows that such independence must be purely nominal, masking the reality of continued economic control. If it can be shown that human beings do not behave in such a way that the arrangements envisaged for the final "era of communism" can actually work, this is only because behavior at present is determined by the economic relations of capitalism—and, even in the Soviet Union, by curiously tenacious "survivals of capitalism"—that will eventually be swept away; and so on. (This very ability to "explain" with equal facility events exactly opposed to each other, in fact, demonstrates the doctrine's lack of validity to the sophisticated observer who is not already committed.)

It should also be noted that part of the appeal of official Marxism-Leninism lies not in its content, but in its form and style, as it were. The very authority with which the occupants of the Kremlin make their pronouncements, as well as the certainty that is claimed for the "scientific" principles and predictions of Marxism, make the doctrine attractive to those whose psychological constitution requires the assurance of certainty. And the more or less steady expansion of Soviet power since 1917 and the confidence with which Communists regard the eventual victory as theirs hold out the promise that those who join them will be "riding the wave of the future."

However, acknowledgement of the strength of Soviet doctrine should not lead one to overlook its serious weaknesses. For example, although the flexibility of Soviet doctrine provides it with many advantages, at the same time an excessive use of that flexibility has often provoked substantial numbers of defections from the Communist cause abroad. This has been the case in some of the spectacular shifts of policy line that the Soviet Union has made at various times; perhaps the classic instance was the shift in 1940, with the signing of the Hitler-Stalin pact, from a policy of active and vigorous opposition to fascism to one of coexistence and even collaboration with it. There is no doubt that the magnitude and suddenness of this shift in policy cost communism very great numbers of adherents. The present writer is inclined to guess that there are many more ex-Communists than there are Communists in some countries outside the Chinese and Russian orbits.

It is also true, of course, that because the Communist image of the world deviates from reality the doctrine provides the Soviet leadership, on occasion, with mistaken policy guides. In its Chinese policy during the 1920s, for example, the Russian leadership gave the signal, time after time, for attempted revolts among the proletariat of the cities in the belief that this was the correct Marxist thing to do, only to have each uprising put down with ease by the Nationalist government while many valuable party militants were killed. At the same time Mao Tse-tung urged the idea that communism in China should seek to base itself on the peasantry rather than the urban workers—to no avail, because Marx had said that the peasantry constituted a reactionary rather than a progressive force.[3]

IS THE COLD WAR AN IDEOLOGICAL STRUGGLE?

One of the most notorious clichés of the discussion of current international politics is that "We are engaged in a battle for men's minds." Graduation speakers at a loss for a theme, politicians trying to look like

---

[3] Indeed, blunders of this type have been so numerous in the course of the development of Soviet foreign policy that some Western observers (for example, Leonard Rowe) have been tempted to argue that they must have been deliberate acts, designed to weaken foreign Communist parties that would not be subject to Russian control if in power.

statesmen, a legion of writers in the weekly magazines, insistently state the case that the Cold War is a conflict of ideologies. With all due respect to this persistent notion, the present writer inclines to the view that the ideological aspect of the current struggle has been greatly exaggerated, and that the basic conflict is simply between one powerful state attempting to extend the sphere of its control and influence and another powerful state reluctant to see this happen—that is, the Cold War is explicable largely in terms of simple political dynamics.

There are many features of the world situation that raise suspicions that this is the case. One does not need a very long memory to recall that only twenty years ago the great ideological struggle in the world was between fascism and the democracies; at the time, because she was fighting on the side of the Allies, the Soviet Union was regarded as a democracy more or less in good standing—a rather strange sort of democracy to be sure, a state whose "democracy" took strange forms—a "people's democracy"—but a democracy nevertheless. Since then, the Soviet Union has changed only in the sense that its dictatorial features have been softened somewhat by Stalin's heirs; nevertheless, it has been transformed in official Western views from the status of a great and valued ally to that of the chief adversary. At the same time, Fascist states continue to exist— Franco's Spain is of course Fascist, and made little secret of its support of Hitler twenty-five years ago. In the Western Hemisphere itself, until 1960, the Dominican Republic suffered under a totalitarian system as vicious and brutal as any. Meanwhile, the Republic of South Africa is transforming itself under our eyes into a full-fledged Nazi state, complete with racial laws, official withdrawal of the protections of the judicial system from the "inferior" race, and the denial of elementary rights of free expression to opponents of the regime. Nevertheless, today the United States tolerates and, in the case of Spain, is even allied with fascism in a way that would have been unthinkable in the early 1940s. What has changed? Is fascism really not as bad as one used to think? Is communism now worse than one used to think?

Clearly, the difference in international alignment between the period of World War II and the period of the Cold War is simply that today the Soviet Union and Communist China constitute the major threat to the independence of action of the United States and its allies; in Hitler's day the overwhelming menace was posed by Germany and Japan. If tomorrow the split between Russia and China should become an extreme and violent one, and should the Soviet Union seek to ally itself openly with the United States to gain support against the Chinese threat, there would be no lack of publicists ready and eager to interpret the new international alignment as a reflection of the fundamental underlying clash of "ideology" between Europe and Asia, or between countries of the Western philosophical tradition and those of Confucian heritage, or some other plausible, and even true, but strictly secondary conflict.

After all, conflicts of power and interest have always been given ideological meaning. In the days when Britain fought France or Spain, these were represented as and were indeed believed to be inevitable conflicts between the Protestant and Catholic world views. In the days before Henry VIII's secession from Rome introduced the religious difference between France and Britain, clashes between the two states were regarded by British ideologists as expressions of the struggle between the principle of Continental despotism and the principle of English liberties, although a much more liberal England than that of the Plantagenets was later regarded as despotic by the American colonists of the eighteenth century and for that matter by the Roundheads of the seventeenth.

From the middle of the nineteenth century till the first years of the twentieth century, similarly, clashes between British and Russian power from the Crimea to Afghanistan were perceived in Britain as expressions of the conflict between Czarist despotism and constitutional democracy, or, alternatively, between Slavic barbarism and Western civilization. After the arrogant international posture of William II made imperial Germany the leading threat to the peace of Europe, however, Czarist despotism and Slavic barbarism were forgotten by the British as the Russians became in World War I gallant defenders of the Western tradition against Teutonic despotism and barbarism. For its part, however, the Germany of William II regarded itself as defending the values of Western culture, which had reached their highest expression, after all, in the Germany of Goethe and Beethoven, against the Asian barbarism represented by the Czar's armies.

One may, accordingly, be pardoned a certain skepticism as to the importance of the ideological phase of the current international conflict. Certainly, ideological conflict exists in the world; nevertheless, by themselves ideological differences, no matter how great, need not occasion conflict. The clearest example of this is surely the fact that Protestants and Catholics, who three and one-half centuries ago were massacring each other over questions of principle in such numbers as to decimate the population of Europe, today live casually and peacefully side by side. It has been fashionable to say, paraphrasing Lincoln, that a world cannot endure half Communist and half free. There is really little basis for such an assertion. A world can exist half Communist and half free, half Christian and half Buddhist, half devout and half pagan, or divided along any other axis one cares to imagine; conflict results when and only when one half tries—or is thought to try—to dominate the other, regardless of the differences or the similarities in the labels they wear.

One might add to the foregoing the prediction that the extent to which the United States or the Soviet Union dominates the remaining third of the world or parts thereof will depend more on the military and economic power each protagonist can muster, and the extent to which each can contrive a comity of interests between itself and the countries of the uncommitted third, rather than on which side holds the better arguments in the combat of ideologies. Thus, although an ideological dimension to the Cold War exists and has some secondary significance, in the view of the present writer it plays a relatively minor role in originating and maintaining the antagonism between the superpowers.

THE SUBSTANCE
OF THE IDEOLOGICAL CONFLICT

One of the extraordinary things about the ideological conflict is that over the years, although the image that each society has of itself is radically different from the image it has of the other, the differences between the two *realities* have steadily grown less. This has even taken place to some extent in the political realm with the softening, since Stalin's death and Beria's execution, of the most repressive features of life in the Soviet Union, and, on the other hand, a restriction of the area of liberty in the United States because of the real or fancied requirements of internal security; although for all the congressional subcommittees, the blacklists of "controversial" persons, and the crackpot right-wing organizations, the United States is still incomparably freer than the Soviet Union, even a de-Stalinized Soviet Union.

More interesting and more curious tendencies in the direction of convergence between the two systems are proceeding in the realm of economic organization, however. The range of income distribution, for example, is comparable in the two societies; the motto that Marx ascribed to the eventual Communist society, "from each according to his ability, to each according to his needs," does not apply in the stage of "transition to communism" in which the Soviet leadership places Soviet society today. Thus a high party official earns on the order of forty times the wages of an unskilled worker, and leading figures in the world of culture and entertainment may earn even more. Of course, wage and salary figures are not strictly comparable between the two societies; the Soviet citizen receives free or at nominal cost more services than the American, but, on the other hand, high incomes are taxed much more lightly in the Soviet Union than they are in the United States. On the score of income distribution, at any rate, the practical differences hardly justify any ferocious clash of principle.

In the organization of the two economies, the area of difference has been steadily diminishing. In the drive to increase output, the Soviet

Union has allowed much greater initiative to individual factory managers, whose income depends in part on the economic performance of the enterprise they head. In other words, as the Soviet economy becomes more sophisticated, the planners are finding that to increase production they are moving in the direction of a more "capitalist" system of incentive compensation.

Stalin himself introduced the principle that, to the maximum possible, workers should be paid according to their actual output, not by the hour or week. This has resulted in a prevalence of piece-work rates, output quotas, and speedups that no labor union in the United States or western Europe would tolerate for a moment (although the harshness of the Soviet system of norms is mitigated in practice by resourceful evasion on the part of both management and labor).

At the same time greater attention is paid to consumers' wishes and a strong tendency to a free market in food and consumers' goods has set in. It seems likely that as economic rationality makes greater headway in the Soviet Union, and as the satisfaction of consumer desires is accorded higher priority, even greater play will be allowed to free-market forces.

In the United States, on the other hand, the basically free-enterprise economy is overlain with a system of legal regulation and supervision by commissions and boards that, while not adding up to anything like a planned economy, does not add up to anything like the traditional picture of capitalism either. And yet, in its official statements the United States urges the benefits of a "capitalism" it does not have against claims made by Soviet spokesmen for a "communism" and even a "socialism" that their system does not resemble. Adolf Berle appropriately wrote that the United States is opposing the slogans of 1776, the year in which Adam Smith wrote *The Wealth of Nations,* to Soviet slogans of 1848, the year in which *The Communist Manifesto* appeared. Neither has much to do with the world of 1966.

One of the many ironies of this curious situation is that, although spokesmen for both countries urge with great force and conviction the benefits of the economic system that each believe themselves to have, each government, when it confronts its domestic economic problems, is anything but sure of the direction that it should take.

THE SOVIET CRITIQUE
OF THE UNITED STATES

In all humility one should recognize that some of the criticisms of the United States made by the Communists have a factual basis; it is this factor that gives Soviet propaganda much of its potency. At the same time one should not succumb to the self-condemnation to which this realization has led many well-intentioned Americans. Americans are, after all, human, perhaps all too human; but acknowledgment that imperfections exist in no way entails acceptance of more than a fraction of the far-ranging criticism of the United States prompted in such large part by envy and sheer ignorance.

First, take the charge that the United States is imperialist. A certain amount of evidence can be admitted on this score. The Indians who inhabited North America were certainly dispossessed of their land. A great deal of territory was taken from Mexico; attempts were made to annex Canada; Puerto Rico, the Philippines, and some of the minor Pacific islands were brought under the American flag as a result of the Spanish-American War and World War II.

Yet clearly the dominant tendencies of twentieth-century American policy have not been imperialist. No one in the United States today seriously contemplates the conquest of Mexico or Canada—although these were once active issues in United States politics.

Acknowledging these facts, the subtler indictments of the United States as imperialist tend to redefine imperialism in the sense of "economic domination." One should first note that in itself this represents a major concession. Anyone not prejudiced by Marxist preconceptions can surely see that a great difference exists between the exercise of direct political control and that of indirect economic influence. Nevertheless, it is certainly true that by reason of the greater development of the American economy, American business interests are widespread; normally the government of a country in which such interests operate has to take them into account in forming policy, just as it takes into account the interests and desires of domestic business. Only those without knowledge of how political processes work, however, can give credence to the naive theories that conceive of a small group of foreign businessmen "giving orders" to a government. Juan José Arévalo, the former President of Guatemala, the small Central American republic in which the legendary United States–owned United Fruit Company is the leading employer of labor, and author of *The Shark and the Sardines,* a strongly anti-American book that hardly qualifies Arévalo as a friend of the United States, has testified that during his presidency the United States never attempted to dictate policy to him in the interest of United Fruit or of anyone else.[4]

If one regards the evolution of United States policy with an unjaundiced eye, one has to acknowledge that far from being dominated by an imperialist impulse, the United States has, on the contrary, leaned in

---

4 New York *Times,* March 27, 1962.

the direction of isolationism and non-involvement in the affairs of the world; and that this sentiment, moreover, has traditionally found its political home in the same Republican party that is the more sensitive of the political parties to the opinions of business groups. That is, rather than being impelled to imperialism by the desires of business interests, the United States government on the contrary has had to drag the vast majority of representatives of business interests reluctantly along with the most necessary actions involving a positive role for American foreign policy.

To the extent that such a positive role has been undertaken, moreover, it seems clear that considerations of national security rather than of economic interest have been primary. If one examines the motives of the individuals and groups active in encouraging war with Spain, for example, people such as Theodore Roosevelt or Elihu Root, it can be seen that the motives are clearly ones of national strategy. Theodore Roosevelt is even on record as writing that war was desirable since it would constitute excellent training for the Navy. Alternatively, if one looks at the "empire" of Pacific islands that the United States acquired over the years,[5] it is seen that these are clearly without value in any economic sense, but are of use principally as naval bases. The major American "colony" of today, Puerto Rico—which constitutionally enjoys a unique and ambiguous status as a "commonwealth" or free state associated with the United States, a status under which it enjoys almost complete internal autonomy—is maintained in its status of quasi-dependence on the United States not because Americans wish it that way, but because the present administration of Puerto Rico, supported by a substantial majority of the inhabitants of the island, believe that in the commonwealth status they have found a device that permits maximum economic development, allowing as it does many of the economic benefits of United States citizenship with a minimum of accompanying tax obligations.

In keeping with the Marxist image of capitalist society, Soviet propaganda maintains, and to some extent the Soviet leadership believes, that the United States is essentially controlled by the capitalist class, or segments of it, who shape national policy in the interests of their class, exploiting the workers, promoting war hysteria so that they can profit from arms production, and so on. To anyone who knows the United States this picture is, of course, nonsense. Not only do "capitalist" groups fight among themselves, revealing little consciousness of a common class interest, but their power is partly checked by the influence of organized

---

[5] The reference here is not to Hawaii, but to Johnston and Enderbury Islands, Okinawa, Guam, American Samoa, and so forth.

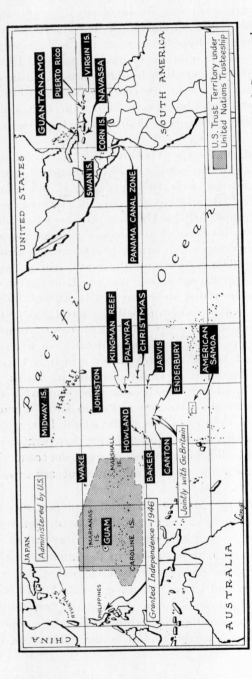

Map 8.1 Dependent Territories of the United States. source: Drawn by Russell H. Lenz, Chief Cartographer of *The Christian Science Monitor.* Reprinted by permission from The Christian Science Publishing Society. All rights reserved.

The Virgin Islands, east of Puerto Rico in the Caribbean Sea, were purchased from Denmark in 1917. Residents are citizens of the United States. They elect a unicameral legislature, but their Governor is appointed by the President of the United States. The Department of the Interior in Washington has responsibility for the islands.

The Panama Canal Zone is a United States reservation granted by a treaty signed in 1904 with the Republic of Panama. The zone is administered by Canal Zone government and the Panama Canal Company. The Governor of the zone and the president of the company are the same person. He reports to the Secretary of the Army.

Guam is the largest of the Marianas Islands in the Pacific. It was ceded to the United States by Spain after the Spanish-American War and now is the chief Pacific base of the Strategic Air Command. The people of Guam are American citizens, but do not vote for President. They do elect a unicameral legislature, however. The Governor of the island is appointed by the United States President.

American Samoa is composed of the seven eastern islands in the Samoan Islands, 2,300 miles southwest of Hawaii. The United States was given possession of them under an 1899 convention with Britain and Germany. The citizens elect a bi-

cameral legislature, but are American nationals, as distinct from American citizens.

Wake Island was annexed from Spain in 1899. With its sister islands, Wilkes and Peale, the group covered only about 2,000 acres. Population in 1950 was 349.

The Midway Islands were discovered by the United States in 1859 and acquired in 1867. They occupy two square miles. Population in 1950 was 416.

Other small islands are Johnston, Canton, and Enderbury Islands (population, 44); Howland, Jarvis, and Baker Islands (population, 10); Kingman Reef; Palmyra; Swan Islands; Corn Islands; and Navassa.

The Caroline, Marshall, and Marianas Islands (except for Guam) are not possessions of the United States, but are administered by Washington under a United Nations Trusteeship. Eniwetok is included in the Marshall Islands group.

The Ryukyu Islands, which include Okinawa, are administered under Article III of the Japanese-American peace treaty. Japan retains what is called "residual sovereignty" over the islands.

SOURCE: Reprinted by permission from *The Christian Science Monitor* © 1961, The Christian Science Publishing Society, All rights reserved.

labor, and by the mechanisms of government control acting in the name of consumers or of the national interest. In fact, far from dictating government policies, business groups typically express the view that government action is antibusiness, for example, in its tax, labor, or antitrust policies. At the same time any unprejudiced observer can see clearly that the American worker is far from living in the state of misery that Marx depicted as the inevitable lot of the proletarian.

Surprisingly enough, many Americans, following in the old agrarian populist tradition of suspicion of eastern business and banking interests, have readily accepted a watered-down version of the Marxist image of American society in conceiving of the United States as ruled by a "power elite"; although when one has stripped away the inconsistencies and factual inaccuracies in this theory, it adds nothing to the truism that the functioning of any complex organization requires the existence of a leadership group.

One must acknowledge that in American society as in most other societies, less than in some, more than in others, money is of political importance. Candidates favorable to business interests are in a better position to raise money for their campaigns, and pressure groups use money in entertaining influential members of Congress, while government attempts not to frighten or to offend business interests for fear that this would undermine investors' confidence. Many of these relations between the possession of money and the exercise of political influence are to be deplored, such as the need of even the most able candidate for office to secure substantial financial backing to defray the expenses of his candidacy. This is, nevertheless, a very long way from saying that the United States is controlled by monied interests, and businessmen in fact typically regard government with suspicion and hostility. Unfortunately the legend of capitalist control of the United States is accepted all too readily by people in countries where the dominance of the well-to-do prepares the ground for the acceptance of a Marxist image of the world.

One of the strongest arguments of those hostile to the United States is the existence in America of racial discrimination—and this certainly offers legitimate grounds on which to criticize American society. The nature and extent of discrimination in the United States is generally quite misunderstood abroad; one frequently meets with conceptions of daily mass lynchings in the South, or with the belief that the federal government prohibits Negroes from exercising the same rights as whites. However, the reality is bad enough and cannot be excused away.

It is paradoxical that so many people abroad should believe that the disorders that have accompanied the Negro's quest for equality in Little Rock, at the University of Mississippi, and elsewhere are black marks against the United States. Viewed in the proper perspective, they are surely signs of hope. In the long decades during which there were no comparable racial disturbances in the South, the oppression of the Negro was complete. That disturbances erupt is a sign that change is under way; it would be unrealistic to believe that a change of this magnitude can take place without the rupture of the normal façade of law and order in the South.

The United States need find no cause for shame in the position its government has taken on questions of human rights, furthermore. Henry Cabot Lodge made this point, which should not be lost sight of, in casting the vote of the United States in the UN Security Council in favor of the discussion of racial problems in South Africa:

> Let me say to the members of the Council that the United States approaches this question with no false pride at all. We recognize that many countries, and the United States must be included on that list, cannot be content with the progress which they have made in the field of human rights and that we must continue our efforts as we are doing to provide full equality of opportunity for all of our citizens.
>
> In many countries unsanctioned violations of human rights continue to occur. But we think there is an important distinction between situations where governments are actively promoting human rights and fundamental freedoms for all without distinction as to race, sex, language or religion, and situations where governmental policy runs counter to this.[6]

A final criticism of American society made by Marxists, and indeed by non-Marxists too—a criticism that the present writer believes contains a great deal of substance—has to do with the fact that under the American economic system, the laws of supply and demand extend not only to manufactured products but in part also to cultural and educational areas. This has reached ludicrous extremes, as for example in the case of television, where the establishment of the medium on a profit-making basis has resulted in the dominance of programming by the advertisers.

Moreover, the exaltation of private enterprise has unfortunately led to a reluctance to support nonprofit public enterprises even in such necessary areas as the schools, which have difficulty raising enough money to support themselves. As a result, the United States is amply supplied with advertising copywriters, small businessmen, and salesmen, but ludicrously short of teachers, nurses, and social workers. John Kenneth Galbraith has written eloquently of this social imbalance in the following words:

---

[6] As reported in the New York *Times,* March 31, 1960.

The contrast was and remains evident not alone to those who read. The family which takes its mauve and cerise, air-conditioned, power-steered, and power-braked automobile out for a tour passes through cities that are badly paved, made hideous by litter, blighted buildings, billboards, and posts for wires that should long since have been put underground. They pass on into a countryside that has been rendered largely invisible by commercial art. (The goods which the latter advertise have an absolute priority in our value system. Such aesthetic considerations as a view of the countryside accordingly come second. On such matters we are consistent.) They picnic on exquisitely packaged food from a portable icebox by a polluted stream and go on to spend the night at a park which is a menace to public health and morals. Just before dozing off on an air mattress, beneath a nylon tent, amid the stench of decaying refuse, they may reflect vaguely on the curious unevenness of their blessings. Is this, indeed, the American genius?[7]

THE AMERICAN CRITIQUE
OF THE SOVIET UNION

For the sake of symmetry, a few words should be inserted here on the validity of United States indictments of the Soviet Union and its ways. These indictments probably need not be treated in detail since they are doubtless familiar to the reader. The focus of the more telling anti-Soviet arguments is surely on the lack of freedom in Soviet life (rather than, for example, on the shortage of consumer goods, which is so much commented on, on both sides of the Iron Curtain). In this regard, it should however be noted that much of what one hears is founded on incorrect information—for example, the common belief that in the Soviet Union personal property is altogether prohibited (private property is allowed, and can indeed be inherited, but not property in productive facilities), or that religious observance does not exist (religious observance is harassed, but continues to exist nevertheless.)

Over and above the false impressions, however, there undeniably exists a high degree of coercion in the system, retaining always the potentiality of again becoming arbitrariness and brutality.

It used to be possible for the apologist for the Soviet Union, Russian or foreign, to maintain that stories of the liquidation on trumped-up charges of "opponents of the regime" were inventions of the capitalist press. This is hardly possible any longer since Khrushchev's revelations at the Twentieth Party Congress of the stupidities and brutalities of Stalin's period. Now that the harsher features of Soviet rule

---

[7] John Kenneth Galbraith, *The Affluent Society*. Boston: Houghton Mifflin Company, 1957, p. 253.

have been mitigated since the death of Stalin, however, it has become more fashionable to argue that the excesses of Stalin's reign were due to the personal foibles of the dictator but are not inherent in the system.

This argument, too, has limited validity. Beneath the surface of Soviet society the essential form of the police state remains, despite the elimination of its more extreme features; with every gesture of "liberalization" the Soviet leaders are careful to point out that these concessions are made only provisionally, and if the narrow degree of freedom conceded is "abused," then the repression can always begin again. In other words, Soviet citizens are allowed a slightly expanded degree of freedom, provided they do not make full use of it. If they should, there seems no doubt that Stalinist methods of repression could then be brought back into action.

There is an apocryphal story that two envelopes of sealed instructions were left by Stalin for his successor. On the outside of the first envelope was marked, "To be opened in case of emergency." On the outside of the second was written, "To be opened in case of extreme emergency." Just before the Twentieth Party Congress, so the story goes, agricultural production was falling, there was unrest in the satellites, and Khrushchev opened the first envelope. Inside was a piece of paper that read, "Blame it all on me." And so Khrushchev made his famous speech denouncing the crimes of Stalin. However, unrest in the satellites grew and led eventually to the Hungarian uprising. Khrushchev opened the second envelope; the message read, "Do as I did," and the tanks were sent into Budapest.

A more fundamental objection exists to the view that the assassinations and executions and forced labor camps of Stalin's reign were due solely to personal idiosyncrasies of the dictator, however. Lenin himself did not shrink from the use of terror against opponents of the regime; while the person originally thought most likely to succeed Lenin, Trotsky, had given every indication that his rule would be as bloody and repressive as that of Stalin later turned out to be. This is especially the case since the absence of stable mechanisms for assuring the succession to high office in the Soviet Union has twice already resulted in a lengthy struggle for power, with a third such struggle recently begun. In this type of competition the odds on survival and ultimate victory lie with the most unscrupulous. The fact that Lenin was succeeded by a ruthless and bloody tyrant was thus no accident, but the logical outcome of a system that provides for no restraints on power.

After all, this is the whole point of constitutional government. A dictator may turn out to be relatively benevolent, as Khrushchev did. He may somehow even be the wisest and most generous of men. But one has no guarantee that anything of the sort will occur. What a constitutional state does is to arrange the structure of powers so that it need take no chances on the fortuitous benevolence of the individuals who will occupy the places of highest power.

It may still be possible to concede that arbitrariness, coercion, and even brutality are necessary features of the system, and yet to maintain that these are justifiable in terms of the idyllic state of affairs that will eventually result. This view must necessarily be based on the sheerest act of faith, however, for there is no basis other than faith for believing that the Soviet Union will evolve into anything substantially different from what it is today.

THE LIMITS OF PROPAGANDA

Before leaving the subject of the ideological conflict, however, several points need to be made about propaganda—since the ideological conflict is, after all, a propaganda war—and how it relates to the Cold War over-all. There are of course technical problems, not completely understood at present, that the conduct of propaganda presents.

There are also limitations to what propaganda can achieve in the implantation of ideas, since the truth has a stubborn way of making itself known; people are, after all, accustomed to a certain amount of falsehood in their own personal relations with others and are always ready to look for the meanings between the lines.

It makes a certain amount of sense, accordingly, to think of propaganda as advertising. Publicity techniques can achieve a great deal, but only within the limits determined by the quality of the product. This should not be lost sight of by concerned Americans; a great deal of improvement of American society is in order before it can legitimately be presented as the ideal that others should strive to emulate.

Yet in a larger sense it must be acknowledged that time and time again what has proved crucial for the assumption of one direction or another in a nation's policy has not been attitudes of attraction or repulsion to another state's way of life or ideology, although these have played a part, but have been the interests that were at stake. The United States allied herself with the Soviet Union in the common struggle against Germany, despite American antipathy to Soviet ideology; currently China is drawing away from the Soviet Union, despite the heritage of a common ideology. The abiding factors of national interest, especially interests in power and security, tend ultimately to be the decisive ones in the formation of policy. This remains true of today's uncommitted states for whose allegiance the United States and the Soviet Union compete. No matter how much they may dislike the Russian repression of the Hungarian uprising on the one hand, or the attitude of American segregationists on the other, no matter how much they are attracted by the principles of Marx or the principles of Jefferson, the policies of the underdeveloped countries will be those that they conceive to be in their interest. Viewed in this light, the task of the United States is thus not so much to talk the uncommitted countries into agreeing with American principles—although this may help, and certainly should not hurt—but rather to show them that American purposes are compatible with their purposes, that a community of interests exists that can be developed to the mutual advantage of both. This subject will be taken up again in a subsequent chapter.

SUGGESTED READINGS

Arnold, Thurman, *The Folklore of Capitalism*. New Haven, Conn.: Yale University Press, 1937.

Berle, Adolf A., *The Twentieth Century Capitalist Revolution*. New York: Macmillan, 1955.

Dahl, Robert, and Charles Lindblom, *Politics, Economics and Welfare*, chapter 1. New York: Harper & Row, 1953.

Fainsod, Merle, *How Russia Is Ruled*. Cambridge, Mass.: Harvard University Press, 1953.

Galbraith, John Kenneth, *American Capitalism: The Concept of Countervailing Power*. Boston: Houghton Mifflin, 1952.

———, *The Affluent Society*. Boston: Houghton Mifflin, 1958.

Marx, Karl, and Friedrich Engels, *The Communist Manifesto*. New York: Appleton, 1955.

Mills, C. Wright, *Listen, Yankee: The Revolution in Cuba*. New York: Ballentine, 1960.

Nove, Alec, *The Soviet Economy*. New York: Praeger, 1962.

Shaffer, Harry G. (ed.), *The Soviet Economy*. New York: Appleton, 1963.

9

Cold War:
The Military Dimension

PRINCIPLES OF MILITARY POLICY

United States military policy is a subject of considerable complexity, if only for the reason that to master its ramifications requires a fair understanding of weapons technology; and accepted strategic concepts are undergoing continual and subtle change. Nevertheless, it is possible to isolate some abiding principles of policy.

1. It is clearly accepted in decision-making circles—despite what some generals and admirals seem to say on occasion, and despite the fears of some nervous publicists in the "peace movement" that are stimulated by such statements—that war is intrinsically undesirable, and that the United States will not "initiate" a war. This is at least true of war in the traditional sense, involving the large-scale use of national forces across international boundaries. It may not be true as far as what might be called "sponsored internal wars" are concerned, as will be seen below. Moreover, it is always possible that a military action intended to fall short of the initiation of war will overreach itself, and result in war. The conscious initiation of world war remains, nevertheless, out of the question.

2. Although the United States disclaims any intention of beginning a war, it is, nevertheless, possible that the Soviet Union or China may do so; accordingly, it is necessary to have forces and weapons that stand ready to repel an aggressive action launched by a member of the Chinese or Soviet camps, or indeed by any other country. The basic military posture of the

United States is thus defensive, and is premised on the purpose of "containing" attempts at the expansion of the area under the control of powers, specifically those under Russian or Chinese leadership, that exhibit intentions inimical to United States security interests.

3. The primary use of United States military forces is therefore as deterrents, that is, their mere existence is intended to convey to a potential enemy the fact that any aggressive action on his part would result in probable defeat of his forces, and in any case in the infliction of heavy losses.

Several comments may be made about this deterrent function of United States military force. One should first note that since the most effective implicit threat of deterrence is that should an aggressor launch a war he would be defeated, then the forces needed to deter the aggressor at any level of possible conflict are the same as those that would be needed to fight and if possible win a war fought at that level. Second, it should be perfectly clear that the creation of United States military forces that are prepared for war is in itself a preparation for peace. At the superficial level this is clearly paradoxical and excites much half-educated scorn, as well as enabling Soviet propaganda to charge that United States military preparations show that Americans want war. Despite this paradox, however, the logic of the Soviet charge does not hold; the maxim, "If you want peace, prepare for war" has a respectable lineage and is based on perfectly reasonable premises. Finally, one should note that the idea of deterrence assumes that the potential aggressor will weigh the likelihood of failure before embarking on an aggressive action, and will refrain from initiating hostilities if these seem doomed to an unsuccessful, or perhaps, a costly though successful outcome. This premise is in turn based on an assumption that the potential aggressor acts rationally; while this is normally the case, it is not so always and inevitably—there have been leaders of aggressive states that have acted irrationally, as some of Hitler's acts show.

4. In addition to the forces required for a mission of deterrence of war, United States military forces are used also to support national foreign policy in lesser actions that fall short of war itself. There is a range of such actions, such as the Fall 1962 blockade of Cuba, or the Berlin airlift of 1948–1949, that demonstrate that armed forces have their uses over and above employment in actual combat, and over and above simple deterrence of outright war.

THE LOGIC OF DETERRENCE

The leading priority, then, in the American military effort is the deterrence of all-out war. Comprehension of what this signifies all too often gets lost amid the paradoxes that the mission entails. It is accordingly necessary to examine the concept with some care.

If a general third world war should actually occur today—a contingency that the present writer believes is unlikely to the point of impossibility—it would presumably begin with an attack on the cities of North America by Soviet long-range missiles launched on the shortest route, which is over the North Pole. The first implication of this premise is that should the leaders of the Soviet Union ever decide consciously to inaugurate such a war they would doubtless begin it in this classic manner, which would take maximum advantage of surprise—an extremely important and perhaps crucial factor in the age of ballistic missiles—and attempt to achieve maximum destructive effect with the first blow. Put in another fashion, it would make no sense whatsoever for such a war to be deliberately initiated by an attack of less than maximum scope, such as an invasion of West Berlin, or an attack on United States warships blockading Cuba. Such lesser ranges of violence could in fact be employed, but in no case as the *deliberate* initiation of a general world war.

If such a general war should occur, one would guess that destruction of life would occur on a colossal scale, which it has become fashionable to describe as the end of human civilization, although the present writer is inclined to take such an evaluation with the proverbial grain of salt. In any case the extent of the damage that would be inflicted on either participant in such a war puts fighting on this scale outside the conventional conception of war as an instrument of policy, and makes the decision to fight under those circumstances quite insane. This leads to the grand paradox of deterrence in the nuclear age: Deterrence is achieved by preparing to fight if attacked, and by conveying to the hypothetical antagonist the impression that one is perfectly sincere in this intention; yet at the same time one shrinks from a commitment, however hypothetical, on this scale, and disbelieves in the possibility that the contingency that it envisions will ever actually arise. One has to be sincere in his intentions to fight, one has to make all the requisite technical preparations to fight, and yet, if one is maximally sincere and well-prepared, the occasion to fight will never arise. This underlying paradox is at the root of the fundamentally schizophrenic situation in which American strategic doctrine finds itself, although it is also complicated by a further series of paradoxes.

One of the major requirements for a deterrent to be effective is that the threat to retaliate be a credible one. If the potential aggressor does not take the threat of retaliation seriously, he is hardly likely to be deterred. Also the credibility of the deterrent is heightened to the degree to which retaliation can be expected to follow automatically on the act of aggression. The more automatically retaliation will be called into play, the more effective the deterrent will be in any case, since the longer the time period after the initiation of hostilities in which the retaliatory force is not used, the greater chance there will be that it will be destroyed by the aggressor's attack. From both points of view, then, the more automatic the deterrent is, the more credible it is.

On the other hand, however, a totally automatic deterrent would be a deterrent removed from the realm of human control and thus more likely to set itself in motion unintentionally. This is a danger that cannot be tolerated, especially in the era of intercontinental ballistic missiles, which cannot be recalled once dispatched,[1] and which could travel from North America to their Soviet targets in less than fifteen minutes. During the period, now ended, in which the American deterrent was composed primarily of long-range bombers, the problem was of course not so acute, and a launching arrangement was developed that minimized most of the difficulties referred to. This was the so-called fail-safe system under which the bombers of the Strategic Air Command take to the air when alerted that an attack is under way, but automatically return after having gone a certain distance between their bases and their targets, unless specifically given a direct order to continue onward. This arrangement attempts to combine speed of response with the requirements of safety. One can, of course, imagine situations in which the arrangement would not work as envisaged, and many publicists and writers of fiction have expended a good deal of energy in this effort.

In the era that we are entering, in which bombers are replaced by missiles in the function of strategic deterrent, the problem has taken on some new dimensions, but at the same time has become simpler to resolve. In the age of missiles effectiveness and credibility of the deterrent suffer if the missiles are highly vulnerable to attack and stand a chance of being wiped out by the initial Soviet strike. In other words, if American missiles were all located above ground in the continental United States, powered by liquid fuels, which require a relatively longer period of time for the launching, it is conceivable that the aggressor might count on destroying them in the initial strike, and they would, therefore, not serve as a completely credible deterrent. Accordingly maximum credibility, and most effective deterrence, is achieved where missiles are powered by solid fuels and are buried in relatively invulnerable emplacements below ground, or are made highly mobile and not possible to pinpoint as targets. Such mobility, for example, might be achieved by mounting rockets on railroad flatcars.

The United States has taken a long stride toward the achievement of an invulnerable and therefore a safe and effective deterrent with the construction of atomic-powered submarines capable of firing Polaris

---

[1] Although it might well be possible to destroy them in the air.

missiles while still submerged below the water's surface. Since such submarines are extremely difficult to destroy in the aggressor's first strike, the problem of the hair-trigger response is avoided; the commander of a Polaris submarine could await the actual destruction of much of the United States before launching his retaliatory rockets, which sharply reduces the possibility that the United States would launch an attack on misinformation or misinterpretation of, say, ambiguous radar signals. At the present stage of weapons technology, the Polaris submarine thus represents an ultimate deterrent in the sense that the aggressor faces the certainty of destruction even if his initial raid on the home territory of his antagonist is totally successful. A fleet of Polaris submarines seems, accordingly, to remove all incentive for a surprise attack on the part of a would-be aggressor by eliminating the advantages of surprise itself. This is so even if future developments in antisubmarine warfare should make such warfare more effective than it is at present; given the destructive power of a single Polaris missile, an aggressor would not dare rationally to launch his attack even if he were able to find and destroy ninety percent of his enemy's Polaris fleet.

The fact that its invulnerability makes a deterrent force such as the Polaris fleet a "second strike" force, able to ride out the enemy's first blow, not only eliminates the "hair-trigger" element in its *response,* but also removes the temptation to *initiate* a war faced by the government that knows that allowing the enemy the first blow is equivalent to accepting defeat. It does, however, complicate the problem of communication with, and control over, the commander with immediate authority over the missiles by the top national leadership.

It was believed for some time that the conversion of the United States deterrent to one based on the atomic-powered submarine would also have immediate political advantages in that—because the submarine can cruise almost indefinitely without refueling—it would eliminate the need for overseas bases, which are often a source of friction with the country in which they are located, and whose existence has been used by some countries as a sort of blackmail weapon to extort political concessions from the United States. It is true that the conversion to Polaris submarines and the phasing out of medium-range bombers as a major component of the deterrent makes it possible to eliminate a large proportion of America's overseas bases; however, it has become clear that even the Polaris submarine can use foreign bases for maintenance and other purposes. It seems, moreover, that there is likely to be greater local resistance to a Polaris submarine base than to air bases because of the widespread fear of radioactive contamination should such a submarine meet with an accident that caused its atomic fuel to be scattered. Needless to say, such anxieties are stimulated and fanned by adherents of the world Communist movement; but they are present in any case and have already led to anti-Polaris demonstrations in Britain, where a Polaris base is already situated, and will doubtless lead to further demonstrations if and when projected bases are developed elsewhere, such as the ones planned in Italy and in Japan.

During the years of Secretary McNamara's tenure at the Defense Department, strategic policy took some steps in the direction of a "counter-force" strategy, that is, a strategy that is designed for the destruction of the enemy's armed forces, weapons, and military installations should war break out, while sparing civilian lives and cities to the extent possible. In this sense it would be possible, at least in principle, for the United States and the Soviet Union to limit a nuclear war that might break out between them should deterrence fail, even if their home territories were involved. Physical and doctrinal capability to act along these lines has now been added to the capability to destroy Soviet and Chinese cities, but has not been substituted for it.

THE ARMS RACE

One of the characteristic features of the current American military effort is the rapid rate of technological change in the weapons that compose the nuclear deterrent, and also in those designed for deterrence, or use, in the limited ranges of conflict. Accordingly an arms race has developed with the Soviet Union in which the stress is less upon the amount of arms and the size of military forces than on the superior technical characteristics of new weapons systems.

Several features of significance need to be pointed out about the contemporary arms race. In the first place, the requirements for secrecy in weapons development are heavy, and scientific and technical espionage has become more important. However, the requirement for secrecy conflicts to a certain extent with one of the necessary features of deterrence, that a possible aggressor be made aware of the damage that could be done to his forces and his homeland should he initiate armed conflict.

The need to demonstrate one's power while at the same time maintaining military secrecy, a dual imperative not new with the Cold War, has led to the heightened salience of several rather curious traditional practices. One is the custom of staging military parades and reviews in which representatives of other states are permitted to look at one's latest weapons. These reviews have frequently caused revisions in the estimates made of one's capabilities by the antagonist; it is an open question whether this increases the degree to which the enemy is deterred, or merely stimulates him to greater efforts and increased military spending. Another paradoxical custom to which this situation gives rise is the practice of sending military attachés to other countries, and of allowing such attachés to serve in embassies on one's own soil. The job of a military attaché is to gather as much information as he can about the military forces and intentions of the country in which he is stationed; he is thus a sort of licensed spy, although if he should go too far and become too zealous in his information-gathering activities he can be expelled from the country for espionage. Nevertheless, the system of military attachés allows states to gain information on each other's capabilities and promotes greater realism and rationality in the estimates of power that enter into policy decisions.

A paradox in weapons procurement policy created by the rapid rate of technological change is that although there in a high rate of obsolescence in weapons systems, with each design rapidly being superseded by a better one, nevertheless the new weapons are so complex that the time lag between the resolution of the theoretical problems involved in designing the weapon and the time at which the weapon is actually ready for use—an average of perhaps four years for the United States—means that very often weapons become obsolete before they have actually been produced. Nevertheless, in order to avoid a gap in the equipment of the armed forces it is often necessary to continue with the production schedules of weapons whose replacement has already been planned.

An arms race conducted at the level of technical proficiency that both protagonists in the Cold War have reached requires the expenditure of fantastic sums of money. On the whole Congress has shown itself prepared to appropriate such sums; in fact it has not been unknown for Congress to appropriate larger sums for certain categories of defense expenditures than were requested by the executive. Now one would think that the greater capacity of the American economy—the United States gross national product, that is, the sum total of all goods and services produced in a given year, is currently about twice that of the Soviet Union, although exact comparisons are for various reasons very difficult to make—means that the United States is better equipped to engage in a sustained arms race than the Soviet Union. However, thus far the Soviet Union has been able to spend an amount roughly comparable to that spent by the United States for military purposes each year; in other words the Soviet Union is spending a much higher proportion of its national product on weapons and men than the United States. A great many other comparisons must enter into an evaluation of the relative potentialities of the two systems for waging sustained Cold War, however. For example, although the Soviet national product is at present about half that of the United States, it is growing at a faster rate; that is, the national product of the United States grows annually at perhaps three or four percent, whereas the Soviet national product typically grows at between four and seven percent. Actually such comparisons are extremely inexact because of the different statistical practices followed by the two countries. Moreover, the Soviet economy has been growing faster than the American only in its early stages of development, and as time passes its rate of growth seems to be slowing down.

When all is said and done there are causes for optimism for Americans who look at the technical factors giving advantage to one side or the other in the arms race. Military spending rises continually, and in recent years the Soviet Union has shown signs of extreme concern that its military expenditures are consuming too great a share of the national product; the commitment of Soviet leaders since Stalin's death to provide larger quantities of consumers' goods is well known. The United States, on the other hand, has a great deal of slack in the economy and could, without a doubt, raise its military spending substantially each year for many years to come. As more expensive weapons are devised, therefore, the Soviet Union may find that it cannot continue to compete with the United States on equal terms. Some observers have suggested that it is economic factors of this type that lie behind the sporadic Soviet attempts to achieve an agreement on disarmament. Whether or not this is the case, it would be difficult to say that the United States is placed at any disadvantage whatsoever in its continuing participation in the arms race. If anything, the signs suggest that the tactic of "peaceful coexistence" is on the road to becoming an economic necessity for the Soviet Union and not simply the current tactical line.

DO ARMS RACES LEAD TO WAR?

One commonly hears it said that arms races inevitably lead to war. If this were the case, the prospects would be discouraging indeed, since United States policy is based on the assumption that deterrent forces are necessary to keep the peace, and yet the attempt to achieve effective deterrence under conditions of rapid technological change implies engaging in an arms race. However, it is not completely true that arms races necessarily lead to war. Arms races in the past have sometimes led to wars, it is true; but they have also led to situations in which one contender in the arms race has realized that it cannot maintain the pace and has given up its attempts to achieve a parity of power.

A classic instance of a state's backing out of an arms race is that of France, which had engaged in a naval arms race with Britain during the 1860s but gave up when it became clear that the British were determined to maintain their lead indefinitely. It is also possible for the political tension that underlies an arms race between two states to be superseded by a different conflict. For example, the British and Russians called off their rivalry in Asia in 1905 in order to create a common front against the aggressive gestures of the Germans; and the traditional Franco-German rivalry was superseded after the end of World War II by the tension between both states and the Soviet Union. It is even possible, although rare, for the hostility that underlies an arms race to evaporate without being superseded by a greater conflict; examples of this are the agreements reached by the United States and Great Britain to eliminate war vessels on the Great Lakes, and by Argentina and Chile to call off an arms race occasioned by disputes over border territory. Nevertheless, one should certainly acknowledge the possibility that the present arms race can lead to war.

It is true that the existence of an arms race in itself can create circumstances conducive to war. This occurs in the case of the so-called preventive war. A preventive war occurs typically when one side is ahead in an arms race but realizes that the other side is about to catch up, overtake it, and maintain a permanent superiority that would enable it to be victorious in any future conflict. In other words, a preventive war is fought when a state believes it currently has its last chance of being able to win a war; or at least that if it begins a war now the terms on which it will fight will be more favorable than those likely at any future time. In the present arms race between the United States and the Soviet Union it is unlikely that such a situation will arise, however. It may have existed, in a sense, during the early post-war years when the United States had the atomic bomb and the Soviet Union did not. If the United States were to launch a preventive war on the Soviet Union, that would have been the time; the fact that the United States did not attack the Russians then supports the thesis that Americans would not start a preventive war so long as there existed the slightest possibility of avoiding war altogether —but so many other factors are involved that the argument cannot be regarded as conclusively settled.

It is highly unlikely that this type of situation will emerge in the current arms race because, given the destructive potentialities of the weapons that even the "weaker" side in the arms race possesses, neither state will be presented with an opportunity of "winning" a war fought with nuclear weapons, no matter at what time hostilities begin. The only time a preventive war situation could again arise would be if one side in the Cold War appeared on the point of developing an absolutely impregnable defense; if such an absolute defense were possible—for example, some means of destroying an enemy's missiles with 100 percent accuracy—it would then be possible for the side possessing such a defense to blackmail the other into making unlimited political concessions, knowing that it could destroy the other's territory while itself being perfectly immune from attack. It might then seem that one of the states involved in the arms race would be tempted to launch a preventive war before the other side could install its "absolute" defensive system. However, this is only a formal possibility. Given the vast damage that would be inflicted on one state by the other's nuclear weapons, it seems most probable that if such a situation should develop, the state without the impregnable defense would simply yield to the inevitable and resign itself to the status of a dependent second-class power.

A further type of situation exists, at least hypothetically—not logically derived from the nature of the arms race itself—in which war might occur between the United States and the Soviet Union. This is the case of the so-called pre-emptive war. Accepted by Soviet military doctrine, and on the margins of acceptance by the United States, although not at the time of writing actually incorporated into United States military policy, is the idea that if certain information should be received that the other side were on the point of launching an attack, it would be rational for the defensive side to launch its own attack first. One can visualize the pre-emptive strike in terms of the classic western hero who draws his gun and shoots the villain after, out of the corner of his eye, he has seen the villain reaching for his own weapon. The concept of the pre-emptive strike need occasion no alarm if only one could be sure that the information that the other side was about to attack was absolutely correct. One fears that if the doctrine of the pre-emptive strike is ever completely accepted as United States policy in the Cold War, there would exist a danger that the hero might draw his gun and shoot his adversary in response to what was only a nervous twitch on the other fellow's part. The development of a completely second-strike, that is, a stable and invulnerable, deterrent force would make adoption of a pre-emptive strategy unnecessary in any case.

LIMITED WAR

Up to this point the use of military force to deter an all-out nuclear war between the United States and the Soviet Union has been discussed. However, the possibility exists that there will continue to be in the years to come military clashes between the forces of the two states, or of other states allied with them, on a less than total scale. The next question one must take up is that of what forces are appropriate to deter, and, if necessary, to fight limited wars.

One has to take some care in delineating the concept of limited war, since it is intellectually difficult for many people to master. Until the Korean conflict broke out in June of 1950 United States military policy tended to assume that any clash between the forces of the Soviet bloc and those of the United States or its allies would be equivalent to a third world war. In fact, nothing seems a priori more implausible than that two sides in a war should try to limit it by refraining from attacking targets of military value, or by refraining to use weapons at their disposal. One would be tempted to say that such a phenomenon were impossible if it had not actually occurred in Korea. During the Korean conflict both sides did impose limitations on their conduct, the Chinese Communists refraining from attacking United States supply vessels and bases outside Korea itself, the Allied forces refraining from attacking Chinese bases across the Chinese–North Korean border. Of course, limiting the war in this fashion was extremely unpopular in the United States and occasioned much political controversy, especially after President Truman relieved General MacArthur of his command in Korea when the general refused to stop speaking out against the strategy of limitation.

Until the North Korean attack on South Korea presented the problem of limited war with such force, United States strategy had been based on the assumption that the forces that acted to deter general nuclear war, if they were capable of inhibiting a major attack, would surely be even more capable of deterring any attack on a lesser scale. During the Eisenhower administration this assumption was revived (even though, paradoxically, it had already been rendered obsolete) and christened "massive retaliation." The doctrine of massive retaliation, as stated by Secretary of State Dulles, took the line that the general nuclear deterrent of the United States, that is, the ability to destroy Moscow or Peking with atomic weapons, would be called into play in the case of any aggressive act initiated by a Communist state, no matter where it occurred or what weapons it employed. In other words, if a limited attack were launched with conventional weapons anywhere in Europe or Asia the United States intimated that it would respond by expanding the scope of the conflict, perhaps even by atom-bombing Moscow or Peking. This was not explicitly stated, but it was implied by Dulles' statement that in the event of such a small attack the United States would retaliate "massively" at places and by means "of her own choosing."

Massive retaliation, understood as the threat to meet a limited challenge with a total response, did not provide an adequate defensive posture for the United States. Dulles himself recognized this, albeit belatedly, before his death. One might even date the obsolescence of the policy from 1949, the year the Soviet Union developed its own atomic bomb. After that date, or at least after the Soviet Union had a supply of deliverable atomic weapons, and especially after the Soviet Union developed nuclear weapons, it had to become a premise of United States policy that a nuclear attack on the Soviet Union would be met by a similar attack on the United States. The button labeled "Moscow" was now also labeled "New York." Accordingly, one became extremely reluctant to press that button. And yet the policy of massive retaliation assumed that American policy makers would stand ready to launch an attack on the Soviet Union itself as a response to, say, a conventional attack by a Soviet satellite on a small state in Southeast Asia. Given the possibility of Soviet retaliation against the United States, this threat by the United States lost its credibility and thus could not be expected to act as a deterrent. It became more than likely that the Soviet Union would believe the threat to begin a third world war over a border incursion into Cambodia to be no more than a bluff, and so would ignore it. Given the horrendous consequences that Soviet nuclear capability now posed, it was also likely that faced with such a limited challenge United States policy makers would fail to retaliate and the threat would in fact become no more than a bluff. This was especially the case given the ability of the Soviet Union and its allies to present such a limited attack in the disputed areas of the world in an ambiguous fashion, so that American policy makers could not be completely sure that the Soviet Union was responsible. If a small Soviet Asian satellite did in actuality cross a vaguely demarcated border with a handful of troops, and if conflicting reports of what had happened reached Washington together with a firm Soviet denial that the Soviet Union had anything to do with the case one can reasonably assume that the threat embodied in the doctrine of massive retaliation would never be carried out.

In early 1965 the Johnson administration nevertheless employed what might be called a limited massive retaliation strategy in the attempt to force a negotiated settlement of the war in South Vietnam. Bombing attacks on Communist North Vietnam were carried out at the same time as the United States stipulated that it did not want a general world war or even a general Southeast Asian war. The failure of these attacks to achieve their aim indicated that "limited massive retaliation" was likely to be as ineffective as the threat of massive retaliation itself had been.

After the lessons taught by the Korean war had made themselves felt, the search began to discover other ways of meeting the challenge of less than total war. The most reasonable conclusion was that to achieve maximum credibility the range of deterrent forces available to the West must be wide and capable of graduation. That is, the appropriate strategy for the West was to command a variety of forces that would make possible a flexibility in retaliation and the threat of retaliation, enabling deterrence or counterattack to be pitched at the same level of force as the attack itself. This is, after all, the military posture most appropriate to a defensive power that necessarily must react to initiatives taken by the aggressor; the aggressor can initiate warfare at times and places and by means of his own choosing; defensive action is by its nature framed in terms of the attack to which it responds. Moreover, the approach that stresses the desirability of range and flexibility in the forces available to the West derives further support from the fact that there are other situations besides attack by a Soviet bloc country that require the use of force. The British, of course, retain residual colonial obligations that can involve them in local police actions from time to time. The United States may be called on to use limited forces in Latin America or Africa in situations in which a Soviet bloc country is not involved. In other words, the necessity of flexibility hardly needs to be argued.

The determination to maintain extensive and flexible forces implies a high level of defense expenditure, and a considerable manpower potential, however. It was no doubt because of reluctance to pay the amounts involved that the Eisenhower administration attempted to prolong the strategic life of the policy of massive retaliation, hoping to use the general nuclear deterrent, which had to be maintained anyhow, to deter threats at every level of violence, and thus to avoid expenditures on forces of less than nuclear capability. Since then, however, the United States and its allies have spent and will, doubtless, continue to spend for as long as it seems necessary to them, increasing amounts for defense.

THE USE OF ATOMIC WEAPONS IN LIMITED WAR

The likelihood that the determination to fight conventional wars if necessary leads to an increase in manpower requirements has fostered concern in some quarters. If one totals the population of the United States and its allies and compares the resulting figure with the number of inhabitants of the Soviet bloc countries, the latter shows a marked preponderance, reflecting the half-billion Chinese that the figures include. Several publicists have suggested that the countries of the West oppose the East's preponderance of manpower with a preponderance of firepower; that is, that the Communist superiority in men be overcome by a Western superiority in weapons.

Essentially, suggestions along these lines have been based on the premise that atomic and/or nuclear weapons can and should be developed for use in limited warfare. The problem immediately arises whether a limited war in which one side uses atomic or nuclear weapons can indeed be kept limited. Now one can conceive of different types of limits being imposed. A war can in principle be limited in terms of the area within which fighting takes place, or in terms of the types of targets attacked. The leading proponents of the use of unconventional weapons in limited warfare, Henry Kissinger and Rear Admiral Sir Anthony Buzzard, while proposing that limits be imposed on dimensions other than that of weapons—that is, in area and target selection— have nevertheless accepted the idea that limited wars should be limited in terms of the weapons used also. Admiral Buzzard proposed a distinction between atomic and nuclear weapons,[2] the former to be allowed in limited wars, the latter, not. Professor Kissinger argued in terms of limiting war to a specified level of destructiveness; thus nuclear weapons up to a certain explosive power could be used and the war still kept limited. Nevertheless, the conceptual difficulties involved in the attempt to conceive of wars that would be limited in terms of the weapons employed and still involve the use of unconventional weapons are overwhelming, and indeed Professor Kissinger himself has appeared in his recent writings to back away from the implications of his original position. In the first place the attempt to limit the fighting in terms of weapons poses the possibility of escalation, that is, that the implicit "rules of the game" will be violated slightly by one side, that the other side will retaliate by increasing the margin by which it violates the rules, and the process will spiral until the fighting passes out of the range of all restraint. Although there are important theoretical reasons, some of them discussed by Thomas Schelling in his able *Strategy of Conflict,* as to why it would be possible to maintain such limitations on warfare, one is, nevertheless, justified in retaining a certain skepticism that under combat conditions it would be possible to maintain such limits indefinitely.

Even if limits could be maintained, however, the use of atomic weapons entails other grim liabilities. The West, for example, playing its characteristically defensive role, would engage in a limited war only after the adversary had launched an attack. The war therefore would presumably be taking place on the soil of the Western ally, in the attempt to drive out the invader. If atomic weapons were used by the United States under those circumstances, the damage caused by the weapons, including the radiation damage, would be largely inflicted on allied populations, a highly undesirable outcome. A foretaste of what this would mean has been provided on a smaller scale by the use by United States and South Vietnamese air forces of napalm (jellied gasoline) in the war in South Vietnam.

Various other objections can be raised to the concept of limited war fought with atomic weapons on grounds ranging from the difficulty of finding appropriate targets in a limited-war situation to the possible propaganda losses suffered by the first power to use atomic weapons in battlefield combat. However, battlefield atomic weapons do exist and, in fact, are already assigned to Allied troops serving in Europe although special safeguards exist with respect to control of their nuclear warheads. This is highly paradoxical when one recalls that the original justification for the use of atomic weapons in limited conflict was to compensate the

---

[2] Nuclear (hydrogen) bombs being those in which nuclear fusion takes place, in addition to nuclear fission.

West for the manpower superiority essentially of the Chinese, who can hardly be expected to be confronting NATO troops in Europe. It is an open question whether the troops of the Red Army and the Warsaw Pact countries in eastern Europe do outnumber those belonging to the NATO alliance stationed in western Europe today; but even if war should break out in Europe the Red Army would have a considerable job on its hands occupying the satellite countries, the peoples of which would, in many cases, seize the opportunity to stage uprisings such as those that have occurred in East Germany, Poland, and Hungary over the last fifteen years. The reliability of the satellite armies is in any case questionable.

One is tempted to say that the occurrence of a limited war like that in Korea, that is, a war begun by the invasion of a pro-Western state by the forces of a neighbor, while certainly more likely to occur than general nuclear war, is likewise highly improbable. Imagine the development of such a limited war situation, consequent on an attack by a Soviet ally. The choice of response to the act of aggression lies with the defensive state and its big power ally. While they may respond in a limited fashion, the level at which the response is pitched would surely be one that would be adequate to repel the aggression. Since the invasion force itself would be a limited-war force, it would presumably be possible for the defensive states to meet it with an equal or somewhat superior force that would also fall within the range of limited capability. The aggressor is then faced with the alternatives of either raising the level of conflict, with the possibility of escalation and expansion of the war, or of accepting a limited defeat. If he had been aware at the outset that these alternatives would face him, however, it seems unlikely that he would have initiated the aggressive move in the first place. Given defensive alliances committed to fighting at less than total levels, it seems unlikely that limited wars in the sense of invasions across frontiers would be undertaken deliberately, except where there is a reasonable expectation of very rapid victory. In other words a limited war between forces of the Communist bloc and forces of the states allied to the West seems likely to occur only when the aggressor miscalculates the intentions of the defensive alliance. The Korean war itself, the exemplar of a limited war, had this type of origin. The North Koreans who invaded South Korea, and presumably their Russian allies, seem clearly to have assumed that the United States would not intervene, an assumption that seemed soundly based on statements of American strategic intentions; the United States had no explicit commitment to defend South Korea and indeed had appeared to exclude South Korea from its defense perimeter, while Congress had shown itself opposed to the maintenance of United States forces on the Korean peninsula.

Khrushchev acknowledged this general thesis explicitly and stated that he considered limited Korean-type wars excluded by reason of the mutual deterrence inherent in the current balance of power, just as general nuclear war was excluded.

"WARS OF NATIONAL LIBERATION"

At the same time, however, Khrushchev indicated that he believed a third type of war would continue to occur, and indeed, from the Soviet point of view, should continue to occur. This is the so-called "war of national liberation." The war of national liberation is essentially civil war, or fighting that does not overtly cross an international boundary; it is most likely to be guerrilla warfare. From the Soviet point of view these wars are an expression of class conflict in which the proletariat attempts to liberate itself from the exploitation of the capitalist class, which is in turn linked with the interests of international imperialism, that is, the United States and its allies.

If one reviews the events of the last few years, it is clear that this type of war has been the type that has occurred and that is still taking place today in many areas of the world. This category would include anticolonial wars, such as the one concluded some years ago in Algeria or those currently in progress in the Portuguese African territories; it also includes civil wars that have as their object the overthrow not of a foreign imperial power but of a native ruling class, or clique, such as Fidel Castro's guerrilla war against Batista, or the civil war waged by the republican forces in Yemen against the royalists. It should be emphasized that the "popular" or "national liberation" forces in such conflicts are by no means necessarily Communist or Soviet-oriented, although the Soviet Union seeks to identify itself with their cause. Indeed in many cases, the sympathies of the United States also lie on the side of the rebels, as was largely the case in Cuba and Algeria.

The United States position is often complicated in the case of anticolonial wars when the colonial power is an ally of the United States in NATO, as are France and Portugal. Nevertheless, Americans should not—and have not—always assumed that because the Soviet Union expresses support for an anticolonial or other popular cause that the United States necessarily has to take the other side; the late President Kennedy, while a Senator, made clear his sympathy for the cause of the Moslems fighting for independence in Algeria, and the American press and people were sympathetic to Fidel Castro's struggle against the government of Batista, even though in both cases the official position of the United States government was neutral or ambiguous.

Nevertheless the Soviet Union and its partisans abroad do use the banner of "national liberation" for their own purely sectarian purposes and the international Communist propaganda apparatus treats a Communist-led movement against a popular and democratic government on the same footing as it does a broad democratic movement against a colonial or dictatorial regime. In Latin America, for example, the "fronts of national liberation" that have been organized, mostly since 1961, are all pro-Soviet and almost all dominated by veteran Communist party members.

The Chinese Communists, too, have been active in lending moral and at times material support to national liberation movements. Only in East Africa and southeast Asia have the Chinese been able to emerge as the chief international sponsors of such movements so far. However, the competition for influence between the Russians and the Chinese is continuing.

For the Soviet Union the acceptance as a fact of mutual deterrence at the levels of both total and limited war creates no doctrinal problems. The limitation of the confrontation between proletarian and capitalist forces to the realm of domestic politics in the "national liberation" struggles is in no way a discouraging development. The forces headed and represented by the Soviet Union have no reason to have misgivings about the ultimate outcome of the struggle; Marx saw in the destruction of capitalism an inevitable process, and thus a good Communist can rest secure in his confidence in the victory of his cause. From the point of view of tactics, on the other hand, the rich experience of the Communist movement in surviving and prospering even under conditions of adversity, in the waging of the political struggle within the boundaries of states, seems to equip it better for the era of "wars of national liberation" than its adversary. And indeed the record of the last fifteen years is encouraging to those of this point of view. The national liberation of the underprivileged peoples is proceeding apace everywhere. The period since World War II has resulted in the granting of independence to the overwhelming majority of non–self-governing territories, which Communists have been taught by Lenin to regard as a drastic blow to the economies of the old colonial powers, even though most of the newly independent states have not identified themselves unequivocally with the camp led by the Soviet Union.

"National liberation" movements that have been led directly by Communists have also achieved a certain number of successes, however. Although most of the states calling themselves Communist were conquered for the bloc by the Red Army, Cuba, North Vietnam, and China itself were "liberated" by guerrilla peasant-based armies, affording enough evidence for the Soviet Union to believe that its interests are identified with those of the national liberation movements.

One should nevertheless not fall into the error of assuming that Soviet or Chinese directives are to blame for the guerrilla forces fighting under banners of national liberation all over the world, although these are joined by Communists where possible. Only in the small Southeast Asian countries that are the present-day successors of French Indochina are national liberation movements *militarily* active on a major scale that are clearly under Communist direction.

Normally, of course, American forces do not get directly involved in the fighting in so-called national liberation struggles. These are either civil wars between different groups of nationals of the country involved, or else anticolonial wars between national forces on the one hand and forces of the colonial power on the other. By their nature these are wars in which foreigners can take part only with difficulty, and their presence is likely to "backfire" and strengthen the guerrillas, whose claim to be fighting a national struggle is thus lent further validity. But in any case these wars are normally fought in the countryside, involving small units of troops whose strength lies in their familiarity with the terrain and their ability to acquire the confidence of the villagers. Clearly the foreigner is greatly handicapped here.

Despite the difficulties cited in the way of productive American participation in other countries' civil wars, defense policy has become sensitized in the last few years to the problem that national liberation wars present. Especially since the accession to office of President Kennedy, American forces have been trained for this type of war. If American troops should get involved in such a war on a large scale, as is now occurring in South Vietnam, a new set of assets and liabilities of American technique will become apparent; it remains to be seen whether the American troops' superiority in health, technical skills, and individual initiative will compensate for unfamiliarity with the area, heavier reliance on equipment that may not always be available, and the disabilities of fighting amid an alien population.

SUGGESTED READINGS

Brodie, Bernard, *Strategy in the Missile Age.* Princeton, N.J.: Princeton University Press, 1959.

Dulles, John Foster, "Challenge and Response in United States Policy," *Foreign Affairs,* October 1957.

Huntington, Samuel P. (ed.), *Changing Patterns of Military Politics.* New York: Free Press, 1963.

————, *The Common Defense.* New York: Columbia University Press, 1961.

Kaufmann, Walter W., *The McNamara Strategy*. New York: Harper & Row, 1964.

King, James E., Jr., "Nuclear Plenty and Limited War," *Foreign Affairs,* January 1957.

Kissinger, Henry A., *Nuclear Weapons and Foreign Policy*. New York: Harper & Row, 1957.

Osanka, Franklin Mark (ed.), *Modern Guerrilla Warfare*. New York: Free Press, 1962.

Osgood, Robert E., *Limited War: Challenge to American Strategy*. Chicago: University of Chicago Press, 1957.

Turner, Gordon B., and Richard D. Challener, (eds.), *National Security in the Nuclear Age: Basic Facts and Theories*. New York: Praeger, 1960.

Wohlstetter, Albert, "The Delicate Balance of Terror," *Foreign Affairs,* January 1959.

IV

Zones of Confrontation: The Permanent Crises

IO

Confrontation in Europe: NATO, Germany, and Berlin

Since the ending of the Korean war and the freezing of Cold War lines in most of the world, East–West relations have attained a certain stability. There have been, however, a few areas of the world where the Cold War battle lines have not stabilized, and where friction between the two superpowers is continual. In each of these areas frictions tend to focus on those symbolic points that one side has not tacitly conceded to the domain of the other, regardless of what the facts of possession may be. It is these sore spots of East-West confrontation that provide the recurring crises of newspaper headlines—the Berlin crises, the Formosan, Laotian, and Vietnamese crises, and, since 1960, the Cuban crises. In discussing each of these perpetual crisis areas, therefore, one must deal not only with the point of crisis itself, but also with the configuration of forces in the surrounding area that gives the passing crises themselves their larger meaning.

THE DIVISION OF GERMANY

The Berlin problem is part of the larger German problem. This grows out of what were thought to be temporary arrangements for the surrender of the German armies and the occupation of German territory by the Allied Powers at the end of World War II. With the onset of the

Cold War, however, the temporary occupation lines took on the character of fixed boundaries. The result has been to create, in effect, four Germanys.

Map 10.1 Map Showing Division of Germany into Western, Central, and Eastern Parts. SOURCE: Reprinted by permission of the German Information Center.

The first of these is the Federal Republic of Germany, usually known as West Germany, and sometimes called the Bonn Republic after the location of its capital. The Federal Republic contains about three fifths of the land area and almost four fifths of the population that it would have if united with Communist East Germany. It is a rich and powerful state of about sixty million people, committed to the Western cause not only by treaty but also by the evident wishes of its population. Perhaps the third state of the world in economic strength, West Germany is increasingly integrated into a European community in which France is its leading partner.

The second Germany is East Germany, the "German Democratic Republic," or DDR after the initials of its German name (*Deutsche Demokratische Republik*) still referred to contemptuously by the West Germans as "the Soviet zone." East Germany is dwarfed by its western neighbor. Nevertheless, with a population of some seventeen million it is perhaps the world's eighth industrial state and a distinct economic asset to the Soviet bloc, of which it is a member. Although the DDR has a Communist government and is linked by treaty to the other Soviet satellite states in the Warsaw Pact, the Eastern European counterpart of NATO, and in COMECON, the Eastern European version of the Common Market, the East German people do not support the political orientation of their government; it is doubtful whether in a free election the Communist party[1] could muster as much as 15 percent of the popular vote. It seems clear that the East German government of Walther Ulbricht remains in power only because of the troops at his disposal, especially the troops of his Russian ally that are stationed in East Germany. The discontent of the people of the DDR is manifested in a host of ways ranging from letters to their relatives in the West, to the heavy flow of refugees who used to pour across the border into West Berlin before escape was cut off definitively by the building of a wall across the divided city during 1961, even to abortive uprisings, which have speedily been repressed.

The third Germany consists of those areas, German before Hitler's conquests, that were annexed by Poland and the Soviet Union in the aftermath of World War II. These are the areas east of the line formed by the Oder and Neisse rivers, which form the actual boundary between East Germany and Poland. They include East Prussia, the home of the Junker caste that ruled Prussia, and then Germany, for so long; in fact East Prussia has been divided between Poland and Russia, so that Koenigsberg, the city on the Baltic immortalized as the home of the great German philosopher Immanuel Kant, is now Kaliningrad, the westernmost city of the Soviet Union.

The former German territories that have fallen to Poland have since been resettled by Poles. The Germans who lived in the areas were largely expelled and most of them seem to have ended up in West Germany, where for a time many of them formed part of an emigré political movement. This has since disappeared as the expellees have been increasingly integrated into West German society. It must indeed be hard for a man who has been employed at a good wage for fifteen years in a factory in Frankfurt to imagine returning to his pig farm in Pomerania.

East Germany, of course, acknowledges the Oder-Neisse line as her eastern frontier. The West Germans, supported by the Western allies, do not regard that boundary as having validity; West German maps identify

---

[1] The ruling party is formally the Socialist Unity party, or SED (*Sozialistische Einheitspartei Deutschlands*).

the lost territories as areas "currently under Polish [or Soviet] administration." It seems clear that if Germany ever were to be reunified in peace, the present eastern frontier would have to be accepted. This seems to be recognized silently by all concerned, although it is something that West German politicians do not say. Since there seems to be no prospect for any foreseeable movement towards reunification, the whole issue remains academic; but even if negotiations for reunification were to take place, the Western states would in any case not recognize the Oder-Neisse frontier in advance but would doubtless hold back in the attempt to extract a reciprocal concession from the Soviet side. There is, however, some merit in the argument that so long as the Oder-Neisse line remains unrecognized by the West, there is a limit to the independence that the Poles can assert in relation to their Russian ally, since the Poles genuinely retain a fear of a German invasion aimed at recovering the lost territories and must, therefore, depend the more heavily on Soviet backing.

The fourth part of Germany is West Berlin—not Berlin as a whole, because East Berlin has been integrated into the East German state, of which it forms the capital. West Berlin, the western two thirds of the city, remains at international law conquered territory occupied by the troops of the three Western Allies, Britain, France, and the United States. Although the military commandants of the Allied troops exercise something like residual sovereignty over West Berlin, in actuality the city's government is carried on by an elected assembly and Lord Mayor. Although not forming a part of the Federal Republic of Germany, West Berlin's over two million people are linked with the West German republic in various ways. West Berlin uses West German currency and has non-voting delegates in the West German Parliament, and West Berlin's Lord Mayor, Willy Brandt, is leader of the West German Social Democratic Party.

THE BERLIN QUESTION

The fact that makes the Berlin problem a peculiarly acute source of irritation in the over-all East-West confrontation is that Berlin lies 100 miles behind the Iron Curtain, that is, 100 miles to the *east* of the border between East and West Germany. It is reached from the west by a route on which Western traffic is sporadically subjected to harassment and interdiction.

In June of 1948, the Soviet Union made a major attempt to force the Western allies out of the city by cutting off access to Berlin from the west by road, rail, and water. The Allied response was to inaugurate the Berlin airlift, a massive effort to keep Berlin supplied with the necessities of life. This fantastic undertaking, in which more than a quarter of a million supply flights were flown to Berlin during the eleven months of the blockade, was a dramatic demonstration of Allied power, and at the same time, of determination not to yield to the Soviet threat. Today, the "air bridge," a monument to the airlift, stands as a symbol of the West Berliners' gratitude to the Western allies for saving their freedom.

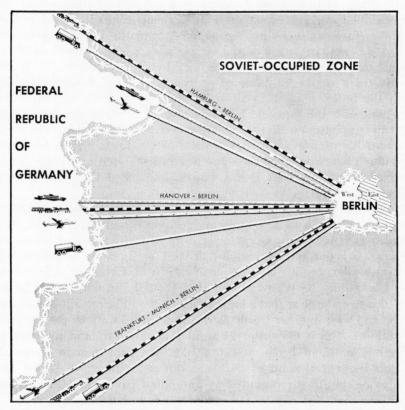

Map 10.2 Main Authorized Access Routes to Berlin from Western Germany. SOURCE: Reprinted by permission of the German Information Center.

It is noteworthy that this attempt to incorporate West Berlin into the Soviet zone was conducted by the Soviet Union as a strictly limited operation. No attempt was made to shoot down the Allied planes flying over the Soviet zone on their way to Berlin, nor indeed to interfere with their radar guidance system. After eleven months of blockade, the Soviet Union tacitly acknowledged that it had been defeated and lifted the restrictions on land and water access to the divided city.

It is clear why Stalin and his successors have been eager to end the Western presence in Berlin. Khrushchev in his vivid manner called West Berlin a "bone in his throat." West Berlin constituted a hole in the Iron Curtain through which East Germans and citizens of the other Soviet bloc countries could escape to the west; until the building of the infamous wall that today divides East from West Berlin, there was a steady drain on East German manpower, especially of the younger and better skilled workers, whom the East Germans could ill afford to lose. West Berlin was also a showcase of freedom to the East Germans who visited the western sector of the city; a visit stiffened their resistance against the repression under which they lived. Needless to say, it also constituted a center for Western propaganda and espionage activities. With the building of the wall across the city in 1961 the world was presented with the fantastic spectacle of a state whose people were so eager to escape from it that they had to be treated like prisoners in a jail. Further edification was provided by the shooting down of those foolhardy individuals who attempted to escape to the west, often under the eyes of horrified visitors to West Berlin who had included the wall on their sightseeing itineraries.

To the leaders of the Western allies West Berlin is necessarily a source of concern because its military position is highly vulnerable. Surrounded as it is by East German territory in which Russian troops are stationed, it is out of the question that West Berlin could be defended at its own borders against an attempt to take it by force. Accordingly, the only surety that the West can give that West Berlin will in fact be defended is to make clear that a local attack on it will be regarded as a cause for general war; in other words, Berlin is defended only by the threat of general war. This is, of course, not an ideal situation from many points of view, one of them being that the West Germans remain somewhat nervous about the extent of the American commitment to Berlin, and need to be continually reassured by an endless parade of United States dignitaries that the United States indeed stands at their side.

Needless to say, the Soviet leadership has no intention of trying to take West Berlin by armed attack. Given the geographic circumstances, the Soviet Union instead has much more sensibly resorted to a policy of gradual attrition, or what Matias Rakosi, formerly the dictator of Hungary, referred to as "salami tactics." That is, the Soviet Union and its East German dependency attempt at periodic intervals to slice away at the West's position in Berlin in the hope that in unguarded moments the West will take the bait and agree to changes in status which, although each in itself of minor significance, will move the Communists step by step closer to control of the western sectors of the city. The West has, however, made no such concessions, although many well-meaning individuals, hopeful for an easing of the tension to which the Berlin problem gives rise, are readily taken in by Soviet proposals. One such Soviet plan, for example, has been to create a "free city" status for West Berlin. This clearly sounds innocuous, and indeed has an attractive ring about it that appealed to some of the neutralist African and Asian leaders. What West Berlin would be free of under the Soviet plan turned out to be Western troops. From time to time, for tactical reasons, the United States presents an appearance of sweet reasonableness over the Berlin question, and indicates its readiness to discuss possible alterations in the *status quo*. Although West German leaders suffer attacks of nerves when this approach is taken, United States diplomats have made it clear that all they are prepared to negotiate are firmer Soviet guarantees of Western access to the city, and other measures designed to stabilize the situation without weakening the Western position.

The form in which Khrushchev used to pose recurrent crises over Berlin was most frequently to announce his intention of concluding a peace treaty with the DDR, no formal peace treaty having yet been signed between Germany and her World War II antagonists. The only meaning that the conclusion of such a treaty could have was expressed in the words of Khrushchev, speaking in Paris on the occasion of what was to have been a summit meeting, but which was aborted by the shooting down of an American U–2 espionage plane flying over the Soviet Union, "Access to Berlin by air, water, or land without permission of the government of the German Democratic Republic will discontinue. Access will be for those who obtain the consent of the government of the German Democratic Republic."

The West regards this possibility askance, primarily because the East German regime would probably attempt to interfere with Allied access to Berlin—hard as it is to visualize the rulers of East Germany taking such action without the Russians' approval—but also because Americans traveling on the *autobahn* would then presumably have to have their papers checked by East German authorities rather than by the Russians. This might be taken by some to imply United States recognition of the authority of the East German regime, a position that the American government has consistently refused to take. The West German government has taken an extremely strong stand against any recognition of the East German government, or the implication in any other way of the legitimacy or the permanence of the division of Germany, and the United States has loyally stood by this position—even though in actuality West Germans traveling to West Berlin do have their papers cleared by the DDR authorities. Indeed, the West Germans have stipulated that they will break diplomatic relations automatically with any state that extends recognition to the DDR. Only one state has actually been able to maintain diplomatic relations with both Germanys—the Soviet Union; Chancellor Adenauer established diplomatic relations with the Soviet Union, even though the latter recognized the government of East Germany, in return for Soviet agreement to repatriate German prisoners of war; but otherwise the policy has held.

THE PROSPECTS FOR REUNIFICATION

It is thus not likely that the status of West Berlin will be changed, by forcible means or otherwise. In the diplomatic formula, the Berlin question will only be resolved as part of the settlement of the division of Germany itself; in other words, the only stable future for Berlin is as capital of a reunified Germany.

No prospect of German reunification exists in the foreseeable future. Nevertheless, every actor, German or foreign, in the drama of German politics must continually protest his unshakable loyalty to the cause of German reunification. This is as true to the east of the Iron Curtain as to the west. The position of the Soviet Union and of its eastern German satellite on the reunification question has been that one must recognize facts, the particular facts in question being that an East German government exists, determined to maintain its hold on its share of the country. Since two German governments do in fact exist, the argument goes on, reunification is only possible through a negotiated agreement between these two governments—which runs head-on into the West German opposition to any act that recognizes, even indirectly, the legitimacy of the Soviet zone authorities. Moreover, the Soviet argument continues, a reunified Germany must retain the "social gains" achieved in the German Democratic Republic, whatever that may mean. The Soviet Ambassador to West Germany, Andrei Smirnov, once went further than this and stipulated that a reunited Germany would have to be "peaceloving," which he defined as meaning that the forces supporting war, the imperialist monopolies, and so forth, would have to be eliminated. In the context of Marxist-Leninist thinking this appears to mean that the only reunited Germany acceptable to the Soviet Union would be one whose social and political organization followed that of the eastern European Communist countries, and that would be pro-Soviet in its orientation.

Of course, this is what one would expect the Soviet position to be. One might translate it as saying that the Soviet Union is willing to see a reunited Germany if it is a Soviet satellite, and it might be willing to settle for a kind of nominal federation between the two governments that exist at present in which the DDR would retain its sovereignty while

East German Communists would be enabled to take a hand in the affairs of West Germany.

The Russians' hope of securing anything like this arrangement is quite a forlorn one, needless to say. In fact, the Communist leadership of the DDR has its hands full trying to maintain control of the rebellious satellite itself without becoming overextended in any all-German ventures. Khrushchev was even quoted in an unguarded moment by a Western journalist as replying to the question whether he would ever agree to the reunification of Germany by saying that half a loaf was better than no bread, a statement he subsequently denied having made, but which of course fitted in with his well-known realistic appraisals of political situations.

Some observers have gone so far as to suggest that the commitment of West German leaders to reunification is hardly more sincere than that of the East Germans, and that the strong position that they take publicly is for popular consumption only. This is so, the argument continues, since the present authorities in West Germany have a strong vested interest in the division of the country. Business men in Frankfurt are fearful of the loss of their central position in West German trade, which would pass to the Berliners in a reunified country. The political position of the dominant Christian Democratic party, strong enough in a West Germany that is almost fifty percent Roman Catholic, might disappear with the addition of the largely Protestant East, it is also alleged.

It seems to the present writer that this conception of the West German leadership and people as only nominally committed to reunification underestimates the powerful force of German nationalism; this is an emotional commitment above and beyond any considerations of interest. As the years have gone by without bringing the day of German reunification nearer, however, the West Germans have adjusted in practice to the apparent permanence of a state of affairs that they cannot accept emotionally as anything more than temporary.

DISENGAGEMENT

A school of thought now mainly confined to Western observers outside Germany, although for a time it included among its adherents many more German Socialists and Liberals than it now does, professes the belief that a solution of the German problem might be possible on the basis of the "disengagement" of the forces of the two superpowers from Germany. This view seems to have originated with a series of lectures given by George Kennan over the British radio in the days following the death of Stalin,[2] when the shape of future Soviet policy was unclear and all things seemed possible. Subsequent to Kennan's espousal of the disengagement thesis, other disengagement proposals were broached by Adam Rapacki, the Polish Foreign Minister, and by Anthony Eden, then Prime Minister of Great Britain. Disengagement was given some plausibility by the fact that in 1955 the Soviet Union, endeavoring to cut its commitments in the reevaluation of the Soviet international position during the years of the post-Stalin interregnum, agreed with the Western allies to conclude a peace treaty with Austria that entailed the withdrawal from that country of all occupying forces, Russian as well as Western.

Proposals for disengagement in Germany envisage a solution comparable to the one agreed to in the Austrian treaty. The major premise of disengagement proposals is that the Russians and their allies in eastern Europe are seriously concerned about the danger presented to them by the rearmament of West Germany, especially given the fact that Russian and American troops confront each other in the center of divided Europe, a situation that may hold the seeds of accidental war; and therefore the Soviet Union might be willing to withdraw its troops a certain distance from their present positions in the center of Germany if the Western allies did likewise, thus making possible a reunification of Germany under the terms of which Germany would be disarmed and permanently neutralized. In other words, West Germany would withdraw from NATO and reduce her armed forces to the minimum necessary for domestic policing, in return for the Soviet Union's agreement to relinquish its hold on East Germany. Various other features complement this basic agreement in the different disengagement plans, but the exchange of the reunification of Germany for her disarmament and neutrality lies at their heart.

Some Western observers, such as Dean Acheson, have professed to see in disengagement a threat to the Western position in Europe, arguing that under its terms the NATO alliance might collapse, a power vacuum would exist in Germany, and a wave of isolationism and neutralism would sweep the Western allies, allowing the Russians to make new advances. There may be something to this thesis, as applied to proposals for disengagement *without reunification*. As far as the present writer can see, however, the chief objection to proposals for a disengagement agreement that included German reunification is simply that the Russians are too wide awake to fall for it, since a reunified Germany, regardless of how carefully its neutrality were safeguarded by treaty, would inevitably be pro-West; the disarmament of Germany could prove to be

---

2 Published as *Russia, the Atom, and the West.*

only temporary—as it did following World Wars I and II, after all; and thus the disengagement hypothesis contemplates that the Russians relinquish a substantial advantage—control of a strategic piece of territory, of an established industrial capacity, and of a large labor force of industrious Germans—in return for concessions that are likely to prove of only temporary advantage. In a word, Germany is not Austria.

NATO

In the absence of any possibility for arriving at arrangements with the Soviet Union that would establish the basis for an unarmed peace in central Europe, United States policy for Europe has instead been based on the deterrence of any Soviet attempt to alter the *status quo* by force. The instrument by means of which the United States and its European allies conduct this policy of deterrence is the North Atlantic Treaty Organization (NATO).

In its early days the North Atlantic Treaty was in essence a guarantee to her western European allies that the United States would come to their defense in case of need; it was a traditional alliance commitment. This was logical given the military thinking of the time, according to which a future war would be a world war in which atomic weapons would be employed. However, after 1950 and the attack on Korea, which had itself been preceded by the first Soviet atomic explosion, it became clear that a situation of atomic stalemate might be created that would open the possibility of limited war.

Accordingly the NATO allies, reacting to the Korean experience, set about to transform the paper NATO agreement into a coordinated mechanism for the local defense of Europe. In line with this conception, rather high force levels were set for the number of troops that each country was to station in western Europe; the United States undertook to provide substantial military assistance to her allies; the basic decision was taken that West Germany was to be rearmed, despite the bitter hostility such a decision would face among the peoples who had so recently and at such cost disarmed German militarism; and the groundwork for a permanent "treaty organization" was created, with a standing multinational command structure.

Many observers were uneasy at this apparent decision to be prepared to fight limited, although large-scale, war in Europe. In their view control of western Europe was too valuable a prize to be met by only a limited defense. Moreover, the superiority of the Soviet bloc in manpower under arms was taken to mean that the decision to be prepared to fight at the conventional level would entail meeting the Russians on their own terms. By the same token it was thought that it might encourage the

Russians into making a conventional invasion of western Europe, secure in the knowledge that the United States would not use her general nuclear retaliatory force. According to this conception, the only forces needed in western Europe were so-called trip wire or plate glass window forces—that is, nominal forces whose purpose it would be to symbolize the American commitment, any attack on which would trigger American massive retaliation.

Nevertheless, for a time at least, the NATO allies struggled to meet the force levels stipulated at the Lisbon Conference. However, these goals have never been met, for substantial economic and political considerations created difficulties for the European powers in living up to their commitments. Military conscription was, of course, universally unpopular, and most of the west European states have either abolished it altogether, or else shortened the term of compulsory service. The economic strain of supporting such large numbers of troops was considerable and created special difficulties for the British balance-of-payments situation. Until a German component of the NATO force was created, however, the Germans were induced to defray the costs of the stationing of Allied troops on West German soil on the principle that these troops were defending Germany; but after West Germany had raised the largest of the NATO contingents, this concept was clearly no longer applicable. In addition, the European allies had commitments outside Europe that on occasion required the use of troops. This was true of colonial or neo-colonial "police actions" the British fought during the period in Kenya, Cyprus, and the Suez area; while as the war in Algeria developed, France withdrew more and more of her troops from their NATO stations.

The underfulfillment of the manpower levels originally hoped for has since been partially compensated for by the development of "small" atomic weapons, designed for battlefield use, which are now stationed with American forces in Europe. The problem remains, nevertheless, as to the strategic function that NATO is designed to serve, since the present levels of force are, on the one hand, too large to serve as a "trip wire" to set off massive retaliation against the Soviet Union and, on the other hand, not large enough to fight successfully a limited war against a Soviet ground invasion of western Europe. Accordingly various rationales have been developed as to the strategic mission of the NATO forces in the attempt to justify their "in-between" character. One such thesis is that the present level of forces serves to ensure that any Soviet invasion of western Europe would have to be a full-scale one. No ambiguous nibbling or "salami" tactics would be possible, and also extensive prior mobilization actions would have to be taken by the Soviet bloc forces, which would serve to reveal Soviet intentions and to reduce the surprise element, making a *blitzkrieg* victory impossible. Another thesis compatible with the one just described is that the purpose of NATO forces at their present level is to gain time, to delay a Russian advance so that the decision whether to retaliate massively can be made, or so that an attempt can be made to use diplomatic and political pressures to bring a halt to the fighting.

This latter conception dovetails with a change of strategy that has taken place in NATO planning in response to political requirements. Originally Western contingency plans called for NATO forces to fall back to the Rhine in the face of a Soviet attack since this would make a more logical defensive line. However, German unhappiness that so much of German territory would be implicitly surrendered to the invader has led instead to adopting the thesis that the line of defense would be as far to the east as possible under the circumstances. This approach is more consistent with the conception that any ground fighting in Europe would only last for a short time, being succeeded by either a political settlement or else by the initiation of general atomic aerial bombardment.

ALLIANCE POLITICS AND MILITARY PROBLEMS

Although it is possible to devise strategic justifications for the present situation, it remains true that the NATO forces in western Europe are not by themselves adequate to deter or defeat a full-scale local Soviet attack. It seems to have become politically very difficult, however, for the United States to initiate reductions that would bring her own forces stationed in Europe closer to the "trip wire" level; any projected reduction of United States forces is strongly resisted, especially in Western Germany, as symbolizing a lessening of the American commitment to defend the continent. American forces thus are cast in the role of hostages, guaranteeing that the United States will not go back on its European commitments. The United States has in turn implicitly accepted this definition of the situation, increasing the number of United States troops in Europe—as at the time of the Berlin crisis of 1961—to signify renewal of the commitment.

Other NATO strategies have, similarly, developed out of the needs of inter-allied politics, rather than from the requirements of the confrontation with Soviet power. Like the example just cited these too stem from a basic unsureness on the part of European members of the alliance that the United States can always be depended on to come to the aid of an invaded Europe, especially given a Soviet nuclear missile capability that implies that New York or Washington would have to be sacrificed to defend Paris or Frankfurt. This unsureness, while unpleasant for Americans to contemplate, is surely understandable, especially in the light of the American reversion to isolationism after World War I.

The uneasiness of the European allies finds repose in one of two directions. One outcome lies in the determination to develop one's own nuclear defense regardless of what the Americans may do; this is the road taken by French policy under General de Gaulle (and having roots in decisions taken before de Gaulle returned to power in 1958), which is bent on creating France's own independent nuclear capability. To pursue this path implies suspicion of one's major ally, and an estrangement between Gaullist France and the United States has indeed developed; it has also led France to refuse to sign the 1963 Treaty of Moscow, which bans atomic tests in the atmosphere, in outer space, and under water. As the estrangement between France and the United States has grown, French participation in NATO has been progressively reduced to a nominal level.

The other avenue out of what might be called "alliance anxiety" is the creation of arrangements that render it extremely difficult for the ally to disengage from his commitment. The stationing of United States troops on the European continent constitutes a less than perfect commitment here from the European viewpoint, since the troops can easily be withdrawn at the discretion of the United States. A more reliable commitment is obtained by devices such as the European Defense Community plan, eventually vetoed by the French National Assembly, under which the troops of the European "Six"[3] would have worn a single uniform and served in integrated units.

As a means of settling European doubts, the United States has tried to revive the integrated unit technique in the project for a mixed-manned surface nuclear fleet under NATO control. This multilateral force, long under consideration in NATO capitals, would comprise surface vessels, equipped with long-range nuclear missiles and manned by crews of mixed nationality under joint NATO command. Strategists have correctly pointed out that such a force would add nothing to the military potential of the Western alliance created by the Polaris submarine fleet of the United States; but of course this is not its intention, which is purely political. An alternative mode of creating a multilateral Allied deterrent favored in some western European circles is for the Allies to be represented directly in the military planning and decision-making echelons in Washington. The United States has made a gesture in this direction by proposing the creation of an Allied "nuclear cabinet," a project that remains under discussion.

Thus the alternative courses of action open to a United States ally have been to heighten its military independence from, or its military interdependence with, the United States; France currently follows the

---

[3] See the discussion in Chapter Six.

former course, West Germany the latter. Th̶
nuclear technology at the same time as the Ame̶
tained their atomic warfare capacity throughout, ̶
follow both lines of action simultaneously, the one reeṅ
Thus the independent British deterrent ensures Britain's̶
fend itself without the United States should that for some reaṡ
necessary; at the same time, however, British possession of aṅ
striking force means that Britain must be closely consulted and giv̶
respectful hearing by Washington, precisely because it maintains a capaċ
ity to go its own way in global strategy if not satisfied with United
States policies.

SUGGESTED READINGS

Acheson, Dean, "The Illusion of Disengagement," *Foreign Affairs,* April 1958.

Cottrell, Alvin J., and James E. Dougherty, *The Politics of the Atlantic Alliance.* New York: Praeger, 1964.

Department of State, *Background: Berlin–1961* (Publication 7257). Washington, D.C.: Government Printing Office, 1961.

Epstein, Klaus, *Germany After Adenauer* (Headline Series No. 164). New York: The Foreign Policy Association, 1964.

Freymond, Jacques, *Western Europe Since the War.* New York: Praeger, 1964.

Heidenheimer, Arnold J., *The Governments of Germany.* New York: Crowell, 1961.

Kennan, George F., *Russia, the Atom, and the West.* New York: Harper & Row, 1958.

———, "Disengagement Revisited," *Foreign Affairs,* January 1959.

Knorr, Klaus (ed.), *NATO and American Security.* Princeton, N.J.: Princeton University Press, 1959.

Osgood, Robert E., *NATO: The Entangling Alliance.* Chicago: University of Chicago Press, 1962.

Plischke, Elmer, *Contemporary Government of Germany.* Boston: Houghton Mifflin, 1961.

Pounds, Norman J. G., *Divided Germany and Berlin.* Princeton, N.J.: Van Nostrand, 1962.

Germany, and Berlin · 173
e British, having started in
ricans, and having main-
are in a position to
forcing the other.
ability to de-
on become
atomic
n a

Conf... n Asia: Laos, Vietnam, and the Two Chinas

AN OVERVIEW

The problems posed in the confrontation with Communist power in Asia are quite different from those met with in Europe. On the continent of Europe the United States is allied with strong and developed states; Soviet power has come face to face with countervailing Allied power and a situation of stalemate has been reached. On the continent of Asia, on the other hand, those countries looking to the United States for protection are most often poor and weak, they face grave problems of maintaining the domestic authority of their governments, and they are confronted with the reality of a powerful and expansionist Communist China.

At times the United States has tried to apply in Asia the formula that has resulted in the successful containment of Communist power in Europe: A powerful military alliance plus an economic recovery program designed to strengthen the loyalties of the peoples of the area to their governments. This dual formula has, however, met with only limited success. The military alliances formed on the continent of Asia, SEATO and the Baghdad Pact, have had disappointing results, being weakened by changes of government and debilitating rivalries among the non-Communist states. Attempts to bolster the authority of pro-Western governments have met with success in some countries but have failed elsewhere, where the capacity to inspire popular confidence, in countries lacking a democratic tradition, has not been present.

The first great setback suffered by the Western position in postwar Asia came in China itself, when in 1949 the Communist movement led by Mao Tse-tung emerged victorious from the long Chinese civil war. The Nationalist government of Chiang Kai-shek, which then transplanted itself to the island of Formosa, had proved unable to command popular support on the mainland, partly as a result of Chiang's belief that measures of social reform could only be undertaken after the successful conclusion of the military struggle. With the advantages of hindsight, it has become commonplace to say that the order of priorities should have been reversed—military victory in a civil war can come only after the loyalty of the population has been secured by appropriate political and economic measures.

With the Communist victory in China, the course of international relations was permanently changed. Although many years will pass before China's economy develops to the point where the country's vast human and material resources can be fully mobilized and brought to bear in international politics, the *status quo* in the Far East is already being challenged on four separate levels.

On the first level the new rulers of China have attempted to reassert traditional Chinese claims of authority over border areas that had at various times in the past owed allegiance to Peking. Chinese initiatives in this category have included the occupation of Tibet and the forced integration of that country into the Chinese political system, and the forcible seizure of border areas long in dispute between China and India. It should be noted that disputes over border areas of this type exist not only between China and countries in South and Southeast Asia, but also between China and the Soviet Union in Central Asia.

On the second level of threat, the Chinese Communists have aided local guerrilla movements in the countries of Southeast Asia with advisors, arms, and other supplies. These movements are currently active in Laos and South Vietnam. The Chinese also participated in the attempt to bring all of the Korean peninsula under Communist control, after United States and United Nations forces had repulsed the original North Korean invasion of South Korea. Today the governments of North Korea and North Vietnam, as well as underground Communist movements in the other countries of the area, are supported materially and politically by the Chinese, and in turn give support to Chinese positions in international diplomacy.

The third type of threat remains today largely potential, but it contains ominous possibilities for the future. It consists of the large number of ethnic Chinese who are living in various countries in Southeast Asia, but whose loyalties are in many cases to China rather than to the countries in which they live. These Chinese populations are of substantial size; Malay fears of dominance by its overwhelmingly Chinese population forced Singapore out of the Federation of Malaysia in 1965. In some of these countries the local Chinese population may in future years come to constitute a real internal security problem if their loyalties should be transferred fully to Communist China. Alternatively, their treatment may serve as a pretext for Communist Chinese intervention, as that of the Sudeten Germans of Czechoslovakia did for Hitler.

At the same time the unfortunate possibility exists that in reacting against internal or external security threats from Communist Chinese, some governments in the area will take retaliatory action against all within their borders who are ethnically or racially Chinese, instituting special legal disabilities or even encouraging popular racism and pogroms.

Finally, on the fourth level of threat, the danger must be faced that as Communist Chinese power grows and is made manifest, non-Communist governments of the area may find it expedient to come to some understanding with the Chinese, allying with them in return for internal autonomy, say, rather than risking the consequences of persevering in their opposition to the growing colossus of the north. Cambodia has clearly moved in this direction, and Thailand and Pakistan may eventually follow. Not only is this type of development plausible in terms of the attitude taken by several European states in response to the growing power of Hitler's Germany, but it finds ample precedent in the policies often followed by neighboring states when Chinese dynasties of past centuries moved to consolidate and expand their power; their rulers acknowledged Chinese suzerainty and rendered tribute in return for being permitted to retain their positions.

THE AMERICAN RESPONSE

In Asia the record of the United States in its goal of containing Communist expansion is mixed, in both its military and its economic-political dimensions. The military problem in Southeast Asia, which has been the major zone of conflict on the continent, is of peculiar difficulty. As was pointed out in the chapter on the military dimension of the Cold War above, military adventures sponsored by the Communist bloc in the area normally take the form of "wars of national liberation," that is, civil and guerrilla wars against established governments. Even the Korean conflict, although launched by an attack across an established boundary line, can be brought into this category, since the components of either side in the early stages of the fighting were Korean.

American military strategists have warned repeatedly of the dangers of the United States' becoming involved in a long-drawn-out war in Southeast Asia. The climate and terrain are inhospitable to North Americans in any case, but a guerrilla war needs to be fought with the support of the local population by people intimately familiar with the countryside in which they are fighting. A foreigner, especially one of another race, is thus placed under substantial handicaps. This is especially true of the United States Army, which is best adapted to fight a highly technical war in which supplies and equipment are of crucial importance, and not a jungle and mountain war in which one must travel light and live off the country. United States "special forces" have nevertheless been trained in counterguerrilla warfare, as of course they should be; it still seems prudent that involvement in such wars should be avoided by the United States wherever possible.

It should not be thought that Communist-sponsored guerrilla forces are invariably invincible, however. The record shows that this is far from the truth; insurrection or guerrilla warfare under Communist auspices was successfully put down following the end of World War II in Indonesia, Burma, Malaya, and the Philippines. In Malaya, then under the British flag, British troops put down the pro-Communist guerrillas; in the other countries mentioned, this was done by local troops.

INDOCHINA: LAOS, VIETNAM, CAMBODIA

Experience in these campaigns indicated that successful counter-guerrilla warfare required a manpower ratio of about ten to one, at least, in favor of the government forces, however. This implied that if the United States were to aid the South Vietnamese government effectively in its campaign against the Communist-led Viet Cong, a commitment of perhaps half a million troops would be required. Moreover it was within the power of the Communist insurgents to raise this figure astronomically by infiltrating additional guerrillas from Communist North Vietnam as required. Understandably, American policy makers turned to techniques of aerial warfare and to threats to widen the war in the attempt to avoid a manpower commitment on this scale—but with little prospect of success.

By the middle of 1965, therefore, the Johnson administration found itself in a discouraging and difficult situation. Feeling itself bound to honor the commitment to defend the independence of South Vietnam made by the Eisenhower administration and reaffirmed by President Kennedy, it faced the prospect of a long, drawn-out war, in which success was not assured, involving heavy American casualties, increasing alienation

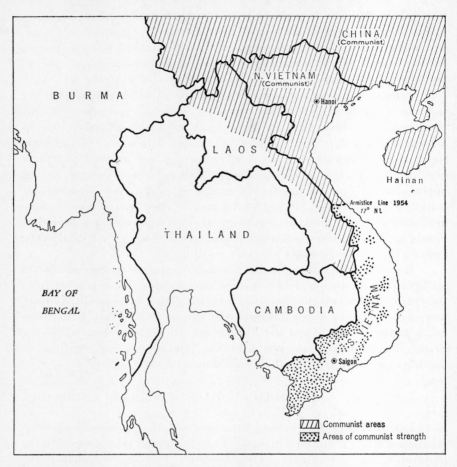

Map 11.1 Southeast Asia Military Situation as of March 1965. SOURCE: © 1964 by the New York *Times* Company. Adaptation © 1965, 1966 by Holt, Rinehart and Winston. Reprinted by permission.

of the public from its policies, and deteriorating relations with allies and with the Soviet Union.

How had this situation come about?

Seen in historical perspective, the Western allies have been conducting delaying actions in the Indochinese area that have, at most, been able to arrest for brief periods the expansion of the area under Communist and pro-Communist control. When fighting began between the French colonial rulers of the Indochinese states and the Vietnamese guerrillas in 1946, it seemed to many just another colonial war. But rather than attempt to arrive at a settlement providing for a French withdrawal and the independence of the states in the area, which would then continue to maintain amicable relations with France, the French resorted to a series of devices, at once cunning and naive, such have so often marked French colonial policy, that only succeeded in making things worse than they would otherwise have been.

After suffering a steady series of military reverses, and failing in a shortsighted attempt to set up a puppet Indochinese government under Bao Dai, the capture of the French stronghold of Dienbienphu by the Vietnamese rebels forced the French to come to terms with the rebel movement.

At a series of meetings in Geneva in 1954 the Western allies proved able to salvage more from the Indochina situation than seemed warranted by the deteriorating military position of the French. Great Britain and the Soviet Union were co-chairmen of the Geneva conference that arrived at the final settlement; the United States, France, and Communist China were also represented.

It may legitimately be asked why the Communist states were willing to conclude an agreement that brought the Indochinese war to an end, since the pro-Communist forces in the fighting had been steadily victorious to that point. The most likely explanation advanced, and one that has been given some support by Pierre Mendès-France, who was Prime Minister of France in the earlier stages of the Geneva talks, is that the Soviet Union was afraid that if the fighting were to continue, the United States would be brought directly into the war and might employ nuclear weapons. This possibility was not as unlikely as it might seem; Dulles was known to favor the commitment of American naval and air forces equipped with atomic weapons, and it may well be that only the opposition expressed by the British and by influential members of Congress induced President Eisenhower to overrule him. The Geneva accords on Indochina thus provide in all probability an instance in which the threat of massive retaliation was, at least for once and at least temporarily, successful.

The solution arrived at, at Geneva, was that the French would withdraw from Indochina, and four independent states would be established. Of these Cambodia and Laos were to be neutral, and Vietnam was to be divided into two parts, a Communist North Vietnam to occupy the territory held by the pro-Communist Vietminh movement, South Vietnam to be in effect an ally of the United States, although foreign "troops" were not to be allowed in the country. It was out of deference to this last proviso that American soldiers in South Vietnam used to be referred to as "military advisors."

Needless to say, the agreement represented not a settlement of the Indochina question but merely a lull in the fighting, as the Communists could be expected to continue to press their local military advantage after a suitable period had elapsed in which the threat of American atomic intervention would have passed.

It should be acknowledged, however, that whatever chance there might have been to stabilize the *status quo* in the key territory of Laos was thrown away by a foolish and shortsighted policy of the United States. After 1954 Laos was given a neutral government in which by 1958 both Communist and pro-Western political forces were represented. Unhappy with a neutralist government in which Communists participated—this was during the period in which Secretary of State Dulles considered neutralism "immoral"—the United States made its disapproval clear and apparently encouraged a right-wing *coup d'état* that overthrew the coalition government. Under a conservative upper-class regime out of touch with the needs of the population, although its international position was impeccably pro-United States, political conditions deteriorated, and the government had to maintain itself in power by blatant rigging of elections.

In 1960 another *coup d'état* was staged, this time by neutralist soldiers in Vientiane, and the able and subtle former Premier, the neutralist Souvanna Phouma, was called back to power; he attempted to reconstruct a broadly-based government that would be representative of all the political forces in the country and that would command popular support. The Communists, however, were excluded from government posts. Many Western observers of the Laotian scene were only too delighted that the West had apparently been given a second chance to become identified with a popular leader and a popular cause in Laos, and France and Great Britain attempted to work amicably with the new government. United States authorities were still unhappy with neutralism, however, regarding it as no better than disguised pro-communism, and, unwilling to settle for the half-loaf that is proverbially to be preferred to no bread, agents of the Central Intelligence Agency and United States military officers stationed in Laos encouraged a right-wing general, Phoumi Nosavan, to revolt against the Souvanna Phouma government and to attempt to establish his own control over all the country. In the fighting that ensued it unfortunately became clear, even to those who had not yet appreciated the real facts of the military situation, that the right-wing forces were impressive only so long as they did not take to the field of combat; that the neutralist forces on which Souvanna Phouma could rely were actually very small in number; and that the pro-Communist Pathet Lao was easily the most capable fighting force. Accordingly the right wing had initiated new fighting that only demonstrated the superiority of the Pathet Lao, which has since gone on to conquer and hold perhaps three fourths to four fifths of the country's land area. The

Western powers, led by a new administration in the United States that did not call neutralism "immoral," now tried desperately to save by diplomatic means whatever possible out of the Laotian situation, hoping that some opportunity would be provided in this direction by the split between the Soviet Union and Communist China. The United States presumably would now be only too glad to settle for the neutralist governments of 1958 or 1960. Unfortunately it is too late; Souvanna Phouma is again Prime Minister, but now hardly holds even the shadow of power; that power lies with the troops of the Pathet Lao. However, fighting in Laos has been in abeyance as Communist efforts have concentrated on South Vietnam.

In South Vietnam, similarly, developments since the Geneva accords were not favorable to the Western position. Irregular pro-Communist forces that remained in South Vietnam after the partition between north and south have been augmented and supplied from the north by a steady and effective guerrilla campaign. Despite a hopeful beginning, and despite substantial United States aid in the form of money, material, and military personnel, the government of South Vietnam under Ngo Dinh Diem repeated many of the errors made by the Nationalist Chinese forces in their civil war against the Communists, in that the arrogant and arbitrary way in which he conducted his government tended to alienate the population. Thus Diem steadily lost the political phase of the war; this was reflected in a steady deterioration in the military situation. During 1963 the political weakness of the regime reached an acute stage as repressive actions taken by the government against Buddhist priests and nuns caused widespread international indignation. The self-destructive path on which the Diem government seemed determined raised the problem of the extent to which the United States should, and indeed could, influence the course of development within an allied country. President Diem seemed to believe, as Chiang Kai-shek and Syngman Rhee of Korea had believed in their time, that the United States was too committed to his cause to be able to object to whatever path of action he chose to follow. Despite the heavy United States commitment to South Vietnam, therefore, the long-run prospects for the maintenance of the country outside the Communist orbit, while better than those in Laos, did not seem very encouraging when late in 1963 a group of military leaders, disturbed at the direction taken in the war against the Viet Cong and doubtless encouraged by expressions of American dissatisfaction with Diem, staged a *coup d'état* in the course of which the President was killed. The change of government briefly raised hopes that a more effective campaign against the pro-Communist guerrilla forces could be mounted. In view of the long-run tendencies at work in the area, however, it seemed all too likely that this would prove merely wishful thinking. Subsequent political turmoil and deterioration of the military situation afforded little room for American optimism, although United States aims were scaled down from complete elimination of the guerrillas from the country to a stalemate and cessation of the fighting. As increasingly heavier bombing raids against Communist North Vietnam failed to produce a Viet Cong willingness to negotiate, the Johnson administration reluctantly increased the number of American ground troops in South Vietnam to over a hundred thousand and began bombing raids on suspected Viet Cong strongholds in the south, even though the brunt of the raids fell on hapless civilians. Even should these tactics lead to a settlement, the possibility emerged that other states in the area might choose to come to terms with Communist China in the attempt to purchase immunity from the fate of Vietnam.

THE TWO CHINAS
AND THE OFFSHORE ISLANDS

Yet even the Chinese civil war that ended in the Communist victory of 1949 continued to exist in vestigial form and to provide its share of international difficulties. Expelled from the mainland, the Nationalist government took up residence in Taiwan (or Formosa), a large island off the coast of Fukien province in Southeast China. The Communist regime on the mainland continued to claim Taiwan as part of the national territory. To protect Nationalist possession of the island against invasion from the mainland, President Truman ordered the Seventh Fleet to patrol the Formosa Straits; to avoid the resumption of fighting in the area, the fleet was also to prevent attempts by Chiang to reinvade the mainland, an attempt thought likely to be forlorn and self-destructive. The opposition to the Truman administration laid heavy stress on this assignment of "protecting" Communist control of the mainland from the Nationalists, and when General Eisenhower took office in 1953 Chiang Kai-shek was "unleashed." No attempt to reinvade the mainland has, of course, been made, despite the Generalissimo's annual prediction on the tenth of October, the anniversary of the inauguration of the republican regime in China, that the year to come will be the year of his return to the mainland.

Although halfhearted attempts to envisage new and permanent modes of settlement of the anomalous condition of Formosa are made from time to time by various students of the situation, it seems overwhelmingly probable that the present situation will continue to exist indefinitely. Neither Nationalists nor Communists contemplate the acceptance of a solution legally establishing a separate republic of Taiwan; each protests that the island is simply a Chinese province. The possibility of the unilateral accession to mainland authority of a Formosa regime that came to power after the passing of the Generalissimo—he is now over seventy—has been suggested in some quarters, but at the present time seems quite unlikely to occur.

The resulting situation is legally awkward, especially at the United Nations, where a government whose authority is limited to Taiwan continues to speak as the voice of China; but in a world habituated to a continual round of crises and accustomed to assign priorities among them on the basis of how many people are being killed or likely to be killed as a result of each, a mere legal anomaly can continue to exist indefinitely without causing much disturbance.

In addition to Taiwan, the Nationalists retain control of a group of smaller islands, the Quemoy and Matsu islands, which lie a few miles off the mainland coast. This circumstance has given rise to one of those never-never-land situations in which the Cold War abounds. In themselves the Quemoy and Matsu islands have no value except in the context of a reinvasion of the mainland in which they would probably be valuable as staging areas. Contemplation of such an invasion is of course unrealistic. At the same time, it is extremely difficult to defend the islands against a determined assault from the mainland, some military authorities having referred to them as "indefensible." The Nationalists have, however, turned the islands into miniature fortresses, partly on principle, and partly against the day when a reinvasion of the mainland may occur. Somewhat baffled as to what attitude to adopt, the United States eventually settled on the principle that Quemoy and Matsu should be defended if an attack were launched upon them as part of an attack on Formosa. Although this formula makes very little strategic sense, it serves as something of a basis for United States policy, despite the fact that it violates one of the criteria for effective deterrence: It does not make clear what United States action would be in the event of an attack on the islands that was *not* at the same time an attack on Formosa. The tendency has been to assume that any threat to Quemoy and Matsu is in some sense a threat to Formosa, and the United States has accordingly assumed menacing postures whenever threats to Quemoy and Matsu were posed from the mainland. This, together with the heavy Nationalist fortification of the islands, has presumably had effect, and despite the occasional occurrence of a Quemoy-Matsu crisis when the danger of an invasion appears especially acute, the Communists have contented themselves thus far with the now desultory bombardment of the islands[1] and seem to have abandoned plans for their "liberation" for the time being, at least.

---

[1] Currently with shells containing leaflets.

THE PROBLEM OF THE TWO CHINAS

Too often the problem faced by the United States with respect to Communist China is regarded as being solely that of deciding whether or not to recognize the Communist government of the Chinese mainland, or how far or in what ways to oppose the admission of Communist China to the UN. These questions have been stewed over, rehashed, and cut and dried to the point that they have become standard themes for high school debates. Clearly the two questions named are only incidental to the central problems posed to United States foreign policy by Communist China, which consist primarily in the military and diplomatic threats to Western positions in Southeast Asia. Nevertheless, the twin problems of recognition and admission to the United Nations do exist, and it is necessary to comment on them.

One should first point out that the two questions are separable. That is, it would be possible for Communist China to be seated in the UN and yet unrecognized by other states that are members of the organization; it would also be possible, although difficult to justify, for a state that recognizes the Peking government to vote against her admission to the UN. The United States has, up to the time of writing, consistently spearheaded the opposition to the admission of Red China to the world organization, while continuing to recognize the Nationalist Chinese government on Formosa as the only legitimate government of China.

The major standing arguments for the admission of the Chinese Communist government to the UN are: that it is the effective government of China, after all; that it is a power whose agreement is necessary to world-wide settlements, on such questions as disarmament; that Peking's aggressive intentions can be modified by bringing the force of world opinion to bear on her in the international organization; that involving the Chinese in the voting on issues that takes place in the UN will make the contours of their policy more apparent, and will compel them to take sides on issues even where this involves the alienation of some states they are trying to cultivate; and finally, that the seating of the Chinese and their participation in UN affairs would tend to bring out in the open, and accentuate, the differences between them and the Soviet Union. It should be noted that the latter two arguments cited are based on the national interest of the United States in weakening the Communist powers; the first three give primacy to more general interests, especially those concerned with the maintenance of world peace. This is a typical feature of viewpoints on matters related to the UN: One can take a strictly national point of view, and urge only what is in the national interest; or one can argue in terms of the interest of the UN itself. While these two criteria often coincide, since the continued existence and strengthening of the world organization is itself part of United States policy, nevertheless they do diverge on occasion.

Against the admission of Communist China to the United Nations, it has been argued that the Chinese are not a "peace-loving" nation, as required by the UN charter; that to admit them would be to sanction their aggressive acts, especially in Korea, where they actually combated forces that were flying the UN flag; that a UN seat would give the Chinese an opportunity to exercise influence on other states, and would serve as a platform from which to spread propaganda; and that Chinese admission, especially in view of the long opposition to it maintained by the United States, would constitute a propaganda victory for the Chinese at American expense.

Without being powerfully moved by the arguments on either side of the issue, the present writer confesses that on the whole he sees more disadvantages than advantages in admitting Communist China to the UN. The argument that Chinese participation is necessary to the solution of important disputes does not move him, since important disputes are in fact not decided in the UN, nor would they be likely to be after the admission of the Peking regime; and he is inclined to believe that the admission of the expansionist Chinese would unnecessarily complicate the existence of a UN, which has a great deal of trouble merely surviving as it is. The long-run tendency seems to be for the admission of Communist China to gather support in the General Assembly, however. If the government of Communist China were admitted, the present writer would regard this as no more than a minor setback for United States policy and not as the major calamity it seems regarded by many Americans.

The recognition of the government of Communist China by the United States raises questions that are comparable to those posed by her admission to the UN. Those in favor of United States recognition have argued that recognition merely entails acknowledgment that the Peking government is actually the effective government of China; that recognition is a necessary prelude to the settlement of problems outstanding between the two states; and that recognition might lessen Red China's aggressive expansionism and perhaps accentuate the division between her and the Soviet Union. Those arguing against recognition normally take the position that to recognize the Communist government of China would imply approval of that government's present and past actions; that it would be regarded by the government of China as an admission of United States weakness, which would only encourage her in her aggressive plans; that it would represent a betrayal of the government of Chiang Kai-shek, and would undermine the morale of the Nationalists and weaken their hold on Formosa; that it would constitute a propaganda victory for the Chinese in Asia; and that it might lead those Chinese scattered throughout Asia to transfer loyalties from the Nationalists to the Communists, thus posing an internal security threat to the countries in which they live.

The present writer is inclined to believe that the arguments in favor of recognition are weaker than those against it—that is, although recognition does not legally imply approval, it tends to be regarded abroad as though it does; and it is possible to negotiate with other states and even to sign agreements with them (such as the Geneva agreements of 1955) without recognizing them. Nevertheless, he would be inclined to support the recognition of Communist China if this meant that the United States would have an ambassador and a full diplomatic staff at Peking permanently, and vice versa, since a great danger in the present situation is the almost total lack of knowledge of each state by the other, and the continued possibility of misunderstanding the other's intentions. It has been argued that Chinese intervention in the Korean war was based on a mistaken Chinese belief that the United States intended to invade China if it should succeed in occupying all of North Korea. Given the policy of deterrence which the United States follows in the Cold War, it seems to the present writer of the greatest importance that there should exist the maximum communication and comprehension of the other's objectives between potential antagonists, so that deterrence can work effectively, and so that the outbreak of war through misunderstanding and miscalculation can be averted. At present American knowledge and understanding of what goes on in China and in the Chinese government is limited and distorted, and the same is even more true of Chinese information about the intentions and capabilities of the United States.

It is unfortunately the case, however, that recognition may not necessarily imply the exchange of ambassadors and full diplomatic missions, and this point would have to be considered most carefully in any decision to recognize the Peking government. For example, the government of Great Britain has recognized Peking and yet the exchange of ambassadors has been blocked by the Chinese.

It goes without saying, moreover, that any recognition of Communist China would have to be handled so that it did not constitute an abandonment of the Nationalist government on Formosa in the sense that it implied the illegitimacy of that government or the right of the Communists to expel it from the island. Thus Formosa might be regarded as an autonomous province, legally part of the Chinese domain, but ruled separately—if the desire for an accord existed on all sides, a legal formula could doubtless be found. However, it is doubtful that the Chinese Communists would desire United States recognition strongly enough to yield, even by implication, their claim to absolute control of Formosa.

In the last analysis, though, the greatest obstacle to United States recognition of the Communist government of China is probably the unpopularity that such a step would have with the American public; this means that for all practical purposes recognition will not come in the forseeable future, regardless of how explicitly Americans come to negotiate with Chinese, even if the other formidable difficulties impeding recognition were resolved.

SUGGESTED READINGS

Barnett, A. Doak, *Communist China and Asia.* New York: Harper & Row, 1960.

———, *Communist Strategies in Asia.* New York: Praeger, 1963.

Brimmell, J. H., *Communism in Southeast Asia.* New York: Oxford University Press, 1959.

Fall, Bernard, *Street Without Joy.* Harrisburg, Pa.: Stackpole, 1963.

Fifield, Russell H., *Southeast Asia in United States Policy.* New York: Praeger, 1963.

Newman, Robert P., *Recognition of Communist China?* New York: Macmillan, 1961.

Scalapino, Robert, *The Communist Revolution in Asia.* Englewood Cliffs, N.J.: Prentice-Hall, 1965.

Scigliano, Robert, *South Vietnam: Nation Under Stress.* Boston: Houghton Mifflin, 1963.

Smith, Roger M., "Laos in Perspective," *Asian Survey,* January 1963.

———, *Cambodia's Foreign Policy.* Ithaca, New York: Cornell University Press, 1965.

Whiting, Allen, *China Crosses the Yalu.* New York: Macmillan, 1962.

I2

Confrontation in the Caribbean: The Case of Cuba

CUBA AND AMERICAN SECURITY

After Fidel Castro came to power in Cuba on January 1, 1959, a situation developed in which the United States found itself confronted with a Communist regime close to home in the Caribbean. The degree of excitement that the American public and political figures in the United States showed over this circumstance occasioned surprise and some alarm among its allies, in view of the fact that Cuba is intrinsically without significance in international relations—an island whose approximately six million people are dwarfed by a United States population thirty times that size. The degree of American concern over the self-described Marxist-Leninist character of the Cuban regime[1] is a striking illustration of the fact that, as far as human behavior is concerned, what is of significance is not the facts of the outside world themselves but perceptions of those facts. There is indeed a marginal diminution in American security created by the existence of a neighboring regime that is hostile and that encourages sabotage and other anti-American activities elsewhere in the Western Hemisphere. This problem will be discussed more extensively below. As a security problem, however, this pales into insignificance by the side of,

---

[1] First stated in these terms by Fidel Castro in a speech on December 2, 1961.

188

say, the traditional security problems of Belgium, existing precariously between two powerful neighbors, France and Germany; or of Finland, which remains independent only by virtue of the most delicate management of relations with her colossal Russian neighbor to the east. In other words the orientation of the current government of Cuba is regarded as a major threat to United States security only because the United States has in the past not had to live with the reality of powerful and unfriendly neighbors, and has thus become accustomed to an extremely high degree of security. Few states have historically enjoyed so high a degree of national security as the United States; it was this situation that made possible American isolationism, and it probably accounts in part for the exaggerated reactions that Americans typically show when confronted with minor and routine threats that are the everyday currency of international relations.

CUBA'S ALIGNMENT
WITH THE SOVIET BLOC

As is customary when United States policy suffers reverses, Americans legitimately ask themselves if there was anything that could have been done to avert the present outcome: Whose fault was it? In the case of Fidel Castro this general question sometimes takes the specific form: Did the United States drive Castro into the Russians' arms? Sometimes the alternative question is posed: Was Castro always pro-Communist, and if so should United States policy makers have known this and have tried to prevent his coming to power? The problem thus becomes one of evaluating how Fidel Castro evolved to his present political position, and of trying to determine whether actions, or failure to act, by the United States contributed to this evolution.

On this difficult range of issues, the present writer has come to the general conclusion that Fidel Castro was not a Communist, in the sense in which the term is normally used in the United States, before he came to power; that, given the circumstances of the time, the United States would not have been justified in trying to prevent his coming to power even if that were possible; and that, although some actions of United States policy makers may have contributed marginally to Castro's evolution towards the Soviet camp, only extraordinarily favorable United States policies, policies the United States could not reasonably have been expected to follow, would have stood any chance of keeping Castro from joining the Soviet camp.

Take first of all the question of Castro's personal orientation. Because of a sensational dispatch transmitted by one of the wire services, most Americans who have views on the problem probably believe that

Castro was a "dedicated Communist" long before his accession to power, but concealed his allegiance to make the road to power smoother. Any intelligent reading of the speech on which the UPI dispatch was based, that of December 2, 1961, however, shows that this interpretation is quite false, and that what Castro actually was saying was that he had opposed the Communists when he was first drawn into politics at the University of Havana, but that as the revolution developed, and as the revolutionary government was faced with the actual problems of ruling Cuba, he began to see the logic in the Communist position and became convinced that the Communist path was the appropriate one for the Cuban revolution to take. "Did I have prejudices? I believe it is good to talk about that. Did I have prejudices about the Communists? Yes. Was I ever influenced by imperialist and reactionary propaganda against the Communists? Yes."[2]

It is noteworthy that the Cuban Communist party interpreted Castro's evolution towards communism in similar terms. In a little-noted speech to the Cuban Communist party, the Popular Socialist party of Cuba, in August 1960, when Castro's political evolution was first taking him close to the Communist position, Blas Roca, the general secretary of the party, said:

> Fidel Castro is that very rare instance in Latin America, among men of his social origin, in that once he had achieved power he did not bend before or get frightened at the offensive of imperialism, nor did he deny his previous revolutionary statements. On the contrary, he developed toward the Left, he became more radical with each experience, and he merged with the popular masses (especially the farmers and the workers) and fulfilled and developed the program of the Revolution.[3]

Here Blas Roca is clearly saying that Castro developed toward the Left and "merged with the popular masses" (that is, aligned himself with the Communist party) only after coming to power and being faced with the problems of ruling Cuba.

Why did Fidel "merge with the popular masses?" Why did he "become more radical with each experience?" It seems clear that although Castro had been a candidate for student office on an anti-Communist ticket in his law school days, and had again run on the ticket of the democratic *Ortodoxo* party as a candidate for congress after receiving

---

2 *Fidel Castro Speaks on Marxism-Leninism.* New York: Fair Play for Cuba Committee, 1962, p. 64.

3 Blas Roca, *The Cuban Revolution.* New York: New Century Publishers, 1961, pp. 43–44.

his law degree, his political position in the years before he came to power was the vague Leftism, sympathy with the underdog, general distrust of the large and affluent United States and the North American companies that loomed large in the national economy, that was and is the typical position of the Latin American student politician. Given this orientation and this set of assumptions, Fidel Castro came to power. As the problems that face anyone involved in the task of actually governing a country arose, Castro came to see the force of the Communist position. For one concerned to change social and economic structures in the interest of improving the lot of the underdog, it was patently simpler to rule by decree than to observe the niceties of democratic procedures; and to Castro's egocentric temperament the natural opposition of business interests to his attempted measures of social reconstruction must have been intolerable. It must have been hard for the man who had been the symbol of the opposition of all decent people to the tyranny of the Batista regime, who had singlehandedly created an opposition movement when the universal opinion was that opposition was hopeless, who had fought for a better Cuba in the face of colossal odds, to credit the good faith of those who raised objections to his policies once in office.

It is probably in temperamental factors of this type that one should look for an explanation of the development of Castro's relations with the United States. In the spring of 1959, a few short months after he had come to power, Fidel Castro visited the United States, a visit that must have been of significance in his evolution towards the Soviet camp. Critics of United States policy have suggested that Castro was offended because the United States did not offer economic aid. This interpretation seems untenable at least as far as the facts can be known to someone who was not directly involved. Castro himself said that he had not come to the United States to ask for money, and his finance minister, who accompanied him on the trip and who has since defected, has said that he was under instructions not to request economic aid. To understand this position one needs to think in terms of the young rebel bent on asserting Cuba's independence, from the economic power of the United States as much as from its political power. It seems much more likely, given Castro's personality, that if anything helped to alienate him from the United States on his visit it was the lack of enthusiasm with which he was greeted; no arrangements were made for him to see President Eisenhower, and his meetings with Secretary of State Herter and Vice President Nixon did not remedy this omission.

In retrospect one can say that United States–Cuban relations might have proceeded along friendlier lines if Fidel Castro had been accorded a reception appropriate to the great man he felt himself to be. Most of the criticisms of United States policy during the period between Castro's coming to power and the end of the Eisenhower administration are of this type, one should note; they allege not that the United States acted incorrectly, or did anything less than the maintenance of cordial relations required, but that under the circumstances this was not enough: that the United States should have made special efforts, should have "gone the second mile."

But why, even granted that he was not enthusiastic about the United States, did Fidel Castro then go on to align himself with the Soviet bloc? Castro has himself given the answer:

> There are some who believe, who presume themselves to be sharp thinkers, when they insist that what the Cuban Revolution should have done was to take money from the Americans and take money from the Russians as well.
>
> That is to say there is no lack of people who preach such a repulsive, such a cowardly, such a cheap and vile political line. What they are saying is: sell yourself, sell the country as if it were any piece of merchandise to the imperialists. Take handouts from imperialism or else scare them with the threat of friendship with the Soviet Union; in other words, be a blackmailer. There were those here who peddled the line of blackmail.
>
> Ah, but how to blackmail? How would they carry out their line of blackmail? There was no room for such blackmail. To have done this would have meant to remain in the *status quo* prevailing in the country, to respect all the interests of imperialism here: all their thousands of acres, all their sugar mills, their electrical monopoly, their telephone company, their control of our foreign and domestic trade, of our banks. On the other hand, any country which decided to free itself from the monopoly grip of North American business, decided to carry out agrarian reform, decided to run its own industries, to carry on an independent policy, would have to take an anti-imperialist position.[4]

In other words, Fidel Castro arrived at two conclusions: social revolution in Cuba would have to be anti-American, since much of Cuban business was in American hands; and since Cuba would take an "anti-imperialist" path, it would necessarily be taking the path of the Soviet Union—there was no middle way. Of course, this shows his naïveté. There are a dozen "middle ways"—Castro is finding this out only too well now that the Communist bloc is itself split.

The thesis that the break with the United States came because Castro did not wish to compromise, did not wish to take American views and interests into account, wanted to tolerate no limits to his own powers

---

4 *Fidel Castro Speaks on Marxism-Leninism*, pp. 59–60.

and his plans for Cuba, is suggested by the fate that was meted out to opposition and potential opposition within the country. The vindictive arrest of Major Hubert Matos on charges of treason,[5] because he had resigned his post after failing to secure an interview with Castro to complain to him personally about the Communist infiltration of the government, was of central significance. Major Matos was sentenced to twenty years' imprisonment for his so-called crime.

Nevertheless, in assigning responsibility for the course Cuba followed to its present status as a member of the Soviet bloc, one must begin by acknowledging the errors committed by United States policy makers. This unhappy catalogue can be begun in the early years of the twentieth century, but this seems hardly necessary in order to make the point. During the period in which Batista ruled Cuba, American policy was far friendlier to the dictator than it need have been in the ordinary course of diplomatic business. After Fidel Castro came to power the United States government showed, in some respects, too little understanding of the problems he was facing, and was negligent in allowing United States territory to be used as a base from which exiles launched commando raids on the island; granted that it may not have been possible to eliminate all such attacks, there seems little doubt that official American attitudes were too casual about these raids during the first year or year and a half of the Castro government.

Yet it seems clear that if Fidel Castro had *wanted* to remain on good terms with the United States, it would have cost him very little to do so—some slowing in the tempo of revolutionary structural reforms, perhaps, hardly a great cost to a thirty-three-year-old who could look forward to an indefinite tenure of office. Other revolutionaries who were with him in the Sierra Maestra or in the government he formed have left him, after all, demonstrating that there was no ineluctable necessity to evolve to the position Castro now holds.

The answer to the riddle is surely that Castro is simply a rebel by temperament, one who had no patience with the niceties of diplomatic usage, and so struck out at the United States because Cuba's many ties with the United States were felt as hampering constraints. In looking back at what has transpired one sees the truth and the relevance of the comment made by President Illia of Argentina, that Fidel Castro is a young rebel who lacks maturity.

Castro's thesis that there was no middle way between the United States and the Soviet Union, between "imperialism" and "socialism," for example, is startlingly naive. Are all non-Communist paths really equivalent? Is there indeed no difference, as Castro has said, between Betancourt

---

[5] In November 1959.

and Pérez Jiménez, between Trujillo and Juan Bosch, between Hitler and Kennedy?

Nevertheless, the congeniality of the Communist framework—vast and rapid structural changes, personal dictatorship, "anti-imperialism"—to Castro's attitudes and temperament is striking.

Since Castro has proclaimed his allegiance to Marxism-Leninism, he must today be accounted a Communist—surely not a Communist in the sense of one who has come to feel that the interests of the Soviet Union as the leading "Socialist" state take precedence over all considerations, nor in the sense that his thinking has been so molded in Marxist forms that they completely determine his outlook on the world; but nevertheless, in some sense, a home-made, self-taught, do-it-yourself Communist. An examination of the propaganda materials put out by the Cuban regime leaves no doubt about the completeness of this new allegiance; the Communist version of history has been adopted *in toto,* complete with a South Korean invasion of North Korea in 1950, a fascist-imperialist attempt at a *coup d'état* in Hungary in 1956 that was put down by the valiant fighting of the proletarian masses, and flat assertions that the United States forces in the Korean war used germ warfare.

CUBA'S RELATIONS
WITH THE SOVIET UNION

Complementary to the evolution of the ideological position of the regime, external relations, both political and economic, have been completely reoriented so that Cuba is today politically a member of the Soviet bloc and economically totally dependent upon aid from the bloc. The United States' economic boycott, poor sugar harvests, mismanagement of the economy, and the loss of great numbers of skilled personnel have been offset somewhat by massive aid from the Soviet Union and her allies, although this constitutes a drain on the Soviet Union out of proportion to the benefit it is bringing to the Cuban economy. This is ironic in many ways; before the Cuban Revolution average *per capita* income in Cuba was one of the highest in Latin America and the highest of any country in the tropics, and life in Havana especially was in many respects more luxurious for the average person than it was in Moscow at the time. It has been said that Cuba's was the first "television revolution"; it was also the first air-conditioned revolution, and the first revolution complete with Coca-Cola.

Cuba's complete economic dependence upon the Soviet Union, from which she receives not only industrial equipment and manufactured goods but now also a substantial part of her food supply, is especially ironic in view of Castro's determination that Cuba be independent of foreign economic domination, since economic domination led to political domination also. In a sense what the Cuban leaders say is true, however, that Cuba's present dependence on the Soviet Union need not lead to political dictation by the Russians. Cuba's close economic ties with the United States in the old days were a natural reflection of Cuba's geographic proximity to the United States and a natural outgrowth of mutually advantageous trading relationships; thus economic ties gave rise to vested political interests (and Cuban sugar interests lobbied with the United States Congress just as North American economic interests tried to defend their positions in Cuba) and also to cultural penetration— Coca-Cola, baseball, American popular music, and so on. Cuba's economic ties with the Soviet Union, on the other hand, have no roots in economic logic or geographic proximity and need not necessarily carry connotations of ties in spheres other than the economic.

What happened was that Castro volunteered to enroll in the Soviet bloc; Khrushchev of course accepted, but found that the offer came with strings attached in the form of very heavy economic assistance. The relationship between Cuba and the Soviet Union thus constitutes another example of the principle that dealings between a large state and a small one are not determined solely by the power of the large state; in this case the commitment that Cuba imposed on the Soviet Union by volunteering to become a satellite made it necessary for the Soviet Union to avoid total collapse of the Cuban economy since this would then reflect unfavorably on the Soviet Union itself.

CUBA AND UNITED STATES POLICY

What should the United States do about a Cuba aligned with the Soviet bloc? Although this is hard for many Americans to accept, the answer is probably that the United States should continue to do what it is doing—in effect, nothing. There is no doubt that the present Cuban regime constitutes an embarrassment for the United States, and to some extent contributes to anti-Yankee activity in other Latin-American countries. As will be seen below, however, the nature of this problem is greatly misunderstood, and it is doubtful that the legend of a martyred Fidel Castro would be any less effective than the encouragement of a Fidel Castro who was Prime Minister of Cuba in fostering anti-American sentiments in the other countries of the hemisphere.

It seems likely that if it were thought worthwhile the United States would be able to remove the Castro regime from power by the direct intervention of United States military forces in Cuba. It is difficult to see that such an effort would be worth a fraction of the cost that it would involve, however, over and above the slim possibility that the Soviet

Union would come to Castro's aid. Such an invasion of Cuba would initially provoke the animosity towards the United States that was felt towards the Soviet Union at the time of its repression of the Hungarian uprising in 1956; but in this case the drain on the popularity and influence of the United States would be a continuous one, since it can be assumed that the supporters of the present regime would simply return to the hills from which they started out and conduct a guerrilla campaign against the occupying United States troops, or against any government that the United States installed or supported in Cuba. The United States would then be faced with a situation similar to the one that confronted the French in Algeria—a long, drawn-out war that could not be "won" in any final sense, that not only resulted in a steady loss of life and constituted a heavy financial burden, but also meant a standing propaganda disadvantage, and at the same time disruption of domestic American political life into the bargain. This all seems quite out of proportion to any advantage to be gained by the removal of the Castro government. It appears more reasonable to the writer at least to permit Fidel Castro to continue to weaken his cause in Latin America by demonstrating the bungling of his administrators, his helpless dependence on Russians who hold the Cubans in thinly veiled contempt, and the steady outward flow of exiles prepared to bear witness to the negative features of his rule. The damage that the latter factor can do to the pro-Soviet cause in the hemisphere was demonstrated by the contribution to the defeat of the Socialist-Communist coalition candidate for President of Chile in 1964 reputed to have been made by Juana Castro's bitter criticisms of her brother's regime.

It does not seem likely that viable alternatives exist between either coexisting with the Castro regime or invading Cuba with American troops. An invasion by Cuban exiles trained by the Central Intelligence Agency has been tried; it failed for a host of reasons that must include the inexperience of President Kennedy and the lack of competence demonstrated, principally by the CIA, in the planning and the execution of the operation. This seems to demonstrate the dangers of success, in that the CIA had presumably been encouraged to believe in the technique of the exile invasion, since an exile invasion conducted under similar auspices and with similar intent had apparently been successful in overthrowing the pro-Communist government of Guatemala in 1954; of course the circumstances were completely different in Guatemala, and the regime of President Arbenz was overthrown less by the invasion itself than by the disloyalty of his own army.

It seems plausible to assume that, other things being equal, Fidel Castro will eventually be overthrown by the Cubans themselves—most Latin American dictators are, after all, even though a Trujillo or a

Porfirio Díaz may last for thirty years. The rate at which the Castro government makes political and economic mistakes suggests that Castro's term of office will be considerably shorter than that of the two gentlemen named.

THE "MISSILE CRISIS" OF 1962

Cuba's role in international politics acquired new significance after the so-called missile crisis of October 1962. To recapitulate the major events of the period: Substantial numbers of Russian military "technicians" (that is, troops) were introduced into Cuba, ascending to a total of between 20,000 and 30,000 men. Medium-range rockets, including ground-to-ground rockets, were shipped into the island secretly and emplaced in launching sites. The presence of these rockets was discovered by flights over the island by U–2 reconnaissance planes, although Soviet representatives denied in general terms that weapons with "offensive capabilities" had been introduced into the island. President Kennedy, under Republican fire for having permitted the evolution of events to this state, and facing a midterm congressional election, responded by imposing a selective naval blockade of Cuba—which he termed a "quarantine," in the attempt to get around the fact that under international law a blockade is traditionally regarded as "an act of war"—under which he proposed to stop and search vessels headed to Cuba that might be carrying "offensive weapons," and not to allow any ships carrying such weapons to proceed. Alternative courses of action that had been considered by the President, and that remained within the bounds of possibility if the selective blockade were without effect, were a tighter blockade that would interdict the shipment to Cuba of the fuel oils that are essential to her economy; the destruction of the missile sites by bombing from the air; or the invasion of the island by United States forces. The troop and weapons movements that were necessary preliminaries to the latter two actions were put into execution.

The Soviet Union capitulated almost instantaneously. Ships carrying missiles to Cuba were ordered to turn around, the missile sites on the island were dismantled, and the withdrawal of the missiles from Cuba begun. The gradual withdrawal of Soviet troops was also initiated.

Although the Russians capitulated 100 percent in the face of the American response to their establishment of missile bases in Cuba, Khrushchev attempted to save face in ways that the United States tried to facilitate. The United States in effect abandoned its early insistence that the former missile sites be inspected to make sure that they had in fact been destroyed. There seems little doubt that this has actually occurred, even though some of those on the extreme Right of political opinion in the United States profess to believe that there are missiles on the island hidden underground or in caves.

In view of the fact that an actual United States invasion of the island to disarm the bases had been considered, and that after the removal of the missiles it was clear that the purpose of such an invasion had disappeared, Khrushchev claimed that his emplacement and subsequent withdrawal of the missiles was a deliberate manuever on his part to secure the abandonment of United States invasion plans; every attempt was made to present what was a complete Soviet capitulation as a clever and complex but successful diplomatic gambit. Nevertheless, the failure of Khrushchev's Cuban missile policy was one of the counts in the indictment drawn up against him by those who removed him from power in 1964.

THE OUTCOME OF THE MISSILE CRISIS

Viewed in retrospect the Cuban missile crisis has the character of the apex of a hill lying on the road that the United States has been following since World War II. It made possible a more accurate and more comprehensive view of the road that had been traveled; it made possible a glimpse of the road that lay ahead; and indeed the road that leads away from the hill heads in a rather different direction from the one it would have taken if the hill were not there.

The missile crisis brought to an end an era in Cuban–United States relations and, more importantly, to an era of Soviet-American relations. What Khrushchev said to try to justify his withdrawal of the missiles from Cuba was in a sense true—he had secured an understanding that the United States would not invade Cuba. It seems clear for several reasons that the termination of the missile crisis marked the acceptance by the Kennedy-Johnson administrations of a policy of coexistence with Castro's Cuba. Until then it had been felt that, in some form or other, Cuba under communism might at some future time pose a direct threat to United States security. With the missile crisis, that threat was posed and defied; the worst was past, and most of the tension subsided.

This *détente* could take place because by withdrawing the rockets the Soviet Union had acknowledged that a limit existed to her forward push in the Cold War. By blockading the island the United States had made clear what she considered to be the limit of permissible Cold War politics short of violence. In accepting the United States' definition of the problem and withdrawing from Cuba in the interests of all concerned, the Soviet Union acknowledged that this was a game that had not been played by the rule book.

Accordingly, it was the paradoxical result of the showdown over the missile bases in Cuba that a new mutual respect and mutual confidence between the United States and the Soviet Union became apparent in their post-October dealings. This is not to say that the solution of any major substantive issues was made possible as a result of the changed international atmosphere. What did happen, however, was that it became possible to make agreements of relatively minor significance, which were in the interest of both sides but which the greater insecurity and lack of definition of the conflict had made impossible to achieve earlier. An agreement growing directly out of the character of the crisis was the arrangement for direct teletype communication between the White House and the Kremlin so as to avoid misunderstandings in the event of a crisis situation in which rapid communication was of importance. Within a year of the missile crisis the treaty pledging that the parties would not test nuclear weapons in the atmosphere was signed and ratified. Thus in the paradoxical fashion of the Cold War, just as safety had been the fruit of mutual deterrence, so now the most vivid of mutual threats gave rise to a relaxation of tension and a sort of understanding.

Another of the long-run effects of the Cuban missile crisis was that it highlighted the different points of view to be found within the Communist and pro-Communist movements. This effect was especially marked in Latin America. In the first place the secret introduction of missiles to Cuba, missiles that remained throughout under Russian control, clearly indicated the extent to which Cuba had become dependent on the Soviet Union. This served to alienate from Castro's cause many people, especially in Latin America, who had favored the Cuban leader as a revolutionary and a patriot, but did not relish Cuba's becoming simply a conveniently situated piece of land to be used for Cold War purposes.

While it may seem strange to Americans long committed to an anti-Soviet position that anyone could still become disillusioned over Soviet behavior at this juncture, so important a Latin American Communist as Carlos Manuel Pellecer, the leader of the Guatemalan Communist party, resigned from the movement over this issue. When Khrushchev ordered the withdrawal of Soviet missiles from Cuba, without even consulting Castro, an interesting difference of opinion was revealed. The long-time, thoroughly committed Communist fell into step with the new change in direction almost as if by reflex, dutifully praising Khrushchev's actions. Even the veteran Cuban Communists took this line. However the "new Communists" in Cuba, that is, those who followed Castro rather than the policies of Moscow, together with the great bulk of pro-*fidelista* opinion in Latin America, condemned the move. This revealed quite clearly that the new Left in Latin America is more extreme, more revolutionary, than the Communists themselves—more "Trotskyite," if one wishes to resurrect the term. The organs of the Chinese Communist party took a similar view. This provided a clear demonstration that the Soviet Union and the Communist parties that continue to follow the Russian lead no longer occupy the extreme Left of the political spectrum.

CASTRO AND THE WESTERN HEMISPHERE

Now that the United States has acknowledged, by its acts if not by its words, that it is prepared to coexist with the Castro regime in Cuba, the focus of the debate over Cuba has shifted from the question of how to get rid of Fidel Castro to the question of how to prevent the spread of his influence in the Latin countries of the hemisphere. As to the precise nature of the threat that Castro represents, one is presented with a wide variety of opinion, ranging roughly from the view that the threat consists of Cuba's demonstrating the social and economic benefits of a Socialist regime, to the view that the threat derives from the possibility of the invasion of other Latin American countries by Cuban troops, or at the least, the shipment of arms and the relaying of orders for insurrection from Moscow.

It seems to the present writer, however, that these conceptions of the nature of the threat of Castro's Cuba are deduced from doctrine, not from fact, and that the distinctively "Castroite" threat to the *status quo* in the hemisphere, or to its evolution in more desirable directions by non-violent paths, is the *fidelista* recipe for revolution. The nature of this formula is clear. It is that a relatively small number of students, using violent means, can overthrow an existing regime. On the one hand, the students establish contact with dissatisfied peasants and begin a rural guerrilla movement that secures and steadily expands a territorial base. On the other hand, the students, through acts of terrorism in the cities, dramatize the struggle and win sympathy from bourgeois elements as the government is forced to use police repression against the urban terrorists. In other words, the essential element that the *fidelistas* have contributed to the current scene is not primarily an ideology, nor a source of material, but a technique. The leading Cuban political exports to the other Latin countries of the hemisphere are three books, and they are not theoretical works by Marx or Lenin. They are General Bayo's *One Hundred and Fifty Questions for a Guerrilla Fighter;* Mao Tse-tung's *Tactics of a Guerrilla Fighter,* a quarter of a million Spanish copies of which have been published by the Cuban government press; and Guevara's booklet on guerrilla tactics, which must also have been printed in the hundreds of thousands.

In many states of the area the conditions necessary for the successful application of the *fidelista* formula do not apply. There is no dissatisfied mass of landless peasants in the pastoral economies of Uruguay and Argentina, or where small holdings predominate or a program of land distribution has begun, as in Costa Rica, Mexico, Bolivia, and Haiti. In Chile peaceful and electoral opportunities of coming to power still exist that must seem more promising to the extreme Left than guerrilla war (although they seem to the present writer unlikely to lead to success).

The attractive power of the Cuban Revolution tends to be overestimated in the United States in any case. A U.S. Information Agency sample survey made in late 1962 in one of the Latin American countries, for example, found that only forty-five percent of the peasants could identify Fidel Castro by name, and of those who could, sixty-three percent had a "negative opinion."[6] This was to be expected: Although Castro's appeal is supposed to be mainly to the peasants, it is precisely the peasants who pay the most attention to the priest; and the clergy has been especially active in condemning Castro for his adherence to communism, which is regarded as primarily an antireligious doctrine.

Nevertheless, the importance of Castroism is much greater than its prospects of coming to power in any given country. It appeals strongly to university youth, and is in all likelihood the dominant ideology on the majority of Latin American campuses (probably followed by Christian Democracy); students are often a strategic political group, although not numerous. At the same time its trouble-making potential for pro-United States governments is serious. One remembers the campaigns of Zapata and Sandino, and the Cacos War against the Marines in Haiti, which make clear the tactical difficulties and the political unpopularity of fighting wars against guerrillas. Castroism can appeal not only to a tradition of guerrilla warfare in many countries, but also to widespread anti-Americanism, some of it earned by past United States policies in the area, most of it not.

It is unlikely that the difficulties created for the hemisphere's governments by the *fidelistas* would diminish measurably if Castro himself were overthrown in Cuba. If the United States were involved, his standing as a martyr would probably rise sharply. The weapons that Cuba is reputedly supplying here and there are not a crucial factor; a great many weapons are in private hands in Latin America, as a result of past epochs of violence diverted from military stocks. In his booklet Guevara makes a special point of stressing that guerrillas must be able to secure their own weapons.

The best hope of containing Castroism lies thus not necessarily in overthrowing Castro, but rather in maintaining an informational and

---

6 Reported by the agency's deputy director in testimony before a subcommittee of the House Foreign Affairs Committee on February 21, 1963.

cultural offensive, especially with regard to the university students, that makes clear the failures of the Castro regime while it tries to soften the harshness of the intellectuals' anti-Americanism; and by giving appropriate support to governments that pursue policies of reform and thus rally popular and especially peasant support to democratic regimes.

SUGGESTED READINGS

Alexander, Robert J., *Communism in Latin America*. New Brunswick, N.J.: Rutgers University Press, 1957.

Blas Roca, *see* Calderío, Francisco.

Burks, David D., *Cuba Under Castro* (Headline Series No. 165). New York: The Foreign Policy Association, 1964.

Calderío, Francisco, *The Cuban Revolution*. New York: New Century Publishers, 1961.

Draper, Theodore, *Castro's Revolution*. New York: Praeger, 1962.

————, *Castroism: Theory and Practice*. New York: Praeger, 1965.

Fidel Castro Speaks on Marxism-Leninism. New York: Fair Play for Cuba Committee, 1962.

Larson, David L. (ed.), *The "Cuban Crisis" of 1962: Selected Documents and Chronology*. Boston: Houghton Mifflin, 1963.

MacGaffey, Wyatt, and Clifford R. Barnett, *Twentieth Century Cuba*. New York: Doubleday (Anchor), 1965.

Pachter, Henry M., *Collision Course: The Cuban Missile Crisis and Coexistence*. New York: Praeger, 1963.

Poppino, Rollie, *International Communism in Latin America: A History of the Movement 1917–1963*. New York: Free Press, 1964.

Seers, Dudley (ed.), *Cuba: The Economic and Social Revolution*. Chapel Hill, N.C.: University of North Carolina Press, 1964.

Szulc, Tad, and Karl Meyer, *The Cuban Invasion*. New York: Praeger, 1962.

V

The Politics
of Amicable Relations

I3

Can the Cold War Be Ended?

Quite naturally, the tensions of the Cold War have led to a continuing search on the part of most people of good will to try to find some alternative approach on which American policy might be based. At the same time the relative success of the policy of containment of Russian expansionism appears to have led to a greater quiescence and lack of aggressiveness in Russian policy that gives encouragement to hopes that a new approach might meet with success. In this chapter a range of suggested new approaches will be considered and an attempt will be made to see what value, if any, they may have.

PROPOSALS FOR STRUCTURAL CHANGE

Proposals have frequently been made for the creation of a world law,[1] compliance with whose dictates would replace the sword as arbiter among nations. Although one might object to this or that aspect of any putative structure of world law—especially, for example, the participation in the making of such laws by people of different legal systems from our own, and of different values and modes of thought—the vision of a world regulated by just laws and not by force of arms is nevertheless an attractive one. The definitive objection to any such proposals, however,

---

[1] Note that this is not the same as "international law," which does exist at present, and has been discussed above.

must be that they are impossible of attainment in any forseeable future; clearly no state, and certainly not the United States, would go so far in voluntarily relinquishing its present powers of self-determination as the creation and maintenance of such a system of law would require. To attempt to *compel* membership of all states in a system of world law, on the other hand, would, given the present stage of arms development, be out of the question.

Similar objections apply to related proposals for the organization of a genuine world government (since the creation of world law-making, -amending, -interpreting, and -enforcing institutions is tantamount to the creation of a world government), and it is difficult to perceive how anyone who has followed the course of international developments over the last fifteen years, or indeed during any other period of history, could believe for a moment that the Soviet Union, say, would consent to the loss of sovereignty that the formation of a world government would require. An authentic world government may, of course, come into existence at some future date; but given the present situation, the most likely manner in which this would occur would be as a result of the accession of a single powerful state to a position of unchallengeable world domination. This has been the manner in which previous "world governments" have arisen, after all.

PROPOSALS FOR PSYCHOLOGICAL CHANGE

A less ambitious attempt to eliminate interstate hostilities aims at the promotion of international understanding and the reduction of tensions among states on the basis of cultural exchange programs and "education for world citizenship." This type of approach bases itself on such premises as that wars derive from hostile feelings that peoples entertain for each other, and that these in turn are based on national stereotypes of the peoples of other states as possessing all kinds of unpleasant attributes, and by a lack of tolerance for other ways of life than one's own. "Wars begin in the minds of men"; accordingly, one must eliminate the putative causes of war by promoting international travel and cultural exchange and by eliminating the biases in the early education of the child that instill in him national chauvinism and prejudices against other peoples.

In themselves these goals are laudable. Whether or not their attainment will eliminate the causes of future wars is another matter, however. The agenda in the first place is a colossal one if it requires nothing less than universal re-education, and the practical difficulties are probably insurmountable. But in any case, the prescription is based on an improper diagnosis of the malady. While it may be possible to discover wars that had their origin in a lack of understanding or in cultural intolerance, it is more typically the case that national stereotypes and prejudices against other peoples are the results of wars rather than their causes; in fact an image of the antagonist as possessing all kinds of unpleasant qualities typically generates itself, or is generated by government propaganda, *after* the conflict has begun. And on the other hand national antipathies, and even sympathies, can be overcome by the pressures of power politics.

Thus American antipathy to the Japanese and their ways, so virulent during World War II, has by now largely evaporated; the centuries-old British aversion to the French, on the other hand, which one can find reflected in the writings of so liberal a person as John Stuart Mill, seemed to be overcome easily when the exigencies of politics made Britain and France allies against Germany before and during World War I. At the same time one finds in German writings, not only in the interwar period but even while World War II was in progress—even in the writings and published conversations of Hitler himself—a steady admiration for British character and ways of acting. There seems to be little justification, accordingly, for believing that wars are based on pre-existing cultural antagonisms or national prejudices.

The writer cannot refrain from adding that it might well be the case (and has indeed occurred in his own experience) that greater acquaintance with other peoples, and travel or residence among them, increases antipathy rather than removes it. The French proverb that to understand everything is to pardon everything, while containing much truth, is not wholly valid.

A more subtle approach to the problem of attaining lasting peace based on comity among states and peoples proposes the taking of a series of steps that steadily reduce tensions that might, if permitted to continue, feed on themselves and create acute hostilities leading to war. This approach is in part based on the sound insight that, given a world organized on the basis of sovereign states, each state must provide for its own defense and this must necessarily be based on the expectation of conflict as normal. The fact that other states are creating armies tends in turn to validate one's suspicions that they do indeed have hostile intentions, and it is thus possible for arms races to develop and even for preventive wars to be launched where in fact no underlying conflict of interest exists. This effect, that the provision of each state for its own security may lead to heightened insecurity, has been called "the security dilemma." Where tensions between states have no ultimate substantive basis, but derive only from the structure of international relations, there can be promise in a program aimed at the deliberate reduction of tension by the making of concrete gestures of good will, such as the renunciation of a territorial claim, or the relinquishment of some good to the other. One must immediately note, however, that such gestures may not disarm suspicions at all but may be interpreted as tricks of some kind to put the other off his guard so that he may be outmaneuvered or so that his demands may be bargained down. This is indeed the intention of many "goodwill gestures." More importantly, such a gesture can also be interpreted as a confession of weakness or a demonstration of incapacity and serve to incite the other state to ambitious undertakings not originally contemplated.

In the present world situation, however, it cannot be said that the tensions that exist between East and West have no substantive basis. It seems fairly clear that the Soviet Union, until checked by the deliberate embarkation of the United States and its allies on a policy of containment, had expansionist goals that it was prepared to realize by violent means where these could be used to advantage. In other words, for the Western states the tensions that exist between the two leading states of the world are functional, just as the creation of anxiety in the individual organism may be functional, in providing the capability to meet the threat. That is, because of Stalin's post-war policies, tensions arose between the Soviet Union and the Western states that led to the creation of NATO and to other initiatives resulting in the frustration of Soviet expansionism, which might not have been possible had the Soviet Union chosen a path of action that was subtler and that did not arouse Western misgivings so strongly. It might actually be more accurate to take the viewpoint that the maintenance of world peace requires not the reduction of tensions but their maintenance, since the *status quo* is currently maintained by a balance of power created out of tension itself. Indeed, as the stalemating of Russian ambitions in Europe has appeared to become definitive over the last ten to fifteen years, some of America's allies have relaxed greatly, not living up to their NATO commitments, for example. The danger remains, however, that should all the states of the West relax and tensions be eased, the Soviet Union may be emboldened to begin again its expansionist policies—a possibility that, in the opinion of the present writer, is more likely to lead to the outbreak of war than the present situation of stalemate.

DISARMAMENT

A perennial favorite and currently a popular prescription for the attainment of permanent peace is disarmament. One should distinguish here between disarmament proper, that is, total disarmament, and "arms control," which may involve the reduction of armaments or their limitation in other ways without the presumption that all arms will be abolished. First total disarmament will be discussed, leaving arms control for later consideration.

The premise on which disarmament is based is deceptively plausible: If men lack the tools with which to fight, they will not be able to fight. The standard rejoinder here is that if all the weapons that exist today could be thrown into the sea it would still be possible for men to fight and to kill each other with sticks, stones, and table knives. This seemingly ingenuous response points at a basic truth: that it will not be possible to abolish weapons until men feel that they will not need them to fight, in self-defense or otherwise. In other words, it is not the possession of weapons that causes men to fight; and thus removal of weapons will in no way remove fighting itself, although if it were possible to effect, it would surely be worthwhile in reducing the number and types of casualties.

A classic illustration of the dichotomy between the belief that disarmament would mean the end of warfare and the realization that self-defense requires the possession of weapons is provided by the following excerpt from a speech of Mrs. Golda Meir, the Israeli Foreign Minister, to the United Nations General Assembly. As reported in the New York *Times* of October 10, 1962, Mrs. Meir said:

> It is the tragedy of our generation that after two World Wars the long drawn-out discussions on disarmament are held as though we had a choice between war and peace.
>
> If only the negotiators in Geneva were to decide unanimously that there was no such choice, it would be a real breakthrough toward disarmament.

However, going on to reply to Arab complaints that Israel was to buy rocket missiles made in the United States, Mrs. Meir said "As long as Arab belligerency continues, Israel will take all necessary measures to be capable of protecting itself."

Even if it should be possible to get all states to agree to disarm, which it clearly is not, difficulties would continue to present themselves. For example, all states have police forces, equipped with weapons, to preserve domestic order. Clearly total disarmament would have to stop short of the disarming of such police forces; and yet the differences between the training and armament of police and soldiers are differences of degree only, and indeed one or two states call a "police" what is in fact an army, for example, the government of East Germany.

Finally, the formidable difficulties that would present themselves to the enforcement of a total-disarmament agreement would make it only too likely that political activists of various persuasions all over the world would attempt to create secret caches of weapons in the hope that everyone else would observe the disarmament agreement, enabling them to emerge subsequently with the concealed arms and be able to effect their various purposes. One thinks of "patriotic" organizations such as the Minutemen in the United States, and their preoccupation with small-arms training. In other words, the more total the disarmament agreed upon, the greater the incentives would be to cheat on the agreement.

At the risk of appearing cynical, one has to conclude that the feasibility of total disarmament is precisely nil. From time to time the great powers reaffirm their support for the principle of total disarmament, but it can hardly be more obvious that the Soviet Union initiates the pledges to total disarmament as the most insincere of propaganda gestures, while other states follow suit only to avoid being placed in a bad light by the Russian initiative.

ARMS CONTROL

Although often confused with disarmament, arms control is based on rather different premises and presents much more practicable possibilities for action. In contrast to disarmament, and instead of ignoring fundamental conflicts of interest and aspirations among states, arms control assumes that conflict will continue to exist; but it goes further, to an appreciation of the fact that common interests exist, even between enemies. This was noted in a previous chapter when it was acknowledged that even though every state attempted to keep the level and condition of its armaments a secret, each nevertheless found it had an interest in allowing other states to station military attachés in their embassies on its soil. The point is that just as foreign states have an interest in finding out the level of one's armaments, each state has an interest in seeing that its own strength is not underestimated—since underestimation weakens the deterrent effect of its forces. Thus even states hostile to each other have a common interest in avoiding misunderstanding and errors of calculation. Similarly, hostile states have a common interest in seeing that war does not break out between them as a result of some accident.

It is possible to conceive of several areas of common interest that exist, even between the Soviet Union or Communist China and the United States, where, at least in principle, it is thus possible to devise acceptable measures of arms control. For example, the testing of nuclear weapons in the atmosphere produces radioactive débris that may be harmful in some measure to all people, and whose creation it is in the interest of all states to prevent. For this and other reasons, it was thus possible in 1963 for the Soviet Union, Britain, and the United States to agree to a ban on nuclear testing in the atmosphere, in outer space, and under water, an agreement that was embodied in the Treaty of Moscow and adhered to by almost all states of the world, the principal exceptions being Gaullist France and Communist China—although military men in the United States, and presumably in Russia too, were unenthusiastic about the treaty.

As was pointed out above, it is to the interest of both sides in an arms race to avoid miscalculation and misunderstanding; thus it was possible for both superpowers to agree to the installation of direct communication links (the "hot-line" teletype) between Moscow and Washington during mid-1963.

Another area in which common interests exist is in limiting the capabilities of third states. It would thus be in the interests of both super powers to conclude an agreement that neither would give nuclear weapons to states that do not now have them. In actuality such an "agreement" does implicitly exist. No treaty that embodies it as a provision has been signed; but none needs to be, and in fact each superpower refrains from fostering the spread of nuclear weapons, to the chagrin of the French on the one side and the Chinese on the other.

It is possible to conceive of other areas in which the Soviet Union and the United States might come to share common interests, at least in principle, although it is difficult to give concrete effect to that common interest without also disadvantaging one side relative to the other; in such a case the country disadvantaged would presumably refuse to conclude the agreement. Nevertheless, there is no intrinsic reason why the Soviet Union and the United States could not again make common cause against a third state, as they did in using pressure to induce the British and French to discontinue their military measures in the Suez Canal area in 1956, when the latter countries combined with Israel in the attempt to bring about the fall of President Nasser. Needless to say, many Americans questioned the wisdom of the decision to oppose the British and French on this occasion. However, similar contingencies may arise in the future, and Russians and Americans may find themselves joining again, in attempts to oppose Chinese expansionism, for example.

Very great difficulties present themselves to the conclusion of any agreements entailing the control or limitation of arms, however. In the first place neither side would agree to measures that would place it at a relative disadvantage. This difficulty is almost insurmountable since, because of their differing geographic situations, resources, and strategic requirements, different states rely in different degrees on any given weapon. Thus a landlocked state will be willing to agree to limitations on naval armaments, while a state possessing limited manpower resources will be eager to put a ceiling on the number of men that can be kept under arms. This point is illustrated by Salvador de Madariaga's charming fable of the disarmament conference of the beasts.

When the animals had gathered, the lion looked at the eagle and said gravely, "We must abolish talons." The tiger looked at the elephant and said, "We must abolish tusks." The elephant looked back at the tiger and said, "We must abolish claws and jaws." Thus each animal in turn proposed the abolition of the weapons he did not have, until at last the bear rose up and said in tones of sweet reasonableness: "Comrades, let us abolish everything—everything but the great universal embrace."[2]

Great difficulties are also presented by the necessity that any agreement not permit the possibility of cheating by either party. On this score a host of technical problems exist, since most weapons are relatively easy to conceal. Moreover, the Soviet Union, as a closed society reluctant to admit foreigners and allow them free contact with Soviet citizens, shrinks instinctively from any arrangement that entails the incursion of numbers of foreign inspectors, some of whom may in any case be disguised spies.

If ever an arms limitation agreement should be concluded, it would have to be carefully drawn indeed. Its provisions would have to be such that if one party to the agreement should break it, then the other could likewise resume its freedom of action without having been placed at a disadvantage during the period in which it observed the agreement. Thus the United States could not afford to agree to refrain from developing a weapon, if it were possible that the weapon could be developed in secret by the Soviet Union, giving her a significant advantage in having gained time. When one contemplates these and other formidable difficulties involved, one is brought to the reluctant conclusion that whatever further arms control measures may be agreed on are likely to be of limited scope.

If the United States should conclude further arms limitation agreements with the Russians, the country's leadership will need to explain the agreement with great care to the American public, and to make clear its limitations, to avoid misunderstanding at home. There would, on the one hand, exist the danger that the more optimistic among us would jump to the conclusion that since an agreement had been reached, the political conflict between the two powers was at an end, and accordingly that the military budget could be reduced and our mutual defense alliances neglected, although this would, of course, not be the case. An even stronger danger, especially in view of the fact that the agreement as a treaty would need to be approved by the Senate, is that the more cynical and suspicious among us would jump to the alternative conclu-

---

[2] Quoted by Ivo D. Duchacek in *Conflict and Cooperation among Nations*. New York: Holt, Rinehart, and Winston, 1960, pp. 502–503, giving Winston Churchill as the original source.

sion that the administration had "sold out," had been duped by the Russians, or perhaps even had willfully betrayed the national interest because of sympathy with communism.[3] It might be possible that this latter type of reaction would occur in the Soviet Union too, with a more extreme Stalinist faction within the Soviet leadership taking the position that the group in control had shown itself to be "soft on capitalism"; this might then lead to a redistribution of power within the party presidium and the repudiation of the agreement. Some of these effects in mild form were visible after the signing of the test-ban treaty.

PACIFISM

Of course the ultimate prescription for ending the Cold War is the approach inherent in pacifism itself. One might characterize true pacifism as the refusal to use violence under any circumstances. This position has surely been misunderstood, both by its opponents and by some individuals who consider themselves pacifists. Pacifism does not and cannot mean simply an aversion to the use of violence; surely everyone except the psychopath prefers to settle problems without violence if possible. Even the most unscrupulous aggressor, so long as he does not enjoy the use of violence for its own sake, prefers to attain his goals by peaceful means if this is possible—this was probably true even of Hitler. Pacifism can thus be understood to mean only the absolute refusal to use violence under any circumstances.

It is the hope of the pacifist that the adoption of his attitude by a whole nation will lead to its being able to avert war—in the first place because international hostility and the fighting to which it gives rise derives solely or principally from the security dilemma that was discussed above; that is, states arm simply because of fear of their neighbors and this in itself provokes their neighbors to arm in turn, even though both would prefer not to have to arm nor to fight the wars that, he believes, the arms race between them generates. Adoption of the pacifist approach would, in this view, break the vicious circle of needless competitive armament that leads to war.

Some pacifists go further than this and acknowledge that peoples and their leaders may harbor aggressive intentions over and above those generated by the security dilemma itself; but they go on to argue that the example of the pacifist state facing the world of international relations with benevolence and good will would prove too powerful to be resisted and would win over the nonpacifist to a similar attitude.

The most sophisticated of the pacifists acknowledge that pacifist means may not be adequate to eliminate threats to the peace and to

---

[3] The Bailey-Knebel book and movie *Seven Days in May* were based on a hypothetical situation of this type.

avoid actual invasion and occupation of the national territory. The true pacifist can maintain his faith while coming to terms with this realization in two ways. The more saintly can acknowledge that suffering may be necessary in the cause of righteousness; they may then find comfort in the biblical precept that suffering is beneficial to the soul, or in the sterner injunction that it is better to suffer evil than to inflict it. The more practically oriented may argue that occupation by an enemy is after all not the end of the world, that life goes on, and perhaps even that the occupying power may withdraw when confronted with the difficulties of governing against the will of a hostile population.

This latter view shades into the defeatism of those Englishmen whose viewpoint has been characterized as "better Red than dead." Many excitable patriots, incensed at this apparent willingness to capitulate to the Communist enemy, have gone to the extreme of proclaiming their preference for being dead rather than Red. In the author's schedule of preferences being dead comes in second best in most of the sets of alternatives he can call to mind; but of course the whole point of American foreign policy in the current age is the belief that one does not have to be either Red or dead, but that other alternatives exist—the leading one being the strategy of deterrence on which United States policy is currently based.

One should surely accord all honor to the genuine pacifist prepared to suffer evil rather than to commit it, prepared perhaps like Thoreau to go to jail rather than to pay a tax whose proceeds would be used to fight an unjust war or, like contemporary civil rights workers and nonviolent racial demonstrators in the South, to be beaten and jailed in a cause they believe just. It may even be that certain special circumstances exist under which the pacifist alternative can in fact be successful in achieving justice without violence. Such cases must, however, be very rare, if they indeed exist. The example often cited of the British withdrawal from India after World War II is not strictly appropriate, despite the fact that most Indians seeking independence from Britain used nonviolent techniques of protest. After all, the British gave independence to a host of other territories after World War II; passive resistance in India may have moved up the date of independence somewhat,[4] but one would be hard put to argue that it was more effective in this regard than was the terrorism practiced by some who favored the end of colonial rule in Israel or Cyprus. And even in India, one has to acknowledge that nonviolence was a more plausible strategy against the highly civilized British than it would have been against the people of any other world power. One can imagine the reaction of a German occupation force to passive resistance

---

[4] Some observers have thought that passive resistance instead actually delayed the date of independence.

techniques; when Indian demonstrators lay down on the railroad tracks in British India, the trains didn't run; in Nazi Germany the outcome would hardly have been so favorable. It is surely not unfair to stress this point since Gandhi did in fact counsel the Jews of Germany to use passive resistance tactics against Hitler—one can imagine what success they would have had!

The fact that the Nazis actually existed and ruled Germany is the most effective answer to the pacifist argument. A war that prevented Hitler's controlling the world was surely a war worth fighting by almost any standard. It remains possible to rejoin that the Communists are not as bad as the Nazis, and that in any case the scope of a war fought today would be much greater and the damage much more terrible than that which resulted from the events of a quarter-century ago. One must point out, nevertheless, that for the Communist powers as much as for Hitler, the adoption of a pacifist attitude by a rival state would in all probability have the effect of encouraging aggressive designs rather than lessening them.

DOES HUMAN NATURE MAKE WAR INEVITABLE?

Even though one may be skeptical as to the effectiveness of pacifist means in achieving or maintaining international peace, or even though one may not personally share the belief that violence is unjustified under any circumstances, it is not necessary to go to the extreme of saying that the fighting of wars is somehow inherent in human nature, although many people do resort to this argument. That such an argument is fallacious is demonstrated conclusively by the fact that whole generations of individuals in some countries have lived their lives without ever engaging in warfare. The Swiss, for example, have not been directly involved in warfare for over a century.

Giving the argument a narrower scope, however, one must acknowledge that aggressiveness *is* in human nature, at least in the sense of human nature in society. It may be that aggressive drives are instinctual; but in any case aggressive feelings certainly arise from the frustration of other basic drives that society imposes on the individual. Social living contains mechanisms for frustrating individual desires; society would clearly be impossible if everyone were free to follow his elementary drives. And the frustrations imposed by society give rise to resentment and aggressive feelings. But there is no reason that these feelings of aggression need issue in warfare. Aggressiveness need not be afforded any outlet whatsoever, as occurs in some societies; it simply takes its toll in a higher level of neuroticism. Or it may find socially acceptable outlet in sports or in social or economic competitiveness.

Even should aggressive feelings give rise to overt violence, however, this is most commonly directed against one's immediate family. One might logically expect this, since the social deprivations against which one reacts are typically inflicted by members of one's immediate family, and aggressive feelings tend to focus either on the individuals inflicting the deprivations, or else on those who come later to occupy similar positions in one's life.

One may even argue that warfare in the twentieth century provides a very unsatisfactory outlet for aggressiveness, in the sense that it is highly structured and highly planned; one fights when he is ordered, not when he is angry; and one fights against perfect strangers who are only remotely to blame for any deprivations one has suffered. It is nevertheless true that generalized feelings of hostility towards other states, which may become a component of national public opinion, and which may influence marginally the direction of national policy, can be derived from free-floating feelings of aggressiveness having their origin in the functioning of individual personality structures.

SUGGESTED READINGS

Clark, Greville, and Louis Sohn, *World Peace Through World Law.* Cambridge, Mass.: Harvard University Press, 1958.

Freud, Sigmund, *Civilization and Its Discontents.* New York: Norton, 1962.

Klineberg, Otto, *The Human Dimension in International Relations.* New York: Holt, Rinehart and Winston, Inc., 1964.

Lefever, Ernest, *Arms and Arms Control: A Symposium.* New York: Praeger, 1962.

Levine, Robert A., *The Arms Debate.* Cambridge, Mass.: Harvard University Press, 1963.

Morgenthau, Hans J., *Politics Among Nations,* 3d ed. New York: Knopf, 1960.

Niebuhr, Reinhold, "The Illusion of World Government," *Foreign Affairs,* April 1949.

Nutting, Anthony, *Disarmament: An Outline of the Negotiations.* New York: Oxford University Press, 1959.

Osgood, Charles E., *An Alternative to War or Surrender.* Urbana, Ill.: University of Illinois Press, 1962.

Spanier, John W., and Joseph L. Nogee, *The Politics of Disarmament.* New York: Praeger, 1962.

Speak Truth to Power: A Quaker Search for an Alternative to Violence. Philadelphia: American Friends Service Committee, 1955.

14

Independent Africa and the Political Problems of the Developing States

Although this book has been organized primarily by topics and not by geographic areas, a sort of *de facto* geographic separation has developed, since the realities of international politics vary from one area of the world to another. Thus this chapter, which deals with the political problems of the less developed states, has reference particularly to Africa, where almost forty states have secured their independence since the end of World War II, although much that is said will apply also to the Middle East and to Southeast Asia.

A GENERAL VIEW OF COLONIALISM

Most of the "underdeveloped" countries of Africa and Asia were until recently colonial or semicolonial territories under the administration or "protection" of foreign powers. The colonial powers were of western Europe, except that the United States administered the Philippines for almost half a century, and many east Asian countries were for a time under Japanese rule. However, the policies followed by the various colonial powers varied substantially one from another, and the effects of these differences are clearly visible in the newly independent states of today.

Colonialism, at least as practiced in the nineteenth century, has now passed into history, beyond recall and, for the most part, unregretted. One should not assume, however, that colonial rule was invariably simple exploitation of the colony in the interest of the mother country. More commonly than not, friendly relations exist between the newly independent state and the former colonial power. An example of this is the Philippines, which is unshakeably pro-American at the popular level as well as at the governmental level. Similarly, one may cite the plaintive comment of the Foreign Minister of Liberia in response to the unflattering comparisons that were drawn between Monrovia, the Liberian capital, and Accra, the capital of Ghana, by many of those in attendance at Ghana's independence ceremonies: that Liberia had never had the advantages of being under colonial rule.

Although it is on the whole true that the more enlightened of the colonial powers did, at least in the later years of colonial rule, follow policies designed in the interests of the colonial peoples, well-meaning welfare measures can never serve as a substitute for national freedom and political self-determination. Even the most well-intentioned colonial administration must consider first the interests of the mother country, and only secondarily those of the colony; the directions the policies of such an administration take, even with respect to the interests of the colonial population, and the priorities assigned to different objectives, are in any case unlikely to be the same as those that would be adopted by a native leadership. But of course colonial rule was never wholly enlightened, and even where welfare programs were initiated, the racial discriminations at least implicit in the system were still deeply resented.

Although colonial policies differed among the various colonial powers, some over-all patterns of colonialism are apparent. The original impulse to establish colonial empires seems in some cases to have been an expression of a national will to power and a desire not to be outdistanced by other European states, and in other cases to have been based on hopes of economic gain. In the latter type of situation the original colonizing adventure was often a strictly commercial enterprise undertaken by a trading company—this was the origin of British rule in India, of Dutch rule in Indonesia, and of Belgian rule in the Congo. In each of these cases popular reaction to abuse of power by company officials led to the abrogation of the companies' charters and the assumption of power in the colonies by the national government itself.

Some of the colonized territories, those with temperate climates, were attractive to European settlers. Where these settlers greatly outnumbered the aboriginal inhabitants of the territory, as in Australia, New Zealand, and Canada, there seemed little reason why the rights that the settlers had enjoyed before leaving the mother country should be taken away from them in the new territories, and these British-held colonies were soon accorded "dominion" status, thus becoming self-governing.

Where European settlers constituted a minority of the total population, however, major political problems ensued. These are visible today in the Republic of South Africa and in Rhodesia (formerly Southern Rhodesia), and were only too painfully apparent in recent years in Kenya and Algeria. In these areas the settlers assumed control of the best land in the territory, as well as the positions of dominance in the local social, political, and economic structures, relegating the native populations to inferior status. In this type of situation the colonial administration, staffed by civil servants on temporary tours of duty from the motherland, was looked to by the indigenous populations to protect them from the worst exactions of the settlers. Because of the tenacity with which the Europeans held on to their privileged positions, Algeria and Kenya became independent only after bitter guerrilla warfare that, while successful in Algeria and unsuccessful in Kenya, in both cases revealed to the colonial power the untenability of its position. Rhodesia and the Republic of South Africa are ruled today by white-settler governments that maintain systems of white supremacy, that of the latter being a racist dictatorship that in many of its features resembles Nazi rule in Germany.

THE VARIETIES OF COLONIAL RULE

The colonial powers differed not only in the extent to which they attempted to develop the economies and the educational systems of the colonial territories, but also in the structure and organization of colonial rule itself. Many of the colonial territories were not acquired as colonies outright but instead came under the control of the colonial power, at least in form, by mutual agreement between it and the native authorities. In cases of this type a "protectorate" would be established, under the terms of which the local structure of authority remained intact, and local customs were respected as much as possible, but in actuality the local rulers were to be merely servants of the resident colonial agents. "Indirect rule," as this was called, was also instituted in many territories that were not protectorates but outright colonies. In the days before colonialism became simply a relic in the museum of history, the relative merits of indirect and direct rule used to be subject to a great deal of argument. Indirect rule tended to be economical in the resources and personnel of the mother country, and elements of it were necessarily adopted by colonial powers of small population administering vast Asian territories, such as the Dutch in Indonesia and to some extent the British in India. Proponents of indirect rule used to defend it on the ground that it interfered to a minimum extent with the local culture, and it did not assume that the social practices of the colonial power were in every respect superior to those in the colony. This was, on the other hand, a defect laid against it by the opponents of indirect rule, who argued that if colonial rule was to be justified at all, it had to bring more civilized practices to the colony; and the barbarity of many of the customs found by the colonizers should not be forgotten. Thus the British suppressed not only slavery and cannibalism in Africa, but also *suttee* in India, the custom that a widow immolate herself on her husband's funeral pyre.

If one excludes the Americans, who were, strictly speaking, colonial rulers only in the Philippines and Puerto Rico and a few sparsely populated islands in the Pacific, British colonial rule seems to have been the most enlightened and the most concerned with the welfare of the inhabitants of the colonial territories. Many of the British colonial administrators showed considerable ability, and their policies were subject to at least intermittent scrutiny by liberal opinion at home. Although British trade benefited from the possession of some of the colonial territories, trade with others constituted a net loss to the British economy; while since 1776 the British followed the rule that the taxes raised within a colony were to be spent within the colony and not to be remitted to the mother country. Where circumstances permitted, the British preferred to follow a policy of indirect rule; this often led to an increase in the authority of local chieftains whose leadership role had been small until buttressed by the authority of the colonial power.

In several territories—India, Palestine, Kenya, Cyprus—lengthy campaigns were waged against British rule, and there is no doubt that in the ensuing "pacification" operations, atrocities were committed in the name of the Crown, especially in Kenya. Since the end of World War II, however, and even earlier in some cases, official British policy has, on the whole, accepted the necessity for giving the colonies independence where possible,[1] and attempts have been made to smooth the path to self-government by a gradual transition process under which local leaders were given steadily increasing amounts of authority. At the same time the process of gradual preparation of the colony for independence by a series of stages has in many cases become a mere façade for a headlong rush towards the abandonment of colonial responsibility under pressure from a newly awakened local population. Moreover, the attempt to instill respect for constitutional procedures by means of this process has already shown a discouraging lack of success in such cases as that of Ghana, where

---

[1] That is, some territories are thought to be too small and poor to be able to manage the burdens of independence.

little time elapsed between the lowering of the Union Jack and the institution of a single-party dictatorship.

It would certainly be wrong to regard British colonial administration as always enlightened and British colonial administrators as always able altruists; compared to the performance of the other colonial powers, however, the British record is not bad.

The colonial policy of France, as is typical of so much of French political life, exhibited sharp contrast between doctrine and reality. The principles of French colonial administration, like the principles of French domestic administration, were centralization and uniformity. The people of the colonies were to be treated exactly like Frenchmen; the colonies themselves were to be considered parts of France. For example, overseas France elected representatives who sat in the National Assembly at Paris.

Reality did not correspond to the blueprint, however; for example, in the elections by means of which overseas France helped participate in its own government and in that of the motherland, suffrage requirements, separate electoral colleges, the screening of candidates, and official interference in the electoral process guaranteed an outcome acceptable to the colonial administration.

The French approach to colonial problems is well typified by colonial education policy. True to the concept that France had a "civilizing mission" in her colonial relations, that France was called to bring to the colonies the benefits of the highest form of Western civilization—her own—educational programs overseas duplicated those in metropolitan France. The French had no patience with attempts like those of the British to try to preserve the indigenous culture, at least in part. The ideal of colonial education in Africa was to create black Frenchmen. The classic example of how this system worked is that of the first-grade class in Senegal whose history books began by recounting the exploits of "our ancestors, the Gauls." But the French system of education was rigorously competitive and selective, and the result was that, although this system turned out some superb products—the President of Senegal, Léopold Senghor, is a poet and philosopher of distinction—the effect was to create a sophisticated elite of Westernized intellectuals who had lost touch with the masses in their own countries. In the former French colonies it is this Westernized elite that is in power today; the political consequences of their estrangement from the masses will doubtless become clear over the next few decades.

Thus in the French colonies, despite the nominal devotion to ideals of liberty, equality, and fraternity, the practical effect did not differ so greatly from the results of British administration, where the colonial populations did not participate in electing representatives until they were thought almost ready for independence, and where an elite of chieftains' sons had long been sent to Oxford and Cambridge.

France made little preparation for the independence of her colonies; during the Third Republic (until 1940) the colonies were regarded constitutionally as parts of France that happened to be outside Europe. Tunisia, Morocco, and the French Indochinese territories were given their independence with reluctance and only under pressure during the Fourth Republic (1946–1958), and Algeria and the African territories were given their independence fairly abruptly during the early years of the Fifth Republic, in the Algerian case only after six years of bitter fighting.

The Belgian Congo had originally been the private estate of King Leopold; rule over it was assumed by the Belgian government in the wake of the scandal caused by the discovery of the atrocities committed by Leopold's overseers against the indigenous population. The administration of the Congo remained, nevertheless, a primarily economic proposition, and even after measures were taken for the benefit of the native population, the Congolese received no political training of any kind whatsoever.

The official Belgian justification of this state of affairs seemed very sophisticated; it was developed after World War II and the founding of the United Nations, and was based on two principles. First, Belgium took the position that a sound economic base had to precede any political superstructure that would be erected. This meant that the economy would be developed, roads built, and power sources tapped, so that political self-government, if and when it came, would be rooted in general economic well-being. It should be said in the Belgians' defense that under their rule the Congolese economy was developed and the African standard of living reached quite a high point compared with other states on the continent. Second, the deliberate decision was taken, and followed almost to the end of the colonial period, to train no Congolese leadership class but instead to try to give elementary education to the entire population before any individuals were educated to a higher level. This policy the Belgians justified with democratic and anti-elitist arguments; it does not seem unfair to conclude, however, that the true aim of Belgian colonial policy was to postpone Congolese independence indefinitely by allowing no opportunities for political participation nor for the emergence of a political class.

What eventually happened was that the Belgian administration of the Congo was engulfed in the tide of African nationalism. The artificial separation of politics and economics broke down, and the authority of the colonial administration collapsed completely. The Belgians were, consequently, forced to give the Congo independence, and a period of chaos and violence ensued that gave the world community cause for much concern. The situation in the Congo was eventually stabilized, for a time at least, by the exercise of a great deal of statesmanship on the part of the Western countries, working through the United Nations, with the aid of political skills developed—despite Belgian policy—by a handful of Congolese leaders. The legacy of Belgian colonial policies still weighs on the unhappy country, however.

Although the Dutch colonial empire has not been completely liquidated, independence has been won by the largest possession of the Netherlands, the former Dutch East Indies, today the republic of Indonesia. Although Dutch rule in the twentieth century was not as rapacious as it had been in the earlier years of colonialism, control of the East Indies remained never any more than a commercial proposition for the Dutch, one out of which they did very well indeed. As colonial rulers the Dutch made no attempt to change Indonesian cultural norms, and probably less of a mark was made in the islands by the Dutch than by any other colonial power on the territories under its control. One might indeed go further and say that the Dutch made no attempt to educate the Indonesians, nor indeed scarcely to administer their affairs. The Indonesians secured independence, partly due to United States mediation, when the Dutch unsuccessfully tried to reimpose colonial rule after the Japanese, who had occupied the islands during World War II, withdrew. A measure of Dutch lack of concern over the development of the archipelago is the fact that independent Indonesia found itself with a population over ninety percent illiterate, with the only indigenous leadership that which had developed during the underground struggle against the Japanese. It is not very surprising that the leadership of independent Indonesia has thus far shown little ability or constructive purpose.

The other principal colonial power today is Portugal. The Portuguese government itself refuses to regard Portugal's overseas territories as colonies, however; in constitutional theory Portugal, rather like France, has no colonies; some parts of Portugal simply happen to be situated outside of Europe, but constitutionally these are as much a part of the motherland as the territory in the Iberian peninsula itself. In some respects constitutional theory here is closer to reality than it was in the French case. That is, the people in the overseas territories are extremely poor, but so is the population of Portugal itself; the people in the overseas territories have few political rights, but hardly fewer than the Portuguese, who have lived under a one-man dictatorship now for thirty-five years. In actuality, however, the status of the indigenous populations of Portugal's overseas territories was at least until very recently considerably worse than that of the people of Portugal. Although some attempts have been made to improve conditions in recent years, under the pressure of the anticolonial movement, the local populations in the overseas territories were heavily exploited and were liable to be conscripted for forced labor under a system in some respects more harsh than slavery itself. Stimulated by the movement for independence in the colonies of other European states, however, the African populations of Angola and Mozambique began guerrilla activities against the Portuguese authorities, which Portuguese forces have largely put down, using drastic measures. The outside world has little awareness of the situation in the Portuguese African territories because the administration takes great pains to keep out foreign visitors, especially newsmen. Nevertheless, the fighting that occurred acquired international implications, as the rebels were supplied and given support and sanctuary by neighboring newly independent states of the continent, especially Tanganyika, Ghana, the former Belgian Congo, and Algeria. The attempt by African and Asian states to bring pressure to bear on Portugal to give independence to her African territories also constitutes one of the staple items on the agenda of the UN General Assembly. The Portuguese have maintained, in keeping with the constitutional fiction that the African territories are part of Portugal itself, that discussion of the issue in the UN constitutes interference in the internal affairs of Portugal in violation of the organization's charter. Although the United States was initially sympathetic to this position—Portugal is after all a NATO ally—its attitude was changed in the later years of the Eisenhower administration, and the United States now regularly supports inclusion of this item on the agenda.

NATIONALISM AND EXPANSION

Their national liberation has, in many of the new states, encouraged a nationalism that, like the nationalisms of Europe, finds expression in expansionist drives. These have been justified occasionally on the basis of the quite valid point that many boundary lines of the new states are arbitrary from an ethnic point of view, cutting across linguistic or tribal demarcations, and often were originally drawn on the map by European statesmen who neither knew nor cared that the lines they were drawing were irrational in ethnic terms. Many of the newly independent states have begun campaigns that seem really neocolonial or neo-imperialist, on the premise that these boundary lines have no validity. Presidents Nasser of Egypt, Nkrumah of Ghana, and Sukarno of Indonesia have been particularly identified with attempts of this type. It is too often assumed by many people that only white Europeans are imperialists, and it seems likely that only the military weakness of some of the newly independent states prevents their embarking on imperialist wars.

The tendency to "rectify" the national boundaries inherited from the colonial era, which has been giving rise to boundary disputes and even to wars of local imperialism, often blends in with another type of problem of the newly established state. This is the attempt to define the constitutional relation between the central government and the local governmental units. Thus disputes arise whether the form of government is to be centralist or federalist, and, if federalist, the extent of the powers to be assigned the member states. All too commonly the latter issue is solved only by violence, as a provincial government attempts to secede while the central government tries to maintain national unity. In Chapter Six, the fate of some attempts at the establishment of federal systems was discussed.

In Southeast Asia, as has already been pointed out, the "border problem" typical of newly independent states is often a problem of either meeting Chinese demands for the rectification of frontiers based on ancient Chinese territorial lines, or alternatively, of putting down guerrilla movements supplied and sustained from Chinese or North Vietnamese territory.

NEUTRALISM AND NONALIGNMENT

Many of the newly independent states have chosen to ally themselves with the United States or with Great Britain or France in mutual security arrangements. However, the more typical international policy of these states seems increasingly to be some form of nonalignment in the Cold War. Many varieties of nonalignment and neutralism exist, however, and it is of some importance to distinguish among them.

A classic type of neutrality is that of Switzerland, whose neutrality is so absolute that it extends to almost complete noninvolvement in international relations; the Swiss have not even joined the United Nations. Although Switzerland enters into no common defensive arrangements with other states, her military posture is anything but pacifist. On the contrary, the Swiss have a large and well-equipped army, established on the basis of universal military training. The Swiss have seen no need to change this policy hitherto (although a large minority is in favor of joining the Western alliance system), and the Swiss have not had to fight an international war since the invasion of the country by Napoleon. One is not sure how much of this security from the European wars of the last century to credit to the reputation of the Swiss army, how much to the difficulties that Swiss terrain would pose for an invading force, and how much to the value that Switzerland has as neutral ground on which belligerents can meet (and from which their intelligence services may operate). Indeed, many thoughtful Swiss entertain doubts as to whether traditional national policy is still relevant to an age of atomic weapons, long-range missiles, and highly trained military forces.

Sweden too is a traditional neutral, but, unlike the Swiss, the Swedes take a very active role in international relations. Sweden coordinates its foreign policy with those of other members of the so-called Nordic bloc—Norway, Denmark, Finland, and Iceland—and has provided troops for United Nations police operations in the Congo and the Middle East, as well as providing the world organization with its second Secretary General, Dag Hammarskjöld. The Swedes maintain a substantial army, and prior to the treaty banning atomic tests in the atmosphere, to which Sweden is a signatory, had decided in principle to equip their forces with atomic weapons. Sweden is nevertheless "neutral" in holding aloof from permanent foreign alliances.

India's foreign policy resembles that of Sweden in entailing an active international role—indeed India accepts economic and even military aid from both the United States and the Soviet Union—while refusing to enter permanent alliances with other states. In the latter respect it may be compared with the early United States policy of shunning "entangling alliances."

The policy of so-called positive neutralism, espoused by such states as the United Arab Republic under Nasser, Ghana under Nkrumah's leadership, and Yugoslavia under Tito, is neutrality in the sense of siding with neither East nor West in the Cold War, but is certainly not a policy of nonalignment on the Swedish or Indian model. Nasser and Nkrumah especially are eager to make allies and to create regional organizations in which they will play leading roles; in fact, it would not be far wide of the mark to qualify the policies of each as imperialist. Nkrumah has been urging for some time a single African federal community, in which he assigns to himself a leading position. Nasser, similarly, has long held the view that Egypt should play a leading role in the three communities of states with which she shares common characteristics—the Arab states, those of Africa, and those of the Moslem world. Indonesia and in recent years a few Latin American states—for example, Brazil—have also on occasion described their foreign policies as "positive neutralism."

The attitude of the United States towards neutralism has undergone change over the years. Secretary Dulles made no secret of his abhorrence of neutralism, characterizing it as immoral, and stating that in the current world conflict it was equivalent to attempting to be neutral between good and evil. One might paraphrase the Dulles attitude as "those who are not with us are against us." The Kennedy and Johnson administrations took a more charitable view of neutralism, trying to adopt the line, albeit with some resistance from Congress, that "those who are not against us are with us."

It is easy to see the attraction that a position of neutralism holds for newly independent states. Concerned almost exclusively with the substantial problems that their own nations face, without a tradition of foreign policy that points to common interests shared with other states, and careful of their newly won independence, it seems easiest not to become involved in a dispute which seems either between two ideologies, capitalism and communism, neither of which exercises a compelling attraction, or else to be about European issues remote from their concerns.

The conception of a world divided into two blocs between which one can stay neutral is regarded by the present writer as unfortunate as well as unsound. The United States, after all, remains primarily a *status quo* power; accordingly, it corresponds much more closely with the underlying realities to regard the world as divided not into an Eastern bloc, a Western bloc, and neutrals, but between imperialist states, those which are bent on expanding the territory under their control by force of arms if necessary, and *status quo* states, those concerned with maintaining their independence and perfectly prepared to accept a world in which change would come about only by peaceful means. In this conception there is, at most, only one "bloc," juxtaposed with an assortment of autonomous states of which the United States happens to be the strongest and therefore the one to which the others look for protection.

This conception of the world is substantially the one generally held in the early years of the Cold War, when the United States reluctantly assumed the burdens of leading the free world. It seems desirable to the author that future United States policy and policy pronouncements should be directed to the end of recreating, as much as possible, this image.

DOMESTIC PROBLEMS
OF THE NEW STATES

Understandably, in view of the colossal tasks that face them, the leadership groups of the emergent states of Africa and Asia are preoccupied especially with domestic problems. Although the attention given to these countries by outside observers focuses primarily on the substantial economic problems with which they are confronted, the strictly political problems are no less severe.

Reference was made above to the fact that as new states these countries must face the issues stemming from questions of basic constitutional organization. These include not only relations between the central government and the provincial governments, complicated by communications difficulties and divergent tribal and religious loyalties, but also the overriding dilemmas derived from the attempt to institute a modern political system in countries that for the most part lack modern cultural and social conditions.

It is natural for democrats to regard with concern the establishment of nondemocratic forms of government in so many of the African and Asian states. Some of these—in Syria, Iraq, and Egypt in the Middle East, and in Burma, Thailand, Pakistan, South Vietnam, and South Korea in South and East Asia—have been military regimes that stemmed from *coups d'état* like those common in Latin America. The more typical form of authoritarian government that has developed, however, has been that of the civilian single-party dictatorship, nationalist, more or less socialist, and led by a dominant figure around whom a "cult of personality" is developed. There is no lack of voices, those both of native propagandists for the regime and of foreign observers, who argue that authoritarianism of some type is necessary, given the circumstances that exist in these countries. There is no tradition of democracy, the argument runs, literacy is low, and racial and tribal rivalries would split the society without the firmest of hands at the helm. The single party, the extreme nationalism, the glorification of the leader, are necessary, in this view, to create the strong sense of community needed to build the nation. Moreover, the argument goes on, the tasks of economic development are so vast that they can be met and solved only by dictatorial techniques; and the trained personnel are so few that it would be a great mistake to divide them between government and opposition, and in this way keep half of them out of office.

The military governments have their own special justifications. The military are normally the most modern element in the society, it is argued; they also comprise the group with modern technical skills, in the handling of equipment as well as in administration and organization. Furthermore, the military are (in this view) the only element that serves the state as a whole, divorced from local and particularistic loyalties.

Although the force of these arguments must be acknowledged, the democrat still has potent arguments that should not be ignored. The failings of dictatorships are well known and clearly established, and they apply with even greater force in the less developed states. The absence of an opposition, for example, means that it is possible for administrative errors, often of gigantic proportions, to go undetected and indeed to be elaborated and compounded. This is especially true of the military regimes, military men being notoriously naive when it comes to economic policy. It is typical of dictatorships to lose touch with reality as opposition is stifled, and as those around the dictator shrink from telling him anything he does not want to hear. In an authoritarian system, moreover, whims of the dictator can be directly translated into policy, often with disastrous results; for example, when the federation of Malaysia, including territory claimed by Indonesia, was established in 1963, Indonesian President Sukarno retaliated by suspending all economic relations with

Malaysia, a move that seemed likely to bring the economy of Indonesia itself to the brink of ruin.

It is also clear that in many cases the arguments for dictatorship in less developed states are exaggerated. The thesis that allowing any opposion to function legally would lead to national disunity and the dissolution of the state—an argument often used by the supporters of Nkrumah in Ghana—seems wide of the mark. It can just as well be argued, in light of the cases of India or Mexico, that since the dominant national party and its leader have such overwhelming support, they can afford to tolerate an opposition that cannot but lack effect so long as the majority will rules. There are many different types of democratic systems, after all, some more effective than others, but all amenable to vigorous and coordinated action where a political party enjoys as much of a popular majority as is the case with most of the governing parties in Africa and Asia. It should also be noted that those who attempt to create national unity by building up the charismatic figure of the national leader only create future difficulties, since the leader is not immortal and national unity will not outlast him if it depends on nothing else. The more sensible path is to strengthen the role of impersonal institutions that do not depend exclusively on the stature of individuals.

Accordingly, there seems little justification for the total outlawry of opposition and the suppression of freedom of speech that has occurred in Ghana, for example. Any political system seeks to protect itself against popular revolt, military mutiny, and terrorism, to be sure; opposition anywhere must stay within reasonable bounds. Restrictions on free political life that go beyond the mere prohibition of the incitement to violence can be justified to the democrat, however, only as regrettably necessary in an interim period of preparation for democracy. A single-party system can be legitimate, accordingly, only where it is explicitly regarded as transitional, and where it allows a steadily widening area of free political activity—at any time the maximum that can be tolerated without the collapse of the political system into violence and turbulence —until the day when the country's social and educational development will have made the single-party system itself obsolete.

SUGGESTED READINGS

Adam, Thomas R., *Modern Colonialism*. New York: Doubleday, 1955.

Alexander, Robert J., *Today's Latin America*. New York: Doubleday, (Anchor), 1963.

Almond, Gabriel, and James S. Coleman (eds.), *The Politics of the Developing Areas*. Princeton, N.J.: Princeton University Press, 1960.

Blackmer, Donald, *et. al., The Emerging Nations.* Boston: Little, Brown, 1961.

Dean, Vera Micheles (ed.), *The Nature of the Non-Western World.* New York: New American Library (Mentor), 1958.

Goldsmidt, Walter (ed.), *The United States and Africa.* New York: Praeger, 1963.

Laqueur, Walter Z., *Communism and Nationalism in the Middle East.* New York: Praeger, 1957.

Nasser, Gamal Abdul, *The Philosophy of the Revolution.* Buffalo: Smith, Keynes and Marshall, 1959.

Needler, Martin C., *Latin American Politics in Perspective.* Princeton, N.J.: Van Nostrand, 1963.

Schmitt, Karl, and David Burks, *Evolution or Chaos: The Dynamics of Government and Politics in Latin America.* New York: Praeger, 1963.

Spiro, Herbert J., *Politics in Africa: Prospects South of the Sahara.* Englewood Cliffs, N.J.: Prentice-Hall, 1962.

Tannenbaum, Frank, *Ten Keys to Latin America.* New York: Knopf, 1962.

I5

Foreign Aid
and the Developing Economies

More problems than it is generally acknowledged deal with purely political questions—questions of position, power, and prestige. It is nevertheless clear that a high proportion of the problems of politics have an economic origin; and certain economic problems are typical of the developing states, giving rise to certain typical political difficulties.

THE FORCES FOR SOCIAL CHANGE

One of the major fuels generating the energy of change in the world today has passed into the lexicon of the discussion of world affairs as "the revolution of rising expectations." As the communications revolution proceeds the peoples of what were once the remotest portions of the globe are brought increasingly into contact with the artifacts of the developed societies, and, more important, with the manipulative attitude towards the world on which the material achievements of the Western societies are based. Even the most conservative rulers of our age, say for example, the King of Saudi Arabia or the former Imam of Yemen, are unable to resist the desire for change that infects leading elements of the population; and in most places even authoritarian rulers themselves are not immune from feeling that desire. Thus the Shah of Iran becomes the great revolutionary leader of his people. This change in expectations, in concepts of what is feasible, creates the pressure that makes it impossible for a government willingly to plan that the economic levels and ways of the future will continue to be those of the past.

The second of the twin motors that powers the engine of change, and an equally beloved cliché of the Sunday supplements, is the well-known "population explosion." For reasons at which demographers can only conjecture, world population is rising at an extremely rapid rate. Part of the causality of the phenomenon doubtless lies in improved public health and sanitation techniques, but there seems more to it than that. Whatever its causes, however, the phenomenon itself is indisputable. The question, moreover, is not only that of a rise in population, but also that of a rise in those age groups—the very young, and, to a lesser extent, the very old—that are not in their productive years, and thus constitute an economic liability rather than an asset. As population increases, therefore, an ever higher proportion of the population is in need of schooling and medical care, to say nothing of the normal requirements of food and clothing, without itself constituting a part of the labor force.

The increase in population takes place in cities and countryside alike, although it is normally higher in the rural areas. In the country, however, economic opportunities are limited by the amount of arable land available and this, together with the rising expectations of the people, stimulates continually increasing numbers to make the trek to the city in the massive world-wide urbanization movement so much in evidence today. The population in the city is itself increasing, however, and the city's capacity to provide jobs, housing, and public utilities has already been strained to, and past, the bursting point. As a result, the urban poor face misery, hopelessness, disease, even slow starvation. The political dangers of such a situation are obvious, quite apart from the human suffering involved.

RELATIONS WITH THE WORLD ECONOMY

In the attempt to expand their economies and to provide both an increased number of jobs and a higher standard of living, the governments of the developing countries face difficulties stemming from the traditional function of their economies in world trade. The less developed countries have historically been specialized suppliers of agricultural and mineral raw materials for the manufacturing economies of North America and Western Europe. To some extent this has been because, as colonial possessions, the economies of most African and Asian territories were organized to function as complements to the economy of the mother country. Their function as raw materials producers had economic as well as political logic, however, and made sense in view of the lack of skills of the labor force and the availability of minerals and qualities of climate and soil that the developed economies lacked. Thus there is a great deal of economic rationality in the specialization in primary products characteristic of most of the developing economies.

Nevertheless, there exists in these countries today a widespread desire, which derives partly from economic and partly from political and psychological motives, to diversify and industrialize their economies. In economic terms production of agricultural and mineral goods for overseas markets has disadvantages in that the country's economy is highly susceptible to economic developments outside its control, an effect that is exaggerated when foreign exchange earnings are derived primarily from the marketing of a single product. Where the principal export is an agricultural product, it may also be the case that agricultural employment is limited to such periods as the planting and the harvest, and much of the labor force is unemployed during the major part of the year.

The economies dependent on the sale of primary products abroad have experienced substantial losses in recent years as a result of the general long-run downward trend in prices for these goods; this problem is accentuated because of a long-term upward trend in the prices of the goods that they must purchase from the developed economies. The causes of these trends are in dispute among economists, and explanations suggested range from sophisticated "structural" arguments to crude pseudo-Marxist theses about capitalist plots, but the existence of the phenomenon itself seems clear. It is also the case that prices were higher during World War II and the Korean war when goods were scarce, and the low level of the prices of primary products reflects in part the fact that most of the world is at peace.

There are also political and psychological reasons for the desire to get away from the classic situation as a primary producer, compounded in part from the feeling that this is an undignified role for a nation to play, in part from patriotic resentment that foreign buyers and often foreign managers make the decisions that affect the level at which one's economy operates and the directions in which its efforts are concentrated.

RELATIONS WITH THE FOREIGN INVESTOR

Despite the widespread prejudice against foreign investment prevalent in the developing countries, it cannot be questioned that such investment has a major role to play. It may seem all very heroic to talk about developing one's economy by one's own efforts, but the inescapable fact remains that in the typical case the developing economy is strained to its capacity in maintaining even the present low levels of existence in the face of the population increase, without being able to devote resources to the investment that will move the economy to higher levels of production in the future. It may well be the unhappy truth that sacrifices of present income in the interests of development will have to be made in any case, enforced through the mechanisms of higher taxation, higher price levels, or even steady inflation. Nevertheless, it is desirable that the necessary sacrifices should be kept to a minimum, and here the securing of foreign loans, grants, and credits can be of great value.

Foreign investment is also desirable in that it introduces technical and managerial skills of which the country's economy stands in need; it provides links with international distribution and marketing systems; and it makes available foreign exchange with which to finance necessary machinery imports. In the best planned of the national economic development programs, such as that of India, there is recognition of the value of foreign investment and provision for its encouragement.

In many countries, however, particularly in Latin America, a great deal of resentment against the foreign investor exists. Some of this undeniably has sound historical roots, it should be noted. In many countries foreign investors heavyhandedly interfered in national politics, bribing government officials, supporting one political faction against another, and even invoking the intervention of their home governments to secure economic ends. In some cases rates of profit have been extremely high and the wages paid to local labor extremely low; often only degrading and unskilled work was available to the local labor force, the higher administrative and technical jobs being reserved for foreign employees.

Thus resentment against foreign business interests has in many cases been earned, and the reasons why nationalistic governments have assumed a posture of hostility to foreign enterprise are understandable. Under today's conditions, nevertheless, this is a luxury that can ill be afforded. It has been possible for statesmanlike leaders willing to let bygones be bygones to work out new ground rules under which foreign businesses are permitted to operate without derogating from national sovereignty, and to the mutual advantage of both parties; many American business interests have been willing and eager to put on their best behavior and to maintain good relations with their host governments and populations. Popular suspicion and antagonism are often present even in such cases, however, and well up especially when governments offer tax and other advantages to try to induce new foreign investment, which often appear to nationalist elements as "selling out" national interests to foreign capitalists.

EXPROPRIATION OF FOREIGN PROPERTY

The accumulated sense of grievance against foreign business interests, together with the nationalist and socialist ideals typical of the developing states, leads frequently to moves to nationalize or otherwise expropriate foreign interests already established in the country. When this occurs, the foreign business interests in question naturally protest, and usually make some kind of appeal to the home government to intervene on their behalf. From time to time the United States government has been confronted with situations of this character and has had to adopt policies with relation to the expropriation of the property of American nationals abroad. The doctrine that has evolved for cases of this type is that although any government in the exercise of its rights as sovereign may legitimately expropriate property within its borders, it is nevertheless under obligation to provide compensation to the former owners that will be reasonably prompt and adequate. This is not only a doctrine of United States policy, but is widely acknowledged among the community of nations. The principle that there should be compensation for expropriated property has even been acknowledged by countries of the Communist bloc, scornful though their official ideology is of the rights of private property; where the Eastern European countries have expropriated foreign property they have acknowledged, at least implicitly, the duty to compensate, and have in most cases made some kind of financial settlement.

Various comments need to be made to put this in proper perspective, however. First, compensation may be given not because one recognizes the validity of the property right itself, but simply in order to maintain amicable relations with the government whose nationals were the former owners of the confiscated property, or to maintain one's reputation for meeting financial obligations in order to be able to continue to participate in international trade arrangements. Nevertheless, the payment of compensation is generally regarded as an implicit acknowledgement of the validity of the claim against which compensation is given. Second, the compensation given may be inferior in amount to that claimed by the former owner of the property in question; the United States government has accepted settlements on behalf of American nationals in amounts ranging down to as low as ten percent of the value set on the property by the former owners. Needless to say, it is reasonable to assume that the amounts that the latter claimed represented higher valuations than might be made by an impartial appraiser. Thus the normal situation that evolves when foreign property is expropriated is that the government representing the former owners attempts to secure a settlement on the best terms possible, while the government that has seized the property attempts to make as little restitution as it can; and on that basis bilateral negotiations proceed, with the matter sometimes being referred to an impartial arbitrator.

Nevertheless, cases occur in which the expropriating government refuses to make any settlement whatever, perhaps justifying its position by alleging that the property was acquired illegally, or that the owners have forfeited it by putting it to illegal uses or by not paying their tax assessments, or by similar arguments, which may or may not be valid ones; alternatively, a government may acknowledge its obligation to make restitution but may pay only a nominal amount, or the compensation given may consist not of cash, but of bonds that bear no interest and that are redeemable only at some time in the distant future. It is because of the possibility that compensation may be given on such terms that the United States has insisted that it be "prompt, adequate, and effective." Congress has elaborated on this traditional position of the United States by stipulating that no economic aid may be given to any country that expropriates American property without paying compensation. This provision of the law was invoked early in 1963 against Ceylon.

The United States is likely to find itself faced increasingly with problems of expropriation as nationalist and socialist sentiments rise in developing nations. While the days are past when business interests could count on the automatic backing of the home country no matter how badly they had abused their position, and while no Western state is likely to do today what Britain, France, Germany, and the United States did in the decades immediately preceding and immediately following the turn of the century, to send gunboats and marines to enforce payments on the bonds held by foreign bondholders, it remains nevertheless a duty of government to protect the interests of its citizens abroad where these interests have been acquired legally and in good faith; how to do this and still to maintain amicable relations with governments attempting to reconstitute their economies on nationalist and socialist lines is one of the major problems facing the United States today. If the foreign government values amicable relations with the United States, however, there seems no reason why solutions cannot be found on the traditional ground of prompt and adequate compensation, or some variant of it. This is in fact what regularly occurs, usually after wire service reports have first created alarm and exaggerated fears in the United States, it should be said.

The problem is complicated somewhat by the fact that in attempting to contribute to the development of the poorer economies, the United States government has tried to encourage its nationals to invest abroad; naturally, prospective investors, an understandably nervous group, are likely to be frightened away by the prospect of expropriation. To try to take account of this problem, the government has established a system of insuring overseas investments against expropriation. Few investors have taken advantage of this insurance program; but in any case it applies only to investments made after the program was begun and not those made before it went into effect.

FOREIGN AID: GENERAL PROBLEMS

This brings us to the problem of foreign aid, a United States policy not yet clearly accepted by all Americans, and a center of a great deal of controversy. It seems to the present writer that any discussion of foreign aid must start from the principle that, although the program may be supported on humanitarian grounds, it should be justified in the first place on the basis of the broadest possible appeal to the American public—in other words in terms of its tendency to promote national interests. The conception that foreign aid is a "give-away" program should yield to the realization that foreign aid is primarily another tool of national policy, directed, like other techniques, to the achievement of national goals. Viewed in this context it is clear that foreign aid is justified if it proves cheaper or more effective than alternative means of promoting national ends.

Although in a specific case aid may act as a substitute for a program of a different type—for example, military aid to an ally that enables him to raise the size of his army can substitute for the dispatch of American troops—it should not be thought that the foreign aid effort *as a whole* can replace other instruments of policy: specifically, foreign aid is not a substitute for a national defense effort. Thus one commonly hears—for example, when a United States rocket has to be destroyed after leaving the launching pad—"Wouldn't it have been better to have spent all that money on foreign aid instead of on weapons?" This is a false dichotomy. Each program must be evaluated and justified in its own terms, independent of others. Specific items of the military budget or of the foreign aid budget may or may not be warranted in terms of national strategic requirements; but each should stand or fall on the basis of its own contribution to national policy, not whether it is more or less attractive than some other item that performs a quite different function.

A second misconception about the foreign aid program is that once a commitment has been given to aid another country, it becomes perpetual. Although there does exist a tendency for any program once instituted to perpetuate itself indefinitely, economic aid programs to various countries have in fact been terminated after their goals have been reached. This was true of Marshall Plan aid for the reconstruction of the western European countries after the end of the war; since then, nonmilitary economic aid programs to Israel, Greece, Japan, and Nationalist China have also been terminated.

The purposes of American *military* assistance are clear. If the United States supplies military equipment to an allied country, or funds with which to pay troops, this reduces the necessity for deploying American troops in the area, and is desirable not only from a budgetary stand-point (since United States troops are invariably better paid than their foreign counterparts), but also from the standpoint of the American soldiers themselves and of their families. The purposes of *economic* aid from the standpoint of the national interest may not be so clear. They are principally the following: First, the economy of the recipient country, thus strengthened, can better support the defense effort necessary to safe-guard national independence against neighboring states with aggressive intentions, or against domestic guerrilla movements; second, as the more prosperous economy that United States aid helps to create is better able to satisfy popular desires, the general satisfaction of the population with the present regime is augmented, and the people are less likely to turn their favor toward communism or to other demagogic anti-United States political movements; third, in addition most types of economic aid act so as to create links between the economy of the United States and the economy of the recipient country that may be of general economic advan-tage to the United States, and, more importantly, will tend to strengthen ties of common interest between the two countries.

This is not the same thing as saying that the purpose of the economic aid program is to "buy friends." One should point out right away that the friendship that can be bought is not worth buying, and that "friends" obtained in this manner would be unlikely to "stay bought" indefinitely. The political purpose to which aid is directed is rather to create situations that are in themselves favorable to United States interests and aspirations, regardless of any feelings of gratitude that may or may not be involved, by strengthening popular well-being and national independence. In other words it would usually be equally valuable for the United States to give aid "anonymously" if equivalent changes were wrought in the recipient economy as a result. Of course, any feelings of gratitude that do result on the recipient's part are all to the good and to be encouraged; nevertheless, it should not be to arouse such transitory and unreliable feelings that aid is given. As a matter of fact, the feelings that aid seems to arouse all too often are of resentment and condescension, and the governments of some states act as though they were doing the United States a great favor by "accepting aid."

It should be noted that United States aid does not consist solely of gifts. An increasing proportion of such aid, now more than half of the total, in fact, consists of loans designed to be repaid, albeit over long periods and at low rates of interest. In addition substantial amounts of the aid given carry the stipulation that they are to be used only to procure goods from the United States—which are generally more expen-sive than goods produced elsewhere—and that higher-cost American ship-ping be used to transport them. Although this is all quite reasonable

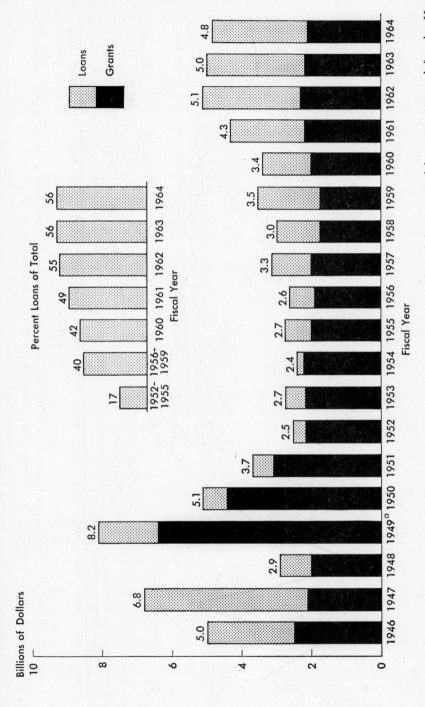

Chart 15.1. United States Economic Assistance—Loans and Grants. SOURCE: Adapted from a special report prepared for the House Foreign Affairs Committee. Washington: D.C.: Government Printing Office, 1964, p. 5. [a] Fifteen months for AID.

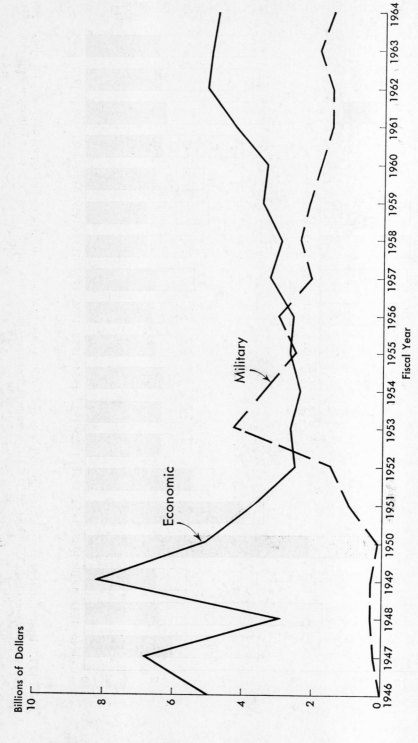

Billions of Dollars

Economic

Military

Fiscal Year

Chart 15.2. Trend of United States Economic and Military Assistance. SOURCE: Adapted from a special report prepared for the House Foreign Affairs Committee. Washington, D.C.: Government Printing Office, 1964, p. 5.

from the American standpoint, of course, it makes American aid much less of a gift than is often assumed. These more direct, more obvious benefits to the American economy are usually cited by foreign aid spokesmen in their testimony before congressional committees and are also inclined to be stressed by anti-Americans abroad, who treat the whole aid program as a "neocolonial" device to tie foreign economies inextricably to that of the United States.

THE SOVIET FOREIGN AID PROGRAM

As one of a series of changes in its policy towards the non-Communist world, the Soviet Union began in the last year of Stalin's rule a program of economic aid competitive with the American program. This represented a new departure for the Soviet Union; during the height of the Stalinist period, economic relations with other states had been dictated by the most narrow and immediate considerations of economic advantage, and the economies of the Eastern European satellites had been heavily exploited.

The fact that now the Soviet Union also has a foreign aid program has helped in the general improvement of the Soviet image abroad, a change that has been going forward since the death of Stalin. It has also made possible a greater freedom of maneuver on the part of underdeveloped countries, which now feel that they do not have to align themselves with United States policies in order to receive aid. As a technique of competing with the West, however, the operation of a foreign aid program contains many drawbacks for the Soviet Union, the principal one being that the Soviet Union is poorer than the United States and has less economic surplus to devote to the program, while the Soviet citizen's consciousness of his low standard of living induces in him resentment against the aid that goes abroad.

The Soviet Union does have a relative advantage in giving aid, however, in that the Russians are less concerned than the United States that the aid given will contribute directly and effectively to the development process. That is, Soviet aid is directed more at the short-run "winning of friends," and the establishment of channels of Soviet influence. Thus Soviet-financed projects in developing countries are more likely than typical United States projects to be designed from the point of view of their propaganda impact, rather than of their actual contribution to development—such as the building of the athletic stadium in Jakarta, for example. The Soviet Union has also been discovering that favorable foreign policies on the part of other states can not be "bought" permanently. However, the Russians also have the advantage that if a Soviet-financed project should, instead of contributing to the development process, contribute to a distortion of the economy or to an accentuation of the gap between rich and poor, for example, this may actually result in an augmentation of the discontent from which the local Communist party draws a large part of its support, and thus represent a net gain for Soviet foreign policy. These are effects that the aid program of a responsible country, such as the United States, cannot tolerate.

A leading characteristic of Soviet economic aid is that it is more highly concentrated in a limited range of selected countries than that of the United States. This is partly because the resources the Soviet Union has to devote to its aid program are more limited, and partly because the program is designed to produce a more immediate political impact. Thus the bulk of Soviet economic aid has gone to about half a dozen countries in the underdeveloped world: Cuba, the United Arab Republic, Indonesia, India, and Afghanistan.

Some misapprehension has developed in the United States, fed by such books as *The Ugly American,* that Soviet economic aid is incomparably better conceived and executed than that of the United States and results in much greater political advantage to the donor. It is highly unlikely that anything of the sort is the case, and there seems to be a great deal of misgiving in Soviet leadership circles over the value to the Soviet Union of its aid program. The Soviet program seems to have resulted in even more spectacular fiascos than that of the United States; the story has now become legendary of how the Soviet Union delivered cement to Burma before warehousing facilities were available, and dumped the cement on the docks in the open air shortly before the beginning of the monsoon season—with the results that could be expected. The Soviet aid program to Guinea, hastily put together in order to capitalize on Guinea's rupture of her ties with France, is reported to have been extremely badly designed and executed, and involved a great deal of heavyhanded Soviet political activity; in disillusionment, Guinea cancelled the Soviet program and turned to the West for aid. The Russian technicians are even targets for the kind of complaint usually leveled at Americans involved in the foreign aid programs—that they keep to themselves and look down on the local inhabitants, and that they create resentment by flaunting a higher standard of living than that of the host country.

CONGRESS AND FOREIGN AID

The United States foreign aid program has met with especially difficult problems in the domestic political arena. Involving as it does the expenditure of substantial amounts of money, the program is a continued source of resentment, and must be rejustified every year to the Congress and the public as the administration faces the annual battle to secure authorizations for expenditures under the program.

Because of the intrinsic unpopularity of spending money, and because the foreign aid program cannot count on the support of a set of clearly defined interest groups in the United States that feel they benefit from it, as is normally the case with domestic programs, it is never an easy matter to get a foreign aid bill through the Congress. And just as success is reputed to feed on itself, so does vulnerability lead to more vulnerability; the aid program must undergo the scrutiny of some ten legislative committees, while inspecting the administration of the United States aid program is one of the commonest purposes—at least nominally—of congressional trips abroad. It is, of course, part of the job of the legislature, under the American system, to scrutinize the acts of the executive, and a certain amount of this is both proper and necessary. But an excess of such scrutiny—such as there is of the foreign aid program—tends to be disruptive of the effective operation of the program, leading to timidity and excessive red tape, as officials become afraid of incurring responsibility in case some project meets with disaster and they become liable to an outpouring of congressional wrath.

In the continuing attempt to "improve the image" of the foreign aid program that is induced by the attack upon it, the program, since its inception at the end of World War II, has been subjected to frequent reorganization, which has only served to complicate its already substantial administrative problems. Unsettling effects result from the periodic expansions and contractions of staff that the program undergoes in line with the widely varying tides of congressional favor and disfavor. New top administrators of the program are continually coming and going as the executive attempts to improve relations with Congress.[1] The name of the agency administering the program has itself been changed from time to time in the attempt to refurbish the agency's "image." Even this creates its own problems: After the agency puts some effort into making itself well known and favorably regarded abroad, it then finds it must begin all over again to try to publicize its new name or initials. At present economic aid is centralized under the Agency for International Development (AID), which has been given a partially autonomous status within the State Department, its regional assistant secretaries having equivalent rank to Assistant Secretaries of State.

---

[1] Thus Representative Otto Passman of Louisiana, a leading congressional opponent of foreign aid, was able to say:

> I've held 800 hours of hearings on this program this year, . . . I think I know more about it than they do at the White House. I think I know more about it than they do at the State Department, for that matter, the way they shift around.

Quoted in the New York *Times,* December 13, 1963.

Because of its general suspicion of the foreign aid program, Congress is more inclined to legislate in detail regarding it than about other aspects of the country's foreign policy. Needless to say, these congressionally-imposed restrictions serve to hamper the executive in implementing national policy in difficult and unusual cases. The limitations placed by Congress on the aid program are not all *designed* to affect the direction of foreign policy, however; some are simply intended to benefit the American economy, or segments of it (even though this may be at the expense of the country being "aided"). Examples of provisions of the latter kind are the requirements cited above limiting the proportion of United States aid that may be spent to procure goods in other countries, or requiring that goods be carried on American shipping, which typically charges higher rates than ships of foreign registry.

But often the restrictions that Congress places on the program *are* designed to change the direction of national foreign policy. Congress sometimes goes so far as to prohibit explicitly aid to designated countries; Poland and Yugoslavia are the usual candidates for a specific ban of this type; Congress takes the position that no aid should be extended to those countries since their governments are Communist, and the administration argues that, Communist or not, aid from the United States enables them to increase their autonomy from Soviet direction and control—an autonomy that is of course absolute in the case of Yugoslavia, and not inconsiderable in the case of Poland—and that this is in the interest of the United States to encourage.

As mentioned above, Congress has stipulated that no aid may be given to a state whose government has expropriated the property of United States nationals without giving them compensation. The executive branch has accepted this limitation, and, as already noted, aid has been discontinued to Ceylon, which did so expropriate American property.

A limitation of this kind adopted by the administration itself early in the first term of President Eisenhower, but dropped at the beginning of Kennedy's term, was that no United States aid would be advanced to state-owned economic enterprises. The rationale for this policy was never very clear, but it seemed to involve an aversion to socialized economic activities on principle, and also a feeling that these were less efficient than enterprises under private control. Unfortunately, the simple truth is that in many countries of the world, cultural factors have militated against the development of an entrepreneurial class, and that if one waits for private enterprise to come forward to do a job, the job will not get done. This is not always the case, and there are potent arguments in favor of having private businessmen rather than governments undertake economic activities; nevertheless, in some cases there are no alternatives to government-run enterprises, while in any event the need may be so vast that the total efforts of both government corporations and private businesses will still be inadequate to perform the task. As was noted above, the Kennedy administration subsequently dropped this line of policy, in order to be able to advance aid to the government-owned Bolivian tin-mining corporation. The Congress seems, however, not to have accepted the logic of the arguments against the original policy, and congressional opposition prevented United States aid being given to a government-owned iron and steel complex in India.

SHOULD "STRINGS" BE ATTACHED TO UNITED STATES AID?

This general line of discussion raises the problem of how much "interference" the United States should permit itself in the internal affairs of the country being aided. Should "strings" be attached to United States aid, and if so, what should they be?

Here the problem becomes one of striking a balance among conflicting pressures. It is clearly the case that continued heavyhanded interference in the domestic affairs of another country as a condition for the continuance of United States aid may lead to a nationalist anti-United States reaction on the part of the government concerned, or is likely to result in popular alienation from the government, which is then regarded as a puppet of the United States; it will in any case lend substance to Soviet claims that the United States aid program is simply a neocolonialist operation, designed to secure United States control over the governments and economies of other states through the payment of "bribes" to unscrupulous government leaders. Interference can thus go too far and can defeat the purposes of the aid program itself.

At the same time there is such a thing as too little American interference, first of all to insure that the aid given is actually spent for the purpose for which it is intended; there have been cases of the diversion of United States funds for private purposes, which not only defeats the aim of the program in that country, but also undermines the confidence of the American people and the Congress in the program as a whole. In the second place a certain measure of United States interference can be justified in areas where the success of the aid program itself requires that various collateral activities be undertaken; for example, a United States program to train teachers will be pointless unless the government's budget makes provision to hire the teachers and pay their salaries after their training is completed—something that was not done in Haiti under the Duvalier dictatorship.[2] In the third place, and this is the area of greatest delicacy, an argument can be made that the granting of large-scale American aid should be contingent on the introduction of various structural social reforms. The argument here runs along these lines: There is no point in the United States providing techniques and resources with which to increase agricultural yield, for example, if the resulting benefits will all go to a small group of large landowners, who are already very rich, and not to the masses of the population. In fact it is possible that such a result would lead to an embittering of relations between the social classes and the creation of a dangerous political situation. In other words social reforms of various types may be necessary before the benefits of United States aid, and the consequent political advantages one hopes will result, can be achieved.

THE ALLIANCE FOR PROGRESS

In the Alliance for Progress program in Latin America, certain key social reforms are envisaged that will enable the United States aid given to the countries of the area to result in the greatest possible political and economic benefit. In this sense the Alliance for Progress program represents the culmination of United States thinking about the effective conception and management of a foreign aid program.

The stress on the program as an alliance, that is, as a cooperative endeavor rather than as a relationship between donor and recipient of aid, was designed to overcome the problem of sensitivity to intervention by outsiders. Although sound in conception, this principle was not at first followed in practice, and the two ex-Presidents who were asked to review the progress of the alliance in 1963, Alberto Lleras Camargo of Colombia and Juscelino Kubitschek of Brazil, both urged that the program be further internationalized by the appointment of a multilateral supervisory committee, a recommendation that was subsequently acted upon. The United States is legitimately afraid that to lose control of the administration of the aid may mean a loosening of the standards applied to the projects for which it is granted. This need not be the case, however, as political pressures from recipient countries, where administration is solely in United States hands, may force a relaxation of standards, while the requirements of effective program planning and development for economic growth are as well understood by economists working for an international body as they are by economists working for the United States government. In fact the multilateralization of the Alliance that took place after 1963 seemed to increase its effectiveness.

Since the Alliance for Progress represents to a great extent the most

---

[2] Aid to Haiti was eventually cut off for a period because of factors of this type.

recent thinking about the most effective ways to conduct an international aid program, it is worth examining in greater detail.

The first point that should be made about the program is that it is in form quite literally an alliance—that is, its principles are embodied in an international agreement, known as the Charter of Punta del Este, whose text was approved at an inter-American conference in August 1961, seven months after the Kennedy administration took office in the United States. The countries that are parties to the alliance are the United States and the nineteen states of Latin America minus Cuba.

In the attempt to dramatize the Alliance and to give it direction, a set of more or less specific objectives was established for the countries of Latin America to reach—such as a minimum annual rate of economic growth of two and one-half percent *per capita,* the elimination of adult illiteracy, the increase of life expectancy at birth by at least five years, and many more. It is the writer's own feeling that these specific objectives should not be taken absolutely literally, and the Alliance adjudged to have failed if they are not met within the ten-year period for which it is initially to run. It makes more sense to regard them as targets set up to be aimed at, the objective being to come as close to them as possible, rather than as magic numbers that determine the difference between success and failure. After all, this is not a situation in which one either succeeds or fails; one improves or retrogresses, and there are degrees of each.

In the effort to attain the objectives established by the Alliance, the parties to the agreement pledge to impose certain criteria of performance on themselves. While some of the standards that are set are desirable in themselves and so from one point of view can be considered "objectives" of the Alliance, others constitute organizational improvements that will help determine whether the other objectives of the Alliance are going to be reached; accordingly the United States has signified that its granting of aid will be in part conditional on the successful adoption of the standards stipulated. These consist of structural changes such as administrative reform, economic planning, tax reform, and land reform, which, while desirable in themselves, are also of worth in that without them the effectiveness of any aid given by the United States is likely to be lessened. That is, an overgrown and incompetent bureaucracy is unlikely to be able to administer an aid program effectively; if land ownership is concentrated in a few hands, the benefits of changes in agricultural productivity are not likely to be distributed most advantageously from a political point of view; and unless a country is already doing as much as it can to help itself through its own tax program, it seems unreasonable to expect the North American taxpayer to help to remedy its deficiencies.

For its part the United States has agreed to supply funds, assuming congressional approval is forthcoming, at the rate of one-billion dollars annually for the ten years of the program, with the hope being that investment funds from other sources, domestic and foreign, would total a similar amount. Congress has thus far shown itself favorably inclined to the program and has tended to reduce Alliance for Progress funds less than it has cut other aid funds.

In the short period since the inception of the Alliance, enough experience has accumulated to make possible an interim evaluation of the program. In the first place there is some question about the wisdom of targeting a flat amount of United States aid that would be of about the same magnitude for the ten years of the program. In view of the problems involved in establishing adequate staffs, and in having projects properly planned, both in themselves and in relation to the country's total development program, it would probably have made more sense to begin the program on a more modest level and to build up over a period of several years to its maximum scope. This is especially true since in many cases the skills and experience necessary to do an adequate job of economic planning must be painfully assembled before the optimum program can be devised. Thus in its early years the Alliance did not face a shortage of public investment funds as much as a shortage of properly conceived and designed projects to which those funds could be devoted.

A more difficult political problem that emerged for the Alliance was that of procrastination on the part of many in government circles in Latin American countries in the initiation of the structural reforms that were intended to be prerequisites for the granting of substantial aid.

In part this has been due to the ambiguities concealed in Alliance goals. What does "tax reform" mean, for example? It must mean at least establishing machinery for effective enforcement, "closing loopholes," and so on; it presumably means rationalization, for example in doing away with taxes that bring in less revenue than they cost to administer, or that have the effect of restricting production without raising much revenue. Over and above this, however, changes in tax structure raise basic policy issues: Should taxes aim to raise revenue, to redistribute income more equally among the population, to stimulate production—or what combination of these aims, since they often contradict each other?

Similar questions can be raised about other Alliance objectives that use the unspecific term "reform"—land reform, for example, or administrative reform. Some of those trying to appraise progress under the Alliance, now that it has been in operation for a little time and has still not solved all of Latin America's problems, have complained about this lack of precision in the "structural change" goals of the Alliance. The present writer is inclined to regard this imprecision rather as a strength, since it has enabled a mobilization of almost the whole spectrum of Latin American political forces, except for the extremes, around the general idea of reform. Although the reforms have not come right away, and although a great deal of domestic political haggling takes place within each country before effective reforms actually are introduced, the Alliance has succeeded in effecting a change in the intellectual environment, which has undermined the pure conservatism that opposes all change on principle. The Alliance for Progress has dictated a new vocabulary for official Latin America, and deeds sometimes have a way of following words.

Naturally there remains great political resistance to specific proposals for land reform, tax reform, and even administrative reform, where these threaten established interests that have a large voice in the political process. The problem has, therefore, arisen of whether to grant funds on the showing of a substantial need only, or to withhold them because of the nonperformance of the reform measures contemplated; political and psychological pressures being what they are, the tendency has been to take the promise of performance for the performance itself and to extend aid before reforms have actually been undertaken.

The most important difficulty faced by the Alliance for Progress in its first years had nothing to do with the Alliance itself, however, but arose from quite different factors. This was that the Alliance had been launched at a time when two major types of economic trends were operating against the cause of the economic development of Latin America, and as a result Alliance funds were outweighed and the whole impact of the Alliance program weakened. The first of these adverse trends was a steady long-term downward tendency in the prices that the Latin American countries received for the commodities they exported, most of them primary—that is, agricultural and mineral—products. The other adverse trend was that the amount of new private investment in Latin American countries, from both domestic and foreign sources, was tending downward, and in some countries more capital was leaving the country than was coming in. The causes of this phenomenon were several, a leading one being the inflationary tendencies that the Alliance itself hoped to overcome; but probably the main reason for the flight of investment funds had to do with the political instability of the area, which has been somewhat on the increase in the years since the Alliance was inaugurated. Thus one has the paradox that the Alliance attempts to achieve a political stability based on democratic premises in the area by dint of attacking its economic and social problems, but is hindered in tackling those problems by the fact of political instability itself.

This does not mean that one should give up hope for the Alliance for Progress. There are now indications that the downward trend in some key commodity prices—especially coffee—has been arrested, perhaps permanently. And even where conditions have deteriorated, the deterioration would clearly have been more rapid if the Alliance did not exist.

It remains true that the greatest social and economic advances have occurred in those states—Mexico, Venezuela, and El Salvador, especially—whose governments are progressive and dedicated to the kind of reform program envisaged by the Alliance. In other words, the Alliance has served to bring social benefits to the populations of several countries, and has strengthened progressive governments by supplying them with funds and with political backing from the United States; nevertheless, it has become clear that the most important variable in determining whether a country will progress socially or not lies in the caliber and intentions of its government, and that without democratic and socially progressive governments there can be little hope for peaceful and democratic social reform.

GUIDELINES FOR A SUCCESSFUL AID PROGRAM

Now that American experience with foreign aid programs has accumulated, something of a consensus has evolved as to the requirements of a successful program, which may be enumerated in summary form as follows.

1. Although it seems truistic to say so, an effective aid program needs efficient and honest administration, on the part both of the United States and of the local country. This most obvious requirement may however be the most difficult to secure. Given the multiplicity of American agencies operating abroad, the danger of specific tasks overlapping and working at cross purposes to each other is always present. A rule of thumb which has helped to meet the problem of administrative efficiency to some extent, however, is that the United States ambassador in each country is given the responsibility of coordinating all American aid activities in the country to which he is assigned.

2. In the substance of the aid program, attention should be given to maintaining its components in balance with each other, and at the same time geared to other programs of the local government and to plans of private industry. A rule of this kind is necessary with respect to the allocation of scarce materials and manpower in order to avoid the creation of delays and bottlenecks.

3. Particular attention should be paid to ensuring that the distribution of benefits from the program is not "skewed" so that only a limited and less needy segment of the population benefits from it. Avoidance of this pitfall is desirable not only in the interests of justice but also to avoid unpleasant political repercussions.

4. Just as the benefits of the program should be spread, so should commitment to it. That is, not only should local people be associated with the program as much as possible so that it becomes a genuinely national effort, rather than an act of charity from outside, but also every effort should be taken to avoid limiting local participation solely to members of the party or group in power; this could of course backfire, since no one's hold on power is permanent.

5. Finally, although the projects to be supported are chosen primarily with a view to their value in promoting the country's economic and social development, it makes sense nevertheless to adopt a bias in program selection in favor of so-called "impact projects," that is, those that are visible to the population and are likely to result in a better public relations position for the United States. The United States should certainly not seek to emulate the Soviet Union in donating funds for projects of great propaganda value but of no social and economic significance whatsoever; one does well, however, to bear in mind the example of the government of Nuri as-Said of Iraq, which inaugurated substantial public works projects of fundamental importance to the country, but whose benefits would not be apparent for some time, and was overthrown partly because of alienation from the population, which knew that money deriving from oil revenues was being spent somehow by the government, but could see no result of it, and so grew increasingly suspicious and restive.

THE PEACE CORPS

No discussion of United States foreign aid would be complete without mention of the Peace Corps. In the long perspective of history the creation of the Peace Corps may well stand out as one of the major achievements of the Kennedy administration. It was surely long overdue for the United States government, whose economic doctrines and national security policies too often appeal only to the tired cynicism of the middle-aged, to try also to engage the idealism of youth in support of national policies. In its first years of operation the Peace Corps proved highly successful in terms of the response both at home and abroad, and congressional favor of the program was reflected in an unaccustomed kindness to Peace Corps budget requests.

In the author's view the Peace Corps has undoubtedly been successful in its purposes, despite the malaise that usually afflicts the Peace Corps volunteer as he comes to grips with his job and begins to realize that changing the world is not as easy as he had thought. The great value of the Peace Corps, however, does not consist simply of the immediate results of the grass-roots work of volunteers in their attempt to aid the less privileged of other lands. Nor does it come solely in demonstrating to tradition-bound villagers that change is possible and one can organize with one's fellows to bring it about, important as this effect is. The writer has been impressed with the impact that the Peace Corps has had on the conscience of the people in the cities of the country aided, especially the better-off, who never go anywhere near the remote parts of the country in which the Peace Corps finds itself working, and whose own national conscience is often awakened by the news of the activities of the Peace Corps contingent, which is reported by a fascinated national press. At the same time the very existence of young Americans such as those who man the Peace Corps is a standing challenge to the stereotype of the United States as a rich, complacent, and greedy materialist society.

It may well be, however, that the most important long-run results of the Peace Corps will be not in its impact outside our borders but in its impact within the United States. As the Peace Corps volunteers return from their overseas assignments, they will constitute a substantial reserve pool of people concerned about the foreign relations of the United States and acquainted with problems of other countries at more than a superficial level, and they will certainly raise the quality of the manpower pool from which public officials are drawn. As Peace Corps volunteers return to their home communities, moreover, one may perhaps be forgiven the wishful thought that they will constitute a leaven that can raise the whole level of popular knowledge about, and concern with, American foreign relations; and perhaps that a newly enlightened citizenry, for whom the intellectual pace is set by the returning Peace Corps volunteer (just as the whole caliber of United States higher education was improved by the returning veterans of World War II), can serve as the public for a foreign policy informed by insight and human concern.

SUGGESTED READINGS

Black, Eugene R., *The Diplomacy of Economic Development*. Cambridge, Mass.: Harvard University Press, 1960.

Gordon, Lincoln, *A New Deal for Latin America: The Alliance for Progress*. Cambridge, Mass.: Harvard University Press, 1963.

Hirschman, A. O., *The Strategy of Economic Development*. New Haven, Conn.: Yale University Press, 1958.

Mason, Edward S., *Foreign Aid and Foreign Policy*. New York: Harper & Row, 1964.

Montgomery, John D., *The Politics of Foreign Aid*. New York: Praeger, 1962.

Rostow, Walt W., *The Stages of Economic Growth*. New York: Cambridge University Press, 1960.

Silvert, Kalman H. (ed.), *Expectant Peoples: Nationalism and Development*. New York: Random House, Inc., 1963.

Staley, Eugene, *The Future of Underdeveloped Countries*. New York: Praeger, 1961.

Urquidi, Víctor, *The Challenge of Development in Latin America*. New York: Praeger, 1964.

White, Gillian, *Nationalization and Foreign Property*. New York: Praeger, 1961.

Wiggins, James W., and Helmut Schoek (eds.), *Foreign Aid Re-Examined: A Critical Appraisal*. Washington, D.C.: Public Affairs Press, 1958.

VI

In Conclusion

16

Understanding Foreign Policy

THE CHANGING AMERICAN ATTITUDE

If one takes a broad historical perspective, it can be seen that the American approach to foreign policy has undergone a drastic shift from its original assumptions. The foreign policies of the United States during the nineteenth century are summed up in the Monroe Doctrine; although usually treated as establishing a line of policy for the United States in the Western Hemisphere, the Monroe Doctrine actually did not establish a policy towards a single problem so much as delineate the scope of the whole range of national foreign affairs activities. In effect the doctrine marked out the Western Hemisphere as the field of action for the United States; and as the European powers were not expected to intervene in the Americas, the United States, for its part, would not intervene in Europe.[1]

The area circumscribed by the Monroe Doctrine was held to for a hundred years; the republic followed a policy of intermittent and limited imperialism with respect to the continent of North America and the adjacent waters, and one of noninvolvement with respect to the politics of the rest of the world.[2] In these respects it resembled the policies of the newly independent states of today.

---

[1] "In the wars of the European powers in matters relating to themselves we have never taken any part, nor does it comport with our policy to do so."

[2] Thus even the United States occupation of Guam and the Philippines was the unanticipated consequence of a war originating in the Caribbean over Cuba.

But the effective arena of action of national arms and statesmanship—the northern part of the Western Hemisphere—had its own peculiar characteristics, and these set their impress on American thinking
about foreign policy. Foremost among these characteristics was the fact
that around most of its perimeter the United States encountered only
power vacuums. The exception was to the north. An attempt had been
made to conquer Canada in the War of 1812, without success; thereafter
the frontier was stabilized on an amicable basis, with the United States to
entertain neither hopes of annexing the British dominions to the north,
nor fears of invasion from that direction. And the Monroe Doctrine
explicitly recognized the possession by the European powers of the
colonies then still in their hands.

To the west, to the southeast and southwest, however, no countervailing power presented itself. To the west only handfuls of primitive
aborigines stood in the path of expansion to the Rocky Mountains; to the
southwest a Mexico in continual political turmoil, corrupt and divided
against itself, could not defend its distant outlying provinces; to the
southeast, in the Caribbean, the small tropical and sub-tropical republics
were not even able to govern themselves, much less to offer resistance to
the incursions of North American power—or so it seemed—while the
decaying remnant of the Spanish colonial empire seemed about to collapse of its own accord.

Given this absence of countervailing power in areas in which
expansion could be contemplated, foreign policy designs could mature
without needing to take the opposition of other states into account. The
foreign and Indian wars in which the United States was engaged in the
century between the War of 1812 and World War I invariably ended in
victory for the United States, and no effective external check to American
expansion presented itself. As the political controversy between the
supporters of imperialism and the anti-imperialists developed, the argument was couched exclusively in terms of American wishes, not in terms
of any realities in the outside world that might present obstacles to the
gratification of those wishes. Thus the anti-imperialists, such as William
Graham Sumner, argued that the United States should refrain from
following the imperialist path not because of the external difficulties
involved in the construction of an empire, but because such a policy
would mean that the republic would not be true to itself, that the
possession of colonies would impair the democratic political system and
the American political personality.

The bond between the views of the simple republican opponents of
imperialism, who judged foreign policy by reference to the norms of
domestic political behavior, and the vulgar self-assertiveness of the super-
patriots of imperialism, like Senator Beveridge, is that both were con-

cerned exclusively with the national self and not at all with any limits placed on American policies by the world outside the national borders. With justification, therefore, the century of simple imperialism and simple anti-imperialism that preceded American involvement in World War I can be regarded as a sort of infantile stage of the development of national policy, in that the United States, like the very young infant, had not yet had to adjust its behavior to take account of the realities of a cold, indifferent, and often hostile world; the country had not yet made the transition from the pleasure principle to the reality principle, as it were.

Of course many differences exist among Americans as they approach questions of foreign policy. Perhaps the major division that exists today, however, is between those who have accepted the realities implied in the American assumption of a great power role in international politics, on the one hand—although they differ among themselves over policies to be followed in specific situations—and, on the other, those who would set foreign policies while ignoring the existence of a world outside the United States. The latter may resemble the imperialists of the turn of the century in believing in American omnipotence, in believing that the simple use of force will produce the desired results without cost—those who meet every problem of foreign policy with the recommendation to send in the Marines or to drop nuclear bombs. But there are also among us successors to the anti-imperialists of seventy-five years ago, who attempt likewise to ignore the realities of the world outside our borders, and who counsel that foreign policy should be set by reference only to the ideals of domestic political life. United States policy to the outside world, in this conception, should be an extension of domestic social policy, and should become a colossal welfare program, supervised by an international legislature. However, it is hardly less naïve to believe that peace and justice can be achieved by treating everyone nicely, campaigning against poverty, and "educating for world citizenship"—desirable though these activities may be in themselves—than to think that policy problems can be resolved by conquering or bombing those who seem to be causing difficulties. There is naïveté on both Right and Left.

A great many commentators on foreign policy have identified their own positions with that of either Right or Left described above, which they have then termed "realistic." The neo-imperialist view passes as realistic because it takes the apparently sophisticated line that issues can be resolved only by force; the welfare-oriented approach to foreign policy passes itself off as more realistic because it is directed at removing the "real" causes of unrest and war: poverty, ignorance, and disease. Actually, however, realism inheres in neither position. The crucial principle of realism as it applies in present American foreign policy is that the field of American international concerns is no longer a power vacuum in which the only determinant of action need be American desires. One is surely entitled to believe that the United States should pursue its "interests" rather than its "ideals," or some interests more than others, or some interests more than some ideals; inevitably, individuals vary widely over the importance that each attaches to a given social or political system, to money, or indeed to the value of human life itself. The criterion of realism, however, is that it values actions not in themselves, but in reference to their consequences, for to be able to estimate the consequences of acts requires some understanding of the realities of the world in which action takes place. Acting with foreknowledge of the consequences of actions is at the same time the definition of responsibility. Whatever the ultimate goals it is designed to serve, a responsible and "realistic" foreign policy is distinguished by its consideration of consequences. It is a policy of forethought, not of emotional reaction; dominated by design, not by slogan; aware of necessary costs, as much as of imagined benefits.

THE CHANGING WORLD SITUATION

The external reality within whose framework policy must be executed is constantly changing. All too often a foreign policy thought to be realistic is addressed not to the reality of the moment but to a reality that has already become obsolete. This danger must especially be guarded against in American foreign policy, since the United States emerged onto the world scene in the midst of a configuration of circumstances that impressed a certain mould on policy, but that is today no longer the dominant pattern of world politics.

The United States participated actively in the whole range of international affairs for the first time with World War I, and indeed the events of that war were what drew the Americans into participation. The style of behavior that the situation imposed on the United States was that of straightforward combat against a clearly defined enemy. After a period of withdrawal, the United States reentered the arena of international politics under a similar set of circumstances; in 1941 the requirement was again for all-out combat against a well-defined enemy. World War II had hardly ended before the familiar pattern imposed itself yet another time, with the Soviet Union assuming the role that had been played twice before by Germany.

The problem for United States policy today is to break out of a conception of world politics limited to that of a straightforward conflict between two camps, and to adjust to a world more complex, more dif-

ficult to understand, yet probably more typical of the normal characteristics of international politics in the long run. Adjustment to this newly
emerging world situation will mark the final attainment by the United
States of maturity as a world power.

THE ERODING OF THE COLD WAR

Let us first consider the recent changes in the theme that has
dominated American thinking about international relations for nearly
twenty years, the confrontation with the Soviet Union. As the world
became set in the pattern that it had assumed by 1949, it became
commonplace to describe the peculiar characteristics of the era as the
bipolarity of power and the rigidity of alliances. American thinking
became dominated by the fact of the military threat posed by the Soviet
Union, and troubles that developed elsewhere in the world were typically
ascribed to the activities of Soviet agents, which was generally plausible,
and sometimes true, but which never gave a complete description of
international reality.

Today the Cold War continues, but its bitterness has softened and
it is becoming merely one among several dominant themes of international relations; it can no longer be regarded as the only one that
matters. Various causes can be adduced for this change. It was certainly
facilitated by the death of Stalin, and the rise of a Communist China;
but the present softening of the Cold War is also the eventual result of
the policy of containment that the United States adopted in President
Truman's day as its response to Soviet expansionism. If it is true that a
powerful state tends to expand into neighboring "power vacuums," it
appears equally true that the expansionist urge steadily atrophies when
opportunities for its gratification are denied it.

The history of the Cold War can thus be told in terms of its increasing moderation as steadily narrowing limits were placed on the scope of
the conflict between the two superpowers. One might say that the code of
Cold-War behavior followed today by the United States and the Soviet
Union represents a sort of "case law" that has grown out of a series of
significant limiting cases that have served to define the boundaries of the
scope of conflict between the two states. The major "cases" in this regard
are the Berlin blockade and the subsequent airlift; the Korean war; the
Soviet repression of the Hungarian uprising of 1956; President Eisenhower's discontinuation of U-2 flights over the Soviet Union; and the
Cuban missile crisis of 1962.

By its action in the Berlin blockade in airlifting supplies to the be-
sieged city, the United States made clear that it would defend the positions it occupied but that it would employ no more force than necessary

to this end; the Soviet Union, in refraining from taking action against the planes that were participating in the airlift, demonstrated that its expansionist moves were likewise limited by considerations of rationality and economy of force. In the case of Korea, the United States showed itself willing to enter actual combat if necessary to hold back Communist expansionism, while both sides showed an appreciation of the importance of limiting the arena of conflict to avoid its escalation into a full-scale world war. By not intervening in the Hungarian uprising of 1956, the United States conceded that it would respect the immediate Soviet security zone of the Eastern European satellites, despite the talk of "liberation" that had been general during the 1952 election campaign. In calling off the flights over the Soviet Union by U-2 planes after the failure of the Paris summit conference of 1960, the United States implicitly acknowledged that the dangers of world conflict inherent in the balance of terror imposed a respect for the territorial integrity of the major antagonist, and an obligation to refrain from humiliating acts. The Cuban missile crisis of fall 1962—when Khrushchev withdrew Soviet missiles already emplaced on the island of Cuba and destroyed their launching sites—parallels in some respects the action of the United States in relation to the Hungarian uprising. That is, the Soviet dictator acknowledged that his attempt to intervene directly in the zone of immediate security of the United States was a bluff that could be called, that is, was an initiative that fell outside the scope of legitimate conflict in the Cold War. It is noteworthy that many commentators understood that there was somehow a connection, however paradoxical it might seem, between the fact that the Soviet Union was forced to back down in the Cuban missile crisis and the improvement of the international atmosphere that made possible the subsequent negotiation of the nuclear test ban treaty. The connection between the two events is simply that in backing down in the Cuban missile crisis the Soviet Union was forced to acknowledge that the Cold War could only be carried on given a set of basic agreements between the two principal protagonists; the fact that each had now accepted the inviolability of the immediate security zone of the other meant that, with respect to a considerable portion of the world's surface, each had, in his own mind, accepted the existence of a *status quo* that he did not favor for its own sake.

One way of looking at the series of events that forms the history of the Cold War is as a learning process for the Soviet Union. Just as the United States, as it became involved in world politics, had to adjust its behavior from the norms consonant with a position of hegemony in North America to those of a participant in world balance-of-power maneuvers, the Soviet Union, similarly, had to make the transition from angry young rebel, bent on self-gratification in defiance of the norms of international society, to responsible middle-aged statesman, conscious of the obligations to world peace and order that rest on his shoulders.

If the Cold War ground rules include: respect for the territory of the opponent and for his immediate security zone; the prohibition of invasions across international boundaries aimed at total conquest; and the limitation to the minimum level of the scope of any overt conflict; then the main dimension in which the Cold War continues today is in the form of "cat's paw" war and *coup d'état,* conflict between the two power blocs disguised as civil war or civil disturbance. Thus the United States tries not to involve its own troops in Cold War fighting; if they should be directly committed, as in South Vietnam, it is only with great reluctance and as a last resort, while every attempt is made to cut short the conflict. Similarly, the Soviet Union has always held back from a direct confrontation of arms. It remains to be seen what norms will guide Chinese conduct as China succeeds an increasingly passive Soviet Union as the principal American antagonist. The author would assume, however, that a similar process of adjustment to a new *status quo* will set in—after it has been possible to stabilize the boundaries to China's expansion.

THE BREAK-UP OF BIPOLARITY

The evolution in the ground rules of the Cold War has been complemented by an evolution in the structure of the Soviet bloc. This has generally been characterized as "polycentrism," that is, the emergence of several centers of initiative and direction within the Communist camp, supplanting the single center of authority allowed during Stalin's reign. Tito's break from the Cominform was followed eventually by a loosening of ties that allowed Poland to pursue independent policies; China and Albania diverged enough from the Soviet line to bring about a series of direct public attacks between their leaders and those of the Soviet Union; the accession of Cuba to the Soviet bloc introduced into the Soviet commonwealth an erratic and idiosyncratic partner; and with the divergence of Romania from the Soviet line on bloc economic policy, it became clear that despite the ideological sympathies that bind the "people's republics" to the Soviet state, divergent national interests continue to exist, and to impose themselves on national policy.

At the same time the ideological bond becomes less significant as the ideology itself becomes less relevant to the needs of domestic policy. Thus, faced with low standards of living and with the desire to improve them, and having learned from the doctrinaire mistakes of the past, the "Leninist" flexibility of the Communist leaderships leads them increasingly to set economic policy in terms of the maximization of production by the introduction of norms of economic rationality. The outcome of this process, however, differs less and less from the mixed-economy pragmatism that characterizes government economic policy outside the Soviet sphere. This resemblance became even plainer under the influence of Khrushchev's dictum that Soviet planners and administrators must build a better economy by learning from advances made in the West, a principle carried even further by Khrushchev's successors.

It is noteworthy that at the same time as the organization of the Soviet economy and the policies of Soviet planners tend to come closer to those found in the West, a parallel development is beginning in the political sphere. The theoretical basis for the political changes that are taking place in the Soviet Union is that of a reinterpretation of the manner in which Soviet society will approach the era of pure communism, the final stage of history in Marxist thought. Under Stalin the attainment of communism tended to be pushed further and further into the indefinite future, or even to be used to justify the extreme political repression of Stalin's day; Stalin even went so far as to announce the thesis that the era of communism would arrive "dialectically," that is, the state would "wither away" only after it had attained its maximum development—in other words, after the apparatus of police oppression had reached its maximum. This doctrine has now been repudiated by the Soviet leadership, which has taken the line that communism is achieved progressively—that is, repression and central direction of Soviet life are steadily to be deemphasized or eliminated in the progressive achievement of pure communism. In practice this means that control of the economy is being decentralized, and the role of the secret police has been limited.

Clearly, if ideology plays a smaller role in the governing of the Soviet Union, and is in any case interpreted so that it counsels policies not very dissimilar from those followed in the West, the whole thesis of ideological conflict with the West is steadily eroded.

A modification in the Soviet concept of conflict with the West has indeed taken place. As the West's policy of containment has taken hold, and as it has become clear that the expansion of Soviet power by military means is no longer possible, the emphasis in Soviet thinking on foreign policy has changed until the coming dominance of communism everywhere in the world is perceived more as a historical development that will evolve of its own accord than as the first imperative of Soviet foreign policy. It appears likely to the writer that this belief in the eventual victory of communism in the world will steadily weaken over time until it comes to resemble the average nominal Christian's faith in the Second Coming—it may be believed in vaguely at some level of consciousness, without in any way affecting day-to-day behavior.

Pressure to abandon an aggressively expansionist foreign policy derives also from the increasing desire among Soviet citizens and the Soviet leadership to limit expenditures on defense, foreign aid, and probes of outer space, in the interest of diverting resources into the production of consumer goods to raise the low Soviet standard of living. The level of national security and space expenditures clearly constitutes a substantial strain for the less than affluent Soviet economy, and with increasing technological sophistication costs in these areas of expenditure tend to rise steeply unless a deliberate decision is made to deemphasize the policies that call for such expenditures.

The tendency is, therefore, for the Soviet Union to become increasingly contented with the territorial *status quo,* in practice if not in principle. This does not mean that the basic prestige-and-power conflict with the United States will disappear, but only that it will subside in significance to become one among the principal conflicts that will dominate international politics, losing its place as the single, most urgent, overriding conflict; and because of the relatively increasing importance of problem areas outside the clash between Soviet and American power, relations between the two states will take on some components of common interest, so that Soviet-American relations will not need to be relations of pure antagonism.

The major dichotomy in international relations will then tend to become not that between the Soviet bloc and states loyal to the American alliance, but between states generally satisfied with the *status quo* and prepared to contemplate changes in it only by peaceful means, on the one hand, and, on the other, revisionist, expansionist, and aggressive states. The states comprised in this latter category will vary, as new personalities or political movements assume leadership; but if it continues to include the Soviet Union in some respects, it will extend at least equally well to embrace Communist China, Indonesia, and perhaps the United Arab Republic or Ghana.

Just as the emergence of polycentrism among Communist states acted to unfreeze the balance-of-power situation of 1949, comparable developments have begun to take place among the states of the Western alliance. The Western alliance was never a "bloc," as the Soviet Union and her allies were, despite the vigorous efforts of Secretary of State Dulles to include all non-Communist states in military alliances with the United States and to regard neutrals outside them virtually as enemies. Dulles' image of the world was never altogether realistic, however, since the United States has always had predominantly defensive policy aims, and has thus shared interests in common with all states that wished to maintain their independence and the formally friendly relations among states normal to diplomatic practice. This was clearly revealed when the United States came to the aid of India after the Chinese attack of 1962, despite the fact that India was not an American ally.

New tendencies have emerged, however, that have weakened the cohesion the Western alliance used to possess. The most salient of these is the development of an independent foreign policy line by France under the leadership of President de Gaulle, which has often taken curious directions, in some cases inimical to the interests of the United States and of the Western alliance. At the same time the coming to independence of most of the former European colonies has meant in many cases that territories once included in the Western alliance are now neutralist; a comparable development has been taking place in Latin America, where such a traditionally staunch ally of the United States as Brazil began under President Quadros to refer to itself as nonaligned.

A NEW BALANCE OF POWER?

In the 1950s it became fashionable to descry in the trends immanent in world politics the emergence of a new balance-of-power system in which the United States and the Soviet Union would be joined, depending on the tastes of the observer, by two or three other new great powers. Communist China was invariably accorded a place in this putative new world system, usually along with a united Europe, sometimes a strengthened British Commonwealth, perhaps a growing India, or some configuration of nonaligned African and Asian states. What was actually occurring, however, was not the revival of a classic European balance of power in which several states of roughly equal power checked the aggressive intentions of others by forming temporary countervailing alliances, but a quite different set of relations.

The more fluid situation that has in fact emerged might more appropriately be described as a "field of power" in which all kinds of influences are exerted in every direction by a variety of states differing widely in size and wealth. It should be noted that in this new "field of power" a state's influence on events is determined not merely by the military and economic power it can muster, but by its symbolic position, its sympathetic ties with other states, the fanaticism of its devotion to a given policy aim, or its strategic position in relation to the world's major alliances—that is, a state's influence is partly determined by its capacity for causing trouble, rather than its capacity for marshalling military and economic resources. For example, the role that Yugoslavia has been able to play in the world, as a Communist state that broke with the Soviet bloc, accepted aid from the West, and maintained its political independence from both blocs, has nothing to do with the size of the country.

Israel's ability to enlist the support of the United States and other powers against hostile moves of the Arab states is constant and reliable, but is based on sympathy for Israel's people and their ideals, not on tangible power factors. Cuba has been able to defy the United States and create difficulties for American policies in Latin America; Romania has forced the Soviet Union to modify her plans for the economic integration of Eastern Europe; Pakistan has succeeded in securing a favorable settlement of a territorial dispute with Communist China.

Why has it been possible for smaller states to exercise this freedom of maneuver and thus obtain some of their foreign policy goals? Why do not the major powers of the world simply arrange affairs to their own liking, coercing the smaller states to fall in line with their wishes willy-nilly? One has to answer, in the first place, that very often the devotion with which an aim is pursued can be a substitute for more tangible factors of power. In other words, a state that is prepared to do more to secure a desired end may be in a stronger relative position than a state nominally more powerful that is not prepared to make similar exertions. An example of the application of this principle is provided by the situation of a large power conducting a military occupation of another country. Normally—at least after its initial enthusiasm has worn off—the people of the occupying state are less than eager about the whole business, which makes it necessary for large numbers of young men to spend tours of duty away from their homes. Normally, one must add to this picture friction with that of the population of the occupied state. If the local population in addition harasses the occupying army, and certainly if it conducts a terrorist or guerrilla campaign, the political pressures on the home government for the withdrawal of troops will be substantial. In a situation of this kind the cards are stacked in favor of the native population of the territory, even if the occupying power is prepared to go to great lengths to maintain its control. A striking illustration of this type of situation was provided by the case of the French in Algeria, who over a period of seven years brought the manpower and economic resources of a large and developed state to bear in the attempt to end the resistance of the Moslem population to French rule, only eventually to yield the point and withdraw.

United States experience is equally instructive. Although the military occupations of Japan and Germany constituted very easy duty for the American soldiers involved, and although no serious difficulties were presented by the attitudes of local populations, the United States never felt comfortable in the role of an occupying power. During the Marine occupations of Haiti, the Dominican Republic, and Nicaragua early in the century, there was indeed resistance from the local populations that became guerrilla war, with the result of extreme alienation from the local population, the unpopularity of the occupations back home, and the eventual withdrawal of American forces. That a similar situation might ensue should be borne in mind by those who advocate American invasion of Cuba to overthrow the government of Fidel Castro; in that case one would have to add to the picture the suitability of the Sierra Maestra for guerrilla operations.

The possibilities of the coercion of small states by the major world powers are also limited by several other factors. The desire of each of the superpowers to avoid an armed conflict with the other may create an area of maneuver for a smaller power—as it did in the case of Yugoslavia. The major Cold War protagonists also make some effort to create a favorable impression of their policies in the "battle for men's minds" (which the present writer believes a vastly overrated component of the Cold War struggle) and for this reason shrink from more obvious acts of coercion, unless they bear directly on national security interests, as in the Hungarian case. In addition to these attitudinal limits presented by the world outside, the larger states tend to be limited in their willingness to coerce smaller states by unfavorable attitudes among their own populations, and indeed among policy makers themselves, who, with the easing of the Cold War, are tending to lose that sense of mission that might otherwise prompt them to support greater costs for the sake of the domination of other states.

THE EMERGING SHAPE
OF THE FUTURE WORLD

As one gains perspective on the changes that have occurred, and are occurring, in the structure of international relations in recent times, it becomes clear that an evolution is taking place in the direction of a world community based on different premises from those of the past. Without any assurance as to exactly how far the process will go, although it clearly will not extend in any forseeable future to the extreme of actual world government in the standard sense, there is a sense in which it can be said that many institutions of a world government are emerging. This semigovernment has its focus in the UN, but its chief characteristic is that it is not limited to any one organization but consists of an interlocking grid of specialized and regional groupings—the OAS,[3] the British Commonwealth, OECD,[4] NATO, GATT,[5] the World Bank, and a host of others. The resulting network of obligations to consult, and of resolu-

---

[3] The Organization of American States.
[4] The Organization for Economic Cooperation and Development.
[5] The General Agreement on Tariffs and Trade.

tions that can be taken by qualified majorities in international organizations, seems to be creating norms of international behavior; the lynchpin of the system is of course the United States as the richest and most powerful nation.

Anyone who has followed the trend of opinion expressed in the standards to which statesmen appeal in public speeches, or in the dominant themes of discussion in the UN General Assembly, can even dimly perceive that a sort of common world ideology is emerging. The principles of this ideology, which constitutes a sort of incipient world conscience, are: the peaceful settlement of disputes, the independence of nation-states, the protection of individual human rights, and the promotion of economic development.

It may still be too fanciful to refer to this web of organizations as a "world government"; but the system at least attempts to perform the major functions that a government has. That is, it tries to maintain order, and when fighting breaks out in an area where the local jurisdiction does not seem able to handle it, some international method of restoring order is attempted. It may well be that U Thant's major achievement as Secretary General will be to achieve the regular use of UN peacekeeping forces in those chronic trouble spots where the major Cold War protagonists do not confront each other.

The system has also been able to make adjustments in the *status quo*, where revisionist claims were felt to be just; it undoubtedly acts to protect and promote trade, and to foster educational, scientific, and cultural activities. Finally, through the various aid and development assistance programs, the emerging world system has begun to perform that characteristic function of modern government: to redistribute income by means of welfare programs from the more well-to-do to the poorer sections of the community.

Clearly, this emerging system of consensus, of interlocking organizations identified by their initials, of fitful and irregular attempts at remedying the world's ills, falls considerably short of government in the normal sense. In response to those who believe in the necessity and possibility of world government in order to meet the world's problems, however, one has to point out that it is perhaps unnecessary to be mechanical or dogmatic, or overly symmetrical, in one's conception of what a "world government" is.

THE UNITED STATES AND WORLD TRENDS

Although specific situations may often have results disadvantageous to the United States, viewed in a long-term perspective the emerging constants of international affairs should on the whole give

Americans cause for satisfaction and not alarm. The world of today is, after all, based increasingly on distinctively American premises, and is guided by characteristically American principles. The very existence of a world organization that tends, albeit slowly, to become the focus of international relations is due eminently to American efforts, is faithful to the tradition of Woodrow Wilson, and conforms to typical American predilections. The norm of national independence on which the dominant anticolonial sentiment in the UN is based is an idea introduced into the practice of the modern world by the American Revolution. The concern for human rights that is increasingly becoming an international norm is in perfect consonance with American attitudes, our own Declaration of Independence and Bill of Rights being among the most important examples of the translation of the concern for individual human freedom from an aspiration to the nominal reality of official documents. The limits that the international community attempts to place upon the outbreak of violence are to be welcomed by all men of good will, and not least by the nation that attempted to make World War I the "war to end all wars." The obsession with economic development that currently dominates all the countries of the globe, and that is embodied in a host of international agencies, is one of the most characteristically American features of today's world, Americans having been long distinguished by their concern with economic and material progress. Even the institutional devices increasingly adopted as the world seeks to organize itself derive from ideas of unmistakably American origin. Federalism, which is emerging among many former colonial states and perhaps in Europe itself, is an American invention; while the intra-American system, which was given impulse from both North America and South America, is the model for the regional organizations that are beginning to take shape in other parts of the globe.

Americans may, therefore, be forgiven if they feel satisfaction as they contemplate the theses and organizational forms prevailing in the world; it is a world largely created on American principles, and in the American image.

POLICY FOR THE FUTURE

What line of policy should the United States take in the changed and changing world that today confronts us? The first of the general considerations that should inform policy is the unequivocal acceptance of the change in the American sphere of action from the quarter of the globe to which it was confined during the nineteenth century to the world scene on which the United States acts today. Acceptance of this change entails in turn acknowledgment that in the sphere in which it must act today the United States is not omnipotent. Paradoxically, the vast increase of the power of the United States has resulted in an appreciation of the limits of national power itself. Even that most creative and ingenious statesman who did more than anyone else to shape the reality of his time, Bismarck, wrote that human beings cannot consciously create the forces that move the world; they can only recognize the tendencies of the time, and, by climbing aboard, may hope to steer them a little this way or that. In George F. Kennan's striking phrase, the maker of foreign policy is not so much a mechanic as a gardener.

Within the range of the limited hopes and expectations defined by recognition of this fact, the United States in its foreign policies should, of course, be concerned to pursue its national interests; but in determining what constitutes American interests, in stressing some elements of the whole complex of national interests rather than others, and in the choice of means that are to be employed, equally knowledgeable and public-spirited people may legitimately differ. While the views that follow are the writer's own, he believes that they will secure a wide measure of agreement.

Preeminent among the national interests of the United States is the interest in the existence of a stable, secure, and ordered world. In the isolationist years it was believed that America was best off in ignoring the rest of the world. Although old-style isolationism is no longer possible, it remains true that the United States will be the better off the less disturbance in the outside world upsets the normal activities of Americans. As the most affluent of the world's states, with the most ramified overseas economic and cultural interests, the United States stands to lose the most by outbreaks of violence and irrational behavior. At the same time, because of American affluence and power, the private individuals who are the bearers of American trade and ideas can in a stable world expect to have their efforts attended by more than average success.

Because of this power and economic strength of the United States, the priority of various national goals is rather different for American policy makers than it is for those of other states. That is, the interest in the preservation of a stable and secure world order is logically accorded higher priority and the interest in defending any specific economic investment is less than for other states, since it is less easy to damage the American economy by damaging any one of its elements.

Because of the American interest in a stable and secure world, the general concern of diplomats to interpret national interests so that they are complementary and not antagonistic to the interests of other states must have special weight with American policy makers. At the same time it is clear that the whole range of national interests can never be absolutely compatible with the interests of all other states, and disagreements are regularly to be expected, even between the United States and her closest allies. The existence of such disagreements over secondary points, however, should not be allowed to interfere with otherwise good relations between them.

A point arrives on the continuum of friendly relations with another state, nevertheless, at which disagreements in objectives between the two become great enough that general amity with occasional minor differences becomes transformed into a policy of settled opposition and antagonism. At what point does this occur? What is it that determines whether the relations between the United States and another country will in general be friendly—despite existing disagreements—or will in general be hostile despite existing common interests? The present writer would suggest that the demarcation of lines between the relations of amity and those of enmity lies at the point where another state opposes *on principle* any policy of the United States, no matter what it is, and refuses even to attempt to negotiate differences in good faith. During most of the administration of Fidel Castro, the government of Cuba has placed itself in this position, as has the government of Communist China. It is an attitude that the government of the Soviet Union used normally to take, but assumes less frequently as time goes on. What this amounts to saying is that the United States can coexist with any state that is prepared to coexist with the United States.

The continuing attempt to coexist peacefully with other states does not, and cannot, mean that the United States is indifferent to what occurs elsewhere in the world, even when what occurs lies clearly within the domestic jurisdiction of other states. Even if one takes the position that it is not the function of United States policy to attempt to impose certain principles of constitutional behavior or economic or social policy on the governments of other states, the United States must necessarily become involved in the internal politics of other countries. Despite all of the principles of international law relative to sovereignty and to the sanctity of a state's domestic jurisdiction, the policies of the world's most powerful state necessarily have repercussions in the domestic affairs of other countries. A change in American tariff or import quota regulations can cause either boom or collapse in the economies of other states; signs of excessive United States friendliness or unfriendliness to an incumbent government can cause its domestic opposition to give up in despair, or to attempt a *coup d'état;* a change in some of the technical requirements for United States foreign aid can cause a drastic shift in the direction of another country's economic growth. Taking into account the magnitude of the effect of United States actions on the domestic situation in other states, therefore, the question becomes not "Should the United States influence developments within other states?" but rather "Should the influence that the United States has be exercised consciously and in keeping with the goals of national policy, or inadvertently and at random?" If one takes the view that responsible action on the part of the United States decision makers entails a consciousness of the effect of their acts, then it seems to the present writer that the only question to be decided is that of the direction in which the United States would like to see the domestic political, economic, and social structures of other states develop.

This question has been squarely and explicitly faced in relation to the Alliance for Progress, which constitutes in part a United States aid program, and in part an agreement among the American states as to the directions in which they wish the structures of their domestic lives to evolve.

In the writer's view there has been an overeagerness among commentators to "write off" the Alliance for Progress before its effects have made themselves felt, and before the initial procedural problems have been overcome. It should surely be acknowledged that the conception of the Alliance has taken a giant step towards meeting the justified charge that, ". . . America's foreign policy headaches around the globe today stem less from information or organization deficiencies than from lack of clearly articulated foreign policy objectives beyond anti-communism."[6]

In a democratic society there are, of course, divergent points of view; and even where general agreement can be secured in principle, formidable difficulties present themselves in the application of principles to specific cases. The author believes nevertheless that recent history suggests that there are certain general ideas with which most Americans agree that provide the framework within which policy can be made. These can be summarized as follows:

States should be encouraged to maintain their autonomy and should be prepared to defend themselves against outside aggression. Their readiness to do so will reduce the possibility of aggressive war. At the same time states should actually take up arms only as a last resort, and should strive to hold to a minimum any fighting that does break out; they should be willing to compromise their differences with other states; and they should be prepared to make financial and other sacrifices to maintain an international organization that can facilitate the process of mutual accommodation. Domestically, a government should be organized on democratic principles where feasible; it should govern in an environment of freedom and respect for individual rights; and, while the presumption should always be in favor of private property and individual

---

6 Harry Howe Ransom, "Secret Mission in an Open Society," New York *Times* Magazine, May 21, 1961.

initiative, the aim of its economic policies should be to help assure the material well-being of the greatest number of people under its jurisdiction.

In the period since the first days of America's involvement in world affairs as a major power, a tradition of national policy has been building up, reflecting the learning processes that have gone on. The general willingness of Americans to accept this tradition was what Senator Goldwater found himself up against, when he urged departures from the standing assumptions of foreign policy during his 1964 presidential campaign.

As time goes on the American foreign policy tradition will be refined and elaborated to meet new situations. If United States policy makers and the American people themselves do not allow the frustrations inherent in the inevitable minor setbacks of policy to weaken their commitment to abiding national principles, then it seems to the present writer that it will become increasingly apparent to the newer nations, whose experience in world affairs is still limited, that the principled yet nonaggressive and compromising spirit that has most often characterized American policy provides the soundest basis for the conduct of world affairs in an era of change, challenge, and hope.

SUGGESTED READINGS

Acheson, Dean, *Power and Diplomacy*. Cambridge, Mass.: Harvard University Press, 1958.

Fulbright, J. William, *Old Myths and New Realities and Other Commentaries*. New York: Random House, 1964.

Kennan, George F., "America and the Russian Future," *Foreign Affairs,* April 1957.

———, *Realities of American Foreign Policy*. Princeton, N.J.: Princeton University Press, 1954.

Kissinger, Henry A., *The Necessity for Choice: Prospects of American Foreign Policy*. New York: Doubleday (Anchor), 1962.

Marshall, Charles B., *The Limits of Foreign Policy*. New York: Holt, Rinehart and Winston, Inc., 1954.

Niebuhr, Reinhold, *The Irony of American History*. New York: Scribner, 1952.

Russett, Bruce, *Trends in World Politics*. New York: Macmillan, 1965.

Wolfers, Arnold (ed.), *Changing East-West Relations and the Unity of the West*. Baltimore: Johns Hopkins Press, 1964.

Index